CONTENTS

1

2

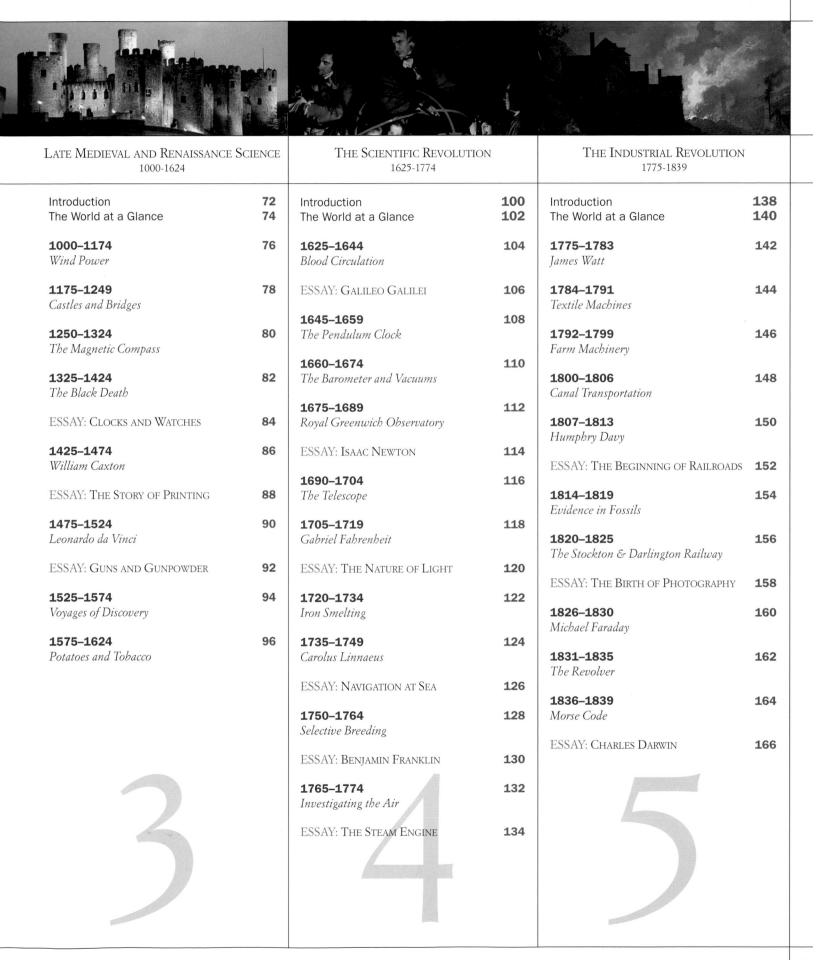

CONTENTS

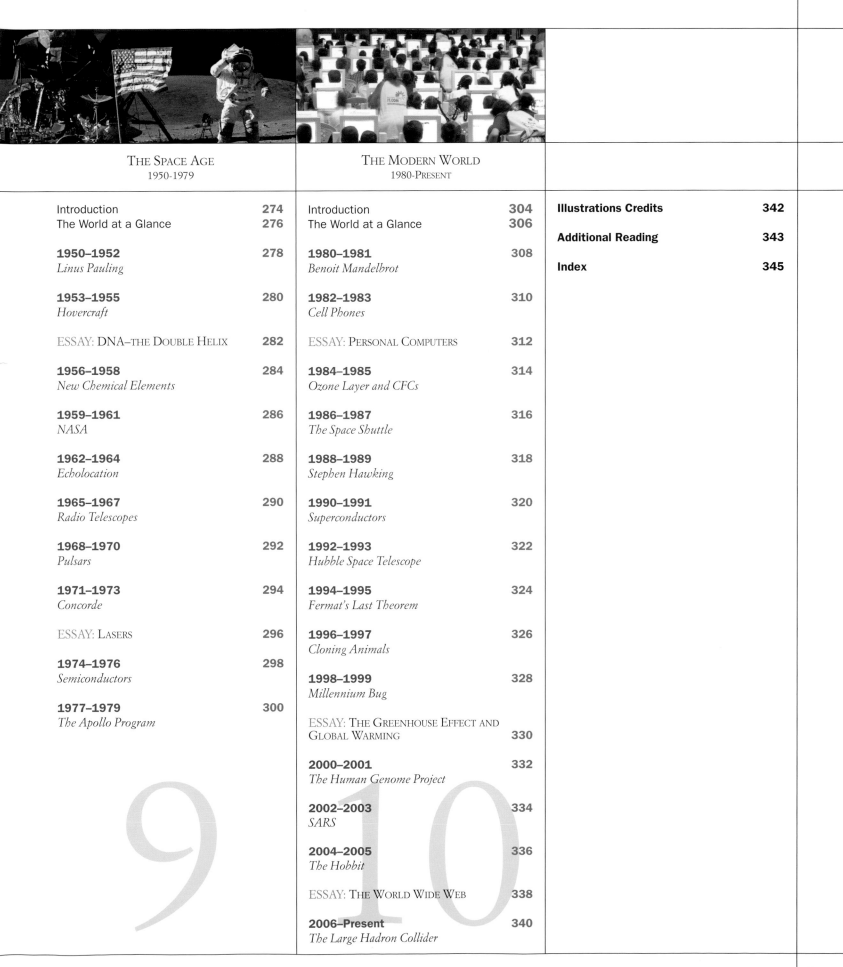

THE SPACE AGE
1950-1979

THE MODERN WORLD
1980-PRESENT

FOREWORD

I
T IS EASY TO THINK OF SCIENCE AS A CHARACTERISTIC OF THE MODERN AGE. WE associate it perhaps with computers or with space exploration. In fact, science is very old: Its history is as long as the history of humankind's attempts to understand the world. In the words of the 19th-century biologist Thomas Henry Huxley, "Science is nothing but trained and organized common sense." As the time line in the *National Geographic Concise History of Science and Invention* shows, the story of scientific and technological advance has for most of the time taken the form of a series of small steps, each based on previous knowledge, rather than a sudden revelation of a new truth. The process began early in human history, when our ancestors first experimented with cultivating crops, domesticating animals, building shelters, and making tools—and it has continued ever since.

"One thing I have learned in a long life: That all our science, measured against reality, is primitive and childlike, and yet it is the most precious thing we have."

ALBERT EINSTEIN

Like all of the publications of the National Geographic Society—since it was established in 1888—this book sets out to promote knowledge of the world and its regions, in our case by providing global perspectives on the growth of human knowledge. This illustrated time line helps readers make sense of the apparently chaotic course of technological development and understand the historical background of cutting-edge scientific innovations. Even the newest scientific and technological advances are often the culmination of processes of discovery that stretch back decades or even centuries.

By tracing this development, the time line and accompanying illustrated essays make complex ideas easier to grasp. They show the reader what happened when and where and highlight the essential facts to understand. In that way, they help the reader avoid the bewilderment that led Nobel laureate Wolfgang Pauli to complain in the 1930s: "Physics is very muddled again at the moment; it is much too hard for me anyway, and I wish I were a movie comedian or something like that and had never heard anything about physics!"

TIME PERIODS AND DATES

The history of science is a multicultural discipline, and scholars and editors working today use terminology that does not impose the standards of one culture on others. This book uses the terms **B.C.E.** (before the Common Era) and **C.E.** (the Common Era). B.C.E. refers to the same period as B.C. (before Christ), and C.E. refers to the same time period as A.D. (*anno Domini*, a Latin phrase meaning "in the year of the Lord"). When a person is mentioned for the first time, his or her birth and death dates are provided where they are available. Dates preceded by r. (reigned) give the reign dates of monarchs. Cases where an exact date is not known are indicated by the use of ca (*circa*, Latin for "about") or fl. (*floruit*, Latin for "flourished").

INTRODUCTION

Each chapter opens with an introductory essay that surveys the major trends in science and invention of the era. The example here, which covers the period from prehistory to 850 B.C.E., describes the earliest technologies and inventions, from making tools and capturing fire to cultivating crops, domesticating animals, and forming early settlements. It also covers the single most important invention for the transmission of human knowledge—writing—and the roots of what many people consider to be the first true science, the study of astronomy.

ABOUT THIS BOOK

NATIONAL GEOGRAPHIC CONCISE HISTORY OF SCIENCE AND INVENTION: *An Illustrated Time Line* chronicles the remarkable story of human knowledge through a versatile design that allows readers to learn in detail about particular periods or regions or to follow themes from prehistory to the modern world. The book traces inventions and discoveries in all fields of science and technology, including math, astronomy, biology, medicine, physics, chemistry, engineering, and invention. The book is divided into ten chapters covering major historical eras. Each chapter begins with an Introduction, outlining the key developments of that era, followed by The World at a Glance, which provides an overview of the chapter. The bulk of each chapter is a time line that traces the most important scientific discoveries and inventions by region and by scientific field. The time lines are supplemented by picture essays, sidebars, and boxes that provide additional detail about particularly important subjects.

Wherever possible, the book provides exact dates for events. However, in some cases it is difficult to say exactly when an invention occurred. This is true of the ancient past, when we rely on archaeological evidence or on written records to trace the development of technology, but it is also true of the modern world. Scientific advance is a continual process rather than a specific event; a breakthrough might be the cumulative result of a series of tiny advances. In such cases, the time lines provide approximate dates or use the dates commonly accepted by experts in the field. Again, it is sometimes not entirely clear who to credit with a specific development or even where it first took place. Scientists in different countries often work on similar subjects at the same time, either in collaboration or in competition. While this book acknowledges differing claims or the work of collaborators, it occasionally uses a degree of necessary simplification in order to place an entry in a particularly place in the time line.

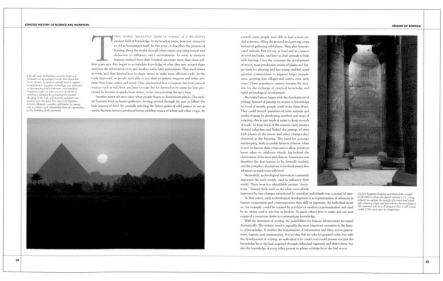

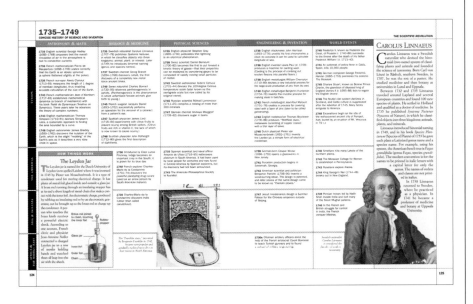

THE WORLD AT A GLANCE

The World at a Glance displays the era's most important scientific developments chronologically from left to right and regionally from top to bottom. The four regions defined here—**Europe**, **The Americas** (North and South America), **Asia & Oceania**, and **Africa & the Middle East**—appear in the same order in the time line. This overview allows for quick comparison of developments occurring in different regions at the same time. The last vertical column here, for example, reveals that while Italian scientist Galileo Galilei was observing moons of Jupiter, ships were beginning to be built in North America and tobacco had reached the Ottoman Empire in western Asia.

TIME LINE

Each time line spread offers a view of scientific developments during the period defined in red at top left. (Time spans may vary in length, depending on the length of the era covered in each chapter.) Four vertical columns cover major areas of science and technology: **Astronomy & Math**, **Biology & Medicine**, **Physical Sciences**, and **Engineering & Invention**. The fifth, **World Events**, provides a broader historical context. Developments within those areas are listed chronologically within each region. At the right of each spread, sidebars highlight significant scientists, technologies, or inventions, and boxed features entitled **Turning Points**, **Inside Story**, and **How Things Work** give extra information on specific entries.

PICTURE ESSAY

Each chapter contains between two and seven picture essays that explore a particularly significant topic. These in-depth articles might focus on the background to a specific invention or discovery, or might describe the influence a particular form of technology had on an entire civilization, such as pyramid construction had on Mesoamerica. This example tells the story of the discovery of the structure of deoxyribonucleic acid (DNA). As here, all picture essays have key dates boxes. Many chapters also have quotes that define the era in the words of scientists, philosophers, and others who embodied their times.

T ODAY PEOPLE FREQUENTLY THINK OF SCIENCE AS A RELATIVELY modern field of knowledge. In its broadest terms, however, science is as old as humankind itself. In this sense, it describes the process of learning about the world through observation, and using reason and deduction to influence one's environment. As soon as modern humans evolved from their hominid ancestors more than three million years ago, they began to accumulate knowledge of what they saw around them and pass the information on to one another and to later generations. They used stones as tools, and then learned how to shape stones to make more efficient tools. As the tools improved, so people were able to use them to fashion weapons and other artifacts from bone, antler, and wood. They also learned how to capture fire from natural sources such as wild fires, and later to make fire for themselves by using the heat generated by friction or sparks from stones, or by concentrating the sun's heat.

Another major advance came when people began to domesticate plants. The earliest humans lived as hunter-gatherers, moving around through the year to follow the best sources of food. By carefully selecting the fattest grains of wild grasses to use as seeds, the first farmers produced better-yielding strains of wheat and other crops. As

Like all early civilizations, ancient Egypt was primarily an agricultural society that depended on its farmers to produce enough food to support its population. Egyptian technology was dedicated to maximizing food production, from building irrigation canals to carry water to the fields to creating a calendar that predicted the annual flooding of the Nile, when fertile sediment was washed over the land. The success of Egyptian farmers allowed a complex civilization to emerge and to achieve such remarkable feats of engineering as the building of the pyramids.

a result, some people were able to lead a more set-tled existence, tilling the ground and growing crops instead of gathering wild plants. They also domesti-cated animals, first for use as food and as a source of wool and hides, and later as draft animals to help with farming. Over the centuries the development of newer, more productive strains of plants and bet-ter tools for planting and harvesting enabled small agrarian communities to support larger popula-tions, growing into villages and towns, even early cities. These population centers became the loca-tion for the exchange of practical knowledge and rapid technological development.

Recorded history began with the development of writing. Instead of passing on stories or knowledge by word of mouth, people could write them down. They could record quantities of farm animals and stocks of grain by developing numbers and ways of counting; this is turn made it easier to keep records of trade. To keep track of the seasons, early peoples devised calendars and linked the passage of time with phases of the moon and other changes they observed in the heavens. The need for accurate timekeeping, both to enable farmers to know when to sow or harvest their crops and to allow priests to know when to celebrate rituals, lay behind the observation of the stars and planets. Astronomy was therefore the first science to be formally studied, and the complex calculations it involved meant that advances in math soon followed.

Meanwhile, technological innovation constantly improved the tools people used to influence their world. There were few identifiable ancient "inven-tions." Instead tools such as the plow were slowly improved by tiny changes introduced by countless individuals over a period of time.

Ancient Egyptian builders constructed the temple at Dendara in about the fourth century B.C.E., using columns to support the weight of a stone roof while still retaining a light and airy interior for worshippers. The structure was so well designed that it still stands nearly 2,500 years after its completion.

To that extent, early technological development is as representative of advances in human cooperation and communication than skill or ingenuity. An individual stone ax, for example, could be created by accident or random experimentation and used by its owner until it was lost or broken. To teach others how to make and use axes required a conscious desire to communicate knowledge.

With the invention of writing, the possibilities for human advancement increased dramatically. The written word is arguably the most important invention in the histo-ry of knowledge. It enables the transmission of information and ideas across genera-tions, regions, and communities. It is an idea that we take for granted today, but with the development of writing, an individual who could read could possess not just the knowledge he or she had acquired through individual ingenuity and observation, but also the knowledge of every other person to whose writings he or she had access.

THE WORLD AT A GLANCE

CONCISE HISTORY OF SCIENCE AND INVENTION

	PREHISTORY	6000 B.C.E.	4000 B.C.E.	3000 B.C.E.	2500 B.C.E.	
EUROPE	ca **750,000** Fire is used by *Homo erectus*. ca **120,000** Neandertals appear in Europe. ca **40,000** Modern humans live alongside Neandertals. ca **28,000** Neandertals die out. ca **25,000** People begin to make ceramic models. ca **6300** Earliest known boat is made.	ca **6000** Scandinavians make sleds to travel on snow. ca **5000** People in Italy make mirrors from obsidian. ca **4300** People in France make canoes.	ca **4000** Horses are domesticated in Ukraine. ca **3100** The first stage of Stonehenge—an earth bank—is built in England.	ca **3000** Copper deposits are found and utilized in Cyprus. ca **3000** Marble sculptures are made in the Greek islands. ca **3000** Grapes and olives are cultivated by town-dwelling people in the Aegean around Greece.	ca **2300** Work begins on aligning the stones at Stonehenge.	
THE AMERICAS	ca **15,000** First settlements appear in America. ca **8,500** North Americans make stone arrowheads.	ca **6000** Pottery is made in South America. ca **5000** Arable farming begins in Mexico and Central America.	ca **4000** Potatoes are cultivated in the Andes.	ca **3000** North Americans begin making baskets and blankets. ca **3000** The llama is domesticated in Peru.	ca **2500** People in the Arctic make flint tools.	
ASIA & OCEANIA	ca **75,000** Modern humans reach Southeast Asia. ca **45,000** Modern humans reach Australia. ca **11,000** Clay pots are made in Japan. ca **6500** Rice is cultivated in China.	ca **5500** The jungle fowl is domesticated. ca **5200** People in Iran make wine.	ca **4000** The Chinese domesticate the water buffalo. ca **4000** Bronze is first made in Thailand. ca **4000** Farmers begin to settle the Indus Valley in India. ca **3500** The plow is invented in both China and Mesopotamia.	**3000** Boats in China are equipped with anchors. **2950** A lunar calendar is developed in China. ca **2900** Cotton is cultivated in India. ca **2700** The Chinese raise silkworms on mulberry leaves. **2637** Year 1 of the Chinese calendar.	ca **2500** The camel is domesticated in Asia. ca **2500** Clay pipes are used as drains in Pakistan. ca **2500** Chinese doctors begin using acupuncture. **2296** Chinese astronomers record the sighting of a comet.	
AFRICA & THE MIDDLE EAST	ca **1,000,000** *Homo erectus* uses stone tools. ca **160,000** *Homo sapiens* (modern man) evolves in Africa. ca **100,000** *Homo sapiens* moves out of Africa. ca **10,000** People in Palestine build houses from sun-dried bricks. ca **10,000** Dogs are domesticated. ca **8000** Goats and sheep are domesticated. ca **7500** Clay tokens are used for record keeping. ca **6500** Cattle are domesticated.	ca **6000** The world's first known city is built in Anatolia. ca **6000** People settle in the Nile Valley in Egypt. ca **5000** Northern African farmers grow millet. ca **5000** Cats are used to catch rodents. ca **5000** Copper is smelted in Egypt. ca **4400** Egyptians weave cloth on looms. **4236** Ancient Egyptians devise a 365-day calendar. ca **4000** The arch is used in construction in Egypt and Mesopotamia.	ca **4000** The Egyptians domesticate the donkey. ca **3500** The Egyptians develop a simple clock. ca **3500** Barges with sails are used in Egypt and Mesopotamia. ca **3500** The wheel is invented in Mesopotamia. ca **3400** Egyptians adopt numerals for quantities more than ten. ca **3200** Bronze is made in Mesopotamia. ca **3100** Egyptians begin using hieroglyphs.	ca **3000** The Sumerians introduce a 360-day calendar. ca **3000** Yams are cultivated in West Africa. ca **3000** Egyptians dam the Garawi River. **2800** Sumerians make soap. **2630** Egyptians begin building pyramids. **2600** Mesopotamians make glass. **2550** The Great Pyramid is completed.	ca **2500** Tin ore is mined and smelted in Turkey. ca **2400** Mesopotamians waterproof boats and buildings with tar. ca **2300** Babylonian astronomers study comets. ca **2300** People in the Middle East keep geese. ca **2300** Egyptians make wine from grapes. ca **2300** The earliest known maps are produced in Mesopotamia.	

2100 B.C.E.	1800 B.C.E.	1500 B.C.E.	1200 B.C.E.	1000–850 B.C.E.
ca 2000 The Minoans build palaces on Crete.	**ca 1700** Central Europeans trade metals and amber. **ca 1600** Bellows are used in glassmaking and metalworking.	**ca 1500** Copper from the Alps is exported to England. **ca 1500** Bathrooms in the Minoan palaces of Crete have running water. **ca 1500** People in the Aegean invent a press to squeeze grapes and olives. **ca 1400** Stonehenge is completed in England.	**ca 1150** Craftsmen in Greece and Cyprus use colored glass to decorate objects. **ca 1050** Ironworking is introduced to Greece.	**ca 1000** Etruscan craftsmen make false teeth from gold. **950** Oats are cultivated in northern and central Europe. **ca 900** Etruscans flourish in Italy.
ca 2000 Copper is mined in North America.	**ca 1750** Peruvians build a long canal to irrigate their crops.	**1400** Cassava (manioc) is grown in South America.	**1200** Fishermen in Peru make rafts and boats from reeds. **1200** Olmec sculptors carve figurines and giant human heads.	**ca 1000** Aleuts and Inuits have now successfully adapted to their Arctic homelands.
ca 2000 Austronesians settle on various islands in the South Pacific.	**ca 1550** Southeast Asian farmers make plowshares from bronze.	**1500** People in Asia make beer. **1450** The Chinese cultivate soybeans. **1361** Chinese astronomers record a solar eclipse.	**1150** Chinese metalworkers cast bronze bells. **1100** The Chinese invent spinning to make yarn. **1000** The Chinese begin writing on bamboo or paper made from bark. **1000** The Hindu calendar of 360 days is introduced in India.	**900** Chinese metalworkers cast coins. **850** The Chinese use natural gas for lighting.
ca 2100 Sumerians build a mud-brick ziggurat. **ca 2000** Babylonian mathematicians introduce a positional number system. **ca 2000** Egyptian armies develop a portable battering ram. **ca 2000** Medicine becomes an important science in Syria and Babylon. **ca 2000** Spoked wheels are made in Egypt and Mesopotamia. **ca 1950** Palestinian farmers make plows.	**ca 1800** Mesopotamian mathematicians discover the "Pythagorean theorem." **1750** Babylonian astronomers compile lists of planets and stars. **ca 1650** Egyptian mathematicians learn to solve simple equations. **ca 1600** Babylonian astronomers recognize the zodiac and the paths of the planets. **ca 1550** Egyptians are using about 700 drugs and medications.	**1500** Professional millers grind wheat in Egypt. **1450** Farmers in Mesopotamia use a seed drill. **1450** The Egyptians devise a water clock. **1350** The symptoms of leprosy are described in an Egyptian text. **1350** Egyptians learn to weld iron.	**1200** The Egyptians dig a canal to join the Nile River to the Red Sea. **1200** Babylonian astronomers make an instrument to determine when a star is due south of their observatory.	**1000** The Phoenicians develop an alphabet. **1000** Farmers use dung to fertilize crops. **975** The Hebrews devise a lunar calendar with 12 months. **950** The Phoenicians make a purple dye. **900** Farmers in Mesopotamia use an irrigation system to water crops. **850** The first-known arch bridge is built in Smyrna.

ASTRONOMY & MATH	BIOLOGY & MEDICINE	PHYSICAL SCIENCES

EUROPE

And God said, "Let the earth put forth vegetation, plants yielding seed, and fruit trees bearing fruit in which is their seed, each according to its kind, upon the earth."

GENESIS 1:11

TURNING POINTS

The World's First City

The settlement at Çatal Hüyük in Anatolia (modern Turkey) dates from about 6000 B.C.E. at the latest. The houses butted closely together and had flat roofs, reached by means of ladders. The people grew crops and irrigated the fields. They supplemented their diet by hunting animals. They wove cloth, made baskets and clay pots, and tanned hides to make leather. Nearby volcanoes produced a hard, glasslike obsidian, which the people of Çatal Hüyük made into knives and other tools. The obsidian was also traded with neighboring peoples. Each house had a religious shrine decorated with figurines and the heads and horns of animals. The dead were left outside exposed to the elements before their remains were buried under the houses.

THE AMERICAS

ca 8000 In Central America pumpkins and squash are domesticated, probably the first fruits cultivated for food.

ASIA & OCEANIA

ca 8000 The woolly mammoth becomes extinct.

ca 6500 Rice is domesticated in the delta of the Yangtze River in China.

Cultivated wheat yields about six times more grain than wild species.

AFRICA & THE MIDDLE EAST

ca 11,000 Hunter-gatherers in northern Syria cultivate rye.

ca 10,000 Dogs are domesticated in Mesopotamia, probably as food.

ca 9000 Einkorn wheat is grown in Palestine.

ca 8000 People in East Africa and Mesopotamia domesticate goats and sheep.

ca 8000 Barley is first grown in the Fertile Crescent in West Asia.

ca 7000 Pigs are domesticated in Turkey.

ca 6500 Cattle are domesticated in Africa and Asia.

The woolly mammoth became extinct about 10,000 years ago. Near-perfect specimens have been discovered in Siberia, preserved in the frozen earth.

ENGINEERING & INVENTION	WORLD EVENTS
ca 750,000 Fire is used by human ancestors, *Homo erectus*, in France.	**ca 120,000** Neandertals live in Europe.
ca 45,000 Stone-headed spears are used in Europe.	**ca 40,000** Modern humans move into Europe and live alongside Neandertals.
ca 25,000 People in central Europe make ceramic images by firing clay models.	**ca 28,000** Neandertals become extinct.
ca 20,000 The wooden bow and arrow are used in Spain and Saharan Africa. People in southern Europe use sewing needles made from bone.	
ca 6300 The earliest surviving dugout boat (hollowed from a tree trunk), found in the Netherlands, dates from this time.	
ca 8500 Indigenous people in North America make stone arrowheads.	**ca 15,000** Likely date for first settlement of America, although some scholars believe people arrived as early as 40,000 B.C.E.
ca 8000 The Folsom people living on the eastern side of the southern Rocky Mountains develop sophisticated tools.	
ca 11,000 The earliest-known clay pots are made in Japan.	**ca 75,000** Modern humans live in Southeast Asia.
	ca 45,000 Modern humans reach Australia.
ca 1,000,000 Human ancestors (*Homo erectus*) begin chipping flakes off stones to sharpen them for tools.	**ca 160,000** First appearance of *Homo sapiens*, the modern human race.
ca 1,000,000 *Homo erectus* use antlers to create tools for cutting and drilling.	**ca 100,000** *Homo sapiens* moves out of Africa.
ca 15,000 In Africa bone harpoons (barbed spears) are used for fishing.	**ca 6,000** Hunter-gatherers settle in farming communities in the Nile Valley in present-day Egypt. They will form the basis of the ancient Egyptian culture.
ca 10,000 People in Palestine make houses of sun-dried bricks and also weave baskets.	
ca 7500 Clay tokens are used for record keeping in Mesopotamia.	
ca 6000 People at Çatal Hüyük in Anatolia (modern Turkey) build the world's first known city.	

THE FIRST CROPS

Modern domestic plants are the result of rapid evolution in response to artificial selection by humans. Characteristics humans prefer, such as large size, flavor, and productivity, are not the same as those favored by natural selection.

The first deliberate cultivation appears to have taken place in West Asia about 10–11,000 years ago (9000–8000 B.C.E.) in the Fertile Crescent, an area running from the Nile Delta up the eastern coast of the Mediterranean and across present-day Iraq to the Persian Gulf. Cereal crops were the first to be cultivated systematically. Barley and wheat were probably first, then rice and oats. People began to sow some of the grain they collected from wild barley and wheat close to home, to make it easier to collect the grain the following year. Cultivation of rice began in China in around 6500 B.C.E. or a little later. The switch from gathering to cultivation made it possible for people to abandon the hunter-gatherer lifestyle in favor of a more settled, more predictable, and so more secure way of life.

A natural mutation produced a variety of wheat known as einkorn, in which the seed head was stable, so the grain did not get dispersed before being harvested. Around 8,000 years ago an einkorn wheat naturally hybridized, or crossed, with a species of wild grass to produce emmer wheat, which was gluten rich and made good flour. Another natural mutation produced durum wheat, in which the grain was easier to separate from the chaff by threshing. Wheat production was still inefficient, however. Farmers only reaped about six ears of wheat for every one they sowed. From about 7,000 years ago in the New World another cereal— corn (maize)—was far more productive. For every kernel planted, a farmer could harvest about 45 times as many.

Between 8,000 and 5,000 years ago came root crops and legumes, such as beets and beans. Later still were fruiting trees, leafy vegetables, and crops grown for feeding livestock.

EARLY HUMANS

THE STORY OF HUMAN EVOLUTION BEGAN more than 5 million years ago. The first hominids, or humanlike creatures, appeared about 2.4 million years ago in Africa. They learned to make fire and shaped tools, mainly as practical aids to survival but also for ceremonial use.

Human ancestors were making tools about 2.3 million years ago in Ethiopia and about 2.25 million years ago in China. Nearly 2 million years ago at Olduvai Gorge, Tanzania, "handy man" (*Homo habilis*) was making choppers by striking one stone against another. Choppers were used for cutting or sawing, and the blunt end of the stone would smash stone or bone.

Leaving Africa

Homo habilis lived only in Africa. A later species, *H. erectus*, migrated out of Africa and spread across Eurasia. *Homo erectus* lived from 1.85 million years ago until about 400,000 years ago and made tools that were more sophisticated than those of its predecessors. The manufacturing technique, however, was the same: striking one stone against another. The earliest tools associated with *H. erectus* were found in Olduvai Gorge and are about 1.4 million years old. Flint was the preferred stone of *H. erectus*, but flint is not found everywhere. When flint was not available, the toolmakers used other rocks, including quartz.

Instead of shaping one stone by striking identical stones together, *H. erectus* toolmakers used stone hammers to make cleavers and hand axes, with longer, straighter cutting edges than the old choppers. By about one million years ago they had discovered a new technique—using hammers made from deer antlers. This development allowed them to work with greater precision to make a much wider range of tools.

Neandertal people (*H. sapiens neanderthalensis*) lived in Europe, the Mediterranean region, and parts of the Middle East at the same time as modern humans, and in some places side by side with them. They first appeared about 100,000 years ago and became extinct about 30,000 years ago. Neandertals made a variety of simple stone tools.

Modern humans, *Homo sapiens*, were making much more efficient tools by 40,000 years ago. At two sites in France, they produced up to 80 different kinds of stone implements. People were also making tools with stone blades fixed to bone or antler handles. Cro-Magnon people living from 35,000 to 10,000 years ago made beautifully engraved bone tools that were probably used for ceremonial purposes. Among other things, they made chisels, awls, and tools with blades for scraping animal skins to make leather.

Stone tools survive indefinitely, allowing archaeologists to trace their development, but humans have also used other materials to make tools, such as wood and plant fibers, that decompose and disappear soon

KEY DATES

2,000,000 B.C.E.
Homo habilis makes stone tools

1,400,000 B.C.E.
Earliest-known *Homo erectus* tools

1,000,000 B.C.E.
H. erectus uses hammers made from deer antlers

20,000 B.C.E.
Leaf-shaped stone blades made in France

8000–7000 B.C.E.
European rock carving depicts a framed boat

5000 B.C.E.
Baskets made in Egypt

2700 B.C.E.
Silk woven in China

Bluefish Cave 15–12,000

Laurentide Ice Sheet

Marmes 10,500

Folsom 9,000

Clovis 11,200

Little Salt Spring 12,000

Tepexpan 11–10,000

Pedra Pintada 11,200–10,500

Guitarrero Cave c.10,000

Monte Verde 12,500

Fell's Cave 11,000

range of early hominids

range of *Homo erectus*, ca 500,000 years ago (y.a.)

range of modern humans by 10,000 y.a.

Selected fossil sites

Ardipithecus ramidus

Australopithecus

Homo habilis

Homo erectus

Homo sapiens neanderthalensis

anatomically modern humans, with date (y.a.)

other early modern human sites, with date (y.a.)

migration of modern humans, 100,000–18,000 y.a.

range of Neandertals, ca 100,000 y.a.

Limit of ice cap

18,000 y.a.

10,000 y.a.

ancient coastline 18,000 y.a.

Rift Valley

after they are thrown away. Arrows and spears had wooden shafts, and arrows needed wooden bows to fire them. None of the wood survives.

People also began wearing clothes. The first garment may have been a woman's skirt made from cords hung from a belt. It is likely that people were twisting fibers into cord and ropes by 20,000 years ago. By that time they were also weaving willow stalks into baskets and fish traps and using twisted cords to make fishing nets. These techniques were adapted to making cloth. The earliest evidence of basket weaving, using palm leaves, split reeds, and other plant fibers, dates from about 5000 B.C.E. at Fayoum, Egypt. By about 2700 B.C.E. silk was being woven into cloth in China.

Fish were an important part of the diet of most communities. In small rivers, hunters could wade across to set traps and spear fish. Wider rivers and lakes called for an alternative method. A rock carving from northern Europe, made between 9,000 and 10,000 years ago, shows a boat carrying hunters in pursuit of swimming reindeer. The boat seems to have a frame, in which case it would have resembled a kayak or coracle, which consists of a strong wooden frame covered in animal skin.

This map shows where early hominids lived and the migration of Homo sapiens *around the world from about 100,000 years ago.*

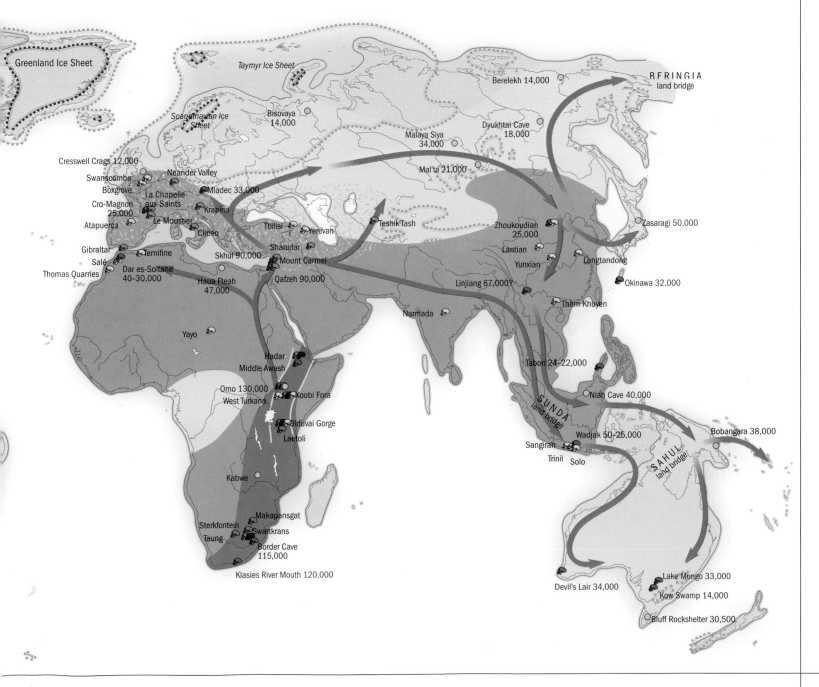

MAKING FIRE

CAPTURING AND MAKING FIRE CHANGED THE lifestyle of early humans. It gave them warmth and a means of defense and allowed them to settle in previously inhospitable areas. Cooking food enabled them to expand their diet and grow stronger. Sitting around the shared warmth of a fire, early humans were also able to develop communication skills that advanced their mental and social development.

Fire was essential for the growth of human civilization. People used it to cook their food, warm their homes, clear woodland or scrubland for cultivation, make pottery, and eventually smelt metals from ores. Historians usually give credit for the first use of fire, around 750,000 B.C.E., to *Homo erectus*, a race of early humans who lived between 1.85 million and 400,000 years ago, gradually spreading from Africa to areas of Asia and Europe.

Early humans likely saw how lightning set fire to dry trees and grass and, in some parts of the world, observed vegetation become ignited by molten lava or hot ashes from erupting volcanoes. At first people probably simply "captured" fire from these natural occurrences. They then kept a campfire burning nonstop, throughout day and night. They may have kept glowing coals or charcoal in a brazier; later, people would keep a lamp or a candle burning so that they were never without a source of fire. It was easier to keep a fire going than to start a new one.

Making fire from scratch is difficult, and all early methods relied on friction. When two surfaces rub together, they become hot. Early ways of making fire involved rubbing two pieces of wood together until they got hot enough to start a fire. The techniques—beginning about 7000 B.C.E.—included the use of fire sticks and fire drills. A fire stick is a stick of dry wood, one end of which has a blunt point that is turned in a small hollow dug in a larger piece of wood. The stick can be rotated between a person's hands by rubbing the palms together back and forth very rapidly. This method is still used by traditional peoples in Africa and Australia, and occasionally by hikers in wilderness areas. The friction between the pieces of wood gradually raises them to burning temperature, and the resulting heat ignites pieces of dry grass (tinder) in the hollow. The stick-and-groove method is a variation on the fire stick, in which a fire stick is rubbed hard back and forth along a groove in another piece of wood.

Alternatively, a bow can be used to rotate the fire stick more rapidly. Using a fire drill, the string of the bow makes a couple of turns around the fire stick, which spins first one way and then the other as the bow is pulled backward and forward.

Other Sources of Fire

Early humans also created fire by using sparks produced when a piece of flint strikes a piece of pyrite (a mineral form of iron sulfide). The sparks fall on tinder, such as dry grass or sawdust. Vigorous blowing then causes the smoldering tinder to burst into flame. A tinder box—which was in use for more than 2,000 years—holds all the necessary equipment to create a fire: flint, steel to strike it on, and tinder to get the fire going. Some later tinder boxes incorporated a candleholder to "capture" the new flame. Another method of making fire, apparently known to the ancient Greeks, used a lens or curved mirror to focus and concentrate the sun's rays—the idea of the burning glass. The final breakthrough in fire production came with the invention of friction matches in the 19th century.

KEY DATES

750,000 B.C.E.
Homo erectus uses fire

7,000 B.C.E.
Modern humans learn to make fire

1827 C.E.
Friction matches invented

The fire drill was probably one of the earliest human inventions. It uses a wooden bow to rotate a blunt-ended fire stick in a hollow in a piece of softer wood. The stick spins one way and then the other as the bow is pulled back and forth.

A tribesman from Kenya, Africa, builds up a fire, which he made with fire sticks, into a blaze by adding dried grass.

ASTRONOMY & MATH	BIOLOGY & MEDICINE	PHYSICAL SCIENCES

EUROPE

ca 4000 Domestication of horses occurs in Ukraine, for food, as beasts of burden, and also for riding.

Dating the Past: Pottery

Because pottery lasts well, ceramic objects, such as pots and fragments of pottery, are common and valuable archaeological finds. The study of pottery artifacts helps archaeologists build up a picture of a culture, including its social organization, daily habits, diet, wealth, and religion.

For cultures that left no written records, pottery is one of the main ways of dating them. One technique is by comparison: Archaeologists can get a rough estimate of when a culture thrived from the style of its ceramics and how it compares with the style of other ancient cultures. A more accurate source of dating is known as thermoluminescence. It analyzes electrons to determine when the clay was fired. In addition, trace element analysis can be used to pinpoint the precise source of the clay, revealing whether it was local or had been transported over a distance.

THE AMERICAS

ca 5000 Arable farming begins in Mexico and Central America, with people growing an early type of corn.

ca 4500 In Central America avocados are grown, and cotton is cultivated.

Yangshao pot from China. The Yangshao culture flourished along the Yellow River from about 5000 to about 3000 B.C.E.

ASIA & OCEANIA

ca 5500 The jungle fowl is domesticated in Southeast Asia. The red jungle fowl of India is the ancestor of today's chicken.

ca 5200 People in northern Iran make wine from wild grapes. The fermentation process relies on natural yeasts.

ca 4000 The water buffalo is domesticated in China.

AFRICA & THE MIDDLE EAST

4236 Ancient Egyptians introduce a 365-day calendar (12 months of 30 days plus a 5-day holiday). This is the first precisely dated calendar until the Sumerian calendar of about 3000 B.C.E.

ca 6000 People in southwestern Asia cultivate flax to get fibers for making cloth.

ca 5000 Farmers in northern Africa and Ethiopia grow various types of millet as the principal grain crop.

ca 5000 People in settlements in the Middle East use cats for catching rats and mice.

If I die you will weep, but if the water buffalo dies, you will starve.

CHINESE PROVERB

ENGINEERING & INVENTION	WORLD EVENTS
ca 6000 In Scandinavia wooden sleds are used to travel over snow. Cave paintings from 1,000 years later show people on skis. **ca 5000** People in Italy make mirrors out of the mineral obsidian, probably taken from the island of Melos. **ca 4300** People living near present-day Paris, France, make oak canoes up to 16 feet (5 m) long.	**ca 5400** Central European farmers begin the Bandkeramik culture, named for the linear patterns on their pottery. **ca 4300** The first megalithic tombs are built of huge stones in western Europe.
ca 6000 The oldest-known pottery in the Americas is produced in Santarém on the Amazon River Basin in present-day Brazil. **ca 5000** Permanent villages begin to spring up in Central America, following the development of corn as a crop.	
ca 4000 People in modern-day Thailand are the first in the world to make bronze, an alloy consisting of 90 percent copper and 10 percent tin.	**ca 6500** Farming begins in the Indus Valley in modern-day Pakistan and western India. **ca 5000** In China the Yangshao culture produces pottery painted with images of people and animals or geometric patterns.
ca 6000 People in Asia Minor (present-day Turkey) produce clay pottery, weave cloth, and make rope. **ca 6000** Palestinians start using mortar to bind together sun-dried bricks for construction. **ca 5000** Copper is smelted in Egypt and used to make weapons and other tools. **ca 4400** Egyptians weave cloth on a loom, usually linen made from wild flax. **ca 4000** The brick-built arch is used in construction in Egypt and Mesopotamia. **ca 4000** The door lock is invented in Mesopotamia. People there employ a harness to use oxen as draft animals. **ca 4000** Egyptians make boat hulls by joining planks of wood together, allowing them to make larger vessels.	**ca 5500** First archaeological evidence of Sumerians in Mesopotamia. **ca 4000** Village culture emerges in the Nile Valley.

DOMESTICATION OF ANIMALS

Ancient humans hunted wild animals for thousands of years. As humans evolved, animals became a source not just of food, but also of fur, hide, sinew, horn, and bone.

The domestication of livestock probably began about 10,000 years ago (8000 B.C.E.), when wild goats and mouflon (sheep), followed by wild pigs (7000 B.C.E.), were captured in eastern Asia and Mesopotamia and kept close to settlements. As these animals bred, their descendants became more accustomed to human proximity.

By about 8,500 years ago (6500 B.C.E.) cattle were kept under domestication in Africa and India. Chickens were domesticated in Southeast Asia in about 5500 B.C.E. Evidence suggests that by about 4000 B.C.E., people in the Middle East were harnessing the strength of animals to drag heavy loads or pull plows. At the same time, Europeans began to keep horses, first for meat and milk, but soon also for riding: Some 6,000-year-old horse teeth found in Ukraine show signs of wear possibly caused by a bit.

By 2000 B.C.E. horses were animals of status, ridden by wealthy or important people. They were also used in war to intimidate the enemy, ridden by cavalry soldiers or used to pull chariots. Bactrian camels were domesticated in northern Afghanistan by about 2500 B.C.E. In the New World the llama was domesticated in about 3000 B.C.E. and the guinea pig (cavy) in 2000 B.C.E. The latter was bred for meat long before it became a pet.

Domesticated cattle in a 4,000-year-old cave painting in Algeria

THE COMING OF THE WHEEL

OPPOSITE: *Inspiration for the vehicular wheel may have come from the potter's wheel, which was developed a few centuries earlier.*

KEY DATES

3500 B.C.E.
First potters' wheels appear in Mesopotamia

3200 B.C.E..
First axled vehicular wheel appears (also in Mesopotamia)

2800 B.C.E.
Chinese develop the wheel (probably independently)

85 B.C.E.
Waterwheel is developed in Greece

500–1000 B.C.E.
Spinning wheel is developed in China

THE WHEEL HAS BEEN INVENTED AND reinvented several times throughout history. The details of its first appearance, at least 5,000 years ago, are lost in the distant past. About 6,000 years ago humans were already using drag technology such as plows and sledges. In some parts of the world, heavy objects such as rocks and boats were moved using log rollers. As the object moved forward, rollers were taken from behind and replaced in front. Rollers may have been the starting point for the invention of the cartwheel.

After a set of logs had been used for some time, they would become worn where they scraped against the sledge. Eventually the sledge would settle into the worn section of the rollers, and this may have given people the idea for the axle wheel. Because an axle has a small circumference, it takes less energy to turn than a whole wheel. However, there are some problems with the theory that the wheel evolved from rollers—whole logs split and fall apart quite easily when rolled under pressure, and the tall, straight trees that were needed to make rollers were not abundant in the Middle East, where the first solid evidence for vehicular wheels appears.

The development of a wheel constructed to rotate on a fixed axle is used by archaeologists as an indicator of relatively advanced civilization. The earliest evidence of axled wheels dates back to about 3200 B.C.E. The Sumerian people of Mesopotamia (modern-day Iraq) produced pictures of carts with solid wheels, apparently made from two pieces of plank bracketed together and cut into a circular shape. The axles went through the center of each wheel and were fixed in place by lynchpins. Similar wheels appeared on war chariots also built by the Sumerians in Mesopotamia in about 2500 B.C.E. By 2000 B.C.E. the Sumerians had developed spoked wheels, which made chariots much lighter and more maneuverable. The design later spread and was refined by other civilizations, including the Egyptians and the Romans. In China, the wheel appeared independently in about 2800 B.C.E.

Not Just Transportation

The first wheels were probably not intended for transportation. Evidence from around 3500 B.C.E. shows that potters were using simple turntables to help them create smooth, evenly shaped pots. These early potters' wheels were developed further by the Greeks and Egyptians into flywheels that could convert pulses of energy, such as the pressing of a treadle, into smooth, continuous motion. The flywheel was to become just as important as the vehicular wheel. The Greeks also came up with other variations on the wheel. The fourth and third centuries B.C.E. saw the development of cogs, gearwheels, and pulleys. The waterwheel was another important variation on the basic axled design. First developed around 85 B.C.E., waterwheels allowed humans to harness the power of water to drive millstones for grinding grain.

Since ancient times there have been several more wheel innovations. The Chinese began using spinning wheels for manufacturing yarn between 500 and 1000 C.E. The flywheel also played a key role in the Industrial Revolution. When connected to pistons driven by a steam engine, it converted pulses of raw power into smooth movement that could be used to drive machines and power locomotives. Later still came wheel-based innovations including turbines, gyroscopes, and castor wheels—all variations on an ancient piece of technology still going strong today.

War has long been a driving force of invention, and the wheel may be another example. The Sumerians were the first to develop wheeled chariots, closely followed by the ancient Egyptians.

WRITING AND NUMBERS

PEOPLE HAVE ALWAYS NEEDED TO KEEP records of important events, goods stored or traded, and taxes collected. A drawing is the simplest type of record. Scientists believe that the cave paintings in the Lascaux Grotto in France, made between 17,000 and 15,000 years ago and depicting various animals and a man, record a religious ritual. Early drawings signified exactly what they represented—a picture of a deer meant "deer." Gradually, the symbols acquired more abstract meanings, and eventually they developed into writing.

Writing developed as a way of keeping records. At first, representational drawings became simpler in form. "Sun" might be a small circle inside a larger circle, and water might be depicted as a wavy line. Such simple signs could be drawn quickly and remained clearly recognizable even when they were made very

small. In time they came to have more than one meaning. The sign for "sun" also meant "day," or in Egypt the sun-god Re (or Ra).

In the next stage each sign came to represent a sound as well as an object, or simply a sound. This type of writing, in which pictures represent sounds, is called "hieroglyphic," and the best-known type was developed in Egypt, where it first appeared around 3100 B.C.E. By about 2700 B.C.E. Egyptian hieroglyphic writing had been more or less standardized, and it remained in use for some 3,000 years.

At about the same time another system of writing was emerging in Mesopotamia, the region between the Euphrates and Tigris rivers, in what is present-day Iraq. It also began as a system of stylized pictures, but it developed very differently from Egyptian hieroglyphs because of the tools used to write it. Whereas

ABOVE: *Cuneiform script —seen here on a stone wall—fell into disuse around the beginning of the Common Era. It was deciphered by scholars in the 19th century.*

Egyptian scribes wrote on papyrus paper with reed pens and ink, Mesopotamian scribes pressed a writing tool called a stylus into a tablet of soft clay, making a wedge or round shape. This type of writing is called cuneiform. It came into use in about 2400 B.C.E. Cuneiform was the writing system used by the Sumerians, the Assyrians, and the Babylonians. It spread to Persia and remained in use for nearly 2,000 years. The first real alphabet (the Proto Canaanite) emerged in the Middle East in about 1700 B.C.E. It used 30 symbols to represent single sounds. From this the Phoenician alphabet of 22 letters developed by about 1000 B.C.E., eventually giving rise to Arabic, Hebrew, Latin, and Greek scripts.

Chinese writing also developed from pictures. They were inscribed on bones and seashells that were then thrown into the air. People believed that the pattern in which they fell conveyed messages from the gods or from ancestors. These symbols were in use from about 1700 B.C.E. They became more abstract during the Zhou Dynasty (ca 1122–256 B.C.E.).

Writing Numbers

Record keepers also needed a way to write numbers. A picture of one cow can represent one cow, but it would be impractical to represent 60 cows by drawing each one. In about 30,000 B.C.E. in what is now the Czech Republic someone carved 55 notches (11 groups of five) on a bone from the leg of a wolf. They may refer to the number of animals killed in a hunt, although no one really knows, but the bone is clearly a numerical record. A stick or bone used in this way is called a tally stick.

Numerals for quantities greater than ten were first used in Egypt in about 3400 B.C.E., Mesopotamia in about 3000 B.C.E., and in Crete in about 1200 B.C.E. Using ten as a base was an obvious choice because humans have ten fingers, and most cultures adopted this counting system. The Babylonians and Sumerians were the major exceptions: They calculated to base 60. Egyptian and cuneiform numbers used different

symbols for 1; 10; 100; 1,000; 10,000; 100,000; and 1,000,000, and indicated higher values by repeating them, as in Roman numerals, where X is 10, XX is 20, and XXX is 30; C is 100, and CCC is 300. However, none of these systems had a symbol for zero.

Clay was plentiful, and cuneiform writing has survived on thousands of Babylonian tablets. As long as the clay was soft, a tablet could be smoothed and used again. Some of the tablets found were students' exercise books. They include multiplication tables and complex calculations. Egyptians, however, used only addition and the two times table. They performed multiplication by repeatedly doubling or halving and then adding the results. Nevertheless, surviving Egyptian papyri describe such tasks as dividing a given number of loaves among a given number of people and finding the area of a right-angled triangle.

Proto Canaanite	Early letter names and meanings	Phoenician	Early Greek	Early monumental Latin	Modern English
	alp oxhead				A
	bêt house				B
	gaml throwstick				C
	digg fish				D
	hô(?) man calling				E
	wŏ mace				F
	zê(n) ?				
	hê(t) fence?				H
	tê(t) spindle?				
	yad arm				I
	kapp palm				K
	lamd ox-goad				L
	mêm water				M
	nahs snake				N
	cên eye				O
	pi't corner?				P
	sa(d) plant				
	qu(p) ?				Q
	ra's head of man				R
	taan composite bow				S
	tô owner's mark				T

Most of the letters in our modern English alphabet can be traced back to the Phoenician alphabet, as shown here. However, the Phoenicians made no distinction between the letter J and the letter I.

KEY DATES

3400 B.C.E.
Numbers (base 10) used in Egypt

3100 B.C.E.
Egyptian hieroglyphs

2400 B.C.E.
Cuneiform writing

1700 B.C.E.
Early Chinese writing

1700 B.C.E.
Proto Canaanite alphabet

1000 B.C.E.
Phoenician alphabet

ASTRONOMY & MATH	BIOLOGY & MEDICINE	PHYSICAL SCIENCES

EUROPE

ca 3000 People establish towns in the Aegean region of Greece, based on the cultivation of olives and grapes.

ca 3000 Copper ore deposits are found on the Mediterranean island of Cyprus, which soon becomes the major source of the metal in the ancient world.

South Americans have used the llama as a beast of burden and for meat and fiber production for about 5,000 years.

Acupuncture remains in regular use over 4,500 years since its invention in China.

THE AMERICAS

ca 4000 Potatoes are cultivated in the Andes, where it is too cold to grow corn.

ca 3000 People in Peru domesticate the llama.

ca 2500 The peanut becomes a food crop.

ASIA & OCEANIA

2950 In China a lunar calendar is developed.

2637 According to later tradition, this is year 1 of the Chinese calendar.

ca 2900 Cotton is cultivated in the valley of the Indus River to weave into cloth.

ca 2700 In China silkworms are cultured on mulberry leaves. Strands of silk are unwound from their cocoons to make cloth.

ca 2500 People in Iran and Afghanistan domesticate the Bactrian camel.

ca 2500 Chinese doctors use acupuncture to heal ailments.

AFRICA & THE MIDDLE EAST

ca 3500 The Egyptians use a simple shadow clock, or gnomon, a vertical stick or obelisk that casts a shadow.

ca 3400 The Egyptians adopt numerals for quantities greater than 10 (with base 10).

ca 3000 The Sumerians introduce a 360-day solar calendar with 12 months of 30 days. They add an extra month roughly every eight years to keep in step with the seasons.

ca 2500 Sumerian traders introduce a system of standard weights, including the shekel and the mina.

ca 2600 Egyptian builders use a set square for setting out right angles and a plumbline for checking verticals.

ca 4000 In Egypt the donkey is domesticated as a beast of burden.

ca 3000 In West Africa yams are cultivated; palm trees are also grown for producing oil.

ca 2600 In Egypt priests begin the practice of embalming dead dignitaries such as pharaohs to create mummies.

ca 2500 Egyptian physicians begin practicing surgery and develop a range of surgical instruments for the purpose.

ca 3200 Bronze, the copper–tin alloy, is first used in Mesopotamia (present-day Iraq). The use of bronze spreads throughout the Middle East and Europe. By 2500 B.C.E. the Sumerians cast ax heads out of copper and bronze.

ca 3200 The Egyptians use a "nilometer" to measure the annual Nile flood.

ca 3000 To create an artificial lake for water for irrigation, Egyptian engineers build a 328-foot (100-m) dam across the Garawi River Valley.

ca 2600 People in Mesopotamia make glass by melting together sand (silica) and soda (sodium carbonate). At first it is used for glazes on pots and vases; later they learn to shape molten glass and make bottles.

ENGINEERING & INVENTION	WORLD EVENTS
ca 3100 The first stage of construction of Stonehenge—an earth bank with a ring of holes—begins in southern England. **ca 3000** An industry making marble sculptures develops on the Greek islands in the Aegean Sea (the Cyclades).	**ca 3000** Megalithic tombs are built on the island of Malta. **ca 2500** The Beaker people spread from the Low Countries to France.
ca 3000 People in North America create rock shelters and produce items made of feathers, including blankets and baskets.	**ca 3500** The Haida culture begins in Canada. **3372** In the calendar of the later Maya, this year marks the beginning of time.
ca 3500 Farmers in Mesopotamia and China use a primitive plow. **ca 3000** Chinese and Egyptian sailors equip their boats with anchors. **ca 2500** Clay water pipes are used for drains at Mohenjo-Daro in Pakistan and in Knossos, Crete.	**ca 4000** Farmers begin to settle on the Indus Valley floodplain and build irrigation systems with dams and canals. **ca 2600** The first cities emerge in the Indus Valley.
ca 3500 River barges with sails are used in Mesopotamia and Egypt. **ca 3500** The wheel appears in Mesopotamia, first as a potter's wheel. **ca 3400** The Sumerians use simple picture writing that later develops into cuneiform. **ca 3200** Wheeled vehicles with axles are used in the Near and Middle East. **ca 3100** Egyptian scribes begin using hieroglyphs as a form of writing. **ca 2800** The Sumerians make soap. **2630** Work begins on the stepped pyramid of Djoser (r. ca 2630–ca 2611) at Saqqara in Egypt. **2550** The Great Pyramid of King Khufu (r. ca 2589–ca 2566) is completed at Giza in Egypt.	**ca 3500** The Sahara region suffers from prolonged desertification. **ca 3200** The first acknowledged civilization emerges between the Tigris and Euphrates Rivers, known in Greek as Mesopotamia or "land between the rivers." The Sumerians farm the fertile valley, build cities, and organize government and religion. **3100** Upper (southern) and Lower (northern) Egypt are united under the kings of the Predynastic period. **2950** The Dynastic Period begins in Egypt when the First Dynasty is formed by Pharaoh Menes.

ANCIENT MEDICINE

Throughout history, people have tried various ways to heal the sick. Some were not particularly medical: Healers, for example, often predicted the course of a disease by examining the liver of a sacrificed animal.

Seeking advice or using herbal remedies to treat minor complaints—"folk medicine"—was widespread. However, people believed that more serious illness was caused by angry gods or by demons entering the body. Treatments involved physical manipulation of the patient, herbal medicines, and incantations to drive the demons away. Drilling a hole in the top of the skull—a procedure called trepanning—was often used to allow whatever caused an illness to escape.

Chinese medicine, including acupuncture, began over 4,500 years ago. Chinese doctors believed that illness was caused by imbalances between the female (yin) and male (yang) cosmic principles, and they aimed to correct the imbalance with herbal remedies.

Ayurvedic medicine, based on religious writings, is still used in India, where it began about 3,000 years ago. It aims to prevent illness through lifestyle, hygiene, and yoga, and to cure complaints by diet and preparations of herbs and minerals. In ancient Greece, there were hundreds of temples to Asclepius, the god of healing. Sick people spent the night at the temple and described their dreams to the priests, who then advised them on a cure.

Ayurvedic yoga is still widely practiced today.

31

THE AGRICULTURAL REVOLUTION

THE HISTORY OF FARMING DATES FROM ABOUT 11,000 years ago, when people gradually gave up nomadic foraging—the hunter-gatherer way of life—and began to form more settled communities. At first using slash-and-burn techniques, people began to live in settlements where they could cultivate, or grow, crops and domesticate, or tame, animals. The need to store or prepare the food they grew or raised to survive times when food was hard to find also led to new discoveries, such as grinding grain to make flour or salting and curing meats. This shift, often called the agricultural revolution, occurred independently in West and East Asia, the Americas, and Africa.

In the fertile valley of the Nile River in Egypt and in Mesopotamia between the Tigris and Euphrates Rivers (in present-day Iraq) early farmers used digging sticks and hoes to prepare the soil for planting and sickles to harvest crops. The plow, invented in about 3500 B.C.E. by farmers in Mesopotamia and China, greatly extended the areas of land that could be prepared to cultivate crops.

Selective Breeding

Over years, selective breeding—choosing which plants or animals (usually the most useful) can reproduce—resulted in higher-yielding strains of cereal plants such as wheat and barley. People also began to domesticate useful animals and selectively bred them for certain characteristics, such as strength or docility. Beasts of burden, such as horses, oxen, camels, llamas, and buffalo, began to replace human muscle power to carry loads, draw plows, and pull carts. Other animals, such as sheep, goats, pigs, chickens, and other poultry, were also domesticated not only for their meat, milk, or eggs, but also for their skin, fiber (hair or wool), and feathers.

It was difficult to keep food over winter, although people did store dried grain. Stored grain became infested with rats and mice, which in turn attracted wildcats. Farmers in the Near East recognized the

usefulness of the cats in controlling the rodent pests, which led to the domestication of the cat. Pulses (edible seeds), such as lentils, peas, and beans, could also be dried and easily stored.

Farmers tended to slaughter many of their animals in late fall because they had insufficient food for the livestock to survive through winter. Because meat would spoil if not soon eaten, people in early settlements needed to find ways to preserve animal carcasses as a supply of meat into the following year. The initial methods for preserving meat included simply

KEY DATES

ca 8000 B.C.E.
Barley first grown and harvested in West Asia

ca 7000 B.C.E.
Pigs domesticated in West Asia

ca 6500 B.C.E.
Cattle domesticated in Africa and Asia

ca 6000 B.C.E
Farmers begin to favor emmer wheat

ca 5500 B.C.E
Chickens domesticated in Southeast Asia

ca 5000 B.C.E.
Corn first cultivated in South America

ca 4000 B.C.E.
Horses first captured and used for riding

ca 3000 B.C.E.
Llamas domesticated in South America

ca 2500 B.C.E.
Camels domesticated in Afghanistan

allowing the carcasses to dry in the wind or in cold climates storing them in caves—in a similar way as we now refrigerate meat. New technologies eventually arose to preserve food in other ways. One method involved smoking meat or fish over a wood fire, a method still widely used today (more often to improve flavor than out of necessity). Fish and meat were also salted. A combination of curing (smoking) and salting pig meat (pork) created ham and bacon.

People also began to use grindstones to make flour from harvested grains and to make clay pots to store food as well as for cooking. The earliest-known pottery dates from about 11,000 B.C.E. in Japan. It was invented independently in the Middle East about 5,000 years later. As the potters grew more skillful, they built ovens for baking the clay.

By about 5000 B.C.E. some communities were producing a food surplus that they could trade or barter for other goods, such as tools or pottery. Once they had reached that stage, people were poised to take the next leap forward: The urban revolution and the establishment of what we call civilization.

This painting from the tomb of an Egyptian artisan called Sennedjem shows him using a simple plow pulled by a pair of oxen. It dates from the reign of pharaoh Rameses II (ca 1303–1213 B.C.E.).

BUILDING THE PYRAMIDS

THE GREAT PYRAMID AT GIZA IS THE ONLY one of the Seven Wonders of the Ancient World to survive today. That it is still standing after 4,500 years is testament to the technological sophistication, ingenuity, and organizational skills of the ancient civilization that built it.

Humankind seems compelled to create tall buildings. Four thousand years ago the only shape for such a structure was a broad base tapering to the top—giving stability and a means of transporting building materials upward. Smooth-sided pyramids seem to have been a natural progression from another type of building, known as a ziggurat. Ziggurats were built by the ancient civilizations of Mesopotamia and Persia (Sumerians, Babylonians, and Assyrians) between 3000 and 500 B.C.E. A ziggurat was a sort of stepped temple-tower built in several levels, each smaller than the one below. Ziggurats were built with a core of unfired mud bricks and an outer covering of fired bricks, often glazed with elaborate colors. They had between two and seven tiers. Among the most famous are the beautifully preserved ziggurat at Ur in Iraq and the ziggurat of Marduk in Babylon.

Egypt's Pyramids

The first pyramid in Egypt was built at Saqqara starting in about 2630 B.C.E. to honor King Djoser (reigned 2630–2611 B.C.E.). It had a stepped structure not unlike that of a ziggurat, but it was made of stone rather than mud. Within 30 years the Egyptians had refined the design and were beginning to build smooth pyramids, such as the Red Pyramid at Dashur, generally taken as the first "true" pyramid. The core was still made of massive structural blocks, but they were cased in smaller blocks to smooth the outline into something more pleasing to the eye.

The pyramids were burial structures built to honor the kings (or pharaohs), who were regarded by their people as living gods. The site for a pyramid would have been chosen by the king himself. Detailed plans were drawn up by skilled draftsmen working on sheets of papyrus. Sometimes the pyramids were built over significant natural features such as rocky outcrops. This meant that fewer materials had to be imported, but it must have posed challenges for the architects, since uneven ground is much more difficult to survey and measure precisely, and precision was imperative.

All Egyptian pyramids are built along a precise north–south axis, but this was achieved thousands of years before the magnetic compass existed. Instead, the Egyptians used a surveying tool called a *bay* to determine the direction of true north from the stars. The perfection of symmetry in the finished pyramids shows that the Egyptians also had a firm grasp of geometry, allowing them to mark out the base of the pyramid as a perfect square. Anything less than perfect right angles would mean that the four sides would fail to form a neat point at the apex. The same perfection was required of the individual blocks, the shape of which was honed by skilled masons.

How Were the Pyramids Built?

For years the questions that have puzzled archaeologists most about the pyramids are: How did the builders transport the enormous blocks of stone used in construction and how did they raise them to such great heights? The blocks used to build the Great Pyramid at Giza weigh from 2.5 to 15 tons (2–14 tonnes) each, and those at the top have been lifted 480 feet (147 m) above ground level. The answer to the first question is that the stone was quarried as locally as possible. Anything brought from far away was carried by boat along the Nile River. To carry the stone to the top the builders used ramps—gentle gradients up which it would have been possible to drag the blocks on wooden sleds. Once at the top, it is assumed that wooden and bronze levers were used to maneuver the blocks into position.

While technology obviously played a key role in the construction of the pyramids, perhaps the real secret of the Egyptians' success was in organizing a vast workforce. Estimates of the numbers of people involved vary from 100,000 to just a few thousand. It seems unlikely that these people were slaves. There is archaeological evidence of thriving communities centered on the construction sites, providing accommodation and services for a huge workforce.

OPPOSITE: *The Giza pyramid complex includes the Great Pyramid (back), the Pyramid of Khafre (center), and the Pyramid of Menkaure, along with numerous temples, cemeteries, and the smaller "queens" pyramids (front).*

KEY DATES

2630 B.C.E.
First pyramid built in Egypt at Saqqara

2600 B.C.E.
First true pyramid built, the Red Pyramid at Dahshur

2550 B.C.E.
Great Pyramid at Giza completed

2250 B.C.E.
Last pyramid built for Pharaoh Pepi II at Saqqara

ASTRONOMY & MATH	BIOLOGY & MEDICINE	PHYSICAL SCIENCES

EUROPE

ca 2300 Work begins on the largest stone circle in Europe at Avebury in southern Britain. The precise alignment of its stones suggests that it may have had an astronomical purpose.

ca 1700 In central Europe, people trade widely in precious amber and metals such as copper and tin.

The large stones of Stonehenge were probably shaped before being dragged to the site on rollers. Using ropes, levers, and props, workers pulled each 28-ton (25-tonne) stone upright and rammed small stones around its base to make it stable.

THE AMERICAS

ca 2000 Copper is mined in the Great Lakes region of North America.

INSIDE STORY

Stonehenge

Stonehenge is a megalithic (meaning made of large stones) monument on the Salisbury Plain in southern England. It was built in three phases from about 3100 B.C.E. The upright stones were erected in about 2300 B.C.E. and joined along their tops by lintels to form a circle 100 feet (30 m) across. It must have taken hundreds of people many years to drag the stones to the site. The purpose of the monument is not known, but it may have been a temple linked to the worship of the sun and the moon.

ASIA & OCEANIA

2296 Chinese astronomers record a sighting of a comet.

ca 2000 Chinese emperors establish an early zoo, called the Park of Intelligence.

AFRICA & THE MIDDLE EAST

ca 2300 Astronomers in Babylon study comets and observe the constellations.

ca 2000 Mathematicians in Babylon introduce a positional number system (in which the value of a digit depends on its position in a number) using base 60.

ca 1800 Mathematicians in Mesopotamia discover what is now called Pythagorean theorem (concerning the lengths of the sides of a right-angled triangle).

1750 King Hammurabi of Babylon authorizes astronomers to compile catalogs of stars and planets.

ca 1650 Egyptian mathematicians learn how to solve simple equations, as indicated in the Rhind Papyrus, which was written at about this time.

ca 1600 Astrologers in Babylon recognize the zodiac, the path that the sun, moon, and planets (except Pluto) appear to take as they move across the sky.

ca 2400 The Egyptians domesticate cats. Some cats are regarded as sacred and made into mummies.

ca 2300 People in the Middle East keep geese. They collect and eat the eggs.

ca 2300 The Egyptians make wine from cultivated grapes. They add resin to improve the taste.

ca 2000 In Syria and Babylon medicine (based largely on astrology) becomes an important science. Recipes for ointments and poultices are recorded on clay tablets.

ca 1550 A papyrus known as the Ebers Papyrus—named for 19th-century German Egyptologist Georg Ebers (1837–98)—describes Egyptian medical practices and gives details of 700 drugs and other medications.

ca 2500 Tin ore is mined and smelted in Göltepe (in present-day Turkey). It becomes a source of the metal for alloying with copper to make bronze.

ca 2400 People in Mesopotamia use naturally occurring tar, or bitumen, to waterproof buildings and boats.

ENGINEERING & INVENTION	WORLD EVENTS
ca 1600 Bellows are used in metal and glassmaking around the Mediterranean.	**ca 2000** The Minoan culture on Crete builds palaces at Knossos.
ca 1500 Interior bathrooms with running water are built in the palace of Minos on the Mediterranean island of Crete.	**ca 1700** Trade routes across Europe carry luxury goods such as amber and raw materials such as copper and tin.
	ca 1600 The Mycenaean culture emerges on Crete.
ca 2500 People in the Arctic begin to chip delicate tools from flint.	**1600** The Poverty Point culture, named for a site in Louisiana, emerges in North America.
ca 1750 People living in the settlement of La Florida in the Rimac River Valley in Peru construct a long canal to irrigate their farmland.	
ca 1550 Farmers in Southeast Asia make plowshares with bronze.	**2333** A legendary ruler named Tangun forms the first Korean kingdom.
	1766 The Shang Dynasty begins in China.
	ca 2500 About 40,000 people live in the Indus Valley city of Harappa.
	ca 2000 Austronesians, sailing on outrigger boats, reach and settle on various islands in the South Pacific.
ca 2400 The parasol or umbrella is invented in Mesopotamia.	**ca 1950** Elamites seize Ur, ending the great period of Sumerian civilization.
ca 2300 The earliest known map is produced on a clay tablet in Mesopotamia. It probably shows a nobleman's estate.	**ca 1792** Under Hammurabi I (ca 1792—50), Babylon becomes the center of an empire that stretches into Assyria and Persia.
ca 2300 King Sargon I of Akkad produces maps of his kingdom in Mesopotamia to calculate land taxes.	**ca 1750** The earliest literary classic— *The Epic of Gilgamesh*—is written down in Mesopotamia.
ca 2100 The Sumerians construct a ziggurat (temple) near Ur using mud bricks.	**ca 1595** Hittites led by Mursilis I (r. ca 1556–26) sack Babylon and bring its power to an end.
ca 2000 Egyptian military engineers develop a portable battering ram.	**ca 1550** The people of the city of Mittani, in Mesopotamia, begin to build an empire.
ca 2000 Spoked wheels are used in Egypt and Mesopotamia, and bridles on horses.	**ca 1550** Ahmose (r. ca 1550–25) establishes the 18th Dynasty and begins Egypt's New Kingdom.
ca 1950 Farmers in Palestine make plows with iron plowshares.	**ca 1504** Amenhotep I (r. ca 1526–06) is the first pharaoh to be buried in the Valley of the Kings.
ca 1500 The Egyptians invent the shaduf—a bucket counterbalanced on a lever—for raising water from a well, a ditch, or a river.	

Egyptian king in a papyrus boat

THE FIRST BOATS

The dugout canoe was the first purpose-built boat. It was made from a hollowed-out log. The oldest-known dugout boat was found in the Netherlands and dates from 6300 B.C.E. Later canoes were made by stretching leather or bark over a wooden frame. Oars provided propulsion. The next development was the sail, invented by the Egyptians in about 3500 B.C.E.

At first Egyptian boats were made from woven papyrus reeds, but they later used wooden planks bound together with strips of leather or papyrus. The first sailboats were square-rigged, with a square sail set at more or less right angles to the direction of travel, which was with the wind. The boats were steered using oars. They were used for many centuries. Later Egyptian vessels abandoned sails and reverted to banks of oars for propulsion. By about 700 B.C.E., the Phoenicians were using biremes, which had two banks of oars; later they built triremes with three banks of oars.

In the first century C.E., the Chinese invented the rudder, a pivoted vertical plank that steers the boat. Another breakthrough was the triangular lateen sail, invented in about the third century C.E. by the Arabs. A lateen sail can be swung through an angle so that the wind does not have to come from behind for the ship to make progress.

Mediterranean vessels also used lateen sails in combination with square sails on the masts. The descendants of these craft were used by Spanish and Portuguese explorers on their voyages of discovery.

MAKING USE OF METALS

THE CLASSICAL POET HESIOD DIVIDED GREEK history into five ages. The first was a perfect "Golden Age." There followed Silver and Bronze Ages, then a Heroic Age, before the Iron Age, in which Hesiod himself lived. With each passing age, the lives of humans become harder and more miserable. Hesiod's choice of different metals to identify four of the five ages reflected the changing use of metals in ancient society.

The importance of gold and silver is well attested by finds buried in ancient graves. For example, at the prehistoric city of Mycenae in Greece, archaeologists found treasures including the gold Cup of Nestor, crafted sometime between 1600 and 1500 B.C.E., and a star-tling death mask said to portray the Greek warrior king Agamemnon (although few historians take the claim seriously).

The Egyptians also produced gold ornaments. The mask of Tutankhamun, the boy king who reigned from 1333 to 1323 B.C.E., is made from gold inlaid with lapis lazuli. It was found in his tomb. Gold and silver vessels, masks, ceremonial weapons, and ornaments have been found in graves throughout the eastern Mediterranean region and Near East. Many are of a very high standard. By about 1600 B.C.E., Mycenaean metalworkers were producing daggers with bronze blades inlaid with gold, electrum (an alloy of silver and gold), silver, and niello (a black substance formed when sulfur is mixed with lead, silver, or cop-

This gold funeral mask was unearthed at Mycenae, Greece, in 1876 by German archaelogist Heinrich Schliemann (1882–90). It was made about 1500 B.C.E. and is known as the Mask of Agamemnon, although it predates the believed time of the Trojan War.

KEY DATES

ca 5000 B.C.E.
Egyptian weapons and tools made of copper

ca 3200 B.C.E.
Bronze produced in the Middle East

ca 2000 B.C.E.
Iron produced in southern India

ca 1600 B.C.E.
Mycenaean daggers with bronze, gold, and silver

ca 200 B.C.E.
Early steel production

per). Copper, silver, and gold occur naturally as nuggets. These can be pried from rocks or found lying on the surface or in the sand and gravel of riverbeds. Small nuggets of gold can be merged together by hammering; but on its own or alloyed with silver to make electrum, gold is too soft for making tools or weapons. Gold and silver were therefore purely decorative.

Copper was different. Hammering does not fuse copper nuggets. In order to make useful articles from copper, the lumps of metal must be melted and then cast in molds. Hammering then hardens the copper, allowing it to be used to make blades with a sharp edge. Weapons and tools were being made from copper in Egypt by 5000 B.C.E., and copper axes were being made and used in the Balkans before 3000 B.C.E. It was around then that people discovered, probably by accident, that they produced much more copper if they melted it in the presence of a particular kind of bright blue stone heated to red heat. They had begun to extract a metal from its ore, in this case azurite.

Bronze: The First Alloy

Many ore minerals contain more than one metal, and some time after 4000 B.C.E., people began to mix a little tin into the copper. At first it may have happened accidentally when metalworkers used stannite, a rare mineral that contains copper, tin, and iron. An alloy of copper and tin is called bronze. It is much harder than copper, and bronze implements retain a sharp edge much longer than those made of copper. Bronze was first made in what is now southern Iraq between 3200 and 2500 B.C.E. Its use spread throughout the Middle East and Europe and probably China. As it did, the Copper Age gave way to the Bronze Age.

Iron was also available. Certain meteorites are made mainly of iron, and melting them releases the metal. But meteorites are rare, and it is more difficult to obtain iron from hematite, its most widespread ore. Copper melts at 1,982.1°F (1,083.4°C), but iron only melts at 2,795°F (1,535°C)—a temperature that is much harder to achieve. Smelting hematite produces a spongy mass mixed with waste products, called slag. Changing this into workable iron requires repeated melting and hammering. Nevertheless, iron was being produced in southern India by about 2000 B.C.E. An iron dagger blade dating from about 2200 B.C.E. was found at Alaca Hüyük in Anatolia (present-day Turkey), although it was a precious and almost certainly ceremonial object. Iron was becoming important to the Hittites by 1400 B.C.E., and by 1000 B.C.E. its use had spread across Europe.

Iron is soft, and an iron blade has to be straightened after each blow struck with it, so iron could not compete against bronze. Then smiths discovered that iron becomes much stronger if it is kept for a long time at bright-red heat in a charcoal fire. By absorbing carbon from the charcoal, iron is converted into steel, and steel can be made stronger still if it is plunged into water while red hot. Steel was first made in India in about the third century B.C.E. and was exported widely. Stories about swords with special powers probably refer to steel blades that were tougher and sharper even than bronze.

Chinese craftsmen made complex shapes, such as bowls and bells, by casting them in molten bronze. The mold itself was made from fireclay in several pieces, which were assembled around a central core to make the mold and then carefully taken apart again after the casting process. In this way, the mold could be used again and again to produce a series of identical objects.

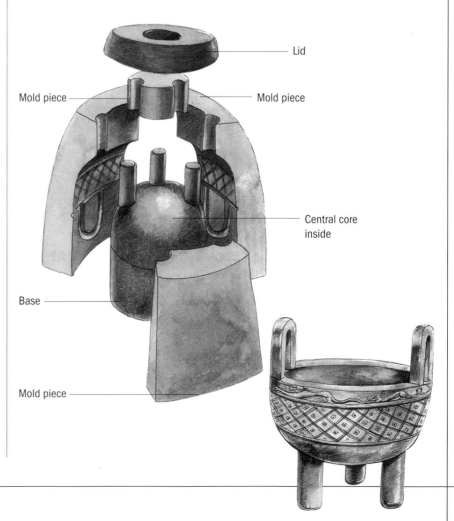

Lid

Mold piece

Mold piece

Central core inside

Base

Mold piece

ASTRONOMY & MATH	BIOLOGY & MEDICINE	PHYSICAL SCIENCES

EUROPE

When tillage begins, other arts follow. The farmers, therefore, are the founders of human civilization.

DANIEL WEBSTER

1000 Etruscan craftsmen in northern Italy make false teeth from gold, probably more for show than for function.

950 Farmers in northern and central Europe cultivate oats, a cereal crop better suited than wheat to the wetter, cooler climate of the region. It was soon grown in northern Britain and is still associated with Scotland, where people make it into porridge.

ca 1500 Copper from the Alps is imported to England and used to make jewelry.

ca 1050 Dorian invaders from Anatolia introduce ironworking into Greece.

ca 900 The Etruscans of central Italy prosper thanks to their rich supplies of copper and tin.

THE AMERICAS

1200 The Olmec develop a lunar calendar.

1400 South American farmers grow cassava (manioc).

1200 Offshore fisherman in Peru use rafts and boats (*cabalitos*) made from reeds.

ASIA & OCEANIA

1361 Chinese astronomers record the sighting of a solar eclipse.

1360 Chinese mathematicians introduce a nonpositional number system (with no zero). It was multiplicative (e.g., 300 was written as 3 together with the symbol for 100) and additive (1,975 was written as 1,000 + 900 + 70 + 5).

1000 The Hindu calendar of 360 days (12 lunar months of 27 or 28 days) is introduced in India.

1500 Chinese people make beer. Also people in various parts of Asia produce alcohol (for drinking) by distilling wine.

1450 People in Manchuria, China, cultivate soybeans. They eat the beans fresh or dry them and store them for use in the winter. They also let them germinate and eat the bean sprouts or allow them to ferment and make them into soy.

1350 Chinese farmers are growing more than one crop in the same year on the same land.

1000 People in Siberia in northern Russia keep herds of domestic reindeer.

The Chinese invented the kite about 1000 B.C.E., arguably the first heavier-than-air flying object made by humans.

AFRICA & THE MIDDLE EAST

1200 Astronomers in Babylon construct an instrument for determining when a star is due south of their observatory.

975 The Hebrews introduce the Gezer lunar calendar (with 12 months of 27 or 28 days).

1500 In Egypt, the first professional millers begin grinding wheat.

1450 Mesopotamian farmers use a single-tube seed drill, in which seeds trickle down a tube into a groove plowed in the soil.

1350 An Egyptian text describes the symptoms of leprosy.

1000 Farmers in Egypt and Mesopotamia fertilize their crops using animal dung.

900 Farmers in Mesopotamia (present-day Iraq) use irrigation systems to improve the yields of their crops.

1500 Egyptian engineers in Syria dam the Orontes River Valley to create a 19-square-mile (50-sq-km) lake.

1350 Egyptian workmen weld iron at about the same time as the Hittites begin working with iron. Ironworking spreads to India by 1200 B.C.E. and Europe by 1000 B.C.E.

1200 The Egyptians join the Nile River to the Red Sea with a canal at Lake Timsah.

ENGINEERING & INVENTION	WORLD EVENTS
1500 People in the Aegean, around Greece, invent the beam press, which uses a weighted lever to squeeze juice from grapes for wine-making or oil from olives.	**ca 1400** People begin to cremate rather than bury their dead.
ca 1400 The last stage of construction of Stonehenge is finished in southern England.	**ca 1200** Proto-Celtic people of Indo-European origin migrate to Central Europe.
1150 Craftsmen in Cyprus and Mycenae (in Greece) decorate objects with vitreous enamel (colored glass).	**ca 1100** Indo-Europeans settle in Italy.
	ca 900 Etruscan culture flourishes.
	ca 850 Greek epic poet Homer writes the Iliad and the Odyssey.
1200 From this time Olmec sculptors in Mesoamerica carve human–animal figurines and giant human heads at sites at La Venta and San Lorenzo near the Gulf coast. Many are ritually destroyed in 900 B.C.E.	**ca 1500** The Olmec culture develops in Central America.
	ca 1100 Andean society flourishes in South America.
	ca 1000 Aleuts and Inuits have now adapted to life in their Arctic environment.
1150 Chinese workmen cast bells in bronze.	**ca 1500** The Jomon period peaks in Japan.
1100 Chinese craftsmen introduce spinning to produce yarn from wool and cotton.	**1300** The Shang rulers of China make Anyang their capital.
1000 Chinese scribes use brushes and black ink made from soot and gum to write on bamboo strips or paper made from tree bark.	**ca 1000** Aryans in India settle between the Himalayas and the Ganges River.
900 Chinese people use cast metal coins in the shape of shovels or knives.	**ca 1000** The Hindu caste system organizes people into four varnas: Brahmins (priests), Kshatriyas (warriors and aristocrats), Vaishyas (farmers, craftsman, and merchants), and Shudras (peasants).
850 The Chinese use natural gas for lighting, conveying it along bamboo "pipes." The gas is probably methane from underground deposits of petroleum.	
1450 The Egyptians make a water clock that measures time by the rate at which water flows out of a hole in a vessel.	
1000 The Phoenicians of the Mediterranean develop a 22-letter alphabet.	
950 The Phoenicians make Tyrian purple dye from the *Murex* sea mollusk. It is so expensive that only kings and emperors have clothes dyed with it.	
850 Smyrna (now Izmir, Turkey) becomes the site of the first known arch bridge.	

EARLY CALENDARS

People have always needed to count the passage of time, partly to know when to sow and harvest crops. The Lebombo bone from Swaziland was marked with 29 notches about 35,000 years ago to record the passage of the lunar month.

All early calendars were based on the lunar cycle. The Egyptians developed a lunar calendar in about 4236 B.C.E. However, it could not predict the most important event in the Egyptian year—the annual flooding of the Nile. They later devised a calendar based on a solar year that could predict the flooding.

In about 1800 B.C.E., the Sumerians of modern-day Iraq produced a lunar calendar with a year that had 12 months alternating between 29 and 30 days. They inserted an extra month so that the calendar coincided with the seasons. The Babylonian and Assyrian empires later adopted the Sumerian calendar. The ancient Chinese, the Hindus in India, and the Hebrews developed their own lunar calendars too.

The zodiac—and the practice of casting horoscopes—originated in ancient Babylon.

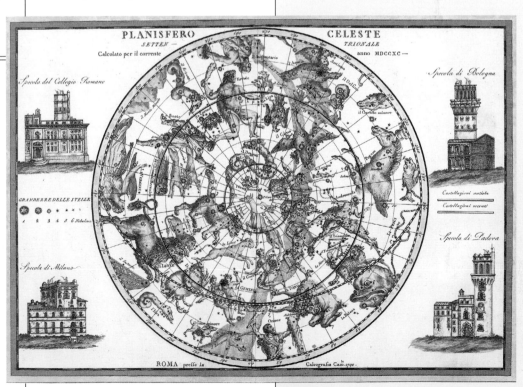

CHAPTER 2

CLASSICAL AND EARLY MEDIEVAL

THE FIRST PEOPLE WE IDENTIFY WITH SCIENCE AND WHOSE NAMES WE know for certain were Greek philosophers who lived in the fourth century B.C.E., such as Plato (ca 428–ca 348) and Aristotle (384–22). Euclid (fl. 300), their contemporary, and Archimedes (ca 287–12), who flourished about a century later, have become famous as early mathematicians, although Archimedes was also an accomplished engineer. In the second century C.E. Greek astronomer Ptolemy (90–168) established geography as a major scientific discipline. The word *philosopher* means "lover of wisdom," and the Greek philosophers attracted numbers of students to whom they passed on their wisdom. Their schools, or academies, were the first universities, where they also established libraries in which recorded knowledge could be stored and referred to.

The Greeks were also practical people, and they applied scientific principles to architecture, constructing great temples and other buildings in their homeland and the regions they settled, such as the Mediterranean island of Sicily. This tradition was continued by the Romans who became the Mediterranean region's next dominant power. The Romans built great aqueducts for water supply and a system of stone roads that extended for a total of 50,000 miles (80,000 km) across a vast empire that at its height

The first major source of mechanical power came from water. Huge wooden waterwheels named norias *were used throughout the Arab world to lift water from rivers to irrigate fields. Up to 40 feet (12 m) across, they were turned by the current of the river itself, making them the first machines that did not need to be driven by animal or human power.*

Throughout the classical world, astronomers studied and recorded the movements of the heavens in order to create accurate calendars. They could predict regular events such as equinoxes and eclipses. They often saw unexpected astronomical events, such as the appearance of a comet, as supernatural omens of events that might occur on Earth.

in the first century C.E. stretched from Scotland in the north to Syria in the south, and from Iberia in the west to the borders of modern Russia in the east. Like the Greeks, Roman engineers also constructed practical machines as diverse as clocks, cranes, catapults, and waterwheels.

At the same time, and independently of the Mediterranean countries, science and technology developed among civilizations elsewhere in the world. In Mesoamerica people built pyramids that rivaled those of the ancient Egyptians; in northern India complex canal systems served huge cities; and in China advances in astronomy and math were matched by technical developments such as improved plows and ships and the invention of paper and printing. The last, in particular, would have a profound impact on the history of science. From now on, knowledge could not just be passed on from one generation to the next; it could also be multiplied and widely shared.

The technique of glassblowing—heating glass until it is soft and then blowing in air to enlarge its shape—was discovered by craftsmen in Syria in about 30 C.E. and soon adopted by the Romans, who used it to make bottles and other glass objects.

THE WORLD AT A GLANCE

CONCISE HISTORY OF SCIENCE AND INVENTION

	849 B.C.E.	500 B.C.E.	250 B.C.E.	0 C.E.	150 C.E.	
EUROPE	**ca 600** Greeks make the first solder. **ca 560** Xenophanes of Colophon deduces that land rises when he find fossils of seashells on mountaintops. **ca 550** Pythagoras observes mathematical relationships between the length of vibrating strings and the notes they produce. **ca 535** Greek physician Alcmaeon studies anatomy by dissecting animals. **ca 515** The sundial is introduced in Greece for telling time.	**424** The Greeks record the use of an early flamethrower in a war between Sparta and Athens. **ca 400** Hippocrates of Kos describes human anatomy. **387** Plato opens his Academy in Athens. **ca 350** Metalworkers in Greece and Italy use coal as a fuel. **330** Aristotle suggests that the sun and planets orbit the Earth. **300** Greek mathematician Euclid writes a book on geometry.	**ca 235** Eratosthenes calculates the circumference of Earth. **200** Greek astronomers in Alexandria invent the astrolabe. **ca 110** The Romans begin using nailed horseshoes. **ca 100** Roman builders use a type of concrete that sets underwater. **ca 80** Overshot waterwheels, more efficient than undershot wheels, are introduced in Mediterranean countries. **46** Julius Caesar introduces the Julian calendar.	**50** Farmers use watermills to grind grain in Italy. **77** Pliny the Elder summarizes natural history as known to the Romans. **80** The Colosseum—a four-story amphitheater—is built in Rome. **100** Roman physician Soranus writes a book on pregnancy and disorders that affect women. **128** The domed Pantheon is built in Rome. **150** Ptolemy writes the *Almagest*, a standard guide to astronomy for over a thousand years.	**226** The Romans build a 14-mile (22-km) aqueduct to carry water into Rome. **ca 250** Parchment replaces papyrus as the standard writing material around the Mediterranean. **250** Greek mathematician Diophantus invents algebra.	
THE AMERICAS	**ca 600** The Maya use cacao to make a chocolate drink.	**ca 400** Mayan mathematicians develop a number system, using base 20, that includes a symbol for zero. **ca 300** The Maya build pyramids in Mexico.	**ca 200** The Nazca Lines are drawn in the desert in southern Peru. **ca 200** South American furnaces produce alloys of gold and silver.	**ca 0** The Anasazi culture begins in the American Southwest.	**ca 200** The Moche civilization in Peru build huge terraced tombs from adobe mud bricks.	
ASIA & OCEANIA	**ca 733** Chinese astronomers record a solar eclipse.	**ca 400** The Chinese use a counting board with bamboo rods to do calculations and keep records.	**240** Chinese astronomers record an appearance of what is now called Halley's comet. **214** The main section of the Great Wall of China is completed. **ca 100** Chinese astronomers begin to use negative numbers. **ca 55** The Hindu Ayurveda appears; the medical treatise is still in use. **28** Chinese astronomers begin to keep a record of the appearance of sunspots.	**1** Chinese mathematician Liu Hsin introduces decimal fractions. **8** Horizontal waterwheels are recorded in China. **ca 100** The wheelbarrow is invented in China. **105** Chinese court official Ts'ai Lun invents a way to make paper. **105** The Chinese use powdered chrysanthemum flowers to kill insects. **132** In China, Zhang Hen invents the first seismograph.	**263** Mathematician Liu Hui correctly calculates the value of pi to five decimal places. **ca 265** Huang Fu-Mi writes a major treatise on acupuncture. **271** The compass is first used in China.	
AFRICA & THE MIDDLE EAST	**ca 800** Egyptians use incubators to hatch eggs. **763** Babylonian astronomers observe an eclipse of the sun. **700** Phoenicians develop biremes, warships with two rows of oars. **691** Assyrians build an aqueduct to carry water to their capital Nineveh.	**283** At Alexandria, in Egypt, Greeks build the 380-foot (115-m) Pharos lighthouse, one of the Seven Wonders of the Ancient World.	**ca 30** Ironworking reaches parts of sub-Saharan Africa. **ca 30** Craftsmen in Syria discover the technique of glassblowing, which soon spreads through the Roman empire. **ca 10** King Herod the Great builds a huge harbor of stone blocks at Caesarea in Palestine.	**100** Nichmachus of Gerasa writes *Introduction to Arithmetic*.	**190** Ironworking spreads as far south as the Limpopo Valley. **269** The library at Alexandria is partly destroyed by fire.	

300 C.E.	500	700	800	900–1000
ca 300 Roman emperor Diocletian builds a palace using arches supported by freestanding columns.	**ca 500** Silk production begins in Byzantium using silkworms smuggled from China.	**ca 700** Europeans adopt the use of stirrups for riding horses.	**ca 800** The use of the blast furnace to produce cast iron spreads through Europe.	**975** Scholar Gerbert of Aurillac builds a hydraulic organ.
ca 300 The Romans begin burning coal as fuel.	**520** Boethius translates the works of Aristotle into Latin.	**750** Arab scholars begin to settle in Spain, bringing knowledge from the Islamic world.	**834** The use of a hand crank to turn a wheel is pictured in an illustrated manuscript.	**982** Viking longships cross the North Atlantic Ocean and reach Greenland.
350 A water-powered sawmill is built in France to cut marble.	**532** The church of Hagia Sophia is designed.	**789** Charlemagne, the Holy Roman emperor, introduces standard weights and measures.	**860** Viking seafarers venture as far west as Iceland.	
365 Mechanical cranks are used to set broken bones in Greece.	**537** Roman engineer Belisarius builds a floating watermill.			
410 Hypatia of Alexandria invents the hydrometer.	**ca 680** Dutch farmers begin building dikes to protect land from the sea.			
	685 The *Ravenna Cosmography* lists all countries, rivers, and towns in Europe.			
ca 400 The wheel is introduced in Mesoamerica, but only for children's toys—the region has no beasts of burden for pulling wheeled vehicles.	**ca 500** Potters in Costa Rica and Panama produce vividly colored ceramics.	**ca 720** Mayan builders at Tikal construct Pyramid IV, one of the tallest buildings in the Americas.	**ca 800** Metalworking techniques from South America are adopted by peoples in Central America.	**ca 900** The Mayan civilization collapses in the lowlands of the Yucatán.
			ca 800 The Hohokam of Arizona build canals to irrigate their fields.	
304 The Chinese use ants to control other pest insects.	**534** Chinese math is adopted in Japan.	**725** Chinese engineers construct a water clock with an escapement mechanism.	**812** Bank drafts are introduced in China—the first form of paper money.	**960** Chinese authorities begin to print paper money as a means of exchange.
310 Chinese astronomers produce a comprehensive star map.	**535** Chinese engineers invent a device for sifting flour.		**ca 855** A Chinese writer describes an early form of gunpowder, or "fire drug."	**976** The Chinese invent a chain-drive mechanism for the astronomical clock.
ca 400 The Chinese invent the umbrella.	**577** Chinese women invent matches.		**868** The earliest book is printed in China.	
405 Chinese craftsmen beat wrought iron and cast iron together to make steel.	**610** In India, a number system is introduced using base ten.		**876** Mathematicians in India introduce a symbol for zero.	
415 Indians use iron chains to build suspension bridges.	**628** *Brahmasphuta Siddhanta* is written by Indian astronomer Brahmagupta.			
497 Indian Aryabhata proposes that the Earth rotates on its axis.				
ca 350 The world's first street lighting is introduced at Antioch in modern-day Turkey.	**622** First year of the Muslim calendar, commemorating the flight of Mohammad to Medina.	**760** The use of Arabic numerals reaches Baghdad.	**ca 820** The House of Wisdom (Bayt al-Hikma) is founded in Baghdad to encourage scholarly research.	**ca 900** Arab scientists distill wine to make alcohol, mainly for use in medicine.
ca 400 Scholars at Alexandria, Egypt, use the Arabic term *al-kimiya* to describe a change of state in matter; it is the root of the English word *alchemy*.	**674** Syrian-born Callinicus invents Greek fire, a burning substance used as a weapon.	**780** Arabs in Baghdad begin making paper.	**ca 820** An Arab writer describes an astrolabe.	**ca 900** Persian physicians use plaster of Paris to set broken bones.
	685 The Dome of the Rock is begun in Jerusalem.		**850** An Arab physician writes a treatise about the eye, including eye disorders and treatments.	**972** A university is founded in Cairo.

ASTRONOMY & MATH	BIOLOGY & MEDICINE	PHYSICAL SCIENCES

EUROPE

550 Greek mathematician and philosopher Pythagoras (ca 580–ca 500) determines the relationship between the length of a vibrating string and the pitch of the note it produces.

434 Ionian philosopher Anaxagoras (ca 500–ca 428) postulates that the sun is a ball of hot rock.

430 Greek mathematician and philosopher Zeno of Elea (ca 490–ca 430) expresses four mathematical paradoxes.

387 In Athens Greek philosopher Plato (ca 428–ca 348) opens an academy for the pursuit of philosophical and scientific teaching and research.

330 Greek scientist and philosopher Aristotle (384–322) proposes that the Earth is at the center of the universe and that the sun, moon, planets, and stars orbit around it.

300 Greek mathematician Euclid (fl. 300) writes *Elements*, a geometry book.

560 Greek poet Xenophanes of Colophon (fl. sixth century) accounts for the presence of fossil seashells on mountaintops by deducing that the land surface must have risen from below sea level in the past.

535 Greek physician and philosopher Alcmaeon (fl. sixth century) uses dissection to study the anatomy of animals.

ca 400 Greek physician Hippocrates of Kos, traditionally thought to be the originator of the doctor's Hippocratic Oath, (ca 460–ca 377) describes human anatomy and various diseases.

350 Greek scientist and philosopher Aristotle draws up a classification scheme for animals and plants.

340 Greek physician Praxagoras of Kos (fl. fourth century) distinguishes between arteries and veins.

600 Greek artist and metalworker Glaucus of Chios (fl. fifth century) makes an alloy that melts easily and uses it to solder metals.

350 According to Greek philosopher Theophrastus of Eresus (ca 372–ca 287) metalworkers in Greece and Italy begin using coal as a fuel.

INSIDE STORY

Ancient Paradox

The classic version of Zeno's racecourse paradox involves a race between the Greek hero Achilles and a tortoise. Achilles can run ten times as fast as the tortoise so he gives the animal a 33-foot (10-m) head start. By the time Achilles reaches the 33-foot (10-m) mark, the tortoise has shuffled along to 36 feet (11 m). Then when Achilles reaches 36 feet (11 m), the tortoise is already at 36.5 feet (11.1 m). And so on, halving the remaining distance to be covered an infinite number of times. It seems to demonstrate that Achilles will never catch up with the tortoise.

THE AMERICAS

400 Mayan mathematicians use a place-value number system, to base 20, that includes a symbol for zero.

600 Mayan people of Central America make a chocolate drink using pods of the cacao plant.

ASIA & OCEANIA

400 Chinese people use a counting board with bamboo rods for calculations and record keeping.

One of the Seven Wonders of the Ancient World, the Pharos lighthouse at Alexandria was 380 feet (115 m) tall. This is a 19th-century artist's impression of the lighthouse.

AFRICA & THE MIDDLE EAST

763 Babylonian astronomers observe and record an eclipse of the sun. About 30 years later Chinese astronomers do the same.

800 Egyptians use artificially heated incubators to hatch eggs.

ENGINEERING & INVENTION	WORLD EVENTS
530 Greek engineer Eupalinus of Megara (fl. sixth century) builds a 3,600-foot (1,100-m) tunnel through a mountain on Samos to carry water across the island.	**800** The Celts spread westward into central Europe.
515 Ionian philosopher Anaximander of Miletus (ca 611–ca 547) introduces the sundial to Greece for telling time.	**800** The Greeks establish independent city states, including Athens and Sparta.
424 In the war between Athens and Sparta (in Greece), the attackers of Delion use a flamethrower consisting of a tube containing burning charcoal, sulfur, and tar, mounted on a wheeled carriage and "powered" by bellows to blow the flames forward.	**776** The first Olympic Games are held at Olympia, Greece. **ca 700** The Etruscans flourish in northern Italy and trade widely. **490** Greek forces halt a Persian incursion at the Battle of Marathon.
312 Roman politician and general Appius Claudius Caecus (fl. fourth century) authorizes the building of the Aqua Appia aqueduct. He also commissions the Via Appia (Appian Way), the first of the great Roman roads.	**399** Greek philosopher Socrates is sentenced to death in Athens. **336** Alexander the Great (r. 336–323) becomes king of Macedon.
283 The Greeks build the 380-foot (115-m) Pharos lighthouse at Alexandria (Egypt), one of the Seven Wonders of the Ancient World.	**ca 300** Rome becomes the dominant power in modern-day Italy.
	ca 300 Zapotec society develops in the Oaxaca Valley in Mexico. **ca 300** The Maya construct monumental pyramids in modern-day Mexico.
	ca 563 Siddhartha Gautama (ca 583–ca 483) is born in the foothills of the Himalaya. He is later known as Buddha. **ca 450** Confucianism spreads in China.
700 Phoenician sailors use biremes (boats with two rows of oars) as warships. **691** Assyrian King Sennacherib (r. 705–681) builds an aqueduct to carry water 50 miles (80 km) from a tributary of the Greater Zab River to supply his capital city Nineveh (present-day Mosul) with water. **513** Persian King Darius (r. ca 549–ca 486) builds a 2,000-foot (600-m) pontoon bridge to carry his invading army across the Bosporus (near present-day Istanbul).	**750** The Phoenician city of Carthage flourishes in North Africa. **ca 300** Ptolemaic rule begins in Egypt and lasts nearly 300 years.

The chief forms of beauty are order and symmetry and definiteness, which the mathematical sciences demonstrate in a special degree.

ARISTOTLE, *METAPHYSICS*

GREEK TEMPLES

In ancient Greece people believed in many gods. Each god possessed particular attributes, and worshippers approached whichever gods they thought most likely to answer their particular prayers.

When the Greeks began to represent their gods with large statues, the statues had to be protected from the weather. The buildings erected to house them were called *naoi*, literally "dwellings." At first these temples were made from wood and mud brick; but as the temples decayed, they were rebuilt with stone and brick. The buildings were rectangular and built on an east–west axis with an entrance porch at one end covered with a roof supported by columns. Later temples had a porch at either end and were surrounded by columns. The first-known example of a temple surrounded by columns is the Temple of Hera (Heraion) at Samos, built in 750 B.C.E.

The Parthenon, built of white marble on the hill of the Acropolis at Athens, is the largest and most famous of all Greek temples. It was built under the supervision of the Greek sculptor Phidias. Work began in 447 B.C.E., and the building was completed in 438 B.C.E., although the exterior decoration was not finished until 432 B.C.E. The Parthenon was dedicated to Athena Parthenos (Athena the Virgin).

The Parthenon was a temple dedicated to Athena. In ancient times, a huge gold and ivory statue of the goddess dominated the interior.

MESOAMERICAN PYRAMIDS

DESPITE THEIR APPARENT SIMILARITIES THE pyramids of Egypt and those in central America are not related. The Mesoamerican pyramids were constructed thousands of years later. Rather than serving as private tombs for rulers, like the Egyptian structures, they were used mainly as public temples for ritual and celebration.

In 1922 archaeologists in the Valley of Mexico found the ruins of Cuicuilco, a city buried by volcanic eruption in about 30 C.E. They discovered the lower part of a circular pyramid, built in four tiers with a core made from clay and rubble faced with blocks of volcanic rock. Ramps on opposite sides of the pyramid led to the temple that once stood on the top. Circular temples were usually dedicated to the Feathered Serpent god, known to many Mesoamerican peoples as Kukulkan and to the Aztec as Quetzalcóatl. He may have been the most important god in Cuicuilco.

A Tradition of Pyramids

Pyramid building had become widespread throughout Mesoamerica long before the Cuicuilco pyramid was built. The earliest pyramid known was built by the Olmec people near La Venta in the Mexican state of Tabasco some time around 900 B.C.E. The Olmec was the most prominent civilization of Mesoamerican culture until about 600 C.E. Olmec cities grew around a central mound where religious ceremonies were conducted. Pyramids replaced the mounds from about 900 B.C.E. There is no evidence of a ramp or stairway used to reach the top of the La Venta pyramid, so historians suspect it was more like a sculpture than a building. It may have represented the mountain that the Olmec believed reached to heaven and was the source of the corn on which agriculture depended.

After the Olmec, the Maya also built pyramids, usually from stone blocks bonded with lime mortar and with steep stairways that only priests were permitted to climb. Tikal, in Guatemala, is the largest and possibly oldest Mayan city. Occupied between

about 800 B.C.E. and 900 C.E., at one time it was home to about 100,000 people. The center contained a number of small pyramids and six very large pyramids, each with a temple at the top. Archaeologists have numbered the pyramids from I to VI in the order they were built. Pyramid I, topped by the Temple of the Jaguar, was built in 695 C.E. and Pyramid VI was built in 766 C.E. The tallest structure, Pyramid IV, is approximately 230 feet (70 m) high and is topped by the Temple of the Two-Headed Serpent. A chamber in the temple was designed to amplify the voice of the priest standing in it, so the people in the square below could hear him.

Although prominent people were sometimes buried in them, Mesoamerican pyramids were not primarily tombs. They represented the three levels of

KEY DATES

ca 900 B.C.E.
Olmec pyramid built at La Venta, Tabasco

ca 30 C.E.
Eruption of Xitle buries Cuicuilco

ca 500 C.E.
Teotihuacán at its peak

695 C.E.
Pyramid I built at Tikal

720 C.E.
Pyramid IV, one of the tallest buildings in Mesoamerica, built at Tikal

750 C.E.
Teotihuacán destroyed by fire

766 C.E.
Pyramid VI built at Tikal

the universe: the subterranean, terrestrial, and celestial. The subterranean level is represented by buried shrines beneath some pyramids.

A New Center

The people who fled from Cuicuilco in about 30 C.E. settled in Teotihuacán, about 30 miles (50 km) northeast of modern Mexico City. The new arrivals stimulated rapid urban expansion. At its peak in about 500 C.E. Teotihuacán covered some 8 square miles (21 sq. km), and its population of up to 200,000 made it one of the world's largest cities. Teotihuacán was destroyed by fire in about 750 C.E. When the Aztec discovered the ruins centuries later, they believed the city had been built by supernatural beings. They named it Teotihuacán, meaning "Place of the Gods."

The ceremonial Street of the Dead runs through the center of the city. The Pyramid of the Moon sits at its northern end. The pyramid is 140 feet (43 m) tall and built with a core of rubble covered by a larger pyramid and with a third pyramid covering that. In 1998 archaeologists found burial pits with many rich burial goods deep inside the Pyramid of the Moon.

The Temple of the Feathered Serpent stands on top of another pyramid at the southern end of the street. It contained the remains of 18 men, apparently soldiers who had been ritually sacrificed.

The Pyramid of the Sun, standing on the eastern side of the street, is the biggest of all the pyramids, rising to 216 feet (66 m) and measuring about 720 by 760 feet (220 by 232 m) at its base. A cave beneath the pyramid was probably a shrine.

Pyramid I towers above the plaza at the Mayan city of Tikal, in present-day Guatemala. It has nine levels rising to the Temple of the Jaguar on top: Nine was a sacred number for the Maya.

ASTRONOMY & MATH	BIOLOGY & MEDICINE	PHYSICAL SCIENCES

EUROPE

235 Greek mathematician Eratosthenes of Cyrene (ca 276–ca 194) calculates the circumference of the Earth. Ten years later he devises the sieve of Eratosthenes as a method of finding prime numbers (numbers that can be divided only by 1 and themselves).

230 Greek mathematician Apollonius of Perga (ca 262–ca 190) writes his treatise *Conics*, dealing with conic sections (i.e., the circle, ellipse, parabola, etc.).

200 Astronomers of the Alexandrian school, founded by pharaoh Ptolemy I (r. 323–283), develop astronomical instruments, including the astrolabe.

150 Greek astronomer Hipparchus of Nicaea (ca 180–125) calculates the distance from the Earth to the moon and discovers the precession of the equinoxes.

100 Roman entrepreneur Gaius Sergius Orata develops a system for heating seawater in order to rear oysters to sell to wealthy people in Rome.

75 Greek physician Asclepiades of Bithynia (ca 120–ca 30) teaches that disease comes from discord in the corpuscles of the body.

There are hundreds of designs, or geoglyphs, of figures in the Nazca Desert, including this hummingbird. The largest geoglyphs are more than 650 feet (200 m) across.

THE AMERICAS

200 At about this time the Nazca people in southern Peru begin "drawing" huge outlines of animals and plants on the surface of the Pampa Colorada desert. Later they add lines and geometric shapes. The purpose of the figures is unknown but they are thought to have astronomical or religious significance.

ASIA & OCEANIA

240 Chinese astronomers make the first records of what becomes known as Halley's comet.

165 Chinese naked-eye astronomers record the existence of sunspots.

100 Chinese mathematicians begin to use negative numbers.

52 Chinese astronomer Ken Shou-Ch'ang makes a form of armillary ring (a metal ring representing the equator, used to observe the stars).

125 Chinese traveler Chang Ch'ien (ca 172–ca 114) introduces wine grapes into China from the West.

55 Hindu medical system the Ayurveda is developed at about this time and becomes the basis of medical teaching in India for centuries.

In Chinese the Great Wall of China is known as Wan-li Ch'ang-ch'eng, which means "10,000-li-long wall." One li equals about 1640 foot (500 m).

AFRICA & THE MIDDLE EAST

INSIDE STORY

Great Wall of China

One of the greatest surviving examples of ancient building construction, the main section of the Great Wall of China runs for 1,400 miles (2,250 km) along the crests of mountains and hills from the Shan-hai Pass (on the Gulf of Chihli) in the east to the Chia-yu Pass (in modern Gansu Province) in the west. Secondary branches add about another 2,600 miles (4,180 km) to the structure, which ranges in height from 20 to 50 feet (6–15 m). It had its origins in the seventh century B.C.E., and the main section was completed in 214 by emperor Shi Huang-di as a defense against northern invaders. It was added to and repaired many times, culminating in major restoration by the Ming emperors (1368–1644).

ENGINEERING & INVENTION	WORLD EVENTS
250 Greek scientist and mathematician Archimedes (ca 287–212) invents the screw pump (a coarse screw rotated inside a sloping tube) for raising water for irrigation.	**218** Rome battles Carthage in the Second Punic War (ca 218–201).
150 Greeks and Romans use a screw press for crushing olives to make olive oil.	**216** Hannibal (247–183) defeats the Romans at the Battle of Cannae.
110 Romans begin to use nailed horseshoes.	**214** Rome goes to war against the Macedonians in the First Macedonian War (214–205). After winning the war, Rome dominates the western Mediterranean.
100 Roman builders use concrete made from crushed stones and pozzolana (volcanic ash) cement, which sets underwater.	**197** Hispania (Spain) becomes a province of the Roman Empire.
80 Vertical undershot waterwheels, used for grinding wheat, are introduced in eastern Mediterranean countries.	**149** The Third Punic War (149–146) begins.
	102 Uprisings by the Germanic Cimbri and Teutones tribes are ruthlessly put down by the Romans.
	58 Julius Caesar (r. 49–44) begins a 10-year campaign to conquer Gaul (France).
	55 Julius Caesar briefly invades Britain on what amounts to a military reconnaissance trip.
200 Metalworkers in South America use blowpipes to create the draft for furnaces to make alloys of gold and silver.	**ca 200** Development starts on the North Acropolis at Tikal, Guatemala, with the construction of a massive stone platform that will subsequently provide a foundation for several Mayan pyramid temples.
214 The main part of the Great Wall of China—a section 1,400 miles (2,250 km) long—is completed.	**221** King Zheng of the Qin state conquers rival states and becomes emperor of unified China (r. 221–210).
105 Traditional date for the invention of paper, made from scraps of cloth and wood chips, in China. For the next two centuries paper will only be used for wrapping and packing, not for writing.	**206** The Han dynasty comes into power in China.
	ca 150 Austronesians arrive and settle in Tahiti and the Marquesas Islands.
	141 Han Wudi (r. 141–87) becomes emperor of China and expands Chinese influence abroad during his long reign.
	ca 100 Buddhism begins to spread along the Silk Road into Central Asia.
ca 250 Ironworking reaches sub-Saharan Africa, probably brought across the desert from southern Mauritania to the Niger Valley.	**ca 200** The Nok Culture reaches its height in Central Nigeria.
250 Egyptian pharaoh Ptolemy II (r. 283–246) rebuilds the canal linking the Nile River to the Red Sea.	**ca 171** Mithridates I (r. ca 171–138) takes control of the Parthian Empire and eventually conquers much of the Seleucid Empire, including Mesopotamia.
210 Egyptian pharaoh Ptolemy IV (r. ca 221–205) builds a huge galley that needs 4,000 oarsmen and a crew of 3,250 others.	**104** Jugurtha, ruler of Numidia (in modern Algeria), dies in prison after an unsuccessful rebellion against Roman rule.
ca 200 Glassblowing is refined in Syria.	**83** Syria becomes part of the Roman Empire.

GANGES VALLEY TECHNOLOGY

The Indian civilizations that developed along the valleys of the Ganga (formerly Ganges) and Indus Rivers were masters of the technologies involved in managing an erratic water supply and working with metals.

About 1500 B.C.E. Aryan people began migrating southwestward into the broad plain of the Ganga River, in what is now northern India. Rice was their staple food. In the hills rice is watered by the rain. In the lowlands it is raised in seedbeds then transplanted into flooded fields called paddies, which are drained before harvesting. Paddy rice produces bigger yields than upland rice, but successful cultivation depends on careful management of the water supply. Water management is especially important in India's monsoon climate, where nearly all the rain falls during the summer.

Dams, artificial lakes, and irrigation systems were being used by 300 B.C.E. Inundation canals were widely used in Bengal (also in northeastern India). Monsoon rainwater and meltwater from the mountains flowed along the canals and through openings in their sides into channels leading to the fields.

A tank built in the first century B.C.E. at Sringaverapura near Allahabad in northern India is a remarkable example of water harvesting. It is 800 feet (244 m) long, 60 feet (18 m) wide, and 12 feet (3.7 m) deep and lined with brick. Water from the Ganga River flowed downhill and through two deep earthen tanks, where silt settled at the bottom. Water left each of these tanks from outlets near the top, which fed into the main tank.

Indian metal working was advanced too. Beside the Quwwat-ul-Islam (Might of Islam) Mosque in Delhi stands a cast-iron pillar more than 23.5 feet (7 m) tall and 16 inches (40 cm) in diameter. It was commissioned by Kumara Gupta (r. 415–55 C.E.) in honor of his father Chandra Gupta II. Not until late in the 19th century were Europeans capable of casting a single piece of metal of that size.

ARCHIMEDES

ARCHIMEDES IS CONSIDERED TO BE ONE OF THE greatest mathematicians not just of the Classical period but of all time. His theories and philosophies became known the world over, and his inventions brought him fame that lasts to this day.

Archimedes (ca 287–212 B.C.E.) was the greatest mathematician and physicist of the ancient world. He was born in Syracuse, Sicily (then a Greek colony), the son of an astronomer named Phydias. The family was friendly with Hieron II, king of Syracuse, and possibly related to him. Archimedes studied in Alexandria, Egypt, where his teacher was a former pupil of the Greek mathematician Euclid (fl. ca 300 B.C.E.). His studies completed, Archimedes returned to Syracuse, where he remained for the rest of his life.

Archimedes was the first person to work out the principle underlying levers, and how they were able to multiply force. He said that if he had somewhere to stand and a lever long and strong enough, he could move the world. The claim led King Hieron to challenge Archimedes to move a very heavy object. Archimedes is said to have assembled a system of levers and pulleys with which Hieron himself was able to pull the royal ship—loaded with passengers and cargo—out of the dry dock, across land, and into the harbor.

Archimedes is said to have designed a planetarium and also the screw pump to help with irrigation of crops (although the Egyptians may have had this much earlier). It is a spiral screw inside a cylinder which, when turned, raises water. It is still used today.

Archimedes' Weapons

Archimedes invented weapons that are said to have struck terror into the hearts of the Romans who laid siege to Syracuse in 215 B.C.E. Anticipating the attack, the king ordered Archimedes to design defenses for the city. He rebuilt the walls to accommodate powerful catapults, cranes that lifted large boulders and dropped them onto the troops below, and also several novel weapons. His weapons held the invaders at bay for three years, turning the siege into a battle between the Romans and Archimedes.

The "claws of Archimedes" were among the most fearsome of these weapons. It was said that they would seize hold of any vessel that came close, and shake it violently until all the soldiers were shaken out of it. No one knows how the claws worked, but the device was probably a large grappling hook lowered by a crane. The hook gripped the bow of a ship and then rose, lifting the vessel until it was almost upright before suddenly releasing it.

Legend also tells of a focusing mirror that worked as a burning glass. It was said that it set fire to the sails of any ship that approached close enough for its archers to be within range of the city wall, but it is far from certain that such a weapon existed.

These inventions made Archimedes famous and gave rise to many legends, but he seems to have thought his mechanical devices were unworthy of him, and he published only his mathematical work. Consequently, it is impossible to say whether he really built all the machines credited to him.

Archimedes was primarily a mathematician. He calculated a value for pi, the relation between the circumference and radius of a circle, that is very close to the modern value, and also devised methods for calculating the volume and surface area of a body with a curved surface—anticipating integral calculus by 2,000 years. He found a way to express very large numbers, demonstrating it with a calculation of the number of grains of sand that exist in the universe.

The Romans finally took Syracuse in about 212 B.C.E., and the general, Marcellus, ordered that Archimedes and his house should not be harmed. A Roman soldier found Archimedes working on a mathematical problem. When the soldier demanded that Archimedes accompany him, the mathematician told him not to disturb the circles he had drawn in the sand. Impatient, the soldier killed him.

Archimedes's Principle

One of the most famous stories about Archimedes concerns his principle. Hieron of Syracuse had commissioned a new crown of gold, but when it was delivered, he doubted its purity. He asked Archimedes to determine, without damaging the crown, whether the gold had been mixed with cheaper silver. Archimedes could think of no way of doing this until one day he overfilled his bath. When he stepped into it, it overflowed. He realized that when an object is immersed in water it displaces its own volume of water. He was so excited that he is said to have run naked through the town shouting "Eureka!" ("I've got it!"). He measured the precise volume of the crown by immersing it in water, and then borrowed a piece of gold weighing exactly the same as the crown and measured its volume the same way. Silver is less dense than gold and therefore bulkier, so when Archimedes found that the crown displaced more water than the same weight of pure gold, he was able to tell the king that the goldsmith had cheated him.

Archimedes's principle can be demonstrated by immersing a heavy object in water. The water exerts an upward force (buoyancy) on the item, and the item's weight decreases. The water displaced by the item flows out of a spout into a bowl. The buoyancy is equal to the weight of the displaced water.

ASTRONOMY & MATH	BIOLOGY & MEDICINE	PHYSICAL SCIENCES

EUROPE

46 B.C.E. Roman emperor Julius Caesar (r. 49–44 B.C.E.) introduces the Julian calendar.

ca 62 C.E. Greek mathematician Hero of Alexandria describes the calculation of various areas and volumes.

110 Greek mathematician and astronomer Menelaus of Alexandria introduces spherical geometry in his book *Spherica*.

150 Greek geographer Ptolemy (ca 100–ca 170) compiles a compendium of astronomy called the *Almagest*. It remains a standard textbook until the Renaissance.

250 Greek mathematician Diophantus (ca 200–284) invents algebra.

30 C.E. Roman physician Aulus Cornelius Celsus publishes *De Medicina*, the first Latin treatise on medicine.

77 Roman Pliny the Elder summarizes natural history as known to the Romans in *Historia Naturalis*. He is killed in 79 by the eruption of Vesuvius, which also destroys Pompeii.

77 Pedanius Dioscorides writes a guide to medicinal herbs and drugs that remains authoritative until the 17th century.

100 The Roman physician Soranus of Ephesus writes *Gynecology*, dealing with pregnancy and disorders that affect women.

27 B.C.E. Roman architect Marcus Vitruvius Pollio describes gold amalgam, a gold–mercury alloy.

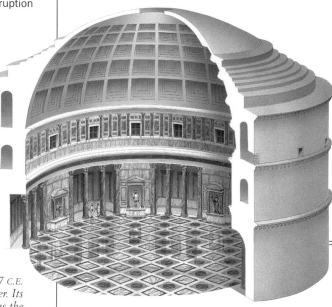

THE AMERICAS

The Pantheon in Rome was begun in 27 C.E. and completed nearly 100 years later. Its 142-foot (43-m) concrete dome was the largest in the world; its thickness tapered to only about a foot at the top to keep it light.

ASIA & OCEANIA

28 B.C.E. Chinese astronomers begin keeping records of sunspots.

1 C.E. Chinese mathematician Liu Hsin introduces decimal fractions.

185 Chinese astronomers observe a supernova in the constellation Centaurus, which continues to shine for 20 months.

263 Chinese mathematician Liu Hui calculates the value of pi as 3.14159 (correct to five decimal places).

ca 50 B.C.E. The Ayurveda, a Hindu medical treatise, establishes a holistic medical system that is still in use today.

105 C.E. Chinese people use powdered chrysanthemum flowers to kill insects.

132 In China Zhang Heng (ca 78–ca 139) constructs a seismograph for detecting the direction of an earthquake.

AFRICA & THE MIDDLE EAST

100 C.E. Mathematician and philosopher Nicomachus of Gerasa (fl. ca 100) writes *Introduction to Arithmetic*, a collection of knowledge about number theory.

The brilliant glow of a supernova—the central ring in this image—is caused by the explosion of a dying star and can last for months. Chinese astronomers called the supernova a "guest star," because it appeared only temporarily.

ENGINEERING & INVENTION	WORLD EVENTS
50 C.E. Farmers use grain-grinding watermills in Italy.	**44 B.C.E.** Julius Caesar (r. 49–44 B.C.E.) is assassinated in Rome.
50 Hero of Alexandria describes a simple steam turbine built as a toy or novelty.	**31 B.C.E.** The Roman navy defeats the forces of Antony and Cleopatra at the Battle of Actium.
80 The Colosseum, a four-story amphitheater, is completed in Rome.	**27 B.C.E.** Octavian takes the title Augustus, marking the start of the Roman Empire.
128 The Pantheon—a Greek-style temple with a concrete dome—is completed in Rome.	**117 C.E.** Under Hadrian, the Roman Empire reaches its greatest extent.
226 The 14-mile (22-km) Aqua Alexandriana aqueduct is completed, carried mostly on arches into the city of Rome.	
ca 250 Parchment supersedes papyrus as a writing material in Mediterranean countries.	
ca 200 C.E. People of the Moche civilization on coastal Peru build two huge terraced platform tombs from molded adobe brick: one is dedicated to the sun, the other to the moon.	**ca 0** The first phase of Anasazi culture begins in the American Southwest.
	ca 150 Tikal becomes the main lowland center of the Mayan empire.
8 C.E. Horizontal waterwheels are used in China.	**ca 50** The Kushans of Central Asia gain control of northwestern India.
ca 100 Chinese farmers sow seed using a multitube seed drill. At about this time they also introduce the tandem hitch so that two horses can pull plows and carts.	**ca 100** Buddhism begins to spread in China.
	184 The Yellow Turban rebellion seriously weakens the Han Dynasty of China.
ca 100 The wheelbarrow appears in China and is used for carrying goods and people.	**ca 200** The Hinduized kingdom of Champa is founded in modern-day central Vietnam.
105 Chinese court official Ts'ai Lun (ca 50–ca 118) describes a technique for making paper using tree bark, rags, and other materials.	**220** The last Han emperor is deposed in China, which splits into three kingdoms.
ca 30 B.C.E. Craftsmen in Syria discover the technique of glassblowing, which the Romans soon adopt for making bottles and other objects.	**ca 50** The Greek influenced Kingdom of Axum is founded in Ethiopia.
	ca 190 Ironworking in Africa spreads as far south as the Limpopo Valley.
10 B.C.E. King Herod the Great (r. 31–4) of Judea builds an open-sea harbor of concrete blocks to serve the city Caesarea of Palestine (in present-day Israel).	

Carving of a Mayan god from Chichén Itzá

MAYAN SCIENCE

The Maya of Mexico and Central America appeared in about 300 B.C.E. and flourished until about 900 C.E. Mayan astronomers used observations to discern cycles in astronomical phenomena. They calculated the length of a lunar month as 29.5302 days. The length accepted today is 29.53059 days. The Maya could predict solar eclipses and calculated the movements of Venus with great accuracy. In the late Maya period, astronomers maintained an observatory in the great city of Chichén Itzá in the Yucatán.

To record dates and perform calculations, the Maya used a number system. They introduced two important concepts: Place values, which allowed them to write large numbers clearly, and a symbol for zero, represented by a picture of a shell. They were already using this notation by about 400 B.C.E.

The Mayan calendar was in fact three calendars. The first was based on a sacred year of 260 days arranged in two overlapping cycles. It was used to maintain ritual practices. For everyday use there was a calendar based on a solar year. It was divided into 18 months each of 20 days plus five extra "unlucky" days. People born on those days were considered cursed. The third calendar, used for "long counts," dated events from a zero date equivalent to August 13, 3114 B.C.E.

ROMAN ENGINEERING

FROM THE FOURTH CENTURY B.C.E. THE Romans built roads throughout their empire to replace the earlier tracks that consisted of clinging mud in winter and choking dust in summer.

At their peak Roman roads totaled over 50,000 miles (80,000 km)—enough to stretch twice around the world. There were 29 great military roads spreading out from Rome. A system ran from Carthage in North Africa along the southern coast of the Mediterranean; in Gaul (France) roads radiated from Lyon; and in Britain London was the hub of the road system.

The first Roman road was the Via Appia (Appian Way) built southward from Rome in 312 B.C.E. by Roman general Appius Claudius Caecus (fl. fourth century B.C.E.). It eventually ran to the coast at Brundisium (present-day Brindisi). Other roads soon followed in the Italian peninsula, such as the Via Aurelia to Genua (Genoa) and the Via Flaminia to the Adriatic coast, each named after a different Roman dignitary.

The Romans built roads mainly for couriers, merchants, and administrators such as tax collectors. They were also useful for moving troops rapidly. The army provided the labor to build many of the roads when there was no fighting. Wherever possible, the roads followed a straight line set out by surveyors using a sighting staff called a *groma*, and the roads tended to turn (if they had to turn at all) at high points with good visibility.

KEY DATES

312 B.C.E.
Via Appia begun

ca 20 B.C.E.
Pont du Gard built in France

ca 50 C.E.
Aqueduct built in Segovia, Spain

52 C.E.
Aqua Claudia completed, Rome

Structure of a Road

For a major highway engineers first dug parallel drainage ditches about 40 feet (12 m) apart, then excavated a shallow trench between them, which they filled with sand, mortar, and a succession of stone courses to form a foundation. They topped a watertight layer of crushed stone with a surface pavement of stone slabs or cobbles set in mortar. They made concrete from crushed stones, pozzolana (volcanic ash) cement if available, and lime. On marshy ground the whole road was raised above the surrounding land.

Some of the major roads in Italy had stone curbs 8 inches (20 cm) high and 2 feet (60 cm) wide on each side, with side lanes outside them that operated as one-way streets. Drivers of two-wheeled chariots could achieve 75 miles (120 km) a day, with eight-horse freight wagons covering a more modest 15 miles (25 km) a day. As the Roman Empire crumbled, so did its roads owing to a lack of maintenance. Later road builders sometimes followed Roman routes, as shown by the straight stretches on any road map of England.

Water Engineering

As Roman towns and cities increased in size, there was growing demand for water for the people to drink and to wash in—public baths and fountains were features of many Roman towns. To bring in the water, Roman engineers built aqueducts. An aqueduct is any permanent channel for carrying water. It may be an open or closed culvert, a tunnel through a hill, or—at its most spectacular—a bridge across a valley.

Between 312 and 200 B.C.E., engineers built 11 aqueducts to take water into Rome, some from more than 56 miles (90 km) away. They built them with a gentle downward slope, and the water flowed by gravity. Roman aqueducts in Italy, Greece, and Spain are still in use today. The aqueduct at Segovia, Spain, for example, was authorized by Roman emperor Trajan (53–117). It is made from 24,000 granite blocks that form a 2,400-foot (730-m) series of 165 arches.

The layered structure of Roman roads gave them great stability, which is one reason why some are still in use today, some 2,000 years after they were built. The surface stones allowed rainwater to drain into ditches at either side of the roadway.

Large surface stones
Curb stones
Gravel
Bank
Ditch
Foundation of stone slabs

The three-tiered Pont du Gard was built over the Gard River to carry water to the French city of Nîmes. It was built in about 20 B.C.E. by Roman general Marcus Agrippa (63–12 B.C.E.).

ASTRONOMY & MATH	BIOLOGY & MEDICINE	PHYSICAL SCIENCES

EUROPE

340 Greek mathematician Pappus of Alexandria (fl. fourth century) publishes his *Synagoge*, a collection of geometry problems. It also includes commentaries on the *Elements* of Greek mathematician Euclid (fl 300 B.C.E.) and the *Almagest* of Greek astronomer and geographer Ptolemy (ca 100–ca 170).

460 Greek mathematician Proclus of Constantinople (ca 410–85) states that, through a given point, only one line can be drawn parallel to an existing line. This becomes known as Playfair's postulate after its rediscovery by Scottish mathematician John Playfair (1748–1819) in 1795.

520 Roman philosopher Boethius translates many of Aristotle's works into Latin, thus providing the main source of these works to later medieval scholars.

500 Cultivation of silkworms begins in Byzantium (present-day Istanbul), using silkworms smuggled from China by Christian monks.

300 At about this time Romans observe the British using coal as a fuel and soon adopt it for heating their villas.

TURNING POINTS

The Library at Alexandria

The greatest collection of documents in classical times was kept in a library in Alexandria, northern Egypt. The library was founded by pharaoh Ptolemy I Soter (r. 323–283 B.C.E.) at the beginning of the third century B.C.E. and built up by his son Ptolemy II Philadelphus (r. 283–46 B.C.E.). Established as part of the research "department" of the Alexandrian Museum, it had a smaller section, the Serapeum, located in the nearby Temple of Serapis that was established by Ptolemy III Euergetes (r. 246–22 B.C.E.). The hundreds of thousands of vellum and papyrus scrolls included nearly all the works of the Greek poets and dramatists, based originally on copies of the works in Aristotle's library in Athens. The large staff included translators, editors, and scribes, who kept adding texts to the collection. Fire damaged part of the library in 269 C.E., and rioting during a civil war led to its final destruction. The Serapeum was pillaged by a Christian mob in 391.

THE AMERICAS

ASIA & OCEANIA

310 Chinese astronomer Chen Zhuo combines the maps of earlier astronomers into a comprehensive star map.

ca 350 An Indian account of astronomy, the *Surya-Siddhanta*, is published with tables of trigonometrical sines.

369 Chinese astronomers observe a supernova (a so-called guest star) that remains bright for five months.

465 Chinese mathematician Tsu Ch'ung Chi (429–501) uses a circle three meters across to calculate π (pi) to ten decimal places.

497 Indian astronomer Aryabhata proposes that the Earth rotates on its axis.

265 Chinese physician Huang Fu-Mi writes a major treatise on acupuncture, a method of medical treatment that involves inserting fine needles through the skin.

304 Chinese writer Hsi Han describes the deliberate use of ants to control other insects that attack mandarin orange trees (the ants are sold at markets in woven straw baskets).

305 Chinese craftsmen use coal instead of wood in making cast iron.

405 Chinese craftsmen make steel by beating together wrought iron and cast iron.

An umbrella seller in China sells paper parasols that are more protection against the sun than the rain.

AFRICA & THE MIDDLE EAST

400 Scholars in Alexandria use the Arabic term *al-kimiya* to describe what takes place when matter changes. The derived word "alchemy" did not enter English until the early 1600s.

Reserve your right to think, for even to think wrongly is better than not to think at all.

HYPATIA OF ALEXANDRIA

ENGINEERING & INVENTION	WORLD EVENTS
300 Roman emperor Diocletian (r. 284–305) builds a palace at modern-day Split in Croatia that employs the new technique of arches supported by freestanding columns.	**286** Troubled by barbarian attacks, the Emperor Diocletian (r. 284–305) divides the Roman Empire into western and eastern parts.
300 The Romans build a flour mill in France, driven by 16 overshot waterwheels.	**313** The Edict of Milan tolerates Christianity in the Roman Empire.
350 A water-powered sawmill is installed in France for cutting marble.	**402** Ravenna replaces Rome as capital of the western empire.
365 The first reference to mechanical cranks appears in a Greek text that describes their use to set broken bones.	**ca 450** Angles and Saxons from northern Germany and Denmark begin to settle in eastern and southern England.
410 Greek mathematician and philosopher Hypatia of Alexandria (d.415) invents a hydrometer for measuring the density of liquids, consisting of a sealed tube weighted at one end and graduated with densities. She calls it a hydroscope.	**476** Odoacer (r. 476–93) declares himself king of Italy, marking the end of the Roman empire in the west.
	486 Clovis (r. 481–511), king of the Franks, begins to expand his kingdom southward.
ca 500 Ceramics in vivid colors are produced in many parts of Costa Rica and Panama.	**ca 450** With an estimated population of 200,000, the city of Teotihuacán dominates central Mexico.
271 A compass is first used in China.	**ca 300** Yamato kings in Japan extend their power through Honshu island.
302 A Chinese pottery figure depicts a horseman using metal stirrups.	**320** Chandragupta I (r. ca 320–ca 335) creates a powerful Hindu kingdom on the Ganges plain and founds the Gupta Dynasty.
ca 400 The umbrella, for protection against the sun as well as the rain, is used in China.	**372** Buddhism reaches Korea.
415 Indian engineers use iron chains to build suspension bridges.	**ca 400** Indian traders spread Hinduism into Southeast Asia.
489 Chinese artists carve 165-foot (50-m) statues of Buddha into a rock face at Yungang.	**ca 400** Polynesian seafarers settle the Hawaiian Islands.
495 Chinese writer Zu Chong Zhi describes a paddleboat with several paddle wheels along each side.	**439** The state of Wei controls all of northern China.
350 Antioch becomes the world's first city to have a system of street lighting.	**ca 270** Saint Anthony becomes a hermit in the Egyptian desert.
510 In about this year craftsmen construct an elaborate chiming water clock at Gaza (in present-day Palestine).	**ca 303** Armenia becomes the first country to adopt Christianity as its official religion.
	439 Vandals from Spain make Carthage their capital.

KEEPING COUNT

As society and its economy grew more complex, traders needed to keep accurate records of transactions. Officials also had to keep records of such things as land holdings, stored foods, and the size of armies. Records had to be written down, and so ways were found to represent numbers.

The simplest way was to carve a series of notches on the edge of a stick or scratch marks onto a stone or piece of bone, but this was not practical for writing large numbers. Numerals came into use in Egypt in about 3400 B.C.E. They consisted of a straight vertical mark for 1 and different symbols for powers of 10 (100, 1,000, 10,000, and so on) and could be written on papyrus paper. At about the same time the Sumerians were using shapes that looked like arrowheads. By about 2400 B.C.E. this system had developed into cuneiform writing. The Cretans began to use numbers in about 1200 B.C.E., with a vertical line for one and a horizontal line for ten.

Systems of this type worked by grouping. If | means 1, then 2, 3, and 4 are ||, |||, and ||||. The alternative is to allocate individual symbols to all numerals up to a given value. The Chinese devised a system of this type in the fourth century B.C.E. with symbols from 1 to 9 and for 10, 100, and 1,000. Roman numerals were simple to use. Students needed to memorize only the symbols I (1), V (5), X (10), L (50), C (100), D (500), and M (1,000). I, V, X, and L were sufficient for most purposes. The Hindu-Arabic numerals we use today originated in India, probably in the fourth century B.C.E. Arab scholars began using them in the eighth century C.E.

Ancient mathematicians performed complex calculations using a counting board, or abacus, a device that was probably invented in Babylon. The Chinese had also invented the counting board by the fourth century B.C.E. and were using the familiar abacus with beads on wires by 1500 C.E. The lines, grooves, or rods represent values (tens, hundreds, thousands) or units of money or measure.

CHINESE SCIENCES

SOME OF THE WORLD'S MOST IMPORTANT early inventions originated in China, including the kite, the spinning wheel, the compass, the crossbow, gunpowder, and the wheelbarrow. The camel's-hair brush for writing appeared in about 250 B.C.E. At the time, people wrote on cloth, but the popularity of the brush led to a demand for a cheaper medium. In about 105 C.E. a court official made sheets of writing material from a mixture of tree bark, waste from hemp manufacture, rags, and worn-out fishnets: He had invented paper. The oldest-known printed book (a Chinese translation of the *Diamond Sutra*, a Buddhist text) is also Chinese, made in 868 C.E.

Chinese books on alchemy, also from the ninth century, contain formulas for making mixtures that burn with a flash—precursors of gunpowder. A text written in about 83 C.E. mentions a *sinan*, a magnetic ladle balanced so that its handle always points south. It is thought to have been used as a primitive compass from about 300 B.C.E. In 132 C.E. a scholar invented an "earthquake weathercock," or seismograph.

Chinese Astronomy

Astronomy was vital because the Chinese believed that the emperor must preserve harmony in the cosmic order by the correct performance of ritual. This required a reliable calendar. The present Chinese calendar emerged in the 14th century B.C.E. after a period of development that began 1,500 years earlier.

The calendar counted days, months, and years in cycles of 60. A year had 12 months of 29 or 30 days beginning at the new moon and an additional month every two or three years to reconcile the lunar year with the solar year. As well as marking the equinoxes, solstices, and agricultural seasons, the calendar noted the dates of predictable events such as lunar eclipses and the positions of the planets. Irregular and unpredictable heavenly events were seen as omens.

Chinese astronomers kept detailed records of eclipses, novas, comets, and sunspots. From as early as the fourth century B.C.E., they noted the positions

In the 12th century firework displays became popular in China. One witness recorded that they made "a noise like thunder."

of stars in star tables, and there is a continuous record from about 70 B.C.E. Not all records survive, but there exists a table of ephemerides—the positions of the sun, the moon, and planets—and a table of planetary motions from 244 to 177 B.C.E.

Chinese Math

Astronomy is a mathematical science, and the earliest-known Chinese mathematical text is the *Zhou Dynasty Canon of Gnomic Computations*, written sometime between 400 and 200 B.C.E. but based on earlier texts that are now lost. It deals mainly with astronomical calculations and also contains instructions in arithmetic and geometry, including a statement of the Pythagorean theorem.

Early Chinese mathematicians also noticed the relationship between the pitch of a sound and the physical processes producing it. This led to Chinese harmonics—used to tune stone chimes and bells employed in rituals—and then to the development of music performed at court. In 1978 archaeologists discovered 65 bronze bells with gold-inlaid inscriptions in a tomb from the fifth century B.C.E. Each bell makes two different tones, depending on where it is struck.

Chinese Medicine

Medicine based on the balance between the cosmic principles of yin and yang is said to have begun in about 2953 B.C.E. Much of Chinese medical literature is based on the text *Nei Ching*, traditionally attributed to the legendary Yellow Emperor, Huang Ti (ca 2698–2598 B.C.E.) but more probably written in the third century B.C.E. Doctors relied mainly on administering herbal, animal, and mineral substances. They also used massage, physical exercises, controlled breathing, and dietary adjustments. Acupuncture and moxibustion—burning cones of substances on the skin—were minor branches of therapy. Their studies of therapeutic materials covered thousands of ingredients and gave the people of China an extensive knowledge of natural history.

The crossbow was in use in China by the sixth century B.C.E. The mechanical trigger meant that, unlike other bows, the crossbow did not depend on the strength of the archer, so that many bolts could be fired in succession.

63

ASTRONOMY & MATH | BIOLOGY & MEDICINE | PHYSICAL SCIENCES

EUROPE

685 The *Ravenna Cosmography* is published in Italy, an index of all known countries, rivers, and towns in the Roman Empire.

750 Knowledge from the Alexandrian school spreads to Europe as Arab scholars begin to settle in Spain.

542 An epidemic of bubonic plague breaks out and eventually kills a quarter of the population of eastern Mediterranean countries.

640 Greek surgeon Paul of Aegina (fl. 640), who practiced in Alexandria, writes *Epitome Medicae Libri Septum* (Seven Books of Medicine).

700 About this time workers in Spain employ a blast furnace for iron smelting, using hand bellows to provide a draft of air to raise the temperature of the furnace.

750 Craftsmen in Italy cast large church bells out of bronze

In 635 Chinese astronomers observed that the tail of a comet always points away from the sun.

THE AMERICAS

> *As the sun eclipses the stars by its brilliancy, so the man of knowledge will eclipse the fame of others… if he proposes algebraic problems, and still more if he solves them.*
>
> BRAHMAGUPTA

ASIA & OCEANIA

534 Japanese mathematicians adopt Chinese math.

610 Indian mathematicians introduce a number system using base ten.

628 Indian astronomer Brahmagupta (598–ca 660) writes *Brahmasphuta Siddhanta*, a work about astronomy that also contains chapters on mathematics, including algebra and trigonometry.

680 The symbol 0 for zero appears in mathematical calculations in Cambodia and Sumatra, although not necessarily as a number but merely as a place holder.

752 Chinese physician Wang Tao writes *Wai Tai Mi Yoo* (The Extra Important Secret), in which he describes various ailments and their remedies, including diabetes and goiter.

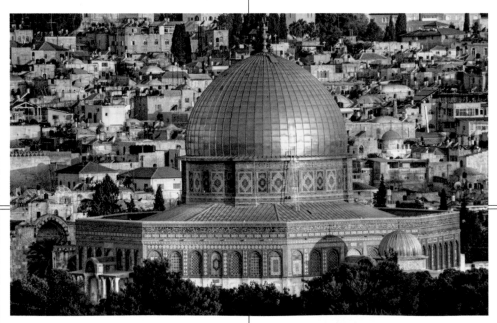

AFRICA & THE MIDDLE EAST

540 Eutocius of Ascalon (ca 480–ca 540) writes commentaries on works by the Greek mathematicians Apollonius of Perga (ca 262–ca 190 B.C.E.) and Archimedes (ca 287–212 B.C.E.)

622 This year marks the start of the Muslim calendar, commemorating the flight of the prophet Muhammad from Mecca to Medina.

760 The use of Arabic numerals, which originated in India, spreads as far as the region of Baghdad in the Middle East.

The Dome of the Rock in Jerusalem was begun in 685 and finished in 691. The Islamic shrine is built on land sacred to both Jews and Muslims.

ca 770 Arab scholar Abu Musa Jabir ibn-Hayyan (ca 721–815), also known as Geber, describes how to make ammonium chloride, white lead, nitric acid, and acetic acid.

ENGINEERING & INVENTION	WORLD EVENTS
532 On the orders of Emperor Justinian I (r. 527–565) Byzantine architect Isidorus of Miletus designs the church of Hagia Sophia in Byzantium (present-day Istanbul). **537** Roman engineer Belisarius (ca 505–65) constructs a floating watermill. **680** Farmers in the Netherlands build dikes to protect their low-lying fields from the gradual rise in sea level. **700** Riders in Europe adopt the use of stirrups for mounting and riding horses.	**561** Civil war erupts among the Merovingians in France. **570** Byzantium and Persia agree to 50 years of peace. **602** Vikings invade Ireland. **675** Bulgars—originally from Asia—establish their first kingdom south of the Danube. **ca 700** Vikings invade Britain. **711** Muslim armies invade southern Spain.
720 The Mayan people of Tikal (Guatemala) build a huge pyramid, Pyramid IV, one of the tallest buildings in Mesoamerica.	**ca 700** The Moche and Nazca civilizations (based in present-day Peru) collapse.
535 Chinese engineers make a machine for sifting flour. **577** Chinese women invent a type of match for starting cooking fires. **610** Chinese engineer Li Ch'un constructs a segmented arch in the Great Stone Bridge over the Chiao Shui River; it still stands. **618** Printed newspapers are reputed to have been produced in China. **725** Chinese engineer Liang Ling-Zan and Buddhist monk Yi-Xing construct a water clock with a proper escapement mechanism. The clock's purpose is to display various astronomical events (such as the phases of the moon) rather than tell the time.	**535** The Gupta Empire in India collapses. **587** The Soja clan champions Buddhism in Japan. **607** Tibet is unified under king Songstan Gampoh (r. ca 605–ca 649). **710** Nara is made capital of Japan.
605 Farmers in Persia (modern Iran) use windmills with horizontal sails to grind cereal grains. **674** Syrian-born Greek architect and chemist Callinicus, or Kallenikos (b. ca 620), invents Greek fire, a mixture of sulfur, resin, pitch, and saltpeter. **685** The 525-foot- (160-m-) high Dome of the Rock is begun in Jerusalem, made of wood and brass and covered overall with gold.	**550** Muhammad (500–632), the Prophet and future messiah of Islam, is born in Mecca. **622** Muhammad and followers flee from Mecca to Medina. **630** Muhammad conquers Mecca. **651** Muslim armies conquer Persia.

WATER POWER

Ancient machines worked by the muscle power of draft animals or people. The first major source of mechanical power came from water, which was harnessed by waterwheels from about 80 B.C.E.

A waterwheel is fitted with paddles that make the wheel turn when water flows past them. Early waterwheels were usually mounted horizontally; later waterwheels were mounted vertically. They used a gear arrangement to turn a horizontal shaft to perform tasks such as turning millstones.

An undershot wheel is a vertical wheel in which the water hits its base. In the more efficient overshot waterwheel, the water arrives at the top of the wheel; the paddles are angled to create small "buckets" to catch the water. The weight of falling water makes the wheel turn.

By 300 C.E. the Romans were building flour mills with several wheels that could process many tons of grain each day. Waterwheels were also used to drive saws for cutting stone and wood, and for lifting water for irrigation purposes.

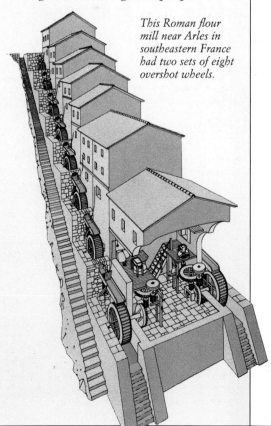

This Roman flour mill near Arles in southeastern France had two sets of eight overshot wheels.

ARABIC SCIENCES

FROM ABOUT 750 C.E. SCIENCE FLOURISHED under the Abbasid caliphs of Baghdad. Drawing on Greek and Hindu texts, early Islamic scholars collected the greatest body of scientific knowledge in the world, to which they added their own important discoveries.

After the death of the prophet Muhammad in the seventh century, his followers spread his teachings throughout an empire that eventually extended from central Asia to Spain.

Damascus was the first Muslim capital, but in 750 the Abassid caliphs moved the capital Baghdad. The seventh caliph, Abdallah al-Ma'mun (786–833) was one of the greatest. In about 820 he ordered the establishment of an astronomical observatory and library as part of an academy called Bayt al-Hikma (The House of Wisdom). His astronomers calculated the inclination of the plane of the ecliptic—the angle between Earth's rotational axis and its orbital plane—to within a few minutes of the modern value. The caliph's geometers calculated the circumference and radius of Earth as 20,400 miles (32,824 km) and 6,500 miles (10,459 km) respectively. The correct values are 24,875 miles (40,030 km) and 3,959 miles (6,371 km).

Arabian alchemist Abu Musa Jabir Ibn-Hayyan (ca 721–815), known later in Europe as Geber, expanded the Greek idea that all matter is made from four elements: earth, air, fire, and water. He lived during the reign of the fifth Abassid caliph, Harun al-Rashid (786–809). Geber believed that the Greek elements combine to form sulfur and mercury. These two substances could be combined to make any metal, including gold, with the help of a substance called *al-iksir*, from which we derive the word "elixir."

Abu-Bakr Muhammad ibn-Zakariya al-Rhazi (ca 865–923), or Rhazes, became chief physician at the main hospital in Baghdad. Rhazes prepared plaster of Paris and described its use for making casts to hold broken limbs in place. He was possibly the first person to classify all substances as being animal, vegetable, or mineral.

Math and Astronomy

We owe our system of numerals to an Arabic mathematician, Abu Jafar Muhammad ibn-Musa al-Khwarizmi (ca 780–ca 850). Al-Khwarizmi studied Hindu and Greek sources and used Hindu numerals, including zero, in his own works, which were later translated from Arabic into Latin. He lived most of his life in Baghdad, where he was chief librarian at the House of Wisdom. In about 830 Al-Khwarizmi wrote *Hisab al-jabr w'al-muqabala* (Calculation by Restoration and Reduction), a treatise on mathematics. Translated into Latin, *al-jabr* ("restoration") became "algebra." Al-Khwarizmi's name gave us our word "algorithm."

Arabian astronomers preserved the ideas of the Greek astronomer Ptolemy (ca 100–170 C.E.), which Ptolemy expounded in a book written in 150 now known as the *Almagest*, from the Arabic phrase meaning "the greatest."

Most astronomers accepted Ptolemy's work, but in about 880 Abu-Abdullah Muhammad ibn-Jabir al-Battani (ca 850–929) observed that when the sun appeared at its smallest—when it is farthest from Earth—its position in the sky was not where Ptolemy said it was. He deduced that the position changes slowly and calculated fairly accurately the rate of its motion. This allowed him to measure the length of the year more accurately: Calendar makers were still using his measurement centuries later. Al-Battani calculated the time of the equinoxes to within an hour or two.

Arabian science depended heavily on scholars who translated works from Greek into Arabic. One of the greatest was a Christian living in Baghdad. Honain ben Isaac (809–873) was a physician as well as a translator. He translated the works of Greek physician Hippocrates of Kos (ca 460–ca 370 B.C.E.) and practiced medicine according to Hippocratic principles.

KEY DATES

622
Mohammad's flight from Mecca to Medina

630
Mohammad's return to Mecca

750
Umayyad Dynasty overthrown; capital moves from Damascus to Baghdad under Abassid caliphs

ca 820
Bayt al-Hikma (The House of Wisdom) established in Baghdad

ca 830
Hindu numerals introduced

ca 860
Medicine according to principles of Hippocrates practiced in Baghdad

ca 880
Al-Battani (Albategnius) calculates the length of the year and the times of the equinoxes

ca 900
Plaster of Paris used to support fractured bones

Algebra—the use of mathematical equations or relations to determine unknown quantities—probably had its roots in Hindu math. It's most important statement in the early medieval period, however, came in an Arabic text the title of which (al-Jahr wa'al-Muqabalah) gave us the English word "algebra."

This 16th-century manuscript illustration shows astronomers in Istanbul using different astronomical devices, including an astrolabe, telescope, and sextant. Many instruments developed by Arab astronomers were used in navigation until the 17th and 18th centuries.

| ASTRONOMY & MATH | BIOLOGY & MEDICINE | PHYSICAL SCIENCES |

EUROPE

975 French cleric, scholar, and natural scientist Gerbert of Aurillac (ca 945–1003) builds a hydraulic organ that produces a steady extended level of sound. Its pipes are matched mathematically, providing better harmonics. He also reintroduces Hindu-Arabic numerals and the abacus into Europe. In 999 he becomes Pope Sylvester II.

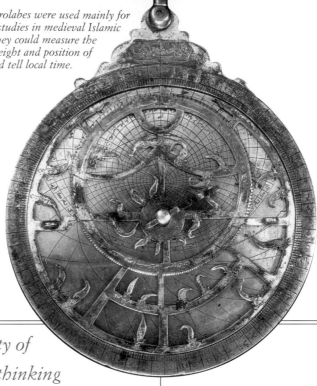

Astrolabes were used mainly for astronomical studies in medieval Islamic countries. They could measure the angular height and position of stars and tell local time.

THE AMERICAS

Gentility of character, friendliness, and purity of mind are found in those who are capable of thinking profoundly on abstruse matters and scientific minutiae.

RHAZES

ASIA & OCEANIA

876 People in Gwalior, India, use a place-value number system with a symbol for zero.

ca 855 In China the pamphlet *The Classified Essentials of the Mysterious Tao of the True Origin of Things*, attributed to Zheng Yin, describes a primitive form of gunpowder, called the "fire drug."

According to popular legend, a goatherd named Kaldi in East Africa discovered the coffee plant in about 850 C.E.

AFRICA & THE MIDDLE EAST

ca 820 In Baghdad Abdallah al-Ma'mun (786–833) founds Bayt al-Hikma (The House of Wisdom), in which scholars translate astronomical and other scientific texts into Arabic.

ca 820 Arab mathematician Abu Jafar Muhammad ibn-Musa al-Khwarizmi (ca 780–ca 850) describes the astrolabe.

880 Arab astronomer Abu Abdullah Muhammad ibn-Jabir al-Battani (850–929), also known as Albategnius, introduces trigonometry to Arab astronomy.

850 Arab physician Hunayn ibn-Ishaq (809–73) writes *The Book of the Ten Treatises on the Eye*, describing eye anatomy, disorders, and treatments.

ca 900 Persian-born Arab physician Rhazes (c.865–923) distinguishes between the diseases measles and smallpox. He also uses plaster of Paris to hold broken bones in place while they heal.

900 Arab chemists make alcohol by distilling wine, for use mainly in medicine.

ENGINEERING & INVENTION	WORLD EVENTS
789 In Europe Emperor Charlemagne (r. 764–814) introduces standard weights and measures.	**795** Viking raiders attack the coast of Ireland.
800 The use of the blast furnace for producing cast iron spreads from Spain to Scandinavia.	**799** First Viking raids along the coast of France.
834 The hand crank is first used in Europe to impart rotary motion to a wheel. It is pictured in the *Utrecht Psalter*, a graphic codex produced near Reims (in present-day France).	**800** Charlemagne, king of the Franks, is crowned Holy Roman Emperor by the pope in Rome on Christmas Day.
	825 Arabs expelled from Spain conquer Crete.
860 Viking longships from Norway and Sweden venture as far as Iceland. Norwegians make settlements there 14 years later.	**840** Viking settlers in Ireland found Dublin as a trading center.
	841 Viking raiders invade Normandy.
	874 Danish Vikings settle in Iceland.
982 Viking longships from Iceland under the command of Erik Thorvaldson (950–ca 1003), known as Erik the Red, cross the North Atlantic Ocean and discover Greenland. Four years later 400 Norse people establish a settlement there.	**888** Charlemagne's empire breaks up on the death of Roman emperor Charles the Fat (r. 881–88).
	930 Settlers in Iceland establish the Althing, the world's oldest parliament.
	987 Hugh Capet (r. 987–96) is crowned king of France, founding the Capetian Dynasty.
800 People in Central America adopt metalworking techniques from South America.	**ca 850** The Toltec people establish military supremacy in the Valley of Mexico.
ca 800 The Hohokam people of Arizona construct an irrigation network of canals and dams. Bows and arrows are used for the first time by hunters in the Mississippi Valley.	**ca 900** Mayan civilization finally collapses in the southern lowlands, and the surviving cities are abandoned.
812 In China paper bank drafts, or money certificates, are introduced for limited use.	**780** The Chinese writer Yu Lu writes *The Classic of Tea*, describing the use of tea.
868 The earliest surviving printed book (a scroll), called the *Diamond Sutra*, is made in China.	**791** The Tibetans defeat the Chinese at the Battle of Tingzhou, forcing the Tang emperors to abandon their gains in Central Asia.
954 Chinese emperor Shih Tsung authorizes the creation of the Great Lion of Tsang-chou, a cast-iron statue weighing about 44 tons (40 tonnes). It is the largest single piece of cast iron ever made in ancient China.	**ca 800** The first Polynesian seafarers, perhaps from the Society Islands, arrive on Aotearor ("the Land of the Long White Cloud"), later to be known as New Zealand.
960 Authorities in the Chinese province of Szechuan begin to print paper money as a means of exchange.	**907** The last Tang emperor of China is deposed, and China splits into ten separate states (the Ten Kingdoms).
976 Chinese engineer Chang Ssu-Hsun invents a chain-drive mechanism for an astronomical clock.	
780 Arabs in Baghdad begin making paper, using a method learned from Chinese craftsmen in Samarkand (present-day Uzbekistan).	**ca 800** Arab merchants found trading towns on the East African coast, including Kilwa Kisiwani (in present-day Tanzania).
800 Arab caliph Harun al-Rashid (ca 766–809) presents a water clock to Emperor Charlemagne.	**ca 871** Ibn Abd al-Hakam writes the first known history of the Arab conquest of Egypt.
	935 Algiers is founded by Arabs.
820 The Moors (Arabs) in Spain produce copper by smelting sulfide ores.	**972** A university is founded in Cairo.

MAKING PAPER

As soon as people learned to write, they needed something to write on. Walls, pillars, and tablets were used but were not very portable. The Egyptians invented papyrus, but real progress was made when Chinese craftsmen invented paper.

From about 2800 B.C.E. the Egyptians made papyrus from reeds. They peeled the reeds and sliced the inner pith into strips, which they criss-crossed and pounded into a flat sheet. Other early writing materials included tree bark, cloth, and thin animal skins, the latter made into parchment or vellum.

The first Chinese reference to paper comes in about 105 C.E. It describes paper being made from rags and other materials, such as bark. Chinese craftsmen also made paper from leaves and other vegetable matter. One method involved taking young bamboo fibers and the inner bark of a mulberry tree and pounding them together in water. The resulting slurry was poured through a piece of coarse cloth stretched on a wooden frame to act as a kind of filter. The water trickled through, leaving the fibers on the cloth, which dried to form paper. They also used hemp fibers to make a fine paper, but the most expensive kind was made from silk. Coarse paper was used for wrapping and soft paper used as toilet paper.

Other cultures invented paper independently of the Chinese. Mesopotamians developed a reed paper resembling papyrus. In Central America by about the sixth century inhabitants in Teotihuacán, Mexico, were making paper from the fibers of fig bark.

Knowledge of Chinese papermaking spread across Asia, and by the eighth century had reached the Middle East. Arab traders spread the technique to Egypt by the tenth century. The first European papermaking plant was built in 1150 near Valencia, Spain. By then paper factories were called mills, either because waterwheels provided the power for the pulping machines or because they used grindstones to crush vegetable materials.

CHAPTER 3

LATE MEDIEVAL AND RENAISSANCE

THE THOUSAND OR SO YEARS FOLLOWING THE FALL OF THE ROMAN EMPIRE in the West in 476 C.E. were once commonly referred to as the Dark Ages because of the perceived lack of learning during the period. To Europeans looking back from the Renaissance, it seemed that the great cultural and technological achievements of the classical Greeks and Romans had been lost. In fact, the period was marked by steady scientific development, artistic and architectural achievement, and the spread of literacy, particularly in Europe's monasteries. Supposedly "lost" knowledge was preserved in the libraries of the Islamic world. Technology advanced as it had for centuries, through a succession of small improvements. Windmills provided a new source of power to supplement the waterwheels that already existed, and the wind also powered a new generation of sailing ships. Together with the introduction of the magnetic compass from East Asia, such ocean-going ships enabled a host of European adventurers to travel the world, taking them to America and eventually around the entire globe.

Increased travel also led to the more rapid spread of ideas around the world. The compass originated in China, which was also a source of the secret of how to make gunpowder (although its manufacture may have been discovered independently in Europe). Printing with movable type, also first developed in the East, was reinvented in Europe, so books no longer had to be copied laboriously by hand. Books spread knowledge, leading to what contemporaries heralded as a renaissance—literally a "rebirth"—of learning in the 14th and 15th centuries. Many of the classical texts that fueled this rebirth of learning arrived in Europe from the Islamic world.

The typical Renaissance man was Leonardo da Vinci (1452–1519), the Italian artist, architect, and engineer, whose inventions anticipated technical developments that came three or four centuries later. Leonardo's contemporary Nicolaus Copernicus (1473–1543) suggested that the sun is at the center of the solar system, with the planets orbiting around it, laying the foundation of modern astronomy.

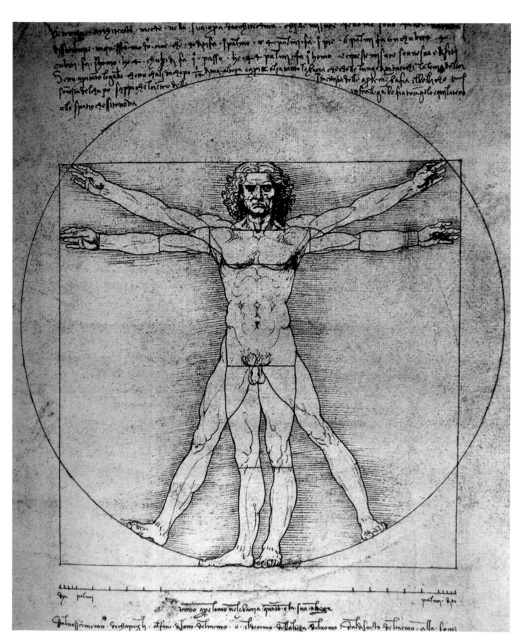

Leonardo da Vinci's "Vitruvian Man." This drawing, a sketch in one of his notebooks, is a study on the principles of ideal human proportions described by classical architect Marcus Vitruvius Pollio (ca 80–20 B.C.E.). This combination of old and new is characteristic of the Renaissance.

Windmills transform wind power into mechanical power, which is used to grind grain or, as in the case of this set of windmills in the Netherlands, to pump water into a drainage canal in order to reclaim low-lying land from the sea.

Outside Europe the so-called Dark Ages were not a time of intellectual stagnation; the Islamic world, which spread from from Cordoba in Spain to Bukhara in Uzbekistan, contained many great centers of learning. Islamic rulers encouraged intellectual activity. Many of them kept extensive libraries, built observatories for accurate astronomical studies, and offered their patronage to physicians, astronomers, mathematicians, and philosophers. In this climate great scientists such as Ibn Sina (980–1037), Ibn Rushd (1126–98), and Ibn al-Haytham (995–1039) had both access to existing scientific texts and the ability to test scientific knowledge through experimentation. In the West, they are known by their Latin pseudonyms: Avicenna, Averroës, and Alhazen, respectively.

One of the earliest figures who can be called a Renaissance man, the English theologian and scientist Roger Bacon (ca 1214–94), demonstrates the link between the rebirth of European science and its contact with the Islamic world. In his surviving works, such as the *Opus Majus* and the *Opus Tertium*, Bacon describes his extensive knowledge of the Arabic language and his study of the work of Islamic scientists and philosophers. He also asserts that without knowledge of Arabic no European intellectual could consider himself properly educated.

The magnifying-glass, made by grinding and shaping a piece of glass to form a convex lens, was first described by the 10th-century Arab physicist Alhazen in his Book of Optics, *which was translated into Latin in 12th-century Spain. Alhazen's work strongly influenced the later studies of English scientist Roger Bacon.*

THE WORLD AT A GLANCE

CONCISE HISTORY OF SCIENCE AND INVENTION

	1000	1100	1200	1300	1350
EUROPE	**1030** Italian Benedictine monk Guido d'Arezzo invents a form of musical notation (for writing down music). **1066** Halley's comet is sighted in England and is associated with the Norman Conquest of that year. **ca 1075** Female obstetrician Trotula of Salerno gives lectures on women's disorders.	**1135** Scholars in Toledo, Spain, translate the medical works of Persian scholar Avicenna into Latin. **1140** Construction begins on a new basilica at the Abbey of Saint-Denis, France, the first building to use flying buttresses in its structure. **1150** A papermill is built in Spain. **1180** European boatbuilders make ships steered by a rudder at the stern.	**1209** The 20-arch Old London Bridge over the Thames River is completed. It is lined with houses to provide rent for its upkeep. **1242** English scientist and philosopher Roger Bacon gives precise instructions on how to make gunpowder. **1286** Eyeglasses are invented in Italy.	**1316** Italian anatomist Mondino de' Luzzi publishes the first Western account of anatomy. It becomes a standard work until the writings of Belgian anatomist Andreas Vesalius become available. **1340** Avoirdupois weights are introduced in England and France. **1345** Dutch engineers use windmills to pump water when reclaiming land from the sea.	**1363** French physician Guy de Chauliac describes how to treat fractures and hernias in his book *Chirurgia Magna* (Great Surgery). **1364** Italian clockmaker Giovanni di Dondi makes an astronomical clock. **1380** Military rockets are fired in Europe for the first time at the Battle of Chioggia between Genoese and Venetian armies.
THE AMERICAS	**1000** Viking longships commanded by Leif Eriksson cross the North Atlantic Ocean and reach North America, establishing a colony.	**1116** According to legend the Aztec leave their homeland, Aztlan, and begin to migrate south into Mexico.	**ca 1200** The Anasazi begin to use a sun calendar that divides the year into four seasons.	**ca 1325** The Hohokam begin to build Casa Grande, a large structure in modern-day Arizona.	**ca 1350** Aztec craftsman are renowned for their technological capability. **ca 1360** The Aztec divide their capital, Tenochtitlan, in quarters based on the four cardinal directions.
ASIA & OCEANIA	**1000** Persian philosopher and physician Ibn Sina, also known by the Latin name Avicenna, writes his medical textbook *Canon of Medicine*. **1044** A Chinese military treatise describes the use and making of gunpowder. **1086** Chinese scientist Shen Kua describes a magnetic compass used for navigation.	**1105** Persian mathematician Omar Khayyam solves cubic equations. **ca 1105** Chinese potters make porcelain, a fine white ceramic that Europeans soon call "China." **1155** Chinese cartographers print maps of western China, the oldest known printed maps.	**ca 1200** Chinese mathematicians introduce a symbol for zero. **1220** The Chinese military use gunpowder bombs with outer cases that shatter on explosion, acting like a type of shrapnel. At about the same time they employ kites to carry messages across enemy lines.	**1313** Chinese printer Wang Chen produces *Nong Shu* (Treatise on Agriculture), using more than 50,000 movable type characters carved from hardwood. (Wooden type replaces the clay characters used previously.)	**1395** Chinese astronomers calculate the length of the solar year as 365.25 days. (A solar year is the time Earth takes to make a complete orbit of the sun, modern value 365.242 days.)
AFRICA & THE MIDDLE EAST	**1013** Arab builders complete the large al-Hakim Mosque in Cairo, Egypt, with a courtyard big enough to hold half the city's male population. **1021** Arab mathematician Alhazen publishes a treatise on optics, describing lenses, curved mirrors, and the refraction of light.	**1150** Hebrew astronomer Solomon Jarchus compiles the first celestial almanac, giving details about the stars.	**1205** Arab scholar Abu al-Iz Ismail ibn al-Razaz Al-Jarzi gives instructions for building 50 machines in his *Book of Knowledge of Ingenious Mechanical Devices*. **1240** Arab physician Ibn al-Baytar lists 1,400 different medications in *The Comprehensive Book on Materia Medica and Foodstuffs*.	**1331** Arab traveler Ibn Battuta visits east Africa as part of a long voyage through the Islamic world.	**ca 1350** Muslim architects adopt the four-liwan style for mosques and schools of four vaulted halls around an open courtyard. **ca 1360** The Ottoman timar system establishes a degree of centralized control over agriculture and manufacture.

1400	1450	1500	1550	1600–1625
1405 Triangular lateen sails come into use on Spanish ships and soon spread throughout the Mediterranean region.	**1450** European metalworkers devise a way of separating silver from lead ores such as galena (silver sulfide); some lead contains up to 10 percent silver.	**1502** German clockmaker Peter Henlein makes the first spring-driven pocket clock, or watch.	**1551** English mathematician Leonard Digges invents the theodolite for measuring angles during surveying.	**1608** Dutch eyeglass-maker Hans Lippershey makes a refracting telescope (using two lenses).
1407 In London, England, Bethlehem Hospital becomes an institution for the insane; it is popularly known as Bedlam.	**1457** The first four-wheel passenger coach is built in Hungary.	**1503** The Spanish begin using mines during warfare.	**1573** Danish astronomer Tycho Brahe publishes *De Nova Stella*, describing a new supernova in the constellation Cassiopeia (often called Tycho's Star at the time).	**1609** German Johannes Kepler draws up his first two laws of planetary motion.
1425 German philosopher Nicholas Krebs maintains that the Earth rotates on its axis once a day and orbits the sun once a year.	**1474** English printer William Caxton produces the first printed book in the English language, *Recuyell of the Historyes of Troye*.	**1513** Swiss artist Urs Graf invents metal etching.	**1590** Dutch optician Zacharias Jansen builds a compound microscope.	**1610** Italian scientist Galileo Galilei observes four of Jupiter's moons and craters on the moon.
1430 Germans use a flywheel to even out the motion of rotating machinery.		**1515** The wheel-lock pistol is introduced in Germany.	**1592** Italian scientist Galileo Galilei makes a thermometer.	**1622** English mathematician William Oughtred invents the slide rule.
		1517 Italian physician and poet Girolamo Fracastoro proposes that fossils are the petrified remains of once-living organisms.	**1595** Geraldus Mercator publishes the first atlas.	**1623** German mathematician Wilhelm Schickard makes a wooden adding machine.
ca 1400 The Inca use quipu, knotted strings, to keep trade records.	**ca 1450** The Inca construct a road system 20,000 miles (32,200 km) long to unite their empire.	**1520** Smallpox decimates the Aztecs.	**1555** Tobacco from the Americas is imported to Spain.	**1598** Spanish colonists begin to grow wheat, apricots, and peaches, north of El Paso.
ca 1400 The Mississippians build large earth mounds in North America.		**1520** Spanish voyagers take turkeys and corn from America to Europe.	**ca 1560** Mercury is discovered in Peru and used in a new process to refine silver ore.	**1607** The first American ship is constructed in Sagadahoc, Maine.
ca 1405 Improvement works begin on China's Grand Canal.	**1483** Russian pioneers begin to explore Siberia.	**1500** Chinese scientist Wan Hu attempts to make a flying machine by tying 45 rockets to the back of a chair. He is killed when the device explodes.	**1543** The Portuguese introduce firearms to Japan.	**ca 1600** The tradition of building huge stone statues dies out on Easter Island.
1408 *Yongle dadian*, a wide-ranging encyclopedia, is published under the patronage of the Chinese emperor Yongle.	**1495** The Chinese divert the Yellow River to a new course near the Shandong Peninsula.	**1514** The Chinese open silver mines at Yunnan.	**1574** *Taiping Guangzhi* is the first Chinese book printed with movable type.	**1602** Italian missionary Matteo Ricci publishes a Chinese atlas of the world.
1414 From this year Chinese trading fleets sail to India, the Middle East, and as far as Africa, using large oceangoing junks.		**1520** The Chinese buy cannon from the Portuguese.		
1410 Hebrew astronomer Hasdai ben Abraham Crescas writes *Or Adonai* (The Light of the Lord). He disagrees with Aristotle that there are no worlds other than Earth.	**1453** At the siege of Constantinople (present-day Istanbul), Ottoman forces use a huge cannon that fires cannonballs weighing up to 1,345 pounds (610 kg).	**1511** The Ottomans begin providing gunpowder weapons to their allies such as Egypt and Mesopotamia. Ottoman gunmakers are in demand as far away as Delhi, in India.	**ca 1550** The Ottomans build aqueducts to carry water into their growing capital city at Istanbul.	**ca 1600** The Ottomans introduce tobacco from the Americas.
1420 Tartar prince, astronomer, and Turkish ruler of Maverannakhr (modern Uzbekistan) Ulugh Beg begins construction of a three-story observatory in Samarkand.	**1471** Portuguese navigator Fernão do Po discovers the island of Fernando Póo (now Bioko) in Equatorial Guinea, West Africa.	**1513** The Ottoman geographer Piri Reis draws a map of the world that includes what is then known of the Americas.	**1569** Ottoman engineers attempt to construct a canal between the Don and Volga Rivers.	

ASTRONOMY & MATH

EUROPE

1050 Arab astronomers and navigators introduce the astrolabe to Europe.

1066 Halley's comet is sighted in England and is associated with the Norman Conquest of that year.

1142 English philosopher Adelard of Bath (ca 1080–ca 1160) translates *Elements* (books about geometry) by Greek mathematician Euclid (ca 300 B.C.E.) from Arabic into Latin.

1145 English scholar Robert of Chester translates *Hisab al-jabr w'al-muqabala* (Calculation by Restoration and Reduction) by Arab mathematician Abu Jafar Muhammad ibn-Musa al-Khwarizmi (ca 780–ca 850) into Latin.

ASIA & OCEANIA

ca 1000 Indian astronomers introduce a calendar of 360 days with 12 months of 27 or 28 days; an extra month is added every five years to bring the calendar in step with the seasons.

1006 Astronomers in China, Egypt, Europe, and Japan record a supernova that remains visible for several months.

1105 Persian mathematician and poet Omar Khayyam (1048–1131) solves cubic equations (algebra equations of the degree 3).

1150 Hindu mathematician Bhaskara Acharya (1114–85) sums up Indian knowledge of algebra and math in *Siddhanta Siromani*.

AFRICA & THE MIDDLE EAST

1075 Arab astronomer al-Zarqali (1028–87), also known by the Latin name Arzachel, proposes that the orbits of the planets are ellipses rather than circles.

1150 Hebrew astronomer Solomon Jarchus compiles the first celestial almanac, giving details about the stars.

BIOLOGY & MEDICINE

ca 1075 Italian obstetrician Trotula of Salerno lectures at a university (unusual for a woman) and writes books on hygiene and women's disorders.

1135 Scholars in Toledo, Spain, translate the medical works of Persian scholar Ibn Sina (980–1037), also known as Avicenna, into Latin.

1140 King Roger II of Sicily (r. 1130–54) introduces government licenses for physicians; only those with licenses may practice medicine.

1150 In Spain Arab physician Avenzoar (ca 1091–1162) introduces blood-letting as a medical treatment.

A modern fireworks display. Fireworks were developed soon after the discovery of gunpowder, and became a popular entertainment in 12th century China.

1000 Avicenna writes his medical textbook *Canon of Medicine*, which remains a standard work for centuries.

The knowledge of anything, since all things have causes, is not acquired or complete unless it is known by its causes.

AVICENNA (IBN SINA), *CANON OF MEDICINE*

PHYSICAL SCIENCES

1120 French-born Prior Walcher of Malvern Abbey, England, begins using degrees to express latitude and longitude on maps.

ca 1000 The Chinese dig the first coal mines.

1086 Chinese scientist Shen Kua writes *Dream Pool Essays*, in which he anticipates earth science by discussing the principles of sedimentation, uplift, and erosion.

1155 Chinese cartographers create maps of western China, the oldest known printed maps.

1160 Persian mathematician Sharaf al-Din al-Tusi of Damascus invents the sighting rod or linear astrolabe, which is much easier to make and use than the regular astrolabe.

1021 Arab mathematician Alhazen (ca 965–ca 1040) publishes a treatise on optics, describing lenses, curved mirrors, and refraction of light.

ENGINEERING & INVENTION	WORLD EVENTS
1030 Italian Benedictine monk Guido d'Arezzo (ca 991–1050) invents a form of musical notation (for writing down music).	**1016** The Danish king Canute (r. 1016–35) becomes undisputed king of England.
1080 The swingletree allows two horses side by side to pull a plow or wagon.	**1000** Bohemia and Moravia are united.
1105 A major arsenal is established in Venice, Italy.	**1066** William of Normandy (1066–87) invades England and becomes king.
1110 European military engineers invent the gravity-powered catapult.	**1096** The first Crusade begins as European knights set out to expel Muslims from the Holy Land.
1140 Construction begins on a new basilica at the Abbey of Saint-Denis, France, the first building to use flying buttresses in its structure.	**1149** Oxford University is founded.
1150 The first European papermill is built in Valencia, Spain.	**1152** Frederick Barbarossa (r. 1155–90) becomes Holy Roman Emperor.
1000 Viking longships commanded by Leif Eriksson (ca 970–ca 1020) cross the North Atlantic Ocean and reach North America, establishing a colony there.	**1116** According to legend the Aztec leave their homeland, Aztlan, and begin to migrate south into Mexico.
1044 A Chinese military treatise describes the use and making of gunpowder.	**1115** The Jurchen from Manchuria found China's Jin dynasty.
1045 In China, Bi Sheng invents movable type made from baked clay.	**1156** The Taira and Minamoto clans fight for control of Japan.
1086 Chinese scientist Shen Kua describes a magnetic compass used for navigation.	
ca 1100 Fireworks become popular in China.	
ca 1105 Chinese potters make porcelain, a fine white ceramic that Europeans soon call "china."	
1013 Arab builders complete the large al-Hakim Mosque in Cairo, Egypt, with a courtyard big enough to hold half the city's male population.	
1075 Arab astronomer al-Zarqali (1028–87), working in Spain, builds several complex astronomical water clocks in Toledo.	

WIND POWER

Windmills arrived in western Europe in the 12th century: Crusaders probably brought the idea from the Holy Land. But European windmills differed in one important respect: Instead of being mounted on a vertical axis, their sails radiated from a horizontal axis, supported on the side of a post or a stone tower. This design makes much more efficient use of available air currents.

Using an upright mill to turn millstones required the use of gears to move the turning force through 90 degrees. Windmills also had to be adjustable so that the sails faced into the wind. Inland mills, known as post mills, were small and mounted on a stout post that could be turned to face the wind. By the 15th century windmill sails were mounted in a free-rotating cap that was separate from the main tower. When the miller needed to change the direction of the sails, he only had to turn the cap, not the whole structure. This advance meant that the size of windmills was no longer restricted by the need to turn them around. Mill towers could be built of brick or stone, several stories high.

On the coasts and islands of the Mediterranean, windmills could be built facing the direction of the prevailing wind, from the sea. Inland, more variable winds required windmills that could be moved.

ASTRONOMY & MATH

BIOLOGY & MEDICINE

PHYSICAL SCIENCES

EUROPE

1175 Italian scholar Gerard of Cremona (1114–1187) makes Latin translations of the Arabic versions of older texts, including the *Almagest* by Greek astronomer Ptolemy (ca 100–70 C.E.) and the works of the Persian physician Avicenna (980–1037).

1202 Italian mathematician Leonardo Fibonacci (ca 1170–1250) introduces the Fibonacci series, in which each number is the sum of the previous two.

1217 Scottish scholar Michael Scot (ca 1175–ca 1235) introduces the ideas of Greek philosopher Aristotle (384–322 B.C.E.) into European astronomy.

1225 Mathematician Jordanus Nemorarius, in his *Arithmetica*, uses letters to denote variable quantities (as in modern algebra).

1240 English mathematician Johannes de Sacrobosco publishes *De Sphaera Mundi* (On the Sphere of the World), a standard astronomical text for the next four centuries.

1180 Italian physician Roger of Salerno publishes *Practica Chirurgica* (Practice of Surgery), the first European book devoted entirely to surgery.

1193 Italian scholar Burgundo of Pisa translates the medical works of Greek physician Galen of Pergamum (ca 129– ca 216) from Greek into Latin. This has a profound effect on the teaching and practice of medicine for the next two centuries.

1205 European farmers begin to grow buckwheat as an alternative to emmer wheat, barley, and oats.

1240 Dissection of human corpses is permitted in a decree issued by the Holy Roman Empire.

1180 English scholar and cleric Alexander Neckam (1157–1217) writes *De Naturis Rerum* (Concerning Natural Things), which contains the first reference to the magnetic compass in Western writing.

1209 Italian engineers build a 31-mile (50-km) irrigation canal from the Ticino River near its outlet at Lake Maggiore to the suburbs of Milan. It is later (1269) enlarged into the Naviglio Grande (Grand Canal) for navigation.

1225 Scientist and mathematician Jordanus Nemorarius, in his book *Elementa super demonstrationem ponderis* (Elements for the Demonstration of Weights), includes laws for calculating the displacements produced by levers.

1242 English scientist and philosopher Roger Bacon (ca 1214–1292) gives precise instructions on how to make gunpowder.

THE AMERICAS

ca 1200 The Anasazi begin to use a sun calendar that divides the year into four seasons, using patterns of sunlight falling on rock carvings to identify the first day of each season.

ca 1200 A Maya codex records information about the cycles of the planet Venus.

ASIA & OCEANIA

1181 Chinese and Japanese astronomers report a new supernova that stays visible for about 183 days.

ca 1200 Chinese mathematicians introduce a symbol for zero.

The Citadel at Aleppo, Syria, was constructed between 1193 and 1215 under the supervision of Saladin's son Malik az-Zahir.

AFRICA & THE MIDDLE EAST

1240 Arab physician Ibn al-Baytar (1179– 1248) lists 1,400 different medications in *The Comprehensive Book on Materia Medica and Foodstuffs*.

1198 Arab scholar Ibn Rushd (1126–98), also known as Averroës, dies after becoming a world-renowned commentator on the works of Aristotle.

ca 1200 Arab geographer Abdallah al-Rumi writes his encyclopedia *Mu'jam ul-Buldan*, a survey of geographical knowledge.

ENGINEERING & INVENTION	WORLD EVENTS
1180 Western boatbuilders start making ships steered using a rudder at the stern instead of steering oars at the sides. **1205** Ironworkers in Catalonia, Spain, improve the Catalan forge, which employs a draft of air in the smelting furnace (a forerunner of the blast furnace). **1209** The 20-arch Old London Bridge over the Thames River is completed. It is lined with houses to provide rent for its upkeep. **ca 1220** The main structure of Chartres Cathedral, France, is rebuilt around this time following a fire of 1194 that destroyed all but the western front of the original building. **1225** French master mason Villard de Honnecourt makes detailed drawings of various mechanisms, including a water-powered machine for sawing timber.	**1189** Richard I (r. 1189–99) becomes king of England. **1204** Amsterdam is founded in Holland. **1215** King John of England (r. 1199–1216) signs Magna Carta, a document that grants English nobles certain rights in their dealings with the king; the document becomes a cornerstone of constitutional government. **1220** Several universities are founded in Europe at about this time, including Padua (1222), Naples (1224), Toulouse (1229), Cambridge (1231), and Rome (1244).
ca 1200 The Anasazi make sandals by weaving together the leaves of yucca plants.	**ca 1175** Toltec power fades in Mexico. **ca 1200** Inca leader Manco Capac founds the city of Cuzco in Peru. **ca 1200** Chichen Itza's dominance of the Yucatán is overtaken by that of Mayapán.
1185 Chinese craftsmen invent the rotary disk cutter (for cutting jade). **1189** Construction of the 770-foot (235-m) Marco Polo Bridge begins across the Yongding River in China; it survives today. **1220** The Chinese military use gunpowder bombs with outer cases that shatter on explosion, acting like a type of shrapnel. At about the same time they employ kites to carry messages across enemy lines. **1227** Japanese artisan Kato Shirozaemon (1169–1249) returns from China with the secret for making porcelain.	**1185** Minamoto Yoritomo (1147–99) sets up a military government in Japan, and later becomes shogun. **ca 1200** While Islam spreads into India, Zen Buddhism begins to become popular in Japan. **1206** Genghis Khan (born ca 1162) becomes leader of the Mongols and begins an expansion of the Mongol Empire across Asia that ends with his death in 1227. **1220** The kingdom of Sukothai is established in Thailand.

1205 Arab scholar Abu al-Iz Ismail ibn al-Razaz Al-Jarzi gives instructions for building 50 machines in his *Book of Knowledge of Ingenious Mechanical Devices.*

1209 The Persian Al-Razi dies after a lifetime of writing on philosophical subjects, including a compendium of science.

CASTLES AND BRIDGES

In the Roman Empire, fortifications and bridges were common. After the empire's collapse it was not until the 11th century that they were again built on the same scale. They were simple structures—motte and bailey castles made from earthworks and wooden palisades, and bridges built from wooden piers and beams. Over the 11th and 12th centuries, however, engineers matched the work of their forbears.

Castles became massive, with high towers, secret tunnels, and walls up to 100 feet (30 m) thick. They were often built on steep hillsides or coastal cliffs and dominated the landscapes of Europe and the Middle East for centuries. Castles were continually upgraded to match the advances in weaponry. By the 15th century, however, artillery had become so powerful that no castle could defend itself adequately.

Bridges also grew more complex. Some, such as the Pont Valentré on the Lot River in France, were fortified. Others had stores, chapels, tollhouses, or homes all the way across. Old London Bridge was the first stone bridge with masonry foundations to be built across a swift-flowing tidal river—the Thames. Constructed between 1176 and 1209 and lined with houses and shops, it survived for more than 600 years.

An illustration of the Old London Bridge, which was continually in use as a major transport route until its demolition in the early 19th century.

ASTRONOMY & MATH

EUROPE

1272 After 10 years' work, the Alfonsine Tables of astronomical data are completed, sponsored by King Alfonso X of Léon and Castile (ca 1221–84). The first set of astronomical tables prepared in Christian Europe, they are used for several centuries.

1275 William of Moerbeke (1215–86) translates works of Greek mathematician and philosopher Archimedes (ca 287–212 B.C.E.) from Greek into Latin. He also translates the medical works of Greek physician Galen of Pergamum (ca 129–ca 216).

1321 French–Hebrew mathematician and philosopher Levi ben Gershon (1288–1344) introduces the mathematics of permutations and combination.

BIOLOGY & MEDICINE

1267 In his *Opus Majus* (Great Work) English scientist and philosopher Roger Bacon (ca 1214–92) describes the magnification of objects by convex lenses, and suggests that magnifying glasses could enhance "weak sight."

1276 Italian theologian Giles of Rome (d. 1316) writes *De Formatione Corporis in Utero* (On the Formation of the Body in the Uterus), in which he discusses the role of both parents in procreation.

1316 Italian anatomist Mondino de' Luzzi (ca 1275–1326) publishes his *Anatomia*, the first Western account of anatomy and a standard work until the writings of Belgian anatomist Andreas Vesalius (1514–64) become available.

1320 In his book *Chirurgia* (Surgery) French pioneer surgeon Henri de Mondeville (1260–1320) recommends the cleansing and stitching of wounds to aid healing.

PHYSICAL SCIENCES

1250 German Dominican monk, scholar, and alchemist Albertus Magnus (1193–1280) isolates arsenic.

1269 In *Epistola de Magnete* (Letter about Magnets) French soldier Petrus Peregrinus introduces the idea that a magnet has "poles" that influence a compass needle.

1300 Spanish alchemist known as False Geber (b. ca 1270), who took his name from the eighth-century Arab scholar Jabir ibn-Hayyan (ca 721–ca 803), describes sulfuric acid.

1304 German scientist Theodoric of Freibourg (d. 1310) investigates the role of raindrops in forming rainbows. He also discovers that refraction causes a colored spectrum, as he records in *De Iride* (Concerning the Rainbow).

1315 According to tradition, Spanish cleric and philosopher Ramón Llull (ca 1232–1315), also known as Raymond Lully and Doctor Illuminatus, discovers ammonia gas.

THE AMERICAS

ASIA & OCEANIA

1270 To observe the positions of the stars, Chinese astronomer Kuo Shou-Ching (1231–1316) constructs an armillary sphere on an equatorial mount, which he calls his "simplified instrument."

1276 Chinese astronomer Zhou Kung erects a 40-foot (12-m) gnomon (shadow clock) for accurate timekeeping.

ca 1300 Hawaiians begin to farm popular food fish in giant ponds.

INSIDE STORY

Roger Bacon

Englishman Roger Bacon (ca 1214–94) was not only a philosopher but also one of the first experimental scientists. Among his many interests he experimented with light and lenses, the branch of science now known as optics, building on the work of Islamic scientists such as Alhazen, whose *Book of Optics* had revolutionized the science of light and vision around 100 years earlier. Bacon is also occasionally credited with the invention of eyeglasses, although glasses were also invented independently in Italy at about this time. Among Bacon's other achievements was the first account in western Europe, in 1242, of the precise composition of gunpowder. Bacon did not suggest any uses for the explosive, however, and guns and cannon were not made in Europe until around 50 years later.

AFRICA & THE MIDDLE EAST

1262 Arab astronomer and mathematician Nasir al-Din al-Tusi (1201–74) designs and builds a well-equipped observatory at Maragheh (in present-day Iraq), which includes a quadrant 12 feet (3.6 m) across. Twelve years later he publishes a set of precise astronomical tables.

1255 Carrier pigeons are used to convey messages in the Middle East. The 400 miles (640 km) between Cairo and Damascus is covered in about a day (using relays of birds).

1260 Arab physician Ibn al-Nafis describes the pulmonary circulation of the blood (the loop of the main circulation that passes from the heart to the lungs and back).

1284 Mamluk Sultan Qala'un (r. 1279–90) builds the Mansuri Maristan in Cairo, Egypt, a hospital with separate wards for different medical disorders.

The workings of the magnifying lens were explained by the optical experiments of Roger Bacon and Alhazen.

1280 A book on warfare by Syrian al-Hassan al-Rammah refers to saltpeter and rockets, suggesting a knowledge of the composition of gunpowder.

ENGINEERING & INVENTION

1250 Armorers in Bohemia (in present-day Czech Republic) make armor using tinplate (steel coated with a layer of tin) to prevent rust.

1250 In Paris the main part of Notre-Dame Cathedral is completed.

1272 Italian mechanic Borghesano of Bologna invents a machine for forming silk threads.

1286 Eyeglasses are invented in Italy at about this time. The invention is often attributed to physician Salvino degli Armati.

ca 1310 Portuguese sailors produce portolan charts to aid coastal navigation.

1315 Italian immigrants establish a silk industry in Lyons, France.

1323 Waterwheel-driven bellows are described for the first time in a French manuscript.

1290 South American people living in the Andes mountains build cable bridges to cross deep gorges.

ca 1325 The Hohokam begin to build Casa Grande, a large structure in present-day Arizona.

1288 Chinese military engineers make the first gunpowder cannon, which they call "erupters."

1313 Chinese printer Wang Chen produces *Nong Shu* (Treatise on Agriculture), using more than 50,000 movable type characters carved from hardwood. (Wooden type replaces the clay characters used previously.)

ca 1275 Building begins at Great Zimbabwe in southern Africa of a large ceremonial enclosure constructed of stone without the use of mortar.

Armillary sphere, similar to that constructed by Kuo Shou Ching in 1270

WORLD EVENTS

1271 Aged 17, Venetian Marco Polo (ca 1254–1324) sets off with his father and uncle on a four-year journey across Asia to China.

1283 The Teutonic Knights complete the conquest of Prussia.

1284 After destroying the Pisan navy at Meloria, Genoa emerges as the major Italian rival of Venice.

1291 The last Crusade ends when the Knights of Saint John of Jerusalem settle in Cyprus.

1306 Robert the Bruce (r. 1306–29) is crowned king of Scotland and leads attacks on the English.

ca 1315 The so-called Little Ice Age, a prolonged period of lower than normal average temperatures, leads to poor harvests and famine across Europe.

ca 1260 The Aztec settle in the Valley of Mexico.

ca 1275 Drought drives the Anasazi away from Mesa Verde in present-day Colorado.

ca 1300 The Toltec domination of Mesoamerica comes to an end.

1279 Kublai Khan (1215–94) reunites China under the Yuan dynasty.

1281 The Mongols launch an unsuccessful invasion of Japan.

1296 The Khalji dynasty of Delhi takes control of much of India.

1320 Tughlak leader Gharzi Khan becomes sultan of Delhi.

1250 Mamluks take power in Egypt after assassinating the Abuyyid caliph.

1291 The Mamluks seize Acre.

1301 Osman (r. 1299–1326), the first ruler of the Ottoman Turks, defeats the Byzantines in battle.

1312 Mansa Musa (r. 1312–37) comes to power in Mali, which he makes a center of Islamic culture.

THE MAGNETIC COMPASS

As compasses function using the Earth's magnetic field, the development of the compass is closely linked with the understanding of magnetism. People were aware of magnetism thousands of years ago, when they realized the unusual properties of rocks they called lodestones. Lodestones are rich in the mineral magnetite, a mixed iron oxide (Fe_3O_4) that is naturally magnetic.

Like a simple bar magnet, Earth's magnetic field has two poles: north and south. Place a bar magnet under a sheet of iron filings, and the filings line themselves up along the field lines that radiate from the poles. A magnetized object such as a lodestone or compass needle will try to align itself to the Earth's magnetic field lines in just the same way.

Compasses were first made in the first century C.E. by Chinese mystics but were not used for navigation until the 11th century. There is some evidence to suggest that the Vikings used compasses on their voyages around northern Europe in the 11th century, but the first clear reference to a magnetic compass in Europe comes from *De Naturis Rerum* (Concerning Natural Things), published in about 1180 by English scholar Alexander Neckam (1157–1217).

Early European compasses consisted of a magnetized needle thrust perpendicularly through a straw that was then floated upright in a dish of water. By 1250 the needle was mounted on a pivot so that it hovered beneath a circular card marked up with the cardinal directions. When the needle moved, so did the card. Further refinements in compass technology included mounting the needle and dial inside a box. Early compass cases were made of wood or ivory—materials that did not interfere with the magnetic forces acting on the needle. Later models used brass for the same reason. They were later mounted on gimbals so that the needle was not affected by the roll of a ship at sea.

ASTRONOMY & MATH

EUROPE

1328 In an attempt to improve on the laws of motion proposed by Aristotle (384–322 B.C.E.), English theologian Thomas Bradwardine (ca 1290–1349) publishes his theory of proportions in *De Proportionibus Velocitatum in Motibus* (Dealing with Proportions), without great success.

1336 Authorities at the University of Paris make mathematics a compulsory subject for all students.

1355 French philosopher Jean Buridan (ca 1300–ca 58) comes up with the idea of "impetus," which keeps celestial bodies continuously in orbit. The idea is close to the modern concept of inertia, the property that makes an object resist a change in its motion.

1365 French cleric and philosopher Nicole d'Oresme (ca 1330–82) publishes a wide-ranging mathematical text, *Latitudes of Forms*, that anticipates ideas such as analytic geometry and calculus.

THE AMERICAS

ca 1360 The Aztec divide their capital, Tenochtitlan, in quarters based on the four cardinal directions.

ca 1400 The Aztec universe combines three types of time: two belong to the gods—transcendent time and active time; the remainder is the time of humans.

ASIA & OCEANIA

1395 Chinese astronomers calculate the length of the solar year as 365.25 days. (A solar year is the time it takes Earth to make a complete orbit of the sun, modern value 365.242 days.)

AFRICA & THE MIDDLE EAST

1410 Hebrew astronomer Hasdai ben Abraham Crescas (ca 1340–1412) writes *Or Adonai* (The Light of the Lord). He disagrees with Aristotle that there are no worlds other than Earth.

1420 Tartar prince, astronomer, and Turkish ruler of Maverannakhr (modern Uzbekistan) Ulugh Beg (1394–1449) begins construction of a three-story observatory at the new university in Samarkand. In 1437 he produces the *Zij-i Gurgani*, a catalog of 992 stars.

BIOLOGY & MEDICINE

1333 Europe's first medieval botanical garden is opened in Venice.

1363 French physician Guy de Chauliac (ca 1300–68) describes how to treat fractures and hernias in his book *Chirurgia Magna* (Great Surgery).

1377 As a measure against the spread of plague, authorities at the port of Ragusa (present-day Dubrovnik, Croatia) establish a quarantine station on a nearby island. Suspected carriers of the disease have to stay there for 30 days.

1407 In London, England, Bethlehem Hospital becomes an institution for the insane; it is popularly known as Bedlam.

1410 Italian physician Benedetto Rinio writes *Liber de Simplicibus*, a catalog of more than 500 medicinal plants.

Architect Filippo Brunelleschi's great dome for Florence Cathedral was finished by 1434, but he continued to be involved with the building of the cathedral until his death in 1446.

1410 People in Ethiopia make and drink coffee from the berries of the wild Ethiopian coffee plant. Coffee does not become a popular drink in Europe until about 200 years later.

PHYSICAL SCIENCES

1340 Avoirdupois weights (using pounds and ounces) are introduced into England from France.

ca 1350 At about this time ironfounders at Liège, Belgium, build a blast furnace for extracting iron from its ores.

1398 A 7.2-mile (12-km) canal from Lake Mölln to the Delvenau River in Germany is built. It links with the Elbe River to provide a tortuous route between the Baltic and the North seas.

HOW THINGS WORK

The Longbow

In 1415 the massively outnumbered English army of King Henry V defeated the French army at the Battle of Agincourt. One of the decisive factors in the English victory was the use of the English longbow, a weapon that allowed archers to fire arrows at high enough speeds to penetrate the thick armor of the French knights. The arrows the weapons fired had narrow barbed heads that were nearly impossible to remove without making a wound worse. The longbow, as the name suggests, was a huge weapon between 4 and 6 feet (1.2–1.8 m) in length. The weapon required around four times the strength as a normal bow to fire accurately. In order to be able to use the longbow effectively, archers had to be trained from a very young age and continue to practice throughout their lives. Archery practice became a standard part of English life. Examination of the skeletons of medieval English longbowmen reveals that they usually had one arm significantly longer than the other, caused by the massive compression of the bow's draw.

ENGINEERING & INVENTION	WORLD EVENTS
1391 *A Treatise on the Astrolabe*, possibly by poet Geoffrey Chaucer (ca 1342–1400), is the first technology book in English.	**1333** Islamic culture reaches its height in Granada, Spain, under Caliph Yusuf I (1318–54).
1345 Dutch engineers use windmills to pump water in land reclamation projects.	**1337** Edward III of England (r. 1327–77) claims the French throne, sparking the Hundred Years' War.
1364 Italian clockmaker Giovanni di Dondi (1318–80) makes an astronomical clock.	**1346–50** The Black Death (plague) kills at least 25 million people, more than a quarter of Europe's population.
1380 Military rockets are fired in Europe for the first time at the Battle of Chioggia between Genoese and Venetian armies.	**1371** The Stewart dynasty comes to the Scottish throne.
1405 Triangular lateen sails come into use on Spanish ships and soon spread throughout the Mediterranean region.	**1381** Venice defeats Genoa and begins a golden age of commerce and culture.
1420 A manual for gunners, *The Book of Fireworks*, is published in Germany and becomes the standard work for 200 years.	**1415** Henry V of England (r. 1413–22) defeats the French at the Battle of Agincourt, part of the Hundred Years' War.
1420 Architect Filippo Brunelleschi (1337–1446) begins supervision of the building of the dome of the Florence Duomo, or cathedral, Italy.	
ca 1350 Aztec craftsman are renowned for their technological capability.	**ca 1350** The Aztec demand tribute from their subject peoples.
ca 1400 The Inca use quipu, knotted strings, to keep trade records and to preserve oral histories.	**1410** Viracocha Inca expands the Inca empire from its base at Cuzco, Peru.
ca 1400 The Mississippians build large earth mounds in North America.	
1395 Printers in Korea use metal type; in 1403 King Taejong (reigned 1400–18) orders type to be cast in bronze.	**1336** The Ashikaga shogunate is established in Japan.
ca 1405 Improvement works begin on China's Grand Canal.	**1368** The Ming dynasty is founded in China, with its capital at Nanjing.
1408 *Yongle dadian*, a wide-ranging encyclopedia, is published under the patronage of the Chinese emperor Yongle.	**1398** Tamerlane (r. 1370–1405) invades India and sacks the capital at Delhi.
1414 From this year Chinese trading fleets sail to India, the Middle East, and as far as Africa, using large oceangoing junks.	**ca 1405** Chinese admiral Zheng He (1371–1433) leads seven huge naval expeditions around the India Ocean.
	1420 Emperor Yongle (r. 1402–24) moves the Chinese capital to Beijing.
ca 1350 Muslim architects adopt the four-liwan style for mosques and schools of four vaulted halls around an open courtyard.	**1331** Arab traveler Ibn Battuta (1304–ca 1368) visits East Africa as part of a long voyage through the Islamic world.
ca 1360 The Ottoman timar system establishes a degree of centralized control over agriculture and manufacture.	**1354** The Ottoman empire reaches across the Bosporus to Europe.
ca 1390 Tamerlane reconstructs Samarkand as his capital.	**1396** An Ottoman army led by Sultan Bayezid (r. 1389–1402) defeats a Christian army led by Sigismund of Hungary (r. 1433–1437) at Nicopolis.
	1402 The Ottomans are defeated by the Mongols led by Tamerlane.
	1421 The Ottoman sultan Murat II (r. 1421–44) resumes a policy of expanding the empire.

THE BLACK DEATH

In the 1340s Europe and the Middle East were struck by an outbreak of the Black Death. The disease—most likely bubonic plague—spread rapidly around the trading centers of the medieval world, killing millions of people. The symptoms of the disease were black spots on the skin, fever, and swollen glands. It was spread by the bites of fleas carried by rats, although the people of the time did not know this.

The disease spread rapidly in the unsanitary conditions of the cities and merchant ships that traveled between them. People panicked, set fire to their homes, and fled, taking their animals— and often their animals' infected fleas— with them.

By the time the pandemic had run its course, the Black Death had killed more than one-quarter of the population of Europe. Across the continent, building projects and road construction came to a halt, and harvests failed for lack of workers. In the aftermath of the disease came social change, as workers who had been tied to the land could now hire themselves out to the highest payer.

A plague doctor. The beak at the front of the hood contained strong-smelling herbs that were believed to prevent infection.

CLOCKS AND WATCHES

THE SHADOW CLOCK, THE FIRST TIMEKEEPER, was in use in ancient Egypt by about 3500 B.C.E. The device consists of a vertical stick in the ground, and time is indicated by the position of its shadow, which changes during the day with the apparent movement of the sun across the heavens. By the eighth century B.C.E. the shadow clock had evolved into the sundial, in which a triangular "fin" (gnomon) replaced the stick. Sand clocks also date from ancient times. The most common type was the hourglass, so called because it took exactly one hour for dry sand to run through a narrow neck from the upper section to the lower section. The British Royal Navy used hourglasses to keep time onboard ships at sea until the 1820s.

At night the ancient Egyptians used a water clock to tell the time. Called a *clepsydra*, the simplest type consisted of a vessel full of water with a graduated scale marked on the inside. Water dripped out of the vessel through a hole in the bottom, and the water level on

The ornate 24-hour clock (dating from 1344) at the Capitanio Palace in Padua, Italy, displays the date as well as the phases of the moon and the positions of the sun in the zodiac.

KEY DATES

725
First mechanical water-driven clock

996
Clock escapement

1380s
Weight-driven clocks

1502
Spring-driven clock

1656
First pendulum clock

1675
Hairspring regulator

the scale inside indicated the time. The Greeks added a float mechanism that moved a pointer to show the time. Chinese inventors also made a version of the clepsydra, sometimes using mercury instead of water.

In 725 C.E. Chinese engineer Liang Ling-Zan and Buddhist monk Yi-Xing (683–727) made the first mechanical clock, based on the regular movement of a huge 33-foot (10-m) paddlewheel. Each "paddle" consisted of a cup and, as it filled with water, it rotated the wheel by exactly one thirty-sixth of a turn. A system of gears gave readings of the time of day, as well as the day of the year and the phase of the moon. In about 1090 Chinese imperial minister Su Sung (1020–1101) built a huge water-driven clock, or "Cosmic Engine," which indicated the apparent movement of the stars as well as the time.

Mechanical Clocks and Watches

The first mechanical clocks were driven by the action of a slowly falling weight at the end of a cord wrapped around a drum. A horizontally oscillating bar controlled the rotation of a cogwheel on the drum and slowed its rotation—this was the first example of a clock escapement. At hourly intervals a hammer rang a bell to indicate the passing of time (there were no hands or dials). The word *clock* comes from the German *glock*, meaning bell. This type of clock is said to have been invented by the French cleric and scholar Gerbert of Aurillac (ca 945–1003) in about 996, before he became Pope Sylvester II in 999. Similar clocks dating from the 1380s still exist in the cathedrals at Rouen, France, and Salisbury, England.

In 1502 German clockmaker Peter Henlein (1480–1542) invented a spring-driven clock, which had a horizontal face with a single hour hand. Then in 1656 Dutch scientist Christiaan Huygens (1629–95) designed the pendulum clock, the first of which was made a year later by a clockmaker in The Hague named Salomon Coster (1620–59). The anchor escapement was the next major improvement in the design, invented in 1660 by English scientist Robert Hooke (1635–1703). Since it was a regular timekeeper, the pendulum could be applied to both weight-driven and spring-driven clocks.

Henlein made the first portable timekeeper, or watch, a year or two before he died in 1542. Spring-

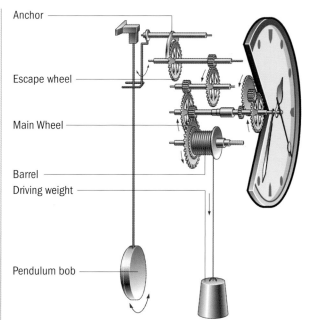

The mechanism that controls the speed at which a clock runs is the escapement. The anchor escapement was used in long-case clocks from about 1670. The swinging pendulum causes a horseshoe-shaped anchor to rock from side to side, allowing the escape wheel to make a fraction of a turn at each half-swing. This action allows the driving weight to fall slowly, rotating the barrel and turning the hands of the clock.

driven, it had a single hour hand that showed through holes in the front of the case. It was highly inaccurate, however. The oscillating balance wheel and hairspring regulator were invented in about 1675; they are still used in mechanical clocks and watches today. In 1680 English clockmaker Daniel Quare (1648–1724) invented a repeating watch that chimed the hours and repeated the last set of chimes when the owner pressed a lever at the side. That made it possible to find out at any time the last hour that had struck.

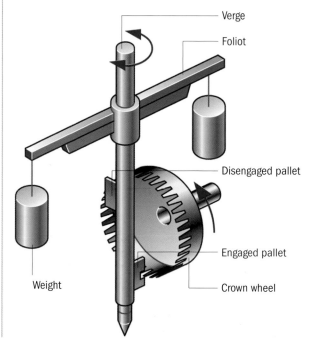

The verge-and-foliot escapement was used on lantern clocks until about 1800. The verge was controlled by two teeth (pallets) that engaged a vertical crown wheel. As the foliot swung in one direction, a pallet disengaged the crown wheel, allowing the weight to fall and turn the hand. The foliot swung back, and a pallet engaged the crown wheel, stopping the fall of the weight. The foliot then swung in the other direction, allowing the weight to fall again.

ASTRONOMY & MATH	BIOLOGY & MEDICINE	PHYSICAL SCIENCES

1425 German philosopher Nicholas Krebs (1401–64), known as Nicholas of Cusa, maintains that the Earth rotates on its axis once a day and orbits the sun once a year.

1435 Italian architect and artist Leon Alberti (1404–72) publishes a book that includes the scientific laws of perspective, which are the basis of projective geometry.

1460 Austrian astronomer Georg von Peuerbach (ca 1421–61) begins work on a version of Ptolemy's *Almagest*. After his death, it is finally published in 1496.

1464 German mathematician Regiomontanus (Johann Müller, 1436–76) writes *De Triangulis Omnimodis* (Concerning Triangles of All Kinds), an overview of trigonometry.

1472 Regiomontanus describes a comet, which we now know as Halley's comet. Two years later he publishes his *Ephemerides Astronomicae* (Astronomical Ephemeris), in which he gives the positions of the stars.

1451 Nicholas of Cusa prescribes eyeglasses with concave lenses for nearsighted people.

1453 A professional association for midwives is established in Regensburg, Germany.

1460 German physician Heinrich von Pfolspeundt publishes *Bündt-Ertzney*, the first German book on surgery.

1473 In Italy the *Canon of Medicine* by Persian physician Avicenna (980–1037) is published. It is the first complete version available in Europe.

1474 *Da Buch der Natur* (The Book of Nature), written by Conrad von Megenburg in 1350, appears in print. It contains the first woodcut images of plants.

1450 European metalworkers devise a way of separating silver from lead ores such as galena (silver sulfide); some lead contains up to 10 percent silver. Miners from central Europe are encouraged to work in England to improve mining there.

1453 Pope Nicholas V (ca 1397–1455) authorizes major repairs to the Aqua Virgo aqueduct (destroyed in 537) so that it can once more be used to carry water into Rome.

1462 Italian writer Giovanni da Castro describes the alum mines at Tolfa, Italy, showing the increasing importance of the mineral.

TURNING POINTS

Avicenna

The first European printing of the *Canon of Medicine* was a milestone in the development of medicine. Its author, Ibn-Sina—whose name was Latinized for publication in a field still dominated by the ideas of ancient Roman and Greek physicians—was a Persian philosopher and physician. He was born in a village near Bokhara (now Bukhara in present-day Uzbekistan). He studied there and traveled widely. He learned all the classical Arab texts and mastered astronomy, Greek, mathematics, and all the available texts on medicine. At age 18 he became a court physician, then vizier (advisor) at the Buyid court in Hamadan, and from 1024 was physician to several sultans. As well as introducing the works of Aristotle to the Islamic world, Ibn-Sina also wrote more than 100 works on science, philosophy, and religion. His pioneering medical work, however, was his most important contribution to the spread of knowledge. The *Canon of Medicine*, written in 1000, remained a standard medical textbook for centuries. It contains instructions for testing medications, guidelines for diagnosing disease by examining the patient, and advice to surgeons to learn anatomy from observation and dissection, rather than from textbooks.

ca 1470 Inspired by Ali Kusai (ca 1400–74) and Ulugh Beg (ca 1390–1449), the Ottoman Empire is home to many advances in the field of mathematics.

A reconstructed Portuguese caravel. Based on an earlier Arabic design, the caravel was capable of performing long ocean crossings. As a result, it was the type of ship chosen by Christopher Columbus for his voyage to the Americas.

EUROPE

THE AMERICAS

ASIA & OCEANIA

AFRICA & THE MIDDLE EAST

ENGINEERING & INVENTION	WORLD EVENTS
1430 German mechanics use a flywheel to even out the motion of rotating machinery.	**1428** Joan of Arc (1412–31) leads French armies against the English; she is executed in 1431.
ca 1430 The matchlock is introduced as the firing mechanism for small arms.	**1434** Cosimo de Medici (1389–1464) comes to power in Florence.
1442 German inventor Johannes Gutenberg (ca 1400–68) sets up a printing press using movable type.	**1453** The French defeat of the English at Castillon ends the Hundred Years' War.
1445 Portuguese shipbuilders develop the caravel, a two- or three-masted ship that will be used by many navigators over the next two centuries.	**1455** The families of Lancaster and York begin the Wars of the Roses, a struggle for the throne in England.
1457 A four-wheeled wagon with strap suspension—the first passenger coach—is constructed at Kocs in Hungary.	**1477** The wedding of Maximilian of Austria (1459–1519) and Mary of Burgundy (1457–82) launches the Hapsburgs on their rise to dominate much of Europe.
1461 Breech-loading cannon are first made experimentally in Europe.	
1474 English printer William Caxton (ca 1422–91) produces the first printed book in the English language, *Recuyell of the Historyes of Troye.*	
ca 1450 The Inca construct a road system 20,000 miles (35,000 km) long to unite their empire.	**1440** Moctezuma (1440–69) becomes ruler of the Aztec Empire.
	1470 Cuzco defeats the coastal empire of Chimu and absorbs its territory into its growing empire.
1428 The Timurid ruler Ulugh-Beg builds an observatory at Samarkand to carry out astronomical observations.	**1434** The Khmer of modern Cambodia move their capital from Angkor to Phnom Penh.
ca 1430 The Ottomans become experts at making cannon.	**1433** Tuareg nomads occupy Timbuktu on the edge of the Sahara.
1432 Portuguese navigator Gonzalo Cabral rediscovers the Azores islands in the Atlantic Ocean (probably first discovered in 1427 by Diogo de Sevilla).	**1453** Ottomans led by Mehmed II (r. 1444–46 and 1451–81) seize Constantinople, bringing the Byzantine empire to an end.
1453 At the siege of Constantinople (present-day Istanbul), Ottoman forces employ a huge cannon that fires cannonballs weighing up to 1,345 pounds (610 kg).	**1464** Sonni Ali Ber (r. 1464–92) overthrows the Tuareg in Timbuktu on behalf of the empire of Songhai.
1471 Portuguese navigator Fernão do Po discovers the island of Fernando Póo (now Bioko) in Equatorial Guinea, West Africa.	

WILLIAM CAXTON

William Caxton was the first printer to produce a book in the English language. His work is credited with beginning the standardization of written and spoken English, changing it from a language composed of a large number of highly varied dialects. Caxton was born in southern England and took an apprenticeship with a London merchant whose business was the import and export of mainly woolen goods to continental Europe.

In about 1441 Caxton went to the Belgian city of Bruges, where he became prosperous. He made translations to produce fine manuscripts for noble patrons. After a change in the political climate he went to Köln in Germany to learn about printing, based on the kind of press first developed by Johannes Gutenberg (ca 1400–68). Caxton returned to Bruges and, with Flemish calligrapher Colard Mansion, set up a printing firm. In 1474 they produced the first printed book in the English language, *Recuyell of the Historyes of Troye* (which Caxton himself translated from French).

An engraving of a 16th-century printing shop. It shows the printing press (on the left), the proofreaders (bottom left), and the typesetters (right). Caxton's press concentrated on making books for the wealthy and powerful.

Two years later Caxton returned to England and established a printing shop with a wooden press near Westminster Abbey, London, in 1477. His first publication in England was *Dictes or Sayengis of the Philosophers.* Over the next 15 years he produced 73 books and 33 other printed works from what became known as the Caxton Press (a name that is still trading in Britain).

THE STORY OF PRINTING

P RINTING ORIGINATED IN CHINA. IN ABOUT the ninth century printers there made paper money and books, with each page of characters carved from a single block of wood to make a printing "plate." By 1045 Chinese printer Bi Sheng was making movable type of baked clay and within ten years was printing books with it.

Printing from cast-metal type began in Korea in the 1390s. In 1403 Korean King Taejong authorized the casting of metal type in bronze. Other printers adopted woodcuts for printing, often carving the type for whole pages out of a single piece of wood. There are thousands of different characters in the Chinese language, and in 1313 printer Wang Chen used more than 50,000 movable wooden characters to print *Treatise on Agriculture*. By 1438 Dutch printer Laurens Koster (ca 1370–1440) of Haarlem is thought to have used movable wooden blocks for printing.

Gutenberg's Bible

Metal type was reinvented in Europe by German inventor Johannes Gutenberg (ca 1400–68) in the 1440s. Gutenberg brought together the ideas of making copper molds in which to cast the type, a low-melting lead alloy to do the casting, a special oil-based printing ink, and a printing press to squeeze the paper against the inked plates. He adapted the screw press previously used for crushing grapes to make wine. (Asian printers did not use a printing press. Instead, they placed the paper on the inked type and used a brush or a roller to push the two into contact.)

Gutenberg set up his first press in about 1442 in Strasbourg, France, but in about 1450 he returned to his hometown of Mainz, Germany, and established a press. Gutenberg's first book—the world's first book to be printed using movable metal type—was a Latin Bible, which he produced in 1455. It is sometimes known as the Forty-Two Line Bible, because its Latin text was printed in 42-line columns. Like other publications of the time, Gutenberg's Bible had no page numbers, no title page, and nothing to indicate who had published it. The first printed book in Europe to carry the name of its printer was a book of psalms produced in 1457 by one of Gutenberg's backers, Peter Schöffer (ca 1425–1502). It was also the first book to be printed in two colors.

Printing Spreads

Printing presses soon began to appear in other parts of Europe. The first press in Italy, at Subiaco near Rome, was established in 1465, and by 1470 the university in Paris had its own press. In 1471 German astronomer and mathematician Regiomontanus (Johann Müller, 1436–76) set up a press at his Nuremberg observatory for printing astronomical tables.

Metal-type printing was introduced to England by William Caxton (ca 1422–91). In 1474 Caxton was the first person to print a book in English, while living in Belgium. Called *Recuyell of the Historyes of Troye*, it had been translated from French by Caxton himself. He printed his own translation from French of *The Game and Playe of the Chesse* a year later. Caxton returned to England in 1476 and established a printing press in London a year later. In 1481 he published the first illustrated book in English. The Caxton Press published more than 100 works over the next 15 years. Many of the books were translations, mainly from French, made by Caxton himself.

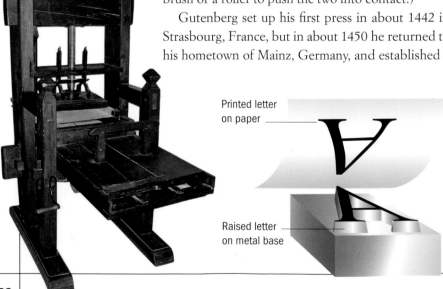

A reproduction of Gutenberg's printing press shows how closely it was based on presses used to crush grapes for wine and olives for oil.

Printed letter on paper

Raised letter on metal base

Nearly all early printers used letterpress printing. The characters to be printed are carved or cast as raised, mirror-image letters. The letters are arranged as text and locked into a frame (called a chase). The printer applies ink to the type, usually with a roller, then places a sheet of paper on the inked type, and squeezes them together in a press. When the paper is peeled off the type surface, it retains the printed image. This method —called flatbed letterpress—remained the standard form of printing into the 19th century.

A page from the Gospel of Saint Paul in the Gutenberg Bible.

Incipit epistola sancti iheronimi ad paulinum presbiterum de omnibus diuine historie libris· capitulū primū.

Rater ambrosius tua michi munuscula pferens detulit· sīl et suauissimas lr̄as· q̄ a principio amiciciaꝝ· fide pb̄a̅re iam fidei ⁊ veteris amicicie noua· pferebant· Vera eni illa necessitudo e̅· ⁊ xp̄i glutino copulata· q̄m non vtilitas rei familiaris· nō pñcia tantum corpoꝝ· nō sbdola ⁊ palpās adulaco̅· sed dei timor· et diuinaꝝ scripturarū studia conciliant· legimꝰ in veteribz historijs· quosdā lustrasse puincias· nouos adijsse p̄plos· maria trāsisse· ut eos quos ex libris nouerant· coꝛa q̄qz viderent· Sicut piragoras memphiticos vates· sic plato egiptū ⁊ architā tarentinū· eandemqz oꝛam ytalie· que quondā magna grecia dicebat· laboriosissime ptaffuit· et ut qui athenis mgr̄ erat· ⁊ potens· cuiusqz doctrinas achademie gignasia psonabāt· fieret peginus atqz discipulus· malēs aliena verecūde discere· q̄m sua ipudent̄ ingere· Denicz cū lr̄as quasi toto orbe fugientes psequit̄· capt9 a piratis ⁊ venundatus· tyrāno crudelissimo paruit· duct9 captiuus vinct9 ⁊ seruus· Tamē quia philsus maior emente se fuit· ad tytum liuiū lacteo eloquêcie fonte manantē· de vltimis hispanie galliaruqz finibz· quosdam venisse nobiles legimus· ⁊ quos ad c̄templacionē suī roma nō traxerat· uni9 hois fama pduxit· Habuit illa etas inauditū ōnibz seculis· celebranduqz miraclm· ut urbē tanta

ingressi· aliud extra urbem quererent· Apolloni9 siue ille mag9 ut vulg9 loquit̄· siue ph̄us· ut pitagorici tradunt· intrauit psas· ptāsiuit caucasū· albanos· scithas· massagetas· opulentissima indie regna penetrauit· et ad extremū latissimo physon ampne trāsmisso puenit ad bragmanas· ut hyarcam in throno sedentē aureo et de tantali fonte potantem· inter paucos discipulos· de natura· de moribz· ac de cursu dieꝝ et siderum audiret docentem· Inde p elamitas· babilonios· chaldeos· medos· assyrios· parthos· syros· phenices· arabes· palestinos· reuersus ad allexandriā· perrexit ad ethiopiā· ut gignosophistas ⁊ famosissimam solis mensam videret in sabulo· Inuenit ille vir ubiqz q̄ discerer· et semp proficiens· semp se melior fieret· Scripsit super hoc plenissime octo voluminibus· phylostratus·

Quid loquar de secli hominibz· cū apl̄us paulus· vas electio̅nis· ⁊ magister gentiū· qui de consciencia tāti ī se hospicis loquebat· dicēs· An experimentū queritis eius qui in me loquit̄ xp̄c· Post damascu arabiāqz lustratā· ascēdit iherosolimā ut videret petrū ⁊ māsit apud eū diebz quindeci· Hoc eni misterio ebdomadis et ogdoadis· futur9 gentiū p̄dicator instruendus erat· Rursūqz post ānos q̄uordecim assumpto barnaba et tyto· exposuit cū aplis euāgeliū· ne forte in vacuum curreret aut cucurrisset· Habet nescio q̄d latentis energie· viue vocis actus· et in aures discipli de auctoris ore transfusa· fortius sonāt· Vnde et eschineus cū rodi exulareret· ⁊ legeretur

ASTRONOMY & MATH

EUROPE

1478 The first popular book on math, the *Treviso Arithmetic*, appears in Italy with rules for common types of calculations.

1482 Italian mathematician Johannes Campanus (1220–96) publishes his Latin translation from the Arabic of *Elements* by Greek mathematician Euclid (fl. 300 B.C.E.).

1494 Italian mathematician Luca Pacioli (1445–1517) describes double-entry bookkeeping in an early printed book on math, *Summa de Arithmetica, Geometrica, Proportioni, et Proportionalita* (Everything about Arithmetic, Geometry, and Proportion).

1497 Polish astronomer Nicolaus Copernicus (1473–1543) records a star being occluded by the moon (which occurs when the moon passes in front of the star).

1519 Portuguese navigator Ferdinand Magellan (ca 1480–1521) observes the Magellanic clouds, the two nearest galaxies to our own galaxy, the Milky Way.

THE AMERICAS

1515 German astronomer Johannes Schöner (1477–1547) makes the first globe to include the name America.

BIOLOGY & MEDICINE

1490 A temporary demonstration theater opens in Padua, Italy, where human dissections are performed.

1517 Italian physician and poet Girolamo Fracastoro (ca 1478–1553) proposes that fossils are the petrified remains of once-living organisms.

1518 English humanist and physician Thomas Linacre (ca 1460–1524) founds the Royal College of Physicians in London.

The origins of fossils were first correctly understood by Italian physician Girolamo Fracastoro.

1493 Italian explorer Christopher Columbus (1451–1506) observes that Native Americans use tobacco as a medicinal herb.

1518 Smallpox reaches the Americas with Europeans. In 1520 it decimates the Aztecs.

1520 Spanish voyagers take turkeys and corn from America to Europe.

PHYSICAL SCIENCES

1477 First recorded mention of a gun with a rifled, or grooved, barrel (with internal grooves to impart spin to the bullet), although rifling did not become standard until the 16th century.

1490 Italian artist and inventor Leonardo da Vinci (1452–1519) explains capillary action (the way in which a liquid rises up a very narrow tube, or capillary).

1492 In England graphite is used for the "lead" in pencils.

ASIA & OCEANIA

1495 The Chinese divert the Yellow River to a new course near the Shandong Peninsula.

1514 The Chinese open silver mines at Yunnan.

AFRICA & THE MIDDLE EAST

1513 The Ottoman geographer Piri Reis draws a map of the world that includes what is then known of the Americas.

An early map of the Americas, drawn using information gathered from the early voyages of Columbus and Magellan.

ENGINEERING & INVENTION

1495 French gunners begin using cast-iron cannonballs rather than stones.

1499 German abbot Johannes Trithemius (1462–1516) writes *Steganographia*, a major work on cryptography (codes).

1502 German clockmaker Peter Henlein (1480–1542) makes the first spring-driven pocket clock.

1503 The Spanish successfully explode a series of mines under castles at Naples, establishing a new form of land warfare.

1513 Swiss artist Urs Graf (ca 1485–1527) introduces the technique of metal etching.

1515 The wheel-lock pistol is introduced in Germany.

1500 Chinese scientist Wan Hu attempts to make a flying machine by tying 45 rockets to the back of a chair. He is killed when the device explodes.

1520 The Chinese buy cannon from the Portuguese.

1522 Fine, pale blue porcelain is made in China during the Chia-Ching period.

1511 The Ottomans begin providing gunpowder weapons to their allies such as Egypt and Mesopotamia. Ottoman gunmakers are in demand as far away as Delhi, in India.

WORLD EVENTS

1485 Henry VII (r. 1485–1509) is victorious over Richard III (r. 1483–85) at Bosworth Field, marking the start of the Tudor dynasty in England.

1492 The Spanish seize Granada, the last Muslim kingdom in Spain.

1508 Maximilian I (r. 1508–19) becomes Holy Roman Emperor.

1509 Henry VIII (1509–47) becomes king of England.

1517 German monk Martin Luther (1483–1546) protests against practices of the Catholic Church, beginning the religious upheaval of the Reformation.

1522 The expedition of Portuguese navigator Ferdinand Magellan (ca 1480–1521) completes the circumnavigation of the globe, although Magellan himself was killed the year before in the Philippines.

1492 Italian navigator Christopher Columbus (1451–1506) sails to islands in the Caribbean.

1500 Portuguese navigator Pedro Cabral (ca 1467–ca 1520) claims Brazil for Portugal.

1513 Spanish explorer Vasco Balboa (1475–1519) crosses the Isthmus of Panama and sees the Pacific Ocean.

1483 Russian pioneers begin to explore Siberia.

1498 Portuguese navigator Vasco da Gama (1460–1524) sails around the Cape of Good Hope and crosses the Indian Ocean to reach India.

1511 The Portuguese conquer Malacca in Malaysia.

1514 Portuguese travelers reach China.

1523 The Chinese expel Portuguese traders.

1488 Portuguese navigator Bartholomew Diaz (ca 1450–1500) sails around the Cape of Good Hope at the southern tip of Africa. He calls it the Cape of Storms.

1514 The Ottomans defeat the Persians at the Battle of Chaldiran.

1515 The Songhai empire, based in Timbuktu, reaches the height of its power.

1517 Ottoman Turks defeat the Mamluks of Egypt and take control of Egypt and the Arabian pensinula.

1520 Süleyman I (r. 1520–66), called the Magnificent, becomes Ottoman emperor.

Leonardo's design for a helicopter.

LEONARDO DA VINCI

Leonardo in many ways sums up the spirit of the Renaissance. Born in the small town of Vinci in 1452, at age 16 he was apprenticed to painter and sculptor Andrea del Verrochio (1435–88). Leonardo became well known not only as a painter and sculptor but also as an architect, engineer, and inventor. He worked for some of the most powerful rulers of the time, including Cesare Borgia (ca 1476–1507), the ruler of Florence, and the French kings Louis XII (r. 1498–1515) and Francis I (r. 1515–47).

Throughout his life Leonardo made sketches and plans of a range of fortifications, civil engineering schemes, and mechanisms. He described pulleys and belt drives to transmit power, a treadle-operated lathe, a paddlewheel boat, and a machine for grinding and polishing glass lenses. He designed pumps, mechanized vehicles, and a machine for digging canals. From the study of birds in flight, he designed a flying machine with flapping wings. (It could never work because a human could not produce enough power.) There were also impractical designs for a tank, a submarine, and a helicopter. His 1485 drawing of a parachute was more practical, and he is even thought to have made some small model parachutes and to have tested them.

When Leonardo died in 1519, his friend Francesco Melzi (1493–1570) gathered up his paintings, papers, and models. However, after Melzi's death many were lost or destroyed. Today only about 7,000 of the original 13,000 pages of notes have survived, but they are more than enough to testify to Leonardo's genius.

GUNS AND GUNPOWDER

*This manuscript from
the 15th century shows
a soldier firing a "hand
gonne." These early hand
cannon were so heavy
they had to be rested on a
portable stand to be fired.*

GUNPOWDER IS A CHINESE INVENTION dating from the 11th century. One or two Europeans also claimed to have invented gunpowder. They may have reinvented it, or they may have learned the secret of how to make it from travelers who had visited China. Either way, gunpowder and the firearms that used it changed the course of history.

The origins of gunpowder are shrouded in mystery, mainly because the people who invented it wanted to keep it a secret. The first written mention comes from Chinese writer Tseng Kung Liang in 1044 when he gives a formula for what he calls the "fire drug." Gunpowder is a mixture of charcoal, sulfur, and saltpeter (potassium nitrate). When mixed in the correct proportions it burns rapidly, with 40 percent of the products being gases and the rest solids that take the form of smoke. The hot gases produced expand; and if confined inside a container, explode with a loud bang. If burned at the closed end of an open-ended tube, the expanding hot gases will push out a ball or bullet, and this is the principle of the cannon and all firearms.

With the advent of gunpowder, fireworks became popular in China in the 1100s. A document from about 1100 describes "a noise like thunder," although more often fireworks came in the form of strings of firecrackers. Gunpowder bombs were more dangerous. In about 1220 the Chinese military made bombs with outer casings that shattered on explosion, producing a kind of shrapnel to kill or maim the enemy. A Japanese woodcut of 1292 illustrates a bomb exploding, showing that gunpowder had reached Japan by this time. In 1126 Chinese soldiers used grenades and "fire arrows" in the defense of Kaifeng. The fire arrows were presumably rockets, made by packing gunpowder into bamboo cases. The packing had to be fairly loose or the rockets would have exploded. This knowledge spread abroad, and there is a reference to saltpeter and rockets in a 1280 book on warfare by Syrian writer al-Hassan al-Rammah.

Cannon

The gunpowder cannon first turns up in the late 1280s, when the Chinese military employed what they called "erupters" to fire stones at their enemies. By about 1300 Arab technicians made cannon barrels from bamboo tubes bound around with iron bands. Metal barrels were made from a bundle of wrought-iron rods bound with iron, rather like wooden barrels. In 1346 the English used these wrought-iron cannon against the French at the siege of Calais. A year later European gunsmiths made arrow-firing cannon. The first cannon barrels cast as a single piece in bronze can be dated to German gunsmiths in 1378. Bronze became the material of choice, especially for ships' cannon, because bronze does not corrode as readily as iron. Cast iron was not used for barrels because the castings were often flawed, resulting in bomblike explosions of the barrels themselves. When a bronze cannon barrel failed it usually tore or ruptured, with less tragic results. French gunners used cast iron to make cannonballs from about 1495, and safe cast-iron barrels were first made in England in 1543.

The first "small arm," as opposed to a cannon, was called variously arquebus, harquebus, or hackbut.

This gun was invented in Spain in the mid-1400s. The shooter propped its barrel on a support and fired the weapon from the shoulder. He inserted the gunpowder charge, dropped a ball down the barrel, and ignited the charge with a matchlock—a length of glowing wick on an S-shaped lever. The weapon was inaccurate, with a range of about 200 yards (200 m). It was used widely, including in the conquest of Mexico in the 1520s. Within a hundred years the musket replaced the arquebus, and the wheel lock and then the flintlock replaced the matchlock. The flintlock was more reliable and could be fired in the rain.

To fire a flintlock, the musketeer first poured a charge of gunpowder down the muzzle of the musket, followed by a lead ball and a felt wad that he rammed down to keep the ball and charge in place.

He then put some fine powder in the pan at the side of the lock, and cocked the weapon by pulling back the cock, which held a piece of flint. When he pulled the trigger, the flint sprang forward, hit the steel, and made sparks that ignited the powder in the pan. This action in turn lit the main charge, and the musket went off. If the main charge did not light, it was just a "flash in the pan."

The musket had a smooth bore and gradually gave way to the rifle, which had a spirally grooved barrel to give a spin to the ball or bullet. The final development was the breech-loading rifle and cartridges to go with it. Handguns also followed the same line of development from muzzle-loading flintlock pistols to cartridge weapons, with multishot revolvers being yet another advancement.

A contemporary illustration of the Siege of Calais in 1346. The cannon in the foreground are aimed at the city walls; the stone cannonballs they fired are lying on the ground beside them.

	ASTRONOMY & MATH	BIOLOGY & MEDICINE	PHYSICAL SCIENCES

EUROPE

1525 German mathematician Christoff Rudolf (1499–1545) introduces the mathematical sign for square root.

1541 German mathematician Rheticus (Georg von Lauchen, 1514–74) publishes a set of trigonometrical tables.

1543 Polish astronomer Nicolaus Copernicus (1473–1543) expounds his idea of a sun-centered universe in *De Revolutionibus Orbium Coelestium*.

1569 Flemish cartographer Gerardus Mercator (1512–94) introduces the Mercator map projection. Two years later his compatriot Abraham Ortelius (1527–98) publishes *Theatrum Orbis Terrarum*, the first compendium of maps, later called an atlas.

1573 Danish astronomer Tycho Brahe (1546–1601) publishes *De Nova Stella*, describing a new supernova in the constellation Cassiopeia (often called Tycho's Star at the time).

1528 Swiss-born alchemist Paracelsus (1493–1541) writes the first modern book on surgery.

1530 Italian Girolamo Fracastoro (ca 1478–1553) describes syphilis, introduced to Spain by sailors returning from America.

1540 French surgeon Ambroise Paré (1510–90) makes jointed artificial limbs.

1542 French physician Jean Fernel (1497–1558) explains the condition appendicitis.

1543 Belgian anatomist Andreas Vesalius (1514–64) publishes his seven-volume *De Humani Corporis Fabrica* (On the Structure of the Human Body).

1551 Italian anatomist Gabriello Fallopio (1523–62) discovers the Fallopian tubes (from the ovaries to the womb).

1573 Italian anatomist Costanzo Varoli (ca 1543–75) describes the optic nerves.

1531 German theologian and cosmographer Sebastian Münster (1488–1552) publishes *Horologiographia*, which describes the construction of sundials. In 1544 he publishes a book on world geography entitled *Cosmographia Universalis*.

1533 *De Principis Astonomiae et Cosmographie* by Dutch cosmographer Regnier Gemma Frisius (1508–55) gives the first published explanation of the use of triangulation in surveying and mapmaking. He also points out that latitude can be found by comparing the time given by a clock with that given by the sun.

1537 Italian mathematician Niccolò Tartaglia (1499–1557) invents the gunner's quadrant for aiming cannon.

1556 *De Re Metallica* by German mineralogist Georgius Agricola (1494–1555) is published after his death. It describes the formation of minerals and has information about mining and metal smelting.

THE AMERICAS

Finally we shall place the sun himself at the center of the universe. All this is suggested by the systematic procession of events and the harmony of the whole universe, if only we face the facts, as they say, "with both eyes open."

NICOLAUS COPERNICUS

1532 Sugarcane is first grown in Brazil.

ca 1550 Spanish farmers import European cattle to the pampas or plains of Argentina.

1555 Tobacco from the Americas is exported to Spain.

1545 The Spanish begin silver mining at Potosí in Peru and Zacatecas in Mexico.

1550s Gold is discovered in Chile and Colombia.

ca 1560 Mercury is discovered in Peru and used in a new process to refine silver ore.

ASIA & OCEANIA

1573 Crops from the Americas, including sweet potatoes, corn, and peanuts, are grown in China.

1555 A huge earthquake in northern China kills more than 800,000 people.

1570 Silver from the Americas reaches China.

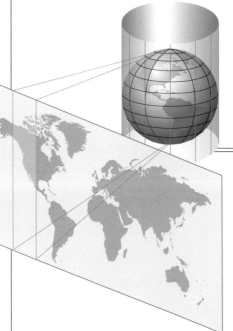

The Mercator projection, as devised by Gerardus Mercator, allows Earth's landmasses to be depicted on a flat map in a similar way to their appearance on a spherical globe.

AFRICA & THE MIDDLE EAST

1543 Copernicus uses theorems in mathematical astronomy developed by Arabian scientists.

1554 Turkish admiral Sidi Ali Reis includes astronomy and mathematics in his writings about the Indian Ocean.

ca 1560 Crops including peanuts and manioc arrive in Africa from the Americas.

ca 1530 Africa exports iron and steel to Portugal.

1539 The Ottoman architect Mimar Sinan builds the first of the 80 mosques, 34 palaces, and many other public buildings that establish him as the leading architect of the Islamic world.

ca 1535 The traveler Motrakci Nasru makes a survey of the route between Istanbul and Baghdad.

ENGINEERING & INVENTION

1525 The fusée comes into use for spring-powered clocks; it equalizes the pull of the clock's spring as it slowly runs down.

1535 The diving bell comes into use in Europe for working on bridge foundations.

1551 English mathematician Leonard Digges (1520–ca 1559) invents the theodolite for measuring angles during surveying.

ca 1555 Trucks running on rails, pushed by hand, come into use in mines in Germany.

1567 The Santa Trinità Bridge, with an elliptical arch, is constructed over the Arno River in Florence, Italy.

1570 Italian architect Andrea Palladio (1508–80) publishes *Four Books on Architecture*.

1573 English sailor Humphrey Cole devises the ship's log for measuring a vessel's speed; it measures "knots" in a rope attached to a log.

1556 The Spanish develop a more efficient process for separating silver from silver ore.

1543 The Portuguese introduce firearms to Japan.

1574 *Taiping Guangzhi* is the first Chinese book printed with movable type.

ca 1550 The Ottomans build aqueducts to carry water into their growing capital city at Istanbul.

1569 Ottoman engineers attempt to construct a canal between the Don and Volga Rivers.

WORLD EVENTS

1530 The Schmalkaldic League is formed by German princes to oppose the Holy Roman emperor Charles V (r. 1519–56) and promote Protestantism.

1547 Ivan IV (the Terrible; r. 1533–84) becomes tsar of Russia, having reigned as Grand Prince of Moscow since 1533.

1555 Religious wars in Germany are ended for a time by the Peace of Augsburg.

1556 Holy Roman Emperor Charles V abdicates in favor of his brother, Ferdinand I (r. 1558–64).

1558 Elizabeth I (r. 1558–1603) becomes queen of England.

1572 As part of the French Wars of Religion, two thousand Protestant Huguenots are massacred on St. Bartholomew's Day.

1572 Dutch nobles begin fighting for independence from Spain.

1532 Spanish soldier Francisco Pizarro (ca 1475–1541) invades Peru and later kills the Inca leader Atahualpa (r. 1532–33).

1536 French navigator Jacques Cartier (1491–1557) claims Canada for France.

1565 The Spanish found St. Augustine in Florida.

1556 Akbar (r. 1556–1605) becomes emperor of India and begins a policy of unifying his Hindu and Muslim subjects.

1550 Mongols besiege Beijing.

ca 1550 Conflict between warlords causes upheaval in Japan.

1569 In Thailand, the kingdom of Ayutthaya is overthrown by the Burmese.

1570 Japan allows Westerners to trade from the port of Nagasaki.

VOYAGES OF DISCOVERY

Until the beginning of the Age of Exploration, the only way Europeans could make contact with India and China was overland by way of the Silk Road through the mountains and deserts of central Asia. The journey by sea was not possible in the small square-sailed ships of the time. In about 1445 Portuguese shipbuilders developed a new type of vessel called a caravel, capable of longer sea journeys. It had two or three masts with one square sail and a set of triangular sails similar to the lateen sails of an Arab *dhow*.

The map below shows the important voyages of the Age of Exploration. They began with an accidental voyage round the horn of Africa by Bartholomew Diaz (ca 1450–1500) after his ship was blown off course in a storm. This was followed by the voyage to the Caribbean made in 1492 by Christopher Columbus (1451–1506). After Columbus's expedition, Italian John Cabot (1450–98) became the first navigator to reach continental North America. In 1498 the Portuguese Vasco da Gama (1460–1524) followed Diaz's route, then crossed the Indian Ocean to reach India. Another voyage, led by Ferdinand Magellan (ca 1480–1521), set out to circumnavigate the globe in 1519. Although Magellan died during the voyage, one of his five ships, captained by Juan del Cano (1486–1526), successfully returned to Spain, completing the first circumnavigation of the globe.

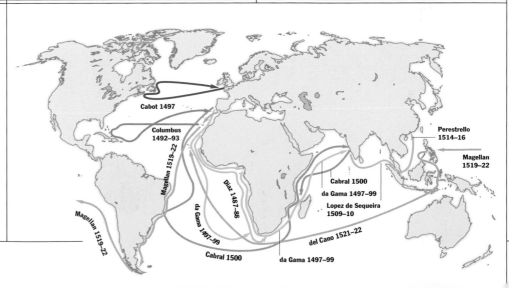

Most of the early voyages of exploration were made in the 30 years between 1492 and 1522.

ASTRONOMY & MATH

EUROPE

1576 Danish astronomer Tycho Brahe (1546–1601) establishes a purpose-built observatory on the Baltic island of Hven.

1582 The Gregorian calendar replaces the Julian calendar; it has a more accurate year length.

1584 Italian philosopher and monk Giordano Bruno (1548–1600) posits his theory of an infinite universe.

1585 Flemish mathematician Simon Stevin (1548–1620), also known as Stevinus, introduces decimal fractions to common use.

1609 German Johannes Kepler draws up his first two laws of planetary motion.

1610 Italian scientist Galileo Galilei (1564–1642) observes craters on the moon and discovers four of Jupiter's moons.

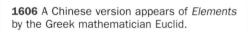

1606 A Chinese version appears of *Elements* by the Greek mathematician Euclid.

This engraving shows Danish astronomer Tycho Brahe and his assistants stargazing in Brahe's observatory on the island of Hven.

AFRICA & THE MIDDLE EAST

1577 Turkish astronomer Takiyuddin founds an advanced observatory at Galatu and begins to correct existing astronomical tables.

BIOLOGY & MEDICINE

1580 Italian botanist and physician Prospero Alpini (1553–1617) distinguishes between male and female flowers.

1583 Italian botanist and physician Andrea Cesalpino (1519–1603) devises a system of classifying plants by their structure in his book *De Plantis*.

1597 Italian surgeon Gaspare Tagliacozzi (1545–99) practices rhinoplasty (skin grafting to reshape the nose).

1603 Italian anatomist Hieronymus Fabricius ab Aquapendente (1537–1619) gives the first clear description of the valves in veins.

1614 Italian physician Sanctorius (1561–1636) writes *De Statica Medicina* (On Medical Measurement) and founds the study of metabolism.

THE AMERICAS

1598 Spanish colonists begin to grow wheat, apricots, and peaches, north of El Paso.

1612 Colonists in Virginia first grow tobacco to sell commercially.

ASIA & OCEANIA

1578 A treatise on pharmacology, *Bencao gangmu*, is published in China.

AFRICA & THE MIDDLE EAST

ca 1600 The Ottomans introduce tobacco from the Americas.

PHYSICAL SCIENCES

1581 Galileo Galilei begins to investigate the properties of the pendulum.

1592 Galileo Galilei makes an air-filled (open-ended) liquid-in-glass thermometer.

1595 Gerardus Mercator publishes the first atlas identified as such, from its cover image of the Greek deity Atlas carrying the globe on his shoulders.

Named for the Italian scientist, a Galileo thermometer is a glass cylinder containing clear liquid and objects (such as liquid-filled glass bulbs) that sink in sequence as the clear liquid warms and decreases in density.

1584 China's tempered musical scale is defined.

ca 1590 With the development of an economy based on coinage, mining fever hits China.

1602 Italian missionary Matteo Ricci (1552–1610) publishes a Chinese atlas of the world.

It is a custom loathsome to the eye, hateful to the nose, harmful to the brain, dangerous to the lungs, and in the black stinking fumes, nearest resembling the horrible smoke of the pit that is bottomless.

JAMES I OF ENGLAND,
A COUNTERBLASTE TO TOBACCO (1604)

ENGINEERING & INVENTION	WORLD EVENTS
1588 English cleric William Lee (ca 1550–ca 1615) invents a machine for knitting hosiery.	**1579** The English and Dutch form an alliance against Spain.
1590 Dutch optician Zacharias Jansen (1580–ca 1638) invents the compound microscope using two lenses.	**1588** England defeats the Spanish Armada.
1598 Dutch inventor Cornelis van Drebbel (1572–1633) patents a "self-winding" clock.	**1590** William Shakespeare (1564–1616) begins writing plays in London.
1608 German-born Dutch eyeglass-maker Hans Lippershey (ca 1570–ca 1619) makes a refracting telescope (using two lenses).	**1603** Queen Elizabeth (r. 1558–1603) of England dies.
1622 English mathematician William Oughtred (1574–1660) creates the slide rule, which uses logarithms to perform multiplication and division.	**1605** The Gunpowder Plot is uncovered in which Catholic plotters try to blow up the Houses of Parliament in London.
1623 German mathematician Wilhelm Schickard (1592–1635) builds a wooden adding machine ("calculating clock").	**1606** Italian opera becomes popular.
	1611 The King James Bible is published.
	1611 Germans plant potatoes—from the New World—as crops.
	1612 Miguel de Cervantes Saavedra (1547–1616) completes publication of *Don Quixote*.
ca 1570 People living in the Rimac River Valley in Peru construct a long canal to irrigate their farmland.	**1600** The Poverty Point culture, named for a site in Louisiana, emerges in North America.
1607 The first American ship is constructed in Sagadahoc, Maine.	**1575** Spanish America begins to import 1,250 African slaves each year.
1619 Virginia colonists fail in their attempt to build an ironworks in the colony.	**1616** Pocahontas (1595–1617) sails for England with English husband John Rolfe (ca 1585–1622).
ca 1575 In Japan, castle-building reaches a peak.	**1581** Under Akbar (1556–1605), India conquers neighboring Afghanistan.
1598 The Koreans invent the turtle ship, an iron-covered warship.	**1591** Territorial lord Toyotomi Hideyoshi (1537–1598) unites Japan.
ca 1600 The tradition of building huge stone statues dies out on Easter Island.	**1600** Ieyasu (r. 1603–05) becomes the undisputed ruler of Japan and founds the Tokugawa shogunate.
	1605 The Mughal emperor Jahangir (r. 1605–27) becomes ruler of India.
	1624 The English begin settling in eastern India.
ca 1590 The Royal Mosque becomes the centerpiece of urban planning in the rapidly growing Persian city of Isfahan.	**1588** Shah Abbas (r. 1588–1629) becomes ruler of Safavid Persia and begins reforming the empire.
	1591 The Songhai Empire is overthrown by Morocco.
	1598 Isfahan becomes the Safavid capital.
	1623 Queen Nzinga Nbandi drives the Portuguese from Ndongo, present-day Angola.

POTATOES AND TOBACCO

Natives of South America have been eating potatoes for at least 10,000 years. At first they were collected from the wild, but around 6,000 years ago people began to cultivate them as a staple crop. Potatoes can grow in high-altitude, cold environments in which other staple crops, such as wheat or corn, would not survive. Potatoes can be easily transported, stored for long periods of time, and are a rich, easily prepared, source of carbohydrate.

The first European to see a potato was probably the Spaniard Juan de Castellanos in about 1537, who described them as "truffles." The potato was first introduced to England in 1563. Across most of Europe it was met with suspicion and considered dirty and primitive. Ireland, however, quickly embraced the potato, which arrived there in about 1600, as it grew well in the country's cool, damp climate. By the early 1780s the population was almost entirely dependent on it. In 1845 the potato crop succumbed to a disease, known as potato blight, resulting in more than one million people starving to death.

Tobacco leaves have been chewed or smoked by Native Americans for at least 2,000 years. The Arawaks of the Bahamas gave Italian explorer Christopher Columbus tobacco leaves when he arrived in 1492. Columbus did not understand that the leaves should be smoked: He threw them away. When explorers later learned its use, tobacco was taken to Europe.

Europeans began cultivating tobacco in South America as early as 1531. Tobacco was introduced to much of Europe from the 1550s. By the late 16th century it was being grown extensively in South America and eastern North America and was regarded as something of a cure-all. The addictive nature of tobacco was recognized early. In the 17th century there was plenty of anti-tobacco feeling: Public smoking was banned in many places.

CHAPTER 4

THE SCIENTIFIC REVOLUTION

IN MANY WAYS, MODERN SCIENCE BEGAN IN THE 17TH AND 18TH CENTURIES. It was marked not only by a flood of discoveries and inventions, but also by the adoption of new methods of studying all aspects of the world and using rational analysis to draw conclusions from the available evidence. So great was the change in approach that the period is commonly described as the Scientific Revolution. The term is somewhat misleading. Knowledge still tended to advance in a series of gradual steps, and by trial and error, rather than in moments of dramatic revelation. Although reason became the universal basis for trying to understand the world, both superstition and religious faith persisted throughout the period. The period itself is difficult to define with a precise start and finish.

According to legend, Galileo dropped cannonballs of unequal sizes from the Leaning Tower of Pisa to demonstrate that their speed of descent is the same and independent of mass.

Nevertheless, over the space of only about a century and a half, a revolution of sorts in scientific knowledge did take place. Near the start of the period, in 1633, the pioneering Italian scientist Galileo Galilei (1564–1642) was put on trial by the Roman Catholic Church for supporting the idea that the sun lay at the center of the solar system, put forward in the previous century by Polish astronomer Nicolaus Copernicus (1473–1543). The church still maintained that the Earth lay at the center not only of the solar system but of the whole universe, a notion first proposed by Greek philosopher Aristotle (384–22 B.C.E.). At the Inquisition, the religious court established to enforce orthodox beliefs, Galileo was found guilty and sentenced to house arrest for the last eight years of his life. By the end of the period, in the 1660s, the English scientist and mathematician Isaac Newton (1642–1727) had explained the invisible force that attracted objects toward the Earth and kept the planets in their orbits around the sun. That force is called gravity.

Galileo and Newton—and many of their contemporaries—shared one essential quality: They were not just thinkers, but experimenters. They gathered information and tested their ideas by close observation, recording, and analysis. Galileo developed his ideas about pendulums by using his pulse rate to time the swings of a chandelier in Pisa Cathedral. The story goes that Galileo tested his theory about falling weights by dropping cannonballs from the Leaning Tower of Pisa. Newton used a glass prism to split white sunlight into a spectrum when formulating his ideas about light.

Accurate observation required the development of accurate instruments. Dutchman Antonie van Leeuwenhoek (1632–1723) invented the microscope, while Galileo himself made significant improvements to the telescope and was the first person to use it to observe heavenly bodies. He identified spots on the sun, hills and craters on the moon, and four satellites of Jupiter. Enthusiastic astron-

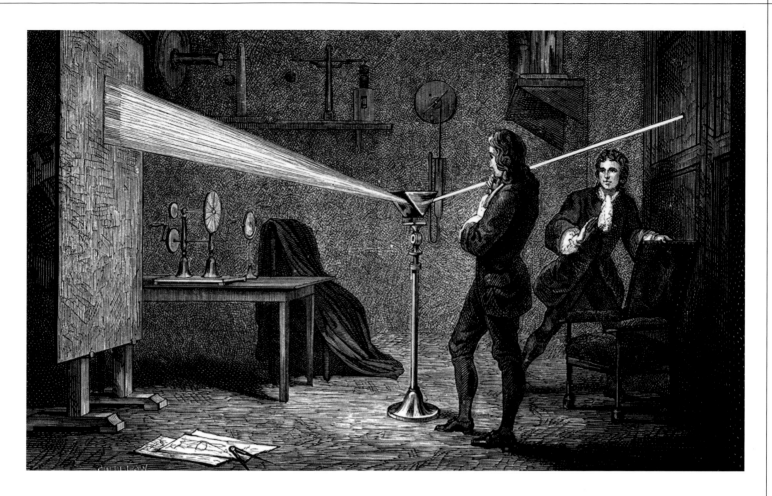

omers throughout Europe recorded a wealth of new observations: A transit of Mercury across the sun, Saturn's rings, and the regular return, or periodicity, of comets. Meanwhile, van Leeuwenhoek's invention allowed the study of another previously invisible world: the internal structure of matter. Newton's contemporary Robert Hooke (1635–1703) coined the word *cell* to describe the "little boxes" he saw when looking at plant tissue under a microscope.

Science did not solely belong to Europeans. The American tradition of practical ingenuity, which continues at the start of the 21st century, began with the towering figure of Benjamin Franklin (1706–90). Franklin combined a career as a printer with politics—he was America's ambassador in France during the American Revolution—and a series of scientific discoveries and inventions. He showed that lightning was a discharge of static electricity and invented bifocal eyeglasses and a nonsmoking woodburner. Franklin's friend Thomas Jefferson (1743–1826) also displayed a flair for practical problem solving, inventing the dumbwaiter to get easy access to his wine cellar.

By the end of the Scientific Revolution, many of the principles of modern science had been explained. Natural philosophers, as these amateur enthusiasts were known, had made huge strides in all areas of science. In biology, for example, they had learned about the circulation of the blood; in physics, they formulated laws about the behavior of gases; and in chemistry, they identified the first elements, the chemical building blocks of the universe. In mathematics, French philosopher René Descartes (1596–1650) invented coordinate geometry, and German philosopher Gottfried Leibniz (1646–1716) introduced binary arithmetic.

Isaac Newton made many breakthroughs in the understanding of mathematics, astronomy, and physics. In the engraving above, he demonstrates that a beam of white light from the sun can be split by a glass prism into the colors of the rainbow.

THE WORLD AT A GLANCE

CONCISE HISTORY OF SCIENCE AND INVENTION

	1625	1645	1660	1675	1690	
EUROPE	**1626** Saint Peter's Basilica in Rome is completed after 120 years. **1628** English physician William Harvey explains the circulation of blood in the body. **1632** The first modern observatory is built in Germany. **1633** Italian scientist Galileo Galilei is condemned by the Roman Catholic Church for his theories. **1633** French mathematician Pierre de Fermat proposes that light always travels in straight lines. **1642** French scientist Blaise Pascal constructs a wooden calculating machine.	**1645** Flemish cartographer Michael Langrenus publishes the first map of the moon. **1645** Italian physicist Evangelista Torricelli makes a mercury barometer. **1649** English physician Henry Power discovers capillary blood vessels. **1654** German physicist Otto von Guericke invents an air pump. **1655** Dutch scientist Christiaan Huygens observes the rings around Saturn with a homemade telescope. **1656** Christiaan Huygens designs a pendulum clock. **1658** Dutch naturalist Jan Swammerdam describes red blood cells.	**1663** Scottish mathematician James Gregory designs a reflecting telescope. **1664** English scientist Robert Hooke describes Jupiter's giant red spot. **1665** Robert Hooke coins the word *cell* after studying plant tissues. He also proposes the wave theory of light. **1666** French engineer Melchisedech Thévenot invents the spirit level. **1669** Jan Swammerdam describes metamorphosis in insects. **1671** English scientist Isaac Newton discovers that a prism splits white light into a spectrum of rainbow colors.	**1675** Royal Greenwich Observatory is completed near London, England. **1675** Isaac Newton theorizes that light travels in particles. **1676** Dutch scientist Antonie van Leeuwenhoek observes bacteria, using a simple microscope. **1676** Robert Hooke invents the universal joint for connect two shafts. **1679** German mathematician Gottfried Leibnitz devises binary arithmetic, which is now used by all computers. **1679** English botanist Nehemiah Grew describes the male and female parts of flowers. **1687** Isaac Newton publishes his major work *Principia*.	**1690** French engineer Denis Papin builds a basic steam engine. **1691** English naturalist John Ray suggests fossils are ancient life-forms. **1698** English engineer Thomas Savery invents a steam pump, a forerunner of the atmospheric steam engine. **1701** English astronomer Edmond Halley publishes a map showing the magnetic variations of Earth. **1701** English agriculturalist Jethro Tull makes a seed drill. **1704** Isaac Newton publishes his theories on light in *Optiks*. **1704** Italian clockmaker Nicolas Fatio de Duiller makes a clock with jewel bearings.	
THE AMERICAS	**1630** The bark of the South American cinchona tree is brought to Europe to treat malaria. **1630** Glassworks are built in Massachusetts. **1644** Ironworks are built in New England.	**1645** The first hospital in North America is founded in Montreal, Canada.	**ca 1670** New Spain takes over from Peru as the major source of silver. **1672** North American wildlife is described in *New England's Rarities Discovered*. **1673** A road is laid between Boston and Philadelphia.	**ca 1680** Rice fields are planted in South Carolina.	**1690** A paper mill is established in Pennsylvania. **1690** North Americans begin making paper money. **1700** Making liquor becomes a significant part of the New England economy.	
ASIA & OCEANIA	**1637** An encyclopedia of Chinese technology is published. **1644** Western telescopes are used by Chinese astronomers.	**1653** The Taj Mahal—a gigantic marble mausoleum—is completed in India.		**1678** Japanese chrysanthemums are brought to the Netherlands. **1681** The Chinese adopt Western farming practices. **1681** The use of determinants is introduced in Japanese mathematics.	**1699** The Russians adopt the same calendar used in the West, starting the year on January 1.	
AFRICA & THE MIDDLE EAST	**1630s** Large areas of Africa are deforested to provide fuel for iron smelting. **1641** A chimpanzee is transported to the Netherlands. It is the first great ape seen in Europe.	**1652** The Dutch plant gardens near the Cape of Good Hope to provide food for passing sailors.			**1702** Islamic observatories begin using European telescopes.	

1705	1720	1735	1750	1765–1774
1709 English physicist Francis Hawksbee describes capillary action. **1712** English engineer Thomas Newcomen invents an atmospheric steam engine that uses a piston. **1712** English astronomer John Flamsteed publishes a catalog of the positions of 3,000 stars. **1714** Dutch physicist Gabriel Fahrenheit makes a mercury thermometer. **1717** English astronomer Abraham Sharp calculates π (pi) to 72 decimal places. **1717** Italian physician Giovanni Lancisi correctly links malaria to mosquito bites. **1719** German printer Jakob Le Blon invents four-color printing.	**1728** French dentist Pierre Fauchard invents the dental drill. **1729** English physicist Stephen Gray distinguishes between electrical conductors and insulators. **1730** English mathematician John Hadley invents the quadrant as a navigational aid. **1730** French surgeon George Martine performs the first tracheostomy. **1731** English astronomer John Bevis discovers the Crab Nebula. **1733** French mathematician Abraham de Moivre discovers the normal distribution. **1733** English engineer John Kay patents the flying shuttle.	**1735** Swedish naturalist Carolus Linnaeus introduces the binomial system of naming of plants and animals. **1738** Swiss scientist Daniel Bernoulli proposes a kinetic theory of gases. **1735** English clockmaker John Harrison unveils his chronometer. **1737** Swedish chemist Georg Brandt discovers cobalt. **1742** Swedish astronomer Anders Celsius devises the 100-degree Celsius scale. **1743** French mathematician Jean d'Alembert establishes mathematical dynamics. **1745** French surgeon Jacques Daviel successfully removes a cataract from a patient's eye.	**1753** Scottish engineer Charles Morrison invents a 26-wire telegraph. **1756** English engineer John Smeaton invents cement that can set underwater. **1760s** English agriculturalist Robert Bakewell uses selective breeding to improve farmstock. **1761** Scottish chemist Joseph Black introduces the concept of latent heat. **1762** English astronomer James Bradley publishes a catalog containing the positions of 60,000 stars. **1763** German botanist Josef Kölreuter discovers the role insects play in pollination. **1764** English mechanic James Hargreaves invents the spinning jenny.	**1765** Scottish engineer James Watt builds a steam engine with a separate condenser. **1766** English scientist Henry Cavendish identifies hydrogen. **1767** Swiss mathematician Leonhard Euler establishes the rules of algebra. **1772** Scottish chemist Daniel Rutherford discovers nitrogen. **1773** English astronomer William Herschel figures out that the sun is moving through space. **1774** English chemist Joseph Priestley identifies oxygen. **1774** Swedish chemist Karl Scheele discovers barium, chlorine, and manganese.
1709 A model hot-air balloon is made in Brazil. **1716** The first lighthouse in North America is built in Boston Harbor.	**1721** Smallpox inoculation is carried out in North America. **1728** The first botanical garden in North America is opened near Philadelphia. **1723** A house in Rhode Island is built with indoor plumbing.	**1740** The drug curare is discovered by French explorer Charles-Marie de la Condamine in South America. **1742** American inventor Benjamin Franklin invents a wood-burning stove.	**1751** Cartographers begin to make accurate maps of the frontiers of North America. **1752** Benjamin Franklin demonstrates the electrical nature of lightning. **1760** Threshing machines are used in rice production.	**1765** The first medical school in the United States is established at the College of Pennsylvania. **1769** American astronomer David Rittenhouse builds the United State's first astronomical telescope.
1709 Magnolias are brought to England from Japan.	**1720s** Jaipur City in India is built on a grid system. **1729** Movable type is used to print an encyclopedia in China.	**1736** India rubber is discovered by Charles-Marie de la Condamine. **1747** Jesuit missionaries design a summer palace for the Chinese emperors.	**1762** A flightless bird called the solitaire becomes extinct on Rodriguez Island in the Indian Ocean.	**1769** Captain James Cook observes a transit of Venus—when the planet passes in front of the sun—in Tahiti.
1717 Smallpox inoculation is witnessed in Turkey and the idea is brought to Britain.	**1729** Ottoman printer Ibrahim Müteferrika publishes descriptions of European life. **1732** The Ottomans build an aqueduct to supply Istanbul with water.	**1730s** A school of military engineering is established by a French aristocrat in Turkey.	**1750** French astronomer Nicolas de Lacaille travels to the Cape of Good Hope to study parallax—the relative position of celestial bodies as seen from different parts of Earth.	**1767** The Ottoman army establishes a cannon foundry and a military school.

ASTRONOMY & MATH

1627 German astronomer Johannes Kepler (1571–1630) publishes tables describing the motions of the planets; they become known as the Rudolphine Tables.

1631 French mathematician and astronomer Pierre Gassendi (1592–1655) makes the first observation of the transit of the planet Mercury across the sun's disk.

1632 The first modern astronomical observatory is built at Leyden (now spelled Leiden) in the Netherlands.

1633 Italian scientist Galileo Galilei (1564–1642) is condemned by the Roman Catholic Inquisition for refusing to withdraw his statement that the sun—and not the Earth—is at the center of the universe.

1639 English astronomers William Crabtree (1610–44) and Jeremiah Horrocks (1617–41) make the first observation of the transit of the planet Venus across the sun's disk.

1642 French scientist Blaise Pascal (1623–62) builds a wooden mechanical calculating machine.

1644 Polish scientist and astronomer Johannes Hevelius (1611–87) observes that Mercury shows phases, like the moon.

BIOLOGY & MEDICINE

1628 English physician William Harvey (1578–1657) explains the circulation of blood—the way in which blood is pumped by the heart through the lungs and around the body.

1641 German anatomist Franciscus Sylvius (1614–72) identifies the Sylvian fissure in the brain, which separates the temporal lobe (at the side) from the rest of the brain.

1642 German anatomist Johann Wirsung (1600–43) discovers the pancreatic duct, which carries digestive juices from the pancreas to the small intestine.

PHYSICAL SCIENCES

1640 French mathematician Pierre de Fermat (1601–65) proposes that light always travels in straight lines.

1642 French scientist Blaise Pascal (1623–62) puts forward Pascal's law, which states that the pressure within a liquid is the same everywhere. The principle underlies the working of all hydraulic machinery.

1644 German chemist Johann Glauber (1604–68) makes impure water glass (sodium silicate), a chemical later found to have many uses (including the preservation of eggs).

Consecrated in 1626, St. Peter's Basilica in Rome stood as the world's largest Christian church for more than 250 years.

1630 The bark from the South American cinchona tree is introduced to Europe by Jesuit priests. It contains the drug quinine, used to treat malaria.

1644 Jesuits in China reform the Chinese calendar on Western lines and introduce Western telescopes to Chinese astronomy.

1631 Persian metaphysician Mir Damed dies, leaving pioneering works that will later influence the development of psychology.

1630s Cutting trees to burn in furnaces for iron smelting causes deforestation in Africa.

1641 Dutch naturalist Nicolaas Tulp (ca 1593–ca 1674) describes the first chimpanzee (*Pan troglodytes*) brought to the Netherlands.

HOW THINGS WORK

Pascal's Law

A hydraulic press works according to the principles of Pascal's law of 1642. A large piston is connected to a small piston, and the setup is filled with an oily liquid. Because pressure is transmitted equally throughout a liquid, a small force on the small piston creates a greater force on the large piston. However, the larger piston will only move a fraction of the distance of the smaller one.

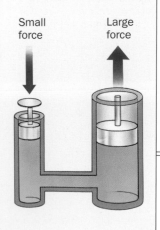

Small force

Large force

EUROPE

THE AMERICAS

ASIA & OCEANIA

AFRICA & THE MIDDLE EAST

ENGINEERING & INVENTION	WORLD EVENTS
1626 St. Peter's Basilica in Rome is finally consecrated, having taken 120 years to build.	**1625** Vincent de Paul (1581–1660) sets up the religious order of the Sisters of Mercy.
1629 Italian engineer Giovanni Branca (1571–1640) manufactures a primitive steam turbine.	**1626** The French impose the death penalty for duelists who kill their opponents.
1631 French mathematician Pierre Vernier (1580–1637) invents the vernier measuring scale, which allows precise measurements to be made.	**1627** Heinrich Schütz (1585–1672) composes *Dafne*, the first German opera.
1638 English astronomer William Gascoigne (ca 1612–44) and Frenchman Adrien Auzout (1622–91) invent the eyepiece micrometer independently, which enables accurate measurements to be made with telescopes and microscopes.	**1629** Charles I (r. 1625–49) dissolves the English Parliament.
	1630 Public advertisements of goods is first used in France.
	1630 Sweden becomes involved in the Thirty Years' War (1618–48).
	1636 Tea drinking arrives in Paris.
1640 French coachbuilder Nicolas Sauvage introduces the horse-drawn cab in Paris.	**1639** The Académie Française compiles a dictionary to try to standardize French spelling and language.
1641 Italian inventor Vincenzo Galilei (1606–49) tries (but fails) to make a pendulum clock, using a design produced by his father, Galileo Galilei (1564–1642).	**1640** Frederick William (1620–88), the Great Elector, becomes elector of Brandenburg.
1642 German engraver Ludwig von Siegen (1609–ca 1680) devises the mezzotint process, in which effects of light and shade are produced by scraping away parts of a roughened metal printing plate.	**1642** Puritans shut down the theaters in London.
	1642 Charles I begins fighting against Parliamentary forces led by Oliver Cromwell (1599–1658).
1639 A glassworks built in Plymouth, Maryland, is one of the first "factories" in the American colonies.	**1630** English Puritans colonize Massachusetts Bay.
1639 North America's first printing press is opened.	**1636** Harvard College is established in Massachusetts.
1644 Ironworks are constructed in American colonies, including Massachusetts, Connecticut, and Rhode Island.	**1643** New Sweden (present-day Delaware) is founded.
1635 Jesuit missionaries collaborate with the Chinese to publish a collection of scientific works called *Ch'ung-chen Li-shu*.	**1628** Dutch settlers occupy the renowned "Spice Islands," Java and the Moluccas.
1637 An encyclopedia of Chinese technology, the *Tiangong Kaiwu*, is published.	**1642** Dutch navigator Abel Tasman discovers Tasmania, New Zealand, and Fiji.
	1644 Invaders from the northern region of Manchuria conquer China and overthrow the Ming dynasty. The Manchus establish the Qing dynasty.
	1625 The kingdom of Dahomey is created in the region that is now southern Benin.
	1626 The French begin to colonize the Senegal River.

BLOOD CIRCULATION

While studying animals, English physician William Harvey (1578–1657) began thinking about the circulation of blood around the body. He noticed that in a single hour the heart forces out far more blood than the total amount that is in an animal's body. The blood must, Harvey reasoned, be going around in a continuous loop in what he referred to as "a circle of ceaseless motion."

Harvey announced his discovery in 1628 and published diagrams (below) in order to prove his point. He tied a ribbon around the upper arm—which modern doctors call a tourniquet—to make the veins stand out, with the valves showing up as swellings. They are one-way valves that allow the blood to flow back to the heart but not in the other direction. Harvey demonstrated that pressing one of the valves stops the blood flowing along a vein until the pressure is released.

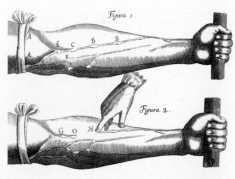
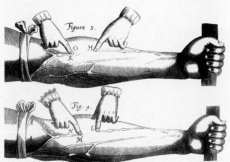

In these woodcuts from William Harvey's book Exercitatio Anatomica de Motu Cordis et Sanguinis in Animalibus (On the Motions of the Heart and Blood), *published in 1628, he shows the one-way system of valves in the veins.*

GALILEO GALILEI

GALILEO GALILEI (1564–1642), GENERALLY known as Galileo, was an Italian scientist who made important advances in astronomy, mathematics, and physics. Galileo's work is important both for his discoveries and for the methods that he used to prove they were right. He was different from most previous scientists because he based his theories on his observations of natural phenomena and confirmed them using carefully arranged experiments. This is known today as the scientific method, and Galileo was one of the first in the Western World to practice it.

Galileo was born in Pisa in northern Italy and educated at a monastery school in Florence. At age 17, he began attending the University of Pisa to study medicine. He soon switched to mathematics and philosophy but left school in 1585 without a degree and began working as a teacher. His reputation spread, and in 1589 he became professor of mathematics at Pisa despite his lack of formal qualifications. He moved to Padua in 1592 and taught there until 1610.

Pendulums and Cannonballs

While attending a service in Pisa Cathedral in 1582, Galileo noticed the regular movements of a lamp swinging above his head. From his observations of the lamp, he created his own simple pendulum, consisting of a weight at the end of a length of string, and then timed its swings. At the time accurate clocks did not exist, so he used his heartbeat to time the swings. He found that the time of each swing depended only on the length of the pendulum and was independent of the mass of the weight. He realised that a pendulum could be used to measure time accurately but did not make a clock himself.

Since the time of the Greek philosopher Aristotle (384–322 B.C.E.) people thought that the speed at which an object fell depended on its weight. Galileo tested this idea in about 1602. According to legend, he dropped two cannonballs of different weights from the Leaning Tower of Pisa and showed that they hit the ground at the same time.

The invention of the telescope in the early 1600s stimulated Galileo's interest in astronomy. He observed the moon, recording in numerous drawings its mountains and craters at different times during the month. He then turned his attention to Jupiter and in 1610 announced that the planet had four moons of its own. A year later he studied the sun and noted that sometimes black spots moved slowly across its surface. The movement of these spots convinced him that the sun was rotating slowly on its axis.

Galileo's discoveries about the celestial bodies finally convinced him that the sun was at the center of the solar system, a theory that had first been published in 1543 by Polish astronomer Nicolaus Copernicus (1473–1543). The idea was contrary to the teachings of the Roman Catholic Church, which postulated an Earth-centered universe. The Church asked Galileo not to spread the idea, but in 1632 he published it in a book, called *Dialogo sopra i due massimi sistimi del*

Galileo demonstrated that objects of different weight fall at the same speed. He also tried to show that they fall at a constant acceleration. As an object falls farther, it moves faster, but the acceleration is constant —the rate of acceleration increases 32 feet (9.8 m) per second every second.

KEY DATES

1582
Constancy of pendulum's swing

1602
Law of falling bodies

1610
Observes four of Jupiter's moons

1611
First views sunspots

1633
Condemned by the Inquisition

Object falls from here

16 feet (4.9 m)

After 1 second

0 feet (0 m) per second

32 feet (9.8 m) per second

48 feet (14.7 m)

After 2 seconds

64 feet (19.6 m) per second

80 feet (24.5 m)

96 feet (29.4 m) per second

After 3 seconds

mondo, tolemaico e copernico (Dialogue Concerning the Two Chief World Systems—Ptolemaic and Copernican). The book was banned because it was seen as a personal insult to Pope Urban VIII (1568–1644), who up to that point had been one of Galileo's supporters. In 1633 Galileo was arrested by the Inquisition and, under threat of torture, made to recant his views.

Old and in failing health, Galileo spent the rest of his life under house arrest in Florence. He became blind in 1637, possibly because of eye damage caused by looking at the sun. When he died in 1642, Pope Urban VIII refused to forget his feud with Galileo, and he was buried unceremoniously in the Church of Sante Croce in Florence.

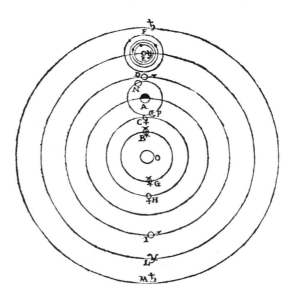

An artist's depiction of Galileo's appearance before the Inquisition.

Galileo made his own diagram of the sun-centered universe proposed by Copernicus (left). He also included his own discovery: the four moons of Jupiter.

ASTRONOMY & MATH

1645 Flemish cartographer Michael Langrenus (1600–75) publishes the first map of the moon.

1650 Italian astronomer Giovanni Riccioli (1598–1671) identifies the first binary (double) star, Mizar, in the constellation Ursa Major (Great Bear).

1653 French scientist Blaise Pascal (1623–62) devises Pascal's triangle of numbers, in which each number is the sum of the two numbers above it. It is later to have important applications in mathematics, such as the binomial theorem.

1655 Dutch scientist Christiaan Huygens (1629–95) uses a homemade telescope to observe the rings around the planet Saturn. He also discovers Titan, the largest of Saturn's moons.

1657 Christiaan Huygens writes the first book on mathematical probability theory.

1659 German mathematician Johann Rahn (1622–76) introduces the division sign (÷) to mathematics.

BIOLOGY & MEDICINE

1645 English physician Daniel Whistler (1619–84) first diagnoses the childhood disease rickets. It is later (1651) also independently described by his compatriot Francis Glisson (1597–1677).

1647 French anatomist Jean Pequet (1622–74) describes the thoracic duct in animals. This duct carries the fluid lymph from the lower body to a vein in the neck. In 1653 Swedish scientist Olof Rudbeck (1630–1702) discovers the lymphatic vessels in humans.

1649 English physician Henry Power (1623–68) discovers the extremely narrow capillary blood vessels.

1658 Dutch naturalist Jan Swammerdam (1637–80) describes red blood cells (erythrocytes).

1659 English physician Thomas Willis (1621–75) first describes typhoid fever.

1659 Italian anatomist Marcello Malpighi (1628–94) discovers the lymph nodes, enlarged structures where lymph vessels come together. Two years later he confirms the existence of capillary blood vessels.

PHYSICAL SCIENCES

1645 Italian physicist Evangelista Torricelli (1608–47) constructs the first mercury barometer. He also discovers the Torricellian vacuum, produced by inverting a tube full of mercury into a dish (the vacuum forms in the space at the closed top end of the inverted tube).

1646 English scientist Thomas Browne (1605–82) coins the word *electricity* (which at that time was limited to static electricity).

1646 Blaise Pascal demonstrates the existence of atmospheric pressure and confirms that it varies with altitude.

1649 French mathematician and philosopher Pierre Gassendi (1592–1655) publishes *Syntagma Philosophiae Epicuri*, a study of Greek philosopher Epicurus (ca 342–270 B.C.E.), who holds that all matter is made up of atoms.

1650 German scholar and inventor Athanasius Kircher (1601–80) demonstrates that sound will not travel in a vacuum.

1650 The first properly equipped chemistry laboratory is established at the University of Leyden in the Netherlands.

1645 The Hôtel-Dieu de Montreal, the first hospital in North America, is founded by French nurse Jeanne Mance (1606–73).

The planet Saturn surrounded by its rings. These were first observed by Dutch astronomer Christiaan Huygens.

People almost invariably arrive at their beliefs not on the basis of proof but on the basis of what they find attractive.

BLAISE PASCAL, THE ART OF PERSUASION

1652 The Dutch East India Company begins planting gardens near the Cape of Good Hope to provide fresh fruit and vegetables for sailors on routes to and from the East Indies.

EUROPE

THE AMERICAS

ASIA & OCEANIA

AFRICA & THE MIDDLE EAST

ENGINEERING & INVENTION	WORLD EVENTS
1647 Blaise Pascal invents a primitive roulette wheel to test his ideas on probability.	**1648** Dissenting preacher George Fox (1624–91) founds the Society of Friends, also known as the Quakers.
1652 Dutch engineer Cornelius Vermuyden (1595–ca 1683) completes the drainage of a large area of the Fens—marshy lands in the east of England—for farmland.	**1652** War begins between Britain and the Netherlands with a series of naval battles off the British coast.
1654 Polish scientist Johannes Hevelius (1611–87) makes a closed-ended thermometer.	**1653** Puritan leader Oliver Cromwell (1599–1658) becomes the Lord Protector of the English commonwealth. During this time the nation is ruled by military governors.
1654 German physicist Otto von Guericke (1602–86) of Magdeburg invents an air pump. As a demonstration, he removes the air from between two copper hemispheres. Two teams of horses fail to pull them apart, because of the force of atmospheric pressure.	**1655** Pope Innocent X (1574–1655) dies in Rome. During his tenure as pope, Innocent involved the Catholic Church directly in a number of wars and diplomatic disputes. He also attacked those whom he considered heretics or political enemies.
1656 Christiaan Huygens designs a pendulum clock.	

1658 English scientist Robert Hooke (1635–1703) has the idea for a watch regulated by a hairspring (the power from the main spring is released very gradually, controlled by the oscillations of the hairspring).

The Taj Mahal in Agra, India, was built as a mausoleum for a Muslim princess.

1653 The first Jewish immigrants arrive in the settlement of New Amsterdam, which later becomes New York City.

1653 The Taj Mahal, a gigantic and complex marble mausoleum, is completed in Agra, India. The structure took 22 years to complete.	**1656** A devastating fire destroys most of the Japanese city of Edo, as well as its castle, and kills tens of thousands of people.
	1650 A Venetian blockade halts Ottoman sea trade for four years.
	1657 The Dutch defeat the local Khoikhoi population for control of territory in southern Africa.

THE PENDULUM CLOCK

The Chinese constructed the first mechanical clocks, which were in effect large, slowly turning waterwheels made of wood. Metal clocks powered by falling weights date from the 1300s, but they were unreliable and inaccurate. In 1582 Italian scientist Galileo Galilei (1564–1642) demonstrated that a pendulum always swings at a constant rate. He also proved that the rate of swing depends only on the length of the pendulum and not on the mass of the weight swinging at its end. A pendulum 39 inches (99 cm) long takes one second to complete one swing (forward and back), and so can be used to mark the passage of time.

In 1641 Galileo instructed his son Vincenzo (1606–49) how to make a clock regulated by a pendulum. Vincenzo did not complete the job, and it was not until 1657 that the first pendulum clock appeared. It was designed by the Dutch scientist Christiaan Huygens and assembled by clockmaker Salomon Coster (ca 1620–59) in The Hague. It kept time to within five minutes a day and was much more accurate than any earlier clocks.

The metal rod of a pendulum expands and contracts with changes in temperature, which changes the speed at which it swings and causes inaccuracy. Various methods were devised to overcome this problem. In 1722 English inventor George Graham (1673–1751) designed the mercury pendulum, which had a glass jar of mercury as the pendulum's weight. When the pendulum expanded downward because of a rise in temperature, the change was counterbalanced by the upward expansion of the mercury in the jar. Another solution, the gridiron pendulum, was invented by English clockmaker John Harrison (1693–1776) in 1728. Harrison's design had a grid of alternate brass and steel rods. Brass expands more than steel, so the expansion of the brass compensated for the lesser expansion of the steel.

ASTRONOMY & MATH	BIOLOGY & MEDICINE	PHYSICAL SCIENCES

EUROPE

1664 English scientist Robert Hooke (1635–1703) describes Jupiter's Great Red Spot (now known to be due to a gigantic storm in the planet's atmosphere). In the same year Hooke proposes that the planets are held in their orbits by their own gravity and the gravity of the sun.

1665 English scientist and mathematician Isaac Newton (1642–1727) introduces the binomial theorem—a key concept in algebra that allows the expansion of the expression $(x + y)^n$. This was only one of many advances in math made by Newton at about this time.

1666 Italian astronomer Giovanni Cassini (1625–1712) observes the polar ice caps on Mars. (We now know that the "ice" is mainly frozen carbon dioxide.)

1670 French astronomer Jean Picard (1620–82) measures the length of part of the meridian (a line of longitude), thus allowing accurate calculation of the circumference of the Earth.

1671 Giovanni Cassini discovers Iapetus, Saturn's third-largest moon (after Titan and Rhea).

1660 French physicist Edmé Mariotte (1620–84) discovers the blind spot on the retina of the eye (at the place where the optic nerve joins the retina).

1665 Robert Hooke coins the word *cell* to describe the "little boxes" he observes in plant tissues using a compound microscope of his own invention.

1669 Dutch naturalist Jan Swammerdam (1637–80) describes metamorphosis in insects—the sequence of changes from egg to larva to pupa to adult or imago (as in butterflies).

1670 English physician Thomas Willis (1621–75) detects the presence of sugar in the urine of patients with diabetes.

1672 Jan Swammerdam identifies the human ovaries. In the same year anatomist Regnier de Graaf (1641–73) uncovers egg-containing follicles (known as Graafian follicles) in the ovaries.

1673 Dutch scientist Antonie van Leeuwenhoek (1632–1723) begins writing letters to the newly formed Royal Society of London describing what he has observed under a microscope.

1661 Irish scientist Robert Boyle (1627–91) defines chemical elements for the first time. A year later he formulates Boyle's law: that at a fixed temperature the pressure of a gas is inversely proportional to its volume.

1665 Robert Hooke proposes the wave theory of light, but his proposal is largely ignored until championed by Dutch scientist Christiaan Huygens (1629–95) in 1678.

1668 English mathematician John Wallis (1616–1703) proposes the law of conservation of momentum: The momentum (mass x velocity) of objects before a collision equals their combined momentum afterward.

1669 German alchemist Hennig Brand (ca 1630–92) discovers phosphorus (in urine). This was the first discovery of a new element since prehistoric times.

1669 German chemist Johann Becher (1635–82) proposes the (incorrect) phlogiston theory of combustion (which states that materials get lighter in weight by releasing "phlogiston" when they burn).

1671 Isaac Newton demonstrates that a glass prism splits, or disperses, white light into a spectrum of rainbow colors.

THE AMERICAS

1672 John Josselyn describes North American wildlife and plants in *New England's Rarities Discovered*.

ca 1670 New Spain surpasses Peru as the major producer of silver in the Spanish Empire.

ASIA & OCEANIA

AFRICA & THE MIDDLE EAST

INSIDE STORY

Champagne

Dom Pierre Perignon ("Dom" is a title given by the Roman Catholic Church) was a French Benedictine monk who developed the process for making champagne wine. He entered the Benedictine order when we was 19, and within ten years he became cellarmaster at the Abbey of Hautvillers. People in southern Europe have made wine since the time of the ancient Greeks and Romans, and the district along the valley of the Marne River became famous for its chardonnay grapes that result in a fine white wine. To make champagne, the winemakers allow chardonnay to ferment in large vats. Then they usually blend it with wines from previous years and add sugar and yeast before putting it in bottles made from thick, dark-green glass. The wine ferments for a second time in the bottles, and the gas (carbon dioxide) produced results in an effervescence that gives champagne its famous bubbles.

Jan Swammerdam demonstrated that insects have four different life stages: egg, larva, pupa, and adult. In butterflies and moths, such as the monarch butterfly shown above, the larval stage is known as a caterpillar.

ENGINEERING & INVENTION

1660 Robert Hooke devises the anchor escapement to regulate a pendulum-driven clock.

1661 Christiaan Huygens invents the manometer, a device for measuring gas pressure.

1663 Scottish mathematician and inventor James Gregory (1638–75) proposes a design for a reflecting telescope.

1664 Italian engineer Giuseppe Campani (1635–1715) creates a lens-grinding lathe (for making lenses for optical instruments).

1666 French engineer Melchisedech Thevenot (ca 1620–92) makes the spirit level.

1667 Robert Hooke (1635–1703) invents the anemometer to measure wind speed.

1668 Isaac Newton builds a reflecting telescope.

1670 French winemaker Dom Pérignon (1638–1715) creates champagne.

1674 English glassmaker George Ravenscroft (1618–81) develops lead crystal glass.

1674 Dutch engineer Menno von Coehoorn (1641–1704) invents the trench mortar.

WORLD EVENTS

1660 Charles II (r. 1660–81) is crowned king of England. His restoration marks the end of Oliver Cromwell's (1599–1658) puritan protectorate.

1662 The scientist, architect, and astronomer Christopher Wren (1632–1723) designs his first major building: the Sheldonian Theater in Oxford.

1663 The second Navigation Act is passed by the British Parliament. This act places restrictions on trade between the American colonies and any nation other than Britain, causing significant resentment and unrest in the American colonies.

1665 Bubonic plague strikes London. Many flee the city, but around 80,000 (a fifth of the city's population) die of the disease. The following year sees the city decimated by a massive fire that destroys around 13,000 houses and many public buildings.

1673 The Test Act is passed by the British Parliament, banning catholics and religious dissenters from holding any public office.

1673 American colonials build the Boston Post Road, a major route linking Boston and Philadelphia.

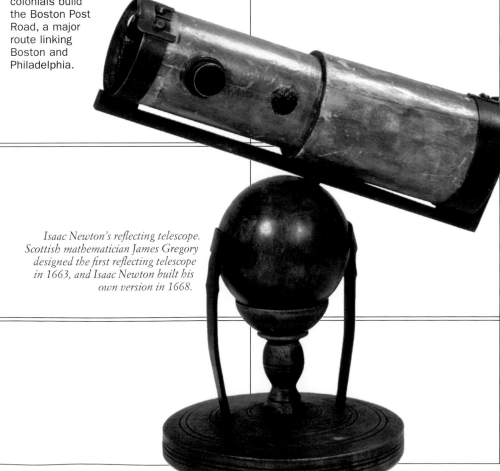

Isaac Newton's reflecting telescope. Scottish mathematician James Gregory designed the first reflecting telescope in 1663, and Isaac Newton built his own version in 1668.

THE BAROMETER AND VACUUMS

It is now common knowledge that air has mass, and that atmospheric pressure results from the weight of the atmosphere pressing down on Earth. In the 1640s an Italian scientist set out to measure air pressure; in doing so, he proved the existence of the vacuum and invented the barometer. Evangelista Torricelli (1608–47) trained as a mathematician and in 1641 went to work as an assistant to the aged Galileo (1564–1642), who always maintained that there was no such thing as a vacuum.

In 1645, aided by his assistant Vincenzo Viviani (1622–1703), Torricelli took a 6.6-foot (2-m) glass tube, sealed at one end, and filled it with mercury. Keeping his thumb over the open end, he upended the tube in a dish full of mercury and removed his thumb, while keeping the end of the tube below the surface of the mercury in the dish. Some of the mercury ran out into the dish, and the mercury level in the tube dropped to a height of about 30 inches (76 cm).

Torricelli reasoned that the weight of the atmosphere (air) pressing on the surface of the mercury in the dish equaled the weight of the mercury left in the tube. The height of the mercury column above the mercury in the dish was therefore a measure of air pressure. The whole device is known as a barometer. Torricelli also noticed that the height of the column varied from day to day depending on the weather and deduced that atmospheric pressure must also vary daily. In 1647 French thinker René Descartes (1596–1650) added a vertical scale to a Torricelli barometer and used it to record weather observations.

The space above the mercury in Torricelli's experiment was a vacuum, a volume of space without matter. In modern terminology it would be referred to as a partial vacuum, filled with extremely low-pressure gas, as a perfect vacuum with a gaseous pressure of zero is now understood to be an impossibility.

ASTRONOMY & MATH

1675 Italian astronomer Giovanni Cassini (1625–1712) discovers the major gap in Saturn's rings, now known as the Cassini division.

1675 The Royal Greenwich Observatory is completed near London and gives its name to the Greenwich Meridian (at longitude 0°).

1679 German mathematician Gottfried Leibniz (1646–1716) introduces binary arithmetic, which uses only two digits. Today it is employed by all computers.

1682 English astronomer Edmond Halley (1656–1742) plots the course of Halley's comet. In 1705 he correctly predicts that it will return in 1758.

1684 Giovanni Cassini discovers Dione and Thetys, two of Saturn's moons.

BIOLOGY & MEDICINE

1676 Dutch scientist Antonie van Leeuwenhoek (1632–1723) reports his observations of bacteria, using a simple microscope made with lenses that he ground himself. A year later he observes human sperm.

1682 English botanist Nehemiah Grew (1641–1712) describes the male and female parts of flowers.

1683 English physician Thomas Sydenham (1624–89) gives the first full description of the disorder gout.

1683 The wild boar (*Sus scrofa*) becomes extinct in the British Isles.

PHYSICAL SCIENCES

1675 English scientist and mathematician Isaac Newton (1642–1727) proposes that light travels as a series of minute particles. He does not publish his theory until 1704.

1676 English scientist Robert Hooke (1635–1703) proposes Hooke's law, which states that when an elastic object stretches, the stress (force per unit area) in it is proportional to the strain (change in dimensions).

1678 Dutch scientist Christiaan Huygens (1629–95) takes up the wave theory of light proposed by English scientist Robert Hooke (1635–1703) in 1665.

1679 Robert Hooke proposes the inverse square law of gravity.

1687 Isaac Newton publishes his major work *Principia*, in which he sets out his various theories in astronomy, mathematics, and physics.

HOW THINGS WORK

Hooke's Law and Metals

Robert Hooke's law of elasticity, which was first proposed in 1676, states that stress is proportional to strain. When a piece of metal is stretched, the elongation (strain) is at first proportional to the load applied (stress)—in this phase the metal obeys Hooke's law. But beyond a certain point—called the elastic limit—the metal is permanently stretched and cannot return to its original length. With more stress, the metal reaches its yield point, when it yields and stretches rapidly with very little extra load until it breaks.

1678 Thomas Thatcher publishes the first American medical treatise, *A Brief Rule in Small Pocks or Measles*.

ca 1680 Rice fields are planted in coastal areas of South Carolina.

1683 Japanese mathematician Seki Kowa (1642–1708) introduces the use of determinants into mathematics. A determinant is a square array of numbers (elements) useful in solving simultaneous equations and other mathematical problems.

1678 Japanese chrysanthemums are exported to the Netherlands.

1681 On the Indian Ocean island of Mauritius the dodo (*Raphus cucullatus*), a large flightless bird of the pigeon family, becomes extinct.

1681 Jesuits bring Western farming practices to China, including irrigation, and make three, rather than two, crops of rice each year possible.

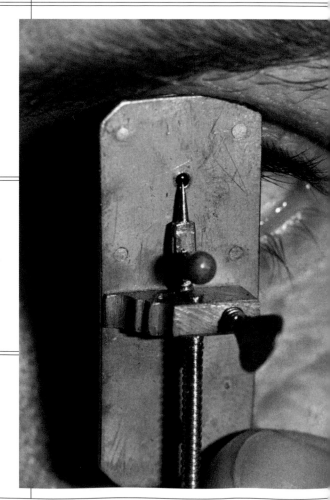

EUROPE

THE AMERICAS

ASIA & OCEANIA

AFRICA & THE MIDDLE EAST

ENGINEERING & INVENTION	WORLD EVENTS
1675 Christiaan Huygens makes an oscillating balance and hairspring regulator for clocks.	**1675** Frederick William (r. 1640–88), Elector of Brandenburg, goes to war against the Swedish in Germany.
1675 Irish scientist Robert Boyle (1627–91) devises a hydrometer (an instrument for measuring the relative density of a liquid).	**1678** English writer and preacher John Bunyan (1628–88) finishes the first part of *The Pilgrim's Progress*.
1676 Robert Hooke invents the universal joint (for connecting two driven shafts joined at an angle).	**1680** Crops begin failing in many parts of Europe, causing widespread famine.
1679 French physicist Denis Papin (1647–1712) produces a steam digester, the forerunner of the pressure cooker.	**1682** Peter the Great (r. 1682–1725) becomes the tsar of Russia.
1680 Robert Boyle invents a match that uses a mixture of sulfur and phosphorus.	**1683** Englishman William Dampier (ca 1651–1715) begins a circumnavigation around the world.
1687 French physicist Guillaume Amontons (1663–1705) invents a hygrometer (an instrument for measuring the humidity of the atmosphere).	**1684** Street lighting is installed in parts of London.
1689 German musical instrument maker Johann Denner (1655–1707) develops the clarinet (as a single-reed instrument with no keys).	**1685** James II (r. 1685–88) succeeds his brother Charles II (r. 1660–85) as king of England. James II is deposed in 1688.
	1685 Huguenots are exiled from France.
	1675 King Philip's War breaks out between Native Americans and English Colonists in New England.
	1680 Spaniards are driven from New Mexico by Pueblo tribes in the Pueblo Revolt.
	1679 The Cambodians and Vietnamese go to war, with Cambodia losing the Mekong delta.
	1680 The French set up a trading station at Pondicherry, southern India.
	1683 The Qing—the last ruling dynasty of China—occupy Taiwan.
	1685 China opens ports to Europeans.
	1689 The Treaty of Nerchinsk between China and Russia defines borders and trading.
	1683 The Ottomans unsuccessfully besiege Vienna but are defeated by the Austrians.
	1689 Natal is made a Dutch colony.

Antonie van Leeuwenhoek's early microscopes, such as this one in which a single lens is mounted on a flat sheet of metal, could magnify objects up to x200. This allowed Leeuwenhoek to see microorganisms for the first time, which he named "animalcules."

ROYAL GREENWICH OBSERVATORY

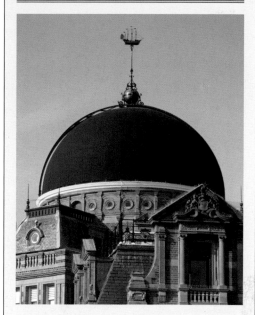

Founded in 1675 by King Charles II, England's Royal Greenwich Observatory was built primarily to help navigation at sea by fixing longitude and improving the determination of star positions. It was also charged with the improvement of timekeeping. The observatory was built on a hill overlooking the Thames River and designed by Sir Christopher Wren (1632–1723), himself an astronomer as well as an architect.

In 1766 the observatory published its first Nautical Almanac, which predicted the position of celestial bodies for the year ahead to allow sailors to fix their position. While this made it easy to determine latitude, or how far north or south a vessel was, calculating longitude remained open to error, which often led to ship wrecks. Finding longitude requires knowing the difference between local time and a reference time. It was not until the latter half of the 18th century that an effective timekeeper was invented by English clockmaker John Harrison (1693–1776) and enabled sailors to measure longitude at sea. In 1884, the Greenwich meridian—a line of longitude passing through Greenwich—was adopted as the Earth's prime meridian, with a longitude of 0°, and the starting point for the international time zones.

ISAAC NEWTON

ONE OF THE FIRST SCIENTISTS WHOSE achievements brought him widespread recognition was Isaac Newton (1642–1727). He made fundamental breakthroughs in mathematics and established the basic laws that became the cornerstones of modern astronomy and physics. The first scientist to receive a knighthood, his name lives on as the newton, the modern International System of Units (SI) unit of force.

Isaac Newton was born in eastern England. He was brought up by his grandmother and educated at a local school before going to Trinity College (Cambridge University). He received his bachelor's degree

ABOVE: William Blake's depiction of Newton (1795)

in 1665 and was forced to remain in the countryside because of the plague that raged in London at that time. At first he concentrated on mathematics, working out the principles of "fluxions," which were to lead to differential calculus.

In 1667 Newton received a fellowship of Trinity College and became professor of mathematics in 1669. He turned his attention to what happens when objects move—what makes them start moving and what stops them. His conclusions are summed up in Newton's three laws of motion. All of the laws can be observed by watching a game of pool, although you do not have to be a physicist to play it!

Newton's next contribution was to have a profound effect on astronomy. According to the well-known story, he was sitting in an orchard when he saw an apple fall. Why did it fall? Newton concluded that it was attracted toward the Earth by a force, which we now call gravity. He also deduced that every object behaves as if its mass were concentrated in one place, its center of gravity (now called the center of mass). Applying his own laws of motion, he figured out that all objects in the universe are affected by such gravitational forces—it is gravity that keeps the moon in orbit around the Earth and the Earth in orbit around the sun. He produced a formula, the universal law of gravitation, that states the gravitational force between any two objects—two pool balls or even two stars—is equal to the product of their masses and inversely proportional to the distance between them.

The English scientist Robert Hooke (1635–1703) also devised a law of gravity in about 1678 and published his ideas a few years later. This led to a bitter dispute between the two great men.

In the branch of physics we now call optics, Newton's main studies concerned the nature of light. By allowing a narrow beam of white light from the sun to pass through a glass prism, Newton split the light into a multicolored spectrum, the sequence of colors seen in a rainbow. He showed that white light is made up of a variety of colors. (Today we say that it is made up of many different wavelengths.) Telescopes of the day produced images that were surrounded by a spectrum of colors because the poor-quality lenses brought different colors into focus in different places. Newton overcame the problem by using mirrors instead of lenses and in 1668 produced one of the first reflecting telescopes with mirrors he made himself.

Newton was convinced that light is composed of a "flux" of minute particles, which he called "corpuscles." The theory was soon challenged by Dutch Scientist Christiaan Huygens (1629–95) and others, who postulated that light travels as waves. The argument raged until the 20th century, when physicists finally concluded that light has properties of both particles and waves; but this had to await the development of quantum theory.

In 1703 Newton was elected president of the Royal Society, and two years later he was knighted. As Sir Isaac Newton he continued to be showered with honors. His final tribute was a state funeral and burial in Westminster Abbey, London. His name lives on in the SI unit of force, which is called the newton (the force that gives 1 kilogram an acceleration of 1 meter per second per second).

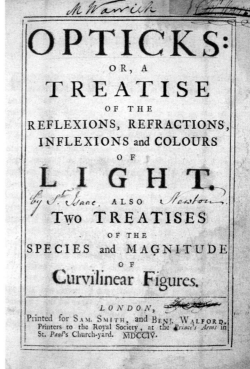

Newton's second major work Opticks, *published in 1704, outlined his theories on optics and the refraction of light.*

NEWTON'S LAWS

Newton formulated laws about two major topics in physics: gravity and motion. His law of gravity deals with the attractive force (gravitation) that exists between any two objects that have mass. The strength of the force depends on how close they are (illustrated below; the nearer they are, the stronger the force pulling them together) and how massive they are (illustrated below; the more massive they are, the stronger the force between them). In mathematical terms the gravitational force is proportional to the product of the masses and inversely proportional to the distance between them.

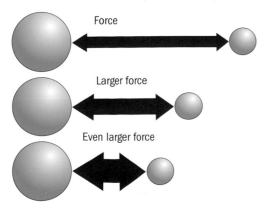

Force

Larger force

Even larger force

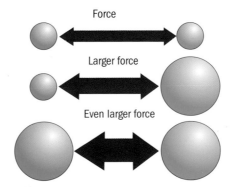

Force

Larger force

Even larger force

KEY DATES

1665
Binomial theorem (math)

ca 1665
Law of gravity and center of gravity

1668
Newton's reflecting telescope

1671
White light into a spectrum

1675
Corpuscular theory of light

1687
Book *Principia* published

1704
Book *Opticks* published

ASTRONOMY & MATH	BIOLOGY & MEDICINE	PHYSICAL SCIENCES

EUROPE

ca 1690 English naturalist John Ray (1627–1705) distinguishes between monocotyledons (plants with one seed leaf) and dicotyledons (plants with two seed leaves).

1691 John Ray suggests that fossils are the remains of creatures from the distant past.

1694 German botanist Rudolf Camerarius (1665–1721) establishes that plants have male and female parts.

1696 Dutch scientist Antonie van Leeuwenhoek (1632–1723) describes microorganisms.

1699 English botanist John Woodward (1665–1728) shows that plants grow best if other substances are added to their water.

1701 Italian physician Giacomo Pylarini (1659–1715) inoculates three children with smallpox to prevent more serious disease when they are older.

1694 Italian scientist Carlo Renaldini (1615–98) suggests that both the freezing point and boiling point of water should be used as "fixed points" on thermometers.

1697 German chemist Georg Stahl (1660–1734) champions the (incorrect) phlogiston theory of combustion devised by Johann Becher (1635–82) in 1669.

1700 German mathematician Gottfried Leibniz (1646–1716) founds the Berlin Academy, the first major national academy of science.

1701 Dutch chemist Wilhelm Homburg (1652–1715) discovers boric acid (sometimes called boracic acid).

1701 English astronomer Edmond Halley (1656–1742) publishes a map showing the magnetic variations of Earth.

1704 English scientist and mathematician Isaac Newton (1642–1727) publishes his book *Opticks*, in which he champions the corpuscular (particle) theory of light and explains the actions of lenses and prisms.

INSIDE STORY

The Sex Life of Flowers

Rudolf Camerarius was a German botanist who identified the reproductive parts of flowering plants. Camerarius described the function of the male and female parts of flowers in fertilization in 1694. The male organ—the stamen—consists of a pollen-filled anther at the end of a stalk, or filament. The female organ—the carpel—is made up of a stigma, style, and ovary, which contains the egg cells, or ovules.

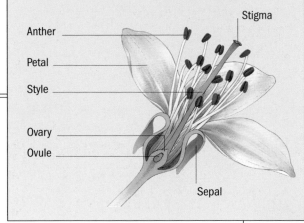

Anther · Petal · Style · Ovary · Ovule · Stigma · Sepal

THE AMERICAS

This 17th-century watercolor depicts a lock on the Canal du Midi in southern France. The canal, completed in 1692, connected the Mediterranean Sea with the Atlantic Ocean.

ASIA & OCEANIA

1699 As part of his program to modernize Russia, Tsar Peter the Great changes the Russian calendar so that the year begins on January 1, as in the West, and not September 1 as previously.

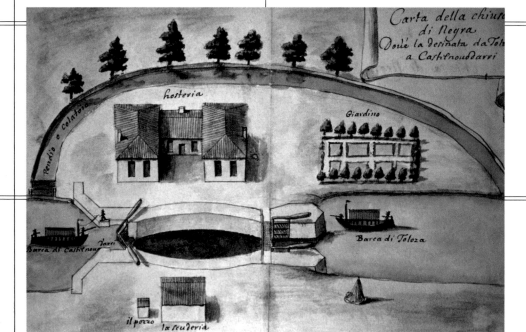

AFRICA & THE MIDDLE EAST

1702 Observatories in Islamic countries begin using European scientific instruments, including telescopes.

ENGINEERING & INVENTION

1690 French engineer Denis Papin (1647–1712) constructs a primitive steam engine.

1692 In France the 46-mile (74-km) Orléans Canal from Orléans to Paris is completed, as is the 32-mile (51.5-km) Canal du Midi, linking the Mediterranean Sea with the Atlantic Ocean.

1694 English clockmaker Daniel Quare (1648–1724) makes a portable barometer.

1698 English engineer Henry Winstanley (1644–1703) completes the first lighthouse at Eddystone Rocks in the English Channel.

1698 English mining engineer Thomas Savery (ca 1650–1715) invents a steam pump, which becomes the forerunner of the atmospheric steam engine.

1701 French mechanic Charles Plumier (1646–1704) publishes his book *L'Art de Tourner* (The Art of Turning), in which he describes a lathe for turning iron.

1701 English agriculturist Jethro Tull (1674–1741) invents a mechanical seed drill for sowing seeds.

1704 Italian clockmaker Nicolas Fatio de Duiller (1664–1753) makes a clock with jewel bearings.

1690 A paper mill is set up in Pennsylvania.

1690 North American colonies begin printing paper money and bills of credit because of a scarcity of coins.

1700 Liquor distilling becomes a significant part of the economy in New England.

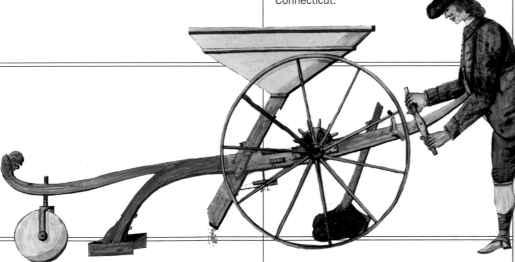

Jethro Tull's seed drill allowed farmers to sow their crops evenly with little wastage of seeds.

WORLD EVENTS

1690 William III of England (r. 1689–1702) invades Ireland to stifle a rebellion led by supporters of the deposed James II (r. 1685–88).

1697 Tsar of Russia Peter the Great (r. 1682–1725) travels around western Europe—often incognito—to study.

1699 English explorers travel to the South Seas and scout Australia.

1700 Peter the Great begins a campaign to westernize Russia.

1702 The English go to war against the French and their Habsburg allies in the War of the Spanish Succession (1701–14).

1702 Street lighting is provided in many German cities.

1704 German composer and organist Johann Sebastian Bach (1685–1750) writes his first cantata.

1692 The Witch trials in Salem, Massachusetts, convict and execute 19 people.

1693 The College of William and Mary is founded by royal charter.

1701 Yale University is established in New Haven, Connecticut.

1696 The Ashante kingdom spreads in West Africa.

1700 The Ethiopian Empire breaks up into feudal states.

THE TELESCOPE

Hans Lippershey (ca 1570–ca 1619), a Dutch eyeglass maker, made a refracting telescope in 1608. Other scientists, including Italian Galileo Galilei (1564–1642), refined the design. Among Galileo's discoveries were sunspots, craters on the moon, and four moons of Jupiter. Lenses of the time had various defects, such as chromatic aberration, which occurs because a lens cannot focus all colors to the same point and results in colored fringes around images. In 1655 an improved lens allowed Dutch scientist Christiaan Huygens (1629–95) to see the rings of Saturn. A century later optical instrument makers learned to make achromatic lenses by sticking together two lenses of different types of glass—flint glass and crown glass.

Another method of avoiding chromatic aberration involved using lenses with only slight curvature and therefore a long focal length (meaning the length of the telescope's light path from the main mirror or object lens to the focal point—the location of the eyepiece). This meant making telescopes very long. Telescopes measuring 33 feet (10 m) long were common.

A better way to view images is with a reflecting telescope, which uses mirrors instead of lenses, because mirrors do not cause chromatic aberration. James Gregory (1638–75), a Scottish mathematician, realized this in 1663 when he published a design for a telescope that had a small, curved secondary mirror to reflect the light back through a hole in the primary mirror to an eyepiece. English scientist Robert Hooke (1635–1703) later improved the design. In 1857 French physicist Léon Foucault (1819–68) devised a method of silvering glass to make curved mirrors. They were easier to manufacture, and could be resilvered if accidentally damaged. Since then telescopes have been made larger and more powerful. Most modern telescopes are reflecting telescopes since it is easier to make a big mirror than it is to make a big lens.

ASTRONOMY & MATH	**BIOLOGY & MEDICINE**	**PHYSICAL SCIENCES**

EUROPE

1706 Welsh mathematician William Jones (1675–1749) introduces the symbol π (Greek letter pi) for the ratio of the circumference of a circle to its diameter (π = ca 3.1416).

1712 First volume of *Historia Coelestis Britannica* (cataloguing the position of 3,000 stars) by English astronomer John Flamsteed (1646–1719) is published.

1712 Italian mathematician Giovanni Ceva (ca 1647–ca 1734) publishes *De Re Numeraria* (Concerning Money Matters), the first clear application of math to economics.

1717 English astronomer Abraham Sharp (1651–1742) calculates the value of π (pi) to 72 decimal places.

1718 English astronomer Edmond Halley (1656–1742) identifies stellar proper motion, the apparent movement of a star that results from the star's very gradual movement relative to the sun (not relative to the Earth).

1718 French mathematician Abraham de Moivre (1667–1754) produces *The Doctrine of Chances*, his first book on probability.

1719 English mathematician Brook Taylor (1685–1731) demonstrates the principle of the vanishing point in perspective.

1707 English physician John Floyer (1649–1734) produces a special watch for counting patients' pulse rates.

1711 Italian naturalist Luigi Marsigli (1658–1730) shows the animal nature of corals (formerly held to be plants).

1714 French physician Dominique Anel (1679–1730) invents a fine-point syringe for use in treating fistula lacrymalis (an abnormal opening in the cheekbone near the eye).

1717 Italian physician Giovanni Lancisi (1654–1720) blames malaria on the bite of the mosquito in his book *De Noxiis Paludum Effluviis* (Concerning the Noxious Effluvia of Marches).

1709 English physicist Francis Hawksbee (ca 1666–1713) describes capillary action, the phenomenon that causes a liquid to rise up a very narrow tube and a sponge or blotting paper to soak up liquids.

1710 French chemist René-Antoine Ferchault de Réaumur (1683–1757) presents a material completely woven from glass fiber to the Academy of Sciences in Paris.

Thomas Newcomen's atmospheric steam engine was the first practical steam-driven device to produce mechanical work. The engines were widely used for pumping water out of mines.

THE AMERICAS

In 1712 English inventor George Graham built an orrery—a clockwork model of the solar system.

ASIA & OCEANIA

1709 Magnolias from Japan are introduced into England.

1707 Mount Fuji in Japan erupts.

AFRICA & THE MIDDLE EAST

1717 The use of inoculation against smallpox in Turkey is witnessed by Lady Mary Wortley Montague, who introduces it to Britain.

ENGINEERING & INVENTION

1709 English iron founder Abraham Darby (ca 1678–1717) introduces the use of coke for iron smelting.

1709 Polish-born Dutch physicist Gabriel Fahrenheit (1686–1736) invents the Fahrenheit temperature scale.

1712 English engineer Thomas Newcomen (1663–1729) invents an atmospheric steam engine that employs a piston.

1712 English inventor George Graham (1673–1751) constructs an orrery, which is a working clockwork model of the solar system.

1714 Gabriel Fahrenheit makes a mercury thermometer.

1714 The British government offers £20,000 reward for a method to determine longitude at sea. In 1759 clockmaker John Harrison (1693–1776) claims the prize but has to wait 14 years to be paid in full.

1716 French engineer Hubert Gautier (1660–1737) publishes *Treatise on Bridges*, which has a lasting influence on bridge design.

1719 German printer Jakob Le Blon (1667–1741) develops a four-color printing process based on superimposing the primary colors blue, yellow, and red plus black.

1709 Brazilian Jesuit priest Bartholomeu de Gusmao (1685–1724) makes a model hot-air balloon.

1715 Sybilla Masters (d. 1720) of Pennsylvania invents a corn mill and a new process for weaving hats.

1716 A lighthouse in Boston Harbor is the first to be constructed in North America.

In the year 1456, a comet was seen passing retrograde between the Earth and the sun. Hence I dare venture to foretell, that it will return again in the year 1758.

EDMOND HALLEY, *A SYNOPSIS OF THE ASTRONOMY OF COMETS*, 1705

WORLD EVENTS

1707 England and Scotland unite to create Great Britain.

1713 Britain and France sign the Treaty of Utrecht, which ends the War of the Spanish Succession and leads to an exchange of territory in Europe and North America.

1715 Prince James the Younger arrives in Scotland as part of a failed campaign to win back the British throne for the Stuart dynasty.

1710 Mohawk leaders travel to England to ask Queen Anne (r. 1702–14) for help.

1710 The British take Acadia in modern Canada from the French.

1713 The Treaty of Utrecht cedes Acadia, Newfoundland, and other French colonies to Britain. Britain now has exclusive rights in supplying the Spanish colonies with slaves.

1715 30,000 slaves are used to work the gold fields of Minas Gerais in Brazil.

1708 The British East India Company and the New East India Company merge as the East India Company.

1712 India is split by a war of succession after the death of Shah Bahadur.

1714 Burma begins a 20-year period of economic and cultural development.

Scientists generally use the Celsius scale—as on this thermometer—to measure temperature.

GABRIEL FAHRENHEIT

Gabriel Fahrenheit was born in 1686 in the seaport of Danzig (Gdansk), Poland, of German descent. He is known for making the first reliable thermometers and devising the temperature scale named for him.

After both of his parents died from mushroom poisoning in 1701, the young Fahrenheit was apprenticed to a shopkeeper in Amsterdam, in the Netherlands. Four years later, he turned his interests to physics and became a meteorological instrument maker and glassblower. In 1709 Fahrenheit made an alcohol thermometer and also devised the Fahrenheit temperature scale, based on 32°F for the freezing point of water and 212°F for the boiling point of water.

In 1714 Fahrenheit invented the mercury thermometer, which gave more accurate readings than an alcohol thermometer. His scientific experiments led to the discovery that the boiling point of water varies with atmospheric pressure. He also discovered supercooling—the phenomenon in which water can remain liquid below its usual freezing point.

Other precision instruments Fahrenheit devised included a constant-weight hydrometer for measuring the density of liquids and a thermobarometer for reading barometric pressure by determining the boiling point of water.

Fahrenheit spent most of his life in the Netherlands but traveled widely in Europe. He gave lectures in chemistry in Amsterdam beginning in 1718 and also spent much of his time in London, where he became a member of the Royal Society.

Mercury thermometers are still commonly used in meteorology, but their use in medicine is now being phased out. The Fahrenheit temperature scale is still widely used in the United States, although the Celsius—also known as centigrade—scale, which is named for the Swedish astronomer Anders Celsius (1701–1744), is generally used by scientists worldwide.

THE NATURE OF LIGHT

EARLY SCIENTIFIC INVESTIGATIONS REVEALED various properties of light—how it is bent by lenses, how it casts shadows, even how fast it travels—but fundamental to understanding those properties is a knowledge of the nature of light itself. In particular, does light consist of a stream of minute particles, like bullets being fired from a machine gun? Or does light consist of waves that are capable of rippling across the endless vacuum of outer space?

It is clear that parallel rays of light bend as they go through a lens and come to a focus. The concentration of the rays allows a magnifying glass to be used as a burning glass, an application known since ancient times. In 212 B.C.E. Greek scientist Archimedes (ca 287–212) is said to have used a burning glass to destroy ships of the Roman fleet at Syracuse, on the island of Sicily. The first person to measure the bending of light in this way was the Dutch mathematician Willebrord Snell (1580–1626). In 1621 he found that when a ray of light passes through a piece of glass, the angle of incidence (at which the ray enters the glass) is related to the angle of refraction (the angle through which the ray is bent) by a property of the glass now known as the refractive index.

Fermat's Principle

It was another mathematician, the Frenchman Pierre de Fermat (1601–65), who figured out how light casts shadows. Fermat stated that it is because light always travels in straight lines—it will not "go around corners" to illuminate a shadow. Known as Fermat's principle, it was proposed in 1640. He also observed that light travels slower in a denser medium such as water or glass.

The first attempt to measure the speed of light was made in 1676 by Danish astronomer Ole Rømer (1644–1710). He was checking the predictions made by Italian astronomer Giovanni Cassini (1625–1712) about the timing of eclipses of Jupiter's moons (when they move out of sight behind the planet). He discovered that the eclipses seemed to happen earlier than predicted when the Earth was moving toward Jupiter and later when the Earth was moving away. Rømer accounted for the differences by assuming that the light had to travel a shorter or longer distance, and that light must therefore have a finite speed, which he calculated as 140,000 miles (225,000 km) per second—75 percent of the actual value. It was nearly 200 years before French physicist Armand Fizeau (1819–96) obtained a more accurate value—5 percent too high —of 195,737 miles (315,000 km) per second. This in turn was improved on by American physicist Albert Michelson (1852–1931) in 1882, who calculated it as 186,325 miles (299,853 km) per second. The value that is used today is 186,288 miles (299,793 km) per second.

In 1675 English scientist Isaac Newton (1642–1727) postulated that light travels as a stream of minute particles ("corpuscles"). Over the years various physicists challenged this idea, the first being his great rival Robert Hooke (1635–1703), who had already proposed the wave theory of light in 1665. The fact that light is refracted by glass and that it travels more slowly in water than it does in air, for example, were cited as evidence that light travels as waves.

Snell's law is named for the Dutch mathematician Willebrord Snell (1580–1626), who discovered it in 1621 when he was professor of mathematics at Leyden (now Leiden) University. It concerns refraction of light, which is the way a ray of light changes direction when it goes from one transparent medium to another—for example, moving from air into a block of glass. The amount of refraction depends on an optical property of the denser medium, called its refractive index. The law says that the sine of the angle of incidence divided by the sine of the angle of refraction equals the refractive index.

In about 212 B.C.E. Greek scientist Archimedes is said to have used a giant lens as a burning glass to defend Syracuse against attacking Roman ships.

The final nail in the coffin of Newton's corpuscular theory came in 1801, when English physicist Thomas Young (1773–1829) discovered the interference of light, a phenomenon in which white light shining through a narrow slit is split into the colors of the rainbow. At that time it could only be explained if light was assumed to travel as waves. Young published his findings in 1804. That is how the argument on the nature of light remained until the beginning of the 20th century, when German physicist Max Planck (1858–1947) put forward his quantum theory. It postulated that all forms of energy, including light, travel in finite "packets," or quanta, similar in fact to Newton's corpuscles. But as modern physics continued to develop, French physicist Louis de Broglie (1892–1987) suggested in 1924 that moving particles can also behave like waves, and this was soon proved to be the case.

So Newton, Hooke, and the others were all correct, and one of the great arguments in the history of science melted away.

In 1849 French physicist Armand Fizeau made the first fairly accurate measurement of the speed of light.

He bounced a light ray between two mirrors 5.6 miles (9 km) apart, directing the ray between the teeth of a fast-rotating cogwheel. The returning ray went between the next pair of teeth and then through a semi-silvered mirror to the observer.

Fizeau adjusted the speed of the cogwheel so that there was no flicker as the light traveled to the mirror and back. Using the wheel's speed and the distance traveled by the light, Fizeau was able to calculate the speed of light.

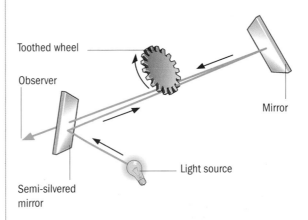

Toothed wheel

Observer

Mirror

Semi-silvered mirror

Light source

ASTRONOMY & MATH

EUROPE

1729 English astronomer James Bradley (1693–1762) discovers the aberration of starlight, an apparent shift in a star's position that results from a combination of the motion of the Earth and the fact that light travels at a finite speed.

1731 English astronomer John Bevis (1695–1771) discovers the Crab Nebula. In 1758 it is rediscovered by French astronomer Charles Messier, who catalogues it as M1. Most known nebulae have Messier numbers.

1733 French mathematician Abraham de Moivre (1667–1754) discovers the normal (bell-shaped) distribution curve, soon to become of major importance in statistical studies.

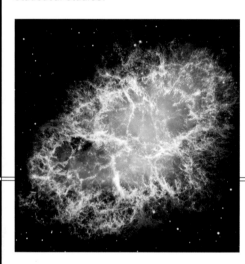

THE AMERICAS

The Crab Nebula was first seen by English astronomer John Bevis in 1731. The nebula (Latin for "cloud") is a remnant of a supernova —the gigantic explosion of a star.

BIOLOGY & MEDICINE

1727 English botanist Stephen Hales (1677–1761) writes *Vegetable Staticks*, the first book on plant physiology.

1730 French surgeon George Martine (1702–41) performs the first tracheostomy, an operation to make an opening in the trachea (windpipe) to help a patient with life-threatening breathing difficulties.

1731 English agriculturist Jethro Tull (1674–1741) publishes *The New Horse-Hoeing Husbandry*, a book that recommends harrowing the soil, growing crops in rows, removing weeds by hoeing, and using manure as fertilizer.

1734 French chemist René-Antoine Ferchault de Réaumur (1683–1757) founds the science of entomology with his book *Mémoires pour Servir à l'Histoire des Insectes* (Memoirs Serving as a Natural History of Insects).

1721 American physician Zabdiel Boylston (1676–1766) carries out the first smallpox inoculation in North America.

1728 The first botanical garden in North America is opened by naturalist and explorer John Bartram (1699–1777) at his home near Philadelphia.

PHYSICAL SCIENCES

1724 Dutch scientist Hermann Boerhaave (1668–1738) publishes his book *Elementa Chemiae* (Elements of Chemistry), the first major chemistry textbook.

1725 The St. Petersburg Academy of Sciences is founded in Russia by Peter the Great (r. 1682–1725).

1725 German physician Johann Schulze (1684–1744) observes that daylight turns certain silver salts dark (later to have significance in photography).

1729 English physicist Stephen Gray (1666–1736) distinguishes between electrical insulators and conductors.

1730 French scientist Pierre Bouguer (1698–1758) demonstrates the Bouguer anomaly: that gravitational attraction decreases with altitude.

1733 French chemist Charles du Fay (1698–1739) distinguishes two types of static electricity: "vitreous" (positive) and "resinous" (negative).

HOW THINGS WORK

The First Piano

The pianoforte (meaning "soft–loud") was a development of the harpsichord. Both instruments were based on a harp lying on its side. In a harpsichord the string is plucked by a small plectrum (originally made of quill), but the instrument lacks the ability to provide contrast between loud and soft notes. However, the strings of a piano are struck by a felt-covered hammer, producing a very different sound and giving performers control over both the volume and length of a given note.

ASIA & OCEANIA

AFRICA & THE MIDDLE EAST

Since we are assured that the all-wise Creator has observed the most exact proportions, of number, weight, and measure, in the make of all things; the most likely way therefore, to get any insight into the nature of those parts of the creation, which come within our observation, must in all reason be to number, weigh, and measure. And we have much encouragement to pursue this method, of searching into the nature of things, from the great success that has attended any attempts of this kind.

STEPHEN HALES, *VEGETABLE STATICKS*

ENGINEERING & INVENTION	WORLD EVENTS
1720 Italian harpsichord maker Bartolomeo Cristofori (1655–1731) invents the pianoforte.	**1721** Bubonic plague breaks out for the last time in Europe.
1725 French clockmaker Antoine Thiout (b. 1692) constructs a clock that displays solar time.	**1721** Robert Walpole (1676–1745) becomes the first British prime minister.
1726 English inventor George Graham (1673–1751) invents the mercury pendulum for clocks, which does not change in length with changes in temperature.	**1721** A regular mail service is set up between London and New England.
1728 English clockmaker John Harrison (1693–1776) creates the gridiron pendulum for clocks.	**1727** The Society of Friends—also known as the Quakers—in England advocates the abolition of slavery.
1728 French dentist Pierre Fauchard (1678–1761) invents the first dental drill and introduces fillings.	**1730** John Wesley (1703–91) and Charles Wesley (1707–88) form the Methodist Church at Oxford, England.
1730 English mathematician John Hadley (1682–1744) devises the quadrant, a navigational instrument that was the forerunner of the sextant.	**1730** Russia, Persia, and the Holy Roman Empire go to war against the Ottomans.
1730 René-Antoine Ferchault de Réaumur makes an alcohol thermometer and devises the Réaumur temperature scale.	**1733** The War of the Polish Succession begins when France and Spain reject the claimant to the Polish throne backed by Austria and Russia. Most fighting takes place in the Hapsburg lands in Italy.
1733 English engineer John Kay (1704–64) patents the flying shuttle, which increases the speed at which a loom makes cloth.	**1734** The Koran is translated into English by English Orientalist George Sale (1697–1736).
1723 A house in Newport, Rhode Island, is built with indoor plumbing.	**1730** English colonies begin to experience a religious revival known as the Great Awakening.
1724 Levees are built along the Mississippi River in Louisiana to protect against floods.	**1732** George II of Great Britain (r. 1727–60) grants a charter to British general James Oglethorpe (1696–1785) to found the colony of Georgia.
1725 The Principio Company constructs Accokeek Furnace in Virginia. The company exports its iron to England.	
1720s In India, Jaipur City is built on a geometric grid.	**1720** The Chinese expel the Dzungars from Tibet, and it becomes a Chinese protectorate.
1729 *T'ushu ji cheng*, a 1,000-page encyclopedia printed in movable type, is published in China.	**1722** Dutch explorers arrive on Easter Island.
	1729 Opium smoking is prohibited in China by Emperor Yongzheng (r. 1722–35).
1729 Transylvanian-born Ottoman printer Ibrahim Müteferrika (1674–1745) publishes descriptions of European governments, military, and geography.	**1720** The Ottomans begin sending ambassadors to Europe to learn about European culture.
1732 The Ottomans build a new system of aqueducts to bring water into Istanbul.	**1729** The Ottomans end the ban on printing books in Turkish or Arabic.
	1729 Arabs drive the Portuguese out of Dahomey.

IRON SMELTING

Iron is made in a blast furnace—a furnace in which combustion is forced by a current of air. Early blast furnaces were holes in the ground covered with a chimney. The furnace was filled with a mixture of iron ore, limestone, and charcoal, and set on fire. Bellows forced a blast of air through the furnace. Impurities rose to the top and molten iron was tapped through a hole at the bottom.

By the 14th century England was Europe's main iron-producing country. With bellows driven by waterwheels, blast furnaces could produce up to 3.3 tons (3 tonnes) of iron a day. This output required large amounts of charcoal, produced by burning wood. As a result, most of Britain's forests were destroyed.

In 1709 English iron-founder Abraham Darby (ca 1678–1717) began using coke (derived from coal) instead of charcoal. Darby's development had a dramatic effect on production. Cast-iron pans, kettles, and other utensils became commonplace in homes.

Darby built his furnaces at Coalbrookdale on the banks of the Severn River. His grandson Abraham Darby III (1750–91) built a lasting memorial to the family. In 1779, using prefabricated cast-iron sections, he completed a bridge across the river. It is 98 feet (30 m) long and stands 39 feet (12 m) above the water. It still carries foot passengers, but it was closed to traffic in 1934.

The iron bridge built by Abraham Darby III

ASTRONOMY & MATH	BIOLOGY & MEDICINE	PHYSICAL SCIENCES

ASTRONOMY & MATH

1735 English scientist George Hadley (1685–1768) proposes that the overall circulation of air in the atmosphere is due to convection currents.

1736 French mathematician Pierre de Maupertuis (1698–1759) states correctly that the Earth is an oblate spheroid (a sphere flattened slightly at the poles).

1736 French surveyor Alexis Clairaut (1713–65) measures the length of 1 degree of meridian (longitude), thus enabling accurate calculation of the size of the Earth.

1743 French mathematician Jean d'Alembert (1717–83) establishes mathematical dynamics (a branch of mechanics) with his book *Traité de Dynamique* (Treatise on Dynamics). Three years later he advances the theory of complex numbers.

1743 English mathematician Thomas Simpson (1710–61) devises Simpson's rules, a systematic approach to finding the area bounded by a curve.

1748 English astronomer James Bradley (1693–1762) discovers the nutation of the Earth, which is the slight "nodding" of the Earth's axis as it describes a very slow circle in space.

BIOLOGY & MEDICINE

1735 Swedish naturalist Carolus Linnaeus (1707–78) publishes *Systema Naturae*, in which he classifies objects into three kingdoms: animal, plant, or mineral. Later (1749) he introduces binomial naming (genus and species names).

1737 Swedish chemist Georg Brandt (1694–1768) discovers cobalt, the first discovery of a completely new metal since ancient times.

1740 Swiss naturalist Charles Bonnet (1720–93) observes parthenogenesis in aphids. (Parthenogenesis is the phenomenon in which unfertilized female animals give birth to young.)

1745 French surgeon Jacques Daviel (1693–1762) successfully performs an operation for the removal of a cataract from a patient's eye.

1747 Scottish physician James Lind (1716–94) experiments with citrus fruits to prevent scurvy among British sailors. (Citrus fruits are rich in vitamin C, the lack of which is now known to cause scurvy.)

1748 Scottish physician John Fothergill (1712–80) gives the first description of diphtheria.

PHYSICAL SCIENCES

1735 English physicist Stephen Gray (1666–1736) postulates that lightning is an electrical phenomenon.

1738 Swiss scientist Daniel Bernoulli (1700–82) becomes the first to put forward a kinetic theory of gases—that their properties can be explained by considering gases to be composed of rapidly moving small particles of matter.

1742 Swedish astronomer Anders Celsius (1701–44) devises the 100-degree Celsius temperature scale (later known as the centigrade scale but now called by its original name).

1745 Russian scientist Mikhail Lomonosov (1711–65) compiles a catalog of more than 300 minerals.

1747 German chemist Andreas Marggraf (1709–82) discovers sugar in beets.

HOW THINGS WORK

The Leyden Jar

The Leyden jar is named for the Dutch University of Leyden (now spelled Leiden) where it was invented in 1745 by Pieter van Musschenbroek. It is a type of condenser used for storing electrical charge. It has plates of metal foil glued inside and outside a glass jar. A brass rod running through an insulating stopper has at its end a short length of metal chain that makes contact with the inner foil. An electrostatic charge, produced by rubbing an insulating rod or by an electrostatic generator, can be brought up to the brass rod to charge up the condenser. A person who touches the brass knob receives a powerful electric shock. According to one account, French cleric and physicist Jean-Antoine Nollet connected a charged Leyden jar to a row of monks holding hands and watched them all leap into the air with the shock.

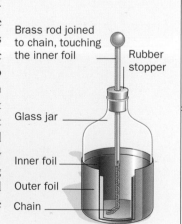

Brass rod joined to chain, touching the inner foil

Rubber stopper

Glass jar

Inner foil

Outer foil

Chain

1738 Introduced by Eliza Lucas Pinckney, indigo becomes an important crop in the South; it is grown for its blue dye.

1740 French explorer Charles-Marie de la Condamine (1701–74) discovers the powerful paralyzing drug curare (used as an arrow poison by South American Indians).

1736 Charles-Marie de la Condamine discovers India rubber (then called *caoutchouc*).

1735 Spanish scientist and naval officer Antonio de Ulloa (1716–95) rediscovers platinum in South America. It had been used by local people for centuries and was found in Central America by Spanish explorers, but its discovery had not been announced.

1743 The American Philosophical Society is founded.

The "Franklin stove," invented by Benjamin Franklin in 1742, became very popular and gradually replaced open fires to heat rooms in North America.

ENGINEERING & INVENTION

1735 English clockmaker John Harrison (1693–1776) unveils his first chronometer, a clock so accurate it can be used to calculate longitude at sea.

1738 English inventor Lewis Paul (d. 1759) produces a machine for carding wool. (Carding is the process of combing out woolen fleeces into parallel fibers.)

1738 English metallurgist William Champion (1710–89) devises a new industrial process for the large-scale production of zinc from its ores.

1740 English metallurgist Benjamin Huntsman (1704–76) invents the crucible process for making steel in batches.

1742 French metallurgist Jean-Paul Malouin (1701–78) creates a process for covering steel with a layer of zinc (later to be called galvanizing).

1743 English metalworker Thomas Boulsover (1706–88) produces "Sheffield plate," metalware consisting of copper coated with a thin layer of silver.

1745 Dutch physicist Pieter van Musschenbroek (1692–1761) invents the Leyden jar, a simple form of electrical condenser.

1740 Frederick II, known as Frederick the Great, of Prussia (r. 1740–86) succeeds to the throne after the death of his father Frederick William I (r. 1713–40).

1741 An outbreak of yellow fever in Cádiz, Spain, kills 10,000 people.

1741 German composer George Frederick Handel (1685–1759) premieres his oratorio *The Messiah*.

1745 Charles Stuart, known as Bonnie Prince Charlie, the grandson of deposed king of England James II (r. 1685–88) fails to regain the English throne.

1746 The feudal clan system declines in Scotland, and Celtic culture is suppressed after the rebellion of 1745. Many Scots emigrate to America.

1748 Excavations begin on the site of the rediscovered ancient city of Pompeii, Italy, buried by an eruption of Mt. Vesuvius in 79 C.E.

1739 German-born Caspar Wistar (1696–1752) opens a glassworks in New Jersey.

1741 Porcelain production begins in Savannah, Georgia.

1742 American scientist and politician Benjamin Franklin (1706–90) invents a wood-burning stove. The design is patented, and later stoves of the same design come to be known as "Franklin stoves."

1740 Smallpox kills many Lakota of the northern plains.

1742 The Moravian College for Women is established in Pennsylvania.

1743 Russians explore Alaska.

1744 King George's War (1744–48) breaks out in New England.

1747 Jesuit missionaries design a Summer Palace for the Chinese emperors outside of Beijing.

1739 Persian troops led by Nadir Shah invade India and loot many of the finest Mughal palaces.

1746 In the French and British struggle for control in India, the French conquer Madras.

1730s Ottoman artillery officers enlist the help of the French aristocrat Count Bonnerai to teach Turkish gunners and to found a school of military engineering.

CAROLUS LINNAEUS

Carolus Linnaeus was a Swedish naturalist who devised the binomial (two-name) system of classifying plants and animals and founded the science of taxonomy. Born Carl von Linné in Råshult, southern Sweden, in 1707, he was the son of a pastor. He studied medicine and then botany at universities in Lund and Uppsala.

Between 1732 and 1735 Linnaeus traveled around Lapland and several European countries and found 100 new species of plants. He settled in Holland and qualified as a doctor of medicine. In 1735 he published *Systema Naturae* (Systems of Nature), in which he classified objects into three kingdoms: animals, plants, and minerals.

Linnaeus introduced binomial naming in 1749, and in his book *Species Plantarum* (Species of Plants) of 1753 he gave each plant a Latinized genus name and a species name. For example, using his system, the American beech tree is *Fagus grandifolia* (genus *Fagus*, species *grandifolia*). The modern convention is for the names to be printed in italic letters with a capital letter for only the genus. The names of orders and classes are not printed in italics.

In 1738 Linnaeus returned to Sweden, where he practiced as a physician. In 1741 he became a professor of medicine and botany at Uppsala University.

Swedish naturalist Carolus Linnaeus is considered the founder of modern taxonomy.

NAVIGATION AT SEA

THE CREW OF A SHIP IN THE MIDDLE OF AN open ocean needs to know in what direction the ship is going and exactly where it is. A compass can indicate direction, and the magnetic compass was in regular use by the 1100s. But accurate positioning needs a knowledge of latitude and longitude, which proved to be much more difficult to determine.

Latitude indicates a position in terms of its distance north or south of the equator. It is measured in degrees. For example, Philadelphia is at a latitude of 40° north. Latitude can be found by measuring the angle of a particular heavenly body above the horizon and consulting books of tables or almanacs. At night the angle of the polestar or during the day the angle of the sun at noon can be measured and compared with tables. Early sailors had various instruments for measuring these angles. Using a cross-staff, a sailor sighted along a 3-foot- (1-m-) long staff while moving a cross-piece until the lower end lined up with the horizon and the upper end coincided with the star or the sun. The staff was calibrated in degrees from which the sailor could read off the angle. It was first described in about 1330 by French astronomer Levi ben Gershon (1288–1344) and used in Europe until as late as the 18th century.

In 1594 English sailor John Davis (ca 1550–1605) invented the backstaff. It was pointed in the opposite direction, and the operator did not need to look directly into the sun. The quadrant was a similar

This illustration shows a ship's navigator taking a reading of latitude from the shore using a variant of the cross-staff.

KEY DATES

1594
Backstaff

1731
Octant

1735
Harrison's early chronometers

1757
Sextant

1759
Harrison's prize-winning chronometer

instrument, also used by astronomers and by gunners to set the correct angles for aiming artillery pieces.

Then in 1731 English mathematician John Hadley (1682–1744) invented the octant, incorrectly named Hadley's quadrant at the time. Anglo-American inventor Thomas Godfrey (1704–49) of Philadelphia invented an almost identical instrument independently. In the octant a pivoted arm carries a mirror that can be moved to bring an image of the sun in line with another mirror. The second mirror also gives a view of the horizon. The maximum angle it could measure was 45°. From there it was a simple step to the sextant (which measured up to 60°), introduced by Scottish naval officer John Campbell (ca 1720–90) in 1757. It remained the standard navigational instrument for 250 years. It was even used on aircraft until it was finally supplanted by radio beacons and the satellite-based GPS (global positioning system).

The Search for Longitude

Finding the longitude of a ship's location—its position east or west of the Greenwich meridian (longitude 0°)—proved to be far more difficult than calculating latitude. For centuries sailors measured the angle between the moon and another heavenly body, and consulted tables called ephemerides that gave the day-to-day positions of the moon. German astronomer Johann Müller (1436–76), also known as Regiomontanus, drew up the first tables in 1474. They were published in 1766 in the *Nautical Almanac* by English astronomer Nevil Maskelyne (1732–1811) and revised every year.

The solution to the longitude problem lay in finding an accurate way of measuring time, which varies locally depending on longitude. For example, at 12 noon in London, England, it is 7.00 A.M. in Philadelphia (longitude about 75° west). If we know the exact time at a given place when it is noon in London,

we can calculate its longitude. To do this we need a chronometer, or very accurate clock. In 1714 the British government offered a prize of £20,000 to anyone who could produce such an instrument. A condition of the competition was that the "sea clock" had to gain or lose no more than two minutes after a six-week voyage to the West Indies and back.

English clockmaker John Harrison (1693–1776) took up the challenge and in 1735 introduced his first chronometer. But it was his fourth instrument of 1759 that won the prize (or half of it, since the government retained half the money until Harrison could prove that the chronometer could be duplicated). He did not receive the remainder until 1773, and then only after King George III intervened on Harrison's behalf. Chronometers based on Harrison's H4 were rarely used at first as they were very expensive, costing about a third of the price of a new warship.

Chronometers are precision timepieces used to keep accurate time and help calculate longitude at sea.

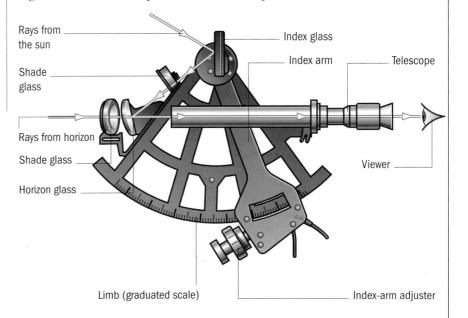

A sextant measures the angle of the sun or a star above the horizon. Special tables convert the angle into the navigator's latitude, the angular distance north or south of the equator.

The index glass (in fact, a mirror) reflects the sun's rays onto a second mirror called the horizon glass. It is a half-mirror that reflects the rays along a telescope to the navigator's eye. A shade glass cuts down the brightness and prevents eye damage. The navigator also looks through the plain (unsilvered) half of the horizon glass at the horizon and adjusts the angle of the index glass until the sun's image appears to be on the horizon. The graduated scale on the limb of the sextant then indicates the angle of the sun above the horizon.

Rays from the sun — Index glass — Index arm — Telescope — Shade glass — Rays from horizon — Shade glass — Horizon glass — Viewer — Limb (graduated scale) — Index-arm adjuster

1750–1764

CONCISE HISTORY OF SCIENCE AND INVENTION

| ASTRONOMY & MATH | BIOLOGY & MEDICINE | PHYSICAL SCIENCES |

EUROPE

1750 French astronomer Guillaume Legentil de la Galaisière (1725–92) discovers the Trifid Nebula (M20) in the constellation Sagittarius. It is named by English astronomer John Herschel (1792–1871) for the three dark rifts that appear to divide the nebula and join at its center.

1755 German philosopher Immanuel Kant (1724–1804) explains his theory for the formation of the solar system in his *Universal Natural History and Theory of the Heavens*. He postulates that it is created from a spinning gaseous nebula and that our galaxy is just one of many in the universe.

1758 German astronomer Johann Palitzsch (1723–88) observes Halley's comet when it returns as predicted by English astronomer Edmond Halley (1656–1742) in 1682.

1761 Russian scientist Mikhail Lomonosov (1711–65) observes a transit of Venus across the sun's disk and deduces that Venus has an atmosphere.

1762 English astronomer James Bradley (1693–1762) produces a star catalog with measured positions of 60,000 stars.

1752 French chemist René-Antoine Ferchault de Réaumur (1683–1757) discovers the part played by gastric juices in the digestion of foods.

1760s English agriculturist Robert Bakewell (1725–95) uses selective breeding to produce improved varieties of farm animals.

1761 Austrian physician Leopold Auenbrugger (1722–1809) introduces the diagnostic technique of percussion, which involves tapping the patient's chest and listening to the quality of the sound produced.

1761 Italian physician Giovanni Morgagni (1682–1771) founds the science of pathology with his book *On the Seats and Causes of Disease*.

1762 The École Nationale Vétérinaire is established in Lyons, France, the world's first national veterinary college.

1763 German botanist Josef Kölreuter (1733–1806) discovers the role of insects in the pollination of flowers.

1751 Swedish chemist Axel Cronstedt (1722–65) discovers nickel.

1758 German chemist Andreas Marggraf (1709–82) introduces flame tests as a method of chemical analysis. (Various metallic elements burn with a characteristic color in a gas flame.)

1760 German physicist Johann Lambert (1728–77) formulates Lambert's law, which states that the illuminance provided by light striking a surface at right angles is inversely proportional to the square of the distance between the surface and the light source.

1761 Scottish chemist Joseph Black (1728–99) introduces the concept of latent heat. Latent heat is the "extra" heat that must be added to an object at its melting point before it actually melts (or to a liquid at its boiling point before it boils).

1762 English physicist John Canton (1718–72) demonstrates that contrary to previous beliefs, water is a compressible liquid.

THE AMERICAS

A single worker could spin many threads at the same time with James Hargreaves's spinning jenny, invented in 1764.

1762 The flightless dodo-like bird called the solitaire (*Pezophaps solitaria*) becomes extinct (on the Indian Ocean's Rodriguez Island).

1751 English surveyors Charles Mason and Jeremiah Dixon begin to accurately map the frontiers of North America.

1752 American scientist and politician Benjamin Franklin (1706–90) demonstrates the electrical nature of lightning in his famous kite-flying experiment.

This hand-colored engraving depicts a stretch of the Bridgewater Canal, in England, crossing the River Irwell in an aqueduct. The canal, completed in 1761, carried coal from the duke of Bridgewater's mines to Manchester.

ASIA & OCEANIA

AFRICA & THE MIDDLE EAST

1750 French astronomer Nicolas de Lacaille (1713–1762) leads an astronomical expedition to the Cape of Good Hope to study parallax, or the relative position of celestial objects seen from different points on Earth.

ca 1750 Zahn al-Umar plants cotton and exports the product, marking the start of the cotton industry in Palestine.

THE SCIENTIFIC REVOLUTION

ENGINEERING & INVENTION	WORLD EVENTS
1753 Scottish engineer Charles Morrison invents a 26-wire telegraph (one wire for each letter of the alphabet).	**1751** In France, Denis Diderot begins to publish the multivolume *Encyclopédia*, a key work of the Scientific Revolution.
1756 English engineer John Smeaton (1724–92) invents cement that sets underwater (for building lighthouses).	**1755** An earthquake in Lisbon, Portugal, kills more than 60,000 people.
1757 English clockmaker Thomas Mudge (1715–94) devises a lever escapement for a watch, although it is not used until 1770.	**1755** Russia's first university, the University of Moscow, is founded.
1758 English cotton weaver Jedediah Strutt (1726–97) invents the stocking frame, a machine for making ribbed hosiery.	**1756** The Seven Years' War (1756–63) breaks out between Britain and France.
1758 English optician John Dollond (1706–61) makes achromatic lenses that consist of two pieces of different glass types.	**1759** Jesuits are expelled from Portugal and its colonies.
1761 English engineer James Brindley (1716–72) completes the Bridgewater Canal.	**1759** King Ferdinand of Spain (r. 1746–59) dies and is succeeded by his half-brother Charles III (r. 1759–88).
1762 English nobleman John Montagu, earl of Sandwich (1718–92), invents the sandwich (so that he did not have to leave the gambling tables to take his meals).	**1759** Voltaire publishes *Candide*.
1764 English mechanic James Hargreaves (d. 1778) invents the spinning jenny for spinning many cotton or woolen threads at the same time.	**1760** George II of England (r. 1727–60) dies and is succeeded by his grandson George III (r. 1760–1820).
ca 1760 About this time, rice planters in the American South start using threshing machines in rice production.	**1754** The French and Indian War (1754–63) breaks out between Britain and France, resulting in the British conquest of Canada.
	1763 Chief Pontiac (1720–69) of the Ottawa leads a rebellion against British settlers.
Science is organized knowledge. Wisdom is organized life. IMMANUEL KANT	**ca 1750** About this time, the Dutch begin spreading Western learning in Japan.
	1760 Canton becomes the only Chinese port allowed to trade with foreigners.

SELECTIVE BREEDING

Choosing which animals can breed together in order to improve the quality of cattle, sheep, and other types of livestock is called selective breeding. The technique was pioneered by Robert Bakewell (1725–95), who ran his own farm in Leicestershire, England.

Previously, farm animals of both sexes were kept in the same enclosures and allowed to breed randomly. This resulted in offspring with random characteristics. Bakewell separated the sexes and only allowed animals with specific characteristics to breed. This inbreeding resulted in exaggerated traits.

Bakewell created a breed of sheep with fatty meat—popular in those days—and a quality fleece called the New Leicester from the Lincolnshire breed. He hired out his best rams to neighboring farmers so that they could improve their stock, too. Bakewell also improved the Longhorn cattle breed, making it more meat productive.

With changes in taste, Bakewell's New Leicester breed of sheep eventually declined in popularity, and Longhorn cattle were superseded by Shorthorn breeds. However, Bakewell's selective breeding methods became widespread across the world in creating not only hundreds of productive breeds of sheep, cattle, goats, pigs, poultry, and other farm animals but also other domestic animals, such as pet cats and dogs.

The New Leicester breed of sheep was created by Robert Bakewell by selectively breeding sheep with fatty meat and long wool.

BENJAMIN FRANKLIN

BENJAMIN FRANKLIN (1706–90) WAS A complex character, an unusual combination of statesman and scientist. He played an important part in the development of the United States and made major discoveries in physics. He also was a talented inventor, and some of his inventions are still in use throughout the world today.

Born in Boston into a family of 17 children, Benjamin Franklin left school at the age of ten. Two years later he was apprenticed to his older brother James, a printer. When he was just 18, he took over publication of the *New England Courant*, a weekly newspaper founded by his brother. Franklin did not stay for long; instead, he went to Philadelphia and worked as a printer himself. In 1724 he set sail for England. He returned home two years later and published the first volume of *Poor Richard's Almanac* in 1733, a collection of articles on a wide range of subjects to "convey instruction among the common people." Franklin held various public offices and helped draft the Declaration of Independence in 1776. He traveled to France to raise help for the American cause in the War of Independence (1775–82). He was also a staunch supporter of the abolition of slavery. Franklin retired from public life in 1788.

Electrical Nature of Lightning

During his lifetime Franklin also conducted scientific experiments. The best known, in 1752, was one of the most dangerous experiments ever undertaken. He attached a metal key to the moistened string of a kite, which he flew during a thunderstorm. Electric "fluid" flowing down the string caused sparks to jump between the key and a Leyden jar (a primitive electrical condenser). Franklin had established the electrical nature of lightning and coined the words *positive* and *negative* to describe the two types of static electricity. Several European scientists who tried to repeat the experiment were struck by lightning and killed. As a result of his discovery Franklin invented the lightning rod—sometimes still called a Franklin rod —a pointed conductor located at the top of a building and connected to the ground by a thick wire attached to a plate buried in the soil.

BENJAMIN FRANKLIN.
THE STATESMAN AND PHILOSOPHER.

Franklin made many scientific discoveries, wrote a number of bestselling books, and was a key figure in the formation of the United States.

KEY DATES

1733
Poor Richard's Almanac first published

1742
Franklin stove

1752
Kite experiment and lightning rod

1784
Bifocal eyeglasses

In 1742 Franklin invented the so-called "Franklin stove" designed to make more efficient use of fuel. In later life, Franklin, who was nearsighted, had the first pair of bifocal eyeglasses made for him. They had split lenses—the upper half for distance vision and the lower half for near vision. Franklin chose not to patent any of his inventions, believing that ideas should be exchanged freely.

Franklin had many other scientific interests. Unlike most of his contemporaries, he rejected Isaac Newton's corpuscular theory of light (that light travels as particles), favoring the wave theories of Robert Hooke and others. He suggested that the rapid heating of air near warm ground causes it to expand and spiral upward, producing tornadoes and waterspouts. He investigated the course of the Gulf Stream, the current of warm water that flows across the Atlantic Ocean, and he suggested that ships' captains should use a thermometer to locate and benefit from the current (or avoid it, depending on the direction in which they were sailing). In 1824 the Franklin Institute was founded in Philadelphia in his honor.

OPPOSITE: *An artist's romantic depiction of Franklin's famous experiment. He flew a kite in a thunderstorm and found that electricity from the storm was conducted along the kite's wet string. During the experiment Franklin charged a Leyden jar, which was connected to the string by a thin wire and a key.*

ASTRONOMY & MATH	BIOLOGY & MEDICINE	PHYSICAL SCIENCES

EUROPE

1767 English astronomer Nevil Maskelyne (1732–1811) edits the *Nautical Almanac*, a book of astronomical and other tables.

1767 Swiss mathematician Leonhard Euler (1707–83) sets out the rules of algebra in his book *Vollständige Anleitung zur Algebra* (Complete Instruction in Algebra).

1773 French mathematician Pierre-Simon de Laplace (1749–1827) uses Newton's law of gravity to show that the solar system is inherently stable.

1773 German-born English astronomer William Herschel (1738–1822) studies the motions of distant stars and figures out that the sun is gradually moving through space.

1774 German astronomer Johann Bode (1747–1826) founds *Astronomisches Jahrbuch* (Astronomical Yearbook).

1774 Nevil Maskelyne determines the gravitational constant (the constant that appears in Newton's law of gravitation) and is thus able to calculate the average density of the Earth.

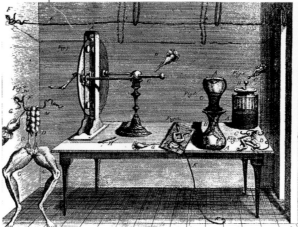

Luigi Galvani used animals such as frogs and sheep in his experiments with electricity in 1771.

1766 English scientist Henry Cavendish (1731–1810) identifies hydrogen, calling it "inflammable air."

1769 English chemist Joseph Priestley (1733–1804) suggests that electrical forces follow an inverse square law.

1771 Swiss geologist Jean Deluc (1727– 1817) uses a barometer to find the heights of mountains (atmospheric pressure decreases with altitude).

1771 Italian physician and physicist Luigi Galvani (1737–98) shows that the muscles of a dissected frog twitch when they are stimulated by electricity.

1772 Scottish chemist Daniel Rutherford (1749–1819) discovers nitrogen.

1774 Joseph Priestley identifies oxygen.

1774 Swedish chemist Karl Scheele (1742–86) discovers barium, chlorine, and manganese.

1774 French chemist Antoine Lavoisier (1743–94) demonstrates the law of conservation of mass (in a chemical reaction).

THE AMERICAS

1765 Colonial American scientist John Winthrop (1714–79) includes calculations of comet masses in his book *Account of Some Fiery Meteors*. In 1772 he presents Harvard University with its first telescope.

1773 In Colombia, botanist Mutis is put on trial for heresy after giving a series of lectures about Copernicus's theory of the sun-centered universe.

ca 1765 Planters in the southern colonies of North America begin rice cultivation, which forms the basis of a period of economic growth.

ASIA & OCEANIA

1769 English explorer James Cook visits Tahiti to observe a transit of Venus (when the planet Venus passes in front of the sun's disk); German naturalist Peter Pallas (1741–1811) travels to the border between China and Russia for the same purpose.

INSIDE SCIENCE

Manganese

Manganese is a gray-white, hard but brittle metal. It occurs as a free element and as a part of many minerals. Swedish chemist Karl Scheele first recognized manganese as an element in 1774. Later that year, Scheele's colleague Johann Gottlieb Gahn (1745–1818) isolated the metal from manganese dioxide. Not long after its discovery, manganese became a key ingredient in iron and steel production because it produced harder alloys. Manganese and its compounds have many other industrial uses, including in batteries, as oxidizers, as pigments, and as an additive in gasoline to boost octane rating and reduce engine knocking. The metal is also essential to all forms of life, as a cofactor of a broad range of enzymes.

AFRICA & THE MIDDLE EAST

ENGINEERING & INVENTION	WORLD EVENTS
1765 Italian naturalist Lazzaro Spallanzi (1729–99) devises a method of preserving food using hermetically sealed containers.	**1767** Catherine II of Russia, also called Catherine the Great (r. 1762–96), commissions a new code of laws.
1765 Scottish engineer James Watt (1736–1819) builds a steam engine with a separate condenser.	**1767** The Russians go to war against Ottoman Turks.
1768 French chemist Antoine Baumé (1728–1804) invents a hydrometer (which he calls an aerometer) and a new density scale for graduating it.	**1770** Fifteen-year-old Marie Antoinette (1755–93), daughter of the Austrian Empress Maria Theresa, marries Prince Louis, later Louis XVI of France (r. 1774–93).
1769 English manufacturer Richard Arkwright (1732–92) produces the spinning frame for spinning strong cotton thread.	**1771** Plague kills more than 50,000 people in Moscow, Russia.
1770 Joseph Priestley invents the pencil eraser.	**1772** Poland is partitioned by Russia, Prussia, and Austria.
1770 French inventor Jacques de Vaucanson (1709–82) constructs textile machinery that incorporates a chain drive.	**1772** Pope Clement XIV (1705–74) dissolves the Jesuit order.
1770 French watchmaker Abraham-Louis Perrelet (1729–1826) develops a watch with automatic winding.	**1773** A Cossack soldier, Yemelyan Pugachev (ca 174–75), declares himself to be Peter III (r. 1762), Catherine the Great's assassinated husband, and leads a popular uprising in southern Russia.
1774 English engineer John Wilkinson (1728–1808) patents a precision cannon-boring machine, also used for making cylinders for steam engines.	**1774** Louis XVI becomes king of France after the death of his grandfather, Louis XV (r. 1715–74).
1765 The first medical school in the United States is established at the College of Pennsylvania.	**1765** The Spanish begin loosening restrictions on American trade.
1769 American astronomer David Rittenhouse (1732–96) constructs the first astronomical telescope in the United States.	**1773** Guatemala City becomes the capital of Guatemala after the former capital, Antigua, is destroyed by an earthquake.
	1765 The Chinese invade Burma.
	1768 English explorer Captain James Cook (1728–79) begins exploring the Pacific.
	1771 The Tay Son Rebellion begins in Vietnam.
1767 Hungarian Baron do Tott (1733–93) is placed in charge of the Ottoman Army. He builds a modern cannon foundry and a new military school and introduces a rapid-fire artillery corps.	**1769** Egyptians revolt against Ottoman rule.
	1772 Scottish explorer James Bruce (1730–94) finds the source of the Blue Nile.

Theologian and scientist Joseph Priestley is credited with the discovery of oxygen, which he called "dephlogisticated air."

INVESTIGATING THE AIR

In the 1760s and 1770s scientists discovered several new elements. Among them were the gas hydrogen and the two most common atmospheric gases, oxygen and nitrogen.

English scientist Henry Cavendish identified hydrogen from a metal–acid reaction in 1766. He called the gas "inflammable air" and later discovered that, on burning, hydrogen produces water. The gas was not named until 1783. French chemist Antoine Lavoisier called it hydrogen, which is Greek for "water producer."

Scottish chemist Daniel Rutherford discovered nitrogen, which makes up about 78 percent of the air, in 1772. Scientists had long suspected that a large portion of the air did not support combustion. For that reason, scientists at first referred to nitrogen as burnt, fixed, noxious, or mephitic (meaning "lifeless") air. The name *nitrogen* means "saltpeter producer."

In 1774 English chemist Joseph Priestley identified oxygen, which makes up almost 21 percent of the volume of air. The gas had been discovered by Swedish chemist Karl Scheele in 1772, but since he did not publish his findings until 1777 Priestley is usually credited with its discovery. Lavoisier further characterized the gas and gave oxygen its name, which means "acid producer," because he mistakenly believed that all acids contained oxygen.

The understanding of carbon dioxide (about 0.04 percent of the air) also improved in the 1700s. Flemish chemist Jan Baptist van Helmont (1580–1644) had recognized carbon dioxide in the 1600s and coined the word *gas*. Scottish scientist Joseph Black (1728–99) further studied the properties of carbon dioxide in the 1750s, and Joseph Priestley also added to its understanding.

THE STEAM ENGINE

An old pumphouse above a disused mine in Cornwall, southwestern England. Steam engines were first used to pump water out of these coastal mines.

FROM THE TIME OF THE ANCIENT EGYPTIANS until the end of the 17th century only wind and water power provided an alternative to the muscles of animals and humans. But the situation changed dramatically with the invention of the steam engine, which involved a sequence of events beginning in 1690 and culminating in 1765 with the work of James Watt (1736–1819).

The earliest steam engines did not use the pressure of steam to provide power. Instead, they used the pressure of the air. For that reason they are more accurately called atmospheric engines. The first was devised by Denis Papin (1647–1712), a French physicist working in England. A vertical, open-ended cylinder with a close-fitting piston had water inside its base. A fire heated the base of the cylinder, causing the water to boil and turn into steam. Steam pressure lifted the piston, which remained raised while the cylinder cooled. The steam condensed back to liquid water, creating a partial vacuum in the cylinder. Then atmospheric pressure on the upper end of the piston pushed it down again. A rope connected to the piston and moving over a pulley could be used to lift a load or work a pump.

A similar arrangement, patented in 1698 by English mining engineer Thomas Savery (ca 1650–1715), made the atmospheric engine into a practical steam pump. It had no piston or other moving parts, just hand-operated valves to provide continuous operation. Steam from a boiler passed into a working chamber that was sprayed with cold water to condense the steam. The partial vacuum that was created as a result lifted water through a one-way valve into the chamber. Steam was then let in again, which forced the water out and up through another one-way valve.

Beam Engines

In 1712 English engineer Thomas Newcomen (1663–1729) perfected the first engine to use steam pressure to work a piston. Because of the way they were constructed, people generally referred to Newcomen's engines as "beam engines." Newcomen could not patent his engine because its principle was too close to that of Thomas Savery's, so the two men went into partnership and built engines together. This was the stage that steam power had reached in 1764, when Scottish engineer James Watt received a model of a Newcomen engine to repair. He realized how much energy is wasted by first heating the cylinder and then cooling it. In 1765 he hit on the idea of adding a separate external condenser. In addition he used steam to push up the piston and then—by admitting low-pressure steam on the other side—to push it down again. This double action greatly improved the efficiency of the machine.

By their very action early steam engines produced an up-and-down motion, but most machines of the time, except pumps, required rotary motion and most were driven by waterwheels. Then in 1781 James Watt invented the sun-and-planet gear to make his engines provide a rotary final drive. The steam engine became a vital part of most industrial facilities.

In a Newcomen engine, steam from a boiler (1) forced a piston up an open-ended cylinder (2). Cold water was sprayed into the cylinder to condense the steam (3). The water then ran out of the cylinder (4). That created a partial vacuum, which sucked the piston down again (5) and also pulled down one end of a long beam connected to the piston rod (6). The other end of the beam was connected to a pump. As the piston went up and down, the beam rocked and worked the pump continuously. A Newcomen engine could produce about 12 strokes a minute.

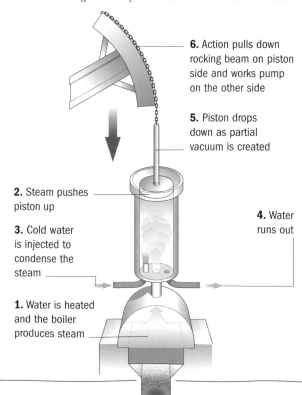

6. Action pulls down rocking beam on piston side and works pump on the other side

5. Piston drops down as partial vacuum is created

2. Steam pushes piston up

3. Cold water is injected to condense the steam

4. Water runs out

1. Water is heated and the boiler produces steam

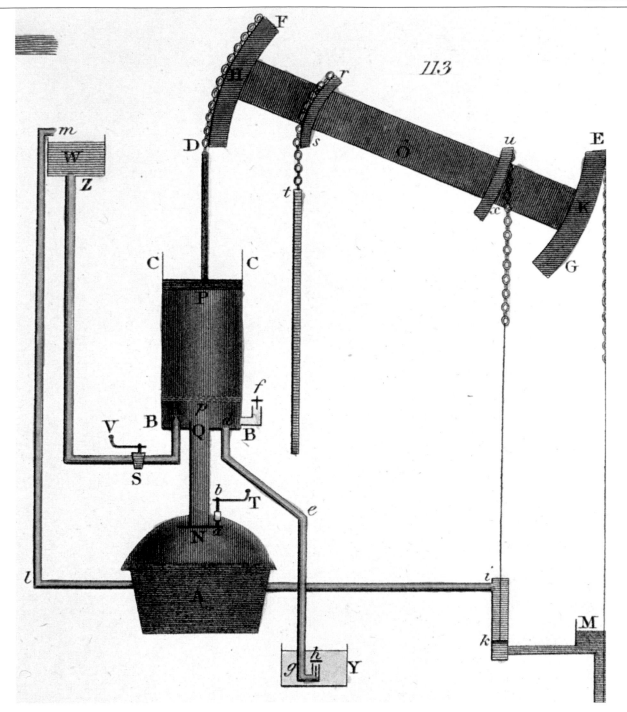

113

This colored engraving shows the various parts of a Newcomen's engine, including the boiler (A), *piston* (P), *cylinder* (C), *and beam* (O).

High-pressure Engines

The next development was an increase in the pressure of steam in the engine—in the terminology of the day, "strong steam." This had to await the introduction of improved cylinders with better-fitting pistons and boilers that were safe at high steam pressures. They became available by 1800, when Watt's master patent expired. The following year English inventor Richard Trevithick (1771–1833) started building his own double-action, high-pressure engines. Trevithick removed the separate condenser and used the waste steam to preheat the water entering the boiler. Within four years he built nearly 50 engines that were used mainly in mines in many parts of Britain and South America. It was the high-pressure engines pioneered by Trevithick that made the steam engine a viable source or power for an even greater number of purposes. Although Trevithick's own experiments with locomotives were not successful, engines based on his designs were used in the earliest successful locomotives.

KEY DATES

1690
Papin's primitive engine

1698
Savery's atmospheric steam pump

1712
Newcomen's atmospheric steam engine

1765
Watt's engine with external condenser

1801
Trevithick's high-pressure engine

CHAPTER 5

THE INDUSTRIAL REVOLUTION

J. M W. Turner's landscape "Rain, Steam and Speed," painted in the mid-1800s, shows a locomotive crossing the Thames River in England above a barge, a symbol of the previous age of transportation. First built in 1803, steam locomotives—and the railroads they chugged along— soon became a common sight across the Western world and a symbol of the industrial revolution.

THE BEGINNING OF THE PERIOD COVERED BY THIS CHAPTER WAS A TIME of widespread political revolution, with major social upheavals in America—the Revolutionary War (1775–83)—and France—the French Revolution (1789–99). Just as influential on the course of history was the industrial revolution that followed the development of the steam engine by Scottish inventor and mechanical engineer James Watt (1736–1819). It opened the way to large-scale manufacture, freed transportation from its dependence on animal and wind power, and heralded significant social changes. The industrial world had begun.

Steam engines evolved from steam pumps, and the first applications of the new engines continued to be in mines, where they were employed to pump out water. They were then used in factories to drive textile machinery and other machines. In 1785 English inventor Edmund Cartwright made the first steam-powered loom. But the steam engine came into its own when it was applied to transportation. Various inventors tried fitting a steam engine to a road vehicle to create a "horseless carriage." English engineer Richard Trevithick (1771–1833) constructed in 1803 the first successful steam locomotive to run on rails. The first railroad to carry passengers and freight was the Stockton & Darlington Railway, which opened in 1825. It used steam locomotives built by English engineer George Stephenson (1781–1848). By 1840 there were railroads in England, Ireland, France, Germany, the Netherlands, and the United States.

In the early days of the industrial revolution—before the spread of the railroads—canals were used to transport raw materials, such as coal, iron ore, and timber, to the factories and also to carry finished products. Horses towed the barges along the canals. When the railroads took off, the canals fell into disrepair.

While people flocked to the towns and cities to work in the factories, advances in farming helped cope with the shortage of workers in the countryside. Cast-iron was used to make better plows. Machines were invented to reap and thresh (separate the seeds from the harvested crop). The combine harvester—invented in 1838—reaped, threshed, and bundled straw into sheaves.

In science a different kind of revolution took place in the field of biology. Scientists had come to recognize that fossils are the remains of long-dead plants and animals. The ages of the fossils correspond to the ages of the rocks in which they are found. But why did fossil animals become extinct? Based on observations made during his voyage on H.M.S. *Beagle*, English naturalist Charles Darwin (1809–82) came up with the theory that animal life is not static but gradually evolves into new forms. The dominant species are those that are best equipped—the fittest—to cope with their environment. Those that cannot adapt to environmental changes become extinct.

Another key development toward the end of this period was the birth of photography. Experiments with light-sensitive chemicals enabled Frenchman Joseph Niépce (1765–1833) to take the first photograph, in 1826. Another Frenchman, Louis Daguerre (1787–1851) improved on Niépce's techniques to make his own photographs, known as daguerrotypes. Electricity was sparking other scientists. English chemist Humphry Davy (1778–1829), English physicist and chemist Michael Faraday (1791–1867), and French physicist, chemist, and mathematician André-Marie Ampère (1775–1836) all improved our understanding of electricity and magnetism.

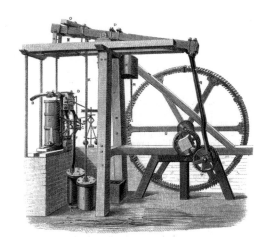

Steam engines powered the industrial revolution. James Watt's steam engine was first used to pump water out of mines. Watt later modified it to drive machinery in factories. Further improvements, notably by Richard Trevithick, led to the steam engines that powered locomotives.

Charles Darwin's voyage on H.M.S. Beagle *in the 1830s took him to many far-flung places, including South America and Australia. In the Galápagos Islands, off the coast of Ecuador, his study of similar species, including tortoises, on the different islands helped him formulate his groundbreaking theory of evolution.*

THE WORLD AT A GLANCE

CONCISE HISTORY OF SCIENCE AND INVENTION

	1775	1785	1795	1800	1810	
EUROPE	**1778** English inventor Joseph Bramah patents a flushing toilet. **1778** Italian physicist Alessandro Volta discovers methane. **1779** French astronomer Antoine Darquier discovers the Ring Nebula. **1779** British scientist Jan Ingenhousz describes photosynthesis. **1781** British astronomer William Herschel discovers the planet Uranus. **1782** Scottish engineer James Watt invents a steam engine in which steam enters each side of the piston alternately. **1783** French brothers Joseph and Jacques Montgolfier, invent the hot-air balloon. **1783** English physicist John Mitchell predicts the existence of black holes.	**1785** French balloonist Jean-Pierre Blanchard invents the parachute. **1785** English physician William Withering introduces the use of the drug digitalis. **1785** English inventor Edmond Cartwright invents a steam-powered loom. **ca 1787** French physicist Jacques Charles proposes Charles's law: that, at constant pressure, the volume of a gas is proportional to its absolute temperature. **1789** German chemist Martin Klaproth discovers uranium and zirconium. **1789** French physician Joseph Guillotin invents the guillotine.	**1795** French chemist Nicolas Conté invents a pencil with a graphite "lead." Pencils of this type have remained in use ever since. **1795** The French adopt the metric system. **1795** English inventor Joseph Bramah devises a hydraulic press. **1796** English physician Edward Jenner introduces the smallpox vaccination into Europe. **1796** German printer Aloys Senefelder invents lithographic printing. **1798** English economist Thomas Malthus discovers a relationship between the size of a population and the available food supply.	**1800** Italian physicist Alessandro Volta invents the voltaic pile battery for producing a continuous electric current. **1805** French inventor Joseph Jacquard constructs a loom that is controlled by punched cards. **1806** English engineer William Congreve builds solid-fuel rockets. **1807** English chemist Humphry Davy uses electrolysis to isolate sodium and potassium. **1808** Humphry Davy invents the arc lamp. **1809** French naturalist Jean-Baptiste Lamarck proposes that characteristics acquired during life are inherited by offspring—a now discredited theory known as Lamarckism. **1809** French chemist Nicholas Vauquelin discovers nicotine in tobacco.	**1810** French chef Nicolas Appert invents food canning (originally for Napoleon's army). **1810** German engineer Friedrich König invents a steam-powered printing press. **1811** Schoolgirl Mary Anning discovers the first fossil of an ichthyosaur (a prehistoric fishlike marine reptile). **1811** Scottish anatomist Charles Bell distinguishes between motor and sensory nerves. **1811** English scientist William Wollaston invents the camera lucida. **1811** English engineer John Blenkinsop invents a steam rack locomotive that uses toothed wheels and track. **1813** English engineer Bryan Donkin begins producing canned meat.	
THE AMERICAS	**1776** American inventor David Bushnell builds the *Turtle*, one of the first submarines. **1780** American physician Benjamin Rush describes dengue fever.	**1786** Long-fibered sea-island cotton is planted in the United States for the first time. **1793** American engineer Eli Whitney invents the cotton gin, a machine that automates the separation of cottonseed from cotton fibers.	**1799** A 12-year-old boy, Conrad Reed, finds a 17-pound (7.7-kg) gold nugget near his home in North Carolina, beginning the first gold rush in the United States.	**1807** American engineer Robert Fulton builds a successful paddle steamer, *Clermont* (originally named the *North River Steam Boat*). **1809** American surgeon Ephraim McDowell performs the first successful ovariotomy (removal of an ovary) to treat a tumor.	**1812** Russian explorers moving south from Alaska establish the town of Fort Ross in Northern California.	
ASIA & OCEANIA	**1779** English explorer James Cook is killed by local people in Hawaii in the course of his exploration of the Pacific Ocean.	**1793** The remains of a mammoth are discovered preserved in the permafrost in Siberia.	**1797** Explorer George Bass leads an expedition along the coast of eastern Australia, recording the geographic and geological features he encounters.	**1805** Japanese physician Seishu Hoanoka performs the first surgery on a patient using general anesthesia.	**1813** European explorers first cross the Blue Mountains in Australia, an area that is home to many unique and ancient species of animals and plants.	
AFRICA & THE MIDDLE EAST	**1775** Scottish explorer James Bruce returns to England having become the first European to discover the source of the Blue Nile.	**1794** The explorer Mungo Park embarks on an expedition to discover the source of the Niger River in central Africa.	**ca 1799** West African cultures begin to manufacture gunpowder, as well as repairing and replicating weapons obtained from European merchants and explorers.	**1807** It is estimated that there are about 20 million guns in use in Africa, fueling a number of wars and uprisings.	**1811** Construction begins on a water supply and sewer system in Cape Town, South Africa.	

1815	1820	1825	1830	1835–1839
1815 Humphry Davy invents the miner's safety lamp.	**1820** Danish physicist Hans Ørsted discovers electromagnetism.	**1825** English chemist and physicist Michael Faraday discovers benzene.	**1831** Scottish botanist Robert Brown describes the nucleus of a cell.	**1836** English naturalist Charles Darwin completes his five-year voyage on H.M.S. *Beagle*.
1815 English scholar Peter Roget devises a slide rule with two logarithmic scales.	**1821** Swedish botanist Elias Fries draws up a systematic classification of fungi.	**1825** The Stockton & Darlington Railway, the first steam railroad to offer a regular service, opens in northern England.	**1831** Michael Faraday makes a simple dynamo.	**1836** Swedish chemist Jöns Berzelius discovers catalysts.
1815 French physicist Augustin-Jean Fresnel demonstrates that light consists of transverse waves.	**1822** Englishwoman Mary Ann Mantell discovers teeth from one of the first fossils later to be recognized as a dinosaur.	**1826** French chemist Joseph Niépce takes the first photograph.	**1831** English explorer James Ross locates the position of the north magnetic pole.	**1837** French mathematician Simon Poisson discovers the Poisson distribution curve.
1815 Scottish engineer John McAdam devises a method of making paved roads using crushed rock.	**1822** English mathematician Charles Babbage makes his "Difference Engine," a type of mechanical adding machine.	**1827** French mathematician Joseph Fourier suggests that world climate is affected by human activities.	**1832** French chemist Pierre Robiquet discovers codeine.	**1837** French physiologist René Dutrochet describes the role of chlorophyll in photosynthesis.
1816 Scottish engineer Robert Stirling invents a two-cylinder external combustion engine that makes use of the expansion of hot gas.	**1822** Jean-Baptiste Lamarck distinguishes between vertebrates and invertebrates.	**1828** French physiologist Pierre Flourens explains how the semicircular canals in the inner ear control balance.	**1833** English mathematician Charles Babbage begins work on his "Analytical Engine," a mechanical computer, but the work is never finished.	**1838** The paddle steamer *Sirius* becomes the first steamship to cross the Atlantic Ocean under steam power alone.
1819 French physicist Jean-Louis Poiseuille invents a mercury manometer for measuring blood pressure.	**1822** French physicist André-Marie Ampère formulates the laws of electrodynamics.	**1829** French teacher Louis Braille, blind himself from the age of three, invents the Braille alphabet to enable blind people to read using touch.	**1834** Michael Faraday formulates the laws of electrolysis.	**1839** French painter and physicist Louis Daguerre invents the daguerreotype, a type of photograph taken on metal plates.
			1834 English architect Joseph Hansom designs the Hansom cab.	
			1832 English physician Marshall Hall discovers the reflex action of certain nerves.	
1819 The SS *Savannah* becomes the first steamship to cross the Atlantic Ocean. The *Savannah* travels under sail for most of the journey, however, only using steam power for the last days of the voyage.	**1821** American engineer Zachariah Allen installs the first hot-air central heating system.	**1825** Scottish botanist David Douglas discovers the Douglas fir in North America.	**1833** American engineer Obed Hussey invents a reaping machine.	**1835** Swedish-born American engineer John Ericsson invents the screw propeller for ships.
	1822 American engineer William Church patents a typesetting machine in England.	**1825** The Erie Canal, which links the Great Lakes with ports of New York and New Jersey, is opened.	**1833** American army surgeon William Beaumont explains the role of gastric juices in digestion (he had studied a patient with a gunshot wound to the stomach in 1822).	**1835** American manufacturer Samuel Colt produces a revolver with interchangeable parts.
		1828 Work begins on the Baltimore & Ohio Railroad.		**1838** American inventor Samuel Morse invents the electric telegraph.
1815 The explosion of Mount Tambora in Indonesia throws enough volcanic ash and dust into the atmosphere to temporarily modify climates throughout the world.				**1837** A whaling station is established in New Zealand.
1816 Factories and other industrial structures are constructed in Egypt. They include lumber mills, sugar refineries, and glass-making factories.				

ASTRONOMY & MATH	BIOLOGY & MEDICINE	PHYSICAL SCIENCES

EUROPE

1777 Swiss mathematician Leonhard Euler (1707–83) introduces the symbol *i* for the square root of -1. In mathematical terms *i* is an imaginary number.

1779 French astronomer Antoine Darquier (1718–1802) discovers the Ring Nebula (which formed 5,500 years ago).

1779 German astronomer Heinrich Olbers (1758–1840) publishes a method of calculating the orbits of comets.

1781 British astronomer William Herschel (1738–1822) discovers the planet Uranus.

1781 French astronomer Charles Messier (1730–1817) publishes the *Catalogue des Nébuleuses et des Amas d'Étoiles* (Catalog of Nebulae and Star Clusters), which gives details of the location in the night sky of 103 visible astronomical objects.

1783 English physicist John Michell (1724–93) predicts the existence of black holes, which he calls "dark stars."

1775 Danish naturalist Johann Fabricius (1745–1808) draws up a classification system for insects in his epic work *Systema Entomologiae*.

1776 Scottish physician John Fothergill (1712–80) describes trigeminal neuralgia (a disorder that causes nerve pain in the face).

1778 German-born physician Friedrich (or Franz) Mesmer (1734–1815) first practices in Paris a form of hypnotism that becomes known as mesmerism. Later (1785) he is denounced as a charlatan and is unable to demonstrate any scientific basis for his technique.

1779 Dutch-born British scientist Jan Ingenhousz (1730–99) describes the process of photosynthesis in plants.

1780 Italian naturalist Lazzaro Spallanzi (1729–99) carries out artificial insemination (in dogs).

1775 German geologist Abraham Werner (1749–1817) proposes the Neptunist theory of the origin of rocks—the now rejected idea that all rocks in the Earth's crust were created by the action of water.

1776 English chemist Joseph Priestley (1733–1804) synthesizes nitrous oxide ("laughing gas"), later to be employed as an anesthetic in dentistry.

1776 Swedish chemist Karl Scheele (1742–86) discovers uric acid.

1776 French chemist Antoine Lavoisier (1743–94) makes three contributions to chemistry: the (incorrect) proposal that all acids contain oxygen; the fact that air is a mixture of gases; and the idea that respiration (breathing) can be regarded as a form of combustion.

1778 Italian physicist Alessandro Volta (1745–1827) discovers methane.

1779 Swiss scientist Horace de Saussure (1740–99) coins the term *geology*.

1781 French mineralogist René Haüy (1743–1822) proposes the existence of "unit cells" in crystals, leading to his theory of crystal structure.

THE AMERICAS

1780 American physician Benjamin Rush (1745–1813) describes dengue fever (then also known as breakbone fever).

The one-person submarine Turtle *carried enough air to last for 30 minutes and was powered by two hand-driven propellers.*

ASIA & OCEANIA

AFRICA & THE MIDDLE EAST

1779 English explorer James Cook (1728–79) is killed by local people in Hawaii in the course of his exploration of the Pacific Ocean.

ENGINEERING & INVENTION

1775 English engineer John Wilkinson (1728–1828) produces a machine for boring cannon—and later cylinders for steam engines.

1777 French physicist Charles Coulomb (1736–1806) invents the torsion balance to measure electrical, magnetic, and gravitational forces.

1778 English inventor Joseph Bramah (1748–1814) patents a flushing toilet.

1779 English weaver Samuel Crompton (1753–1827) builds the spinning mule, which twists strands of fibers into single lengths of yarn and winds them onto bobbins.

1782 Scottish engineer James Watt (1736–1819) invents a steam engine in which steam enters each side of the piston alternately.

1783 Swiss scientist François-Pierre Argand (1750–1803) patents the Argand burner, an oil lamp with an air supply. It burns ten times brighter than an ordinary lamp.

1783 French brothers Joseph (1740–1810) and Jacques (1745–99) Montgolfier invent the hot-air balloon.

The Montgolfier brothers' balloon flew 5.5 miles (8.8 km) on its first crewed flight.

1776 American inventor David Bushnell (ca 1742–1824) builds the *Turtle*, one of the first submarines.

WORLD EVENTS

1772 The first partition of Poland divides Polish territory between Russia, Prussia, and Austria. Further partitions will mean Poland ceases to exist by the end of the century.

1781 Serfdom is abolished in Austria.

1783 Russia annexes the Crimean Peninsula, which gives it access to the Black Sea and thus to the Mediterranean.

1775 The American Revolution begins at Concord and Lexington.

INSIDE STORY

James Cook

The three voyages of exploration conducted by British seaman and navigator James Cook between 1766 and 1779 were important to many branches of science and technology. The first voyage left Britain in 1766 and traveled to Tahiti in order to observe the transit of Venus—an important astronomical event—before mapping New Zealand and eastern Australia. On the second voyage in 1772, Cook's ship was equipped with the *K1*, a copy of John Harrison's revolutionary marine chronometer the *H4*. Accurate clocks allowed precise and reliable calculations of longitude, essential for navigation. The charts Cook drew using the *K1* were so accurate that they were still in use in the early 20th century. On all three of Cook's voyages the ship carried biologists who discovered countless species of previously unknown plants and animals.

JAMES WATT

James Watt was born in Scotland at Greenock on the Clyde River. He was the sixth son of a carpenter and merchant. He was educated at the local school and at Greenock Grammar School, and learned technical skills in his father's workshop. In 1755 Watt went to London and worked as an apprentice to a maker of mathematical instruments. Two years later he was appointed instrument maker at Glasgow University and had his own workshop.

The university had a model of a Newcomen steam engine, and in 1764 Watt was asked to repair it. The engine was heated by steam and then cooled by cold water sprayed into the cylinder to condense the steam. Watt realized that the alternate heating and cooling processes of the cylinder wasted a lot of energy.

In 1765 Watt made an engine that overcame the energy loss by leading the steam into a separate condenser so that the cylinder could remain hot all the time, making the engine three times more efficient. The project was financed by Scottish chemist Joseph Black (1728–99), who taught at the university.

In 1775 Watt went into business manufacturing his new engine, which he had patented in 1769. The first machine needed five years of development before it was reliable enough for quantity production. Most of the engines produced were used as pumps to replace the ageing Newcomen engines in the mines of Cornwall in southwestern England.

ASTRONOMY & MATH	BIOLOGY & MEDICINE	PHYSICAL SCIENCES

EUROPE

1784 Dutch-born English astronomer John Goodricke (1764–86) observes a new type of pulsating variable star (Delta Cephei), the second of the so-called Cepheid variables. Earlier the same year the first—Eta Aquilae—was found by English amateur astronomer Edward Pigott (ca 1753–1825).

1784 French mathematician Adrien-Marie Legendre (1752–1833) determines Legendre polynomials, mathematical functions that arise as solutions to differential equations that relate to various problems in physics.

1786 French astronomer Pierre Méchain (1744–1804) discovers Encke's comet, which was later named for Johann Encke (1791–1865), who studied it in detail in 1819. It has the shortest-known orbital period of all comets—3.3 years—and has been seen about 60 times since its discovery.

1787 German-born English astronomer William Herschel (1738–1822) observes Oberon and Titania, two moons of the planet Uranus (which he had discovered in 1781). Two years later he discovers Saturn's moons Enceladus and Mimas, and in 1790 he identifies the first planetary nebula.

1788 French mathematician Joseph Lagrange (1736–1813) publishes his book *Mécanique Analytique*, which deals with the calculus of mechanics.

1785 English physician William Withering (1741–99) introduces the use of the drug digitalis, made from the foxglove plant, to treat dropsy (fluid retention due to heart disease). The drug is still used to treat certain heart disorders.

1789 English naturalist Gilbert White (1720–93) publishes *The Natural History and Antiquities of Selborne*, a detailed year-long study of the habits of local animals, which is read by naturalists to this day.

INSIDE STORY

Glacier Tables

Early travelers to the Alps were often puzzled by great slabs of rock balanced on top of stems of ice like huge mushrooms. They persist because the rock casts a shadow that keeps the sun's warmth from melting the ice. Swiss geologist Bernard Kuhn figured out in 1787 that they had been slowly moved to their improbable locations by glaciers, most of which had subsequently melted away. They were known as "glacier tables," but modern geologists refer to them as "erratics." The largest known erratic is the Big Rock, a vast 16,000-ton (14,500-tonne), 30-foot (9-m) tall quartzite boulder located in Alberta, Canada.

1784 French chemist Antoine Lavoisier (1743–94) shows that matter can be neither created nor destroyed.

1784 English scientist Henry Cavendish (1731–1810) finds that water is a compound (of hydrogen and oxygen, H_2O) and not an element. A year later he determines the composition of nitric acid (HNO_3).

1784 French mathematician and physicist Gaspard Monge (1746–1818) is the first person to liquefy a substance that is a gas in its normal state—in this case sulfur dioxide.

ca 1787 French physicist Jacques Charles (1746–1823) postulates Charles's law: that, at constant pressure, the volume of a gas is proportional to its absolute temperature.

1788 English physicist Charles Blagden (1748–1820) puts forward Blagden's law: that, for a solution, the lowering of the freezing point of the solvent is proportional to the concentration of the substance dissolved in it.

1789 German chemist Martin Klaproth (1743–1817) discovers uranium and zirconium.

1791 English chemist and clergyman William Gregor (1761–1817) discovers titanium.

THE AMERICAS

1786 Long-fibered sea-island cotton is planted in the United States for the first time. In the next 50 years "King Cotton" becomes the most important crop in the American economy.

As we enjoy great advantages from the inventions of others, we should be glad of an opportunity to serve others by any invention of ours; and this we should do freely and generously.

BENJAMIN FRANKLIN,
THE AUTOBIOGRAPHY OF BENJAMIN FRANKLIN (1791)

ASIA & OCEANIA

AFRICA & THE MIDDLE EAST

The flowers of the foxglove plant. Drugs derived from foxgloves are known as digitalins; they are used to treat arrhythmia and other heart problems.

ENGINEERING & INVENTION	WORLD EVENTS
1784 Scottish engineer William Murdock (1754–1839) constructs a model steam-powered road vehicle.	**1784** English minister John Wesley (1703–91) founds the Methodist Church in England.
1785 English inventor Edmund Cartwright (1743–1823) makes a steam-powered loom.	**1785** The first edition of the *Times* newspaper is printed in London.
1785 English inventor Lionel Lukin (1742–1834) patents a noncapsizing lifeboat.	**1787** A group of ministers, politicians, and industrialists found the *Society for the Abolition of the Slave Trade* in London, one of the first organized abolitionist groups.
1785 French balloonist Jean-Pierre Blanchard (1753–1809) invents the parachute.	
1786 Scottish millwright and inventor Andrew Meikle (1719–1811) makes a threshing machine (patented 1788).	**1789** Large crowds storm the Bastille prison in Paris, marking the beginning of the French Revolution.
1787 English engineer John Wilkinson (1728–1808) builds an iron-hulled boat.	**1790** The population of Europe reaches an estimated 190 million people. Many of them live in the new cities and towns of the industrial revolution.
1788 Scottish banker Patrick Miller (1731–1815) and Scottish engineer William Symington (1763–1831) build a steam paddleboat.	
1789 French physician Joseph Guillotin (1738–1814) invents the guillotine. It is not used for executions until 1792, during the French Revolution.	

1784 American scientist and politician Benjamin Franklin (1706–90) invents bifocal eyeglasses.	**1786** Revolutionary War veteran Daniel Shays (ca 1741–1825) leads an armed uprising against high taxes in Massachusetts, known as Shay's Rebellion.
	1787 The United States Constitution is adopted by the Constitutional Convention.

A modern replica of a guillotine, the execution machine invented by Joseph Guillotin in 1789.

1786 The pirate states of North Africa sign treaties with the United States, agreeing to cease disruption of U.S. merchant shipping in exchange for large sums of money.

1787 A group of freed slaves from the United States settle in Freetown, Sierra Leone.

TEXTILE MACHINES

The development of the textile industry was at the forefront of the industrial revolution. During this period, many new technologies were developed to turn raw materials such as wool into yarn and then fabric.

The first aid to spinning was the distaff—a long stick onto which wool is loosely wound. The spinner held it under his or her arm and teased out a continuous strand of wool, which was spun between the fingers of the other hand. The spun thread wound itself around a rotating spindle at its end. Mesopotamians first used the distaff 7,500 years ago.

The spinning wheel was in use in Europe from the 1200s. It simplified the task by using a large vertical wheel. A belt drive spun the spindle, while the spinner pulled a strand of wool from a vertical distaff. With the other hand he or she turned the wheel.

In the 18th century, spinning became mechanized and mass production was possible. English mechanic James Hargreaves (ca 1720–78) invented the spinning jenny in 1764, and the spinning frame was invented by his compatriot Richard Arkwright (1732–92) in 1769. The spinning jenny allowed one operator to produce eight strands of yarn simultaneously. The spinning frame—powered by a waterwheel—made strong cotton yarn. The two were combined by English weaver Samuel Crompton (1753–1827), whose spinning mule produced 48 strands of fine yarn at the same time.

Once spun, yarn was made into cloth on a loom. A simple loom is a frame that holds a set of parallel threads called the warp. The weaver interweaves them at right angles with another thread—the weft—that is carried in a holder known as a shuttle. In 1733 English engineer John Kay (1704–ca 1780) invented the flying shuttle, a mechanism that enables the weaver to "throw" the shuttle rapidly from side to side. Mechanized looms came next, driven by water power until 1785, when English inventor Edmund Cartwright (1743–1823) made the first steam-powered loom.

EUROPE

ASTRONOMY & MATH

1795 French astronomer Joseph de Lalande (1732–1807) records observations of Neptune, but he does not recognize it as a new planet.

1795 France adopts the metric system.

1796 French astronomer Pierre-Simon de Laplace (1749–1827) proposes his nebular hypothesis for the origin of the solar system. It states that the sun condensed out of a whirling mass of gas that threw off rings that in turn condensed into the planets. Modern theories retain some of these ideas.

1796 German physicist Karl Gauss (1777–1855) proposes the method of least squares for fitting a line or curve to a set of points on a graph. He does not publish it until 1806, when it is independently suggested by French mathematician Adrien-Marie Legendre (1752–1833).

1798 Danish mathematician Caspar Wessel (1745–1818) represents complex numbers as vectors (quantities with magnitude and direction).

BIOLOGY & MEDICINE

1794 English chemist John Dalton (1766–1844) describes color blindness, a condition from which he and his brother both suffer.

1796 English physician Edward Jenner (1749– 1823) introduces smallpox vaccination into Europe.

1796 German physician Samuel Hahnemann (1755–1843) founds homeopathy, a form of unconventional therapeutic medicine. It involves giving a patient minute doses of a drug that produces similar symptoms in a healthy person. It is still practiced today.

1796 German physician Franz Gall (1758–1828) introduces the "science" of phrenology, in which mental ability is purported to be related to the shape of the head.

1798 English economist Thomas Malthus (1766–1834) discovers a correlation between population size and the available food supply—the former always increases faster than the latter.

PHYSICAL SCIENCES

1794 Finnish chemist Johan Gadolin (1760–1852) discovers yttrium.

1794 French chemist Joseph Proust (1754–1826) publishes Proust's law, also known as the law of definite proportions. It states that in any chemical compound the proportions of the components are always the same no matter how it is made.

1797 German chemist Martin Klaproth (1743–1817) and French chemist Nicolas Vauquelin (1763–1829) independently discover chromium. In 1798 Klaproth and Scottish chemist Thomas Hope (1766–1844) independently discover strontium.

1798 French chemist Nicolas Vauquelin (1763–1829) discovers the element beryllium, the lightest metal known.

1793 French naturalist Jean-Baptiste Lamarck (1744–1829) reintroduces the theory that fossils are the remains of extinct plants and animals.

INSIDE STORY

The Metric System

The idea of a system of weights and measures was first proposed by English scientist John Wilkins (1614–72). It was after the French Revolution in 1783 that the system was first worked out and promoted, becoming the official system of France and its colonies. Other countries adopted it, and by the end of the 19th century most of the world's nations were using the system. In 1960 it was adapted to become the *Systèm Internationale d'Unités* (International System of Units), usually abbreviated to SI, the system used in science, engineering, and commerce worldwide. Today only three countries in the world do not use SI units officially: Myanmar, Liberia, and the United States.

THE AMERICAS

Edward Jenner is depicted here vaccinating women and children against smallpox.

ASIA & OCEANIA

1793 The remains of a mammoth are discovered preserved in the permafrost in Siberia.

1797 Explorer George Bass (1771–ca 1803) leads an expedition along the coast of eastern Australia, recording the geographic and geological features he encounters.

AFRICA & THE MIDDLE EAST

The perpetual tendency of the race of man to increase beyond the means of subsistence is one of the general laws of animated nature, which we can have no reason to expect to change.

Thomas Malthus, *An Essay on the Principle of Population* (1798)

ca 1799 West African cultures begin to manufacture gunpowder, as well as repair and replicate weapons obtained from European merchants and explorers.

ENGINEERING & INVENTION

1792 Scottish engineer William Murdock (1754–1839) introduces domestic lighting using coal gas.

1795 French chemist Nicolas Conté (1755–1805) invents a pencil with a graphite "lead." Pencils of this type have remained in use ever since.

1795 English inventor Joseph Bramah (1748–1814) invents a hydraulic press.

1796 German printer Aloys Senefelder (1771–1834) develops lithographic printing using sheets of flat stone as printing "plates."

1797 French aeronaut André Garnerin (1769–1823) produces an improved parachute and demonstrates it by jumping from a balloon.

1797 French physicist Jean Fortin (1750–1831) invents a portable mercury barometer.

1799 Scottish chemists Charles Tennant (1768–1838) and Charles Macintosh (1766–1843) develop a process for the large-scale manufacture of bleaching powder.

1799 French chemist Philippe Lebon (1767–1804) patents a light that burns gas made by heating sawdust at a very high temperature.

1793 American engineer Eli Whitney (1765–1825) invents the cotton gin, a machine that automates the separation of cottonseed from cotton fibers.

1793 French balloonist Jean-Pierre Blanchard (1753–1809) makes the first untethered hot-air balloon flight to take place in the United States.

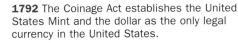

A cotton gin processing raw cotton

WORLD EVENTS

1792 France officially becomes a Republic.

1792 English radical and feminist Mary Wollstonecraft (1759–97) publishes the *Vindication of the Rights of Woman*.

1793 The execution of King Louis XVI (r. 1774–93) takes place in Paris.

1793 One of the leaders of the French Revolution, Maximillien Robespierre (1758–94), begins a series of public executions and persecutions known as the "Reign of Terror" in order to suppress counter-revolutionary plots.

1798 Economist Thomas Malthus (1766–1834) publishes *An Essay on the Principle of Population*, which argues that poverty is caused by the world's population growing at a consistently faster rate than the supply of food and natural resources.

1792 The Coinage Act establishes the United States Mint and the dollar as the only legal currency in the United States.

1799 A 12-year-old boy, Conrad Reed, finds a 17-pound (7.7-kg) gold nugget near his home in North Carolina, beginning the first gold rush in the United States.

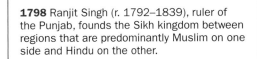

1798 Ranjit Singh (r. 1792–1839), ruler of the Punjab, founds the Sikh kingdom between regions that are predominantly Muslim on one side and Hindu on the other.

1798 Followers of the strict Wahhabi interpretation of Islam seize control of the city of Riyadh.

1799 The Rosetta Stone is found. Its inscription is written in three languages, allowing historians to translate ancient Egyptian hieroglyphs for the first time.

FARM MACHINERY

The earliest known agricultural inventions are the plow—used to prepare the earth for sowing seeds—and the sickle—used to cut down mature plants at harvest time. Although Middle Eastern farmers were using plows with forged iron plowshares as far back as 1900 B.C.E., it was not until the end of the 18th century that similar inventions began to change farming in Europe and the Americas.

In 1785 the English engineer Robert Ransome (1753–1830) invented a cast-iron plowshare. It was first mass produced in 1839 by the U.S. industrialist John Deere (1804–86). Like the wooden plowshare it replaced, it was pulled by oxen or horses, but it was able cut through the soil deeper and faster. Plowing was speeded up by the invention of the steam plow, which used a stationary traction engine to winch a plow from one side of a field to the other. Steam tractors were later used to pull standard plows; they were replaced in turn by gasoline-powered tractors.

In addition to plowing, other labor-intensive or time-consuming processes to be mechanized included sowing seeds, harvesting crops, and threshing the harvest to separate the grain. Sowing was revolutionized by the invention of the mechanical seed drill by Jethro Tull (1674–1741). This machine allowed farmers to sow seeds in parallel rows quickly, which also made harvesting easier. Threshing was a labor-intensive operation until Scottish millwright Andrew Meikle (1719–1811) invented the horse-driven threshing machine in 1786.

Reaping the harvest was the last part of the agricultural process to be mechanized. The first horse-drawn reaper was made in 1831 by U.S. inventor Cyrus McCormick (1809–11) and began mass production around 1879. Subsequent advances in farming technology involved the creation of combine harvesters that could reap and thresh grain as they worked. Early examples were extremely heavy and required dozens of horses to pull.

EUROPE

ASTRONOMY & MATH

1800 Italian astronomer Giuseppe Piazzi (1746–1826) locates Ceres, the first asteroid (minor planet) to be discovered.

1802 German astronomer Heinrich Olbers (1758–1840) discovers Pallas, the second asteroid to be recorded. Juno, the third asteroid, was located in 1804 by his compatriot Karl Harding (1765–1834). To date, more than 25,000 asteroids have been identified.

1802 English scientist William Wollaston (1766–1828) observes dark lines in the sun's spectrum. The discovery went unnoticed until reported again in 1814 by German astronomer Joseph von Fraunhofer (1787–1826). Since then they have been known as Fraunhofer lines.

1806 Swiss mathematician Jean-Robert Argand (1768–1822) devises the Argand diagram for representing a complex number, $z = x + y$, as points on a coordinate plane. The horizontal (x) axis represents the real part of the number, and the vertical (y) axis denotes the imaginary part.

BIOLOGY & MEDICINE

1800 The Royal College of Surgeons is established in London.

1801 English scientist Thomas Young (1773–1829) explains the eye disorder astigmatism.

1802 French naturalist Jean-Baptiste Lamarck (1744–1829) introduces the word "biology" for the study of living things and life processes.

1803 German physician John Otto (1774–1844) describes the inherited blood disorder hemophilia.

1805 French naturalist Georges Cuvier (1769–1832) founds the science of comparative anatomy.

1806 French chemists Nicolas Vauquelin (1763–1829) and Pierre Robiquet (1780–1840) identify the first amino acid: asparagine (in asparagus).

PHYSICAL SCIENCES

1800 English astronomer William Herschel (1738–1822) discovers infrared radiation.

1800 English chemists William Nicholson (1753–1815) and Anthony Carlisle (1768–1840) perform electrolysis for the first time.

1801 German physicist Johann Ritter (1776–1810) discovers ultraviolet light.

1801 French chemist Charles Désormes (1777–1862) establishes the formula for carbon dioxide (CO_2). It had been discovered by Scottish chemist Joseph Black (1728–99) in 1754, but its composition was unknown.

1803 English chemist William Henry (1774–1836) formulates Henry's law: at a constant temperature the amount of gas absorbed by a liquid is in proportion to the pressure of the gas.

1802 English scientist Edward Howard (1774–1816) postulates that meteorites originate outside the Earth (previously they were thought to be terrestrial phenomena).

1804 Two French scientists, Jean-Baptiste Biot (1774–1862) and Joseph Gay-Lussac (1778–1850), study the Earth's atmosphere by ascending in a balloon.

1805 English naval officer Francis Beaufort (1774–1857) devises the Beaufort wind scale for classifying winds in terms of their speed and effects on objects.

THE AMERICAS

INSIDE STORY

Dalton's Elements

English chemist John Dalton (1766–1844) put forward his atomic theory in 1803. He stated that chemical elements are made up of indivisible atoms that combine to form compounds. He also devised a set of symbols to represent the known elements. But his "elements" included several substances that are, in fact, compounds, such as magnesia and lime. We now know them as magnesium oxide and calcium oxide, but it was many years before other chemists separated these metals from their compounds.

A modern reconstruction of the earliest experiments with electrolysis. In the 19th century electrolysis was used to isolate large numbers of new metallic elements.

ASIA & OCEANIA

ELEMENTS

	wt.		wt.
Hydrogen.	7	Strontian	46
Azote	5	Barytes	68
Carbon	54	Iron	50
Oxygen	7	Zinc	56
Phosphorus	9	Copper	56
Sulphur	13	Lead	90
Magnesia	20	Silver	190
Lime	24	Gold	190
Soda	28	Platina	190
Potash	42	Mercury	167

1805 Japanese physician Seishu Hoanoka performs the first surgery on a patient using general anesthesia. Due to the isolationist policies of the Japanese government at the time his achievements were not known to the Western World until 1854.

John Dalton's table of elements from 1803

AFRICA & THE MIDDLE EAST

ENGINEERING & INVENTION

1800 English scientist and politician Charles Stanhope (1753–1816) invents an iron printing press.

1800 Italian physicist Alessandro Volta (1745–1827) invents the voltaic pile battery for producing a continuous electric current.

1801 English engineer Richard Trevithick (1771–1833) constructs a steam-powered road "locomotive." In 1803 he builds the first successful steam railroad locomotive.

1802 Scottish engineer William Symington (1763–1831) builds one of the most successful early steamboats, *Charlotte Dundas*.

1804 English inventor George Cayley (1773–1857) builds and flies a model glider.

1805 French inventor Joseph Jacquard (1752–1834) constructs a loom that is controlled by a "chain" of punched cards.

1805 Scottish clergyman Alexander Forsyth (1769–1843) develops detonating powder for use in firearms. Two years later he patents the percussion cap for muzzle-loading firearms.

1806 English military engineer William Congreve (1772–1828) constructs solid-fuel rockets.

1801 American chemist Robert Hare (1781–1858) invents an oxyhydrogen blowpipe that can produce flames of extremely high temperature.

1804 American engineer Oliver Evans (1755–1819) constructs an amphibious steam dredger.

After passing through

a narrow strip of woodland,

I came suddenly into an

open and boundless prairie.

I say boundless because

I couldn't see the edge of

the plain in any direction.

WILLIAM CLARK,
EXPEDITION JOURNAL, JUNE 19, 1804

WORLD EVENTS

1800 The Act of Union is passed, combining Great Britain and Ireland into the United Kingdom.

1805 After his defeat of the Russians at the Battle of Austerlitz, Napoleon (r. 1804–14 and 1815) dominates continental Europe.

1805 The Royal Navy led by Lord Horatio Nelson (1758–1805) defeats the French and Spanish fleets at the Battle of Trafalgar, ending Napoleon's hopes of invading Britain.

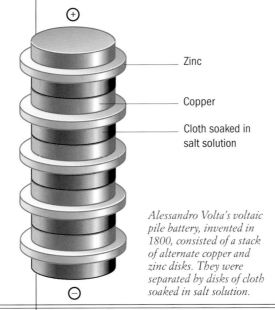

Zinc

Copper

Cloth soaked in salt solution

Alessandro Volta's voltaic pile battery, invented in 1800, consisted of a stack of alternate copper and zinc disks. They were separated by disks of cloth soaked in salt solution.

1803 The Louisiana Purchase doubles the size of the United States.

1804 The Lewis and Clark expedition sets out to explore the interior of the United States.

1803 The first penal colony is established in Van Diemen's Land (now Tasmania).

1803 Ranjit Singh (1780–1839), founder of the Sikh kingdom of the Punjab, declares himself maharaja ("great ruler") at the age of 21.

1805 United States Marines and their Berber allies attack the pirate stronghold of Tripoli, Libya.

CANAL TRANSPORTATION

The main method of moving heavy goods before the coming of the railroads was by canal. By the end of the 18th century timber, coal, and iron ore—all the raw materials needed for the emerging industrial revolution—as well as finished goods were towed on barges along the canals, with horses used as the motive power. The long narrow boats, which were designed specifically for use on canals, could carry a load of 33 tons (30 tonnes), while a wagon could carry just 2.2 tons (2 tonnes).

Chinese engineers built the first canals for transportation more than 2,000 years ago. Extensive canal systems were used for drainage and irrigation in northern India and by the Middle Ages in the Netherlands. Canals for industrial transportation were first used in England in 1757, after the engineer Henry Berry (1720–1812) completed the Sankey Brook Navigation near St. Helens in the north of England.

The first canal of economic importance was the Bridgewater Canal near Manchester, England. It was designed by engineer James Brindley (1716–72) and completed in 1761. The canal followed the contours of the land. A canal that takes a more direct route needs locks for coping with inclines, tunnels for going through hills, and aqueducts for crossing valleys.

In North America the first canal with locks was probably the short waterway at Coteau-du-Lac, Quebec, built in 1779 by English engineer William Twiss (1745–1827) to bypass a stretch of rough water on the St. Lawrence River. In 1825 the Erie Canal was completed to carry grain from the Great Lakes to New York City via the Hudson River. The 362-mile (583-km) canal was 39 feet (12 m) wide and 4 feet (1.2 m) deep, and it needed 83 locks to cross the high ground west of Troy. The enlarged modern canal, now part of the New York State canal system, can carry barges of up to 2,204 tons (2,000 tonnes).

ASTRONOMY & MATH	BIOLOGY & MEDICINE	PHYSICAL SCIENCES

EUROPE

1807 German astronomer Heinrich Olbers (1758–1840) discovers Vesta, the fourth asteroid to be found.

1808 French mathematical physicist Siméon Poisson (1781–1840) puts forward a theory to account for irregularities in the orbits of the planets.

1810 French mathematician Joseph Gergonne (1771–1859) establishes the first privately owned mathematics journal, *Annales de Mathématiques Pures et Appliquées*.

1811 German-born English astronomer William Herschel (1738–1822) proposes a theory that stars develop from nebulae as clouds of gas condense into star clusters.

1812 French mathematician Pierre-Simon de Laplace (1749–1827) publishes *Théorie Analytique des Probabilités*, an exposition of probability theory, which greatly influences the development of the subject.

1809 French naturalist Jean-Baptiste Lamarck (1744–1829) postulates that acquired characteristics (for example, a weightlifter's muscles) are inherited by offspring—a now discredited theory known as Lamarckism.

1811 Scottish anatomist Charles Bell (1774–1842) distinguishes between motor nerves (which are concerned with movement) and sensory nerves (which are concerned with sensations such as touch).

1813 Swiss botanist Augustin de Candolle (1778–1841) devises a plant classification system and describes it as a "taxonomy."

1807 English chemist Humphry Davy (1778–1829) uses electrolysis to prepare the first samples of sodium and potassium. A year later, using the same technique, he isolates barium, calcium, magnesium, boron, and strontium.

1807 Swedish chemist Jöns Berzelius (1779–1848) coins the term *organic* to describe chemicals that are derived from living things. Eleven years later he devises the modern system of chemical symbols for the elements.

1808 Swiss chemist Nicolas de Saussure (1767–1845) determines the composition of ethanol (ethyl alcohol).

1808 French scientist Joseph Gay-Lussac (1778–1850) formulates Gay-Lussac's law: that at the same temperature and pressure combining volumes of gases are in a simple relationship to the volume of the product.

1809 French chemist Nicolas Vauquelin (1763–1829) discovers nicotine in tobacco, which was first taken to France in 1561 by the diplomat Jean Nicot (1530–1600).

1811 Schoolgirl Mary Anning (1799–1847) discovers the first fossil of an ichthyosaur (a prehistoric fishlike marine reptile).

THE AMERICAS

1807 A meteor explodes and falls over Weston, Connecticut. Later American scientist Nathaniel Bowditch (1773–1838) estimates that it originally weighed 6.6 million tons (6 million tonnes).

1809 American surgeon Ephraim McDowell (1771–1830) performs the first successful ovariotomy (removal of an ovary) to treat a tumor.

ASIA & OCEANIA

AFRICA & THE MIDDLE EAST

Lamarck contended that to feed in the trees, giraffes stretched their necks, which made them longer. Parents then passed this acquired trait to their offspring until over many generations very long necks developed. Lamarck's ideas are now discredited.

INSIDE STORY

Lamarckism

The theory of evolution promoted by Jean-Baptiste Lamarck became known as Lamarckism. It suggested that physical and behavioral characteristics acquired during an animal's lifetime could be passed on to its offspring. The giraffe was often used as an example of the hypothetical mechanism of the theory. As giraffes reach up for high leaves, the theory contends, they stretch their necks, which become longer. The longer neck is inherited by the giraffe's offspring, and over several generations giraffes acquire longer and longer necks. Lamarck's theory was not the first to suggest the evolution of species through acquired traits, but it was the most comprehensive. Although now discredited, it remained popular until the explanation of evolution by natural selection was proposed in the book *On the Origin of Species* by the English naturalist Charles Darwin (1809–82)—who studied Lamarck's theories as a young man—gained widespread public and scientific acceptance. Darwin was not willing to discount entirely the possibility that acquired characteristics could be inherited, however, and some research into Lamarck's ideas continued into the 1920s.

ENGINEERING & INVENTION

1807 Two French-born brothers, Henry (1766–1854) and Sealy (1774–1847) Fourdrinier, patent a continuous paper-making machine.

1808 Humphry Davy invents the arc lamp.

1808 English inventor George Cayley (1773–1857) builds a full-sized (unpiloted) glider.

1810 French chef Nicolas Appert (ca 1750–1841) invents food canning (originally for Napoleon's army).

1810 German engineer Friedrich König (1774–1833) invents a steam-powered printing press.

1811 English engineer John Blenkinsop (1783–1831) invents a steam rack locomotive that uses toothed wheels and track.

1812 English scientist William Wollaston (1766–1828) invents the camera lucida, which attaches to a microscope so that the viewer can see at the same time an object and a paper surface on which to draw it.

1813 English engineer Bryan Donkin (1768–1855) begins producing canned meat.

1813 Swiss engineer Johann Bodmer (1786–1864) invents a breech-loading cannon.

1807 American engineer Oliver Evans (1755–1819) invents the conveyor belt.

1807 American engineer Robert Fulton (1765–1815) builds a successful paddle steamer, *Clermont* (originally named the *North River Steam Boat*).

1808 American engineer John Stevens (1749–1838) builds the first steamboat to go to sea, called the *Phoenix*.

WORLD EVENTS

1807 The British Parliament passes the Slave Trade Act, which abolishes the slave trade within the British Empire. This act only covered the trade in slaves however. It was not until the passing of the Slavery Abolition Act in 1833 that slavery itself was abolished.

1807 The system of serfdom, in which farmers were considered part of their landlord's property, is abolished in Prussia.

1811 Britain's King George III (r. 1760–1820) is declared insane; his son the Prince of Wales becomes prince regent.

1812 Napoleon Bonaparte (r. 1804–14 and 1815) invades Russia and advances as far as Moscow before being driven back by a lack of supplies and the fierce Russian winter.

1811 Paraguay declares its independence from Spain.

1812 The United States declares war on Britain (the war of 1812), citing as the cause the continued blockading of its ports and attacks on its commerce. U.S. forces also invade Canada.

The fossilized remains of an icthyosaur, a fishlike reptile that lived in the prehistoric oceans.

1811 Construction begins on a water supply and sewer system in Cape Town, South Africa.

HUMPHRY DAVY

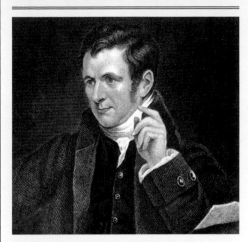

Humphry Davy was an English chemist whose pioneering work using electrolysis led to the isolation of seven chemical elements. After basic education in southwestern England, Davy became apprenticed to an apothecary and surgeon. In 1797 he began to teach himself chemistry. A year later Davy became an assistant at the Pneumatic Institute in Bristol. In 1799 he discovered the anaesthetic effect of nitrous oxide. Two years later he became a chemistry lecturer at the Royal Institution in London.

He began experiments in electrolysis, using the new electric battery invented by Alessandro Volta (1745–1827). Davy broke water down into its component elements, and in 1807 extracted the metals sodium and potassium. The following year, Davy isolated barium, boron, calcium, magnesium, and strontium.

In addition to discovering new chemicals, Davy invented the arc lamp in 1808. He also found that the gas methane caused explosions in coal mines. This led him to invent the miner's safety lamp in 1815. It had a flame surrounded by a gauze that conducted the heat away, keeping the temperature from getting high enough to ignite methane.

THE BEGINNING OF RAILROADS

RAILROADS HAD THEIR ORIGINS IN ANCIENT Greece, where a stone trackway for transporting ships was carved across a narrow strip of land separating two seas. Later, in the 16th century, miners in various European countries used horses to pull wagons along "roads" made from beams of timber, and later iron, laid lengthwise along the ground. Using rails provides a smooth, even surface for the wheels to move along, reducing friction. The sleepers evenly distribute the weight on the rails and allow very heavy loads to be carried.

In the coal mines of the English Midlands at the end of the 17th century, horses pulled the empty trucks up the inclines to the mines; then the loaded trucks took themselves down again under the force of gravity. Stronger cast-iron rails became available in the early 1700s, allowing heavier loads to be carried by the trucks.

The first steam locomotive was built in 1803 by English engineer Richard Trevithick (1771–1833). He ran it along 10 miles (16 km) of cast-iron track from the Pen-y-Darren Ironworks to the Glamorganshire Canal in South Wales. The locomotive and rolling stock had smooth, unflanged wheels, and there was a lip on the outer edge of the track. Four years later he built a circular track in Euston, London, and charged people a shilling to chase their tails on his train—called *Catch Me Who Can*.

RIGHT: *Horse-drawn coaches were common on railroads until public confidence in steam locomotives grew.*

KEY DATES

1803
Trevithick's locomotive

1825
Stockton & Darlington Railway

1830
Liverpool & Manchester Railway

1830
Baltimore & Ohio Railroad

1831
South Carolina Railroad

The First Passenger Railroads

The first railroad to carry passengers regularly as well as freight opened in 1825. With locomotives built by English engineer George Stephenson (1781–1848) the Stockton & Darlington Railway ran for 26 miles (42 km); but until 1833 passengers traveled in horse-drawn coaches, and only freight was steam hauled. The first intercity line, the Liverpool & Manchester Railway, opened in 1830, and the first train was hauled by Stephenson's *Rocket*. The line was constructed to carry cotton from the port of Liverpool to the mills in Manchester in northwestern England.

Railroads also sprang up in other countries. The year 1830 saw the inauguration of the Baltimore & Ohio Railroad, which initially ran for 13 miles (21 km) from Baltimore to Ellicott's Mills. To operate it, U.S.

engineer Peter Cooper (1791–1883) built *Tom Thumb*, the first locomotive to be made in the United States. The Philadelphia & Columbia Railroad opened with horse-drawn vehicles in 1831, but within three years it had steam locomotives. The longest railroad in the world at the time, the South Carolina Railroad, also started operations in 1831. It ran for 154 miles (248 km) from Charleston to Hamburg.

In 1832 the first steam-hauled line in France opened between St. Étienne and Lyons; and in 1835 Germany's first railroad opened between Nürnberg and Fürth with a locomotive called *Der Adler* (The Eagle), built by English engineer Robert Stephenson (1803–59). By 1840 there were railroads in Austria, Ireland, and the Netherlands. As the new railroads appeared, the old barges disappeared and canals fell into disrepair.

Railway Technology

As well as locomotives and rolling stock, railroads need other equipment. The "road" of the original railroads were rails made of cast iron, at first with a right-angled section to keep the wheels on the track. Soon these flanged rails were replaced. The flanges were put on the wheels of the vehicles, which ran on short "fish-bellied" rails that were straight on top but curved beneath to make them thicker (and stronger) in the center. But cast-iron rails were brittle and often broke. From 1858 they were replaced by steel rails, introduced by English steelmaker Henry Bessemer (1813–98).

To enter sidings and branch lines, railroads need switches (known as "points" in Europe). They were invented as early as 1789 by English engineer William Jessop (1745–1814) for primitive tramway systems. As the traffic on railroads increased so did the risk of collisions. Signals were invented to direct drivers and warn them of hazards. At first they took the form of disks or arms that rotated or pivoted like semaphore signals. In 1849 the New York and Erie Company introduced block signaling, which does not allow a train to enter a section of track until the previous train has left it. Soon block signals were linked electrically.

To drum up interest in his new railroad, Richard Trevithick built a circular track on an open space in London. People paid a shilling to ride around in circles on the aptly named Catch Me Who Can.

Passengers ride a steam train on the opening day of the Stockton & Darlington Railway.

EUROPE

THE AMERICAS

ASIA & OCEANIA

AFRICA & THE MIDDLE EAST

ASTRONOMY & MATH

1815 German astronomer Heinrich Olbers (1758–1840) discovers Olbers' comet, which has the comparatively short orbit period of 74.1 years.

1815 German astronomer Joseph von Fraunhofer (1787–1826) makes a detailed map of the solar spectrum first seen by English scientist William Wollaston (1766–1828) in 1802.

1815 English scholar Peter Roget (1779–1869) devises a slide rule with two logarithmic scales, which greatly simplifies multiplication and division.

BIOLOGY & MEDICINE

1814 English surgeon Joseph Carpue (1764–1846) pioneers plastic surgery with the operation known as rhinoplasty (to restructure a patient's nose).

1817 French physician René Laennec (1781–1826) uses a stethoscope—a single-tube device of his own design—to listen to a patient's heartbeat.

1817 English surgeon James Parkinson (1755–1824) describes parkinsonism. At the time it is called "paralysis agitans," or Parkinson's disease.

1817 French chemists Pierre Pelletier (1788–1842) and Joseph Caventou (1795–1877) discover chlorophyll (the light-absorbing pigment in plants) and a year later discover the poisonous alkaloid strychnine.

1818 French chemist Jean Dumas (1800–1884) introduces the use of iodine to treat patients with the thyroid disorder goiter (which is often caused by iodine deficiency).

1819 French physicist Jean-Louis Poiseuille (1799–1869) invents a mercury manometer (pressure gauge) to measure blood pressure.

PHYSICAL SCIENCES

1814 Spanish-born physician Matthieu Orfila (1787–1853) publishes his book *Traité des Poisons* (Treatise of General Toxicology) in Paris and founds the science of toxicology.

1815 French physicist Augustin-Jean Fresnel (1788–1827) discovers the diffraction of light as it passes through small apertures. He also demonstrates that light consists of transverse waves.

1815 English geologist William Smith (1769–1839) publishes a geologic map of England and Wales. He observes that different rock layers contain different fossils and postulates that a fossil must be the same age as the rock in which it is found.

1817 Two new elements are found: cadmium by German chemist Friedrich Strohmeyer (1776–1835) and lithium by Swedish chemist Johan Arfwedson (1792–1841). A year later (1818) selenium is discovered by Swedish chemist Jöns Berzelius (1779–1848).

1819 British astronomer and photographer John Herschel (1792–1871) discovers that sodium thiosulfate can "fix" a newly developed photographic image.

1815 The explosion of Mount Tambora on the island of Sumbawa in Indonesia throws enough volcanic ash and dust into the atmosphere to temporarily modify climates throughout the world.

The green leaves of plants get their color from chlorophyll, discovered in 1817.

ENGINEERING & INVENTION

1815 Scottish engineer John McAdam (1756–1836) devises a method of making paved roads using crushed rock.

1815 French-born engineer Marc Brunel (1769–1849) creates a tunneling shield (for making the first tunnel under the Thames River in London).

1815 English chemist Humphry Davy (1778–1829) and English engineer George Stephenson (1781–1848) independently invent the miner's safety lamp.

1816 Scottish physicist David Brewster (1781–1868) invents the kaleidoscope.

1816 German musician Johann Maelzel (1772–1838) patents the metronome, a clockwork upside-down pendulum that ticks to help students keep time with the music.

1816 Scottish engineer Robert Stirling (1790–1878) invents a two-cylinder external combustion engine that makes use of the expansion of hot gas.

1818 German-born English engineer Rudolph Ackermann (1764–1834) devises a steering mechanism for horse-drawn carriages. Ackermann steering is still the main type used by modern road vehicles.

1819 German inventor Augustus Siebe (1788–1872) develops a pressurized diving suit complete with helmet.

1819 American engineers Stephen McCormick (1784–1875) and Jethro Wood (1774–1834) independently produce a cast-iron plow.

1819 The SS *Savannah* becomes the first steamship to cross the Atlantic. The *Savannah* travels under sail for most of the journey, however, only using steam power for the last days of the voyage.

1819 European and American companies establish industrial-scale whaling around the islands of the Pacific.

1816 Factories and other industrial facilities are constructed in Egypt. They include lumber mills, sugar refineries, and glass-making factories.

WORLD EVENTS

1814 Napoleon Bonaparte (r. 1804–14 and 1815) abdicates and is exiled to the Mediterranean island of Elba. A year later he returns and raises a new army, only to be decisively defeated at the Battle of Waterloo.

1818 Mary Shelley (1797–1851) publishes her novel *Frankenstein*. Written during the cold, dismal summer caused by the eruption of Mount Tambora, the novel explored the ethical issues raised by advances in science and changing social attitudes.

1819 Eleven people are killed when calvary soldiers charge a crowd of protesters in St. Peter's Field, Manchester, England. The event becomes known as the Peterloo Massacre. The protest was calling for greater representation and voting rights for working people.

This miner's safety lamp is based on Humphry Davy's original design but with added improvements.

1814 British troops burn Washington D.C., during the War of 1812 (1812–15), which is ended by the Treaty of Ghent, signed in December 1814. (Although fighting continued into 1815 until news of the treaty reached America.)

1819 The British establish the port of Singapore in Southeast Asia. By allowing unregulated free trade in the port, the Dutch control over trade in the region is broken.

1817 Usman dan Fodio (1754–1817) establishes the Sokoto Caliphate in the Hausa lands of northern Nigeria and southern Niger.

EVIDENCE IN FOSSILS

Fossils are the remains of plants and animals that lived millions of years ago. Most are the hard parts of animals—bones, teeth, or shells—that have changed to rock. Some, such as the outlines of plants in coal or sedimentary rocks, are impressions.

The scientists who study fossils, paleontologists, recognize several ways in which fossils can form. One requirement for fossil formation is quick burial before the carcass can decompose or be eaten by scavengers. The best place for that to happen is in the mud or sediment at the bottom of a lake or sea. Remains embedded in sediment may be dissolved by water, leaving behind a perfect mold. Minerals may be deposited in the mold, forming a cast often made from a totally different type of rock from the sediment. Footprints or animal tracks in mud can be preserved in a similar way. Whole animals are preserved only occasionally, as with insects trapped in amber (fossilized tree resin) or mammoths buried in the frozen ground, called permafrost.

In 1517 the Italian physician and poet Girolamo Fracastoro (1478–1553) was probably the first person to suggest that fossils are animal remains. But it was not until the fossil finds in Europe of the late 18th century that scientists began to realize that fossils can tell us a great deal about the history of living things. In 1793 French naturalist Jean-Baptiste Lamarck (1744–1829) revived the idea that fossils represent ancient organisms.

EUROPE

ASTRONOMY & MATH

1820 English astronomer John Herschel (1792–1871), mathematician Charles Babbage (1791–1871), and others establish the Royal Astronomical Society in London.

1821 French astronomer Alexis Bouvard (1767–1843) observes irregularities in the orbit of Uranus. He hypothesizes that they are caused by a celestial body, later identified as Neptune.

1822 French mathematician Joseph Fourier (1768–1830) proposes the Fourier analysis, a method of analyzing continuous functions in terms of sine and cosine curves.

1824 German astronomer and mathematician Friedrich Bessel (1784–1846) publishes a treatise on the study of planetary perturbations, in which he develops Bessel functions (originally proposed in 1817). Bessel functions form an infinite series useful in solving partial differential equations that occur in astronomy and physics.

BIOLOGY & MEDICINE

1821 Swedish botanist Elias Fries (1794–1878) draws up a systematic classification of fungi. Published as *Systema Mycologicum* (System of Mycology), it takes 11 years to complete.

1821 English naturalist and botanist Joseph Banks (born 1743) dies. During his voyages with the explorer Captain James Cook he was the first to catalog many of the plants and animals of Oceania and South America.

1822 French naturalist Jean-Baptiste Lamarck (1744–1829) distinguishes between vertebrates (animals with backbones) and invertebrates (animals lacking backbones).

1823 English chemist and physician William Prout (1785–1850) identifies free hydrochloric acid in the stomach. Four years later he classifies foods into fats, carbohydrates, and proteins.

1823 The medical journal *The Lancet* is published for the first time in London.

1825 French naturalist Georges Cuvier (1769–1832) puts forward his catastrophe theory of extinction: that sudden worldwide events, such as land upheavals and floods, caused species to become extinct and new ones to appear abruptly to replace them. In keeping with religious doctrines of the time, Cuvier attributed the most recent changes to the great biblical flood.

PHYSICAL SCIENCES

1820 Danish physicist Hans Ørsted (1777–1851) discovers electromagnetism by noticing the deflection of a compass needle in the magnetic field caused by an electric current flowing along a nearby wire.

1820 French chemists Joseph Caventou (1795–1877) and Pierre Pelletier (1788–1842) discover the alkaloid quinine, soon to be used to treat malaria. Two years later they discover caffeine (in coffee).

1822 Englishwoman Mary Ann Mantell discovers teeth from one of the first fossils later to be recognized as a dinosaur; her husband, paleontologist Gideon Mantell (1790–1852), names it *Iguanodon*.

1822 French physicist André-Marie Ampère (1775–1836) formulates the laws of electrodynamics that deal with electricity and magnetism.

1824 French physicist Dominique Arago (1786–1853) discovers magnetic induction —the production of an electric field by a changing magnetic field.

1824 Swedish chemist Jöns Berzelius (1779–1848) discovers silicon; a year later Danish physicist Hans Ørsted (1777–1851) prepares an impure form of aluminum.

1825 English chemist and physicist Michael Faraday (1791–1867) discovers benzene and several of its compounds.

THE AMERICAS

1825 Scottish botanist David Douglas (1798–1834) discovers the Douglas fir in North America.

ASIA & OCEANIA

AFRICA & THE MIDDLE EAST

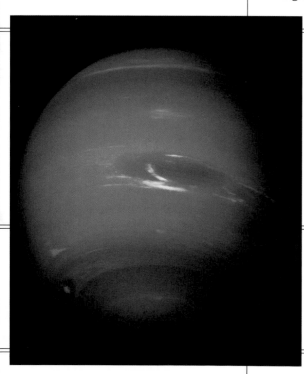

The existence of the planet Neptune was deduced—before any astronomer had seen it—from the effects of its gravitational pull on the orbit of its neighbor Uranus.

TURNING POINTS

Quinine

The isolation of the chemical compound quinine by French chemists Pierre Pelletier and Joseph Caventou in 1820 was a breakthrough with wide-reaching consequences in medicine and politics. Quinine is a compound found in the bark of the cinchona tree in South America. For centuries it was used by the Quecha peoples of Peru as a muscle relaxant to suppress shivering, and missionaries who saw this use brought the bark back to Europe in the 17th century, believing it would relieve the shivering associated with malarial fevers. It proved highly effective, not only stopping the shivering but also halting the advance of the disease. With the isolation of the active chemical component in 1820 quinine could be produced in large quantities and more easily administered. Tropical regions in which malaria was prevalent and therefore inhabitable to Europeans, who have no natural immunity, were now open for colonization, starting the "scramble for Africa" as European powers fought to take control of sub-Saharan Africa.

ENGINEERING & INVENTION

1821 German physicist Karl Gauss (1777–1855) invents the heliograph, which uses an adjustable mirror to reflect sunlight and send messages over a distance.

1822 English mathematician Charles Babbage (1792–1871) makes his "Difference Engine," a type of mechanical adding machine. In 1833 he devises an improved machine, the "Analytical Engine."

1823 Scottish chemist Charles Macintosh (1766–1843) patents waterproof fabric made by impregnating cloth with rubber.

1824 English mason Joseph Aspdin (1778–1855) patents Portland cement, made from a mixture of limestone and clay or limestone and shale.

1825 English physicist William Sturgeon (1783–1850) makes the first electromagnet.

1825 Scottish engineer Thomas Drummond (1797–1840) creates limelight (also called Drummond light), in which a piece of lime is heated to incandescence in an oil or gas flame.

1825 The Stockton & Darlington Railway, the first steam railroad to offer a regular service, opens in northern England. Its engineers are George Stephenson (1781–1848) and his son Robert (1803–59).

1821 American engineer Zachariah Allen (1795–1882) installs the first hot-air central heating system.

1822 American engineer William Church (ca 1778–1863) patents a typesetting machine in England.

1825 The Erie Canal, which links the Great Lakes with ports of New York and New Jersey, as well as the open sea, is formally opened to commercial traffic.

WORLD EVENTS

1821 Greece begins a war to win independence from the Ottoman Empire.

1823 French troops invade Spain to support King Ferdinand VII (r. 1808 and 1813–33) in quelling a rebellion in his country.

1824 Louis XVIII (r. 1814–24), who became king of France on the restoration of the monarchy following the death of Napoleon (r. 1804–14 and 1815), dies. He is succeeded by his brother, Charles X (r. 1824–30). The monarchy continues to rule in France until the beginning of the Second Republic in 1848.

1825 The "Decemberists"—progressive army officers seeking to reform autocratic rules in Russia—stage an unsuccessful uprising.

Charles Babbage's Difference Engine was designed to calculate logarithms and other mathematical functions using a system of cogs and gear wheels.

THE STOCKTON & DARLINGTON RAILWAY

Opened on September 27, 1825, the line between Stockton and Darlington in County Durham, in the northeast of England, was the world's first steam railroad. Thousands of people attended the opening ceremony out of curiosity, most believing that this form of transport would be a passing fad. However, the Stockton & Darlington Railway inspired the construction of railroads all over the world.

The track was the idea of the English businessman Edward Pease (1767–1858) who wanted to build an 8-mile (13-km) line to transport coal from Darlington to the port of Stockton. Pease planned to use horses to pull trucks along a fixed railway. But English engineer George Stephenson took an interest and convinced Pease that he would be better served by a steam engine, which could pull 50 times as much weight as a horse. Steam locomotives had been built before, but the Stockton & Darlington Railway was the first major commercial use.

More than 40,000 spectators lined the route on the day the Stockton & Darlington Railway opened. The train, pulled by a steam engine built by George Stephenson's son Robert in nearby Newcastle, left Darlington at 12.20 p.m. The engine pulled about 38 open wagons weighing a total of 90 tons (90 tonnes) and carrying about 600 passengers. The train reached a speed of 15 miles (24 km) per hour. All did not run smoothly, however. The train broke down three times on its journey, arriving in Stockton at 3.45 p.m.

Although the inaugural Stockton and Darlington train was full of people, the line was not primarily intended as a passenger railroad. Its main function was to bring coal from the pits to the port, where it was was loaded onto barges. Records show that 19,448 tons of coal were carried in 1828.

THE BIRTH OF PHOTOGRAPHY

THE CAMERA AS IT IS KNOWN TODAY IS made from two essential components. The first is the lens or aperture through which the light is focused. The second is a way of capturing the image viewed through this aperture, either with light sensitive chemicals or, as in many modern cameras, with digital image sensors.

The origin of the camera was the camera obscura (Latin for "dark room"), a windowless room with a small hole in one wall. Light entering the hole forms an upside-down image of the scene outside on the opposite wall. Artists used the device as an aid to trace an image, and later it became portable in the form of a large light-excluding box.

In 1725 the German physician Johann Schulze (1684–1744) found that certain silver salts turn dark when exposed to daylight. Fifty years later Swedish chemist Karl Scheele (1742–86) discovered that the darkening effect is due to the presence of grains of metallic silver. As a result, silver salts were to become standard ingredients in photographic emulsions (light-sensitive coatings) for films, paper, and even leather—as tried in the late 1790s by Englishman Thomas Wedgwood (1771–1805). However, a number of other processes were tested before Scheele's method was generally accepted.

The First Successful Photographs

In France, beginning in 1816, Joseph Niépce (1765–1833) also experimented with fleeting silver images. His first successful photograph in 1826 used a polished pewter plate coated with bitumen as the light-sensitive substance. During a long exposure the bitumen turned white. Niépce then removed the bitu-

In 1843 William Fox Talbot set up a professional photogaphic "factory" in Reading, England. The greenhouse shown here was a portrait studio, although there was often much more light available outside.

men from the unexposed areas using a solvent and darkened the metal by exposing it to iodine vapor.

Iodine also figured in the photographic process perfected by Frenchman Louis Daguerre (1787–1851) in 1839. To make his photographic plates, he coated a sheet of copper with silver and left it for a while (in the dark) exposed to iodine vapor; this process created light-sensitive silver iodide. He exposed the plate in a camera and "developed" it in mercury vapor. The resulting image was made permanent, or "fixed," in a solution of common salt. These daguerreotypes, as they came to be called, were mirror images and could not be used to make further copies.

Film and Multiple Prints

Although the discoveries of Daguerre and Niépce allowed images to be taken relatively quickly, the resulting images were as unique and hard to copy as paintings. In 1841 this changed when English chemist William Fox Talbot (1800–77) patented his calotype process, which he had devised six years earlier. It used paper film impregnated with silver nitrate and common salt or potassium iodide. After exposure to light in a camera, the film was developed in a solution of gallic acid and fixed in sodium thiosulfate solution, known as "hypo." The resulting "negative" image (with black and white reversed) was placed in contact with a sheet of light-sensitive paper and changed back to positive. This stage could be repeated to make many positive paper copies of the image.

Frenchman Louis-Désiré Blanquart-Evrard (1802–72) made improvements in 1850 by coating the printing paper with albumen (egg white), which allowed better quality and cheaper prints to be made. Fox Talbot accused him of "scientific piracy" and of stealing his patent.

As soon as the calotypes pioneered by Fox Talbot became popular, Englishman Frederick Archer (1813–57) hit on the idea of making a photosensitive emulsion of silver salts in collodion (a sticky solution of guncotton in ether) and coating it onto glass plates. His wet-collodion process of 1851 soon became paramount until it was superseded by the use of dry plates

by the late 1870s. The dry-plate process used gelatin emulsions, as invented by British physician Richard Maddox (1816–1902) in 1871. American George Eastman (1854–1932) used a dry gelatin emulsion for his first Kodak camera of 1888, initially on paper film and a year later on transparent celluloid. This film was sold in rolls, which greatly simplified the process of photography and turned it into a popular pastime.

The long exposure times of 19th-century photography meant that photographs were generally restricted to posed portraits taken in well-lit studios.

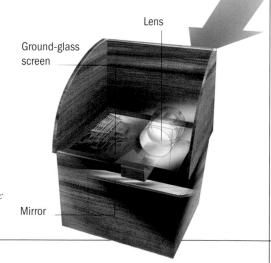

In a portable camera obscura a lens focuses light from a distant scene onto a mirror. The mirror, angled at 45 degrees, reflects the image upward onto a ground-glass screen. An artist can then trace over the image with perfect accuracy. This method is thought to have been used by Italian artist Canaletto (1697–1768) when he made his detailed views of cities. The camera obscura continued as an artist's aid until it was replaced by photographic cameras after the 1850s.

Lens

Ground-glass screen

Mirror

ASTRONOMY & MATH

1826 German astronomer Heinrich Olbers (1758–1840) puts forward Olbers' paradox: Why is the sky dark at night (when the universe is full of stars)? One answer is that light from the most distant objects in the universe has not yet reached Earth.

1827 German physicist Karl Gauss (1777–1855) develops differential geometry.

1830 English mathematician George Peacock (1791–1858) first puts forward the laws of numbers in his book *Treatise on Algebra*.

1830 Scottish writer Mary Somerville (1780–1872) publishes *The Mechanism of the Heavens*, a popularization of *La Mécanique Céleste* by French astronomer Pierre-Simon de Laplace (1749–1827).

Why isn't a starry night full of light?

BIOLOGY & MEDICINE

1827 Scottish botanist Robert Brown (1773–1858) distinguishes between angiosperms—flowering plants with enclosed seeds—and gymnosperms, which have naked seeds, often in cones.

1828 French physiologist Pierre Flourens (1794–1867) explains how the semicircular canals in the inner ear control the sense of balance.

1829 German anatomist Martin Rathke (1793–1860) finds evidence of gill structures in the embryos of birds and mammals.

1827 American ornithologist and artist John James Audubon (1785–1851) publishes the first part of *Birds of America*.

PHYSICAL SCIENCES

1826 French physiologist René Dutrochet (1776–1847) describes the phenomenon of osmosis, in which a solvent passes through a semipermeable membrane separating solutions of different concentrations.

1827 German physicist Georg Ohm (1789–1854) publishes Ohm's law, which states that the voltage across a conductor divided by the current flowing through it is a constant, called the resistance.

1827 Scottish botanist Robert Brown (1773–1858) discovers Brownian motion, the random motion of microscopic particles suspended in a liquid.

1827 French mathematician Joseph Fourier (1768–1830) suggests that world climate is affected by human activities.

1828 German chemist Friedrich Wöhler (1800–82) synthesizes an organic compound from an inorganic compound. This proves that organic compounds are not limited to living things and causes a major rethink among chemists.

1830 Scottish geologist Charles Lyell (1797–1875) begins publication of his most influential book, *The Principles of Geology*.

The Principles of Geology

Between 1830 and 1833 English geologist Charles Lyell published the three volumes of his influential book *The Principles of Geology*, an explanation of Lyell's theories, backed up with his own observations. In this work, Lyell outlined his controversial theory of uniformity. This essentially argued that the world was formed by the same geological processes that can be observed in action today. The consequence of this new theory was that it placed estimates of the Earth's age in hundreds of millions of years, rather than the thousands suggested by biblical chronologies. Naturalist Charles Darwin (1809–82) was given a copy to help him with geological observations in his voyage on the H.M.S. *Beagle*. He was very impressed by Lyell's ideas, and considered them an important influence on his theory of natural selection.

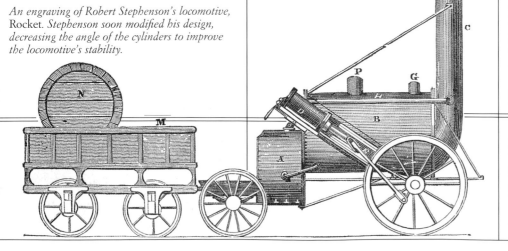

An engraving of Robert Stephenson's locomotive, Rocket. *Stephenson soon modified his design, decreasing the angle of the cylinders to improve the locomotive's stability.*

EUROPE

THE AMERICAS

ASIA & OCEANIA

AFRICA & THE MIDDLE EAST

ENGINEERING & INVENTION

1826 French chemist Joseph Niépce (1765–1833) takes the first photograph on a metal plate.

1827 Two French engineers, Claude Burdin (1790–1873) and Benoît Fourneyron (1802–67), begin work on a design for a practical outward-flow water turbine. It is completed in 1833.

1827 English chemist John Walker (ca 1781–1859) invents the friction match.

1828 Scottish engineer James Neilson (1792–1865) invents the hot-air process for smelting iron.

1829 The *Rocket* steam locomotive built by English engineer George Stephenson (1781–1848) wins the Rainhill Trials, a competition to find a locomotive for the new Liverpool & Manchester Railway.

1829 French teacher Louis Braille (1809–52), blind himself from the age of three, invents the Braille alphabet to enable blind people to read using touch.

1830 French engineer Barthélemy Thimonnier (1793–1857) patents a single-thread stitching machine.

1830 Scottish chemist Andrew Ure (1778–1857) invents the bimetallic strip thermostat.

1828 Work begins on the Baltimore & Ohio Railroad, the first steam-powered railroad in the United States.

1829 American William Burt (1792–1858) patents the first typewriter.

1830 American engineer Peter Cooper (1791–1883) builds *Tom Thumb*, the first railroad locomotive to be made in the United States.

Braille has been a most precious aid to me in many ways. I use Braille as a spider uses its web—to catch thoughts that flit across my mind for speeches, messages, and manuscripts.

HELEN KELLER, 1929

WORLD EVENTS

1829 Greece gains independence from Turkey.

1829 Sir Robert Peel (1788–1850) forms Britain's first official police force.

1830 Revolutions calling for political reform break out in France, Italy, Poland, and Germany.

1830 Belgium breaks away from the Netherlands and proclaims independence.

1828 Uruguay becomes an independent country.

1830 The first wagon trains cross the Rocky Mountains and arrive in California.

1830 The U.S. Congress passes the Indian Removal Act, enabling President Andrew Jackson (1767–1845) to relocate Native Americans from the eastern to the western part of the continent.

1828 Russia declares war on the Ottoman Empire, which is already fighting the revolutionary armies in Greece.

1828 The Dutch claim possession of the western half of New Guinea.

1828 The Zulu leader Shaka (ca 1787–1828), who is showing growing signs of insanity, is assassinated. During his reign Shaka's military leadership greatly expanded the power and influence of the Zulu nation.

MICHAEL FARADAY

Michael Faraday (1791–1867) was a highly influential chemist and physicist whose research into electricity and magnetism were important in the transformation of electricity from a scientific curiosity to a practical technological advance. His experiments founded the sciences of electrochemistry and electromagnetism. Faraday had little formal education and, unlike many of the scientists of his time, had only a limited understanding of higher mathematics. Faraday's success and importance lies in his skill as an empirical experimenter rather than in abstract theorizing.

Michael Faraday, the son of a blacksmith, was born in Newington Butts outside London. He left school at 13 to be apprenticed to a bookbinder. The books he read during this time aroused an interest in science, and in 1813 he left to work as assistant to English chemist Humphry Davy (1778–1829), where part of his job was to set up experiments for Davy's lectures. As Davy's assistant he met many famous scientists, and in 1827 he took over Davy's post of lecturer at the Royal Institution.

Faraday made a number of contributions to the field of chemistry before turning his attention to electricity. He liquified chlorine by heating it in a sealed tube and discovered the flammable hydrocarbon benzene (C_6H_6). His pioneering work with electrolysis established the fundamental laws and principles of the technique. It is his work with electricity and magnetism, however, that has had the greatest influence on everyday life. Faraday made the first primitive electric motor in 1821. He suspended a length of stiff wire alongside a bar magnet that projected vertically from a dish of mercury. When he connected a battery between the mercury and the top of the wire, the lower end of the wire rotated around the magnet. He discovered in 1831 that a moving magnet could induce a current in a coil of wire, a discovery that led to the development of electrical generators.

ASTRONOMY & MATH	BIOLOGY & MEDICINE	PHYSICAL SCIENCES

A screw propeller on a modern merchant ship. The first successful propeller was invented by Swedish–American engineer John Ericsson for use on the U.S.S. Princeton.

1831 French surgeon Guillaume Dupuytren (1777–1835) describes Dupuytren's contracture, an arthritic condition that affects a patient's fingers.

1831 Scottish botanist Robert Brown (1773–1858) describes the nucleus of a cell (in this case a plant cell).

1832 English physician Marshall Hall (1790–1857) discovers the reflex action of certain nerves (such as those involved in the knee-jerk reflex).

1833 Czech physiologist Jan Purkinje (1787–1869) discovers sweat glands in the skin.

1834 French agricultural chemist Jean Boussingault (1802–87) discovers nitrogen fixation—the ability of some plants (such as beans and other legumes) to convert nitrogen from the air into chemicals that the plant can absorb.

1831 English explorer and naval officer James Ross (1800–62) locates the position of the north magnetic pole (which changes continuously).

1832 French chemist Pierre Robiquet (1780–1840) discovers codeine (in opium from poppies).

1833 French chemist Jean Dumas (1800–84) develops a method of determining the nitrogen content in organic compounds. The method is still used today.

1833 French chemist Anselme Payen (1795–1871) discovers diastase, the first enzyme to be identified.

1834 German chemist Justus von Liebig (1803–73) synthesizes melamine, the basis of a range of modern plastics.

1834 English scientist Michael Faraday (1791–1867) formulates the laws of electrolysis.

1835 English geologist Adam Sedgwick (1785–1873) establishes the geology of the Cambrian system of rocks (which were laid down between 540 million and 505 million years ago).

1835 Scottish geologist Roderick Murchison (1792–1871) establishes the geology of the Silurian system of rocks (which were laid down between 439 million and 409 million years ago).

INSIDE STORY

Ada Lovelace

Ada Lovelace (1815–52) was a British mathematician, regarded by many as the first computer programmer. She was born Augusta Byron, the only legitimate child of the aristocratic English poet Lord Byron. Her childhood was dominated by illness, and as a teenager she was left partially paralyzed by a bout of measles. She continued with her education, however, and as a young woman corresponded with many prominent scientists and mathematicians. Through her correspondence with Charles Babbage, she learned of his designs for the "Difference Engine" and later his "Analytical Engine." She was one of the few of Babbage's contemporaries who properly understood the ideas and intentions behind Babbage's designs. In an article discussing the Analytical Engine she wrote a program for the unbuilt device that would allow it to generate a sequence of Bernoulli numbers, which are used in pure mathematics.

1833 American army surgeon William Beaumont (1785–1853) explains the role of gastric juices in digestion (he had studied a patient with a gunshot wound to the stomach in 1822).

The Hansom cab was a one-horse cab with a low center of gravity that allowed safe cornering at high speeds.

EUROPE

THE AMERICAS

ASIA & OCEANIA

AFRICA & THE MIDDLE EAST

ENGINEERING & INVENTION

1831 English scientist Michael Faraday (1791–1867) makes a simple dynamo.

1832 English physicist Charles Wheatstone (1802–75) invents the stereoscope, which produces an image in three dimensions from a pair of stereo photographs.

1832 Belgian physicist Joseph Plateau (1801–83) invents the stroboscope— a rapidly flashing light that can make rotating machinery appear stationary.

1832 The 61-mile (98-km) artificial section of the Gotha (Göta) Canal, which crosses Sweden from west to east, is completed.

1833 English mathematician Charles Babbage (1792–1871) begins work on his "Analytical Engine," a type of mechanical computer, but it is never completed.

1834 English architect Joseph Hansom (1803–82) designs the Hansom cab ("Patent Safety Cab"), a one-horse cab that soon appears in large numbers on the streets of Victorian London.

1834 English phonographer Isaac Pitman (1813–97) invents the system of shorthand writing that bears his name. It is soon adopted throughout the English-speaking world.

1833 American engineer Obed Hussey (1792–1860) invents a reaping machine.

1835 American physicist Joseph Henry (1797–1878) invents the electromagnetic relay.

1835 Swedish-born American engineer John Ericsson (1803–89) invents the screw propeller for ships.

1835 American manufacturer Samuel Colt (1814–62) produces a revolver with interchangeable parts.

Revolvers like this early Colt were used by the U.S. Army between 1873 and 1892. Similar models were popular with lawmen and civilians in the frontier towns of the Wild West.

WORLD EVENTS

1831 The Polish Diet (parliament) declares the nation's independence from Russia; Russian forces put down the revolt at the Battle of Ostrolenka.

1832 The Reform Act gives the vote in Britain to all wealthy men, rather than just those who own significant amounts of land.

1833 After a long campaign by anti-slavery activists and politicians like William Wilberforce (1759–1833), a law is passed abolishing slavery in the British Empire. It comes into effect at the beginning of 1834.

1834 The Spanish Inquisition, which had enforced Roman Catholic orthodoxy in Spain since 1478, was ended by royal decree.

1831 Nat Turner (1800–31) leads a slave revolt in Southampton, Virginia, that leaves 55 whites dead. In the aftermath the state executed 55 slaves believed to be involved with the rebellion; approximately 200 more slaves and former slaves were killed in the mob violence that followed.

1835 Texans declare independence, creating the Republic of Texas—a sovereign state that lasted until 1846, when it joined the United States.

1834 The South Australia Act is passed in the British Parliament, allowing the establishment of a colony there.

1831 The French Foreign Legion is founded in Algeria.

1831 Muhammad Ali (1769–1849), viceroy of Egypt, begins a revolt against his Turkish overlords that will see Egypt become an autonomous entity within the Ottoman Empire.

THE REVOLVER

The first pistols—the original "handguns"—were made in the 1400s. They were muzzle-loading weapons that fired a lead ball or bullet using black powder (gunpowder) as the propellant charge. The means of igniting the charge, called the lock, improved over time from the original matchlock through the wheel lock and the snaphaunce to the flintlock pistols of the late 1700s.

Most of the early pistols could fire only one shot. There were some double-barreled flintlocks, but the only effective way of ensuring more than one shot was to carry more than one loaded pistol. One attempt at increasing the number of shots was the invention of the pepper-box pistol, which had several barrels. They were rotated by hand to bring a new loaded barrel in front of the firing mechanism each time. But these weapons were heavy and poorly balanced, which made them difficult to aim.

Another solution was the revolving pistol, or revolver, which has a cylinder with a number of loaded chambers that can be fired in turn as they align with a single barrel. There are examples of flintlock revolvers (in which the spark from a flint ignites the charge), but the revolver only became a practical weapon when the percussion cap became available after 1807. In this type of weapon each chamber in the cylinder has a narrow hole at the back that holds a tight-fitting percussion cap. When the pistol is fired, the hammer strikes the cap, which explodes and fires the charge.

The first percussion revolvers were made in England after about 1820 by American gunsmith Elisha Collier of Boston. But the first manufacturer to make reliable revolvers in quantity was American Samuel Colt (1814–62), who obtained his first patent in England in 1835. The design was further improved by the invention of metal-cased cartridges, which allowed faster reloading. The first mass-produced cartridge revolvers were made by the Smith and Wesson company in 1857.

ASTRONOMY & MATH	BIOLOGY & MEDICINE	PHYSICAL SCIENCES

EUROPE

1836 English astronomer Francis Baily (1774–1844) describes Baily's beads, a phenomenon during an eclipse when beads of light appear around the moon's rim (caused by the sun shining between mountain peaks).

1837 French mathematical physicist Siméon Poisson (1781–1840) discovers the Poisson distribution curve, a "normal" distribution important in statistical studies.

1838 German astronomer and mathematician Friedrich Bessel (1784–1846) for the first time determines the distance between the Earth and a star (other than the sun), finding that 61-Cygni is about 11.4 light-years from Earth.

1839 French painter and physicist Louis Daguerre (1787–1851) takes the first photograph of the moon.

1839 German astronomer Johann Encke (1791–1865) finds Encke's gap, a division in Saturn's "A" ring.

1836 Czech physiologist Jan Purkinje (1787–1869) discovers the protein-digesting action of juices from the pancreas. A year later he identifies Purkinje cells in the brain (large branched nerve cells in the cerebellum), and in 1839 he coins the word *protoplasm* to describe the viscous fluid within cells.

1836 English naturalist Charles Darwin (1809–82) completes his epic voyage on H.M.S. *Beagle*; his observations during the voyage eventually enable him to propose his theory of evolution by natural selection.

1837 Estonian naturalist Karl von Baer (1792–1876) proposes an early form of the law of biogenesis, which states that a living thing can arise only from other similar organisms ("like gives rise to like") and never from anything nonliving.

1837 French physiologist René Dutrochet (1776–1847) describes the role of chlorophyll in photosynthesis—as the substance that absorbs sunlight and converts its energy to food.

1837 Three scientists independently discover the role of yeast in fermentation: in France Charles Cagniard de la Tour (1777–1859) and in Germany Theodor Schwann (1810–82) and Friedrich Kützing (1807–93).

1839 German biologist Theodor Schwann postulates that all living matter is made up of cells.

1836 English chemist James Marsh (1794–1846) devises the Marsh test for detecting arsenic.

1836 English chemist John Daniell (1790–1845) invents the Daniell cell, a primary cell (battery) with zinc and copper electrodes.

1836 French chemist Alexandre Becquerel (1820–91) identifies the photovoltaic effect (whereby light produces an electric current), the principle of most modern photocells.

1836 Swedish chemist Jöns Berzelius (1779–1848) discovers catalysts—substances that accelerate or slow down chemical reactions without taking part in them. Much of modern industrial chemistry and most natural biochemical processes depend on the action of catalysts.

1836 English chemist Edward Davy (1806–85) discovers acetylene (ethyne). It soon becomes an important gas for fuel and lighting.

1838 French chemist Anselme Payen (1795–1871) identifies cellulose, the basic material of all plants.

1839 Swedish chemist Carl Mosander (1797–1858) discovers lanthanum, one of a series of very similar "rare-earth" elements that are to puzzle chemists for many years.

THE AMERICAS

1839 American astronomer William Bond (1789–1859) becomes the first astronomical observer at the new Harvard College Observatory. Eight years later he installs the world's largest refracting telescope, the 15-inch (38-cm) "great refractor."

1836 American botanist Asa Gray (1810–88) draws up a method for classifying plants based on their fruits and seeds.

1837 American physician William Gerhard (1809–72) distinguishes between typhus and typhoid fever.

1839 American inventor Charles Goodyear (1800–60) develops the process of vulcanizing rubber to harden it (by heating raw rubber with sulfur).

ASIA & OCEANIA

AFRICA & THE MIDDLE EAST

Designed by Isambard Brunel, the S.S. Great Britain *was the first successful seagoing steamship to use a propeller. The original version still carried sails in case of emergency.*

ENGINEERING & INVENTION

1836 English physicist William Sturgeon (1783–1850) invents the moving-coil galvanometer, a sensitive instrument for detecting electric currents.

1837 German-born Russian printer Moritz von Jacobi (1801–74) invents a form of electrotyping in which a whole page of type is made by electroplating a mold taken from a page of type set in the usual way.

1837 English physicists William Cooke (1806–79) and Charles Wheatstone (1802–75) patent a five-needle electric telegraph.

1838 The paddle steamer *Sirius* is the first steamship to cross the Atlantic Ocean under steam power alone (taking 18 days). Only hours later S.S. *Great Western* arrives, having taken four days fewer. Seven years later (in 1845) the S.S. *Great Britain* becomes the first ship driven by a screw propeller to make the crossing.

1839 Scottish engineer Kirkpatrick Macmillan (1812–78) invents a bicycle powered by treadles.

1839 Louis Daguerre invents the daguerreotype, a type of photograph taken on metal plates (with the image reversed left to right).

1837 American industrialist John Deere (1804–86) invents a steel plow.

1838 American inventor Samuel Morse (1791–1872) demonstrates a single-wire electric telegraph over a 10-mile (16-km) circuit at New York University. The electromagnetic receiver "clicks" when telegraph signals arrive.

1838 American engineer Charles Page (1812–68) invents an electric generator with soft-iron electromagnets as field magnets instead of permanent magnets.

The natural history of the Galápagos Islands is eminently curious, and deserves attention. Most of the organic productions are aboriginal creations, found nowhere else.

CHARLES DARWIN,
THE VOYAGE OF THE BEAGLE (1837)

WORLD EVENTS

1836 In Britain the Chartists (backers of the People's Charter calling for the universal right to vote) found the first national movement representing working people.

1837 Victoria (r. 1837–1901) becomes queen of Great Britain.

A portrait of Charles Darwin around the time of his voyage on the H.M.S. Beagle

1838 Nicaragua declares its independence from Spain.

1839 Slaves being transported onboard the schooner *Amistad* rebel off the coast of Cuba, seizing control of the ship.

1837 The first whaling station is established in New Zealand, on a site near what is now the city of Christchurch.

MORSE CODE

Samuel Morse (1791–1872) was an American painter and inventor who made the first electric telegraph in the United States. His name is also remembered in the Morse code, which he helped invent. Morse was born in Charlestown, Massachusetts, the son of a minister. After graduating from Yale in 1810, he became a clerk for a Boston publisher. He traveled to England in 1815 and became a successful portrait artist.

Morse's interest turned to electricity in the 1830s. It was known by this time that the presence of an electric current in a wire could be detected by making it work as an electromagnet. This was the phenomenon that Morse decided to use in an electric telegraph.

Morse applied for a patent for his new telegraph in 1837. In 1843 Congress awarded him a grant for $30,000 to build a 37-mile (60-km) telegraph line between Washington and Baltimore. Morse sent his first message in May 1844.

The Morse code was essential for the success of the telegraph. It is a system of short and long electrical pulses ("dots" and "dashes") that encode the letters of the alphabet. The code was the work of Morse's financial backer Alfred Vail (1807–59), who is said to have consulted a newspaper printer to find out which letters are used most in the English language. Vail assigned the shortest codes to the most common letters.

CHARLES DARWIN

IN 1831 CHARLES DARWIN (1809–82) set sail around the world on H.M.S. *Beagle*; during the voyage he made observations that would eventually prompt him to propose the theory of evolution through natural selection. However, he sailed not as a naturalist or biologist but as a dinner companion for the captain.

Charles Darwin was the grandson of English physician Erasmus Darwin (1731–1802), whose writings contained speculations on the nature of familial inheritance and expressed his support for the now discredited ideas of French naturalist Jean-Baptiste Lamarck (1744–1829). When he was 22 years old and had recently finished his university degree, Charles Darwin joined H.M.S. *Beagle* as company for the captain, Robert Fitzroy. At the time naval captains were forbidden to socialize with their officers or crew, a situation that was believed to be the reason for the suicide of the *Beagle*'s previous captain on another voyage two years earlier.

A newspaper cartoon depicts Charles Darwin as an ape, published during the controversy surrounding the publication of On the Origin of Species.

Observation and Exploration

In addition to his desire for adventure, Darwin also wanted to be a naturalist, and he used the five-year voyage as a unique opportunity to study the plants and animals from the far-flung places he saw. The ship visited Tenerife and the Cape Verde Islands off the western coast of Africa before sailing around Cape Horn and up the western coast of South America. It then called at Patagonia, Chile, Peru, and the Galápagos Islands before sailing across the Pacific to Tahiti and New Zealand, returning to England by way of South Africa. At each port of call Darwin went ashore to make observations and collect specimens of rocks, plants, and animals.

Darwin made more trips ashore in South America than anywhere else on the five-year voyage—in fact, he spent more time on land than on the ship. In addition to exotic plants and animals, he also studied the rocks and geology of the places he visited. In Patagonia he came upon a shore with a 19.6-foot- (6-m-) high gravel cliff containing some huge bones. They were too large to belong to any living creature, including the new ones he had already discovered. He observed that—apart from size—they resembled those of South American armadillos and sloths. He realized that their giant ancestors had become extinct but was unable to find a satisfactory explanation at the time for why this had happened.

Development of the Theory

H.M.S. *Beagle* returned to England in the fall of 1836, and Darwin went to live in London. He studied geology and was convinced by the uniformitarian

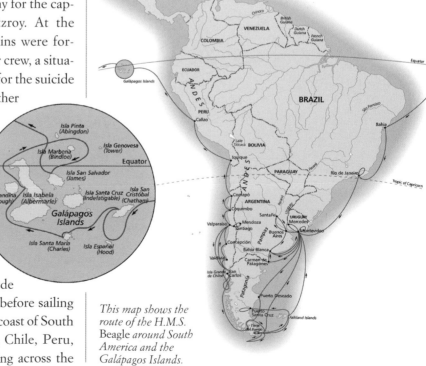

This map shows the route of the H.M.S. Beagle *around South America and the Galápagos Islands.*

ideas of Scottish geologist Charles Lyell (1797–1875), who argued that the world was shaped—and was still being shaped—by the same geological and environmental processes that could be observed in the present. Importantly for the development of Darwin's ideas, this hypothesis suggested that the age of the Earth should be measured in hundreds of millions of years rather than the thousands suggested by biblical chronologies. Darwin also read the works of English economist Thomas Malthus (1766–1834), who described history as a "struggle for existence" in which animal and human populations grow or contract in proportion to variations in available food.

Darwin recognized a similar state among animal species—why do some fish, for example, produce so many offspring when there is insufficient food for all of them? Darwin theorized that in a competitive environment, animals with traits that allow them to take full advantage of available food resources have a better chance of surviving and pass on these beneficial traits to their offspring.

Once Darwin had formulated his theory he set about gathering evidence to support it. In addition to his own observations on the *Beagle*, he consulted with hundreds of individuals—from his fellow zoologists to dog breeders, pigeon keepers, and gardeners—collecting their observations of species variation.

Publication and Further Development

At the same time as Darwin was putting together these ideas on evolution, Welsh naturalist Alfred Russel Wallace (1823–1913) came to very similar conclusions based on his observations of Asian and Australasian animals. He wrote of his theories in 1858 and sent a copy to Darwin. Darwin passed the paper to his friend, the geologist Charles Lyell, who decided to present both Darwin's and Wallace's papers to the Linnean Society at its next meeting. Darwin finally finished his epic work *On the Origin of Species by Means of Natural Selection*, which was published in 1859.

Darwin's theory was that evolution takes place in stages by chance mutations. Favorable mutations are inherited and passed on to offspring, so producing a gradual change in a whole species. Eventually new, fitter species come into existence and old, less fit ones become extinct. Darwin and his contemporaries

Darwin deduced that several species of finches in the Galápagos Islands had a common mainland ancestor. They evolved different beaks to suit their island diet. Finches 1, 3, and 4 have long beaks adapted for eating insects; finch 2 is a fruit-eating species; and the slightly crossed stubby beaks of finches 5 and 6 are best for tackling seeds.

had no idea of exactly how mutations take place. Unknown to them, however, heredity was being studied in the garden of a monastery in Austria by the monk Gregor Mendel (1822–84). He grew successive generations of pea plants and figured out the basic laws of heredity—that offspring receive sets of inherited "factors" that we now call genes. As scientific knowledge has advanced further, Darwin's theories have been vindicated and clarified by more discoveries, such as the discovery of DNA in 1953 and more recently the mapping of the human genome, completed in 2003.

CHAPTER 6

THE AGE OF STEAM

With new railroads spreading across Europe and the United States (and at the same time putting most of the canal companies out of business), engineers began to find even more applications for the steam engine. The most important involved shipping. At first the steam engine drove paddle-wheels, and paddle steamers could be seen plying their trade up and down rivers as far apart as the Danube in Europe and the Mississippi in the United States, where they helped transport settlers to the Midwest. Attempts at building paddle-driven oceangoing vessels met with little success, however, until the new power source was used to drive a propeller. Soon propeller-driven steamships replaced sailing ships on many of the world's oceans. The steam engine also came to displace the waterwheel as a source of power. However, the ancient device received a new lease on life with the invention of high-speed water turbines in the middle of the 19th century. Turbines are still used in hydroelectric power plants throughout the world.

The proliferation of advances in science and technology was celebrated in a number of international exhibitions, beginning with the Great Exhibition of 1851 in the remarkable iron-and-glass structure of the Crystal Palace in London. The electric telegraph carried the good news by way of cables across continents and under the oceans. On the theoretical side, Russian chemist Dmitri Mendeleev (1834–1907) brought

The steam engine was a versatile invention and was soon adapted to power ships. This lithograph depicts a celebrated race between two steamers, the Robert E. Lee *and the* Natchez, *on the Mississippi from St. Louis to New Orleans in 1870. The victorious* Robert E. Lee *made the trip in 3 days, 18 hours, 14 minutes, a record that still stands for a commercial vessel.*

order to chemistry with his development of the periodic table, and Austrian monk Gregor Mendel (1822–84) laid the foundation for the science of genetics when he revealed the laws of inheritance from his studies of garden pea plants. Atomic theory —that everything consists of atoms—became widely accepted, although at first atoms were thought to be just tiny indivisible particles of matter. Further investigation was needed to prove that atoms themselves are made up of even smaller particles.

A major medical breakthrough came with the understanding that infections are caused by parasitic organisms. With the aid of microscopes, scientists such as German doctor Robert Koch (1843–1910) and French chemist Louis Pasteur (1822–95) isolated the bacterial causes of infectious diseases such as typhoid and tuberculosis. Now doctors knew exactly what they were fighting, although it would be many years before the advent of effective drugs—antibiotics—that could kill bacteria.

The invention of the internal combustion engine in the late 19th century heralded the end of the age of steam. Much more efficient than a steam engine and more compact, the internal combustion engine could be adapted to smaller vehicles, including the newly invented automobiles, as well as boats and eventually airplanes.

Russian scientist Dmitri Mendeleev made sense of the known chemical elements by arranging them by atomic weight in his periodic table, as shown above on the wall of a technical school in Moscow. He arranged the table so that elements with similar properties fell in columns, and this allowed him to predict the existence of elements that were still undiscovered.

	1840	1845	1850	1855	1860
EUROPE	**1840** German pathologist Jacob Henle puts forward his germ theory of disease: that infection is caused by parasitic organisms. **1842** English zoologist Richard Owen coins the word *dinosaur* to describe certain prehistoric reptiles. **1842** German physicist Julius von Mayer first states that energy can neither be created nor destroyed. **1843** The first underwater tunnel is completed under the Thames River at Rotherhithe in London. **1843** German physiologist Emil du Bois-Reymond recognizes the electrical nature of nerve impulses.	**1845** Designed by engineer Isambard Brunel, S.S. *Great Britain*, the first successful propeller-driven ship, makes its maiden voyage. **1846** German astronomer Johann Galle is the first person to observe the planet Neptune. **1846** Italian chemist Ascanio Sobrero discovers the explosive nitroglycerin. **1848** Scottish physicist William Thomson, Lord Kelvin, introduces the absolute temperature scale. **1849** French gardener Joseph Monier invents reinforced concrete.	**1850** German chemist Robert Bunsen begins using the Bunsen burner, designed by his assistant Peter Desaga. **1851** French physicist Léon Foucault constructs Foucault's pendulum and uses it to show the Earth's rotation. **1852** English astronomer Edward Sabine establishes the connection between sunspot activity and magnetic storms on Earth. **1853** French chemist Charles Gerhardt derives acetylsalicylic acid (the basis of aspirin) from plants. **1854** English physician John Snow pinpoints a link between cholera and contaminated water.	**1855** Italian physicist Luigi Palmieri designs a seismograph, an instrument that detects and measures the strength of earthquakes. **1856** Workmen digging in the valley of the Neander River near Düsseldorf, Germany, discover remains of Neandertal man. **1857** Léon Foucault devises a method of silver-coating glass for use as mirrors in telescopes. **1858** English engineer Charles Bright organizes the laying of the first transatlantic submarine telegraph cable. **1859** English naturalist Charles Darwin publishes *On the Origin of Species*, the book in which he puts forward his theory of evolution.	**1860** The first fossil of *Archaeopteryx*, a birdlike prehistoric flying reptile, is found. **1860** English nurse Florence Nightingale establishes the world's first nursing college in London. **1860** Robert Bunsen and German physicist Gustav Kirchhoff develop a technique for analyzing substances by their spectra. **1862** German physician Felix Hoppe-Seyler establishes the presence of hemoglobin in blood. **1863** French chemist Louis Pasteur introduces pasteurization. **1864** French engineer Pierre Michaux makes the first pedal bicycle.
THE AMERICAS	**1842** The first U.S. suspension bridge (designed by Charles Ellet) opens over the Schuylkill River in Fairmount, Philadelphia. **1842** American surgeon Crawford Long uses ether as an anesthetic. **1844** American dentist Horace Wells introduces nitrous oxide ("laughing gas") as an anesthetic. **1844** American inventor Samuel Morse sends the first telegraph message in the United States.	**1845** The first clipper ship, the *Rainbow*, is launched in the United States. **1846** American inventor Elias Howe patents a lock-stitch sewing machine. **1846** American John Deere (1804–86) markets a plow with a steel moldboard. **1849** Anglo-American engineer James Francis makes an improved reaction water turbine, in which a jet of water is directed at cup-shaped "paddles."	**1850** American engineer Charles Page builds the first electric locomotive in the United States. **1851** American inventor Isaac Singer patents a single-thread sewing machine that produces continuous and curved stitching. **1852** American inventor Elisha Otis patents the safety elevator. **1854** American chemist David Alter uses atomic spectra as a method of chemical analysis.	**1859** American industrialist George Pullman develops the Pullman sleeping car for use on railroads. **1859** American oil pioneer Edwin Drake drills the world's first productive oil well in Pennsylvania.	**1861** A telegraph line is built in the United States from Omaha, Nebraska, to Carson City, Nevada. **1862** American astronomers Lewis Swift and Horace Tuttle discover comet Swift–Tuttle, which causes the annual Perseid meteor shower. **1862** American inventor and gunsmith Richard Gatling patents a rapid-fire, ten-barrel machine gun.
ASIA & OCEANIA					**1861** Australian astronomer John Tebbutt discovers the long-period Tebbutt's comet. The Earth passes through the comet's tail.
AFRICA & THE MIDDLE EAST					

1865	1870	1875	1880	1882–1884
1865 Austrian monk Gregor Mendel formulates his laws of inheritance. **1865** German botanist Julius von Sachs identifies chloroplasts. **1867** Swedish chemist Alfred Nobel patents dynamite in Britain. **1868** English astronomer William Huggins detects a Doppler shift in the spectrum of the star Sirius and demonstrates that the star is receding from Earth. **1869** Russian chemist Dmitri Mendeleev compiles the first Periodic Table of the elements. **1869** Swiss pathologist Johann Miescher isolates deoxyribonucleic acid (DNA), which he calls *nuclein*.	**1871** Irish physicist George Stoney observes that three lines in the hydrogen spectrum have wavelengths in a simple ratio to one another. **1872** English-born chemist Robert Chesebrough patents the process of making petroleum jelly. **1873** Austrian physician Josef Breuer discovers the sensory function of the semicircular canals in the ear, which help maintain balance. **1873** English mathematician William Shanks calculates π (pi) to 707 decimal places.	**1876** German engineer Nikolaus Otto builds a four-stroke internal combustion engine fueled by coal gas. **1876** Polish-born German botanist Eduard Strasburger describes mitosis. **1877** English physicist Joseph Swan develops the first electric light bulb. **1877** German physiologist Wilhelm Kühne suggests the name *enzyme* for a protein that acts as a catalyst. **1879** English inventor Henry Lawson invents a chain-driven bicycle, which he calls the bicyclette.	**1880** French physical chemist Pierre Curie discovers the piezoelectric effect, which is the production of a voltage in a crystal that is under a mechanical stress. **1880** Louis Pasteur identifies the bacterium *Streptococcus*. **1880** Scottish astronomer George Forbes predicts the existence of "Planet X" orbiting beyond Uranus. **1881** German scientist Hermann von Helmholtz demonstrates that the electric charges of hydrogen atoms occur in whole-number portions.	**1882** German bacteriologist Robert Koch discovers the bacterium that causes tuberculosis. A year later he discovers the bacterium that causes cholera. **1883** Belgian engineer Étienne Lenoir invents the spark plug (for internal combustion engines). **1884** American-born English inventor Hiram Maxim makes the first fully automatic machine gun. **1884** Danish physician Hans Gram introduces a method of classifying bacteria by staining. **1884** Swedish chemist Svante Arrhenius begins to study the dissociation of electrolytes into ions in solution.
1865 A meteorite explodes just before reaching the ground in Vernon County, Wisconsin. **1866** The metric system is introduced in the United States but is largely ignored. **1867** English-born American engineer Andrew Hallidie invents the cable car. **1869** The Union Pacific transcontinental railroad is completed.	**1870** American engineer Lester Pelton designs a new form of water turbine—the Pelton wheel impulse water turbine. **1872** American astronomer Henry Draper photographs Vega's spectrum, creating the first photograph of the spectrum of a star.	**1876** American librarian Melvil Dewey introduces the Dewey Decimal Classification system for cataloging library books. **1876** Scottish-born American engineer Alexander Graham Bell patents the telephone. **1877** American engineer Thomas Edison invents the phonograph. **1877** American astronomer Asaph Hall discovers Phobos and Deimos, the two moons of Mars.	**1881** American astronomer Henry Draper takes the first photographs of comets. **1881** American astronomer Samuel Langley makes a bolometer, a sensitive temperature-measuring device with which he measures the sun's radiation. **1882** American physicist Albert Michelson publishes his first calculation of the speed of light. It is within 0.02 percent of the correct value.	**1882** The first steam-powered electricity-generating plant in the United States, designed by Thomas Edison, opens in New York City. **1884** German-born American inventor Ottmar Mergenthaler invents the linotype machine.
		1879 The first shipment of frozen meat is sent to England from Australia.		**1883** Mount Krakatoa, an active volcano in Indonesia, erupts. The explosion is heard as far away as Perth, western Australia.
1869 The Suez Canal is completed under the supervision of French engineer Ferdinand de Lesseps.				**1883** The world's last quagga (an African animal resembling a zebra) dies in the Amsterdam Zoo.

ASTRONOMY & MATH	BIOLOGY & MEDICINE	PHYSICAL SCIENCES

EUROPE

1843 German astronomer Heinrich Schwabe (1789–1875) declares that sunspots have a cycle of about ten years (they reach a maximum number every ten years). Later Swiss astronomer Rudolf Wolf (1816–93) defines the period as 11 years.

1843 French amateur astronomer Hervé-Auguste Faye (1814–1902) discovers Faye's comet. It has a period of 7.3 years.

1843 Irish mathematician William Hamilton (1805–65) devises quaternions, a system of complex numbers that are not commutative (in which *ab* does not necessarily equal *ba*). They later find use in both theoretical and applied mathematics.

1840 German pathologist Jacob Henle (1809–85) proposes his germ theory of disease: that infection is caused by parasitic organisms invading the body.

1840 Swiss embryologist Rudolf von Kölliker (1817–1905) describes spermatozoa as being cellular in origin and nature.

1842 English zoologist Richard Owen (1804–92) coins the word *dinosaur* (meaning "terrible lizard" in Greek) to describe certain prehistoric reptiles.

1842 Danish zoologist Johann Steenstrup (1813–97) first explains the alternation of sexual and asexual generations that takes place in plants such as mosses.

1842 Scottish anatomist Charles Bell (1774–1842) describes Bell's palsy, a type of facial paralysis.

1843 German physiologist Emil du Bois-Reymond (1818–96) recognizes the electrical nature of nerve impulses.

1840 French chemist Henri Regnault (1810–78) discovers dichloroethylene (dichloroethene), which soon becomes an important industrial solvent.

1840 Swiss-born Russian chemist Germain Hess (1802–50) formulates Hess's law, concerning the heats of reaction of chemical processes.

1840 English physicist James Joule (1818–89) proposes Joule's law, which states that the amount of heat per second that develops in a wire carrying a current is proportional to the electrical resistance of the wire and the square of the current.

1842 German physicist Julius von Mayer (1814–78) first states the principle of conservation of energy (that energy can neither be created nor destroyed, merely changed from one form into another form).

1842 Austrian physicist Christian Doppler (1803–53) describes the Doppler effect—the change in frequency (or wavelength) of a wave motion when the source and the observer move closer to or farther away from each other. Applied originally to sound waves, the effect also relates to any form of wave motion, such as light.

The dark spots visible on the surface of the sun are sunspots—areas of reduced temperature caused by magnetic anomalies.

1841 English-born American scientist John Draper (1811–82) creates Draper's law: that only the radiation that is absorbed by a substance will produce a chemical change in it.

THE AMERICAS

1840 English-born American scientist John Draper (1811–82) takes the first celestial photographs, daguerreotypes of the moon.

1842 American surgeon Crawford Long (1815–78) uses ether as an anesthetic. American dentist William Morton (1819–68) patents it in 1846, and it is used by Scottish obstetrician James Simpson (1811–70) in 1847.

1844 American dentist Horace Wells (1815–48) introduces nitrous oxide ("laughing gas") as an anesthetic.

ASIA & OCEANIA

AFRICA & THE MIDDLE EAST

TURNING POINTS

Safe Anesthetics

For many centuries a major impediment to safe surgical procedures was the problem of pain. The intense pain that accompanied surgery before the introduction of reliable anesthetics not only caused considerable distress to the patient, but also made the surgery more dangerous. The patient's involuntary movements and the need to finish the surgery quickly increased the likelihood of potentially fatal mistakes. Anesthetics such as opium, cocaine, and mandrake had always been available but were not reliable: an underdose or overdose was too easily administered. Sometimes the anesthetic would be insufficient to dull pain; at other times it would kill the patient. The discovery of new anesthetics—including ether, chloroform, and nitrous oxide—in the mid-19th century improved the situation, but almost as important was the methodical research into anesthetic techniques and dosages conducted during this time. Physicians such as John Snow (1813–1858)—better known for identifying the cause of cholera—published dosage advice and designed apparatus for administering these new anesthetics safely to patients of all ages and body sizes.

ENGINEERING & INVENTION

1841 English engineer Joseph Whitworth (1803–87) introduces a system of standard screw threads.

1841 English chemist Alexander Parkes (1813–90) invents a process for cold vulcanizing rubber (using carbon disulfide and no heat).

1843 English engineer Thomas Crampton (1816–88) invents the Crampton railroad locomotive. It has a single pair of large driving wheels located behind the firebox.

1843 The first underwater tunnel is completed under the Thames River at Rotherhithe in London. It is designed by French-born engineer Marc Brunel (1769–1849) and constructed under the supervision of his son Isambard (1806–1859). Although intended for use by pedestrians, it is not a financial success and later (1865) it is acquired for use by railroad trains.

1844 Belgian engineer Égide Walschaert (1820–1901) invents the Walschaert's valve gear. It is used on the majority of steam railroad locomotives until the end of the steam era.

1841 German-born American engineer John Roebling (1806–69) invents a machine for making wire rope (cable). It becomes important in constructing suspension bridges.

1842 The first suspension bridge in the United States opens over the Schuylkill River in Fairmount, Philadelphia, designed by Charles Ellet (1810–62).

1843 African-American inventor Norbert Rillieux (1806–94) designs a vacuum evaporator for extracting sugar from sugarcane (patented 1846).

1844 American inventor Samuel Morse (1791–1872) sends the first message on a telegraph line in the United States (Washington to Baltimore).

WORLD EVENTS

1840 The world's first postage stamp comes into circulation in Great Britain.

1840 Queen Victoria of Great Britain (r. 1837–1901) marries the German Prince Albert (1819–61).

1844 A weavers' uprising in Silesia (now southern Poland) is put down by Prussian troops.

This skeleton is the fossilized remains of a Tyrannosaurus rex, *first discovered in 1874. The dinosaur stood up to 13 feet (4 m) tall.*

1840 A report prepared by Canada's Governor General Lord Durham (1792–1840) recommends the union of Upper and Lower Canada into a single state.

1844 The eastern part of the island of Hispaniola wins independence as Santo Domingo (now the Dominican Republic).

The two passages of the Thames Tunnel at Rotherhithe in London—depicted in this contemporary illustration—were completed by Marc Brunel and his son Isambard in 1844.

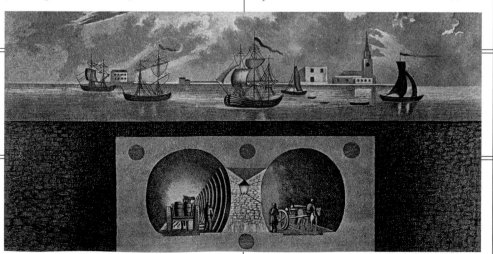

DISCOVERING THE DINOSAURS

The bones of the creatures now known as dinosaurs have been unearthed throughout history. In China the bones were thought to be the remains of dragons, while in Europe they were believed to be those of giants.

The first dinosaur to be scientifically described was *Megalosaurus*, following the discovery of a partial skeleton in Oxfordshire, England, in 1677. By the mid-19th century another two species had been identifed: *Hylaeosaurus* and *Iguanadon*. The term *dinosaur* was coined by paleontologist Robert Owen in 1842.

Public interest quickly grew in these vast ancient creatures, and some fossil hunters became famous for their discoveries. They often used reckless and unscientific techniques, such as blasting fossil beds with explosives. The late 19th-century rivalries among fossil hunters in the United States were dubbed the "Bone Wars." Since then the search for new fossils has expanded to include every continent, including Antarctica. This has led to the discovery of many new species, as well as a far greater understanding of the ecological roles and possible behaviors of these creatures.

ASTRONOMY & MATH

1845 Two French physicists—Armand Fizeau (1819–96) and Léon Foucault (1819–68)—take detailed photographs of the sun.

1846 German astronomer Johann Galle (1812–1910) is the first person to observe the planet Neptune. A few months later English astronomer William Lassell (1799–1880) discovers Triton, Neptune's moon.

1847 English mathematician Augustus de Morgan (1806–71) formulates de Morgan's laws, which are fundamental to the science of logic.

1848 English astronomer William Lassell (1799–1880) and, independently, American astronomers William (1789–1859) and George Bond (1825–65) discover Hyperion, one of Saturn's moons.

1848 French astronomer Édouard Roche (1820–83) calculates the Roche limit—the closest distance to a planet that one of its moons can approach without being torn apart by gravitational forces.

BIOLOGY & MEDICINE

1845 German zoologist Karl Siebold (1804–85) demonstrates that protozoa (protists) are single-celled organisms.

1845 English clergyman and amateur biologist Miles Berkeley (1803–89) shows that the disease potato blight is caused by a fungus. By 1848 the potato famine has killed more than one million people in Ireland.

1845 German pathologist Rudolph Virchow (1821–1902) and English physician John Bennett (1812–75) independently describe the disorder leukemia.

1846 French physiologist Claude Bernard (1813–78) describes the role of the pancreas in digestion.

1846 Italian astronomer and microscopist Giovanni Amici (1786–1863) discovers the circulation of sap in plants.

1847 French physiologist Pierre Flourens (1794–1867) first uses chloroform (trichloromethane) as an anesthetic on small animals. In the same year Scottish obstetrician James Simpson (1811–70) uses it on humans.

PHYSICAL SCIENCES

1845 German chemist Christian Schönbein (1799–1868) discovers the explosive properties of nitrocellulose (guncotton), which was first prepared by French chemist Théophile Pelouze (1807–67).

1845 German physicist Franz Neumann (1798–1895) publishes his first paper outlining his theory of electromagnetic induction, based on the experiments of Michael Faraday (1791–1867) and Joseph Henry (1797–1878).

1846 Italian chemist Ascanio Sobrero (1812–88) discovers nitroglycerin (trinitroglycerol), a powerful but unstable explosive, which is later found to be useful in the treatment of certain heart disorders.

1847 German scientist Hermann von Helmholtz (1821–94) and English physicist James Joule (1818–89) establish the principle of the conservation of energy, first proposed in 1842 by German physicist Julius von Mayer (1814–78).

1848 Scottish physicist William Thomson, Lord Kelvin (1824–1907), introduces the absolute temperature scale. Now known as the Kelvin scale, it is the SI unit of temperature.

1846 American physician Oliver Wendell Holmes (1809–94) coins the term *anesthetic*, meaning "without feeling."

1847 The American Medical Association is founded in Philadelphia.

The Smithsonian Institution in Washington, D.C. The institution was founded with the goal of advancing science and public knowledge in the United States.

INSIDE STORY

Temperature

The Kelvin temperature scale, devised in 1848 by William Thomson, Lord Kelvin, is based on absolute zero. The kelvin is the international standard (SI) unit of temperature.

Fahrenheit	Celsius	Kelvin	
212°	100°	373°	Water boils
176°	80°	353°	
140°	60°	333°	
104°	40°	313°	Average room
68°	20°	293°	temperature
32°	0°	273°	Water freezes
4°	-20°	253°	
-40°	-40°	233°	Mercury
-76°	-60°	213°	freezes
-112°	-80°	193°	
-148°	-100°	173°	
-184°	-120°	153°	Alcohol
-220°	-140°	133°	freezes
-256°	-160°	113°	
-292°	-180°	93°	Oxygen boils
-328°	-200°	73°	
-364°	-220°	53°	Oxygen
-400°	-240°	33°	freezes
-436°	-260°	13°	
-459.4°	-273°	0°	Absolute zero

ENGINEERING & INVENTION

1845 Scottish engineer Robert Thomson (1822–73) patents a pneumatic tire made of vulcanized rubber for horse-drawn vehicles.

1845 Designed by engineer Isambard Brunel (1806–59), S.S. *Great Britain*, the first successful propeller-driven ship, makes its maiden voyage.

1846 Belgian-born French musician Adolphe Sax (1814–94) patents the saxophone.

1848 English inventor John Stringfellow (1799–1883) builds a model steam-driven airplane.

1848 English engineer William Adams (1797–1872) constructs a steam-powered railcar.

1849 French gardener Joseph Monier (1823–1906) invents reinforced concrete (concrete cast around iron or steel reinforcing rods).

1845 The first clipper ship, the *Rainbow*, is launched in the United States.

1846 American inventor Elias Howe (1819–67) patents a lock-stitch sewing machine.

1846 American industrialist John Deere (1804–86) markets a plow with a steel moldboard.

1848 American inventor James Bogardus (1800–74) introduces a method of making cast-iron buildings.

1849 Anglo-American engineer James Francis (1815–92) makes an improved reaction water turbine, in which a jet of water is directed at cup-shaped "paddles."

WORLD EVENTS

1845 Potato blight causes a terrible famine in Ireland that will claim the lives of about a million people and drive many more into exile before its end in 1851.

1846 The Corn Laws, which placed high tariffs on imports of grain to Britain, are repealed, ostensibly to ease the famine in Ireland. Repeal will be significant step in the development of international free trade.

1847 The ongoing famine in Ireland causes an estimated 200,000 people to emigrate in just one year, mostly to the United States.

1848 German political thinkers Karl Marx (1818–83) and Freidrich Engels (1820–95) publish the *Communist Manifesto*, a blueprint for a socialist state created through a revolution of the workers.

1848 Pro-democracy uprisings take place across Europe, including in Italy, France, Germany, Austria, and Hungary. Unrest in France forces King Louis-Phillipe (r. 1830–48) to hand power to the Second Republic.

1849 Pope Pius IX (1792–1878) is returned to power in Italy, forcing revolutionary leader Giuseppe Garibaldi (1807–82) to return to exile in America.

1846 Oregon Territory (Washington, Oregon, and Idaho, with parts of British Columbia) is divided between the United States and Canada, with the border at the 49th parallel.

1846 Hostilities break out between the United States and Mexico when the two nations cannot agree terms on the sale of New Mexico. Mexican forces suffer heavy losses at the battles of Palo Alto and Resaca.

1848 Thousands of prospectors swarm to the California gold rush. Few of them succeed in making a living from the mining, but the influx of people accelerates the growth of the state of California.

A contemporary engraving of the steamship Clermont *in New York Harbor*

STEAMSHIPS

Before the improvements made by James Watt (1736–1819), the steam engine was essentially a piece of specialized mining equipment. The utility of Watt's steam engine made it a vital part of any industrial enterprise. Its popularity brought it to the attention of many engineers and inventors, who modified the design and adapted it to different uses. The early development of locomotives was hindered by the size and weight of steam engines, but this was not a problem for steamships.

Attempts were made to build a steamboat in the late 18th century by inventors in Britain, France, and the United States. These early ships used a variety of methods of propulsion—including paddlewheels, mechanical oars, and suction pumps—but met with only limited success. Some later designs, such as the *Charlotte Dundas*, designed by William Symington (1763–1831), were technical successes but not commercial ones.

It was the U.S. engineer Robert Fulton (1765–1815) who built the first practical steamship—*Clermont*—in 1806. The *Clermont* made the trip up the Hudson River from New York to Albany at a speed of 5 miles (8 km) per hour and went into regular passenger service.

Although they were successful on rivers, and some operated in coastal waters, steamships did not cross the open sea until 1838, when two British steamships crossed the Atlantic. The S.S. *Great Britain*, launched in 1845, was the first transatlantic ship to be powered by an efficient screw propeller.

The total quantity of all the forces capable of work in the whole universe remains eternal and unchanged throughout all their changes.

HERMANN VON HELMHOLTZ

ASTRONOMY & MATH

EUROPE

1851 French mathematician Joseph Liouville (1809–82) publishes his work establishing the existence of transcendental numbers (numbers that are not algebraic).

1851 English astronomer William Lassell (1799–1880) discovers Ariel and Umbriel, two moons of Uranus.

1852 English physicist and astronomer Edward Sabine (1788–1883) establishes the connection between sunspot activity and magnetic storms on Earth.

1854 English mathematician George Boole (1815–64) introduces Boolean algebra, which is later important in the development of computer logic circuits.

1854 German mathematician Bernhard Riemann (1826–66) develops a type of non-Euclidean geometry later to find applications in relativity theory.

THE AMERICAS

1850 American astronomer William Bond (1789–1859) and English astronomer William Lassell (1799–1880) independently observe Saturn's dark inner ring: the crepe ring, or C ring.

Giant sequoias grow naturally only in the western Sierra Nevada, in California.

BIOLOGY & MEDICINE

1850 German scientist Hermann von Helmholtz (1821–94) measures the speed of a nerve impulse.

1850 English physician Alfred Higginson (1808–84) invents the hypodermic needle. It is used initially for extracting samples of blood or other fluid.

1851 Hermann von Helmholtz devises the ophthalmoscope, which enables physicians to look inside a patient's eye.

1851 French physiologist Claude Bernard (1813–78) discovers vasomotor nerves, which regulate the diameter of blood vessels.

1852 English zoologist Richard Owen (1804–92) identifies the parathyroid glands in the neck of a rhinoceros.

1852 German physiologists Georg Meissner (1829–1905) and Rudolf Wagner (1805–64) describe Meissner's corpuscles, which are receptors in the skin that detect slight pressure.

1854 English physician John Snow (1813–58) pinpoints a link between cholera and contaminated drinking water during an epidemic in London.

A contemporary engraving shows the figure of death working a water pump, reflecting John Snow's discovery of the cause of cholera.

1853 The world's largest tree, a giant sequoia, is found in California and named *Wellingtonia gigantea* (now *Sequoiadendron giganteum*).

PHYSICAL SCIENCES

1850 French chemist Auguste Bravais (1811–63) publishes his analysis of crystal lattice structure, in which he identifies 14 different types of lattice.

1850 German physicist Rudolf Clausius (1822–88) formulates the second law of thermodynamics. It states that heat will not, on its own, move from a hot object to a hotter object.

1851 French physicist Léon Foucault (1819–68) constructs Foucault's pendulum and uses it to demonstrate the rotation of the Earth.

1851 Irish-born physicist George Stokes (1819–1903) proposes Stokes's law, an expression for the force acting on a small sphere falling through a liquid.

1853 French chemist Charles Gerhardt (1816–56) derives acetylsalicylic acid (the basis of aspirin) from plants. In the same year, together with his compatriot Auguste Laurent (1807–53), he introduces to organic chemistry the theory of "types"—the idea that certain characteristic groupings always behave in a similar way, even when they occur in different kinds of compounds.

1854 American chemist David Alter (1807–81) studies atomic spectra, the light given off by elements when heated to incandescence, and uses them as a method of chemical analysis.

HOW IT WORKS

Foucault's Pendulum

In 1851 the French physicist Léon Foucault devised an experiment to simply demonstrate the rotation of the Earth. In Foucault's experiment a steel ball, weighing 61 pounds (28 kg), was suspended from a 197-foot (60-m) steel wire in a large indoor space. The weight was drawn back and allowed to swing like a pendulum. The direction of the swing altered gradually, at a rate of around 11° per hour, so that it eventually completed a full rotation. The rotation of the swing around its center is caused by the rotation of the Earth on its axis and shows that the Earth makes one complete rotation every 24 hours. The experiment was soon replicated in locations around the world.

ASIA & OCEANIA

AFRICA & THE MIDDLE EAST

ENGINEERING & INVENTION	WORLD EVENTS
1850 German chemist Robert Bunsen (1811–99) begins using the Bunsen burner, which was probably designed by his assistant Peter Desaga.	**1851** Louis Napoleon, nephew of Napoleon Bonaparte (r. 1804–14 and 1825) and president of France's Second Republic, creates the Second Empire, with himself as Emperor Napoleon III (r. 1852–70).
1850 The French battleship *Napoléon* is launched. It is the first purpose built steam-battleship and the first to be driven by a screw propeller.	**1854** The United Kingdom declares war on Russia, marking the beginning of the Crimean War (1854–56). Later in the year a misunderstood order costs the lives of 150 British soldiers in the infamous "Charge of the Light Brigade."
1850 A tubular railroad bridge is opened across the Menai Strait, North Wales, designed by English engineer Robert Stephenson (1803–59).	**1854** British nurse Florence Nightingale (1820–1910) leaves for the Crimea with a group of 38 nurses she has trained. Her examination of mortality rates and causes—through first hand experience and statistical analysis—leads to revolutionary changes in hospital design and management.
1851 The Crystal Palace, a cast-iron and glass building designed by English architect Joseph Paxton (1801–65), is put up in Hyde Park, London, for the Great Exhibition.	
1852 French engineer Henri Giffard (1825–82) builds a steerable, hydrogen-filled nonrigid airship called a dirigible.	
1853 English inventor George Cayley (1773–1857) constructs a glider capable of carrying a person.	

ENGINEERING & INVENTION	WORLD EVENTS
1850 American engineer Charles Page (1812–68) builds the first electric locomotive in the United States.	**1850** The Fugitive Slave Act requires all states to return slaves to their former masters, increasing tension between the Northern and Southern states.
1851 American inventor Isaac Singer (1811–75) patents a single-thread sewing machine that produces continuous and curved stitching.	**1852** Harriet Beecher Stowe (1811–96) publishes the antislavery novel *Uncle Tom's Cabin.*
1851 American dentist John Allen (1810–92) produces false teeth consisting of porcelain teeth on a platinum plate.	**1854** The Kansas-Nebraska Act destroys the 1820 Missouri Compromise over the creation of new slave states. Fighting breaks out in Kansas territory between supporters and opponents of slavery.
1852 American inventor Elisha Otis (1811–61) patents the safety elevator; the first is installed in Yonkers, New York, in 1857.	
1854 American gunsmiths Horace Smith (1808–93) and Daniel Wesson (1825–1906) produce a single-action cartridge revolver (patented 1856).	

The Menai Bridge in North Wales was one of the first modern suspension bridges.

THE GREAT EXHIBITION

Staged in London in 1851, the first Great Exhibition was a world fair of exhibits designed to celebrate the extent of human achievement. The emphasis was on practical science and technology, and more than half of the exhibits came from Britain or the British Empire.

The exhibition was devised by Queen Victoria's husband, Prince Albert (1819–61), who was at the time president of Britain's Royal Society of Arts. The idea was to mount an exhibition showcasing the "industries of all nations." The exhibition was funded partly by Queen Victoria herself and partly by British manufacturers.

The exhibition was staged in a vast glass-and-iron structure known as the Crystal Palace, designed by architect Joseph Paxton (1801–65). There were about 14,000 exhibitors showing more than 100,000 examples of manufactured goods. They included everything from printing presses, railroad locomotives, and hydraulic machinery, to items as small as cutlery and jewelry. The 560 exhibits from the United States included Cyrus McCormick's reaper and Samuel Colt's repeating revolver. The exhibition remained open for 23 weeks, during which time it received more than 6 million visitors (equivalent to about a third of the population of the United Kingdom at the time).

The profits made by the exhibition were used to found the Victoria and Albert Museum, the Science Museum, and the Natural History Museum in London—which collect and exhibit significant examples of design, technology, and biological and geological specimens respectively.

The original Crystal Palace was taken down in 1852 and rebuilt on a hill at Sydenham, south of London, where it remained in use by the public until it was destroyed by fire in 1936. The London district where it once stood is still known as Crystal Palace.

EUROPE

ASTRONOMY & MATH

1857 Scottish physicist James Clerk Maxwell (1831–79) suggests the true nature of Saturn's rings (that they consist of millions of small orbiting particles).

1857 French physicist Léon Foucault (1819–68) devises a method of silver-coating glass for use as mirrors in telescopes. Glass mirrors will replace the metal mirrors used in earlier reflecting telescopes.

1858 Italian astronomer Giambattista Donati (1826–73) discovers Donati's comet, which has a period of about 2,000 years. It is the first comet to be photographed (by English astronomer William Usherwood).

1859 German astronomer Gustav Spörer (1822–95) establishes Spörer's law. It states that during the course of the sunspot cycle sunspots gradually move toward lower latitudes (nearer the sun's equator).

1859 English astronomer Richard Carrington (1826–75) observes flares in the chromosphere (outer layer) of the sun.

BIOLOGY & MEDICINE

1855 German pathologist Rudolph Virchow (1821–1902) observes that cells originate from the division of other cells.

1855 English physician Thomas Addison (1793–1860) describes the disease of the adrenal glands, which later becomes known as Addison's disease.

1856 German physician Carl Ludwig (1816–95) is the first to keep animal organs alive outside the body by pumping blood through them.

1856 Workmen digging in the valley of the Neander River near Düsseldorf, Germany, discover remains of Neandertal man.

1857 French chemist Louis Pasteur (1822–95) observes that microorganisms cause fermentation.

1858 English anatomist Henry Gray (1825–61) publishes *Anatomy of the Human Body*, commonly known as *Gray's Anatomy*.

1859 English naturalist Charles Darwin (1809–82) publishes *On the Origin of Species*, the book in which he puts forward his theory of evolution.

PHYSICAL SCIENCES

1855 English geophysicist John Pratt (1809–71) demonstrates that gravity remains constant everywhere at sea level (whereas it varies over different altitudes on land).

1855 Northern Irish chemist and physicist Thomas Andrews (1813–85) proves that ozone is an allotrope (molecular compound) of oxygen with three atoms per molecule (O_3).

1856 Scottish physicist William Thomson, Lord Kelvin (1824–1907), coins the term *kinetic energy* to describe energy associated with movement.

1858 Italian chemist Stanislao Cannizzaro (1826–1910) distinguishes between atomic weights and molecular weights, thereby establishing atomic and molecular weights as the basis of chemical calculations.

1859 German chemist Hermann Kolbe (1818–84) synthesizes salicylic acid, leading to the mass production of aspirin, the first synthetic drug.

1859 Scottish physicist and engineer William Rankine (1820–72) devises the Rankine cycle to measure the efficiency of steam engines.

HOW IT WORKS

Cell Division

All cells originate from the division of other cells, as first observed by German pathologist Rudolph Virchow in 1855. There are three different types of cell division: binary fission, mitosis, and meiosis. Binary fission is the type of cell division that single-celled organisms such as bacteria use to reproduce. Mitosis is the process by which a cell divides so that two identical sets of chromosomes appear in the daughter cells. In meiosis, new cells are created with half the chromosomes of their parent cells. This process creates the gametes used in sexual reproduction. Rapid and uncontrolled cell division is the defining characteristic of cancers.

THE AMERICAS

ASIA & OCEANIA

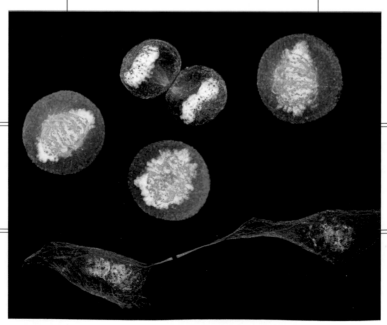

This micrograph shows cancer cells at various stages of division. The image has been enhanced by using antibodies that attach fluorescent dyes to specific structures, thereby illuminating the cells.

AFRICA & THE MIDDLE EAST

ENGINEERING & INVENTION	WORLD EVENTS
1855 Swedish chemist Johan Lundström (1815–88) patents the safety match. **1855** Italian physicist Luigi Palmieri (1807–96) designs a seismograph, an instrument that detects and measures the strength of earthquakes. **1856** English steelmaker Henry Bessemer (1813–98) develops the Bessemer converter for making steel out of iron. **1857** English inventor Edward Cowper (1819–93) creates the hot-blast stove for blast furnaces and improves the steelmaking process. **1858** English engineer Charles Bright (1832–88) organizes the laying of the first transatlantic submarine telegraph cable. **1858** The S.S. *Great Eastern*, designed by English engineer Isambard Brunel (1806–59), is launched in England. At the time it is the world's largest ship. **1859** The first ironclad (wooden-hulled) warship, *La Gloire*, is built in France. **1859** Belgian engineer Étienne Lenoir (1822–1900) devises a gas-burning internal combustion engine.	**1857** An earthquake measuring an estimated 7 on the Richter scale partially destroys the city of Naples in Italy, killing thousands. **1859** The Battle of Solferino is fought between the Austrian Empire and an alliance of France and Italy. The aftermath of the bloody battle is witnessed by Swiss businessman Henri Dunant (1828–1910), who is inspired to found the International Red Cross. Dunant was later an important figure in the drafting of the first Geneva Convention.
1859 American industrialist George Pullman (1831–97) develops the Pullman sleeping car for use on railroads. **1859** American oil pioneer Edwin Drake (1819–80) drills the world's first productive oil well in Pennsylvania.	**1856** The worst railroad accident in the world to date occurs in Fort Washington, Pennsylvania. Around 60 passengers are killed when two trains collide on a single track line. **1858** In the *Dred Scott vs Sandford* case, the United States Supreme Court rules that Dred Scott (1799–1858), a slave, was not a citizen of the United States and that freeing him without the consent of his owner would be an unconstitutional confiscation of property. **1859** Abolitionist John Brown (1800–59) raids the armory at Harper's Ferry, Virginia, to arm a slave revolt; he is captured and hanged.

I often say that when you can measure what you are speaking about, and express it in numbers, you know something about it; but when you cannot express it in numbers, your knowledge is of a meagre and unsatisfactory kind; it may be the beginning of knowledge, but you have scarcely, in your thoughts, advanced to the stage of science, whatever the matter may be.

WILLIAM THOMSON, FIRST LORD KELVIN

NEANDERTAL MAN

Neandertals, also spelled Neanderthals, are an extinct type of hominid that lived about 130,000 to 30,000 years ago in Europe and Asia. In 1856 Neandertal remains were unearthed by quarrymen in a cave in the Neander Valley near Düsseldorf, Germany. Amateur naturalist Johann Carl Fuhlrott (1803–77) took the bones to Herman Schaaffhausen (1816–93), professor of anatomy at the University of Bonn. Together they announced their discovery in 1857. The term *Neandertal Man* was coined in 1863 by Anglo-Irish geologist William King (1809–86).

Early reconstructions of Neandertals portrayed them as stooping and apelike. It is now thought that their posture was upright and similar to modern humans. They did, however, have many anatomical differences from modern humans, such as larger skulls, sharper teeth, and stronger but not very dextrous hands.

Neandertals used fire, made wood, bone, and stone tools, and wore ornaments. They buried their dead in simple graves. Their diet was mainly carnivorous, and they lived in small groups.

A modern facial reconstruction based on a Neandertal skull

MENDEL AND GENETICS

A portrait of Mendel as Abbot of St. Thomas's Abbey, Brno. During his lifetime Mendel was known for his long-standing political disputes with the Austrian government, rather than his work on genetics.

TODAY GENETICS IS ONE OF THE MAJOR scientific disciplines. It has applications in agriculture, biology, medicine, and even law enforcement. But it had very humble beginnings in the garden of a remote monastery in Austria, where a monk named Gregor Mendel (1822–84) experimented by growing pea plants.

Gregor Mendel was born in Heinzendorf in Austrian Silesia (now Hyncice in the Czech Republic). He studied in college before entering the Augustinian order in 1843. By 1868 he was abbot of the monastery at Brünn (now Brno). He became interested in hybrids and began to breed pea plants in 1856. In the next six years he grew 30,000 plants, which he fertilized artificially by manually transferring pollen between flowers. For example, he crossed tall plants with short plants. He then counted the number of tall and short plants in the next and later generations. He found that all first-generation plants were tall, but that the second generation contained tall plants and short plants in the ratio of 3 to 1.

Mendel concluded that every plant receives two "factors" of inheritance, one from each parent. In the first generation of peas each plant receives one factor for tallness from the tall parent and one factor for shortness from the short parent. All the offspring are tall, since the tallness factor is dominant over the shortness factor (which is described as recessive). Recessive factors can, however, make themselves apparent when two occur in a single individual.

Mendel's Laws

These observations led Mendel to propose two laws. The law of segregation states that the two factors controlling each hereditary characteristic segregate and pass into separate germ cells (egg and sperm). The law of independent assortment states that the pairs of factors segregate independently of each other during the formation of germ cells. In 1865 Mendel reported his results to the Brünn Natural History Society and published them a year later in the society's journal. Nobody took much notice, but Mendel's interest continued. However, an increase in monasterial duties meant that science ceased to occupy the central position in his life.

Mendel's "factors" are now called alleles, which are alternative forms of a gene. In any one body cell of an organism there are two alleles of each gene, one inherited from each parent, which occupy the same place on a chromosome. Usually one allele is dominant and the other is recessive. A germ cell (gamete) —egg or sperm—has only one allele. When egg and sperm combine at fertilization, the two alleles come together in a new individual that inherits characteristics from each parent. The appearance of the new individual, however, depends on which characteristic (if any) is dominant.

In the 1890s, after Mendel's death, several European biologists independently studied inheritance in plants. In the Netherlands Dutch botanist Hugo de

The diagram shows how Mendel's laws predict the colors produced by crossing purple-flowered peas with white-flowered peas. Purple is dominant, and the first generation (known as F_1 phenotypes) produced by planting seeds from the cross are all purple. But when this generation is interbred, the second generation (F_2 phenotypes) has purple or white flowers in the ratio 3 to 1.

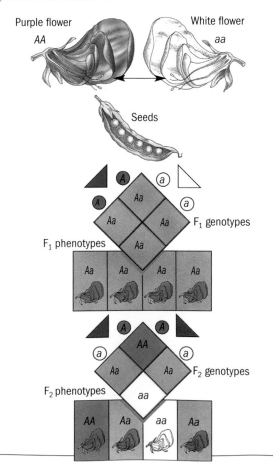

This early photograph of a large 19th century family group shows the clear similarities between parents and children as well as the variation in appearance among the children.

Vries (1848–1935) came up with results identical to Mendel's, and his accidental discovery of Mendel's obscure publication prompted him to announce his results in 1900. De Vries's publication in turn led German botanist Karl Correns (1864–1933) and Austrian botanist Erich von Tschermak-Seysenegg (1871–1962) to publish their observations, which also confirmed that Mendel's theories had been correct all those years before.

Heredity in Practice

The diagram on the opposite page shows the principles of heredity using pea plants (as Mendel did). Initially, a purple-flowered pea is crossed with a white-flowered pea. The seeds resulting from this cross are sown to produce first-generation hybrids, which have what biologists call the F_1 phenotype. (The phenotype is the appearance of a plant or animal that results from its genetic makeup, known as its genotype.) All of these plants have purple flowers.

This can be explained if it is assumed that the allele for purple (A) is dominant over the allele for white (a). If the F_1 generation is allowed to self-fertilize, and their seeds are planted, flowers of both colors are produced. But purple outnumbers white in the ratio of 3 to 1. This is because among the F_2 phenotypes one-quarter is AA and purple in color, two-quarters (one-half) are Aa and also purple (since A is dominant), and one-quarter is white (aa). White turns up only when two a recessives occur together.

Sometimes the gene for a characteristic is located on one of the sex chromosomes (in mammals they are X and Y). For example, a gene on the X chromosome prevents color blindness when functioning properly. If one allele is defective, the condition can develop. More males than females have this disorder, since they have only one X chromosome. In females, however, both alleles—one on each X chromosome—would need to malfunction before they developed the condition. The same applies with hemophilia.

This early photograph of a large 19th century family group shows the clear similarities between parents and children as well as the variation in appearance among the children.

KEY DATES

1856
Mendel begins experiments with pea plants

1865
Mendel reports to Brünn Natural History Society

1866
Mendel publishes his results

1900
De Vries, Correns, and Tschermak-Seysenegg confirm Mendel's findings

ASTRONOMY & MATH	BIOLOGY & MEDICINE	PHYSICAL SCIENCES

EUROPE

1860 English astronomer and inventor Warren de la Rue (1815–89) shows that prominences visible during a solar eclipse are a feature of the surface of the sun.

1862 Swedish astronomer and physicist Anders Ångström (1814–74) identifies hydrogen in the sun's atmosphere (using a spectroscope).

1862 German astronomer Friedrich Argelander (1799–1875) publishes *Bonner Durchmusterung* (Bonn Survey), a catalog of more than 324,000 stars.

1863 Italian Jesuit priest and astronomer Angelo Secchi (1818–78) begins a four-year study of the stars, leading to a system of classifying stars according to their spectral type that is still used today.

1860 The first fossil of *Archaeopteryx* (a prehistoric flying reptile with some birdlike features) is found in a German quarry.

1860 English nurse Florence Nightingale (1820–1910) establishes the world's first training school for nurses in London.

1861 German anatomist Max Schultze (1825–74) defines a cell as a nucleus surrounded by living protoplasm.

1862 English naturalist Henry Bates (1825–92) defines Batesian mimicry, in which a harmless animal gains protection from predators by mimicking the coloration of an animal that is dangerous.

1862 German physician Felix Hoppe-Seyler (1825–95) establishes the presence of hemoglobin, the red oxygen-carrying pigment in the blood.

1862 German botanist Julius von Sachs (1832–97) establishes that starch is produced in plants by photosynthesis.

1863 French physician Casimir-Joseph Davaine (1812–82) identifies the bacterium that causes anthrax.

1860 English chemist and physicist Michael Faraday (1791–1867) presents his paper "Pressure Melting Effect" to the Royal Society, describing an experiment in which he lowers the freezing point of water by applying pressure.

1860 German chemist Robert Bunsen (1811–99) and German physicist Gustav Kirchhoff (1824–87) develop a technique for analyzing substances by their spectra. Using the new technique, they discover the elements cesium and, a year later, rubidium.

1860 German chemist Johann Greiss (1829–88) identifies diazo compounds. He later develops synthetic azo dyes.

1861 Scottish chemist Thomas Graham (1805–69) coins the term *colloid* to distinguish those materials in aqueous solution that will not diffuse through a parchment membrane (e.g., starch) from those that will (crystalloids, such as salt).

1862 Belgian chemist Ernest Solvay (1838–1922) patents an industrial process for making soda (sodium carbonate) from chalk (calcium carbonate) and common salt (sodium chloride).

The eyelike markings on the wings of Caligo eurilochus *butterflies—here on a piece of lemon—are an example of Batesian mimicry, in which harmless animals adopt the markings of harmful ones.*

THE AMERICAS

1862 American astronomers Lewis Swift (1820–1913) and Horace Tuttle (1837–1923) discover comet Swift–Tuttle, which causes the annual Perseid meteor shower.

ASIA & OCEANIA

1861 Australian astronomer John Tebbutt (1834–1916) discovers the long-period Tebbutt's comet. The Earth passes through the comet's tail—the first time this has been observed.

AFRICA & THE MIDDLE EAST

HOW IT WORKS

Spectral Analysis

Robert Bunsen and Gustav Kirchhoff discovered new elements by analyzing their spectra. When a chemical element is heated strongly, electrons in its atoms "jump" to higher energy levels. When they fall back to their original levels, they give off light with characteristic wavelengths. In a spectrograph the wavelengths appear as colored lines (line spectra). Each spectrum has a unique pattern, like a fingerprint, and can be used to identify different elements.

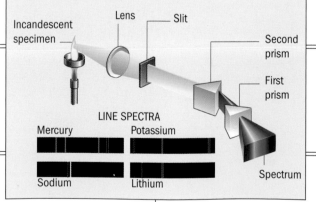

Incandescent specimen · Lens · Slit · Second prism · First prism · Spectrum

LINE SPECTRA

Mercury · Potassium · Sodium · Lithium

ENGINEERING & INVENTION	WORLD EVENTS
1860 H.M.S. *Warrior*, the world's first iron-hulled warship, is launched in England. It is designed by Scottish engineer John Russell (1808–82).	**1860** Italian patriot Giuseppe Garibaldi (1807–82) leads an uprising in southern Italy, initiating unification of the country in 1861.
1860 German botanist Julius von Sachs (1832–97) introduces hydroponics, a method of growing plants without soil but using water and chemical fertilizers.	**1861** The Russian serfs are emancipated.
1863 French chemist Louis Pasteur (1822–95) introduces pasteurization, a process that kills bacteria with heat. At first it is used for treating wine.	**1862** Otto von Bismarck (1815–98) becomes prime minister of Prussia.
1863 Scottish engineer Robert Fairlie (1831–85) invents the Fairlie articulated locomotive, designed specifically for narrow-gauge railroads with tight curves.	**1863** Britain and other European countries adopt a gold standard for their currencies.
1863 The world's first underground railroad, the Metropolitan Line, opens in London using steam-hauled trains.	**1864** Henri Dunant (1828–1910) establishes the Red Cross in Switzerland.
1863 Built by French engineer Simon Bourgeois, *Le Plongeur*, a 140-foot (42.6-m) compressed air-driven submarine, is launched in France.	
1864 French engineer Pierre Michaux (1813–83) makes the first pedal bicycle.	
1860 Designed by American engineer Montgomery Meigs (1816–92), the Cabin John Bridge, the world's longest masonry arch, is completed.	**1860** The Pony Express is established, delivering mail across the western United States.
1861 A telegraph line is built in the United States from Omaha, Nebraska, to Carson City, Nevada. It links to local networks, giving transcontinental coverage.	**1861** The American Civil War (1861–65) starts when Confederate forces attack Fort Sumter, South Carolina.
1862 American inventor and gunsmith Richard Gatling (1818–1903) patents a rapid-fire, ten-barrel machine gun.	**1862** The French try to set up a puppet empire in Mexico.
	1864 Paraguay goes to war against Argentina, Brazil, and Uruguay in the War of the Triple Alliance (1864–70).
1861 Scottish-born Australian James Harrison (1816–93) builds the world's first large-scale meat-freezing plant, in which meat is prepared for export to Britain.	**1860** Robert O'Hare Burke (ca 1820–61) and William John Wills (1834–61) finish the first overland crossing of Australia; however, both die on the return journey.

ALFRED NOBEL

Alfred Bernhard Nobel (1833–96) was a Swedish chemist remembered for the invention of dynamite and for endowing the funds to pay for the annual Nobel prizes. He was born near Stockholm, the son of an inventor and industrialist, and taught mainly by his father after the family moved to St. Petersburg, Russia, in 1842. From 1852 Nobel worked for his father, but bankruptcy forced them to move back to Sweden in 1863.

Nobel soon built a factory in Stockholm. He experimented with producing nitroglycerin—a powerful but volatile explosive, which could be detonated by mild physical shock—but the factory exploded in 1864, killing his brother Emil. He was ordered to move his factory to a more isolated location. The explosives were still highly unstable, and his new factory in Krümmel, Germany, was twice destroyed by explosions.

In 1867 Nobel patented dynamite, which he created by mixing inert absorbent powder with nitroglycerin. Dynamite was relatively safe to manufacture and use. It soon replaced unstable nitroglycerin in mining and railroad construction projects. In 1875 Nobel invented the even safer blasting gelatin, or gelignite.

These inventions and holdings in the petroleum industry earned Nobel a huge fortune, which he left to the Nobel Foundation. Each year the foundation awards cash prizes in the fields of chemistry, physics, physiology or medicine, literature, economics, and peace.

ASTRONOMY & MATH	BIOLOGY & MEDICINE	PHYSICAL SCIENCES

EUROPE

1866 English astronomer William Huggins (1824–1910) and English chemist William Miller (1817–70) discover the gaseous nature of some nebulas by studying their spectra.

1866 Italian astronomer Giovanni Schiaparelli (1835–1910) demonstrates that meteor showers are associated with the orbits of comets.

1866 French geologist Gabriel Daubrée (1814–96) suggests that the Earth's core is made of nickel–iron alloy.

1867 French astronomers Charles Wolf (1827–1918) and Georges Rayet (1839–1906) describe Wolf–Rayet stars. They are very hot stars that rapidly lose mass (as indicated by their irregular spectra).

1868 English astronomer William Huggins detects a Doppler shift (a shift to a longer wavelength) in the spectrum of the star Sirius and thereby demonstrates that the star is receding from Earth.

1865 Austrian monk Gregor Mendel (1822–84) formulates Mendel's laws of inheritance.

1865 German botanist Julius von Sachs (1832–97) identifies chloroplasts, the structures in green leaves that contain chlorophyll.

1865 French physician Jean Villemin (1827–92) discovers the infectious nature of tuberculosis and states that it can be transmitted by contact between humans and animals, as well as from one animal to another.

1866 German anatomist Max Schultze (1825–74) distinguishes between rods and cones in the retina of the eye.

1867 English surgeon Joseph Lister (1827–1912) introduces phenol (carbolic acid) as a disinfectant in the operating room.

1867 German physiologist Julius Cohnheim (1839–84) explains the role of white blood cells in inflammation (in helping to form pus).

1868 In a rock shelter in southwestern France French paleontologist Louis Lartet (1840–99) excavates fossils of Cro-Magnon man, the earliest type of modern man, *Homo sapiens*.

1865 Belgian chemist Jean Servais Stas (1813–91) devises the first modern table of atomic weights using oxygen as a standard (set at 16).

1865 German physicist Rudolf Clausius (1822–88) coins the term *entropy* as a measure of the extent to which the energy of a system is unavailable (increasing the entropy decreases the energy).

1865 German chemist Joseph Loschmidt (1821–95) introduces Loschmidt's number, which is the number of particles (atoms or molecules) of gas per unit volume of the gas.

1866 German physicist August Kundt (1839–94) develops a method for determining the speed of sound in gases.

1866 Russian chemist Aleksandr Butlerov (1828–86) synthesizes isobutane, a gaseous hydrocarbon that later plays an important role in refrigeration.

1868 French astronomer Pierre Janssen (1824–1907) detects a bright yellow line in the sun's spectrum during an eclipse; English astronomer Joseph Lockyer (1836–1920) names this element helium.

THE AMERICAS

It is hard now to realize the dread and apprehension with which formerly even minor surgical operations were regarded. The change in our ideas is due partly to the discovery of anesthetics and perhaps even more to Lister's work.

KING GEORGE V OF THE
UNITED KINGDOM (1927)

1867 American surgeon John Bobbs (1809–70) introduces a surgical procedure called cholecystotomy to remove gallstones.

1866 The metric system is introduced in the United States but is largely ignored.

A cable car on a street in San Francisco, California

ASIA & OCEANIA

AFRICA & THE MIDDLE EAST

1865 In China French missionary and naturalist Armand David (1826–1900) discovers a new species of deer, Père David's deer (*Elaphus davidianus*).

ENGINEERING & INVENTION	WORLD EVENTS

1865 German-born English metallurgist William Siemens (1823–83) and French engineer Pierre Martin (1824–1915) patent the open-hearth process for making steel.

1866 The Royal Aeronautical Society is founded in England.

1866 English engineer Robert Whitehead (1823–1905) builds a self-propelled torpedo, powered by compressed air.

1867 Swedish chemist Alfred Nobel (1833–96) patents dynamite in Britain. (U.S. patent 1868.)

1867 In Germany the first modern cantilever bridge, designed by German engineer Heinrich Gerber (1832–1912), is completed over the Main River.

1868 English inventor John Stringfellow (1799–1883) constructs a steam-powered model triplane.

Sticks of Alfred Nobel's explosive, dynamite

1865 Russian author Leo Tolstoy (1828–1910) publishes the first part of his great novel *War and Peace*, which he completes in 1869.

1867 Austria becomes Austria-Hungary with the establishment of the Dual Monarchy; already emperor of Austria, Francis Joseph I (r. 1848–1916) is now crowned king of Hungary at Budapest.

1867 The Italian revolutionary Giuseppe Garibaldi (1807–82) launches his third attempt to capture Rome for the nation of Italy but is defeated by the papal army and its French allies.

1867 German political philosopher Karl Marx (1818–83) publishes the first volume of his treatise on capitalist economics, entitled *Das Capital* (Capital).

1865 American locksmith Linus Yale (1821–68) perfects the cylinder lock and receives a second patent for it.

1865 American printer William Bullock (1813–67) invents the web-fed rotary printing press, which has the paper supplied to the press on a large roll.

1867 English-born American engineer Andrew Hallidie (1836–1900) invents the cable car, a type of streetcar that is hauled by a cable beneath the road surface.

1868 American engineer Eli Janney (1831–1912) invents the knuckle, or buckeye, coupler for railroad vehicles.

1868 American engineer George Westinghouse (1846–1914) designs the air brake for steam locomotives. It is soon adopted by railroads worldwide.

1865 Confederate forces under Robert E. Lee (1807–70) formally surrender at Appotomax Court House; the American Civil War (1861–65) comes to an end soon after.

1865 United States President Abraham Lincoln (1809–65) is assassinated by John Wilkes-Booth (1838–65).

1867 Russia sells Alaska to the United States for $7.2 million, about 2 cents an acre.

1867 The transportation of convicts from Britain to penal settlements in Australia comes to an end.

THE SUBMARINE

The first recorded attempt to build a submarine dates from about 1620, when Dutchman Cornelis Drebbel (1572–1633) covered a rowing boat with greased leather. It had waterproofed holes covered by leather flaps for the oars. In 1776 American student David Bushnell (ca 1742–1824) built a barrel-shaped, one-person submarine called the *Turtle*. It had a rudder, two hand-operated propellers (one for up-and-down movement and one for forward movement), and a hand ballast pump to allow the craft to surface.

A more successful submarine was built in France in 1801 by U.S. engineer Robert Fulton (1765–1815). The *Nautilus* was a slow, hand-cranked craft. At 21 feet (6.4 m) long, it could hold four people and enough air for three hours underwater. During the U.S. Civil War (1861–65), a replica of the submarine sank the Union ship *Housatonic* in Charleston Harbor, only to sink itself because its ram remained stuck in the ship's hull.

The first practical submarine, the U.S.S. *Holland*, was built in 1898. Designed by Irish-American John Holland (1840–1914), the craft used gas engines for surface propulsion and electric motors when submerged—a standard means of power for submarines until the launch of the nuclear-powered U.S.S. *Nautilus* in 1955.

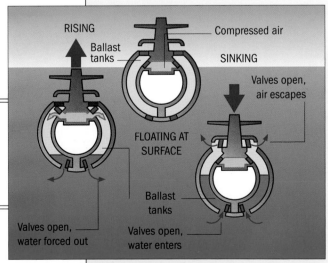

Submarines have twin hulls: the gap between the hulls holds water that acts as ballast to make the vessel rise or sink in the water.

ASTRONOMY & MATH

1870 English mathematician James Sylvester (1814–97) analyzes poetry mathematically in *The Laws of Verse*.

1872 German mathematician Richard Dedekind (1831–1916) publishes his theory of irrational numbers.

1872 The link between meteors and comets is reinforced when Hungarian astronomer E. Weiss predicts a meteor shower associated with a comet that had disappeared six years before. The shower occurs as predicted.

1872 Italian mathematician Luigi Cremona (1830–1903) introduces graphical statics, the use of graphical techniques to study forces in equilibrium.

BIOLOGY & MEDICINE

1869 Swiss pathologist Johann Miescher (1844–95) isolates deoxyribonucleic acid (DNA), which he calls *nuclein*.

1869 English scientist Francis Galton (1822–1911) publishes his book *Hereditary Genius*. It becomes the basis of eugenics—the now disproven belief that genetics can be utilized to improve the physical and mental makeup of the human species.

1869 Norwegian physician Armauer Hansen (1841–1912) identifies the bacterium that causes leprosy, which is also known as Hansen's disease.

1869 German pharmacologist Matthias Liebreich (1839–1908) introduces the use of chloral hydrate as a sedative drug.

1869 French surgeon Gustav Simon (1824–76) pioneers nephrectomy, an operation to remove a kidney that is diseased.

1872 English-born chemist Robert Chesebrough (1837–1933) patents the process of making petroleum jelly. It is sold as a soothing ointment under the name of Vaseline.

PHYSICAL SCIENCES

1869 Russian chemist Dmitri Mendeleev (1834–1907) compiles the first Periodic Table of chemical elements.

1869 Northern Irish chemist and physicist Thomas Andrews (1813–85) publishes the results of his experiments on the liquefaction of gases, including the critical temperature for carbon dioxide.

1870 German physicist Ernst Abbe (1840–1905) introduces the use of his condenser to provide strong, even illumination for microscopes.

1870 German chemist Rudolf Fittig (1835–1910) makes aromatic hydrocarbons by combining two molecules of a halogen compound in the presence of sodium metal. It is known as the Wurtz–Fittig reaction.

1871 Irish physicist George Stoney (1826–1911) observes that three lines in the hydrogen spectrum have wavelengths in a simple ratio to each other. This finding is to be significant in interpreting atomic structure.

1872 German chemist Eugen Baumann (1846–96) prepares PVC (polyvinyl chloride). Much later, it becomes an important plastic.

EUROPE

1869 American astronomer Charles Young (1834–1908) observes that during a solar eclipse the dark lines in the sun's spectrum brighten just before the eclipse is total.

1869 American meteorologist Cleveland Abbe (1836–1916) introduces the use of high-altitude balloons for studying the Earth's atmosphere.

1870 American astrophysicist Jonathan Lane (1819–80) publishes *On the Theoretical Temperature of the Sun*, in which he explains how gravitational contraction of gases in the sun caused it to heat up.

1872 American astronomer Henry Draper (1837–82) takes the first photograph of the spectrum of a star, Vega.

THE AMERICAS

1869 American chemist John Hyatt (1837–1920) makes celluloid. His discovery is independent of the method used earlier by English chemist Alexander Parkes (1813–90) in 1855.

A young man poses on a "penny-farthing" bicycle, invented by James Starley in 1871. The penny-farthing was rendered obsolete by Starley's nephew's chain-driven "safety bicycle," designed several years later.

ASIA & OCEANIA

AFRICA & THE MIDDLE EAST

ENGINEERING & INVENTION

1869 French engineer Pierre Michaux (1813–83) constructs a steam-powered motorcycle.

1871 English engineer Francis Wenham (1824–1908) constructs a wind tunnel for testing airplane wings. It employs a steam-driven fan.

1871 English inventor James Starley (1830–81) patents his "ordinary" bicycle with one large and one small wheel. It is nicknamed "penny-farthing" (a penny was a large coin and a farthing was a small coin).

1871 Belgian engineer Zénobe Gramme (1826–1901) markets a dynamo for heavy industrial use.

1869 The Union Pacific transcontinental railroad is completed.

1869 American engineer Thomas Edison (1847–1931) makes an improved ticker-tape machine.

1870 American engineer Lester Pelton (1829–1908) designs a new form of water turbine—the Pelton wheel impulse water turbine.

1871 American engineer Simon Ingersoll (1818–94) invents a pneumatic rock drill.

1872 American gunsmith Benjamin Hotchkiss (1826–1885) invents a revolving-barrel machine gun.

1869 The Suez Canal is completed by French engineer Ferdinand de Lesseps (1805–94) from original plans by Austrian engineer Alois Negrelli von Moldelbe (1799–1858).

WORLD EVENTS

1870 The Franco–Prussian War (1870–71) breaks out; Prussian forces invade France, defeat the French army at Sedan, and lay siege to Paris. Emperor Napoléon III (r. 1852–70) is taken prisoner, bringing the Second Empire to an end.

1870 The annexation of the Papal States means that the unification of Italy is almost complete; only the Vatican Palace and its immediate environs remain outside the new nation.

1871 Germany's Chancellor Otto von Bismarck (1815–98) declares Germany unified under William I, formerly king of Prussia but now emperor of the Second Reich (r. 1971–88).

1871 The Treaty of Frankfurt brings the Franco–Prussian War to an end. The French give up the disputed provinces of Alsace and Lorraine to Germany.

1872 The secret ballot is introduced for elections in the United Kingdom.

1869 French settlers and French-speaking native peoples in what is now Manitoba rise up against the Canadian Confederation in the Red River Rebellion.

1869 Susan B. Anthony (1820–1906) and Elizabeth Cady Stanton (1815–1902) found the National Women's Suffrage Association to campaign for women's suffrage (the right to vote) in the United States.

1870 The 15th Amendment to the United States Constitution is passed, giving African Americans the right to vote.

1871 The Great Chicago Fire destroys around 2,000 acres of the city of Chicago, leaving around 100,000 homeless.

1869 The sailing clipper *Thermopylae* completes its maiden voyage from London to Sydney in 63 days. The voyage marks the beginning of a period of high-profile races between the fast cargo ships bringing tea from China to Europe.

THE BUILDING OF THE SUEZ CANAL

Located in Egypt and opened in 1869, the Suez Canal provided a waterway between Europe and Asia. Prior to the canal's construction ships traveling between Europe and Asia had to circumnavigate Africa or transport their cargoes over land.

A canal was dug in antiquity but fell into disuse by the eighth century. In 1858 Ferdinand de Lesseps, a French diplomat based in Cairo, was given the concession by the Viceroy of Egypt, Sa'id Pasha (1822–63), to create the Suez Canal Company and construct a canal following the plans made by Austrian engineer Alois Negrelli. The excavation of the canal took 11 years, using the forced labor of up to 30,000 Egyptian workers.

The single-lane canal is around 100 miles (160 km) long. It incorporates several lakes and links the Mediterranean Sea at Port Said to the Gulf of Suez on the Red Sea. The canal has no locks since the terrain is flat.

The canal opened on November 17, 1869. Originally, its width was 200 feet (61 m) with a maximum depth of 24 feet (7.3m). (The canal has since been widened and deepened.) The passage of a ship takes up to 16 hours, traveling at about 8 knots (15 km) per hour. Today about 7.5 percent of the world's sea trade passes through the canal.

ASTRONOMY & MATH	BIOLOGY & MEDICINE	PHYSICAL SCIENCES

EUROPE

1873 French mathematician Charles Hermite (1822–1901) proves that *e* (the base of natural logarithms) is a transcendental number (an irrational number that cannot be represented by an equation in algebra).

1873 English mathematician William Shanks (1812–82) calculates π (pi) to 707 decimal places.

1873 English astronomer Richard Proctor (1837–88) proposes that craters on the moon were caused by the impact of meteorites, not by volcanoes as previously thought.

1874 French astronomer Jérôme Coggia (1849–1919) discovers Coggia's comet. It approaches to within 24,900 miles (40,000 km) of Earth, but will not return for more than 13,500 years.

1874 Russian-born German mathematician Georg Cantor (1845–1918) introduces the theory of transfinite numbers to mathematics.

1875 French astronomer Jules Violle (1841–1923) makes the first high-altitude measurement of the solar constant—the total amount of the sun's energy that reaches the top of the Earth's atmosphere.

1873 Italian physician Camillo Golgi (1844–1926) discovers the "black reaction," a new technique for staining nervous tissue with silver nitrate. Known as Golgi staining, it enables an entire nerve-cell body and its processes to be observed.

1873 Austrian physician Josef Breuer (1842–1925) discovers the sensory function of the semicircular canals in the ear, which help maintain balance.

1875 German physicians Wilhelm Erb (1840–1921) and Carl Westphal (1833–90) discover the knee-jerk reflex. This reflex gives a reaction to a stimulus without the involvement of the brain; it is sometimes used by physicians as a diagnostic aid.

1876 The gray squirrel (*Sciurus carolinensis*) is introduced into Britain from North America. It displaces the native red squirrels (*Sciurus vulgaris*).

1876 Polish-born German botanist Eduard Strasburger (1844–1912) describes mitosis, the process of cell division that results in two new identical cells. Belgian zoologist Edouard van Beneden (1846–1910) discovers centrosomes, the pair of structures that move apart as mitosis begins.

1873 Scottish physicist James Clerk Maxwell (1831–79) publishes *Electricity and Magnetism*, containing his electromagnetic theory of light—that light is a form of electromagnetic radiation (as also are radio waves and x-rays).

1873 Dutch physicist Johannes Van der Waals (1837–1923) derives Van der Waals' equation, which shows the relationship between the pressure and volume of a real gas (previous gas equations applied only to ideal, or perfect, gases).

1874 In his paper "On the Physical Units of Nature" Irish physicist George Stoney (1826–1911) coins the term *electrine* for the fundmental unit of electricity. He later (in 1891) changes it to *electron*.

1874 German chemist Othmar Zeidler synthesizes DDT (dichlorodiphenyl-trichloroethane), but does not realize its value as an insecticide.

1874 German chemist Ferdinand Tiemann (1848–99) synthesizes vanillin (the active taste ingredient in vanilla), the first artificial flavoring.

THE AMERICAS

1873 Canadian physician William Osler (1849–1919) discovers blood platelets (thrombocytes), small cells that are important in blood clotting.

1874 American physician Andrew Still (1828–1913) founds osteopathy, a system of medicine that mainly uses manipulation of bones and joints to treat disorders.

1876 American chemist and mathematical physicist J. Willard Gibbs (1839–1903) introduces the concept of chemical potential, which is important in determining whether a chemical reaction will take place.

ASIA & OCEANIA

Mr. Watson—Come here—I want to see you.

ALEXANDER GRAHAM BELL
FIRST WORDS SPOKEN ON A TELEPHONE, 1876

AFRICA & THE MIDDLE EAST

The European red squirrel has disappeared in many parts of Europe, replaced by the American gray squirrel.

ENGINEERING & INVENTION

1873 French engineer Amédée Bollée (1844–1917) constructs a steam-powered car.

1874 French engineer Jean-Maurice Baudot (1845–1903) patents a five-unit telegraph code, which later supplants Morse Code in continental Europe.

1875 A safe loading level for ships, known as the Plimsoll line, is introduced by an Act of the British Parliament. It becomes internationally recognized.

1876 German engineer Karl von Linde (1842–1934) develops the first practical refrigerator, which uses ammonia as a coolant.

1876 German engineer Nikolaus Otto (1832–91) builds a four-stroke internal combustion engine fueled by coal gas.

1876 Russian engineer Pavel Jablochkoff (1847–94) invents a self-adjusting arc lamp, known as an "electric candle."

1874 The three-arch St. Louis Mississippi Bridge is built, designed by U.S. engineer James Eads (1820–87).

1875 Steam trains begin to run on an elevated railroad in New York City.

1876 Scottish-born American engineer Alexander Graham Bell (1847–1922) patents the telephone.

1876 American librarian Melvil Dewey (1851–1931) introduces the Dewey Decimal Classification system for cataloging library books.

WORLD EVENTS

1874 The first Impressionist exhibition is held in France. Claude Monet's (1840–1926) painting "Impression: Sunrise" gives the style its name, which was originally intended as a criticism.

1875 Rebellion breaks out in Bosnia against Ottoman rule. In Bulgaria the next year a similar uprising is brutally suppressed by the Ottoman army.

1875 A British polar expedition fails to reach the North Pole but succeeds in gathering scientific information and creating public interest in polar exploration, which will peak during the "Race for the Pole" at the end of the century.

1876 German composer Richard Wagner (1813–83) produces the complete *Ring Cycle* of operas for the first time.

1876 A new constitution restores the Spanish monarchy.

1876 The Sioux army, led by Sitting Bull (ca 1831–90), defeat the U.S. forces led by General George Custer (1839–76) at the Battle of the Little Bighorn.

1876 The Molly Maguires, a violent workers' rights movement in the Pennsylvania coalfields, is broken up by the execution of ten of its leaders.

THE PERIODIC TABLE

By 1869, following discoveries using the new techniques of electrolysis and spectroscopy, there were 63 known chemical elements. They were the building blocks from which, in that year, Dmitri Mendeleev (1834–1907) constructed his famous periodic table.

Wishing to find some order in the apparent jumble of chemical elements, Mendeleev wrote the name of each on a card and then arranged the elements in order of increasing atomic weight (the average mass of each atom of the element). He found that if he started a new row of cards every eighth element, those with similar chemical properties fell one above the other in columns. Looking at the rows, he saw that properties tended to recur along each row—the properties possessed what he called "periodicity." He named his new grid the periodic table and even included additional "missing" elements that were still to be discovered. He predicted the chemical and physical properties of these elements, such as their atomic weights and melting points.

Mendeleev could not explain the reason for the periodicity of the elements. That explanation had to wait until scientists developed an understanding of the structure of atoms.

Today's periodic table contains about 50 more elements than in Mendeleev's time. They are arranged in order of their atomic numbers in seven horizontal "periods" of varying length. Two very long series of 14 elements each—the lanthanides following lanthanum (57) and the actinides following actinium (89)—are shown in separate lines at the foot of the table.

ASTRONOMY & MATH	BIOLOGY & MEDICINE	PHYSICAL SCIENCES

EUROPE

1877 Italian astronomer Giovanni Schiaparelli (1835–1910) reports the existence of "channels" on the surface of Mars, but his Italian word *canali* is mistranslated as "canal" and starts a long-standing argument.

1878 German astronomer Johann Schmidt (1825–84) publishes the last detailed map of the moon based on visual observation, hand-drawn by German astronomer Wilhelm Lohrmann (1796–1840).

1879 English astronomer George Darwin (1845–1912) suggests that the moon formed from crustal material flung off by the rapidly rotating Earth, with the moon moving gradually farther away as the Earth slowed down. The theory has been discredited only in the last 50 years. Currently the moon is thought to have formed after an Earth–asteroid collision.

1880 Scottish astronomer George Forbes (1849–1936) predicts the existence of "Planet X" orbiting beyond Uranus. The planet Pluto was found in 1930.

1877 German bacteriologist Robert Koch (1843–1910) develops a method of staining bacteria (in order to study them through a microscope).

1877 German physiologist Wilhelm Kühne (1837–1900) suggests the name *enzyme* for a protein that acts as a catalyst in biochemical reactions.

1878 French physiologist Paul Bert (1833–86) demonstrates that nitrogen dissolved in the blood is the cause of "the bends" (decompression sickness), an illness suffered by divers and miners associated with significant drops in air pressure.

1879 Scottish surgeon William MacEwen (1848–1924) performs the first successful operation for the removal of a brain tumor.

1880 French parasitologist Alphonse Laveran (1845–1922) discovers the microorganism (a plasmodium) that causes malaria.

1880 French chemist Louis Pasteur (1822–95) identifies the *Streptococcus* bacterium.

1880 German bacteriologist Karl Eberth (1835–1926) discovers the bacterium that causes typhoid fever.

1877 French chemist Charles Friedel (1832–99) and U.S. colleague James Crafts (1839–1917) describe the Friedel–Crafts reaction, a method of introducing an alkyl group (such as methyl) into a benzene ring using an alkyl halide (such as methyl chloride) and a catalyst. The reaction becomes extremely important in organic chemistry synthesis.

1877 English physicist John Strutt, Lord Rayleigh (1842–1919), explains the nature of sound waves as alternate regions of high and low pressure in the air or another medium.

1878 German chemist Viktor Meyer (1848–97) identifies oximes, organic compounds characterized by the bivalent grouping C=NOH.

1879 Swedish chemist Per Cleve (1840–1905) discovers holmium and thulium. French chemist Paul Lecoq de Boisbaudran (1838–1912) discovers samarium.

1880 French physical chemist Pierre Curie (1859–1906) discovers the piezoelectric effect, which is the production of a voltage in a crystal that is under a mechanical stress.

THE AMERICAS

1877 American astronomer Asaph Hall (1829–1907) discovers Phobos and Deimos, the two moons of Mars.

1879 American chemists Ira Remsen (1846–1927) and Constantine Fahlberg (1850–1910) discover saccharin, an artificial sweetener 2,000 times sweeter than sugar.

1879 American physicist Edwin Hall (1855–1938) observes the Hall effect, which is the production of a voltage across a conductor through which a current is flowing when it is placed in a magnetic field.

ASIA & OCEANIA

AFRICA & THE MIDDLE EAST

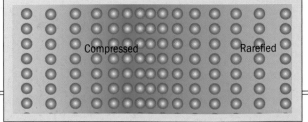

INSIDE STORY

Sound Waves

Sound waves are made by the vibration of an object or the air itself. When sound radiates out from a source, air does not move away from the source. Instead, the molecules in the air vibrate back and forth. Where the molecules are squeezed closer together, they are said to be compressed. Where they move apart, they are described as rarefied. The movement of the sound wave is the movement of this pattern of crowding and spreading out.

Compressed   Rarefied

Aviation pioneer Otto Lilienthal pilots one of his unpowered gliders. He steered by shifting his weight, as in a modern hang-glider.

ENGINEERING & INVENTION	WORLD EVENTS	THOMAS EDISON

1877 English physicist Joseph Swan (1828–1914) and American Thomas Alva Edison (1847–1931) develop the first electric light bulbs, demonstrated in 1878 (Swan) and 1879 (Edison).

1877 Swedish engineer Carl de Laval (1845–1913) devises a centrifugal cream separator, the first practical application of the centrifuge.

1877 German aeronautical pioneer Otto Lilienthal (1848–96) builds his first model glider.

1879 English metallurgist Sidney Thomas (1850–85) and his cousin Percy Gilchrist (1851–1935) develop the basic (Gilchrist–Thomas) steelmaking process.

1879 English inventor Henry Lawson invents a chain driven bicycle, which he calls the bicyclette. It retains a number of features from the penny-farthing, such as the large front wheel, and is not a success.

1877 An explosion caused by firedamp at a coal mine at Ballantyre, Scotland, kills more than 200 miners.

1877 Russia intervenes in the Balkans in support of local Slavs (Serbs and Montenegrins) rising against Ottoman rule. Britain and Austria ally to oppose Russian expansion in the region. A year later, a military standoff compels Russia to back down. The Berlin peace conference confirms the independence of Serbia, Romania, and Montenegro; Austria occupies Bosnia.

Edison's phonograph used grooves etched into a wax cylinder to reproduce sound.

1877 American engineer Ephraim Shay (1839–1916) builds a geared steam locomotive, particularly suited to the steep grades on logging railroads.

1877 Thomas Alva Edison and Frenchman Charles Cros (1842–88) independently invent the phonograph.

1878 English-born American inventor David Hughes (1831–1900) devises the carbon microphone.

1879 American inventor James Ritty (1836–1918) patents the cash register.

1877 Large-scale labor unrest breaks out in the United States, with railroad strikes and riots.

1877 In the "Compromise of 1877" the disputed 1876 presidential election is resolved when the Democrats agree to concede defeat in exchange for the cessation of Reconstruction Republicans' attempts to reform and integrate the Southern states.

1879 The first shipment of frozen meat is sent to England from Australia on board S.S. *Strathleven*. The trip lasts two months.

1879 The Zulu War breaks out in South Africa; British forces suffer a crushing defeat at Isandhlwana. The defeat of a modern British regiment by a Zulu force armed with spears and clubs shocks the colonial powers of the time.

THOMAS EDISON

Thomas Alva Edison is America's most famous inventor. He was born in Milan, Ohio, in 1847. A childhood illness delayed his schooling and left him partially deaf. Edison's curiosity made him a poor student as a young man and later an easily distracted employee. After training as a telegraph operator, Edison patented a number of telegraph-related inventions, such as the quadruplex telegraph and an improved ticker-tape machine.

Many of Edison's initial inventions were successful, and he made a considerable amount of money from them. For example, the Automatic Telegraph Company paid him $40,000 for a machine that transmitted 500 words per minute. Using the money gained from this and other inventions Edison moved to Menlo Park, 24 miles (39 km) from New York in 1876, where he built what he called an "inventions factory" that employed 50 technicians. Edison's Menlo Park laboratory was a commercial research facility in which scientists and engineers developed new technology.

At Menlo Park, Edison developed his most successful inventions. In 1877 he invented the phonograph as a dictating machine for business use. Edison went on to invent a megaphone, the kinetoscope (a type of movie projector), and a storage battery for a planned electric car. The light bulb, patented in 1879, proved his most enduring creation. The direct current electrical transmission method he developed to power his bulbs ultimately lost "the war of the currents" to alternating current systems developed by George Westinghouse (1846–1914) and Nikola Tesla (1856–1943).

GERMS AND DISEASE

URING THE MIDDLE OF THE 19TH CENTURY scientists made the discovery that most diseases were caused by germs (microscopic bacteria or fungi) and not by "evil spirits" or "bad air," as previously assumed. With improved microscopes and new laboratory techniques, they set about tracking down these sometimes deadly microorganisms.

As early as 1546 Italian physician Girolamo Fracastoro (ca 1478–1553), in his book *De Contagione et Contagiosis Morbis* (On Contagion and Contagious Diseases), suggested that germs are the cause of dis-

A view of bacterial cells multiplying. These cells have been stained with a special dye to make them easier to see.

ease. Nobody took much notice, even after 1676, when Dutch scientist Antonie van Leeuwenhoek (1632–1723) first saw bacteria through a homemade microscope. (They were from his own mouth and were probably not disease-carrying.)

Then in 1840 German pathologist Jacob Henle (1809–85) put forward the idea that infection is caused by parasitic organisms, the so-called germ theory of disease, which was later proposed independently by French chemist Louis Pasteur (1822–95). In 1877 German bacteriologist Robert Koch (1843–1910) announced that bacteria could be stained to

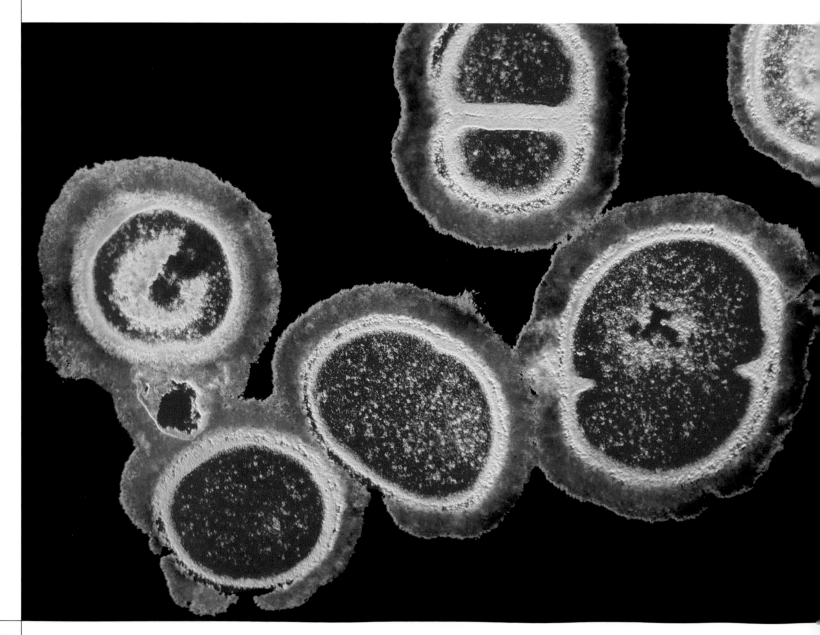

make them easier to study under a microscope. Seven years later Danish physician Hans Gram (1853–1938) extended this idea as a means of classifying bacteria, which since then have been dubbed either Gram-positive or Gram-negative, depending on their capacity to absorb a special stain. Bacteriologists also classify bacteria according to their shapes: coccus (round), bacillus (oval), spirochete (spiral), and so on.

Bacterial Discoveries

Once biologists knew what bacteria looked like, the hunt was on. The scientists who handled cultures of infectious diseases often put themselves at great risk, but results came quite quickly. In 1880 German bacteriologist Karl Eberth (1835–1926) found the bacillus that causes typhoid. In 1882 German bacteriologist Robert Koch found the bacterium that causes tuberculosis, and Germans Friedrich Löffler (1852–1915) and Wilhelm Schütz (1839–1920) identified the cause of the animal disease glanders. Later, in 1897 Danish veterinarian Bernhard Bang (1848–1932) discovered a bacillus that causes spontaneous abortion in cattle, and the Japanese bacteriologist Kiyoshi Shiga (1871–1957) found the cause of endemic dysentery.

Bacteria are not the only parasitic microorganisms to cause human diseases. Protozoans, for example, include the trypanosomes that cause sleeping sickness and Chagas' disease, the amoebas that result in amoebic dysentery, and the *Plasmodium* parasite responsible for malaria. Some microscopic fungi produce diseases that affect the skin or lungs. Most of these microorganisms were tracked down by 19th-century microbiologists.

In 1897 Dutch microbiologist Martinus Beijerinck (1851–1931) demonstrated that the microorganism that causes tobacco mosaic disease escapes through a filter that normally traps bacteria. He had discovered the

French physician Louis Pasteur holds the rabbits that he used for many of his early tests on vaccines. Pasteur confirmed the germ theory of disease and created the first vaccine for rabies.

The various common shapes of bacteria are: monococcus (1), diplococcus (2), staphylococcus (3), vibrio (4), streptococcus (5), spirillum (6), spirochete (7), and bacillus (8).

first virus. A year later the virus that causes foot-and-mouth disease in cattle was discovered. Since then viruses have been found to be responsible for many diseases in humans, including yellow fever, influenza, polio, measles, and AIDS (acquired immune deficiency syndrome). Almost as fast as the bacteriologists found the bacteria that cause diseases, they managed to develop vaccines against them, so that people could be vaccinated and gain immunity. Vaccines for viral diseases proved more difficult but now exist for all the disorders named above except AIDS.

ASTRONOMY & MATH	BIOLOGY & MEDICINE	PHYSICAL SCIENCES

EUROPE

1881 English mathematician John Venn (1834–1923) publishes *Symbolic Logic*, in which he introduces his ideas on logical relationships and develops Venn diagrams.

1884 German astronomer Max Wolf (1863–1932) discovers Wolf's comet, with an orbital period of only seven years.

1882 French anthropologist Alphonse Bertillon (1853–1914) develops the Bertillon system, which uses bodily measurements, physical descriptions, and photographs as a means of identifying criminals.

1882 German bacteriologist Robert Koch (1843–1910) discovers the bacterium that causes tuberculosis. A year later he discovers the bacterium that causes cholera.

1883 Swiss surgeon Emil Kocher (1841–1917) discovers the role of the thyroid gland in myxedema (goiter), and a year later German physiologist Moritz Schiff (1823–96) uses thyroid extract as a treatment for the disorder.

1884 German pathologist Edwin Klebs (1834–1913) and bacteriologist Friedrich Löffler (1852–1915) discover the microorganism that causes diphtheria (*Corynebacterium diphtheriae*).

1884 Danish physician Hans Gram (1853–1938) introduces a method of classifying bacteria by staining them.

1884 German bacteriologist Georg Gaffky (1850–1918) rediscovers the bacterium (*Salmonella typhi*) that causes typhoid fever.

1881 German scientist Hermann von Helmholtz (1821–94) demonstrates that hydrogen atoms have their electric charges in whole-number portions, implying that there is a unit of electrical charge (the charge has a finite minimum value).

1881 English physicist J. J. Thomson (1856–1940) uses Maxwell's equations of 1864 to predict that an object's mass changes when it becomes electrically charged (the concept of electromagnetic mass).

1882 German chemist Viktor Meyer (1848–97) discovers thiophene, an aromatic organic compound whose molecules consist of a ring of four carbon atoms and one sulfur atom. It later finds use as a solvent.

1883 Northern Irish engineer Osborne Reynolds (1842–1912) establishes the Reynolds number, which predicts how fluids will flow through pipes (e.g., whether or not the flow will be turbulent), enabling engineers to scale up models to design prototype machines.

1884 Swedish physical chemist Svante Arrhenius (1859–1927) begins to study the dissociation (splitting up) of electrolytes into ions in solution.

THE AMERICAS

1881 American astronomer Samuel Langley (1834–1906) makes a bolometer, a sensitive temperature-measuring device with which he measures the sun's radiation.

1881 American chemist and mathematical physicist J. Willard Gibbs (1839–1903) introduces a system of three-dimensional vectors.

1881 American astronomer Henry Draper (1837–82) and, a year later, Scottish astronomer David Gill (1843–1914) take the first photographs of comets.

1882 American physicist Albert Michelson (1852–1931) publishes his first calculation of the speed of light as 186,320 miles (299,853 km) per second. It is within 0.02 percent of the correct value and remained the most accurate measurement until Michelson improved on it in 1926.

ASIA & OCEANIA

German doctor Robert Koch (right), along with his contemporary French scientist Louis Pasteur, isolated the causes of many infectious diseases.

1883 Mount Krakatoa, an active volcano in Indonesia, erupts. The explosion is heard as far away as Perth, western Australia.

AFRICA & THE MIDDLE EAST

1883 The world's last quagga (an African animal resembling a zebra) dies in the Amsterdam Zoo.

ENGINEERING & INVENTION

1881 French engineer Charles Lartigue (1834–1907) constructs a steam-powered monorail railroad in Algeria. His design is also used for the monorail from Listowel to Ballybunion in Ireland, which opens in 1886.

1882 German engineer Werner von Siemens (1816–92) builds an electric trolleycar.

1883 Belgian engineer Étienne Lenoir (1822–1900) invents the spark plug (for internal combustion engines).

1884 American-born English inventor Hiram Maxim (1840–1916) makes the first fully automatic machine gun.

1884 English engineer Charles Parsons (1854–1931) develops a multistage steam turbine. It is used initially for powering boats.

1882 The first steam-powered electricity-generating plant in the United States, designed by American engineer Thomas Edison (1847–1931), opens on Pearl Street, New York City.

1884 American engineer Frank Sprague (1857–1934) forms the Sprague Electric Railway and Motor Company.

1884 German-born American inventor Ottmar Mergenthaler (1854–99) invents the linotype machine, which casts a whole line of type at once.

WORLD EVENTS

1881 Reforming Russian Tsar Alexander II (r. 1855–81) is assassinated by revolutionaries. He is succeeded by his reactionary and dictatorial son, Alexander III (1881–94).

1881 Romania becomes a kingdom, ruled by Carol I (r. 1881–1914).

1882 In the Phoenix Park Murders Britain's chief secretary for Ireland and his undersecretary are assassinated in Dublin by Irish nationalists (Fenians).

1883 Germany, Austro-Hungary, and Italy form the Triple Alliance.

1884 At the Berlin Conference European powers divide Africa into spheres of influence.

Inventor Hiram Maxim demonstrates his machine gun.

1881 James Garfield (1831–81) is assassinated by a disgruntled and probably insane campaign worker after less than a year as President of the United States.

1882 The Chinese exclusion act severely restricts Chinese immigration into the United States. Follow-up legislation will effectively end the immigration from eastern Asia.

1883 Chile emerges victorious from the War of the Pacific (1879–83), winning territory from Peru and all of Bolivia's coastal lands.

1882 The Indian Education Commission is established by Lord Ripon (1827–1909) to find ways of extending educational opportunities for Indian children.

1881 The First Boer War (1880–81) concludes with a British defeat at the battle of Majuba Hill. Britain concedes autonomy to Transvaal.

THE INTERNAL COMBUSTION ENGINE

In an internal combustion engine, fuel is burnt in a combustion chamber, causing the expansion of gases in the chamber that directly applies force to a movable part of the engine, such as a piston. This type of engine was devised by Belgian engineer Étienne Lenoir (1822–1900) in 1859 and improved by German engineer Nikolaus Otto (1832–91), who patented a coal-gas engine that worked in four stages, or strokes, in 1876.

In 1879, German engineer Karl Benz (1844–1929) made a two-stroke engine. It was lighter than a four-stroke engine, but less efficient. Benz and German engineer Gottlieb Daimler (1834–1900) independently made the first practical gasoline-burning internal combustion engines in 1885, heralding the age of the motor car.

Rudolf Diesel (1858–1913) designed the diesel engine in 1892, in which the compression cycle spontaneously ignites the fuel. Diesel engines are more efficient and cope better with moisture, making them ideal boat engines.

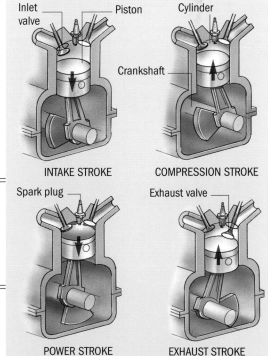

The stages of the four-stroke engine

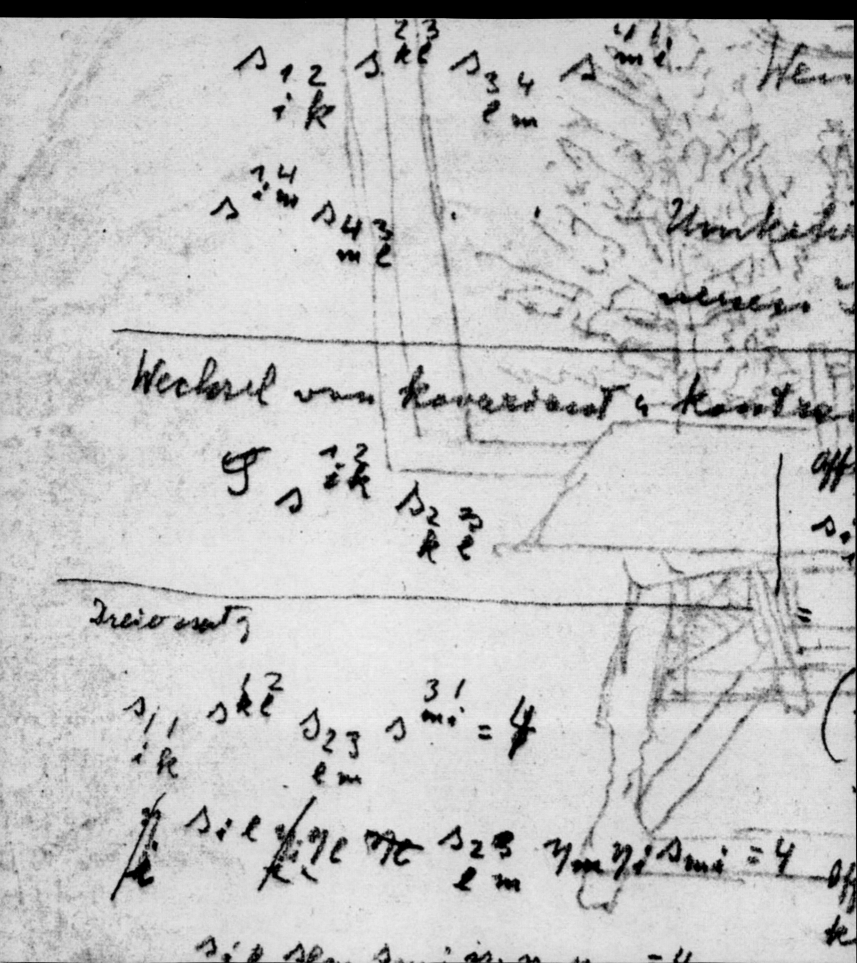

EVER SINCE AMERICAN FOUNDER AND SCIENTIST BENJAMIN FRANKLIN (1706–90) flew his kite in a thunderstorm in the 18th century, scientists had investigated the nature of electricity in order to better exploit this mysterious power. Eventually they established that static electricity is an accumulation of electric charges on an object, while current electricity is a flow of charges along a conductor such as a copper wire. Then in 1897 Cambridge University physicist J. J. Thomson (1871–1937) discovered the electron. The electron, a tiny negatively charged particle, is an essential part of all atoms and the elusive carrier of electric charge. Thomson's breakthrough was followed by the discovery by New Zealand-born Ernest Rutherford—who moved to Cambridge to work with Thomson—of the positively charged proton and predicting the existence of the uncharged neutron, which together nestle in the nuclei of nearly all atoms.

The discovery of the electron gave rise to a new branch of science, dubbed "electronics" in 1910. It began with the invention of radio, a method of transmitting radio waves—discovered by German physicist Heinrich Hertz (1857–94) in 1887—through the air. (The existing telegraph and the telephone were both restricted to places that were linked by wires.) In 1894 English physicist Oliver Hodge (1851–1940) used radio waves to transmit messages in Morse code; within less than a decade, Italian physicist Guglielmo Marconi (1874–1937) was transmitting Morse code messages from Cornwall in England, across the Atlantic Ocean, to Newfoundland in Canada. The first transmissions of music and human speech were made in 1906 by Canadian-born electrical engineer Reginald Fessenden (1866–1932) from a radio station in Massachusetts. Radios themselves meanwhile improved with the invention of electron tubes and the various circuits that employed them.

Another field that saw major advances was transportation. Great airships, the most famous being the Zeppelin—named for its designer Count Ferdinand von Zeppelin (1838–1917)—conquered the skies and established regular routes between continents. Their heyday did not last long. On a December day in 1093 U.S. brothers Wilbur (1867–1912) and Orville Wright (1871–1948) made the first heavier-than-air flight in North Carolina. Their biplane's longest flight that day lasted for just under a minute and covered 300 yards (280 m), but it opened up a new world of possibilities.

An illustrated French postcard from the early 1900s celebrates the achievement of French aristocrat Comte de Lambert, who in 1909 used a Wright brothers' biplane to circle 300 feet (90 m) above the Eiffel Tower, claiming an altitude record of 1,300 feet (396 m).

Financiers and city officials take the first train to run on New York City's subway, which opened on October 27, 1904. The subway used electric trains and served 28 stations.

On the railroads, meanwhile, steam-powered trains continued to rule, although the first electric trains were soon being developed. The first line to use electric trains was the City and South London Railway, a commuter subway that opened in 1890. The New York City subway followed in 1904.

Road transportation was also revolutionized when engineers began building motor cars. Earlier models used steam engines, but with the development of the internal combustion engine more powerful and efficient vehicles could be made. German engineers Karl Benz (1844–1929) and Gottleib Daimler (1834–1900) and U.S. brothers Charles (1861–1938) and Frank Duryea (1869–1967) all produced gasoline-engined cars in the 1890s. But it was U.S. industrialist Henry Ford (1863–1947) who introduced mass-production techniques to car manufacturing at the start of the 20th century and made automobiles a part of everyday life. Sea travel improved, too, when in 1914 completion of the Panama Canal cut a total of 6,000 miles (9,650 km) off the voyage by sea between ports on the east and west coasts of America.

	1885	1889	1893	1897	1901
EUROPE	**1885** Austrian neurologist Sigmund Freud develops psychoanalysis. **1885** French scientist Louis Pasteur produces a rabies vaccine. **1886** German engineer Gottlieb Daimler makes a four-wheel car. **1887** German physicist Heinrich Hertz detects radio waves. **1887** Scottish inventor John Dunlop invents the pneumatic tire for bicycles.	**1889** The Eiffel Tower is completed in Paris. **1889** English inventor William Friese-Greene builds a motion-picture camera. **1891** German astronomer Max Wolf uses photography to discover an asteroid. **1891** Dutch anthropologist Eugène Dubois discovers fossils of human ancestor dubbed "Java man." **1891** English physicist John Poynting calculates the value of the gravitational constant. **1892** English scientist Francis Galton discovers that each human has unique fingerprints. **1892** Scottish physician James Dewar invents the vacuum bottle.	**1893** German inventor Rudolph Diesel builds the first compression–ignition (diesel) engine. **1893** French brothers Auguste and Louis Lumière make a motion-picture camera. **1895** German physicist Wilhelm Röntgen takes the first x-ray. **1896** French physicist Henri Becquerel discovers radioactivity. **1896** New Zealand-born English physicist Ernest Rutherford describes alpha and beta particles. **1896** Swedish physical chemist Svante Arrhenius proposes a link between the levels of carbon dioxide in the atmosphere and global temperatures.	**1897** Dutch botanist Martinus Beijirinck coins the term *virus*. **1897** German physicist Ferdinand Braun develops the cathode-ray tube. **1897** English physicist J. J. Thompson identifies the electron. **1898** English physician Ronald Ross discovers *Plasmodium*, the protozoal cause of malaria. **1900** German physicist Max Planck proposes quantum theory. **1900** The rigid airship *LZ-1*, designed by German engineer Graf Ferdinand von Zeppelin, makes its maiden flight. **1900** German chemist Friedrich Ernst Dorn discovers radon.	**1901** Italian physicist Guglielmo Marconi makes the first transatlantic radio broadcast. **1902** English physiologists Ernest Starling and William Bayliss coin the term *hormone* to describe secretin. **1903** Russian physiologist Ivan Pavlov describes the conditioned reflex. **1903** German surgeon Georg Perthes first uses x-rays to treat cancerous tumors. **1903** Russian rocket pioneer Konstantin Tsiolkovsky proposes the first practical theory of rocket propulsion. **1904** J. J. Thomson puts forward his model of the atom.
THE AMERICAS	**1885** American neurologist James Corning introduces spinal (epidural) anesthesia. **1885** American electrical engineer William Stanley develops the transformer. **1885** American architect William Jenney completes a steel-framed building in Chicago, the world's first skyscraper. **1886** American physician Reginald Fitz advocates appendectomy as a treatment for appendicitis.	**1889** American astronomer Edward Barnard takes the first pictures of the Milky Way. **1889** American undertaker Almon Strowger makes the first automated telephone exchange. **1892** New York City and Chicago are linked by a telephone line. **1892** American pathologists discover the bacterium that causes gas gangrene.	**1893** African-American surgeon Daniel Williams performs the first open-heart surgery. **1895** American astronomer James Keeler observes that Saturn's rings do not all rotate at the same speed. **1895** American inventor King Gillette designs the first disposable double-edged razor.	**1897** American physiologist Walter Cannon devises the barium meal to help diagnose digestive disorders. **1898** Irish-American John Holland builds the first modern submarine. **1900** Austrian-born American Karl Landsteiner discovers the ABO blood group system. **1897** A 40-inch (100-cm) refracting telescope is commissioned for the Yerkes Observatory in Williams Bay, Wisconsin.	**1901** Japanese-born American Jokichi Takamine isolates epinephrine (adrenaline). **1903** American brothers Wilbur and Orville Wright make the first sustained airplane flight. **1904** The first part of the New York City subway opens. **1904** American engineer Charles Kettering invents an electric cash register.
ASIA & OCEANIA		**1891** Australian inventor Lawrence Hargrave builds a successful model ornithopter—a flying machine propelled by flapping wings.	**1895** Australian-born David Bruce shows that the tsetse fly carries the parasite that causes sleeping sickness.	**1897** Japanese bacteriologist Kiyoshi Shiga identifies the bacterium that causes dysentery.	**1904** Japanese physicist Nagaoka Hantaro proposes the "Saturnian" theory of atomic structure.
AFRICA & THE MIDDLE EAST				**1899** Construction of a railroad between Istanbul and Baghdad begins.	**1901** The okapi is discovered by western explorers in central Africa. **1902** The first Aswan Dam is built in Egypt.

	1905	1908	1911	1914	1917–1919

1905 German-born physicist Albert Einstein publishes his special theory of relativity.

1905 French cycling advocate Paul de Vivie invents the derailleur gear system for bicycles.

1906 French mathematician Maurice Fréchet introduces functional calculus.

1906 Austrian physician Clemens von Pirquet coins the term *allergy*.

1906 German chemist Paul Ehrlich establishes the structural formula of atoxyl.

1907 French engineer Louis Bréguet develops an early type of helicopter.

1908 German mathematician Ernst Zermelo introduces set theory.

1908 German chemist Fritz Haber discovers a way of making ammonia.

1908 French anthropologist Marcellin Boule reconstructs a skeleton of a Neandertal.

1909 Danish botanist Wilhelm Johannsen coins the term *gene*.

1909 Danish chemist Sören Sörensen introduces the concept of pH.

1909 French aviator Louis Blériot flies across the English Channel.

1910 Ernest Rutherford proves the existence of the nucleus of an atom.

1911 Dutch physicist Heike Kamerlingh Onnes discovers superconductivity.

1911 Scottish physicist C. T. R. Wilson invents the cloud chamber.

1911 German physicist Ferdinand Braun devises a scanning system for cathode-ray tubes.

1913 French physicist Charles Fabry discovers the ozone layer.

1913 English geologist Arthur Holmes calculates Earth's age as 4.6 billion years.

1913 English chemist Frederick Soddy discovers isotopes.

1913 Danish physicist Niels Bohr proposes his model of the atom.

1914 English physiologist Henry Dale and English chemist Arthur Ewins isolate acetylcholine.

1914 English military engineer Ernest Swinton proposes the concept of a tank.

1914 English astronomer Arthur Eddington recognizes that nebulae are made up of millions of stars.

1915 Scottish astronomer Robert Innes locates Proxima Centauri, the nearest star to the sun.

1916 Albert Einstein publishes his paper on the general theory of relativity.

1916 French physicist Paul Langevin experiments with ultrasound and produces a primitive form of sonar.

1917 Albert Einstein determines the cosmological constant.

1917 English engineer Archibald Low invents an electronic control system for rockets.

1919 Austrian zoologist Karl von Frisch describes the "bee's dance."

1919 British aviators John Alcock and Arthur Brown make the first nonstop flight across the Atlantic Ocean.

1919 Ernest Rutherford reports that he has artificially disintegrated nitrogen atoms by bombarding them with alpha particles.

1905 American surgeon John Murphy pioneers arthroplasty.

1906 Canadian-born American engineer Reginald Fessenden makes AM (amplitude modulation) radio transmissions.

1907 Amercian zoologist Ross Harrison develops *in vitro* tissue culture.

1907 Belgian-born American chemist Leo Baekeland invents bakelite plastic.

1908 The first Model T Ford comes off the assembly line.

1908 American physicist William Coolidge uses tungsten to make an incandescent filament lamp.

1908 American electrical engineer Edward Weston's cadmium cell (battery) is adopted as an international voltage standard.

1911 American airman Calbraith Rogers makes the first flight (with stops) across the United States.

1913 American geneticist Alfred Sturtevant introduces chromosome mapping.

1913 American physicist Robert Millikan calculates the charge on an electron.

1913 American physicist William Burton patents a thermal cracking method for processing crude oil.

1914 American biochemist Edward Kendall isolates thyroxine.

1915 American astronomer Walter Adams identifies Sirius B as the first white dwarf star.

1915 American surgeon Alexis Carrel performs open-heart surgery on a dog.

1916 American chemist Gilbert Lewis describes the nature of covalent chemical bonds.

1917 American nurse Margaret Sanger opens a birth control clinic in the United States.

1917 Black & Decker make their first electric hand drill.

1918 American physiologists William Howell and Luther Holt discover the anticoagulant heparin.

1919 American astronomer George Hale reveals that sunspots reverse their magnetic field every 22 to 23 years.

1905 Astronomer John Grigg observes a comet from his observatory in New Zealand.

1908 The "Tunguska event" occurs in Siberia. It is thought to be the collision of a comet with Earth.

1911 A public demonstration of an aircraft takes place in New Zealand.

1912 The Komodo dragon is found by Europeans in Indonesia.

1915 Coal tar is shown to cause cancer by Japanese researchers.

1916 Japanese physicist Kotaro Honda makes Alnico—an alloy of aluminum, nickel, and cobalt.

1917 A railroad crossing Australia from east to west is completed.

1912 Israeli chemist Chaim Weizmann uses bacteria to produce acetone.

ASTRONOMY & MATH	BIOLOGY & MEDICINE	PHYSICAL SCIENCES

EUROPE

1885 A supernova flares up in the Andromeda galaxy; no other supernova visible to the naked eye will appear until 1987.

1888 German astronomer Heinrich Kreutz (1854–1907) reveals the Kreutz sungrazer comets, which travel very close to the sun and orbit it in the opposite direction to most other comets.

1888 Danish astronomer Johan Dreyer (1852–1926) publishes the *New General Catalogue of Nebulae and Clusters of Stars* (NGC). Astronomers still use Dreyer's NGC numbers.

In the late 19th century the study of comets and their orbits was a very popular branch of astronomy, with many new comets being discovered and named.

1885 Austrian neurologist Sigmund Freud (1856–1939) develops psychoanalysis as a diagnostic procedure.

1885 French chemist Louis Pasteur (1822–95) produces a vaccine against rabies.

1886 French neurologist Pierre Marie (1853–1940) describes the disfiguring disorder acromegaly (caused by the overproduction of growth hormone).

1886 Dutch botanist Hugo de Vries (1848–1935) observes that plants occasionally have offspring that differ markedly from their ancestors and later coins the term *mutations* to describe new forms or varieties of plants that arise randomly.

1887 German cell biologist Theodor Boveri (1862–1915) describes polar bodies (small cells that arise from the division of an unfertilized egg).

1888 German biologist Wilhelm von Waldeyer-Hartz (1836–1921) coins the term *chromosome.*

1885 Austrian chemist Karl Auer von Welsbach (1858–1929) isolates the elements neodymium and praseodymium. They were previously thought to be a single element.

1885 Swiss physicist Johann Balmer (1825–98) deduces a mathematical formula for the lines in the atomic spectrum of hydrogen; it provides important information about atomic structure.

1886 German chemist Clemens Winkler (1838–1904) discovers germanium, whose existence was predicted in 1869 by Dmitri Mendeleev (1834–1907) from one of the gaps in his periodic table.

1887 German chemist Emil Fischer (1852–1919) synthesizes fructose, the sugar found in fruits.

1887 German physicist Heinrich Hertz (1857–94) detects radio waves.

1887 Austrian physicist Ernst Mach (1838–1916) observes that airflow becomes turbulent as it approaches the speed of sound.

THE AMERICAS

1886 American physicist Henry Rowland (1848–1901) maps 14,000 lines of the sun's spectrum, using his improved ultrafine diffraction grating.

1885 American neurologist James Corning (1855–1923) introduces spinal (epidural) anesthesia.

1886 American physician Reginald Fitz (1843–1913) advocates appendectomy as a treatment for appendicitis. A year later physician Thomas Morton (1835–1903) performs the first successful operation in the United States.

1886 American chemist Charles Hall (1863–1914) and, independently, French chemist Paul Héroult (1863–1914) devise a method for the electrolytic extraction of aluminum from its ore. The Hall–Héroult process is the mainstay of the aluminum industry today.

1887 American physicist Albert Michelson (1852–1931) and American chemist Edward Morley (1838–1923) carry out an experiment that indirectly proves that the ether does not exist. (The ether was thought to be needed to "carry" light waves.)

ASIA & OCEANIA

AFRICA & THE MIDDLE EAST

HOW THINGS WORK

The Transformer

The transformer transfers electric energy from one AC (alternating current) circuit to another, either increasing (stepping up) or reducing (stepping down) the voltage. Transformers consist of two coils of wire wrapped around a magnetic core and work on the principle of magnetic induction. The current of the primary coil induces an alternating magnetic field in the core that induces a current in the secondary coil. In a step-down transformer the number of turns of wire on the primary coil is greater than the number of turns on the secondary coil, thus reducing the voltage. In a step-up transformer the secondary coil has more turns and therefore develops a higher voltage.

ENGINEERING & INVENTION

1885 German engineer Karl Benz (1844–1929) builds a three-wheeled car. A year later Gottlieb Daimler (1834–1900) makes a motorcycle. Both independently build internal combustion engines.

1885 German chemist Karl Auer von Welsbach (1858–1929) patents the gas mantle, which produces an incandescent white light in a coal-gas flame.

1886 German engineer Gottlieb Daimler produces a four-wheeled gasoline-engined car.

1887 Scottish inventor John Dunlop (1840–1921) develops the pneumatic tire for bicycles.

1887 German-born engineer Emile Berliner (1851–1929) devises the disk gramophone record. It soon supersedes the cylinder records of Thomas Edison's phonograph.

1885 American architect William Jenney (1832–1907) completes a steel-framed building in Chicago, the world's first skyscraper.

1885 American inventor Tolbert Lanston (1844–1913) patents a "monotype" machine for casting metal-type characters.

1885 American electrical engineer William Stanley (1858–1916) develops the transformer.

1886 American pharmacist John Pemberton (1831–88) invents Coca-Cola.

1886 The town of Montgomery, Alabama, becomes the first in the United States to have an electric trolley system.

Psychiatry is the art of teaching people how to stand on their own feet while reclining on couches.

SIGMUND FREUD

WORLD EVENTS

1885 The Prussian government, encouraged by Otto von Bismarck (1815–98), orders the expulsion of all ethnic Poles and Jews who do not hold German citizenship.

Gottlieb Daimler's 1886 automobile

1885 The Rock Springs Massacre, an outbreak of violence between white and Chinese miners, takes place in Rock Springs, Wyoming. Twenty-eight Chinese miners are killed, and hundreds more are injured or left homeless.

1886 The Statue of Liberty, a gift from the French people, is dedicated by President Grover Cleveland (1837–1908).

1885 The Panjdeh Incident, a military confrontation between Afghanistan and Russia, takes place. This increases tensions between Russia and the British Empire almost to the point of war.

Sigmund Freud's Jewish ancestry forced him to leave Nazi-controlled Vienna in 1938. He settled in London, England, and died the following year of oral cancer.

SIGMUND FREUD

Sigmund Freud (1856–1939) was an Austrian physician who founded the discipline of psychoanalysis. He was born in Freiburg, then part of the Austrian Empire, and studied neurology at Vienna University.

In 1885 Freud left Austria to study with the renowned French neurologist Jean-Martin Charcot (1825–1893). A year later Freud established his own clinic in Vienna and developed his revolutionary "talking cure," in which the patient was encouraged to try and explain his or her problems.

Freud's treatments centered on the concept of the unconscious—a set of desires, fears, and needs that direct people's actions without them being aware of their existence. He divided the human personality, or psyche, into three areas: the *ego*, the *superego*, and the *id*. The *ego* is the realistic, rational mind; the *superego* is the regulating conscience; and the *id* is the home of unconscious drives and desires. Freud believed that dreams were manifestations of these unconscious desires.

In his time Freud's ideas were highly controversial, especially his studies into human sexuality. Although many of his ideas about the nature of the psyche have now been disregarded, Freud's "talking cure" has become an essential part of modern psychoanalysis.

SOURCES OF ELECTRICITY

BEFORE 1800 SCIENTISTS KNEW ONLY ABOUT electricity that was stationary, or static. This static electricity consists of a positive or negative charge on an object, usually produced by friction. Then an Italian count produced an electric current—this was electricity on the move.

In 1791 Italian physician Luigi Galvani (1737–98) reported what he called "animal electricity." While dissecting a dead frog, he found that the animal's muscles twitched when he touched them with two different metals. Then in 1800 Alessandro Volta (1745–1827), an Italian count, replaced the animal tissue with a disk of cardboard soaked in salt solution. He put a piece of copper or silver on one side and a piece of zinc on the other side. Wires connected to the metal plates carried an electric current. Volta found he could obtain higher voltages by making a stack of such disks to form what became known as a voltaic pile, which was the first true battery.

Today scientists call such a battery a primary cell. The pieces of metal are called electrodes, and the solution between them is an electrolyte. In 1836 English chemist John Daniell (1790–1845) produced a more efficient type of primary cell. It consisted of a zinc rod electrode dipped in dilute sulfuric acid, contained in a porous earthenware pot. He immersed the pot in a copper container (which acted as the other electrode) containing copper sulfate solution. In the Daniell cell an electric current flows from the copper (the positive electrode, or anode) to the zinc (the negative electrode, or cathode). It gives a steadier current than Volta's cell and overcomes the problem of polarization—a build-up of hydrogen bubbles on the copper electrode that eventually stops the flow of electrons and causes the voltaic pile to stop working.

The Leclanché Cell

Invented in 1866 by French engineer Georges Leclanché (1839–82), the Leclanché cell also avoids polarization. It too has a zinc cathode, but it dips into an electrolyte of ammonium chloride solution. The anode is a carbon rod surrounded by powdered manganese dioxide. It produces about 1.5 volts. Today's common type of dry battery has the same system, using a zinc case containing a paste of ammonium chloride with a carbon rod surrounded by manganese dioxide down the center.

The German chemist Robert Bunsen (1811–99) also made a zinc–carbon primary cell; using acid electrolytes, it produces 1.9 volts. The cadmium cell,

A primary cell, such as the dry battery for a flashlight, can be used only until its chemicals run out, when it has to be thrown away (carefully). In this type of cell the electrolyte is a paste of ammonium chloride and gum. The zinc cathode forms the case of the battery, and manganese dioxide and carbon surround the central carbon anode.

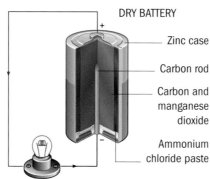

DRY BATTERY

Zinc case

Carbon rod

Carbon and manganese dioxide

Ammonium chloride paste

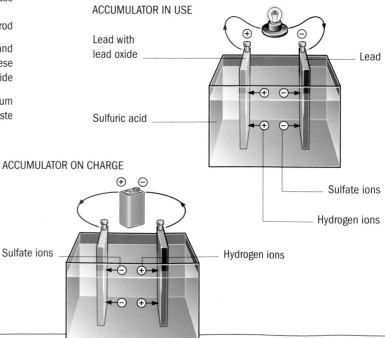

ACCUMULATOR IN USE

Lead with lead oxide

Lead

Sulfuric acid

Sulfate ions

Hydrogen ions

ACCUMULATOR ON CHARGE

Sulfate ions

Hydrogen ions

A secondary cell, or accumulator, can be recharged when it runs down, and reused. It has lead and lead-oxide electrodes in a sulfuric acid electrolyte. When it is in use, sulfate ions react with the lead cathode to produce lead sulfate and release electrons. At the anode hydrogen ions from the acid and sulfate ions react with the lead oxide to produce lead sulfate and water. The reactions produce about two volts.

To recharge the accumulator, current from an outside source is passed through the battery in the opposite direction. This has the effect of reversing the reactions at the electrodes, reforming lead and lead oxide. The accumulator is then ready for use again (for example, car batteries).

Alessandro Volta took every opportunity to demonstrate his new battery. Here he shows it to Napoleon Bonaparte, emperor of France.

invented in 1893 by English-born American electrical engineer Edward Weston (1850–1936), produces 1.0186 volts, and in 1908 the scientific community accepted it as a standard of voltage. Known as the Weston standard cell, it has mercury (cathode) and a cadmium–mercury mixture (anode) as its electrodes, with cadmium sulfate solution as its electrolyte.

Accumulators

A primary cell stops working when it is fully discharged. A different type, called variously a secondary cell, a storage cell, or an accumulator, can be recharged. The lead–acid accumulator, devised in 1859 by a French chemist, Gaston Planté (1834–89), is the earliest and still the most commonly used kind. It has one electrode (or "plate") of lead and one of lead covered with lead oxide, which dip into a sulfuric acid electrolyte. This is the type of battery used in most cars. The alkaline nickel–iron accumulator, or Ni–Fe cell, is another type, devised in 1900 by American inventor Thomas Edison (1847–1931). When any accumulator becomes discharged, it can be connected to a supply of DC (direct current) and recharged. For example, while a car's motor is running the battery is continually recharged.

Primary and secondary cells convert chemical energy into electrical energy. To do so, they "consume" materials in the electrodes or electrolyte. A fuel cell, however, converts the chemical energy of a fuel directly into electrical energy. The first fuel cell that "consumed" hydrogen and oxygen gases was demonstrated in 1839 by Welsh physicist William Grove (1811–96).

KEY DATES

1800
Voltaic pile

1836
Daniell cell

1859
Lead-acid accumulator

1866
Leclanché cell

1893
Weston cadmium cell

1900
Nickel-iron accumulator

CONCISE HISTORY OF SCIENCE AND INVENTION

ASTRONOMY & MATH	BIOLOGY & MEDICINE	PHYSICAL SCIENCES

EUROPE

1889 Italian astronomer Giovanni Schiaparelli (1835–1910) states, incorrectly, that the planet Mercury rotates on its axis so that it always presents the same face to the sun (as the moon always faces the Earth the same way).

1889 German astronomer Hermann Vogel (1842–1907) and American astronomer Edward Pickering (1846–1919) discover spectrographic binary stars, two-star systems that reveal they are double stars by the way their spectrum varies.

1890 English mathematical physicist Oliver Heaviside (1850–1925) introduces operational calculus for studying short-lived electrical phenomena.

1891 German astronomer Max Wolf (1863–1932) locates Brucia, the first asteroid discovered by photography.

1889 French bacteriologists Émile Roux (1853–1933) and Alexandre Yersin (1863–1943) isolate the diphtheria toxin.

1890 German bacteriologist Emil von Behring (1854–1917) and coworkers develop antitoxins against diphtheria and tetanus.

1891 Dutch anthropologist Eugène Dubois (1858–1940) discovers fossils of the human ancestor "Java man," which he names *Pithecanthropus*. Today it is classified as *Homo erectus*.

1891 German physiologist Karl von Voit (1831–1908) demonstrates that the body converts excess sugars into glycogen as an energy reserve.

1892 English scientist Francis Galton (1822–1911) states in his book *Finger Prints* that no two people have the same fingerprints, and advocates the use of such prints in crime detection.

1892 German bacteriologist Robert Koch (1843–1910) introduces filtration of water to control a cholera epidemic in Hamburg, Germany.

1889 English chemist Frederick Abel (1827–1902) and Scottish physicist James Dewar (1842–1923) develop the propellant explosive cordite.

1889 Swedish physical chemist Svante Arrhenius (1859–1927) derives the Arrhenius equation, which provides a way of calculating the speed of a chemical reaction.

1890 Hungarian physicist Roland von Eötvös (1848–1919) demonstrates that gravitational mass and inertial mass are the same.

1891 Irish physicist George Stoney (1826–1911) coins the term *electron* for the fundamental unit of electricity (from his earlier *electrine* of 1874).

1891 English physicist John Poynting (1852–1914) calculates the value of the gravitational constant.

THE AMERICAS

1889 American astronomer Edward Barnard (1857–1923) takes the first photographs of the Milky Way (our galaxy).

1892 Edward Barnard discovers Amalthea, one of Jupiter's moons.

1889 American microbiologist Theobald Smith (1859–1934) discovers the cause of Texas cattle fever, the protozoan parasite *Babesia*, and shows that it is transmitted by a cattle tick.

1892 American pathologists William Welch (1850–1934) and George Nuttall 1862–1937) discover *Clostridium welchii*, the microorganism that causes gas gangrene.

1891 American chemist Edward Acheson (1856–1931) makes carborundum (silicon carbide), an ultrahard compound used as an abrasive.

ASIA & OCEANIA

AFRICA & THE MIDDLE EAST

Each person's fingerprints have a unique pattern. Fingerprints are routinely used by the police to identify suspected criminals.

INSIDE STORY

Fleming's Rules

In 1890 British scientist John Fleming formulated rules relating to electrical machines—the left-hand rule to motors and the right-hand rule to dynamos. When the first finger, second finger, and thumb are extended at right angles to one another, the first finger indicates the direction of the field, the second finger the direction of the current, and the thumb the direction of the force (motion).

ENGINEERING & INVENTION

1889 The Eiffel Tower is completed in Paris, France, designed by French engineer Gustave Eiffel (1832–1923).

1889 English inventor William Friese-Greene (1855–1921) builds a motion-picture camera.

1890 French engineer Clément Ader (1841–1926) builds a piloted steam-powered monoplane. However, it is unsuitable for sustained flight.

1891 German aeronautical pioneer Otto Lilienthal (1848–96) makes a steerable human-carrying glider.

1892 French engineer François Hennebique (1842–1921) develops prestressed concrete, in which the reinforcing rods are tensioned before the concrete is poured.

1892 Scottish physicist James Dewar (1842–1923) invents the vacuum bottle (sold as a flask under the trade name Thermos).

1889 American scientist Franklin King (1849–1911) devises the cylindrical tower silo for storing animal feed.

1889 American undertaker Almon Strowger (1839–1902) makes the first automatic telephone exchange (patented 1891).

1890 American inventor Herman Hollerith (1860–1929) creates a punch-card reader for recording the results of the 1890 United States census.

1891 American inventor George Blickensderfer (1850–1917) patents a portable typewriter.

1892 A telephone line linking New York City and Chicago goes into operation.

1891 English-born Australian inventor Lawrence Hargrave (1850–1915) builds a successful model ornithopter, propelled by flapping wings.

WORLD EVENTS

1889 An attempt to build a canal across the isthmus of Panama envisaged by French engineer Ferdinand de Lesseps (1805–94)—designer of the Suez Canal—fails.

1889 Charles Stuart Parnell (1846–91), leader of the Irish Nationalist cause in the British Parliament, is brought down by a scandal relating to an adulterous love affair.

1890 Kaiser Wilhelm II (r. 1888–1918) dismisses Germany's long-serving chancellor Otto von Bismarck (1815–98).

1889 Emperor Pedro II of Brazil (r. 1831–89) is overthrown in a military coup; the country becomes a republic.

1890 Sioux refugees are massacred at Wounded Knee, South Dakota, by U.S. cavalrymen.

1892 Pitched battles break out between striking workers and the owners of the Homestead Steelworks, Pittsburgh. The eventual outcome is a demoralizing defeat for organized labor in the United States.

Until the construction of the Chrysler Building in New York City in 1929, the Eiffel Tower in Paris was the tallest structure in the world.

1889 Japan's New Constitution establishes a diet or parliament but restricts its powers severely. The emperor will be Japan's true ruler.

1889 New Zealand holds its first democratic general election based on full male suffrage.

1889 British South Africa Company—run by Cecil Rhodes (1853–1902)—is granted a charter to exploit territories to the north of the British Cape Colony in what is now Zimbabwe.

THE EIFFEL TOWER

One of the most famous and instantly recognizable landmarks in the world, the Eiffel Tower (French: *Tour Eiffel*) is a masterpiece of iron construction. The building was designed by French civil engineer Gustave Eiffel and constructed between 1887 and 1889 in time to celebrate the centenary of the French Revolution. At the time of completion the tower—standing 984 feet (300 m) tall—was the tallest artificial structure in the world, nearly doubling the height of the previous record holder: the Washington Monument in Washington, D.C., which was completed in 1884.

The tower was constructed using 7,300 tons (6,600 tonnes) of iron. The structural girders and braces were made from a strong type of iron known as "puddle iron." About 2.5 million rivets were used to create the tower's latticework of girders, bars, and braces. At each of the tower's four corners, a lattice-girder pier tapers inward, with the four meeting to form a single vertical tower. The piers are connected at two levels by girders. These levels serve as viewing platforms for tourists and are accessible by stairways and elevators. A third level toward the summit is accessible only by elevator. The top of the tower can sway up to 3 inches (7.5 cm) in the wind. The tapering design of the tower enhances its resistance to wind. The tower can also lean up to 7 inches (18 cm) due to thermal expansion of the metal on the side facing the sun.

Although it is now an internationally recognized symbol of Paris, the tower was not well received at first by Parisians. A petition calling for its demolition was published in newspapers before it was even finished. In 1909 it was saved from demolition only because it had a useful role as a telecommunications tower.

THE INVENTION OF RADIO

At the beginning of the 20th century the Italian inventor Guglielmo Marconi was the first to develop radio into a reliable means of international communication.

RADIO IS A METHOD OF COMMUNICATION that uses electromagnetic radiation known as radio waves, which travel at the speed of light. It used to be called wireless to distinguish it from telegraphs and telephones, which both needed wires running between the sender and the receiver to transmit their signals.

Radio had its origins in the late 19th century. Scottish physicist James Clerk Maxwell (1831–79) predicted the existence of electromagnetic radiation in 1864 and concluded that light is just one part of the spectrum of electromagnetic radiation. German physicist Heinrich Hertz (1857–94) discovered a new type of radiation—radio waves—in 1887. He made electrical waves (then called Hertzian waves) by letting a high-voltage spark jump between two metal spheres.

In 1890 French physicist Édouard Branly (1844–1940) devised a way of detecting radio waves using a "coherer," a sealed glass tube containing iron filings and an electrode at each end. When radio waves are present, the filings cohere (stick together) and conduct electricity well enough to form part of a circuit. English physicist Oliver Lodge (1851–1940) improved the coherer in 1894 and used it together with a spark transmitter to send Morse code messages a distance of 490 feet (150 m).

Unaware of these developments, Italian physicist Guglielmo Marconi (1874–1937) also began experimenting with radio in 1894 and in the process invented a radio antenna and the use of a ground (earth) with the apparatus. He could soon transmit coded messages more than 1.8 miles (3 km). The invention, known as radiotelegraphy, developed rapidly, especially after Marconi moved to England in 1896. By 1901 he was able to transmit signals in Morse code across the Atlantic Ocean.

So far, radio was better than the telegraph only because it did not need wires. The telephone, which needs wires, can carry speech. Could radio be made to carry the human voice? This question led to the development of radiotelephony. The early work was done by Canadian-born American electrical engineer Reginald Fessenden (1866–1932), who invented modulation. Radiotelegraphy sends out pulses of short and long signals representing the dots and dashes of Morse code. In radiotelephony the transmitter sends out a continuous signal, called a carrier wave, whose amplitude (strength) is varied (modulated) in step with the variations in the sound signals from a microphone. Fessenden first demonstrated AM (amplitude modulation) in 1903, and in 1906 he transmitted speech and music from a radio station in Massachusetts.

Crystal Detectors

The new system needed a better detector. This came in the form of a crystal detector produced by American electrical engineer Greenleaf Pickard (1877–1956) in 1906. It used a crystal of carborundum, galena, or silicon and worked by rectifying the incoming radio signal, converting it from alternating current (AC) to direct current (DC). The detector connected to the radio circuit by an adjustable thin wire—a "cat's whisker."

English engineer John Fleming (1849–1945) had invented an even better rectifier and detector system in 1904. It was a two-electrode vacuum tube called a diode. Two years later American engineer Lee De Forest (1873–1961) added a third electrode to make the audion, a forerunner of the triode, which could be used as an amplifier to boost weak radio signals. With the aid of the new devices radio engineers could build better circuits for transmitters and receivers. In 1917 Marconi

began making VHF (very high frequency) transmissions. By 1924 Marconi was sending speech signals from England to Australia using short-wave radio.

Radio receivers improved in 1912 when Fessenden devised the heterodyne circuit, which allowed more selective tuning. American engineer Edwin Armstrong (1890–1954) improved on this with the superheterodyne circuit in 1918, which can detect very weak signals. But Armstrong's major contribution came in 1933, when he invented FM (frequency modulation). In this technique the frequency (not amplitude) of the transmitted carrier wave is modulated by the broadcast signal, increasing the quality of the received sound.

Radiotelephony depends on a technique called modulation—the changing of one constant signal by another varying one. An audio-frequency signal from a microphone is amplified and made to vary ("modulate") an oscillator's radio-frequency signal, which is amplified again before being transmitted. At the receiver an antenna picks up the transmitted signal. It is amplified before being demodulated by a detector and amplified to reproduce the original audio signal in a loudspeaker.

In amplitude modulation used in AM radio the amplitude (strength) of a constant carrier wave is modulated by the audio signal. In FM radio (frequency modulation) the frequency of the carrier wave is modulated.

KEY DATES

1864
Radio waves predicted

1887
Discovery of radio waves

1890
Coherer for detecting radio waves

1894
Marconi's first radio transmissions

1903
Amplitude modulation (AM)

1904
Diode vacuum tube

1906
Triode vacuum tube

1933
Frequency modulation (FM)

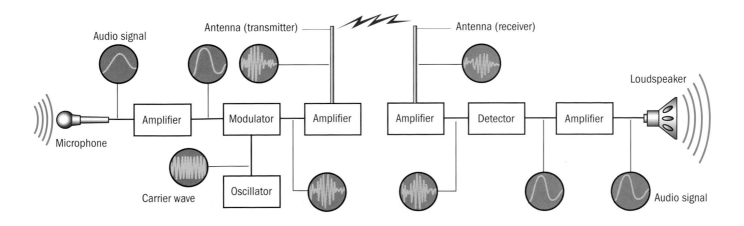

ASTRONOMY & MATH

EUROPE

1893 British astronomer Walter Maunder (1851–1928) studies old records of sunspots and notices that very few were observed between 1615–1745. He deduces that the time (known as the Maunder minimum) corresponds to a "Little Ice Age."

1895 French mathematician Jules-Henri Poincaré (1854–1912) introduces topology as a branch of mathematics. It deals with the general geometrical properties of surfaces and space.

1896 Swedish physical chemist Svante Arrhenius (1859–1927) proposes a link between the levels of carbon dioxide (CO_2) in the atmosphere and global temperatures, a theory that has received much attention with the advent of global warming.

BIOLOGY & MEDICINE

1893 Swiss physiologist Wilhelm His (1863–1934) describes the bundle of His, specialized muscle fibers in the heart that conduct nerve impulses that control the heartbeat.

1894 German chemist Emil Fischer (1852–1919) describes the "lock-and-key" system by which enzymes work.

1894 English physiologist Edward Sharpey-Schafer (1850–1935) demonstrates the existence of the pituitary hormone epinephrine (adrenaline).

1895 English botanist Frederick Blackman (1866–1947) discovers that gas exchange (oxygen and carbon dioxide) in plants takes place through pores in the leaves called stomata.

1896 English bacteriologist Almroth Wright (1861–1947) develops a vaccine against typhoid fever.

1896 German chemist Eduard Buchner (1860–1917) observes that fermentation of sugar (as in brewing and winemaking) is caused by enzymes in the yeast.

PHYSICAL SCIENCES

1894 Scottish physicist James Dewar (1842–1923) makes liquid oxygen, one of the first elemental gases to be liquefied.

1894 English physicist John Strutt, Lord Rayleigh (1842–1919), and Scottish chemist William Ramsay (1852–1916) discover the inert gas argon in air.

1895 Swedish chemist Per Cleve (1840–1905) and Scottish chemist William Ramsay (1852–1916) independently discover helium on Earth.

1895 German physicist Wilhelm Röntgen (1845–1923) takes the first x-ray.

1896 French physicist Henri Becquerel (1852–1908) discovers radioactivity.

1896 New Zealand-born British physicist Ernest Rutherford (1871–1937) describes and names alpha particles (which are helium nuclei) and beta particles (which are electrons).

1896 Dutch physicist Pieter Zeeman (1865–1943) observes the Zeeman effect, which is the splitting of atomic spectral lines in a strong magnetic field.

THE AMERICAS

1894 American astronomer Percival Lowell (1855–1916) sets up his private observatory at Flagstaff, Arizona, and begins the search for a ninth planet. The search ends with the discovery of Pluto by American astronomer Clyde Tombaugh (1906–97) in 1930.

1895 American astronomer James Keeler (1857–1900) observes that Saturn's rings do not all rotate at the same speed, contrary to the prediction in 1857 by Scottish physicist James Clerk Maxwell (1831–79).

1893 African-American surgeon Daniel Williams (1858–1931) performs the first open-heart surgery operation.

1895 Canadian physician Daniel Palmer (1845–1913) establishes the medical procedure of chiropractic.

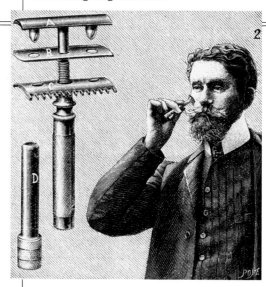

An illustration from an early advertisement for the Gillette safety razor

ASIA & OCEANIA

1895 Australian-born physician and bacteriologist David Bruce (1855–1931) shows that the tsetse fly carries the parasite *Trypanosoma brucei* that causes sleeping sickness.

AFRICA & THE MIDDLE EAST

The Lowell Observatory in Flagstaff, Arizona—home of the discovery of Pluto

ENGINEERING & INVENTION	WORLD EVENTS
1893 German physicists Julius Elster (1854–1920) and Hans Geitel (1855–1923) make the first practical photoelectric cell. **1893** German inventor Rudolf Diesel (1858–1913) builds the first compression-ignition engine (diesel engine), patented in 1892. **1893** French brothers Auguste (1862–1954) and Louis (1864–1948) Lumière invent a motion-picture camera. **1893** The 3.9-mile- (6.3-km-) long Corinth Canal opens. It crosses the Greek mainland from northwest to southeast. **1895** Czech-born Austrian printer Karl Klic (1841–1926) founds the Rembrandt Intaglio Printing Company. It publishes reproductions of illustrations on paper by photogravure—a process invented by Klic in 1878, in which the printing plate consists of hundreds of minute ink-holding pits.	**1893** Scottish socialist Keir Hardie (1856–1915) founds Britain's independent Labour Party; as the Labour Party, it will replace the Liberal Party as one of the two main political parties (the other being the Conservative Party). **1893** Jewish French army officer Alfred Dreyfus (1859–1935) is wrongfully accused of treason in a case that will divide France for over a decade. Convicted by court-martial in 1894, his pardon was eventually won in 1906, after a long campaign by liberals such as writer Émile Zola (1840–1902) against the military establishment. **1894** Tsar Alexander III (r. 1881–94) dies. He is succeeded by his son, Nicholas II (r. 1894–1917). **1896** The first modern Olympic Games are staged in Athens, Greece.
1893 American engineer Whitcomb Judson (d. 1905) patents the "clasp locker," a forerunner of the zipper. **1894** American physician John Kellogg (1852–1943) invents wheat flakes. **1895** American inventor King Gillette (1855–1932) has the idea for the disposable double-edged razor blade. **1896** American aeronautical pioneer Samuel Langley (1834–1906) builds a steam-powered airplane capable of sustained (but uncontrolled) flight. **1896** American engineer and patent lawyer Charles Curtis (1860–1953) invents an impulse steam turbine, later used in ships and electricity power plants.	**1893** The failure of a number of major railroad companies causes panic on Wall Street and plunges the United States economy into a depression that will last another four years. **1894** The United States army imprisons leaders of the Hopi people on Alcatraz Island in San Francisco for sedition. **1895** The "Atlanta Compromise" speech by Booker T. Washington (1856–1915) proposes a cessation of African-American political activity in exchange for new educational opportunities. **1896** In the *Plessy v. Ferguson* case the United States Supreme Court rules that racial segregation is constitutional.
1893 English-born Australian inventor Lawrence Hargrave (1850–1915) invents a human-carrying box kite.	**1893** The Durand Line is created, marking the border between British India and Afghanistan. **1894** Japan invades Korea, triggering the First Sino-Japanese War (1894–95).
	1896 After its forces suffer a crushing defeat at the battle of Adowa, Italy is forced to recognize the independence of Ethiopia at the treaty of Addis Ababa.

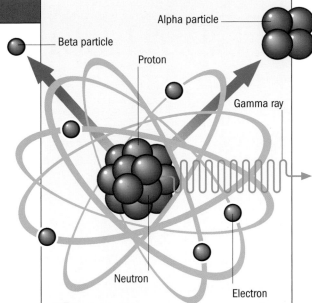

ERNEST RUTHERFORD

Ernest Rutherford (1871–1937) was a New Zealand-born English physicist and one of the pioneers of nuclear physics. After studying in New Zealand, Rutherford won a scholarship to Cambridge University, England. There, he discovered that radioactive uranium gives off three kinds of rays: low-power alpha rays, penetrating beta rays, and highly ionizing gamma rays.

Two years later, during his tenure at McGill University, Montreal, Rutherford worked with English chemist Frederick Soddy (1877–1956) on the process of radioactive decay. They came up with the theory that radioactive decay takes place by a series of "transformations." This work eventually led to Soddy's discovery of the existence of isotopes.

Rutherford moved to Manchester University, England, in 1907. In 1910, he supervised Hans Geiger (1882–1945) and Ernest Marsden (1889–1971). In one experiment Geiger and Marsden fired positively charged alpha particles at a piece of gold foil. Most of the particles went through, but some bounced back. The scientists suggested that this was caused by a positive charge at the center of the gold atoms. This led Rutherford to create a model of the atom with a central, positively charged nucleus surrounded largely by empty space.

THE ELUSIVE ELECTRON

EVERY MODERN SCIENCE STUDENT KNOWS what an electron is and how important it is in understanding electricity and atomic physics. But things were different 100 years ago when an English physicist discovered what was the smallest particle of matter known at the time. Until the end of the 19th century various discoveries in physics had given rise to a host of unanswered questions such as: Objects can be made to hold a charge of static electricity, but what form does the charge take? In an electric current charges flow along a conductor, but what are these charges and are they different from the electrostatic ones? A high voltage across the plates of a vacuum tube produces cathode rays, but what are the rays made of? And if matter is made of atoms, what are atoms made of?

It turned out that the answers to these questions depended on an invention—the vacuum pump—that allowed scientists to remove nearly all the air from a piece of apparatus. One of the first experimenters to use it was the German glassblower and manufacturer of laboratory equipment Heinrich Geissler (1815–79). In about 1850 he sealed metal plates inside a glass vacuum tube containing only traces of a gas (such as neon or argon). He connected the plates to a source of high-voltage electricity and obtained pretty lighting effects as the gas glowed in the container.

The Geissler tubes became a popular novelty but were used for serious experiments by two German physicists: Julius Plücker (1801–68) in 1859 and Johann Hittorf (1824–1914) in 1869. The two scien-

tists maintained that the light resulted from "rays" that left the negatively charged plate, or cathode, of the Geissler tube and traveled in straight lines to the anode. This fact was confirmed in 1879 by English physicist William Crookes (1832–1919), who also suggested that the "rays" may, in fact, be particles. Sixteen years later French physicist Jean Perrin (1870–1942) deflected these cathode rays using magnetic and electric fields, proving that they are made up of negative electric charges.

The Cavendish Laboratory

The scene was set for the pioneering experiments of an English physicist. Joseph John Thomson (1856–1940), always known as J. J. Thomson, was born near Manchester in the north of England. At the age of 14 he began to train as a railroad engineer. He then won a scholarship to Cambridge University, graduating in 1880. He went to work in the Cavendish Laboratory under John Strutt, Lord Rayleigh (1842–1919), and succeeded him to the professorship in 1884.

Thomson also deflected cathode rays with electric and magnetic fields, measured their speed (proving that they travel much more slowly than light waves),

---

KEY DATES

1850
Geissler tubes invented

1874
Stoney predicts existence of electrons

1879
Crookes suggests cathode rays are particles

1891
Electron named

1895
Perrin proves cathode rays are made up of negative charges

1897
Electron discovered

J. J. Thomson carried out research at Cambridge University's Cavendish Laboratory for 39 years, the whole of his working life.

This diagram shows the flow of electricity in a metal wire. Electrons are basic components of all atoms, in which they normally orbit the nucleus. In most metals—such as the copper wire of an electric cable—many of the electrons wander away from their atoms to form a "sea" of free electrons (bottom section of diagram).

When a voltage is applied to the cable (middle section), the free electrons move and become the electric current flowing along the cable. Copper is an example of a metal that is said to have low resistance.

A metal with very high resistance, such as tungsten used for elements in electric heaters, has only a few free electrons (top section). As a result, a voltage causes only a small current to flow, and the metal becomes hot.

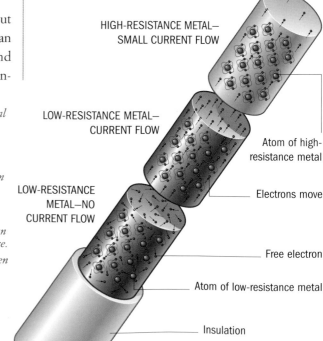

HIGH-RESISTANCE METAL—
SMALL CURRENT FLOW

LOW-RESISTANCE METAL—
CURRENT FLOW

Atom of high-resistance metal

LOW-RESISTANCE
METAL—NO
CURRENT FLOW

Electrons move

Free electron

Atom of low-resistance metal

Insulation

and more importantly, figured out the ratio of their charge (e) to their mass (m). This ratio, e/m, was 1,000 times smaller than that for a hydrogen ion (the smallest charged atom), and so Thomson deduced that cathode rays must consist of minute negatively charged particles. He announced the discovery of these first subatomic particles, which he called "corpuscles," in 1897. Two years later he found that they have a mass equal to about one two-thousandth of the mass of a hydrogen atom. Their existence had already been predicted in 1874 by the Irish physicist George Stoney (1826–1911), who in 1891 had named them "electrons." The electron turned out to be the long-sought-after unit of electricity responsible for electrostatic charges. Also, it became clear that a flow of electrons along a conductor constitutes an electric current. And because electrons come from the metal of the cathode in a discharge tube, they must be a fundamental part of all atoms.

Thomson went on to study canal rays (positive rays emitted by the anode of a discharge tube). This work led in 1912 to a method of separating charged particles, which in turn was developed into the mass spectrograph in 1919 by English physicist Francis Aston (1877–1945). When Thomson retired in 1919, he was succeeded by his former assistant, New Zealand-born English physicist Ernest Rutherford (1871–1937). Rutherford eventually proposed a structure for the atom that included the atomic nucleus. Seven of Thomson's assistants later won Nobel prizes, an award that he received in 1906.

Many notable scientists, including J. J. Thomson, Ernest Rutherford, and Sir Lawrence Bragg, experimented in the Cavendish Laboratory at Cambridge University in England.

ASTRONOMY & MATH	BIOLOGY & MEDICINE	PHYSICAL SCIENCES

EUROPE

1897 Dutch astronomer Jacobus Kapteyn (1851–1922) discovers Kapteyn's star, which has the second-largest proper motion (meaning it is the second-fastest moving star).

1897 Irish-born English geologist Richard Oldham (1858–1936) distinguishes between the primary (P) and secondary (S) seismic waves produced by earthquakes.

1898 German astronomer Gustav Witt (1866–1946) discovers Eros, the first of the so-called near-Earth asteroids (in 1931 it passed within 14 million miles [23 million km] of Earth).

1898 German physicist Woldemar Voigt (1850–1919) introduces tensor mathematics, originally for handling vector transformations in physics problems.

1897 Danish veterinarian Bernhard Bang (1848–1932) discovers *Brucella abortus*, the cause of infectious abortion in cattle.

1897 German bacteriologist Friedrich Löffler (1852–1915) discovers the foot-and-mouth virus. Two years later he produces a vaccine.

1897 Dutch botanist Martinus Beijerinck (1851–1931) proves that tobacco mosaic disease is caused by something smaller than a bacterium. He calls the pathogen a "virus."

1897 Danish physician Niels Finsen (1860–1904) introduces the use of ultraviolet light to treat various skin disorders, such as cutaneous tuberculosis (lupus vulgaris).

1898 English physician Ronald Ross (1857–1932) finds *Plasmodium*, the microorganism that causes malaria, in the stomach of the *Anopheles* mosquito. He shows that the mosquito transfers the parasite from one human to another.

1900 Austrian neurologist Sigmund Freud (1856–1939) publishes his seminal book *The Interpretation of Dreams*.

1897 English physicist J. J. Thomson (1856–1940) identifies the electron, the first known subatomic particle.

1898 French physical chemists Marie (1867–1934) and Pierre (1859–1906) Curie discover the elements polonium and radium.

1898 German chemist Emil Fischer (1852–1919) synthesizes a type of purine. It is later found to be a key constituent of DNA (deoxyribonucleic acid) and RNA (ribonucleic acid).

1899 French chemist André Debierne (1874–1949) identifies actinium.

1899 German chemist Hans Henning prepares cyclonite for medical use. It is later used as the explosive RDX.

1900 German chemist Friedrich Ernst Dorn (1848–1916) discovers radon.

1900 German physicist Paul Drude (1863–1906) reveals that electrons carry electricity in an electric current.

1900 German physicist Max Planck (1858–1947) proposes quantum theory.

THE AMERICAS

1897 A 40-inch (100-cm) refracting telescope is commissioned for the Yerkes Observatory in Williams Bay, Wisconsin. It is still the world's largest refractor.

1899 American astronomer William Pickering (1858–1938) observes Phoebe, one of Saturn's moons.

1897 American physiologist Walter Cannon (1871–1945) pioneers the use of the barium meal to facilitate diagnostic x-rays of the stomach and the intestinal tract.

1900 Austrian-born American pathologist Karl Landsteiner (1868–1943) discovers A, B, and O blood groups and their intercompatability.

1900 Cuban-born American physiologist Aristides Aramonte y Simoni (1869–1931) discovers that yellow fever is transmitted through the bite of a mosquito.

1897 American physicist Robert Wood (1868–1955) observes electric field emission.

1900 Russian-born American chemist Moses Gomberg (1866–1947) prepares triphenylmethyl, the first chemical free radical—a highly active group of atoms with an unpaired electron (later to be important in reactions such as polymerization for making plastic polymers).

1900 American chemist Charles Palmer (1858–1939) invents the basic process for cracking crude oil, increasing the amount of gasoline obtained from a barrel of oil. It gains importance as automobiles become more widely used.

ASIA & OCEANIA

1897 Japanese bacteriologist Kiyoshi Shiga (1871–1957) identifies the cause of endemic dysentery, a bacillus known as *Shigella* for its discoverer.

1898 French scientist Paul-Louis Simond (1858–1947) identifies the plague bacillus in the tissues of dead rats in India.

AFRICA & THE MIDDLE EAST

Count Zeppelin's LZ-2, the successor of the first Zeppelin, LZ-1

Pierre and Marie Curie made many important discoveries in the field of radioactivity.

ENGINEERING & INVENTION

1897 German physicist Ferdinand Braun (1850–1918) develops the cathode-ray tube, later to be used in radar and television sets.

1897 English engineer Charles Parsons (1854–1931) builds a high-speed steam turbine boat, anticipating marine propulsion of the future.

1898 Work begins on the Paris Métro (subway). The first 6.25 miles (10 km) are opened in 1900.

1898 German engineer Wilhelm Schmidt (1858–1924) invents the superheater for steam locomotives, greatly improving their efficiency.

1898 German gunmaker Georg Luger (1849–1923) produces the Luger automatic pistol.

1899 The 165-mile (266-km) Dortmund-Ems Canal is completed across Germany, linking the industrial Ruhr district with the Ems River and the North Sea.

1900 The rigid airship *LZ-1*, designed by German engineer Graf Ferdinand von Zeppelin (1838–1917), makes its maiden flight.

1898 After three years, two months, and two days Canadian sailor Joshua Slocum (1844–1909) completes the first single-handed circumnavigation of the world in his sailboat *Spray*.

1898 Irish-American schoolmaster and engineer John Holland (1840–1914) builds the first modern submarine.

1899 American metallurgist Frederick Taylor (1856–1915) formulates "high-speed" steel (containing tungsten, chromium, and vanadium) for making machine tools.

1900 American engineer Thomas Edison (1847–1931) invents the nickel–iron accumulator (Ni–Fe cell).

WORLD EVENTS

1897 The First Zionist Congress meets in the town of Basle, Switzerland. Representatives from Jewish communities across Europe gather to discuss the creation of an internationally recognized Jewish state in Palestine.

1898 Russia's Marxist revolutionaries join together to form the Social Democratic Party.

1898 At the instigation of Russia's Tsar Nicholas II (r. 1894–1917) representatives of 26 countries gather for the first International Peace Conference at The Hague in the Netherlands.

1897 The Klondike Gold Rush begins: thousands of hopeful prospectors head to the Klondike River region on the Canada–Alaska border.

1898 The U.S.S. *Maine*, an American battleship, explodes in the harbor at Havana, Cuba. The explosion was blamed, wrongly, on a mine and was one of the important triggers of the Spanish–American War.

1898 The Treaty of Paris ends the Spanish–American War. Spain cedes Puerto Rico, Guam, and the Philippines to the United States. Cuba gains independence.

1897 In China, German forces seize the port of Kiaochow Bay. A year later Russia leases the port of Lushun, renaming it Port Arthur.

1899 Construction begins of a railroad from Istanbul to Baghdad: Germany's involvement in the enterprise alarms rival European powers.

1899 The Second Boer War (1899–1902) breaks out between the British and the Boers in South Africa.

BLOOD GROUPS

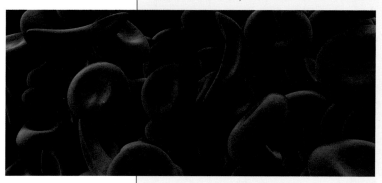

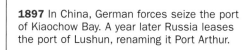

ABO blood group antigens are present on the surface of red blood cells.

Before the development of blood transfusions, surgical operations were very dangerous. Even if the patients avoided infection, there was a high risk of death from loss of blood during surgery. Bleeding was also a common cause of death during childbirth.

In the 19th century some physicians successfully performed blood transfusions. However, medical science could not explain why only about a half of the patients survived. Sometimes the transfusions worked perfectly, but on other occasions a patient's body was seen to attack and break down the infused blood, causing deadly toxic reactions.

In 1901 Austrian physician Karl Landsteiner (1868–1943) discovered that human blood belonged to four primary groups, depending on surface molecules, or antigens, on red blood cells. In addition, three of the blood types contained antibodies that rejected blood of other types. Landsteiner named these types A, B, AB, and O. The discovery transformed blood transfusions into a common and viable medical technique.

There were still problems with blood rejection, however, and Landsteiner continued his work. In 1937 Landsteiner and American physician Alexander Wiener (1907–76) conducted transfusion experiments with rhesus monkeys. They discovered an antigen that was sometimes present on the surface of red blood cells that they named the "rhesus factor." Wiener soon realised that the incompatibility of rhesus-positive and rhesus-negative blood was the cause of many transfusion complications and pregnancy-related blood disorders.

THE FIRST AUTOMOBILES

THE AUTOMOBILE WAS THE RESULT OF A LONG period of trial and error in the quest for a motorized road vehicle. The early machines used a steam engine, the only motive power available at the time. Credit for the first successful attempt goes to a French military engineer.

In 1770 Nicolas-Joseph Cugnot (1725–1804) built his second three-wheel gun carriage (he had built a smaller version in 1769). It was powered by a two-cylinder steam engine mounted on the single front wheel. It achieved a speed of 3 miles (5 km) per hour and was involved in the world's first motor accident when it demolished a wall. German engineer Charles Dietz built another three-wheel machine in 1835. It had a pair of rocking cylinders that worked cranks to move a chain drive to the rear wheels.

Experiments with steam vehicles continued, aimed at producing a tractor or a bus, rather than a smaller form of personal transportation. In England Scottish engineer

William Murdock (1754–1839) ran a model steam-powered road vehicle in 1784, and in 1789 American inventor Oliver Evans (1755–1819) fitted one of his high-pressure engines to a four-wheel land vehicle. English engineer Richard Trevithick (1771–1833) built a similar vehicle in 1801. It had large driving wheels with front wheels that were steered independently, and it could reach a speed of 10 miles (16 km) per hour. In 1829 English inventor Goldsworthy Gurney (1793–1875) began a regular steam coach service from London to Bath that ran at an average speed of 15 miles (24 km) per hour.

New Yorker Richard Dudgeon built a lightweight steam carriage in about 1865, and in 1873 French engineer Amédée Bollée (1844–1917) built a 12-seater carriage that he called *L'Obéissante* ("The Obedient One"). His *La Mancelle* ("The Young Lady from Le Mans") of 1878 had a front-mounted engine driving the rear wheels. It could travel at up to 25

In 1908 Henry Ford produced the Model T, or "Tin Lizzy," as it was affectionately known by millions of Americans.

miles (40 km) per hour. Just as automobiles were becoming efficient, however, steam carriages fell into decline in the face of competition from the railroads.

Benz and Daimler

The next step in the development of the automobile came with the work of engineers Karl Benz (1844–1929) and Gottlieb Daimler (1834–1900) in Germany. They realized the potential of the new gasoline engine as a means of powering road vehicles. Benz's first car, a three-wheeler, dates from 1885. It had a 1-horsepower engine and a maximum speed of 8 miles (13 km) per hour. Daimler built his first car a year later, mounting his gasoline engine in a heavier four-wheel vehicle. At first he concentrated on producing engines for other makers' cars, and by 1889 he had a powerful, reliable 3.5-horsepower unit. By 1891 French engineers René Panhard (1841–1908) and Émile Levassor (d. 1897) were emulating Daimler and building cars with a chassis. The vehicles, known as

système Panhard (Panhard system), had front-mounted Daimler engines to drive the rear wheels. They had modern Ackermann (double-pivoting) steering, a gear box, and a friction clutch. By 1893 Benz was making the more stable four-wheel cars with 3-horsepower engines. The same year saw the first gasoline-engined car built by U.S. inventor Charles Duryea (1861–1938) and his brother Frank (1869–1967). The first U.S.-made cars went on sale in 1896. One year later there was a brief reversion to steam power when the Stanley brothers of Massachusetts—Francis (1849–1918) and Freelan (1849–1940)—launched the Stanley Steamer.

Soon after the turn of the 20th century American industrialist Henry Ford (1863–1947) revolutionized car manufacture by introducing mass-production techniques. As a new chassis moved slowly along an assembly line, workers added the engine, transmission, wheels, and body. In 1908 the method produced the Model T. "You can have it in any color as long as it's black," declared Ford. The motor age was born.

By 1894 French motorists were organizing speed and endurance races for their Panhard and Levassor voitures sans chevaux (horseless carriages).

ASTRONOMY & MATH

EUROPE

1902 English mathematician Bertrand Russell (1872–1970) introduces his paradox questioning contemporary set theory. Russell proposed a set that contains all sets that are not members of themselves. If this set is not a member of itself, then it must be included in itself, thus disqualifying it from being a member of itself.

1902 French meteorologist Léon Teisserenc de Bort (1855–1913) distinguishes the stratosphere and troposphere layers in the Earth's atmosphere.

1904 German astrophysicist Johannes Hartmann (1865–1936) reveals the presence of interstellar matter in space by studying stellar spectra.

THE AMERICAS

1901 American astronomer Annie Cannon (1863–1941) adds spectral subclasses to complete the Harvard classification of stars, a system in which stars are assigned to seven different classes according to their surface temperature.

1904 American-born Argentine astronomer Charles Perrine (1867–1951) locates Himalia, the sixth moon of Jupiter. A year later he finds the seventh, Elara.

BIOLOGY & MEDICINE

EUROPE

1901 French physiologist Charles Richet (1850–1935) coins the term *anaphylaxis* to describe the life-threatening allergic reaction to an antigen to which an individual has become sensitized.

1901 Russian bacteriologist Élie Metchnikoff (1845–1916) determines the role of white blood cells in fighting infection.

1902 English physiologists Ernest Starling (1866–1927) and William Bayliss (1860–1924) isolate the digestive-juice stimulant secretin and later coin the term *hormone* to describe it.

1903 German surgeon Georg Perthes (1869–1927) first uses x-rays to treat cancerous tumors.

1903 German company A. G. Bayer markets Veronal (a barbiturate) as a sleeping pill.

1903 German chemist Eduard Buchner (1860–1917) isolates zymase—the first enzyme—in yeast.

1903 Russian physiologist Ivan Pavlov (1849–1936) develops the concept of the conditioned reflex (the way in which an action can be influenced by previous behavior).

THE AMERICAS

1901 The Rockefeller Institute for Medical Research opens in New York City.

1901 Japanese-born American chemist Jokichi Takamine (1854–1922) reports that he has successfully isolated epinephrine (adrenaline).

The okapi is a large mammal related to the giraffe, with zebralike stripes and an extremely long, flexible tongue.

AFRICA & THE MIDDLE EAST

1901 The first okapi (*Okapia johnstoni*) to be seen by Western explorers is found in the rain forests of central Africa.

PHYSICAL SCIENCES

EUROPE

1901 French chemist François Grignard (1871–1935) presents Grignard reagents (organometallic compounds containing magnesium and a halogen such as chlorine).

1902 English physicist Oliver Heaviside (1850–1925) and American engineer Arthur Kennelly (1861–1939) independently propose that a layer of ionized gases in the atmosphere "bounces" radio waves around the Earth.

1902 German chemist Emil Fischer (1852–1919) determines that proteins are polypeptides.

1903 Scottish chemist William Ramsay (1852–1916) obtains helium from the radioactive decay of radium. This confirms that alpha particles (produced by radium emission) consist of helium nuclei.

1903 Russian rocket pioneer Konstantin Tsiolkovsky (1857–1935) proposes the first practical theory of rocket propulsion.

1904 English physicist J. J. Thomson (1856–1940) puts forward his model of the atom—a spherical mass of positively charged matter with electrons inside it.

ASIA & OCEANIA

1904 Japanese physicist Nagaoka Hantaro (1865–1950) puts forward the "Saturnian" theory of atomic structure, in which small electrons orbit a massive nucleus.

ENGINEERING & INVENTION

1901 German engineer August von Parseval (1861–1942) begins construction of a nonrigid airship (the *Parseval*).

1901 German engineer Eugen Langen (1833–95) builds a suspended monorail railroad in Wuppertal, Germany.

1901 Italian physicist and radio pioneer Guglielmo Marconi (1874–1937) makes the first transatlantic radio transmission.

1901 English engineer Hubert Booth (1871–1955) invents a vacuum cleaner powered by a gasoline engine.

1901 German physicist Ferdinand Braun (1850–1918) invents the crystal detector for tuning a radio. In 1906 it is improved by American engineer Greenleaf Pickard (1877–1956).

1903 Dutch physiologist Willem Einthoven (1860–1927) invents the electrocardiograph for recording the electrical activity of the heart.

1904 English engineer John Fleming (1849–1945) invents the diode valve (vacuum tube).

In 1901 a suspended monorail (Schwebebahn) began running in the German city Wuppertal.

1903 American brothers Wilbur (1867–1912) and Orville Wright (1871–1948) make the first sustained flight in a heavier-than-air airplane.

1904 The first section of the New York City subway opens, with electric trains serving 28 stations.

1904 American engineer Charles Kettering (1876–1958) invents an electric cash register.

1902 The first Aswan Dam is completed in Egypt, based on a design by English engineer William Willcocks (1852–1932).

WORLD EVENTS

Henri Giffard's airship of 1852 flew 17 miles (27 km) on its first flight.

1901 Britain's Queen Victoria (r. 1837–1901) dies and is succeeded by her son Edward VII (r. 1901–1910).

1903 Russia's Social Democratic Party splits between the minority Mensheviks and the majority (and more extreme) Bolsheviks.

1903 In Britain Emmeline Pankhurst (1858–1928) forms the Women's Social and Political Union to campaign for women's suffrage (the right to vote). Its supporters are known as suffragettes or suffragists.

1904 Britain and France become allies in the Entente Cordiale ("Friendly Understanding"), one of a series of defensive pacts formed in the decade before World War I (1914–18).

1901 President William McKinley (1843–1901) is assassinated by an anarchist. Vice President Theodore Roosevelt (1858–1919) succeeds him.

1902 Colombia's War of the Thousand Days (1899–1902) comes to an end, with 100,000 people killed.

1901 Various British colonies join to form the commonwealth of Australia.

1902 Japan allies with Britain to resist Russian expansion in eastern Asia.

1904 The Russo–Japanese War (1904–05) breaks out.

1901 Ashanti in northern Nigeria is annexed to Britain's Gold Coast colony (later Ghana).

AIRSHIPS

Only weeks after the first passengers flew in a Montgolfier hot-air balloon in 1783, a hydrogen gas-filled balloon soared over the rooftops of Paris. Early hydrogen-filled balloons could only travel with the wind and carry a small number of people. In 1852 French engineer Henri Giffard (1825–82) designed a craft that he called a *dirigible* (French for "steerable"). This consisted of a cylindrical gasbag with an open cabin, or gondola, suspended beneath to hold the pilot and engine. The design enabled sustained controlled flight for the first time. As lighter and more powerful engines were developed, airships became a more practical mode of transport.

The first rigid airship—with an internal metal framework that maintained an aerodynamic shape—was built by Austrian David Schwartz (1852–97) in 1897. But it was German engineer Graf Ferdinand von Zeppelin (1838–1917) who turned the concept into a commercially viable design. Zeppelin's first successful airship was the *LZ-3*, built in 1908.

Airships were used by both sides in World War I (1914–18) for both reconnaissance and bombing raids. In the 1920s and 1930s huge airships such as the *Graf Zeppelin* and the *Hindenburg* made frequent transatlantic flights. The disastrous wreck of the *Hindenburg* in 1937, coupled with tensions between the United States and Nazi Germany, ended the period. Soon after, advances in airplane design rendered airships obsolete.

ASTRONOMY & MATH

EUROPE

1906 German astronomer August Kopff (1882–1960) discovers the short-period Kopff comet.

1906 Russian mathematician Andrey Markov (1856–1922) develops the theory of the Markov chain, a sequence of random events whose probabilities depend on previous events in the chain. This theory would later prove important in biology and physics.

1906 French mathematician Maurice Fréchet (1878–1973) introduces functional calculus to mathematics.

1906 Irish-born English geologist Richard Oldham (1858–1936) deduces that the Earth's core is molten.

1906 German astronomer Max Wolf (1863–1932) locates 558 Achilles, one of the so-called Trojan asteroids that orbit just in front of or behind Jupiter.

THE AMERICAS

$$E = mc^2$$

ALBERT EINSTEIN, *ANNALEN DER PHYSIK*, 1905

ASIA & OCEANIA

1905 Astronomer John Grigg (1838–1920) observes the third of the comets that bear his name from his observatory in Thames, New Zealand.

AFRICA & THE MIDDLE EAST

BIOLOGY & MEDICINE

1905 French psychologists Alfred Binet (1857–1911) and Theodore Simon (1873–1961) devise a method of testing intelligence and ascribing an intelligence quotient (IQ) based on the results.

1906 French bacteriologists Albert Calmette (1863–1933) and Camille Guérin (1872–1961) begin work on developing the BCG vaccine (*Bacillus* Calmette–Guérin) against tuberculosis.

1906 German bacteriologist August von Wassermann (1866–1925) develops a blood-serum test for syphilis.

1906 Austrian physician Clemens von Pirquet (1874–1929) shows that hay fever is a reaction to pollen and coins the term *allergy*.

1906 German chemist Paul Ehrlich (1854–1915) establishes the structural formula of atoxyl. Four years later he produces Salvarsan 606, an early synthetic drug.

1906 English biochemist Frederick Gowland Hopkins (1861–1947) concludes that "accessory food factors," later called vitamins, are essential to health.

1905 American surgeon John Murphy (1857–1916) pioneers arthroplasty, an operation to remodel a diseased joint.

1905 American embryologists Edmund Wilson (1856–1939) and Nettie Stevens (1861–1912) independently demonstrate the role of chromosomes in sex determination in insects.

1907 American zoologist Ross Harrison (1870–1959) introduces the technique of *in vitro* tissue culture (growing tissues in glass laboratory apparatus).

Workers pose for a photograph during the digging of the Simplon Tunnel, which links Italy to Switzerland. At the time of its completion, the 12-mile (20-km) tunnel was the longest in the world.

PHYSICAL SCIENCES

1905 German chemist Richard Willstätter (1872–1942) begins the work that will eventually reveal the molecular structure of chlorophyll.

1905 German-born physicist Albert Einstein (1879–1955) publishes his special theory of relativity. He also explains the photoelectric effect in terms of quanta ("packets") of light that strike a metal surface and liberate electrons from it.

1906 Russian botanist Mikhail Tsvett (1872–1919) separates plant pigments using paper chromatography.

1906 New Zealand-born English physicist Ernest Rutherford (1871–1937) measures the ratio of charge to mass for alpha particles and deduces that they are helium nuclei.

1906 German physical chemist Walther Nernst (1864–1941) announces the third law of thermodynamics: that at absolute zero the entropy (a measure of the ability to do work) of a perfect crystalline substance is zero.

ENGINEERING & INVENTION

1905 French cycling advocate Paul de Vivie (1853–1930) invents the derailleur gear system for bicycles, allowing cyclists to climb hills with less effort and travel faster.

1906 Russian physicist Boris Golitsyn (1862–1916) creates an electromagnetic seismograph for detecting earthquakes.

1906 French physicist Jacques d'Arsonval (1851–1940) invents a freeze-drying technique used to preserve foods.

1906 The Simplon Tunnel under the Alps is completed, linking Italy to Switzerland.

1906 The British navy launches H.M.S. *Dreadnought*, the first modern battleship, armed with ten 12-inch (30.5-cm) guns and powered by steam turbines.

1907 A diesel-engined ship, the tanker *Djelo*, is launched at the Koloma Yard in Russia.

1907 French engineer Louis Bréguet (1880–1955) constructs a primitive kind of helicopter, the gyroplane.

1907 The German company Henkel markets the first synthetic household detergent (Persil).

1906 American engineer Lee De Forest (1873–1961) invents the audion tube.

1906 Canadian-born American electrical engineer Reginald Fessenden (1866–1932) makes AM (amplitude modulation) radio transmissions.

1907 Belgian-born American chemist Leo Baekeland (1863–1944) invents bakelite plastic.

1905 New Zealand inventor Richard Pearse (1877–1953) patents various innovations he used in his first flying machine in 1904. Due to his isolation from the centers of early aviation, however, his achievements pass largely unnoticed.

WORLD EVENTS

1905 In St. Petersburg the tsar's troops fire on demonstrating workers on Bloody Sunday, triggering a wider uprising. To quell the unrest, Nicholas II (r. 1894–1917) concedes limited reforms, including the establishment of an elected assembly, the duma.

1906 Russia's duma meets for the first time, only to be quickly dissolved by the tsar, who considers it too radical.

1906 A massive earthquake strikes San Francisco, destroying buildings and starting a fire that devastates the city.

With its heavy armor and huge mobile turret guns, H.M.S. Dreadnought *was the first modern battleship.*

1905 Japanese forces gain control of Manchuria and defeat the Russian Pacific fleet in the naval Battle of Tsushima.

1905 The Treaty of Portsmouth ends the Russo-Japanese War (1904–05). Japan gains northern Sakhalin and is given a free hand to establish a protectorate in Korea.

1906 Mahatma Ghandi (1869–1948) organizes a campaign of civil disobedience and nonviolent protest against discriminatory laws while working as a lawyer in South Africa.

ALBERT EINSTEIN

German-born theoretical physicist Albert Einstein is best known for his theory of relativity, one of the most important contributions in the history of science.

Einstein was born into a Jewish family and educated in Munich, Aarau, and Zurich. After graduating with a degree in physics in 1902, Einstein was unable to find work as a teacher. In 1905 he took a job as an examiner at the Swiss Patent Office while at the same time publishing his four papers on physics. The first dealt with Brownian motion, the random movement of particles suspended in a liquid or gas. In the second paper he explained the photoelectric effect (the production of electrons by a metal surface when struck by light) in terms of the new quantum theory of German physicist Max Planck (1858–1947). The third paper outlined his special theory of relativity, which deals with the relative motion of objects moving with uniform velocity. The fourth paper contained the equation $E = mc^2$, which states the equivalence of mass and energy, and employs c, the speed of light, as a universal constant. The concept was essential to the development of atomic weapons and modern physics. In 1916 Einstein published the general theory of relativity.

When the Nazis rose to power, Einstein left for the United States and began lecturing at Princeton in 1934. He became an American citizen in 1940 and spent his remaining years working toward a unified field theory.

THE AIRPLANE

EVEN BEFORE THE INVENTION OF LIGHTER-than-air flying machines, such as balloons and airships, people wanted to copy birds and fly. For this reason many early designs, such as those drawn by Leonardo da Vinci (1452–1519), had flapping wings. It was almost another 500 years before the ambition was realized.

A flapping-wing machine is called an ornithopter. No such machine was ever built except in model form; even if a full-size version had been built, it would not have worked because it depended on human muscle power for propulsion. (Human-powered aircraft have been built in recent times but aided by modern knowledge of aerodynamics, mechanisms, and materials.)

Kites and Gliders

The first heavier-than-air machines to fly were kites, invented by the Chinese in about 1000 B.C.E. In the late 19th century human-carrying kites were built, including one designed by English soldier Baden Baden-Powell (1860–1937) in 1894 and improved in 1901 by American showman "Colonel" Samuel Cody (1867–1913). Today's ski-kites and microlight aircraft continue the tradition. Real progress did not come, however, until people began to experiment with gliders. One of the first to do so was English inventor George Cayley (1773–1857). In 1808 he flew an unpiloted glider with a wing area of about 320 square feet (30 sq m). Then in 1853 he built a 300-pound (135-kg) person-carrying glider. The passenger was Cayley's footman—unaware that he was the first person ever to fly in a heavier-than-air machine. Three years later French naval officer Jean-Marie Le Bris

Leonardo da Vinci's sketches of a glider—from the early 16th century—was based on his study of bats' wings.

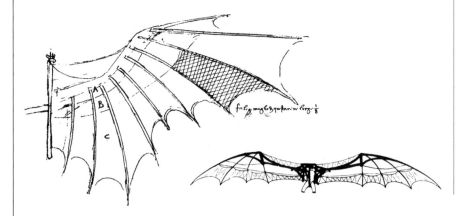

(1817–72) made a short gliding flight on a beach in northern France. In 1895 Scottish aviator Percy Pilcher (1866–99) made a part-controlled gliding flight in his hang glider, the *Bat*. A year later he built his fourth glider, the *Hawk*. It was steered by a tiller attached to a four-vaned rudder. In 1897 Pilcher broke the world record for flight when he flew 820 feet (250 m) in the *Hawk*. He died in 1899 from injuries sustained when the *Hawk* crashed.

German aeronautical pioneer Otto Lilienthal (1848–96) made a piloted flight in a steerable glider in 1891. His early machines copied birds' wings, but later he added a tail for stability and came up with the idea of two pairs of wings, one above the other. The pilot hung beneath the wings, as in a modern hang glider. The two-wing arrangement, later called a biplane, remained a feature of nearly all early flying machines. In 1893 Lilienthal tried birdlike jointed wings, but they failed, and in 1896 he became another glider pilot to crash to his death. In the United States Wilbur Wright (1867–1912) and his brother Orville (1871–1948) read about Lilienthal's pioneering work, which would influence their experiments. Also in the United States French-born American inventor Octave

Chanute (1832–1910) constructed an extremely stable biplane glider in 1896, which again was noted by the Wright brothers. By 1903 they had perfected human-carrying gliders of their own.

Steam Power

By the early 20th century engineers had developed what is now called an "airframe." Now all they needed was a suitable power source. At the time, the steam engine was the only possibility. As early as 1842 English-born American engineer William Henson (1812–1888) took out a patent for a monoplane aircraft with a steam engine, pusher propellers, and a cabin for several passengers. He was only ever to build a nonfunctional model. In 1848 English inventor John Stringfellow (1799–1883) also made a steam-powered model. It flew a short distance before crashing. In France in 1890 engineer Clément Ader (1841–1926) built a full-sized steam-powered monoplane, *Eole*. It flew—uncontrolled—for about 165 feet (50 m).

Another short-lived success was a huge machine built by American-born English inventor Hiram Maxim (1840–1916). His biplane of 1894 had two steam engines, each one driving its own propeller.

Launched along a set of rails, it managed to rise less than 3 feet (1 m) before falling to the ground. Two years later American Samuel Langley (1834–1906) built a large steam-powered model airplane. It flew for about 90 seconds and covered 875 yards (800 m).

In 1903 Langley built a full-sized airplane with a lighter gasoline engine. Two attempts to launch it from a barge in Washington, D.C., failed—each time the machine crashed into the Potomac River. The Wright brothers built their own gasoline engine out of lightweight aluminum and attached it to one of their gliders. The launch of this machine at Kitty Hawk, North Carolina, on December 17, 1903, heralded the start of sustained heavier-than-air flight. For the first time a human flew in a machine that took off and landed under full control. It was three years before Brazilian aviator Alberto Santos-Dumont (1873–1932) achieved the same feat in his own motorized glider.

The next advances mainly involved materials. Steel and other alloys replaced wood for airframes, and aluminum panels instead of varnished cloth were used to cover them. Jets superseded gasoline engines, and just 44 years after the Wright brothers' first flight, an airplane flew faster than the speed of sound.

The Wright brothers' biplane takes off from Kitty Hawk, North Carolina, on December 17, 1903.

KEY DATES

1808
Unpiloted glider

1848
Steam-powered model airplane

1853
Human-carrying glider

1890
Unpiloted steam-powered airplane

1891
Steerable human-carrying glider

1903
Sustained flight in gasoline-engined airplane

EUROPE

ASTRONOMY & MATH

1908 Following his publications of 1905 and 1907, Danish astronomer Ejnar Hertzsprung (1873–1967) introduces a method of classifying stars by plotting a graph of luminosity against temperature. It becomes the basis of the Hertzsprung–Russell diagram, published in 1913.

1908 German mathematician Ernst Zermelo (1871–1953) introduces set theory to mathematics.

1908 English-born Belgian astronomer Philibert Melotte (1880–1961) discovers Pasiphae, one of Jupiter's outer moons.

BIOLOGY & MEDICINE

1908 English mathematician Godfrey Hardy (1877–1947) and German physician Wilhelm Weinberg (1862–1937) independently formulate an equation that describes the genetic equilibrium within a population. It is later known as the Hardy–Weinberg law.

1908 French anthropologist Marcellin Boule (1861–1942) reconstructs the first complete skeleton of an early Neandertal human found in France.

1909 English physiologist Henry Dale (1875–1968) discovers oxytocin, the hormone that causes the womb to contract during and after childbirth.

1909 Danish botanist Wilhelm Johannsen (1857–1927) coins the term *gene* for the factor that carries inheritable characteristics.

1910 French surgeon Alexis Carrel (1873–1944) develops the technique of making tissue cultures.

1910 German chemist Paul Ehrlich (1854–1915) prepares the synthetic drug Salvarsan 606, used in the treatment of syphilis.

PHYSICAL SCIENCES

1908 German chemist Fritz Haber (1868–1934) discovers the catalytic reaction for synthesizing ammonia from nitrogen and hydrogen. Later it is developed by German chemist Carl Bosch (1874–1940) and becomes the basis of industries that make fertilizers and explosives.

1908 French physicist Jean Perrin (1870–1942) calculates the value of Avogadro's number (the number of atoms or molecules in one mole of a substance.

1908 Dutch physicist Heike Kamerlingh Onnes (1853–1926) liquefies helium.

1908 German physicist Hans Geiger (1882–1945), working with New Zealand-born English physicist Ernest Rutherford (1871–1937), devises a method for detecting and measuring ionizing radiation.

1909 Danish chemist Sören Sörensen (1868–1939) introduces the concept of pH, a measure of acidity or alkalinity.

1910 Ernest Rutherford proves the existence of the nucleus of the atom after seeing an experiment by his assistant Ernest Marsden (1889–1970).

In 1908 trees are knocked over and stripped of their leaves and branches in Siberia by the explosion known as the "Tunguska event."

THE AMERICAS

1908 American physicist and astronomer Harold Babcock (1882–1968) detects the sun's weak magnetic field. In the same year American astronomer George Hale (1868–1938) observes the magnetic fields associated with sunspots.

1909 American pathologist Howard Ricketts (1871–1910) finds a new type of small bacteria (Rickettsia) that are often carried by ticks. In the same year he discovers the bacterium that causes typhus, which French bacteriologist Charles-Jules Nicolle (1866–1936) shows is carried from person to person by the body louse.

1910 Brazilian physician Carlos Chagas (1879–1934) first describes Chagas' disease, which is caused by a protozoan parasite (*Trypanosoma cruzi*).

1908 American physicist William Coolidge (1873–1975) uses tungsten to make an incandescent filament lamp.

1908 English-born American electrical engineer Edward Weston (1850–1936) sees the Weston cadmium cell (battery) adopted as an international voltage standard.

1909 American Edward Davidson first uses carbon tetrachloride (tetrachloromethane) as a fire extinguisher.

Aviator Louis Blériot (right) stands in front of the Blériot IX aircraft in which he successfully crossed the English Channel from France and England.

ASIA & OCEANIA

AFRICA & THE MIDDLE EAST

I will build a motor car for the great multitude. It will be large enough for the family, but small enough for the individual to run and care for. It will be constructed of the best materials, by the best men to be hired, after the simplest designs that modern engineering can devise. But it will be so low in price that no man making a good salary will be unable to own one.

HENRY FORD, *MY LIFE AND WORK*

1909 French aviator Louis Blériot (1872–1936) flies across the English Channel. It is the first flight over an ocean in a heavier-than-air craft.

1909 Irish engineer Louis Brennan (1852–1932) builds and demonstrates a gyrostabilized monorail system.

1909 "SOS" is introduced as the international radio distress signal.

1910 French engineer Henri Fabre (1882–1984) builds the first seaplane.

1910 French chemist Georges Claude (1870–1960) invents neon discharge tubes for use in lighting and signs.

1908 Taking advantage of an Ottoman Empire weakened by internal and external troubles, Bulgaria and Crete declare independence. Four years later the Balkan states of Serbia, Montenegro, and Albania join their independence struggle.

1910 A revolution takes place in Portugal: the monarchy is brought down and a republic proclaimed.

1910 George V (r. 1910–36) ascends the British throne at a time when the British Empire is at its peak, covering about a quarter of the globe.

Workers at Henry Ford's Detroit factory add components to a partially assembled Model T.

1908 The first Model T Ford of American industrialist Henry Ford (1863–1947) comes off the assembly line at Detroit.

1908 The American Corning Flint Glassworks funds a research project to develop heat-resistant glass for railroad lanterns.

1908 American musician and physicist Dayton Miller (1866–1941) invents the *phonodeik* system of recording sound photographically.

1910 American airman Eugene Ely (1886–1911) makes the first airplane flight off a ship (the U.S.S. *Birmingham*).

1910 The National Association for the Advancement of Colored People (NAACP) is founded to campaign for the rights of African Americans.

THE HERTZSPRUNG–RUSSELL DIAGRAM

By the early 1900s it was possible to measure a star's apparent magnitude with accuracy. "Apparent magnitude" is the brightness with which a star glows in the sky. It depends on the star's actual luminosity and how far away it is. Danish astronomer Ejnar Hertzsprung (1873–1967) and American astronomer Henry Russell (1877–1957) used these measurements to relate a star's luminosity to its color. A star's color depends on its surface temperature and the range of electromagnetic radiation it gives off, known as its spectrum.

Hertzsprung found that bright blue–white stars seemed to follow the rule that brighter meant hotter, but that stars of the redder, cooler type could be divided into high- and low-luminosity groups. Since these stars have the same temperature, the differences in luminosity must be due to differences in size. Hertzsprung called the larger cool stars "giants." He published his ideas in 1905.

At Princeton, Russell developed similar ideas. By 1913 he had devised a diagram mapping luminosity against temperature. The Hertzsprung–Russell (HR) diagram acknowledged the contributions of both astronomers.

The Hertzsprung–Russell diagram plots stars' luminosity (vertical axis) against surface temperature (horizontal axis). The stars are not randomly scattered. Most of them lie on a line that runs from bright, hot blue stars at the top left to cool, faint red stars at the bottom right.

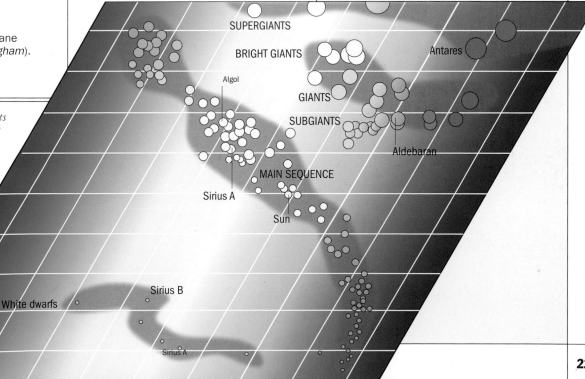

ASTRONOMY & MATH	BIOLOGY & MEDICINE	PHYSICAL SCIENCES

EUROPE

1913 A photographic survey of the sky—206 photographs taken by English astronomer John Franklin-Adams (1843–1912) between 1903 and 1912—is published posthumously.

1913 French physicist Charles Fabry (1867–1945) reveals the existence of the ozone layer in the Earth's upper atmosphere.

1913 English geologist Arthur Holmes (1890–1965) uses rock radioactivity data to calculate the Earth's age as 4.6 billion years (in agreement with the modern value).

1911 English physiologist Henry Dale (1875–1968) identifies histamine, a substance that is released into the bloodstream as part of the immune system response to injury or infection.

1912 German chemist Paul Ehrlich (1854–1915) introduces acriflavine for use as an antiseptic.

1912 German biochemist Heinrich Wieland (1877–1957) begins studying bile acids. He later discovers that they are steroids (complex molecules based on cholesterol).

1912 English geologist Charles Dawson (1864–1916) unearths fossils of prehistoric "Piltdown man" at a quarry in England. In 1953 they are revealed to be a hoax.

1911 Dutch physicist Heike Kamerlingh Onnes (1853–1926) discovers superconductivity—the total loss of electrical resistance that some substances exhibit at very low temperatures.

1912 Austrian chemist Friedrich Paneth (1887–1958) and Hungarian-born chemist Georg von Hevesy (1885–1966) use radioactive substances as tracers to follow the paths of chemical reactions.

1912 German physicist Max von Laue (1879–1960) proves the diffraction of x-rays by crystals, which becomes the basis of x-ray crystallography.

1913 English chemist Frederick Soddy (1877–1956) concludes that some elements can exist in forms that differ only in atomic weight and calls them "isotopes."

1913 English physicist Henry Moseley (1887–1915) proposes that the frequencies of the lines in x-ray spectra of elements are related to their atomic numbers.

1913 Danish physicist Niels Bohr (1885–1962) proposes his model of the atom: a central, positively charged nucleus surrounded by orbiting electrons that are negatively charged.

THE AMERICAS

1912 Austrian-born American physicist Victor Hess (1883–1964) observes cosmic rays, using a hot-air balloon.

1912 American astronomer Vesto Slipher (1875–1969) discovers reflection nebulas (near the Pleiades, an open cluster of stars in the constellation Taurus).

1912 American astronomer Henrietta Swan Leavitt (1868–1921) formulates the period-luminosity law, which is used to measure interstellar distances.

1913 American geneticist Alfred Sturtevant (1891–1970) introduces the technique of chromosome mapping to record the positions of genes along a chromosome.

1913 American biochemist Elmer McCollum (1879–1967) and his coworkers discover vitamin A (retinol).

1913 German-born American chemist Leonor Michaelis (1875–1949) and Canadian physician Maude Menten (1879–1960) develop a mathematical explanation of how enzymes act as catalysts.

1913 Hungarian-born American pediatrician Béla Schick (1877–1967) devises the Schick test for diphtheria. The same year German bacteriologist Emil von Behring (1854–1917) develops a vaccine against the disease.

1913 American physicist Robert Millikan (1868–1953) announces his famous oil-drop experiment, in which he balances the charge on an ionized drop of oil with the charge between two metal plates. From this he calculates the charge on an electron.

1913 American chemist William Burton (1865–1954) patents a high-temperature, high-pressure thermal cracking process for crude oil (breaking it down into simpler compounds using heat).

ASIA & OCEANIA

When it comes to atoms, language can be used only as in poetry. The poet, too, is not nearly so concerned with describing facts as with creating images and establishing mental connections.

NIELS BOHR, 1920

1912 The world's largest extant lizard, the Komodo dragon (*Varanus komodoensis*), is recorded in Indonesia.

The Komodo dragon was discovered by Europeans in 1912.

AFRICA & THE MIDDLE EAST

1912 Russian-born Israeli chemist and statesman Chaim Weizmann (1874–1952) devises a way of using bacteria to produce acetone by the fermentation of grain.

ENGINEERING & INVENTION	WORLD EVENTS

1911 Scottish physicist C. T. R. Wilson (1869–1959) invents the cloud chamber, used for studying subatomic particles.

1911 German physicist Ferdinand Braun (1850–1918) devises a scanning system for cathode-ray tubes, later used in radar and television.

1911 Prince Henry of Prussia (1862–1929) invents the windshield wiper for cars.

1912 The R.M.S. *Titanic* sinks on its maiden voyage, with the loss of 1,517 lives.

1913 German chemist Friedrich Bergius (1884–1949) conceives a method of converting coal to oil using high-pressure hydrogenation. The process is to be of great value to Germany during World War I (1914–18), when demand for oil increases dramatically.

1911 Norwegian explorer Roald Amundsen (1872–1928) becomes the first person to reach the South Pole, beating the British expedition led by Robert Scott (1868–1912).

1912 The military alliance between the states of Germany, Austria–Hungary, and Italy is strengthened and renewed.

1913 The Home Rule Bill granting limited independence to Ireland is passed by Britain's House of Commons but rejected by the House of Lords.

Grand Central Station in New York City has 44 platforms, making it the largest railroad station in the world.

An artist's impression of the R.M.S. Titanic *sinking after striking an iceberg*

THE *TITANIC*

In 1909 construction began on the ship that would become the R.M.S. (Royal Mail Ship) *Titanic*. It was intended to be the biggest, safest, and most luxurious passenger ship ever built. Promotional materials proclaimed the ship to be "practically unsinkable" and described the opulent decor, extensive recreational facilities, and modern technology, including shipwide electric lighting and wireless radio communications equipment.

However, away from the bright lights of the first-class cabins many of the techniques and technologies used in the ship's construction were far from being the best available. Most importantly, the ship did not carry enough lifeboats, and its old-fashioned rudder was barely large enough for the ship to be considered seaworthy.

On its well-publicized first voyage in April 1911—from Southampton, England, to New York City—the *Titanic* struck an iceberg in the northern Atlantic. Although the iceberg was sighted by the ship's lookout, it was too late for the ship—with its poor maneuverability—to avoid. The iceberg gouged a tear in the side of the ship, inundating five of its bulkhead compartments with water.

The passengers and crew were not initially aware of the severity of the impact, and the first lifeboat was not lowered until almost an hour afterward. Distress signals were sent out, but the nearest ship was four hours' travel away. The ship sank in just under three hours. Of the 2,223 people on board, 1,517 died.

1911 American airman Calbraith Rogers (1879–1912) makes the first flight (with stops) across the United States.

1912 American Elmer Sperry (1860–1930) invents an automatic pilot system for ships, which uses his gyrocompass.

1912 American Albert Berry makes the first parachute jump from an airplane.

1912 The largest railroad station in the world—Grand Central Station in New York City—is completed.

1911 Theodore Roosevelt (1858–1919) breaks with the Republicans to lead his own Progressive Party.

1912 U.S. forces invade Nicaragua. The country will remain under U.S. occupation for 20 years.

1912 Democrat Woodrow Wilson (1856–1924) becomes U.S. president.

1911 The first public demonstration of a aircraft in New Zealand takes place near Aukland. By this time New Zealand's own aviation pioneer, Richard Pearse (1877–1953), had abandoned his experiments.

1911 The purpose-built city of New Delhi becomes the capital city of India.

1911 Sun Yat-Sen (1866–1925) leads a nationalist revolution in China.

1912 Tibet and Mongolia both take advantage of the revolution in China to reclaim their independence, expelling Chinese officials.

1912 France imposes a protectorate on southern Morocco; the northern third of the country becomes a protectorate of Spain.

1913 The Native Land Act further reinforces the apartheid system of racial segregation in South Africa.

SYNTHETIC DRUGS

THE MID- TO LATE 19TH CENTURY SAW THE science of chemistry declare war on pain and physical suffering. Some of the new developments had their roots in traditional medicines, others were the result of years devoted to trial and error, and a few were simply pure luck.

Humans have used naturally occurring substances as medicines for thousands of years. Some of them, such as opiates, were used as analgesics (painkillers); but they were never very reliable, and they often had undesirable side effects.

A worker in a pharmaceutical company checks the production of aspirin pills.

The first wholly synthetic drugs were gases. In 1799 English chemist Humphry Davy (1778–1829) discovered the painkilling properties of nitrous oxide, also known as laughing gas. In 1815 similar properties were noted for ether vapor. Both proved to be popular social novelties due to their intoxicating side effects, but it was another 30 years before medical practitioners were to take advantage of their painkilling properties to perform surgery. In 1847 a stronger anesthetic gas, chloroform vapor, was developed by Scottish obstetrician James Simpson (1811–70) and used to help women during childbirth. None of the gases was free from side effects, notably that they made the patient unconscious, or at least insensible, and they were poisonous in large doses.

Salicylic Acid Synthesis

The use of certain plants to treat pain and fever has an extremely long history. Ancient Egyptians used myrtle, ancient Greeks and medieval Europeans used willow and meadowsweet, and Native Americans used birch. It turns out that all these plants contain the same active ingredient, named salicin for the scientific name for willow, *Salix*.

The medicinal use of willow was rediscovered by English clergyman Edward Stone (d. 1768). In 1763 Stone reported that he had successfully used willow bark to reduce fever in 50 of his patients. German pharmacist Johann Buchner (1783–1852) first isolated salicin from willow in 1828. Ten years later Italian chemist Raffaelle Pira extracted the active ingredient, salicylic acid, which took the form of colorless crystals. In 1853 French chemist Charles Gerhardt (1816–56) modified the structure of salicylic acid and created acetylsalicylic acid. But the crucial breakthrough came in 1859, when another German chemist, Hermann Kolbe (1818–84), figured out the chemical structure of salicylic acid and came up with a means of synthesizing it on a large scale—not from plants but from coal tar. Using the Kolbe reaction, the new drug went into mass production.

Salicylic acid was an effective painkiller, but it also caused severe stomach upsets, so there was an incentive to modify it. This was achieved by German chemist

Felix Hoffman (1868–1946) at the chemical company Bayer. Hoffman adapted Gerhardt's earlier formula to synthesize acetylsalicylic acid, and in 1899 the new drug was launched by Bayer as aspirin. At first, aspirin could be administered only by doctors, but in 1915 it became available without prescription.

Another painkilling drug with a bright future was developed at about the same time as aspirin. The analgesic and antifever effects of two very similar compounds, known as acetanilide and phenacetin, were recognized in 1886 and 1887 respectively. Phenacetin was launched as a drug for use in human patients in 1888. In more ways than one it was the direct forerunner of acetaminophen. Acetaminophen is a natural derivative of phenacetin, and the body converts one to the other very quickly. However, the significance of this was not realized immediately, and acetaminophen was not developed as a painkiller and antifever drug in its own right until the 1950s.

Salvarsan and Syphilis

A third important synthetic drug also being developed at the turn of the 20th century was a compound called arsphenamine. Sold under the proprietary name Salvarsan, this arsenic-based drug was used to treat the sexually transmitted disease syphilis. German chemist Paul Ehrlich (1854–1915) knew that some arsenic-containing compounds had antisyphilis

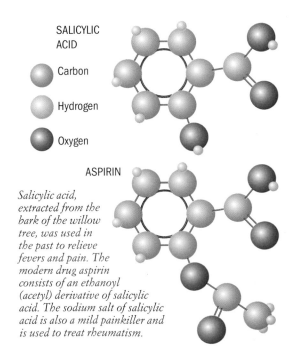

SALICYLIC ACID

Carbon

Hydrogen

Oxygen

ASPIRIN

Salicylic acid, extracted from the bark of the willow tree, was used in the past to relieve fevers and pain. The modern drug aspirin consists of an ethanoyl (acetyl) derivative of salicylic acid. The sodium salt of salicylic acid is also a mild painkiller and is used to treat rheumatism.

Paul Ehrlich used a systematic approach to drug development. His famous "compound 606" was marketed as Salvarsan, a treatment for syphilis, in 1910.

properties, so in 1906 he set about making and testing hundreds more. The 606th preparation turned out to be effective against the bacterium that causes syphilis (*Treponema pallidum*). The drug was improved a little in 1914 and became known as Neosalvarsan. However, the successful treatment of syphilis still needed a long and intensive series of injections.

The therapeutic advancements of the 20th century meant that the science of pharmaceutics had finally come of age. Synthesizing new compounds and tinkering with their structure to modify their effects is the basis of almost all modern drug development.

KEY DATES

1799
Laughing gas as painkiller

1815
Ether as painkiller

1828
Salicin isolated from willow

1847
Chloroform used in childbirth

1859
Salicylic acid in mass production

1899
Aspirin launched

1910
Salvarsan 606

ASTRONOMY & MATH

1914 English astronomer Arthur Eddington (1882–1944) recognizes that many nebulae are, in fact, galaxies made up of millions of stars.

1915 Scottish astronomer Robert Innes (1861–1933) locates Proxima Centauri, the star nearest to the sun.

BIOLOGY & MEDICINE

1914 English physiologist Henry Dale (1875–1968) and English chemist Arthur Ewins (1882–1957) isolate acetylcholine and later establish that it acts as a nerve transmitter, chemically passing on impulses from nerve to nerve.

1915 English bacteriologist Frederick Twort (1877–1950) and French-born Canadian bacteriologist Felix d'Hérelle (1873–1949) independently discover viruses that attack bacteria. Hérelle names them bacteriophages (meaning "bacteria-eaters").

PHYSICAL SCIENCES

1915 German physicist Arnold Sommerfeld (1868–1951) proposes that electrons orbit the atomic nucleus in ellipses, not circles.

1916 German-born physicist Albert Einstein (1879–1955) publishes his paper on the general theory of relativity, which mostly concerns gravity.

1916 French physicist Paul Langevin (1872–1946) experiments with ultrasound and produces a primitive form of sonar.

HOW THINGS WORK

Covent and Ionic Bonds

A covalent chemical bond involves the sharing of electrons between two atoms. The top diagram shows the reaction between two atoms of hydrogen (H) and one of oxygen (O). (Only the outermost electron shells are shown.) As the atoms get close, they share a pair of electrons to form a molecule of water. The number of electrons in the outermost shell of the oxygen atom effectively becomes eight—a configuration that is particularly stable. Hydrogen has two electrons, which is also stable. The bottom diagram shows the reaction between a sodium (Na) atom and a chlorine (Cl) atom. As the atoms get close, an electron switches from the sodium to the chlorine, making a positive sodium ion and a negative chloride ion. The two ions form a molecule of sodium chloride. The component atoms are held together by an ionic bond, and the chlorine atom now has the stable number of eight electrons. The sodium ion is also stable.

COVALENT BOND

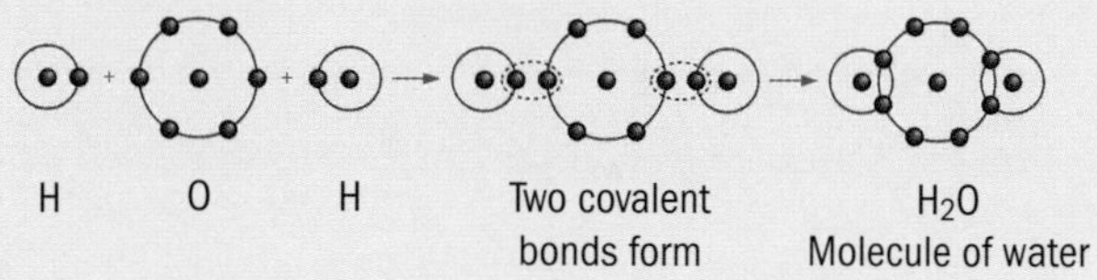

H   O   H   Two covalent bonds form H_2O Molecule of water

IONIC BOND

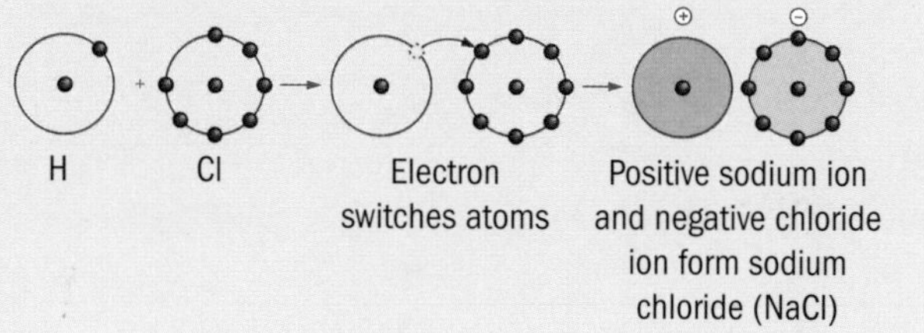

H   Cl   Electron switches atoms   Positive sodium ion and negative chloride ion form sodium chloride (NaCl)

1915 American astronomer Walter Adams (1876–1956) identifies Sirius B as the first white dwarf star. It was first discovered in 1862 by American astronomer Alvan Clark (1832–97).

1916 American astronomer Edward Barnard (1857–1923) finds Barnard's Star, the second-closest star to the sun and the star with the greatest proper motion (the fastest-moving star).

1914 American biochemist Edward Kendall (1886–1972) isolates thyroxine, the principal hormone produced by the thyroid gland.

1915 American medical researcher Joseph Goldberger (1874–1929) reveals that the skin disorder pellagra is a deficiency disease, generally caused by a lack of vitamins, specifically niacin, in the diet.

1915 American surgeon Alexis Carrel (1873–1944) performs open-heart surgery on a dog.

1916 American physical chemist Gilbert Lewis (1875–1946) puts forward the idea that a covalent chemical bond involves a sharing of electrons (not a transfer of electrons as in an ionic bond).

1916 American physicist Robert Millikan (1868–1953) uses the photoelectric effect to confirm the value of Planck's constant.

1915 Japanese researchers Katsusaburo Yamagiwa (1863–1930) and Koichi Ichikawa show that coal tar is a carcinogen (a substance that causes cancer).

1916 Several scientists make special alloys, including Japanese physicist Kotaro Honda (1870–1954), who makes Alnico (a magnetic alloy of aluminum, nickel, and cobalt), and French engineer Pierre Chevenard (1888–1960), who makes Elinvar (a nickel–iron–chromium alloy used for watch springs).

EUROPE

THE AMERICAS

ASIA & OCEANIA

AFRICA & THE MIDDLE EAST

ENGINEERING & INVENTION

1914 English military engineer Ernest Swinton (1868–1951) proposes the concept of a tank.

1914 The Canadian Grand Trunk Pacific Railway is completed.

1914 The world's largest ocean liner, S.S. *Bismarck*, is launched in Germany.

1914 German engineer Oskar Barnack (1879–1936) produces his prototype Leica camera.

1915 English inventor William Mills (1856–1932) invents the Mills bomb, a type of hand grenade used by British troops during World War I (1914–18).

1915 Dutch engineer Anthony Fokker (1890–1939) introduces an interrupter gear, which allows a machine gun to fire through the propeller of an airplane.

1915 The German company Junkers builds the first all-metal cantilever-wing airplane, the *Junkers J-1*.

1916 In Russia the Trans-Siberian Railroad is completed (begun in 1891).

1914 The 40-mile-long (64-km) Panama Canal, joining the Atlantic and Pacific oceans, is completed.

1914 American engineer John Hammer (1888–1965) invents a radio remote-control system.

1914 American inventor Garrett Morgan (1875–1963) produces a practical gas mask.

1915 American inventor Elmer Sperry (1860–1930) devises a high-intensity arc lamp (searchlight).

WORLD EVENTS

1914 Archduke Franz Ferdinand (1863–1914), heir to the Austro–Hungarian throne, is shot dead by a Bosnian nationalist in Sarajevo.

1914 World War I begins, setting the Central Powers—Germany, Italy, and Austria–Hungary—against Britain, France, and Russia.

1916 The Easter Rising is suppressed by British troops in Ireland. Hundreds of Irish civilians and rebels are killed and thousands more wounded or arrested.

1916 The British and German naval fleets clash at the Battle of Jutland. Neither side emerges as a clear victor. It is the only major naval battle of the war.

1916 The Battle of the Somme takes place in northeastern France. The battle begins in July with a failed British attack on German lines in which about 20,000 British soldiers are killed in a single day. By the time the offensive ends in November, the combined number of dead and wounded from both sides has exceeded one million men.

A pilot and gunner perform preflight checks in a World War I fighter plane. Airplane technology developed rapidly on both sides during the war.

Gas! Gas! Quick, boys!–An ecstasy of fumbling,

Fitting the clumsy helmets just in time;

But someone still was yelling out and stumbling

And flound'ring like a man in fire or lime…

Dim, through the misty panes and thick green light,

As under a green sea, I saw him drowning.

WILFRED OWEN, "DULCE ET DECORUM EST"

THE PANAMA CANAL

Soon after the Spanish conquered central America in the 16th century, they saw the advantages of a canal across the Isthmus of Panama. Engineers drew up various plans in the 1530s. However, it was not until after the opening of the Suez Canal in 1869 in Egypt that such a massive engineering project was considered feasible.

In 1878 an international company was granted a concession to dig the canal by the Colombian government, which controlled Panama. The company was led by French engineer Ferdinand de Lesseps (1805–94), designer of the Suez Canal. Poor planning and disease among the workers soon halted the construction.

With the permission of the new state of Panama, the United States took over construction of the canal in 1904. Presidents Theodore Roosevelt (1858–1919) and William Howard Taft (1857–1930) were enthusiastic supporters of the canal route devised by French engineer Adolphe de Brusly (1821–98). His design involved building an earth dam across the Chagres River to create Gatún Lake and linking this reservoir to the oceans through a series of locks.

Although many thousands died in the construction of the canal, efforts by the Surgeon General of the U.S. Army William Crawford Gorgas (1854–1920) to reduce the risk of disease—such as by exterminating mosquitoes—prevented many more deaths. With the help of heavy machinery, about 40,000 workers dug the 40-mile (64-km) canal. The project cost about $336 million in total, and the canal opened in 1920. In 1999 control and ownership was handed over to Panama.

William Crawford Gorgas

ASTRONOMY & MATH

1917 German-born theoretical physicist Albert Einstein (1879–1955) determines the cosmological constant, a term needed to "balance" his universe equation. Later he acknowledges the term is unnecessary and calls it his "biggest mistake."

1919 English theoretical physicist James Jeans (1877–1946) proposes a now discredited theory for the evolution of the solar system. He suggests that a near-collision between the sun and a passing star pulled off matter that later condensed into the planets.

1919 American astronomer Edwin Hubble (1889–1953) begins his study of Cepheid variable stars in the Andromeda galaxy.

1919 American astronomer George Hale (1868–1938) reveals that sunspots reverse their magnetic field every 22 to 23 years.

BIOLOGY & MEDICINE

1917 Austrian neurologist Julius Wagner-Jauregg (1857–1940) successfully treats syphilis by deliberately giving the patient malaria.

1919 Austrian zoologist Karl von Frisch (1886–1982) describes the "bee's dance," the way in which honeybees communicate with one another.

INSIDE STORY

Bee's Dance

When a worker bee finds a good source of pollen, she has to communicate the information to other bees in the hive. Austrian zoologist Karl von Frisch discovered in 1919 that she does this by a "dance" performed on the honeycomb, reenacting the trip she has taken. In the "waggle dance," the bee runs in two semicircles to form a flattened figure eight, waggling her abdomen as she runs along the straight middle section of the figure eight. The length of the straight and the frequency of waggle indicate the distance to the pollen. If the food lies within 80 feet (25 m) of the hive, she performs a "round dance," running several times in a circle with many changes of direction from clockwise to counterclockwise. Von Frisch's discovery significantly improved scientific understanding of the behavior of animals that live in swarms or large communal groups.

1917 American nurse Margaret Sanger (1879–1966) opens the first birth control clinic in the United States. The following year in Britain Scottish paleobotanist Marie Stopes (1880–1958) publishes *Married Love*, a book about feminism and marriage.

1918 American physiologists William Howell (1860–1945) and Luther Holt (1855–1924) discover the natural anticoagulant heparin.

PHYSICAL SCIENCES

1917 German physicist Max Born (1882–1970) and chemist Fritz Haber (1868–1934) devise the Born–Haber cycle, which is a cycle of reactions that can be used to calculate the lattice energy of a crystalline solid.

1918 German physical Chemist Walther Nernst (1864–1941) puts forward his theory of chemical chain reactions. They are important in explaining light-triggered reactions.

1919 English physicist Francis Aston (1877–1945) develops the mass spectroscope for separating isotopes and discovers the two isotopes of neon, thus explaining why the atomic weight of the gas is not a whole number.

1919 German physicist Heinrich Barkhausen (1881–1956) establishes the Barkhausen effect: that the magnetization of iron takes place as a series of steps.

1919 New Zealand-born English physicist Ernest Rutherford (1871–1937) reports that he has artificially disintegrated nitrogen atoms by bombarding them with alpha particles.

1918 American chemist Winford Lewis (1878–1943) develops the poison gas lewisite, an arsenic compound that causes blistering and respiratory irritation.

1919 American physical chemist Frederick Cottrell (1877–1948) devises a way of extracting helium from natural gas.

It was quite the most incredible event that has ever happened to me in my life. It was almost as incredible as if you fired a 15-inch shell at a piece of tissue paper and it came back and hit you. On consideration, I realized that this scattering backward must be the result of a single collision, and when I made calculations I saw a system in which the greater part of the mass of the atom was concentrated in a minute nucleus.

ERNEST RUTHERFORD

The arc welder for steel revolutionized the construction and ship-building industries.

EUROPE

THE AMERICAS

ASIA & OCEANIA

AFRICA & THE MIDDLE EAST

ENGINEERING & INVENTION	WORLD EVENTS
1917 English engineer Archibald Low (1888–1956) invents an electronic control system for rockets.	**1917** Following defeat on the battlefields of World War I (1914–18), Russia undergoes two separate revolutions. The first overthrows Tsar Nicholas II (r. 1894–1917) and establishes democratic government; the second, in November, brings the Bolsheviks, led by Vladimir Lenin (1870–1924), to power.
1918 The German company Junkers builds the world's first all-metal fighter airplane, the Junkers *J-10*.	
1919 English aviator John Alcock (1892–1919) and Scottish aviator Arthur Brown (1886–1948) make the first nonstop transatlantic flight.	**1918** British women aged 30 or more win the right to vote.
1919 Scottish physicist Robert Watson-Watt (1892–1973) patents a short-wave "radiolocator," the forerunner of radar.	**1918** World War I ends with the defeat of Germany and its allies. Both sides are left devastated by economic, political, and social repercussions of four years of war.
1919 The British airship *R-34* is the first airship to cross the Atlantic Ocean. It flies from Edinburgh, Scotland, to Mineola, New York, in 108 hours 12 minutes.	**1919** The Treaty of Versailles imposes harsh peace terms on Germany, including the disbanding of most of the county's military, economic reparations, and the restoration of Alsace and Lorraine to France (captured during the Franco–Prussian War in 1871).
	1919 Spartacists—German communists—stage an unsuccessful uprising in Berlin. In Hungary communists temporarily seize power under Béla Kun (1886–1938).
1917 The American Black & Decker company markets the first electric hand drill.	**1917** The United States declares war on Germany. In all, some two million American soldiers will travel to Europe to fight in World War I; 115,000 will be killed by the war's end in November 1918.
1917 The world's longest cantilever bridge, with a 1,800-foot (549-m) span, is completed over the St. Lawrence River in Quebec.	
1918 American engineer Edwin Armstrong (1890–1954) invents the superheterodyne radio circuit. It is still in common use.	**1919** A peace plan devised by President Woodrow Wilson (1856–1924) is adopted at the Versailles Conference, but the United States Congress rejects the treaty.
1918 A powerful 200-kilowatt radio transmitter begins sending signals from the naval station in New Brunswick, New Jersey.	**1919** The Volstead Act (coming into force in 1920) bans the manufacture or selling of alcohol.
1919 American airman Albert Read makes the first east–west crossing of the Atlantic Ocean—in stages—in a Curtiss flying boat.	**1919** Mexican guerrilla leader Emiliano Zapata (1879–1919) is assassinated.
1919 American engineer Elihu Thomson (1853–1937) invents the arc welder for steel.	
1917 The east–west trans-Australian railroad is completed.	**1919** British forces open fire on demonstrators in Amritsar, India, killing 379 unarmed protesters.
	1919 Ho Chi Minh (1890– 1969) founds the Indochinese Communist Party in the part of French Indochina that will eventually regain its independence as Vietnam.
	1918 The Ottoman authorities negotiate a peace agreement at the end of World War I. Military defeat leads to the disintegration of the Ottoman Empire.
	1919 Britain exiles Egyptian nationalist leaders, sparking an uprising that is put down by force.

The rapid-firing, compact Thompson submachine gun was patented in 1920.

THE MACHINE GUN

Machine guns are small-caliber weapons that keep firing as long as the trigger is pressed and ammunition is available. Some sort of mechanism automatically carries out the cycle of loading, firing, and extracting cartridge cases.

Although there had been some similar weapons in the past, the modern repeating gun had to await the invention of metal cartridges. American gunsmith Richard Gatling (1818–1903) patented the first gun of the type in 1862. It had a set of 10 barrels that were cranked around by hand. A drum on top of the weapon fed in cartridges under the force of gravity. It was used to devastating effect during the American Civil War (1861–65).

In 1883, American-born English inventor Hiram Maxim (1840–1916) patented his machine gun in England. It used energy produced by the weapon's recoil to extract the spent cartridge, recock the gun, and insert the next round into the breech. Early single-barrelled machine guns failed because the barrel soon overheated, causing it to bend. Maxim solved this by adding a water cooling system around the barrel.

During World War I light machine guns (LMG) were developed that could be carried and operated by just one soldier. Lighter still was the submachine gun (SMG). A well-known early example is the "Tommy gun," designed by and named for American army officer John Thompson (1860–1940) in 1920. It had a straight magazine or a higher-capacity drum magazine. Most SMGs have a rate of fire of between 500 and 800 rounds per minute.

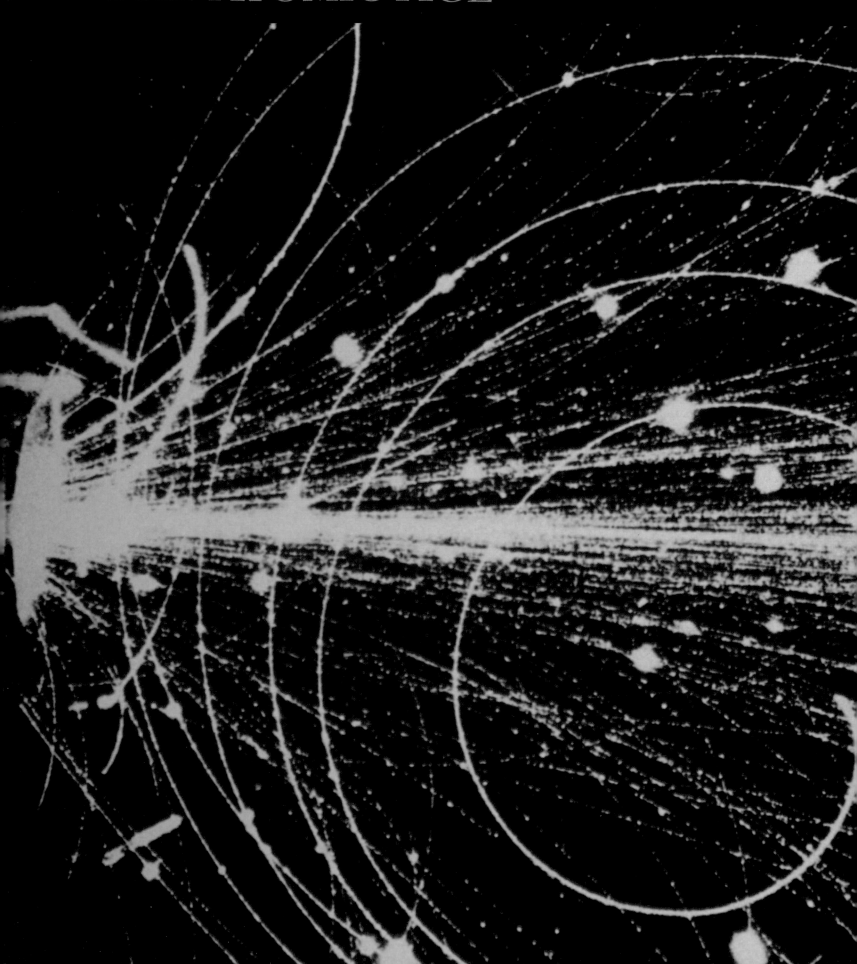

1920-1949

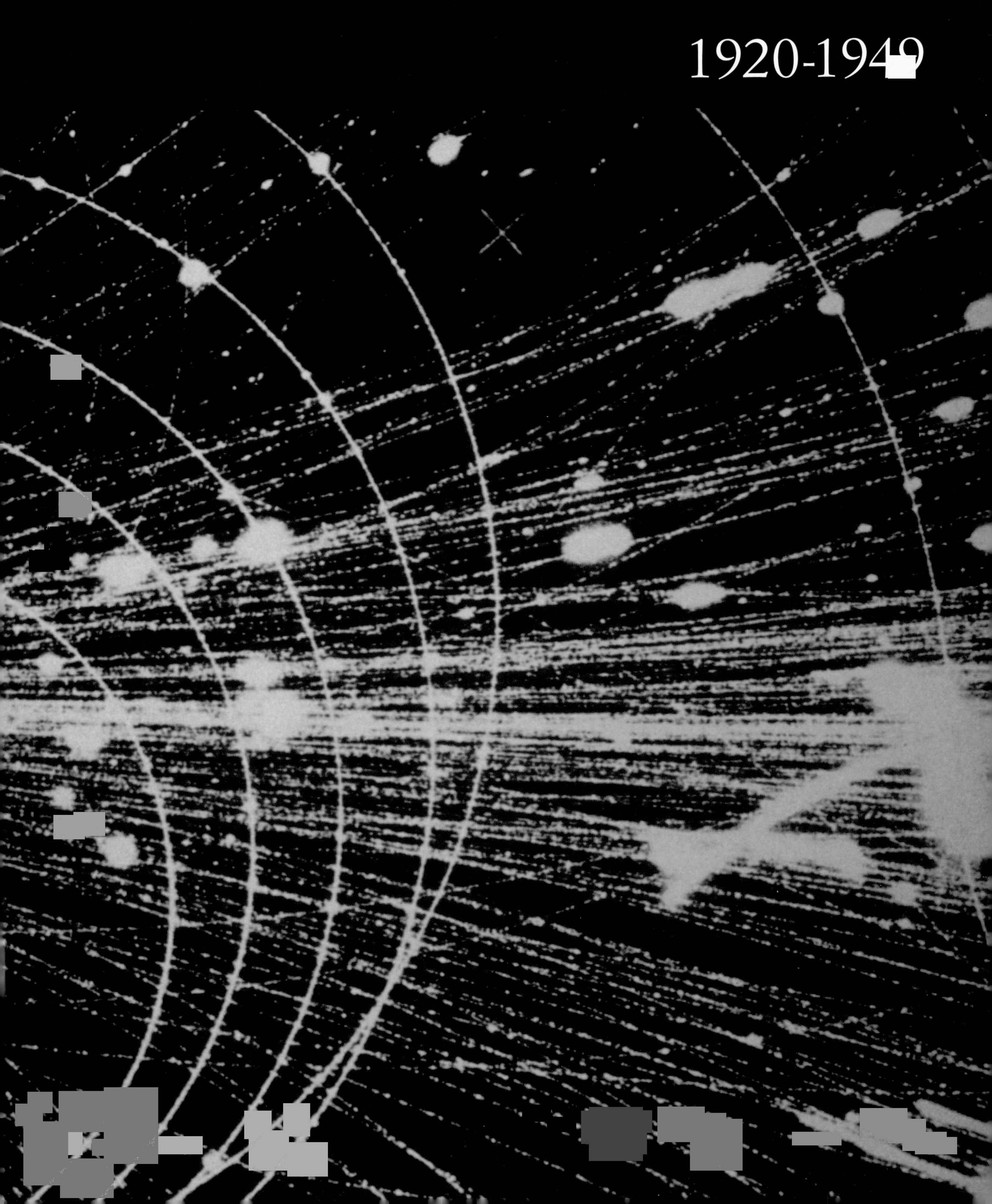

THE INVISIBLE WORLD OF THE ATOM DOMINATED SCIENTIFIC ADVANCE in the first half of the 20th century. The process of understanding atoms and learning how to harness their power produced many positive results, such as the invention of television and the development of radar. For many people, however, the idea of atomic energy became inextricably associated with destruction on an unprecedented scale when atomic bombs devastated the Japanese cities of Hiroshima and Nagasaki in August 1945. The distinctive mushroom cloud released by an atomic explosion—caused by superhot gases dragging dust and debris into the air—became a symbol of a new and frightening age, leaving even scientists concerned. On all sides of World War II (1939–45), academics and theoreticians found themselves questioning their consciences. Albert Einstein, whose work had done much to make the atomic bomb possible, ended up asking U.S. President Harry S. Truman not to use the weapon.

Warfare has always been a major motivation for advances in science. From bows that could fire farther to fortifications that could withstand cannonballs, the side that had the most advanced technology has usually had an advantage in conflict. In the 20th century, warfare became even more scientific. Research into radar, for example, received a boost because of the need to detect enemy aircraft and to aim naval guns

Since 1951 the United States has detonated more than 900 nuclear weapons, mostly underground, at the Nevada Test Site. This photograph from 1953 shows the U.S. nuclear test explosion known as Upshot-Knothole Grable. Currently, nine countries are known to have nuclear weapons.

for long-range battles at sea. Rocket research made huge advances, particularly in Germany, where engineer Wernher von Braun (1912–77) pioneered long-range flying bombs; recruited by the U.S. National Aeronautics and Space Administration (NASA) after the war, von Braun played a key role in the space program.

Other wartime advances included improvements to conventional aircraft, such as the jet engine, and the development of the helicopter, pioneered by Russian-born American engineer Igor Sigorsky (1889–1972). In medicine, scientists came up with ways to mass produce the antibiotic penicillin, "accidentally" discovered in 1928, and needed in large quantities to treat the wounded.

The most significant scientific development of the war, however, was nuclear fission. It was just three years from the first demonstration of a controlled nuclear chain reaction in an atomic pile (an early type of nuclear reactor) in 1942 to the detonation of the atomic bombs in Japan. Within seven more years, U.S. scientists had developed and tested the much more powerful hydrogen bomb.

The year 1947 saw the invention of the transistor, the first solid-state device, which was to revolutionize the electronics industry. It appeared just in time for the first commercial computers, which could be made faster and more powerful now that they no longer depended on unreliable vacuum tubes. Portable transistor radios and electronic calculators soon became commonplace. Clothing and fabrics were revolutionized, too, by the manufacture of artificial fibers, such as nylon and polyester.

The Bell X-1 was the world's first supersonic aircraft. The plane made its first supersonic flight in 1947, piloted by U.S. Air Force Captain Charles "Chuck" Yeager. It was powered by a four-chamber rocket engine and could fly as fast as 1,471 miles (2,367 km) an hour—almost twice the speed of sound.

	1920	1923	1926	1929	1932	
EUROPE	**1920** German astronomer Max Wolf observes dark clouds of matter in the Milky Way. **1920** Dutch airline KLM begins service between England and the Netherlands. **1921** Swiss psychiatrist Hermann Rorschach develops his inkblot test. **1922** New Zealand-born English physicist Ernest Rutherford predicts the existence of the neutron.	**1923** Austrian neurologist Sigmund Freud invents the concepts of the ego and the id. **1923** Germany company Benz makes the first diesel-engined trucks. **1923** Scottish inventor John Logie Baird makes a type of television. **1924** French physicist Louis de Broglie proposes the idea of wave-particle duality.	**1926** Austrian physicist Erwin Schrödinger formulates the wave equation for the hydrogen atom. **1926** Norwegian inventor Erik Rotheim invents the aerosol can. **1927** Belgian astronomer Georges Lemaître proposes the big bang theory for the origin of the universe. **1928** Scottish bacteriologist Alexander Fleming discovers the antibiotic penicillin.	**1929** German biochemist Adolf Butenandt isolates the hormone estrogen. **1929** German engineer Felix Wankel patents his rotary engine. **1930** Swedish biochemist Arne Tiselius invents electrophoresis. **1930** Austrian-born Swiss physicist Wolfgang Pauli predicts the existence of the neutrino. **1930** English engineer Frank Whittle invents the jet engine.	**1932** English physicist James Chadwick discovers the neutron. **1933** Swiss astrophysicist Fritz Zwicky proposes that space must contain invisible "dark matter." **1934** Danish biochemist Henrik Dam discovers a factor needed for blood clotting (vitamin K). **1934** The French company Citroën launches the first mass-produced front-wheel-drive car.	
THE AMERICAS	**1920** American astronomer Vesto Slipher detects redshift in the light from galaxies. **1920** The Panama Canal opens. **1920** Regular radio broadcasts begin in the United States. **1921** German-born American physiologist Otto Loewi discovers the neurotransmitter acetylcholine. **1921** Canadian physiologist Frederick Banting isolates insulin. **1921** American physicist Albert Hull invents the high-frequency magnetron vacuum tube. **1922** American airman James Doolittle makes the first coast-to-coast flight across the United States.	**1923** Russian-born American electronics engineer Vladimir Zworykin invents the iconoscope TV camera tube. **1923** American pilots and their crews make the first flight around the world (with refueling stops). **1925** American physicist Robert Millikan observes cosmic rays in the upper atmosphere. **1925** American pathologist George Whipple finds iron in red blood cells. **1925** African-American biologist Ernest Just demonstrates that ultraviolet radiation can cause cancer.	**1926** American geneticist Hermann Müller uses x-rays to create genetic mutations in fruit flies. **1926** American inventor Robert Goddard launches a liquid-fuel rocket. **1926** American physical chemist Gilbert Lewis coins the word *photon* to describe a quantum of light. **1927** American physicist Clinton Davisson and coworkers confirm that electrons have wavelike properties. **1927** German-born American physicist Fritz London proposes a quantum theory of chemical bonding. **1927** American aviator Charles Lindbergh makes the first solo flight across the Atlantic Ocean.	**1929** German-born American physicist Albert Einstein first announces his unified field theory. **1930** American astronomer Clyde Tombaugh discovers the planet Pluto (now considered a dwarf planet). **1930** American electrical engineer Vannevar Bush builds an analog computer. **1930** American businessman Clarence Birdseye markets the first quick-frozen foods. **1930** The Chrysler Building is completed in New York City. **1931** The Empire State Building in New York City becomes the world's tallest building.	**1932** Synthetic rubber is marketed in the United States. **1932** American physicist Carl Anderson announces the existence of the positron. **1932** American physicist Ernest Lawrence operates one of the first particle accelerators. **1932** American electrical engineer William Kouwenhoven proposes the idea for a defibrillator. **1933** American biochemist George Wald discovers vitamin A in the retina of the eye. **1933** The first modern airliner, the Boeing 247, enters service. **1934** American scientist Royal Raymond Rife tests radio waves to treat cancer.	
ASIA & OCEANIA			**1928** The Flying Doctor Service begins in Australia. **1928** Indian physicist Chandrasekhara Raman describes the effects of a beam of light in a transparent substance.	**1929** Japanese geophysicist Motonori Matuyama theorizes that the Earth's magnetic field has undergone reversals in its history.	**1932** The Sydney Harbor bridge is completed. **1933** The Tasmanian wolf, or thylacine, becomes extinct in the wild.	
AFRICA & THE MIDDLE EAST		**1924** Australian-born South African anthropologist Raymond Dart discovers fossils of possible human ancestor *Australopithecus* in Africa.				

1935	1938	1941	1944	1947–1949
1935 Austrian zoologist Konrad Lorenz discovers imprinting in animals. **1935** Scottish physicist Robert Watson-Watt invents radar. **1936** German engineer Heinrich Focke builds a two-rotor helicopter. **1936** The Spitfire airplane makes its maiden flight. **1937** German-born English biochemist Hans Krebs explains the citric acid cycle.	**1938** German computer pioneer Konrad Zuse constructs a binary digital computer. **1938** German physicists Otto Hahn and Fritz Strassmann induce nuclear fission in uranium. **1939** Swiss chemist Paul Müller discovers the insect-killing properties of DDT. **1939** French physicists Irène and Frédéric Joliot-Curie show that uranium fission can lead to a chain reaction.	**1942** French underwater explorer Jacques Cousteau invents the aqualung, or scuba. **1942** German rocket engineer Wernher von Braun designs the V-1 flying bomb and the V-2 rocket bomb. **1942** English astronomer Harold Spencer Jones obtains an accurate value for the Earth–sun distance. **1943** Dutch-born American physician Willem Kolff constructs a kidney dialysis machine.	**1944** German forces begin launching V-1 flying bombs and V-2 rocket bombs against England. **1945** Soviet physicist Vladimir Veksler designs and builds a particle accelerator, the synchrocyclotron. **1945** Northern Irish engineer James Martin designs the ejector seat. **1946** Scientists obtain radar reflections from the moon.	**1947** English physicist Cecil Powell and Italian physicist Giuseppe Occhialini discover the pion (pi-meson). **1948** The World Health Organization (WHO) is founded. **1949** English computer engineer Maurice Wilkes and coworkers build EDSAC, the Electronic Delay Storage Automatic Calculator. **1949** The first jet airliner, the De Havilland Comet, flies in England.
1935 American seismologist Charles Richter devises the Richter scale to measure earthquake intensity. **1935** Canadian-born American physicist Arthur Dempster discovers the fissile isotope uranium-235 (later used in atom bombs). **1935** American amateur photographers Leopold Godowsky, Jr. and Leopold Mannes invent Kodachrome transparency film. **1936** American physicist Carl Anderson discovers the muon in cosmic rays. **1936** The Boulder Dam is completed. **1937** The world's first pressurized aircraft, the Lockheed XC-35, makes its maiden flight.	**1938** American physicists figure out the series of nuclear fusion reactions that "fuel" stars. **1938** Hungarian-born Argentine inventor Laszlo Biró makes a prototype of the ballpoint pen. **1939** The National Broadcasting Company (NBC) begins regular television transmissions. **1939** American physicist John Atanasoff makes a prototype electronic binary calculator. **1940** American zoologist Donald Griffin announces that bats "echolocate" using ultrasound. **1940** Austrian-born American pathologist Karl Landsteiner describes the Rhesus factor in human blood.	**1941** German-born American biochemist Fritz Lipmann shows the role of ATP (adenosine triphosphate) in the chemistry of cells. **1942** American radio astronomer Grote Reber compiles the first radio map of the universe. **1942** Belgian-born American biologist Albert Claude uses an electron microscope in biological studies. **1942** Italian-American physicist Enrico Fermi achieves the first controlled nuclear chain reaction. **1943** American scientists construct the world's first operational nuclear reactor.	**1944** Canadian-born American Oswald Avery and coworkers show that the cells of nearly all organisms have deoxyribonucleic acid (DNA) as their hereditary material. **1945** American biochemist Melvin Calvin begins his studies of photosynthesis using radioactive carbon-14 to follow the reactions. **1945** American scientists manufacture and test an atom bomb. **1946** American chemist Willard Libby develops radiocarbon dating. **1946** Swiss-born American physicist Felix Bloch and American physicist Edward Purcell develop nuclear magnetic resonance (NMR) spectroscopy.	**1947** American geneticist Joshua Lederberg reports that some bacteria can reproduce by conjugation. **1947** American airman Charles "Chuck" Yeager makes the first supersonic flight. **1947** American inventor Edwin Land demonstrates the Polaroid instant camera. **1948** American electrical engineer Peter Goldmark invents the long-playing phonograph record. **1949** American rocket engineers launch a two-stage rocket. **1949** The American company IBM makes a stored-program electromechanical computer Selective Sequence Electronic Calculator (SSEC).
1936 The last known Tasmanian wolf dies in captivity. **1936** A giant panda is captured alive in the wild.		**1943** Japanese theoretical physicist Sin-Itoro Tomonaga outlines the basic physical principles of quantum electrodynamics.	**1946** The Sony company is founded in Japan.	**1947** Armenian astronomer Viktor Ambartsumian describes stellar associations.
	1938 A thought-to-be-extinct fish, the coelacanth, is discovered off the eastern coast of South Africa.			**1948** English anthropologist Mary Leakey discovers fossils of possible ape ancestor *Proconsul africanus* in Africa.

ASTRONOMY & MATH

BIOLOGY & MEDICINE

PHYSICAL SCIENCES

EUROPE

1920 German astronomer Max Wolf (1863–1932) observes dark clouds of interstellar matter in Earth's galaxy, the Milky Way.

1920 English amateur astronomer and comet-hunter William Denning (1848–1931) discovers Nova Cygni, a star that experiences sudden outbursts of radiant energy.

1921 German mathematician Emmy Noether (1882–1935) begins to develop mathematical axioms ("rules") for algebra.

1921 English economist John Maynard Keynes (1883–1946) publishes his *Treatise on Probability*.

1921 Swiss psychiatrist Hermann Rorschach (1884–1922) introduces the Rorschach inkblot test for examining patients' personalities.

1921 English biochemist Frederick Gowland Hopkins (1861–1947) discovers glutathione, an important requirement for cell metabolism involving oxygen (respiration).

1921 Scottish bacteriologist Alexander Fleming (1881–1955) identifies the bacteria-killing enzyme lysozyme.

1922 English pharmacologist Edward Mellanby (1884–1955) establishes the use of cod-liver oil as a treatment for rickets in children.

1922 Scottish physiologist John Macleod (1876–1935) and coworkers first use insulin to treat patients with diabetes.

1920 Scottish chemist Arthur Lapworth (1872–1941) establishes the role played by electrons in organic chemical reactions.

1920 English physicist Francis Aston (1877–1945) formulates the so-called "whole number rule": that the mass of the oxygen isotope being defined, all the other isotopes have masses that are very nearly whole numbers.

1920 New Zealand-born English physicist Ernest Rutherford (1871–1937) predicts the existence of the neutron.

1922 German chemist Hermann Staudinger (1881–1965) coins the term *macromolecule* and recognizes that substances such as rubber are natural polymers.

THE AMERICAS

1920 American astronomer Vesto Slipher (1875–1969) detects a redshift in the light from galaxies, proving that they are receding (and providing evidence for an expanding universe).

1920 German-born American astronomer Walter Baade (1893–1960) discovers the asteroid Hidalgo, an object 18.6 miles (30 km) in diameter that follows a highly elliptical, cometlike orbit.

1922 Canadian astronomer John Plaskett (1865–1941) identifies the supergiant binary star known as Plaskett's star.

In 1920 Max Wolf used photography to find dark clouds of matter in the Milky Way.

1921 German-born American physiologist Otto Loewi (1873–1961) discovers a chemical released by stimulated nerves, which English physiologist Henry Dale (1875–1968) later identifies as acetylcholine.

1921 Canadian physiologist Frederick Banting (1891–1941) isolates insulin, the hormone that controls the levels of the sugar glucose in the blood.

1922 American biochemist Elmer McCollum (1879–1967) discovers vitamin D (calciferol).

1922 American anatomist and embryologist Herbert Evans (1882–1971) discovers vitamin E (tocopherol).

1922 American psychologist G. Stanley Hall (1844–1924) publishes *Senescence*, one of the first books to discuss the social and psychological aspects of aging.

1920 Belgian-born American chemist Julius Nieuwland (1878–1936) polymerizes acetylene, producing divinyl acetylene.

1921 American chemist Thomas Midgley (1889–1944) discovers the "antiknock" properties of tetraethyl lead (it prevents preignition in gasoline engines).

1921 American physicist Arthur Compton (1892–1962) suggests that ferromagnetism is caused by spinning electrons.

ASIA & OCEANIA

AFRICA & THE MIDDLE EAST

TURNING POINTS

Insulin

Produced in the pancreas by cells called the islets of Langerhans, insulin is a hormone that enables body cells to take up the blood sugar glucose. Glucose is used as an energy source by the body. If the body cannot make insulin, type I diabetes mellitus results. In 1921 Canadian physiologist Frederick Banting (1891–1941) isolated insulin from dogs and found that injecting it cured the symptoms of diabetes in a dog that had had its pancreas removed (and therefore could not produce its own insulin). Using a purer extract from calves, Banting and coworkers successfully treated terminally ill children with type I diabetes the following year. Purified animal insulin was soon available for sale. By the early 1980s insulin could be made by genetically modified bacteria containing the human insulin gene. Banting received the Nobel Prize for Physiology or Medicine in 1923 for his discovery.

ENGINEERING & INVENTION	WORLD EVENTS
1920 KLM, the Dutch National Airline, makes its first scheduled flight between Amsterdam in the Netherlands and London, England.	**1920** Admiral Nikolaus Horthy (1868–1957) leads a counterrevolution in Hungary.
1921 The first expressway in Germany (*Autobahn*) is completed.	**1921** The communist Red Army finally overcomes its White opponents in the civil war that has divided Russia since 1918.
1922 The British Broadcasting Company (later Corporation)—BBC—begins regular broadcasts in Britain.	**1921** Britain concedes autonomy to the Irish Free State, excluding six Ulster counties with a predominantly Protestant population; they remain part of the United Kingdom under the name of Northern Ireland.
1922 Swedish inventor Nils Dalen (1869–1937) patents the Aga solid-fuel stove.	**1922** The Union of Soviet Socialist Republics (USSR) is established; Soviet troops occupy Ukraine.
	1922 Facist leader Benito Mussolini (1883–1945) leads the March on Rome, taking power as Italy's prime minister.

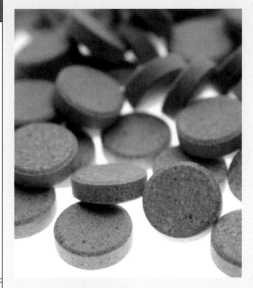

VITAMINS

Vitamins are organic substances, essential in minute quantities, that regulate various chemical reactions in the body. While humans get most of their vitamins from their diet, vitamin D can be made by the body itself, and vitamin K is made by helpful microorganisms living in the intestine. Vitamins are distinct from other nutrients, such as sugars and proteins, that act as building blocks for cells and tissues or as sources of energy to fuel the chemical reactions in the body. Deficiencies of vitamins lead to various disorders.

ENGINEERING & INVENTION	WORLD EVENTS
1920 The Panama Canal is officially opened by U.S. President Woodrow Wilson (1856–1924).	**1920** Mexican generals proclaim the Republic of Sonora, going on to defeat President Venustiano Carranza (1859–1920) and force the surrender of revolutionary leader Pancho Villa (1878–1923).
1920 American gunsmith John Thompson (1860–1940) patents the Thompson submachine gun (Tommy gun).	**1920** The Nineteenth Amendment gives U.S. women the vote.
1920 Station KDKA in Pittsburgh, Pennsylvania, begins the first regular radio broadcasts in the United States.	**1921** Republican Warren Harding (1865–1923) is sworn in as 29th president of the United States. One of his first significant steps is to raise custom barriers against European trade.
1921 American physicist Albert Hull (1880–1966) invents the high-frequency magnetron vacuum tube.	**1921** The Immigration Act (further tightened in 1924) limits the number of foreign nationals who can enter the United States.
1921 American airman John Macready (1887–1979) gives the first demonstration of crop spraying from an airplane.	
1922 American engineer Lee De Forest (1873–1961) creates a sound-on-film optical recording system for movies.	
1922 After five years of research Canadian-born American electrical engineer Reginald Fessenden (1866–1932) makes an improved echo sounder.	
1922 American airman James Doolittle (1896–1993) makes the first coast-to-coast flight across the United States, taking 21 hours 19 minutes.	

In 1912 Polish biochemist Kazimierz Funk (1884–1967) isolated a substance from brown rice that he mistakenly believed to be vitamin B_1 (thiamin). Funk believed that the substance was essential for good health and because a chemical group called an amine was included in its structure, he named it "vital amine," later contracted to "vitamine." As more types of essential micronutrients were discovered, some were found not to contain an amine group and the name was further shortened to vitamin.

A drop from the nose of Fleming, who had a cold, fell onto an agar plate where large yellow colonies of a contaminant had grown, and lysozyme was discovered.

ALEXANDER FLEMING

1920 The map of Central Asia is redrawn as areas in the former empire of the Russian tsars are re-created as autonomous soviet socialist republics (ASSRs) of the Soviet Union.

1920 Britain grants Egypt independence under King Fuad I (r. 1917–36) but retains control over defense and foreign policy, the Suez Canal, and the administration of Sudan.

Almost all the vitamins we know today were discovered, isolated, and artificially synthesized in the first half of the 20th century. They include the fat-soluble vitamins A, D, E, and K, and the water-soluble vitamin C and B complex vitamins.

SUBATOMIC PARTICLES

Italian-American Physicist Enrico Fermi demonstrates the interaction between subatomic particles.

BY 1920 PHYSICISTS KNEW that every atom consists of a nucleus carrying a positive charge surrounded by a cloud of electrons carrying negative charge. This implied that the atom is not an "elementary particle"—an object that cannot be divided into smaller constituents. Before long, scientists were identifying a growing list of particles smaller than atoms.

The Proton and the Neutron

Ernest Rutherford (1871–1937), the New Zealand-born English physicist, found that when he bombarded nitrogen atoms with alpha particles, hydrogen nuclei were released. It followed that a nitrogen atomic nucleus must contain hydrogen nuclei. In 1920 Rutherford suggested the name *proton* for the hydrogen nucleus. The mass of a proton is 1,836 times that of an electron.

Since 1919 Rutherford had been professor of physics at Cambridge University and director of the Cavendish Laboratory. His research continued to center on smashing atomic nuclei by bombarding them with alpha particles (helium nuclei). In 1925 English physicist Patrick Blackett (1897–1974), working under Rutherford's direction, developed a device for recording the disintegration of atoms. But alpha particles were not powerful enough to smash large nuclei, which repelled them without disintegrating. It was not until 1932, when English physicist John Cockcroft (1897–1967) and Irish physicist Ernest Walton (1903–95) built the world's first particle accelerator at the Cavendish Laboratory that these larger atoms could be smashed. The device used powerful electromagnets to accelerate protons that were then directed at a target.

Using these advances, other physicists, such as Irène (1897–1956) and Frédéric (1900–58) Joliot-Curie discovered the existence of very high energy radiation quite unlike gamma radiation. English

physicist James Chadwick (1891–1974), working at the Cavendish Laboratory, suggested that this high-energy radiation consisted of particles with approximately the same mass as the proton, but carrying no electromagnetic charge. Chadwick conducted experiments bombarding the element boron to confirm his hypothesis. Because it carries no charge, the particle came to be called the "neutron." It is stable while it remains inside an atomic nucleus, but outside the nucleus a neutron decays into a proton, an electron, and an antineutrino.

The Neutrino and the Discovery of Antimatter

In 1930 Austrian Wolfgang Pauli (1900–1958) was studying beta radiation—a stream of electrons emitted by unstable atoms. The electrons seemed to lose energy, but no explanation could be found for the loss, which

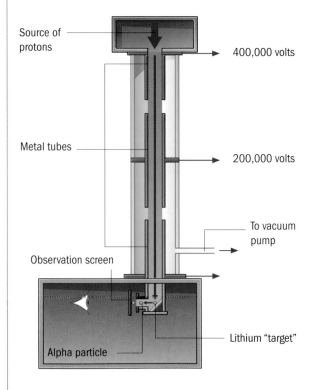

In 1932 John Cockcroft and Ernest Walton created an atom splitter by charging a hollow metal chamber to 400,000 volts and injecting protons into it. The positively charged particles were driven away from the high positive voltage along a series of tubes kept at lower voltages and into a piece of lithium. Alpha particles that were formed in the collision caused flashes on an observation screen and were photographed.

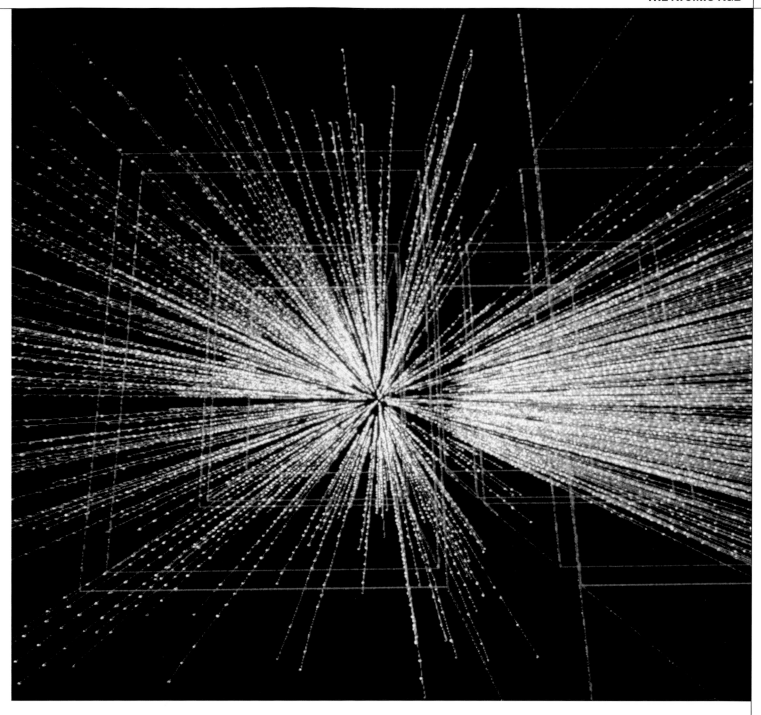

appeared to contradict one of the most fundamental laws of physics: that energy cannot be created or lost. Pauli's solution to the riddle was to propose that beta radiation also contains a previously unknown particle with the unusual properties of possessing no charge and no mass when it is at rest. Italian-American physicist Enrico Fermi (1901–54) confirmed the existence of such a particle in 1934 and called it the "neutrino."

In 1928 English physicist Paul Dirac (1902–84), dissatisfied with the description of the electron, pro-

posed an alternative. The equations describing Dirac's model predicted that it should be possible for an electron to possess a positive charge. American physicist Carl Anderson (1905–91) discovered this particle (later called the "positron") in 1932. It was the first antimatter particle to be identified.

In 1936, in collaboration with graduate student Seth Neddermeyer (1907–88), Anderson discovered the muon—a very unstable particle similar to an electron but 200 times more massive.

The European Organization for Nuclear Research (CERN), in Switzerland, is the world's largest particle physics lab. The image above shows a computer simulation of a lead-ion collision—a proposed experiment using the facility's Large Hadron Collider.

ASTRONOMY & MATH	BIOLOGY & MEDICINE	PHYSICAL SCIENCES
EUROPE		
1923 Austro-Hungarian rocket scientist Hermann Oberth (1894–1989) introduces the idea of escape velocity in his book *The Rocket into Interplanetary Space*. **1924** Danish astronomer Ejnar Hertzsprung (1873–1967) discovers DH Carinae, the first flare star (a red dwarf star that has brief bright episodes). **1924** English astronomer Arthur Eddington (1882–1944) figures out the mass–luminosity relation for stars. **1925** Swedish astronomer Bertil Lindblad (1895–1965) proposes that our galaxy (the Milky Way) is slowly rotating.	**1923** Austrian neurologist Sigmund Freud (1856–1939) introduces his concepts of the ego (the part of the mind in touch with reality) and the id (the instinctive unconscious mind). **1923** German biochemist Otto Warburg (1883–1970) demonstrates that cancerous cells absorb less oxygen than do normal cells. **1924** German psychiatrist Hans Berger (1873–1941) detects the electrical activity of the brain and later (1929) publishes his work on electroencephalography. **1925** Russian-born English biochemist David Keilin (1887–1963) names the important cellular protein cytochrome (which contains heme, a component of hemoglobin).	**1924** English physicist Edward Appleton (1892–1965) demonstrates the existence of the ionosphere, a layer of ionized gases in the upper atmosphere. **1924** French physicist Louis de Broglie (1892–1987) proposes the idea of wave-particle duality: that some entities (such as electrons) sometimes behave like waves and sometimes behave like particles. **1925** German chemist Walter Noddack (1893–1960) and his wife Ida Tacke (1896–1979) discover the element rhenium. **1925** German chemist Franz Fischer (1877–1947) and Czech chemist Hans Tropsch (1889–1935) devise a process for producing oil-type fuels from coal.
THE AMERICAS		
1925 American physicist Robert Millikan (1868–1953) observes cosmic rays in the upper atmosphere. **1925** American astronomer Edwin Hubble (1889–1953) introduces his classification scheme for galaxies.	**1923** American physicians George (1881–1967) and Gladys Dick (1881–1963) isolate the bacterium that causes scarlet fever. **1924** American pathologist George Whipple (1878–1976) and American physicians George Minot (1885–1950) and William Murphy (1892–1987) introduce the use of raw liver as a treatment for pernicious anemia. **1925** American pathologist George Whipple discovers iron in red blood cells. **1925** American psychologist John Watson (1878–1958) publishes *Behaviorism*, in which he sets out his ideas for improving society. **1925** African-American biologist Ernest Just (1883–1941) shows that UV radiation can cause cancer.	**1923** American physicist Arthur Compton (1892–1962) publishes his explanation of the Compton effect, which is the increase in the wavelength (loss in energy) of an x-ray or gamma ray when it collides with electrons. **1923** Dutch-born American physicist Peter Debye (1884–1966) and German physicist Erich Hückel (1896–1980) propose their theory of electrolytes. It states that electrolytes are fully ionized in dilute solution, and that oppositely charged ions are attracted to each other. **1923** American physical chemist Gilbert Lewis (1875–1946) defines an acid as a substance that accepts electrons.
ASIA & OCEANIA		
	Psychoanalysis is based on the ideas of the Austrian physician Sigmund Freud, who published his study of the human psyche, The Ego and the Id, *in 1923.*	
AFRICA & THE MIDDLE EAST		
	1924 Australian-born South African anthropologist Raymond Dart (1893–1988) discovers fossils of *Australopithecus* in Africa. They help establish Africa as the site of humankind's origins.	

ENGINEERING & INVENTION	WORLD EVENTS

1923 Spanish engineer Juan de la Cierva (1895–1936) successfully flies an autogyro, a helicopter-like airplane with a free-rotating horizontal propeller.

1923 German company Benz manufactures the first diesel-engined trucks.

1923 German company Ormig markets a spirit duplicator for making paper copies (using a dye-gelatin process).

1923 Scottish electrical engineer John Logie Baird (1888–1946) invents a television system that uses mechanical scanning.

1924 Swedish chemist Theodor Svedberg (1884–1971) develops the ultracentrifuge. It soon becomes standard equipment in biology and chemistry laboratories.

1923 Hyperinflation devastates the German economy. French troops occupy the coal-rich Rühr region in response to the nation's failure to keep up with the war-reparation payments dictated by the Versailles peace treaty.

1923 Led by Prime Minister Ramsay MacDonald (1866–1937), the Labour Party comes to power in Britain for the first time.

1924 Vladimir Lenin (1870–1924) dies, unleashing a prolonged power struggle in the Soviet Union.

1925 Benito Mussolini (1883–1945) proclaims himself Il Duce ("The Leader") of a Fascist Italy.

1923 Russian-born American electronics engineer Vladimir Zworykin (1889–1982) invents the iconoscope TV camera tube, while working at the Westinghouse laboratory.

1924 American pilots Erik Nelson, Lowell Smith, Leigh Wade, and their crews make the first around-the-world flight (with refueling stops) in three U.S. Navy biplanes.

1924 The American company Kimberly-Clark introduces Kleenex, the world's first disposable facial tissues.

1925 French-born American physicist Henri Chrétien (1879–1956) invents the anamorphic lens, which compresses images sideways. (Twenty-eight years later it is used for CinemaScope movies.)

1923 Republican Calvin Coolidge (1872–1933) succeeds as U.S. president following the sudden death of Warren Harding (1865–1923).

1924 The Coolidge administration is rocked by the Teapot Dome scandal, which forces the resignation of Secretary of the Interior Albert Fall (1861–1944).

1924 Native Americans are granted full U.S. citizenship.

WOLFGANG PAULI

Born in 1900 in Vienna, Austria, Wolfgang Pauli was a theoretical physicist who made important contributions to quantum mechanics—the behavior of matter and radiation at the atomic and subatomic level. Pauli was the son of a professor of physical chemistry, and he studied at Munich University, where he gained a doctorate in 1921. He worked with German physicist Max Born (1882–1970) at Göttingen University and with Danish physicist Niels Bohr (1885–1962) in Copenhagen before moving to Hamburg University in 1923. Five years later he moved to the Federal Institute of Technology in Zurich, where he remained until his death, although he spent World War II (1939–45) at Princeton.

In about 1924 Pauli added a fourth "spin" quantum number to the existing three to account for the anomalous Zeeman effect (the splitting of a spectral line into two or more components of slightly different frequency when the light source is placed in a magnetic field) and in 1925 revealed his exclusion principle (for which he was awarded the Nobel Prize for Physics in 1945). It states that no atom can have two electrons with the same four quantum numbers. In 1930 he postulated the existence of the neutrino, a neutral low-mass subatomic particle that must, he said, be produced during beta decay, the radioactive decay in which a neutron changes into a proton and a beta particle (electron).

Images of elliptical (left), spiral (center), and barred spiral (right) galaxies taken by the Hubble Space Telescope

1923 Mustafa Kemal (1881–1938) establishes a republic in Turkey with its capital at Ankara.

Wolfgang Pauli (right) sits with two other physicists, Enrico Fermi (left) and Werner Heisenberg (center).

INVENTION OF TELEVISION

John Logie Baird examines his mostly mechanical television camera. The circle with holes cut through it is a Nipkow disk.

IN OCTOBER 1925 SCOTTISH ELECTRICAL engineer John Logie Baird (1888–1946) transmitted the first television pictures in his London workshop. The systems designed to capture moving images for broadcast required a very different set of technologies from existing motion-picture cameras. The image had to be broken down into narrow strips, or "lines," which could then be encoded for transmission.

The First Television Pictures

All television cameras have some method of scanning an image. In the early 1920s Baird designed a system which used a rapidly spinning "Nipkow disk," patent-

ed by Polish electrical engineer Paul Nipkow (1860–1940) in 1884. It is a disk—in Baird's case made of cardboard—pierced with a spiral of holes. As the disk rotates, an observer looking through it sees an object as a series of curved lines or scans, each line produced by a different hole in the disk. The first pictures, from 1925, depicted a ventriloquist's doll.

At first, Baird sent his television images along wires. In 1927 he transmitted pictures from London to Glasgow along a telephone line. A year later he sent pictures over the transatlantic telegraph cable to New York. In September 1929 the British Broadcasting Company (BBC; now Corporation) began experimental television broadcasts using Baird's mechanical system. The flickering images consisted of only 30 lines, although this was later increased. In 1932 Baird transmitted pictures by short-wave radio. The experimental broadcasts ended in 1935; and by the time national television broadcasting started in 1937, the BBC had adopted the 405-line electronic system developed by the British company Marconi–EMI. Television broadcasting was suspended during World War II (1939–45) to prevent the transmitters being used to guide enemy aircraft. Baird died before television broadcasting resumed, this time using an all-electronic system.

Electronic Systems

Scottish electrical engineer Alan Campbell-Swinton (1863–1930) figured out the principles of an electronic television system in 1908, although at that time the apparatus was not available to put his ideas into practice. He envisaged using a cathode-ray tube in both the television camera and the receiver. He proposed that a picture signal could be transmitted along wires or received anywhere using the newly invented radio.

In the United States Russian-born electronics engineer Vladimir Zworykin (1889–1982) abandoned Baird's spinning disks and went the electronic route from the beginning. He developed his iconoscope camera tube of 1923 from a cathode-ray tube, using a

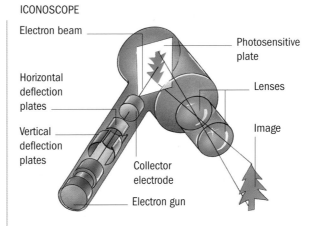

ICONOSCOPE

Electron beam · Photosensitive plate · Horizontal deflection plates · Lenses · Vertical deflection plates · Image · Collector electrode · Electron gun

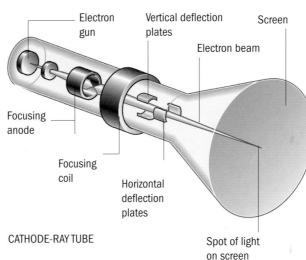

CATHODE-RAY TUBE

Electron gun · Vertical deflection plates · Screen · Electron beam · Focusing anode · Focusing coil · Horizontal deflection plates · Spot of light on screen

The iconoscope was the first successful television camera tube and was developed by Zworykin. A beam of electrons from an electron gun scans an image focused onto a photosensitive plate. Horizontal and vertical deflection plates force the electron beam to scan in a series of lines. Light striking the plate gives it a positive charge, and electrons not held by the charge bounce back to a collector electrode and form the video signal.

A cathode-ray tube, invented in 1897 by German physicist Ferdinand Braun (1850–1918), is the most common type of television receiver. It has an electron gun and deflection plates and a coil to focus the electron beam onto the screen at the front of the tube. Phosphor, which emits light when struck by electrons, coats the inside of the screen on which the scanned image builds up line by line.

beam of electrons for scanning. A lens focused light from a scene onto a so-called signal plate, which was coated with a mosaic of cesium–silver pellets. Each pellet released electrons in proportion to the amount of light falling on it, and the tube's electron beam replenished the electrons as it scanned across the signal plate. The electric current leaving the plate varied in accordance with the variations in light intensity— today we call such an output signal a video signal. American inventor Philo Farnsworth (1906–71) developed a similar camera in 1927 (patented 1930). Though Zworykin joined the Radio Corporation of America (RCA) and improved his system within a few years, from 1939 RCA was required to pay royalties to Farnsworth. In 1941 CBS made experimental color broadcasts from New York, although regular transmissions in color did not begin until 1951.

The Baird Televisor was the first fully operational television set. However, this mechanical device only had 30 lines of display and was soon superseded by higher-definition sets.

KEY DATES

1923
Zworykin invents iconoscope TV camera tube

1925
Baird's first television pictures

1929
BBC begins experimental TV broadcasts

1937
BBC begins national TV broadcasts

1938
Zworykin receives patent for iconoscope TV camera tube

1941
CBS begins experimental color TV broadcasts

ASTRONOMY & MATH	BIOLOGY & MEDICINE	PHYSICAL SCIENCES

EUROPE

1927 Belgian astronomer Georges Lemaître (1894–1966) first proposes what is known as the big bang theory of the origin of the universe.

1927 Dutch astronomer Jan Oort (1900–92) confirms the rotation of the Milky Way galaxy and locates its center (in the constellation Sagittarius).

1927 German astronomers Arnold Schwassmann (1870–1964) and Arno Wachmann (1902–90) discover (using photography) the comet Schwassmann–Wachmann 1, which has a circular orbit just beyond that of Jupiter.

1927 English zoologist Charles Elton (1900–91) publishes *Animal Ecology* and establishes the science of ecology.

1927 Portuguese neurologist António de Egas Moniz (1874–1955) detects brain tumors using cerebral angiography (in which a substance opaque to x-rays is injected into an artery serving the brain).

1928 Scottish microbiologist Alexander Fleming (1881–1955) "accidentally" discovers the antibiotic penicillin.

1926 English chemist Christopher Ingold (1893–1970) discovers mesomerism, a phenomenon in which the structure of a chemical compound "resonates" between two alternative forms.

1926 Austrian physicist Erwin Schrödinger (1887–1961) formulates the wave equation for the hydrogen atom. It is a mathematical expression that describes the behavior of an electron as it "orbits" the atom's nucleus.

1927 English chemist Nevil Sidgwick (1873–1952) introduces the modern theory of chemical valence, concerning the role of electrons in chemical bonds.

1927 German theoretical physicist Werner Heisenberg (1901–76) formulates his uncertainty principle.

Charles Lindbergh crossed the Atlantic in 1927 in his custom-built, single-engine plane, the Spirit of St. Louis.

THE AMERICAS

1927 German-born American physicist Fritz London (1900–54) proposes a quantum theory of chemical bonding.

1928 American astronomer Henry Russell (1877–1957) determines the abundance of elements in the solar atmosphere and finds that hydrogen is the principal element in the sun's atmosphere.

1928 Austrian-born American mathematician Richard von Mises (1883–1953) publishes *Probability, Statistics, and Truth*, a philosophical approach to probability.

1928 Hungarian-born American mathematician John von Neumann (1903–57) publishes a paper outlining his minimax theorem, the basic foundation of game theory.

1926 American geneticist Hermann Müller (1890–1967) uses x-rays to create genetic mutations in fruit flies (*Drosophila*).

1926 American biochemist James Sumner (1887–1955) is the first to crystallize an enzyme—urease.

1926 American biochemist John Abel (1857–1938) and coworkers crystallize insulin and show that it is a protein.

1927 Canadian anthropologist Davidson Black (1884–1934) identifies a new human fossil—Peking man (*Homo erectus*)—by a single tooth.

1928 Greek-born American physician George Papanicolaou (1883–1962) devises the Pap smear test for cancer of the cervix.

1928 American engineers Philip Drinker (1894–1972) and Louis Shaw (1886–1940) first use the iron lung, a respirator for patients with paralyzed chest muscles.

1926 American physical chemist Gilbert Lewis (1875–1946) coins the word *photon* to describe a quantum, or "particle," of light.

1927 American physicist Clinton Davisson (1881–1958) and coworkers demonstrate the diffraction of electrons, an experiment that confirms their wavelike properties.

ASIA & OCEANIA

One sometimes finds what one is not looking for.

ALEXANDER FLEMING

1928 The Flying Doctor Service is introduced in Australia.

1928 Indian physicist Chandrasekhara Raman (1888–1970) describes the Raman effect: When a transparent substance is illuminated by a beam of light of a single wavelength, some of the light is scattered and has frequencies higher and lower than that of the incoming light.

AFRICA & THE MIDDLE EAST

ENGINEERING & INVENTION	WORLD EVENTS
1926 English aviator Alan Cobham (1894–1973) flies around the world, leaving England June 30 and returning October 1.	**1926** Benito Mussolini (1883–1945) takes full control of Italy and bans opposition.
1926 Norwegian inventor Erik Rotheim (1898–1938) invents the aerosol can.	**1926** A. A. Milne (1882–1956) publishes *Winnie-the-Pooh*.
1926 Norwegian explorer Roald Amundsen (1872–1928) and American explorer Lincoln Ellsworth (1880–1951) fly over the North Pole in the airship *Norge*, designed and piloted by Italian engineer Umberto Nobile (1885–1978).	**1927** Joseph Stalin (1878–1953) emerges as the dominant figure in the collective leadership now ruling the Soviet Union.
1928 German aviators Hermann Köhl (1881–1938) and Guenther von Hünefeld (1892–1929) and Irish army officer James Fitzmaurice (1898–1965) become the first to fly across the Atlantic from east to west.	**1927** *In Search of Lost Time* by Marcel Proust (1871–1922) is published posthumously.

1926 American inventor Robert Goddard (1882–1945) successfully launches a liquid-fuel rocket.	**1927** *The Jazz Singer*, starring Al Jolson (1886–1950), inaugurates the era of "talking pictures" in the cinema.
1926 Designed by Polish-born American engineer Ralph Modjeski (1861–1940), the Delaware River Bridge (the world's longest suspension span) opens in Philadelphia. It is renamed the Benjamin Franklin Bridge in 1956.	**1927** Canada is voted into the League of Nations Council.
1927 American inventor Philo Farnsworth (1906–71) makes a television camera tube (patented 1930).	**1928** Brazil's economy collapses as a result of the overproduction of coffee.
1927 American aviator Charles Lindbergh (1902–74) makes the first solo flight across the Atlantic Ocean.	
1928 American inventor Jacob Schick (1878–1937) patents the electric shaver.	

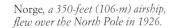

Norge, a 350-feet (106-m) airship, flew over the North Pole in 1926.

1926 Japan's Emperor Yoshihito (r. 1912–26) dies. He is succeeded by his son Hirohito (r. 1926–89).

1928 Latin script replaces Arabic for writing the Turkish language.

ROCKETS

The Chinese first used rockets in the 1100s, both for ornamental fireworks and as weapons of war. Knowledge of rockets spread, and in 1288 the Moors used them in their attack on Valencia in Spain. Multistage rockets (with one rocket mounted on top of another) came next, and by 1715 the Russians had their own rocket factory near St. Petersburg.

Early rockets were solid-fuel rockets that burned gunpowder. In 1806 English engineer William Congreve (1772–1828) started making rockets with an explosive warhead. They could reach targets 1.5 miles (2.5 km) away.

Congreve rockets had a long wooden tail, or stick, like modern fireworks. To improve accuracy and stability in flight, English inventor William Hale (1797–1870) added three angled fins to the rocket exhaust, which made the missile spin in flight. Rockets no longer needed a long wooden tail. Hale rockets were used by the U.S. Army in the Mexican–American War (1846–48) and by both sides in the American Civil War (1861–65).

American inventor Robert Goddard (1882–1945) launched the first liquid-fuel rocket in 1926 and ushered in a new age. The rocket used gasoline and liquid oxygen. By 1935 Goddard's rockets could climb over 7,820 feet (2,400 m) at a speed of 620 miles (1,000 km) per hour.

In Germany, Hermann Oberth (1894–1989) led a research team that developed a gasoline/liquid oxygen rocket by 1931. Wernher von Braun (1912–77) joined the team in 1930 and directed the research that produced the V-1 and the V-2. The V-1 (also known as the Doodlebug) was a pulsejet-powered flying bomb. The V-2, with its 1.1-ton (1-tonne) warhead, was the first rocket-powered guided missile.

After the war von Braun and other German scientists continued their work in the United States. Progress continued rapidly there and in the Soviet Union, resulting in intercontinental ballistic missiles and the space launchers that dominated the space race for 30 years.

ASTRONOMY & MATH	BIOLOGY & MEDICINE	PHYSICAL SCIENCES

EUROPE

1930 Dutch mathematician Bartel van der Waerden (1903–96) publishes what becomes the standard work on abstract algebra, *Modern Algebra*.

1929 German biochemist Adolf Butenandt (1903–95) isolates the female sex hormone estrogen. Two years later he isolates the male hormone androsterone.

1929 German biochemist Hans Fischer (1881–1945) determines the structure of heme (a key part of hemoglobin, the red pigment in blood) and synthesizes it.

1930 Swedish biochemist Arne Tiselius (1902–71) introduces the technique of electrophoresis for separating proteins (later to become a key process in genetic fingerprinting).

1930 Swiss chemist Paul Karrer (1889–1971) determines the structure of carotene, the precursor of vitamin A, and goes on to synthesize both.

1929 Irish crystallographer Kathleen Lonsdale (1903–71) uses x-ray crystallography to prove the hexagonal structure of benzene.

1929 German physicists Walther Bothe (1891–1957) and Werner Kolhorster (1887–1946) use a pair of Geiger counters to detect the direction from which cosmic rays come, and establish that cosmic rays are charged particles.

1930 French physicist Louis Néel (1904–2000) determines the Néel temperature, the temperature above which an antiferromagnetic substance (which is not magnetic) becomes paramagnetic (slightly magnetic).

1930 Austrian-born Swiss physicist Wolfgang Pauli (1900–58) predicts the existence of the neutrino.

THE AMERICAS

1929 American astronomer Edwin Hubble (1889–1953) formulates Hubble's law, which relates the distance of a star to its velocity of recession from Earth.

1930 American astronomer Clyde Tombaugh (1906–97) discovers the planet Pluto (now considered a dwarf planet).

1930 American electrical engineer Vannevar Bush (1890–1974) builds an analog computer.

1931 Indian-born American astrophysicist Subrahmanyan Chandrasekhar (1910–95) calculates the possible Chandrasekhar limit, the maximum mass for a white dwarf star (equal to about 1.4 times the mass of the sun).

1931 Austrian-born American mathematician Kurt Gödel (1906–78) proves that any mathematical system that includes the laws of arithmetic must be inconsistent or incomplete.

1931 Italian-born American physicist Bruno Rossi (1905–93) finds that cosmic rays can travel through lead 3.2-feet (1-m) thick.

1929 Canadian-born American physical chemist William Giauque (1895–1982) determines that natural oxygen consists of three isotopes of masses 16, 17, and 18.

1929 German-born American physicist Albert Einstein (1879–1955) first announces his unified field theory, which attempts to bring all the fundamental forces into a single theory.

1930 Italian-born American physicist Bruno Rossi (1905–93) discovers the composition of cosmic rays—the primary rays being positively charged and the secondary rays being elementary particles and gamma rays.

1930 American chemist Thomas Midgley (1889–1944) demonstrates the properties of Freon, the first CFC (chlorofluorocarbon), invented by his team for use as a refrigerant.

1930 American chemist Wallace Carothers (1896–1937) discovers neoprene (patented 1937). His work leads to the first commercial production of synthetic rubber and nylon.

1931 American chemist Linus Pauling (1901–94) explains that benzene is stable because its molecule has two structures that resonate ("flip" back and forth).

ASIA & OCEANIA

1929 Japanese geophysicist Motonori Matuyama (1884–1958) postulates that the Earth's magnetic field has undergone reversals several times in its history.

Art deco in style, New York's Chrysler Building was the tallest building in the world on its completion in 1930. That record, however, was broken 11 months later with the completion of the Empire State Building, a few blocks away.

AFRICA & THE MIDDLE EAST

ENGINEERING & INVENTION

1929 German engineer Hugo Eckener (1868–1954) commands a Zeppelin airship that makes a 21-day around-the-world flight.

1929 German engineer Felix Wankel (1902–88) patents his rotary engine.

1929 English engineer Robert Davis (1870–1965) invents a decompression chamber for deep-sea divers and in the same year designs an escape apparatus for submarines.

1930 English engineer Frank Whittle (1907–96) invents the gas turbine (jet) engine.

1930 English engineer Barnes Wallis (1887–1979) starts using the geodesic construction technique for aircraft, which uses light, straight structural elements.

1930 American businessman Clarence Birdseye (1886–1956) markets the first flash-frozen foods.

1930 American chemist Waldo Semon (1898–1999) invents a plastic called PVC (polyvinyl chloride).

1930 American naturalist William Beebe (1877–1962) and American engineer Otis Barton build a bathysphere submersible for deep-sea studies.

1930 The 1,048-foot- (319.4-m-) tall Chrysler Building is completed in New York City, designed by American architect William van Alen (1883–1954).

1931 American physicist Robert Van de Graaff (1901–67) invents the Van de Graaff high-voltage generator, which is later used as an atom smasher.

1931 The Empire State Building in New York City becomes the world's tallest building.

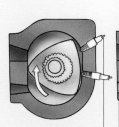

Frank Whittle (right) explains the workings of his jet engine to a journalist.

WORLD EVENTS

1929 The Kingdom of Serbs, Croats, and Slovenes is renamed Yugoslavia.

1929 Joseph Stalin (1878–1953) confirms his position as ruler of the Soviet Union by forcing his chief rival, Leon Trotsky (1879–1940), into exile. He launches the first five-year plan, aimed at modernizing the Soviet economy.

1930 The Nazis (National Socialists) led by Adolf Hitler (1889–1945) run second in elections to the Reichstag (Germany's parliament), winning 107 seats.

1931 King Alfonso XIII (r. 1886–1931) leaves Spain as his country declares itself a republic.

1929 Republican Herbert Hoover (1874–1964) becomes U.S. president.

1929 The Wall Street Crash: American shares lose more than $40 billion in value in a single month. The crash contributes to the beginning of the Great Depression of the 1930s.

1930 Revolution in Brazil brings dictatorial powers to Getúlio Vargas (1882–1954).

1929 Tajikistan—previously treated as part of Uzbekistan—becomes a separate Soviet republic.

1931 Japanese troops occupy Manchuria in northern China.

1929 The Riotous Assemblies Act is passed by the South African parliament to suppress protests by the country's black majority.

WANKEL ENGINE

Invented by German engineer Felix Wankel, the Wankel engine is the most widely used type of rotary engine. A Wankel engine works on a four-stroke cycle, and it is lighter and has fewer moving parts than the usual piston engine of similar power output. Instead of pistons it has a revolving rotor, so there is no need for a crankshaft to convert the up-and-down motion into rotary motion. Wankel first conceived his idea for a rotary engine in 1924 and received his first patent in 1929. However, it was not until 1957 that he built his first fully functional engine. The Wankel engine is still widely used in cars, notably by Mazda, and also in some go-carts, motorcycles, boats, and airplanes.

Gasoline/air mixture enters

Chamber containing fuel/air mixture

Inlet port | Rotor

Rotor

Induction

A gasoline/air mixture enters one of the chambers as the tip of the rotor goes past the inlet port.

Compression

The chamber containing the mixture decreases in size as the rotor turns, compressing the mixture.

Exhaust port

Spark plugs | Burned gases escape

Power

A pair of spark plugs ignites the mixture, which explodes and expands, "pushing" the rotor around.

Exhaust

Burned gases escape out of the exhaust port as the leading lobe of the rotor goes past.

PENICILLIN AND ANTIBIOTICS

I N THE EARLY PART OF THE 20TH CENTURY millions of people died every year from bacterial infections such as diphtheria, pneumonia, and septicemia. But the discovery of a mold that could kill germs would change all that.

From the late 19th century, thanks to the work of French chemist Louis Pasteur (1822–95) and others, scientists and medical practitioners recognized a new type of enemy—bacteria, or "germs." Many bacteria had been identified, and the conditions they caused were better understood. For example, staphylococci gave rise to boils and other skin infections, food poisoning, septicemia, and pneumonia; streptococci caused throat infections and various feverish conditions; and several bacilli produced tetanus, anthrax, diphtheria, and food poisoning.

The same kinds of organisms caused untold suffering when they infected wounds. Wound infection was the specialized area of Scottish bacteriologist Alexander Fleming (1881–1955). Unlike other medical researchers of the time, Fleming believed that the way to tackle infection was not to douse it with chemicals but to harness natural processes to do the job instead.

KEY DATES

1877
Pasteur observes anthrax-killing bacteria

1921
Fleming discovers lysozyme in living cells

1928
Fleming identifies penicillin

1940
Mice and humans treated with penicillin

c.1943
Penicillin in mass production

While the German chemist Paul Ehrlich (1854–1915) devoted himself to isolating chemical therapies, Fleming was in search of biological cures. By the mid-1920s he had already made a name for himself by discovering the enzyme lysozyme (1921), produced by living cells to break down other organic material. He thought that this kind of naturally occurring substance could hold the key to fighting bacterial infection.

Strange Mold

In 1928, after returning from vacation to his laboratory at St. Mary's Hospital in London, Fleming noticed something unusual about a culture of *Staphylococcus* that he had left developing in a petri dish. In his absence, a mold had grown in the dish, and it appeared to be killing the *Staphylococcus*. Fleming identified the strange mold as a species of *Penicillium* and discovered that the liquid it produced (penicillin) was equally effective at destroying a large number of different bacteria. More exciting still, it appeared to have no effect on healthy living tissue, so Fleming thought it could be safe to use on humans. But there were drawbacks. For a start, there were several disease-causing bacteria—notably those responsible for plague and cholera—on which it had no effect at all. (In fact, penicillin only works on gram-positive bacteria, in which the cell walls contain a thick layer of peptidoglycan—a substance that gives the bacteria shape and strength. Penicillin inhibits the formation of the peptidoglycan layer and thereby weakens the cell wall.) Even more disheartening was the fact that penicillin turned out to be very difficult to produce. For every milliliter of fluid secreted from the *Penicillium* mold, only about 0.000002 ml was active penicillin, and what tiny amounts could be extracted deteriorated easily.

The problems seemed insurmountable, but in 1939 a group of scientists at Oxford University in England led by Australian pathologist Howard Florey (1898–1968) and German biochemist Ernst Chain (1906–79) began following up Fleming's discovery. By 1940 they extracted penicillin and began

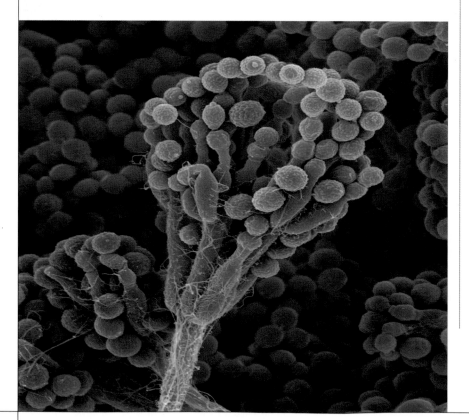

The image left shows a fruiting body of the mold Penicillium chrysogenum, *which is used to make penicillin antibiotics. Other species of* Penicillium *are used to make blue cheeses. Magnification x 500.*

testing it on mice. The results were startling. A dose of penicillin enabled mice to fight off infections that otherwise would have killed them. Florey then began treating a human patient who was dangerously ill with staphylococcal septicemia (blood poisoning). The patient improved a little; but the doses required were too large, and Florey's laboratory was unable to produce enough to keep up the treatment. The patient died, but the results were impressive enough to convince several pharmaceutical companies of penicillin's importance. Thanks to refinements in the production technique developed by English biochemist Norman Heatley (1911–2004), the "miracle drug" was being mass-produced in the United States and Britain by about 1943.

The development could not have come at a more crucial time. World War II was raging, and wounded Allied servicemen were the first to benefit. Thousands of lives were saved. After the war the benefits of penicillin were spread more widely. Deaths from diseases such as anthrax, pneumonia, and tetanus and from blood infections were cut dramatically. Fleming, Florey, and Chain received the 1945 Nobel Prize for Medicine. Heatley remained an unsung hero until 1990, when his contribution was recognized by an honorary degree from Oxford University.

Fleming's accidental discovery of penicillin marked the beginning of modern antibiotics. He also found that some bacteria could build up resistance to penicillin if exposed to repeated low doses.

ASTRONOMY & MATH	BIOLOGY & MEDICINE	PHYSICAL SCIENCES

EUROPE

1932 German astronomer Karl Reinmuth (1892–1979) observes the first Earth-crossing Apollo asteroid. It is lost soon after and not rediscovered until the 1970s.

1933 Swiss astrophysicist Fritz Zwicky (1898–1974) proposes that space must contain invisible "dark matter" (to account for the total mass in the universe).

1934 Swiss astrophysicist Fritz Zwicky and German-born American astronomer Walter Baade (1893–1960) predict the existence of neutron stars from their analysis of supernovas.

1932 German bacteriologist Gerhard Domagk (1895–1964) discovers the first sulfa drug, sulfanilamide. It is first used in 1935 against a streptococcal infection.

1933 Austrian-German chemist Richard Kuhn (1900–67) and coworkers isolate vitamin B_2 (riboflavin). The same year American chemist Roger Williams (1893–1988) discovers another B complex vitamin, pantothenic acid.

1934 German biochemist Adolf Butenandt (1903–95) identifies the female sex hormone progesterone.

1934 Danish biochemist Henrik Dam (1895–1976) discovers a factor needed for blood clotting, which a year later he calls vitamin K. American chemist Robert Williams (1886–1965) isolates vitamin B_1.

1932 English physicist James Chadwick (1891–1974) discovers the neutron.

1932 English physicist John Cockcroft (1897–1967) and Irish physicist Ernest Walton (1903–95) carry out the first nuclear fission by bombarding lithium with protons, using a linear accelerator they have invented.

1933 English chemist Charles Coulson (1910–74) and German physicist Erich Hückel (1896–1980) independently propose the molecular orbital theory to describe the behavior of bonding electrons in compounds.

1933 Polish chemist Tadeus Reichstein (1897–1996) and, working together, English chemists Norman Haworth (1883–1950) and Edmund Hirst (1898–1975) synthesize vitamin C (ascorbic acid).

THE AMERICAS

1932 American physiologist Walter Cannon (1871–1945) introduces the concept of homeostasis, in which the body's systems act together to maintain a condition of balance.

1932 American physician Armand Quick (1894–1978) develops the Quick test for blood clotting.

1932 Hungarian-born American biochemist Albert Szent-Györgyi (1893–1986) and American biochemist Charles King (1896–1986) independently prove that hexonuric acid is vitamin C; it is isolated and renamed ascorbic acid.

1933 American biochemist George Wald (1906–97) discovers vitamin A in the retina of the eye, later shown to be a precursor of rhodopsin (a red photosensitive pigment).

1934 American scientist Royal Raymond Rife (1888–1971) tests a cancer-curing treatment using radio waves on human patients.

1932 Anthropologist George Lewis discovers fossils of the hominoid *Ramapithecus* in northern India.

1933 The Tasmanian wolf (or thylacine) becomes extinct in the wild.

1932 American chemist Harold Urey (1893–1981) and coworkers isolate deuterium (heavy hydrogen, the hydrogen isotope of mass 2). Two years later Australian physicist Mark Oliphant (1901–2000) discovers tritium (the hydrogen isotope of mass 3).

1932 Synthetic rubber is first marketed in the United States (by the DuPont Company) under the name Duprene, later renamed Neoprene.

1932 American physicist Carl Anderson (1905–91) announces the existence of the positron (positive electron). It is the first example of a particle of antimatter.

ASIA & OCEANIA

AFRICA & THE MIDDLE EAST

INSIDE STORY

Neutron Stars

A tiny neutron star lies at the very center of the Crab nebula, the remnant of a supernova explosion that was observed by Chinese astronomers in 1054. Fritz Zwicky and Walter Baade predicted the existence of such stars in 1934. They are the densest and smallest stars, consisting of tightly packed neutrons (so-called degeneracy matter). They have a mass similar to that of the sun but are only about 12 miles (20 km) across. Rapidly spinning neutron stars become pulsars, emitting high-energy pulses of radio waves.

The cat's eye, a road safety device invented in 1934, consists of reflective glass spheres set in rubber and surrounded by cast iron.

ENGINEERING & INVENTION

1932 Dutch physicist Frits Zernike (1888–1966) invents the phase-contrast microscope.

1933 English engineer Alan Blumlein (1903–42) patents a system of stereophonic sound recording.

1934 The French company Citroën launches the first mass-produced front-wheel-drive car.

1934 The *Queen Mary*, the world's largest ocean liner, is launched in Glasgow, Scotland. The liner's maiden voyage takes place in 1936.

1934 English inventor Percy Shaw (1890–1976) patents "cat's eyes" (reflecting road markers).

1932 American physicist Ernest Lawrence (1901–58) successfully operates the first cyclotron, one of the first particle accelerators, or atom smashers.

1932 American electrical engineer William Kouwenhoven (1886–1975) has the idea for a defibrillator to restart the heart of a patient with a heart attack.

1933 The first modern airliner, the Boeing 247, enters service.

1934 American engineer Laurens Hammond (1895–1973) designs the electronic organ that bears his name.

1934 American firearms engineer John Garand (1888–1974) designs the semiautomatic Garand M1 rifle, soon to become standard issue in the U.S. Army.

1934 American psychologist B. F. Skinner (1904–90) invents the Skinner box for studying the behavior of animals.

1932 The Sydney Harbor Bridge, designed by English engineer Ralph Freeman (1880–1950), is completed. At the time it has the longest single span of any bridge in the world.

WORLD EVENTS

1932 Famine in Ukraine follows the attempt of Soviet ruler Joseph Stalin (1878–1953) to impose the collectivization of agriculture.

1932 António Salazar (1889–1970) comes to power in Portugal. His Estado Novo ("New State") dictatorship will rule the nation for the next 36 years.

1933 Adolf Hitler (1889–1945) becomes chancellor of Germany; he assumes dictatorial powers and outlaws all political parties except the Nazi Party.

1934 Stalin eliminates political enemies in the Soviet Union; many are found guilty of invented crimes in "show trials" and shot, while millions more are deported to labor camps (gulags).

1932 The Chaco War (1932–35) between Bolivia and Paraguay begins. It is fought for possession of the disputed Northern Chaco region. Paraguay emerges victorious three years later.

1932 In the United States the Great Depression is at its worst, with more than 15 million workers unemployed.

1933 Prohibition (of alcohol) ends in the United States.

1934 After a drought in the Midwest, many U.S. farmers leave the "Dust Bowl."

1934 Lázaro Cárdenas (1895–1970) becomes president of Mexico, introducing a program of social reform.

Skinner boxes are used to study animal behavior and learning. This box has a lever inside, which the rat learns to press to get a reward of food.

ARTIFICIAL FIBERS

The first attempts at creating an artificial fiber tried to copy silk, the most expensive of natural fibers. Natural silk contains cellulose, which is also found in plants. Methods of copying it involve dissolving cellulose (in the form of wood pulp or cotton) to make a solution that is forced through a tiny hole to make a strand. Chemicals harden the strand to form a fiber. The first patent for such a process—in the early 1800s—went to a Swiss chemist named Georges Audemars. In 1883, while searching for a material to make the filaments for his newly invented electric lamp, English physicist Joseph Swan (1828–1914) patented a process for making cellulose fibers by dissolving nitrocellulose (guncotton) in acetic acid (ethanoic acid) and forcing it through small holes.

In 1884 French chemist Hilaire de Chardonnet (1839–1924) made cotton waste into cellulose acetate (ethanoate) and dissolved it in a solvent. He forced the sticky solution through a mesh of small holes to make Chardonnet silk, later called acetate rayon. Cellulose was also used to make *Glanzstoff* in Germany and viscose rayon in Britain.

The first totally artificial fiber was produced in 1935 by American chemist Wallace Carothers (1896–1937). It was a polymer named nylon 66. His company, DuPont, released the top-secret product in 1938. Since then DuPont and other companies have produced several other kinds of nylon. In 1941 a different type of polymer, a polyester with the trade names Dacron and Terylene, was created. It is often blended with a natural fiber such as wool.

In 1964 both American and British researchers independently reinvented carbon fibers (originally invented by Joseph Swan). Manufacturers mix them with plastics to make materials of great strength and versatility. These composites are made into leisure products such as golf clubs, tennis rackets, and sailboat masts, as well as industrial items such as helicopter rotors and turbine blades.

	ASTRONOMY & MATH	BIOLOGY & MEDICINE	PHYSICAL SCIENCES

EUROPE

1936 English mathematician and logician Alan Turing (1912–54) "invents" the hypothetical Turing machine, which determines whether or not a problem can be solved using a computer. A year later he devises a mathematical theory of computing and publishes his paper "On Computable Numbers."

1937 Russian mathematician Ivan Vinogradov (1891–1983) proves that every large even number can be expressed as the sum of four prime numbers.

1935 Austrian zoologist Konrad Lorenz (1903–89) discovers imprinting in animals.

1935 Portuguese neurologist António de Egas Moniz (1874–1955) introduces prefrontal lobotomy to treat personality disorders.

1937 German-born English biochemist Hans Krebs (1900–81) explains the citric acid cycle, also called the Krebs cycle. It is a series of reactions fundamental to the metabolism in aerobic (oxygen-consuming) organisms.

1937 Swiss-born Italian pharmacologist Daniel Bovet (1907–92) identifies the first antihistamine effective in treating allergies.

1937 Italian physician Ugo Cerletti (1877–1963) introduces electroconvulsive, or "shock," therapy (ECT) to treat schizophrenia.

1935 Swiss chemist Paul Karrer (1889–1971) determines the structure of vitamin B_2 (riboflavin) and synthesizes it.

1935 British chemists at ICI (Imperial Chemical Industries) develop a reproducible high-pressure synthesis of polyethene (also known as polyethylene or polythene).

1936 Danish physicist Niels Bohr (1885–1962) proposes a liquid-drop model of the nucleus.

1936 Danish seismologist Inge Lehmann (1888–1993) proposes that the Earth's inner core is solid and surrounded by liquid metal.

THE AMERICAS

1935 American radio engineer John Dellinger (1886–1962) confirms that sunspot activity causes interference with radio signals on Earth.

1935 American oceanographer William Ewing (1906–74) starts a seismic (earthquake) study of the seabed.

1935 American seismologist Charles Richter (1900–85) devises the Richter scale to measure earthquake intensity.

1935 German-born American astronomer Rupert Wildt (1905–76) detects that the large planets have ammonia and methane in their atmospheres.

1936 American mathematician Alonzo Church (1903–95) demonstrates that there is no single way in which a mathematical statement can be verified or proven.

1937 American electrical engineer George Stibitz (1904–95) of Bell Laboratories makes a binary adding machine (the Model K).

1935 American biochemist Wendell Stanley (1904–71) crystallizes tobacco mosaic virus.

1935 German-born American biochemist Rudolf Schoenheimer (1898–1941) uses deuterium (heavy hydrogen) as a tracer to follow biochemical reactions.

1937 American chemist Michael Sveda (1912–99) accidentally discovers the artificial-sweetening properties of cyclamates.

The giant panda is part of the bear family. This rare animal is found wild only in China.

1935 German-born American physicists Fritz (1900–54) and Heinz (1907–70) London announce the so-called London equations concerning superconductors.

1935 Canadian-born American physicist Arthur Dempster (1886–1950) discovers the fissile isotope uranium-235. It is used later in atom bombs.

1935 American biochemist William Rose (1887–1985) discovers threonine, the last of the so-called essential amino acids.

1936 American chemist Robert Williams (1886–1965) announces the structure of vitamin B_1 (thiamin) and its synthesis.

1936 American physicists Russian-born George Gamow (1904–68) and Hungarian-born Edward Teller (1908–2003) put forward a theory to account for beta decay by a radioactive isotope.

1936 American physicist Carl Anderson (1905–91) discovers the muon (mu-meson) in cosmic rays. The muon is a negatively charged particle some 200 times as massive as the electron.

ASIA & OCEANIA

1936 The last-known Tasmanian wolf, or thylacine (*Thylacinus cyanocephalus*), dies at Hobart Zoo in Tasmania, Australia.

1936 The first giant panda (*Ailuropoda melanoleuca*) is captured alive in the wild by clothing designer Ruth Harkness, widow of adventurer William Harkness.

AFRICA & THE MIDDLE EAST

The Boulder (Hoover) Dam was built on the Colorado River between 1931 and 1935. The hydroelectric power it produces is distributed among three states: Nevada, Arizona, and California.

ENGINEERING & INVENTION	WORLD EVENTS

1935 German engineer Willy Messerschmitt (1898–1978) designs the Bf-109 single-seat fighter airplane.

1935 Scottish physicist Robert Watson-Watt (1892–1973) invents radar, which is also being developed in Germany.

1936 German engineer Heinrich Focke (1890–1979) builds and successfully demonstrates a two-rotor helicopter.

1936 The Supermarine Spitfire fighter airplane, designed by English engineer Reginald Mitchell (1895–1937), makes its maiden flight.

1937 The Swiss company Nestlé begins marketing instant coffee (Nescafé).

1936 The Spanish Civil War (1936–39) breaks out between right-wing forces led by General Francisco Franco (1892–1975) and the leftist Popular Front government. It will end in victory for Franco.

1938 Pablo Picasso (1881–1973) paints "Guernica" to protest the bombing of the Basque town of that name in the Spanish Civil War.

1935 The coin-operated parking meter, invented by American editor Carlton Magee (1873–1946), is introduced in the United States.

1935 American musicians and amateur photographers Leopold Godowsky, Jr. (1900–83) and Leopold Mannes (1899–1964) invent Kodachrome transparency film.

1936 The Boulder Dam is completed on the Colorado River.

1937 The world's first pressurized aircraft, the Lockheed XC-35, makes its maiden flight.

1937 San Francisco's Golden Gate Bridge, designed by American engineer Joseph Strauss (1870–1938), is completed.

1937 American physicist Chester Carlson (1906–68) invents xerography, a dry photocopying process (patented 1940).

1936 African-American athlete Jesse Owens (1913–80) wins four golds at the Berlin Olympics.

1937 *Gone with the Wind* by Margaret Mitchell (1900–49) is published.

1937 American aviator Amelia Earhart (1897–1937) disappears on a flight across the Pacific.

HOW THINGS WORK

Early Photocopiers

The earliest types of photocopiers used the xerography process. The item to be copied is moved across the light source (instead of the light moving to scan the item as in most modern machines). A lens focuses an image of the item onto a drum (1), where it produces an electrostatic copy as a pattern of electric charges. Particles of charged toner powder stick to the pattern (2) and transfer to a sheet of blank paper as the drum rotates (3). A heater partly melts the toner to "fix" the image onto the paper (4).

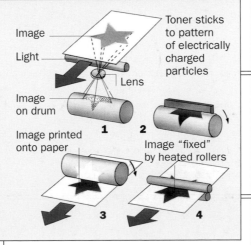

HELICOPTERS

As early as 1480 Italian artist Leonardo da Vinci (1452–1519) sketched a design for an aircraft that carried a large, vertically mounted screw. He reasoned that if the screw rotated fast enough, the craft would rise into the air. However, he did not know about the phenomenon of torque, which would actually make the craft rotate while the screw remained still.

Four centuries later, Italian Carlo Forlanini (1847–1918) and Frenchman Gustave de Ponton d'Amécourt (1825–88) made models of steam-powered helicopters. Forlanini's model had a pair of rotors turning in opposite directions on the same shaft. Driven by a small steam engine, they lifted the craft to a height of 49 feet (15 m), where it hovered for nearly a minute.

By the beginning of the 20th century gasoline engines powered machines that could hover a short distance off the ground for a short time. These early helicopters were not directionally stable, which is crucial for sustained flight. Many engineers tried to solve this problem, including Russian-born American Igor Sikorsky (1889–1972) and German Heinrich Focke (1890–1979). Focke's Fa-61 twin-rotor machine could fly backward as well as forward at a speed of 75 miles (120 km) per hour and a height of more than 7,800 feet (2,400 m). It set an endurance record of 1 hour 20 minutes in the 1930s.

Finally, in 1939 Sikorsky flew the first practical single-rotor machine. It could take off vertically and reached a forward speed of 43 miles (70 km) per hour. It had an enclosed cabin and a latticework tail carrying a small vertical propeller. The second propeller overcame the long-standing problem of torque in a single-rotor machine, since it kept the whole machine from rotating. The U.S. and British forces used improved versions of the Sikorsky VS-300 helicopter. The military helicopter came into its own during the Korean War (1950–53), transporting troops and casualties, and in the Vietnam War (1954–75), as aerial artillery.

ASTRONOMY & MATH	BIOLOGY & MEDICINE	PHYSICAL SCIENCES

EUROPE

1938 The asteroid Hermes—first located in 1937 by German astronomer Karl Reinmuth (1892–1979)—approaches within 485,000 miles (780,000 km) of Earth, closer than any other observed asteroid at the time.

1938 German computer pioneer Konrad Zuse (1910–95) constructs a binary digital computer (the Z1).

1939 Under the pseudonym Nicolas Bourbaki, a group of French mathematicians publishes *Elements of Mathematics*, the first of many books on contemporary mathematics.

1939 Danish astrophysicist Bengt Strömgren (1908–87) identifies Strömgren spheres, regions of ionized gas (mainly hydrogen) surrounding a hot star.

1938 May & Baker pharmaceutical company produces sulfapyridine, the sulfa drug used to treat pneumonia.

1939 Swiss chemist Paul Müller (1899–1965) determines the insect-killing properties of DDT.

1940 German-born British biochemist Ernst Chain (1906–1979) and Australian pathologist Howard Florey (1898–1968) extract and purify penicillin and perform the first clinical trials of the drug.

1940 Swiss psychologist Carl Jung (1875–1961) publishes *The Integration of Personality*.

1938 German physicists Otto Hahn (1879–1968) and Fritz Strassmann (1902–80) induce nuclear fission in uranium.

1939 German chemist Richard Kuhn (1900–67) and coworkers isolate vitamin B_6 (pyridoxine) in yeast and synthesize it within a few months.

1939 French chemist Marguerite Perey (1909–75) discovers the radioactive element francium. (She calls it actinium K and changes its name to francium in 1945.)

1939 French physicists Irène (1897–1956) and Frédéric Joliot-Curie (1900–58) show that uranium fission can lead to a chain reaction.

THE AMERICAS

1938 American astronomer Seth Nicholson (1891–1963) discovers Lysithea, a small moon of Jupiter.

1938 Russian-born American astrophysicist Otto Struve (1897–1963) establishes the presence of hydrogen ions in space.

1938 German-born American physicist Hans Bethe (1906–2005) and colleagues determine the series of nuclear fusion reactions that "fuel" stars.

1939 American physicist John Atanasoff (1903–95) makes a prototype electronic binary calculator (the Atanasoff-Berry Computer, or ABC).

1939 German-born American geophysicist Walter Elsasser (1904–91) postulates the existence of eddy currents in the Earth's semiliquid outer core to account for the Earth's magnetism.

1938 American physician Florence Seibert (1897–1991) isolates and purifies tuberculin used in the skin test for tuberculosis.

1939 French-born American bacteriologist René Dubos (1901–82) isolates tyrothricin. Tyrothricin (Gramacidin) is the first commercial antibiotic to be marketed.

1939 American zoologist Victor Shelford (1877–1968) introduces the concept of biomes (major geographical areas, such as tundra or desert, that support their own range of organisms).

1940 American zoologist Donald Griffin (1915–2003) announces that bats "echolocate" using ultrasound.

1940 Austrian-born American pathologist Karl Landsteiner (1868–1943) describes the Rhesus (Rh) factor in human blood.

1938 American chemist Roy Plunkett (1910–94) synthesizes the "nonstick" plastic PTFE (polytetrafluoroethylene, or Teflon).

1939 German-born American physicist Albert Einstein (1879–1955) advises President Franklin Roosevelt (1882–1945) that the discovery of nuclear chain reactions would lead to the atomic bomb.

1940 Canadian-born American chemist Martin Kamen (1913–2002) discovers the isotope carbon-14.

1940 Three heavy radioactive elements are identified this year: astatine by Italian-born American physicist Emilio Segrè (1905–89) and coworkers, neptunium by American physicist Edwin McMillan (1907–91) and coworkers, and plutonium by American physical chemist Glenn Seaborg (1912–99) and coworkers.

1940 American physical chemist Philip Abelson (1913–2004) introduces the diffusion method for separating the isotopes of uranium, an early enrichment process.

1940 Austrian-born American physicist Maurice Goldhaber (1911–) introduces the use of beryllium as a moderator (neutron-absorber) in a nuclear reactor.

ASIA & OCEANIA

American shipyards built about 2,750 Liberty ships during World War II.

AFRICA & THE MIDDLE EAST

1938 American professor J. L. B. Smith (1897–1968) identifies a coelacanth (*Latimeria chalumnae*)—a fish previously thought to be extinct—off South Africa.

The farther an experiment is from theory, the closer it is to the Nobel Prize.

Frédéric Joliot-Curie,

ENGINEERING & INVENTION

1938 The British steam locomotive *Mallard* gains the title of the world's fastest steam engine, with a speed of 126 miles (203 km) per hour. The record still stands.

1938 Italian Achille Gaggia (1895–1961) files a patent for an espresso coffee machine (not manufactured until 1946).

1938 German engineer Ferdinand Porsche (1875–1951) designs the Volkswagen "Beetle" car.

1939 English radio engineers John Randall (1905–84) and Henry Boot (1917–83) invent the cavity magnetron UHF radar tube.

1940 German engineer Paul Schmidt invents the pulsejet engine. It is later used to power V-1 flying bombs.

1938 German-born American engineer Anton Flettner (1885–1961) constructs his Fl-265 "synchropter," a small helicopter with counter-rotating rotors; it first flies in 1939.

1938 American radio engineers Russell (1898–1959) and Sigurd Varian (1901–61) invent the klystron UHF radar transmitter tube.

1938 American physicist Katherine Blodgett (1898–1979) creates nonreflective glass.

1938 Hungarian-born Argentine inventor Laszlo Biró (1899–1985) makes a prototype of the first ballpoint pen.

1939 The National Broadcasting Company (NBC) begins regular television transmissions in the United States.

1940 Hundreds of Liberty ships, designed by American engineer William Gibbs (1886–1967), are built to replace ships lost to German submarines.

1940 The Tacoma Narrows suspension bridge in Washington State collapses owing to oscillation (resonant vibration). The phenomenon is explained by Hungarian-born American engineer Theodore Kármán (1881–1963).

WORLD EVENTS

1938 German troops take over Austria and the Sudetenland region of Czechoslovakia.

1939 The first Nazi concentration camp is established at Dachau in Germany.

1939 The Axis powers—Italy and German—sign a formal treaty of cooperation, the "Pact of Steel."

1939 Adolf Hitler (1889–1945) and Joseph Stalin (1879–1953) sign the German–Soviet Nonaggression Pact.

1939 Germany invades Poland; Britain and France declare war on Germany, beginning World War II (1939–45).

1940 Germany occupies Denmark, Norway, the Netherlands, and France.

1938 The 40-hour working week is established in the United States.

1939 The U.S. economy begins to rebound after the recession of 1938. It is mainly due to European demand for weapons and war materials.

1940 Leon Trotsky (1876–1940) is assassinated in Mexico on Stalin's orders.

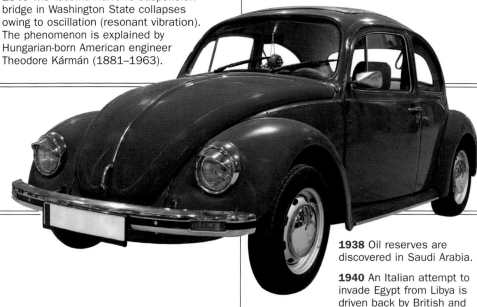

Ferdinand Porsche's design for the German "people's car" (Volkswagen Type 1) dates from 1938.

1938 Oil reserves are discovered in Saudi Arabia.

1940 An Italian attempt to invade Egypt from Libya is driven back by British and Australian forces.

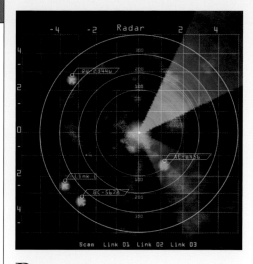

RADAR

During the 1920s and 1930s radio engineers in the United States and Europe reported that passing aircraft distorted their broadcasts. Part of the radio signal had "bounced" off the airplane. Researchers realized that this type of radio reflection could provide a way of detecting planes and other objects such as ships and icebergs.

Radar stands for "**ra**dio **d**etecting **a**nd **r**anging." To detect a plane, a radar set transmits a pulse of very-high-frequency radio waves. A receiving antenna picks up any radio echoes that return. The direction of the returning signal reveals the direction of the target and its range can be calculated from the time it takes for the signal to travel out and back.

In 1904 German engineer Christian Hülsmeyer (1881–1957) took out the first patent for a radar set. Research continued in various countries. By World War II (1939–45) Britain had built a chain of radar antennas along the eastern and southern coastline of England to detect incoming German planes. In Germany engineers adapted radars to aim guns, particularly antiaircraft guns.

Radar has since had many peacetime applications. Astronomers have picked up radar signals reflected back from several planets. The National Aeronautics and Space Administration (NASA) used radar signals from orbiting space probes to map the bottom of Earth's oceans. In addition, weather forecasters make extensive use of satellite radar images.

ASTRONOMY & MATH	BIOLOGY & MEDICINE	PHYSICAL SCIENCES

EUROPE

1941 Russian astronomer Dmitri Maksutov (1896–1964) builds a new type of reflecting telescope with a wide angle of view.

1942 English astronomer Harold Spencer Jones (1890–1960) obtains an accurate value for the Earth–sun distance—equal to 1 astronomical unit, or 93,000,626 miles (149,670,000 km).

1942 English physicist Stanley Hey (1909–2000) discovers that sunspots are a source of ultrashort radio waves.

1943 English engineer Thomas Flowers (1905–98) and English logician and mathematician Alan Turing (1912–54) build Colossus, an all-electronic stored-program computer, for breaking German military codes.

1943 Physicians at the University of Stockholm, Sweden, introduce the use of xylocaine as a local anesthetic.

1943 Swiss chemist Albert Hofmann (1906–2008) accidentally discovers the hallucinogenic properties of the drug LSD (lysergic acid diethylamide).

1943 Dutch (later American) physician Willem Kolff (1911–) constructs the first kidney dialysis machine (secretly in German-occupied Netherlands).

1941 The German company I.G. Farbenindustrie begins to manufacture polyurethane plastics.

1941 Soviet nuclear physicist Georgii Flerov (1913–90) observes spontaneous nuclear fission in uranium.

1942 Swedish physicist Hannes Alfvén (1908–95) suggests that plasmas such as ionized gases and liquid metals passing through magnetic fields in space create electromagnetic waves.

THE AMERICAS

1941 American mathematician Abraham Albert (1905–72) begins formulating his theories on nonassociative algebra, which he publishes in 1942.

1942 American radio astronomer Grote Reber (1911–2002) compiles the first radio map of the universe.

1942 American physicist John Atanasoff (1903–95) and coworkers complete the development of the ABC, a vacuum-tube electronic calculator with a memory. However, work is interrupted by World War II.

1943 American astronomer Carl Seyfert (1911–60) discovers Seyfert galaxies, which have active nuclei and spectra that indicate a high degree of ionization.

1941 German-born American biochemist Fritz Lipmann (1899–1986) shows the role of ATP (adenosine triphosphate) as the carrier of chemical energy in cells.

1941 American biochemists George Beadle (1903–89) and Edward Tatum (1909–75) observe cell reactions that are controlled by genes.

1941 Canadian-born American surgeon Charles Huggins (1901–97) uses female sex hormones to treat prostate cancer in men.

1942 Belgian-born American biologist Albert Claude (1898–1983) first uses an electron microscope in biological studies.

1942 Italian-born American microbiologist Salvador Luria (1912–91) obtains the first high-quality electron micrographs of a bacteriophage (a virus that attacks bacteria).

1943 American biochemist Britton Chance (1913–) establishes the existence of enzyme-substrate complexes in explaining how enzymes work.

1942 American chemist Louis Fieser (1899–1977) develops napalm for use as an incendiary weapon dropped from the air.

1942 Italian–American physicist Enrico Fermi (1901–54) achieves the first controlled nuclear chain reaction, at the University of Chicago.

1942 American biochemist Vincent du Vigneaud (1901–78) establishes the structure of biotin, one of the B complex vitamins.

1943 The American company Dow Corning is established and begins manufacturing silicone plastics.

1943 American scientists complete the world's first operational nuclear reactor at Oak Ridge, Tennessee.

ASIA & OCEANIA

1943 Japanese theoretical physicist Sin-Itiro Tomonaga (1906–79) publishes a paper on the basic physical principles of quantum electrodynamics.

AFRICA & THE MIDDLE EAST

At Oak Ridge, Tennessee, Enrico Fermi and his colleagues developed a nuclear reactor to make plutonium. The plutonium was used in the atomic bomb dropped on Nagasaki, Japan, in 1945.

ENGINEERING & INVENTION	WORLD EVENTS
1941 German rocket engineer Walter Dornberger (1895–1980) designs the A-4 liquid-fuel rocket.	**1941** Germany invades the Soviet Union; the Germans advance to Moscow by December but are forced back by the cold weather.
1941 English chemists John Whinfield (1901–66) and James Dickson produce the plastic Dacron (Terylene).	**1942** The Nazis adopt the "final solution," a genocide campaign aimed at the total extermination of the Jews; mass deportations to the death camps follow.
1942 French underwater explorer Jacques Cousteau (1910–97) invents the aqualung, or scuba (self-contained underwater breathing apparatus).	**1942** Defeat at Stalingrad, Russia, ends further German expansion in the east.
1942 German rocket engineer Wernher von Braun (1912–77) designs the V-1 flying bomb and the V-2 rocket bomb.	**1943** The Nazis suppress a Jewish uprising in the Warsaw ghetto in Poland.
	1943 Allied forces land in Italy.
1942 The German air force flies the Me-262, the first operational jet airplane, designed by engineer Willy Messerschmitt (1898–1978).	**1943** The Battle of Kursk, the biggest tank battle in history, ends in a narrow victory for the Soviet army against the Germans.
1941 French-born American electrical engineer Henri-Gaston Busignies (1905–81) invents a high-frequency direction finder for plotting the positions of aircraft.	**1941** At a secret meeting off the coast of Newfoundland President Franklin Roosevelt (1882–1945) and British leader Winston Churchill (1874–1965) set out the terms of the Atlantic Charter for the future of postwar Europe.
1942 The Manhattan Project, to make an atom bomb, begins in the United States.	**1941** The Japanese bomb the American naval base at Pearl Harbor in Hawaii.
	1942 Japanese troops advancing through Burma (Myanmar) reach the border with India.
	1943 Famine spreads through Bengal in India.

The 47-foot (14-m) V-2 rocket bomb had a launch speed of 2,500 feet (760 m) per second to carry it high into the upper atmosphere. It came down silently 200 miles (320 km) away at more than three times the speed of sound.

WERNHER VON BRAUN

Wernher von Braun was an engineer and pioneer rocket scientist. He was born in 1912 into a prosperous German family and attended universities in Berlin and Zurich, where he studied engineering. From 1930 he made experimental rockets. The ballistics and munitions branch of the German army, under rocket engineer Walter Dornberger (1895–1980), noticed his work. With the backing of Adolf Hitler (1889–1945), von Braun went to the newly established rocket research center at Peenemünde on the Baltic Sea coast, where in 1936 he became director. There he worked on the "vengeance weapon" 2 (V-2). This huge rocket used liquid oxygen and alcohol, weighed more than 11 tons (10 tonnes), and delivered a warhead containing 1.1 tons (1 tonne) of explosives. Many of the 4,300 V-2s launched from 1944 fell in Belgium and England.

At the end of the war von Braun surrendered to the U.S. Army and went to work in the United States. There he adapted a V-2 to carry a nuclear warhead. He was recruited by the National Aeronautics and Space Administration (NASA) and in 1958 oversaw the successful launch of *Explorer I*, the United States's first artificial satellite. He also headed the team that built the Mercury capsules for the piloted spaceflight program, culminating in the orbital flight of John Glenn (1921–) in 1962. In 1960 von Braun became director of the Marshall Space Flight Center, developing the three-stage Saturn V rocket for NASA's Apollo missions. The climax of this work came in 1969 when astronauts landed on the moon.

ASTRONOMY & MATH

EUROPE

1944 Dutch physicist and radio astronomer Hendrik van de Hulst (1918–2000) predicts that interstellar space emits microwave radio waves at a wavelength of 21.1 cm.

1944 German physicist and astrophysicist Carl von Weizsäcker (1912–2007) proposes a theory for the origin of the solar system, a version of the nebular hypothesis first proposed by French astronomer Pierre-Simon de Laplace (1749–1827) in 1796.

1946 English physicist Edward Appleton (1892–1965) detects radio emissions from sunspots.

1946 Hungarian physicist Zoltán Bay (1900–92) and investigators at the U.S. Army Signal Corps Laboratory independently obtain radar reflections from the moon.

BIOLOGY & MEDICINE

1946 Swedish pharmacologist Ulf von Euler (1905–83) identifies the hormone norepinephrine (noradrenaline).

1946 British surgeon Thomas Cecil Gray introduces (1913–2008) the use of curare (a Native American arrow poison) in general anesthesia.

PHYSICAL SCIENCES

1944 English biochemists Archer Martin (1910–2002) and Richard Synge (1914–94) complete the development of their paper chromatography technique.

1944 German biochemist Hans Fischer (1881–1945) determines the structure of the bile pigment bilirubin and synthesizes it.

1945 English crystallographer Dorothy Hodgkin (1910–94) uses x-ray crystallography to determine the structure of penicillin.

1945 Soviet physicist Vladimir Veksler (1907–66) designs and builds a particle accelerator called the synchrocyclotron.

1946 English chemist Robert Robinson (1886–1975) figures out the structure of the alkaloid drug strychnine.

THE AMERICAS

1944 German-born American astronomer Walter Baade (1893–1960) classifies stars into two types: Population I (younger stars in galaxy arms) and Population II (older stars in galaxy nuclei).

1944 American mathematician Howard Aiken (1900–73) and coworkers from IBM complete the Harvard Mark I, an automatic sequence-controlled calculator.

1944 Hungarian-born American mathematician John von Neumann (1903–57) and German-born American mathematician Oskar Morgenstern (1902–76) establish that game theory has a mathematical basis.

1944 American pioneer computer engineers John Eckert (1919–95) and John Mauchly (1907–80) devise the mercury delay line store (a computer memory device). Two years later they complete ENIAC (Electronic Numerical Integrator And Computer), a fully electronic computer.

1944 Canadian-born American bacteriologist Oswald Avery (1877–1955) and coworkers demonstrate that nearly all organisms have DNA (deoxyribonucleic acid) as their hereditary material.

1944 Ukrainian-born American biochemist Selman Waksman (1888–1973) discovers the bacteria-killing drug streptomycin.

1944 American pediatrician Helen Taussig (1898–1986) and American surgeon Alfred Blalock (1899–1964) introduce a pulmonary bypass operation to treat the heart defect in "blue babies."

1945 American biochemist Melvin Calvin (1911–97) begins his studies of photosynthesis using radioactive carbon-14 as a tracer to follow the reactions.

1946 In the United States, German-born biologist Max Delbrück (1906–81) and biologist Alfred Hershey (1908–97) independently find that genetic material from two different viruses can combine to form a new virus.

1944 American physical chemist Glenn Seaborg (1912–99) and coworkers isolate the radioactive elements americium and curium.

1944 American chemist Robert Woodward (1917–79) and coworkers synthesize the antimalarial drug quinine.

1946 American chemist Willard Libby (1908–80) begins work on radiocarbon dating—perfected a year later—which estimates the age of old organic material from the amount of radioactive carbon-14 isotope it still contains.

1946 American experimental physicist Luis Alvarez (1911–88) designs a proton linear accelerator.

1946 Swiss-born American physicist Felix Bloch (1905–83) and American physicist Edward Purcell (1912–97) develop the technique of nuclear magnetic resonance (NMR) spectroscopy, which becomes a powerful tool in chemical analysis.

ASIA & OCEANIA

1946 The Japanese company Sony is founded (originally as Tokyo Tsushin Kogyo) by Japanese engineer Akio Morita (1921–99).

AFRICA & THE MIDDLE EAST

Aeronautical inventor Igor Sikorsky stands beneath the helicopter he designed.

ENGINEERING & INVENTION	WORLD EVENTS
1944 The German air force employs the unsuccessful Messerschmitt Me-163B Komet rocket-powered airplanes as interceptors. **1944** German forces begin launching V-1 flying bombs and V-2 rocket bombs against southeastern England. **1945** Engineers working for the British Rolls-Royce company develop the afterburner for jet engines. **1945** Northern Irish engineer James Martin (1893–1981) designs the ejector seat for aircraft, which will save the lives of thousands of pilots.	**1944** On D-Day (6 June) Allied troops commanded by General Dwight D. Eisenhower (1890–1969) land in Normandy, France, at the start of the campaign to liberate Europe. **1945** Adolf Hitler (1889–1945) commits suicide as the Soviet Red Army reaches Berlin. **1945** Germany surrenders on May 7, ending the war in Europe; the next day, May 8, is celebrated as VE (Victory in Europe) Day. **1946** Italy becomes a republic after a referendum decides in favor of abolishing the monarchy.

NUCLEAR MAGNETIC RESONANCE

Nuclear magnetic resonance (NMR) is a phenomenon based on the magnetic properties of an atom's nucleus; NMR also refers to the technique used to study the magnetic resonance of molecules.

NMR was first discovered and measured in molecular beams by Galacian-born American physicist Isidor Rabi (1898–1988) in 1938. In 1946 Americans Felix Bloch and Edward Purcell used Rabi's technique on liquids and solids. The technique involves exposing a chemical in solution simultaneously to high-frequency radio radiation in a surrounding coil and a very strong magnetic field provided by powerful magnets. A second coil detects the radio frequencies that are absorbed by the chemical. They are analyzed in a signal detector and plotted as a spectrum. In the example below the NMR spectrum distinguishes between the hydrogen atoms (H) in two different chemical groupings within the chemical bromoethane (CH_3-CH_2-Br). The peaks on the chart correspond to the CH_3 and CH_2 groups.

One application of NMR, magnetic resonance imaging (MRI), is used for diagnosing medical conditions.

1944 The Delaware Aqueduct, part of New York City's water-supply system, is completed. It includes an 85-mile (137-km) tunnel, later extended to 105 miles (169 km)—at the time the world's longest tunnel. **1944** Russian-born American engineer Igor Sikorsky (1889–1972) sets the design of the modern helicopter with the VS-36A, which has an adjustable-pitch main rotor and a single vertical tail rotor for stability. **1944** American physicist Robert Dicke (1916–97) makes a radiometer for detecting microwave radiation. **1945** American government scientists make and test an atom bomb. **1945** Austrian-born American electrical engineer Rudolf Kompfner (1909–77) invents the traveling-wave amplifier for microwave signals, such as those used in radar. **1946** American engineer Percy Spencer (1894–1970) invents the microwave oven while working for the Raytheon Company.	**1945** President Franklin Roosevelt (1882–1945) dies in office less than six months after becoming the only U.S. president in history to be reelected to a fourth term. **1945** Argentine Juan Perón (1895–1974) is released from jail and made president of Argentina.

Dorothy Hodgkin's research using x-ray crystallography determined the structure of various natural molecules, including penicillin (1945), vitamin B_{12} (1954), and insulin (1969).

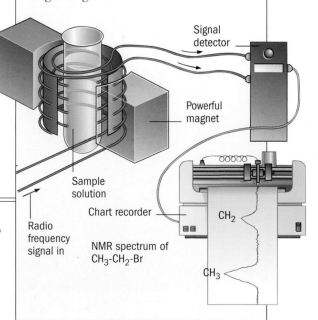

Signal detector

Powerful magnet

Sample solution

Chart recorder

Radio frequency signal in

NMR spectrum of CH_3-CH_2-Br

CH_2

CH_3

	1945 One month after atomic bombs are dropped on Hiroshima and Nagasaki, Japan surrenders to the Allies.
	1945 The Arab league is founded with seven initial members; it aims to speak for all Arab nations. **1946** Syria and Transjordan win independence from, respectively, France and Britain.

NUCLEAR FISSION

Ernest Walton, photographed in 1932, sits in a protective cage away from the particle accelerator that he and John Cockcroft designed at the Cavendish Laboratory, Cambridge.

IN THE EARLY 20TH CENTURY PHYSICISTS WERE learning what happens when atoms are bombarded with subatomic particles. Their experiments led them to realize that under certain circumstances such bombardment could release huge amounts of energy through nuclear fission in nuclear reactors, which could be used to generate electricity. In January 2005 there were 439 operational reactors worldwide, producing 16 percent of all electricity.

In 1932 Irish physicist Ernest Walton (1903–95) and English physicist John Cockcroft (1897–1967) began experimenting with high-energy protons in the particle accelerator they had built in Cambridge, England. In Paris in 1934 French physicists Irène (1897–1956) and Frédéric (1900–58) Joliot-Curie found that proton bombardment sometimes produced radioactive isotopes of the target atoms. Two years later Italian-American physicist Enrico Fermi (1901–54), working in Rome, found that neutrons—discovered in 1932 by English physicist James Chadwick (1891–1974)—were more effective than protons at smashing atoms.

Uranium Bombardment

Neutron bombardment usually produced heavier atoms through neutron absorption; but when Fermi bombarded atoms of certain heavy elements, especially uranium, he found that much lighter nuclei were produced. In 1939 German physicists Otto Hahn (1879–1968) and Fritz Strassmann (1902–80) identified the products of uranium bombardment as elements with about half the mass of uranium. Hahn and Strassmann had demonstrated that the uranium nuclei had broken apart. Fission had occurred.

The same year Lise Meitner (1878–1968), an Austrian-born physicist working in Stockholm, and her Austrian nephew Otto Frisch (1904–79), working in Copenhagen with Danish physicist Niels Bohr (1885–1962), explained this result. The uranium nucleus absorbed a neutron, causing it to vibrate violently and then divide into two parts with the release of about 200 million electron volts of energy (= 3.204 x 10^{-11} joules). Hahn and Strassmann then found that, in addition to a large amount of energy, uranium fission released neutrons that could trigger fission in other uranium nuclei, raising the possibility of a chain reaction that would release a prodigious amount of energy. The Joliot-Curies and Leo Szilard (1898–1964) confirmed this experimentally. Szilard was a Hungarian-born American physicist working with Fermi, then at Columbia University, New York.

Three isotopes of uranium occur naturally, always in the same proportions: Uranium-238 (U-238)

chain reaction by ensuring that enough of the neutrons released strike other uranium nuclei. Perrin also introduced the idea of adding a substance that absorbs (rather than slows) neutrons as a way to control the rate of the fission reaction. Rudolf Peierls (1907–95), a German-born physicist working in England, extended these ideas. Designed by Fermi and called "an atomic pile," the first working reactor began operating on December 2, 1942, at the University of Chicago. In 1951 the Experimental Breeder Reactor, built at Idaho National Engineering Laboratory near Idaho Falls, Idaho, became the first reactor to generate electricity.

The Manhattan Project

It became apparent that a sustained fission reaction could be used to create a bomb of immense power. Work to develop an atom bomb began in Britain and the United States. The two programs merged in August 1942 to form the Manhattan Project, with American physicist J. Robert Oppenheimer (1904–67) as scientific director. The first successful test took place in New Mexico on July 16, 1945.

Research in the Soviet Union had been proceeding independently, and by 1940 Soviet scientists also understood the principles of fission. But it was 1942 before Stalin became convinced that a bomb could be developed, and a program led by nuclear physicist Igor Kurchatov (1903–60) began. The first Soviet reactor entered operation in 1948, and the first Soviet bomb was detonated in August 1949.

American physicist J. Robert Oppenheimer, sometimes referred to as "The Father of the Atomic Bomb," was the scientific director of the Manhattan Project, which created the world's first nuclear weapons.

accounts for 99.28 percent, U-235 for 0.71 percent, and U-234 for 0.006 percent. Bohr calculated that fission would occur more readily in U-235 than in either of the other isotopes. This meant that a way had to be found to separate the isotopes—a technique now known as "enrichment." Bohr also figured out that fission would be more effective if the neutrons were slowed down. Szilard and Fermi suggested surrounding the uranium with a "moderator"—a substance such as graphite or heavy water that slows neutrons.

Just before the outbreak of war in 1939 Bohr and American physicist John Wheeler (1911–2008) published a paper describing the complete fission process. Also in 1939 French physicist Francis Perrin (1901–92) showed that a certain "critical mass" of uranium is needed to sustain a

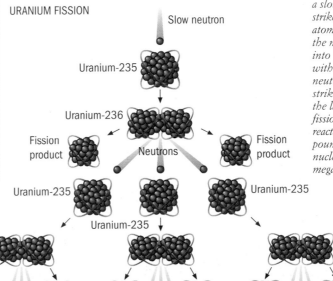

Fission occurs when a slow-moving neutron strikes a U-235 atom. The atom's nucleus absorbs the neutron and divides into two lighter nuclei with the release of neutrons. If the neutrons strike other U-235 nuclei the latter also undergo fission, setting up a chain reaction. The fission of 2.2 pounds (1 kg) of U-235 nuclei releases 20,000 megawatt-hours of energy.

URANIUM FISSION

Slow neutron

Uranium-235

Uranium-236

Fission product — Neutrons — Fission product

Uranium-235 — Uranium-235

Uranium-235

ASTRONOMY & MATH	BIOLOGY & MEDICINE	PHYSICAL SCIENCES

EUROPE

1948 English astronomer Fred Hoyle (1915–2001) and Austrian-born English astronomers Hermann Bondi (1919–2005) and Thomas Gold (1920–2004) propose the steady-state theory of the universe (i.e., that it is not expanding—it maintains a constant average density).

1949 English computer engineer Maurice Wilkes (1913–) and coworkers build EDSAC, an Electronic Delay-Storage Automatic Calculator.

1947 Italian biologist Rita Levi-Montalcini (1909–) finds nerve growth factor (NGF) in chick embryos.

1948 The World Health Organization (WHO) is founded.

1947 English physicist Cecil Powell (1903–69) and Italian physicist Giuseppe Occhialini (1907–93) discover the pion (pi-meson), a heavy subatomic particle, in cosmic rays.

1948 Scottish biochemist Alexander Todd (1907–97) synthesizes ADP and ATP (adenosine diphosphate and adenosine triphosphate).

1949 English chemists George Porter (1920–2002) and Ronald Norrish (1897–1978) study ultrafast chemical reactions, using pulses of light in the technique known as flash photolysis.

1948 Hungarian-born English electrical engineer Dennis Gabor (1900–79) puts forward the principles of holography.

THE AMERICAS

1948 Dutch-born American astronomer Gerard Kuiper (1905–73) locates Miranda, a small inner moon of Uranus. A year later he finds Nereid, Neptune's moon.

1948 American mathematician Norbert Wiener (1894–1964) coins the term *cybernetics*.

1948 American astronomers Harold (1882–1968) and Horace (1912–2003) Babcock detect the sun's magnetic field.

1949 German-born American astronomer Walter Baade (1893–1960) discovers the asteroid Icarus, which passes very close to the sun (and the Earth).

1949 American pioneer computer engineers John Eckert (1919–95) and John Mauchly (1907–80) construct BINAC, a BINary Automatic Computer.

1949 The American company IBM makes a stored-program electromechanical computer Selective Sequence Electronic Calculator (SSEC).

1949 American astronomer Fred Whipple (1906–2004) proposes the "dirty snowball" theory of comets, suggesting that they consist mainly of ice with accumulated rocky debris.

1947 German-born American biochemist Fritz Lipmann (1899–1986) isolates coenzyme A (CoA), a substance needed to ensure the effectiveness of certain enzymes.

1947 Microbiologist Mildred Rebstock discovers the antibiotic chloramphenicol (Chloromycetin) in a sample of soil from Venezuela.

1947 American geneticist Joshua Lederberg (1925–2008) reports that some bacteria can reproduce by conjugation (joining together as in sexual reproduction).

1948 American biochemists Philip Hench (1896–1965) and Edward Kendall (1886–1972) introduce the use of cortisone to treat patients with rheumatoid arthritis.

1948 American organic chemist Karl Folkers (1906–97) and coworkers isolate vitamin B_{12} (cyanocobalamin), the factor that prevents pernicious anemia.

1949 American microbiologists John Enders (1897–1985) and Frederick Robbins (1916–2003) culture the virus that causes poliomyelitis.

1947 American physicist Willis Lamb (1913–2008) observes the Lamb shift, a small difference in energy between two levels in the atomic spectrum of hydrogen.

1948 Karl Folkers determines the structure of the bacteria-killing drug streptomycin.

1948 American theoretical physicist Richard Feynman (1918–88) and coworkers and, independently, American physicist Julian Schwinger (1918–94) formulate new versions of quantum electrodynamics.

1949 American physical chemist Glenn Seaborg (1912–99) and team produce the radioactive element berkelium by bombarding americium with alpha particles (helium nuclei).

1949 German-born American physicist Maria Goeppert-Mayer (1906–72) proposes the "shell" theory of the atomic nucleus (which pictures its component protons and neutrons moving in shells analogous to those occupied by electrons).

ASIA & OCEANIA

1947 Armenian astronomer Viktor Ambartsumian (1908–96) describes stellar associations, groups of stars in the galaxy's spiral arms (but not as closely linked as a star cluster).

Mary Leakey and her husband Richard Leakey examine fossil finds from Olduvai Gorge in the Serengeti plains of northern Tanzania, Africa.

AFRICA & THE MIDDLE EAST

1948 English anthropologist Mary Leakey (1913–96) discovers fossils of the hominoid *Proconsul africanus* in Africa.

ENGINEERING & INVENTION

1947 The first nuclear reactor in Europe is built at Harwell, England.

1947 Soviet gunsmith Mikhail Kalashnikov (1919–) produces the AK-47 assault rifle (used by Soviet forces from 1949).

1948 Swiss-born Belgian physicist August Piccard (1884–1962) designs the bathyscaphe submersible craft.

1948 The first turboprop airliner, the Vickers Viscount, makes its maiden flight in England.

1949 The first jet airliner, the de Havilland Comet, flies in England.

1947 American airman Charles "Chuck" Yeager (1923–) makes the first supersonic flight, in a Bell X-1 rocket-propelled airplane.

1947 American inventor Edwin Land (1909–91) demonstrates the Polaroid instant camera.

1947 American architect Richard Buckminster Fuller (1895–1983) devises the geodesic dome construction for large buildings.

1947 American physicists John Bardeen (1908–91) and Walter Brattain (1902–87) and English-born American William Shockley (1910–89) build the point-contact transistor. A year later Shockley conceives the junction transistor.

1948 American electrical engineer Peter Goldmark (1906–77) invents the long-playing phonograph record.

1948 American instrument maker Leo Fender (1909–91) and coworkers market the first solid-body electric guitar.

1949 American rocket engineers launch a two-stage rocket (a German V-2 with a small rocket mounted on its nose) in New Mexico.

WORLD EVENTS

1947 Britain's Labour Government introduces a free, tax-financed National Health Service.

1949 Two separate states are formed in Germany: the democratic Federal Republic of Germany (West Germany) and the communist People's Republic of Germany (East Germany).

1949 The Greek Civil War (1946–49) between communists and monarchists ends in victory for the monarchists.

1949 The North Atlantic Treaty Organization (NATO) is set up to defend Europe and North America from the threat of Soviet aggression.

1947 President Harry S. Truman (1884–1972) commits the United States to support free peoples in the struggle against communist totalitarianism (the "Truman Doctrine"); immediate aid is given to Greece and Turkey.

1947 Secretary of State George Marshall (1880–1959) announces a plan to help Europe rebuild its war-shattered economies (the Marshall Plan).

1947 Congress's investigations into communist influence in the movie industry lead to the imprisonment of 10 Hollywood screenwriters and directors who have refused to cooperate with the House Un-American Activities Committee.

1948 The Organization of American States is formed to promote regional peace and security.

1947 India and Pakistan separate; violence mars the partition, with about 500,000 deaths.

1948 The Jewish state of Israel declares itself an independent nation.

1949 The South African National Party introduces apartheid, separating white from black South Africans.

INSIDE STORY

Comets

Fred Whipple likened the nucleus of a comet to a dirty snowball and suggested that it consists of a collection of ice and small solid particles, together extending a few miles across. A bright coma develops around the nucleus as it evaporates on approaching the sun. There may be one or two tails pointing away from the sun, one made of dust or gas and one consisting of ions.

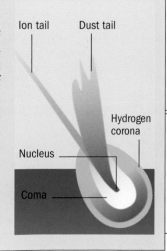

Ion tail • Dust tail • Hydrogen corona • Nucleus • Coma

WORLD HEALTH ORGANIZATION

Established on April 7, 1948 (the first World Health Day), the World Health Organization (WHO) is one of the original agencies of the United Nations (UN). Headquartered in Geneva, Switzerland, WHO was set up to improve international cooperation for better health conditions across the world. It took over from the Health Organization of the League of Nations (created in 1923) and the International Public Office of Health at Paris (set up in 1909). Those two organizations had focused on the control of epidemics, quarantine measures, and the standardization of drugs.

An African boy is vaccinated against smallpox and measles. By 1980 WHO had eradicated smallpox —the first disease to be eliminated by humans.

WHO's mission is to help all people attain "the highest possible level of health." WHO defines health not merely as the absence of disease or infirmity but as "a state of complete physical, mental, and social well-being."

WHO collects and distributes health information. It monitors many diseases and helps control many infectious diseases through education or by promoting mass vaccination programs. It helps improve sanitation to prevent disease. This work has helped reduce the incidence of many diseases, including malaria, sexually transmitted infections, and cholera. The organization also helps governments set up long-term national health plans.

THE FIRST COMPUTERS

The stored-program computer built at Manchester University in 1949 occupied an entire laboratory. Despite its size, it had far less computing power than a modern laptop.

A COMPUTER IS AN ELECTRONIC MACHINE that can perform various tasks involving the processing of information or data under instructions from a program. Today the term most often applies to a digital computer, which handles its data in the form of digits or numbers expressed in binary notation.

Binary is a number system that uses only two digits, 1 and 0, represented in the computer's activities and memory as on and off pulses of electric current. According to the definition above, the first computers were used by the U. S. Army and Navy toward the end of World War II (1939–45). They were massive vacuum-tube machines developed from electronic calculating machines of the late 1930s, which in turn derived from earlier mechanical calculating machines. The first calculator was the abacus, a frame with beads invented around 3,000 B.C.E. and still used in parts of China and Japan. The task of multiplication is simplified by logarithms, invented in 1614 by Scottish mathematician John Napier (1550–1617) and "mechanized" in the slide rule designed in 1622 by English mathematician William Oughtred (1574–1660).

French scientist Blaise Pascal (1623–62) probably invented the first mechanical adding machine in 1642. It had a system of intermeshed cogs, a method also adopted by English mathematician Charles Babbage (1792–1871) in his "Analytical Engine" of 1833. Babbage's machine could be programmed for a particular calculation and was therefore technically a computer (although not electronic). Calculating machines with keyboards—called comptometers—were developed from the 1880s by inventors such as the American William Burroughs (1855–98).

Most early methods of feeding data into programmable machines used punched tape or punched cards. In about 1805 French inventor Joseph Jacquard (1752–1834) designed a loom that could weave various patterns in carpets by following instructions on an endless belt of punched cards. American inventor Herman Hollerith (1860–1929) employed similar cards to record and analyze the results of the 1890 U. S. census. The company that Hollerith formed later became part of International Business Machines (IBM).

Electronic Computers

Electromechanical calculators appeared in the 1930s, invented by American scientists such as Vannevar Bush (1890–1974) and John Atanasoff (1903–95). By 1942 Atanasoff had constructed an electronic calculator (the ABC), using vacuum tubes, that could also be programmed for processing data. Two years later at Harvard, American mathematician Howard Aiken (1900–73) had a manually operated digital machine controlled by punched paper tape, and in 1946 the all-electronic ENIAC (Electronic Numerical Integrator And Calculator) computer was in service, although it too still employed vacuum tubes.

A machine built at Princeton in 1946 by John von Neumann (1903–57), a Hungarian-born American mathematician, was the first with a stored program that used binary numbers. The idea was incorporated into UNIVAC I, designed by American computer engineers John Eckert (1919–95) and John Mauchly (1907–80) and in 1951 the first computer to be manufactured in bulk in the United States. They modified

The women above hold circuit boards from a range of early electronic computers. As technology improved circuit boards became smaller.

it to use magnetic tape storage a year later. In 1949 a team at Manchester University, England, also built a stored-program machine under the guidance of English mathematician Alan Turing (1912–54), who had worked at Princeton. The Manchester machine was so successful that the British government commissioned the Ferranti company to manufacture it.

After the invention of the transistor in the late 1940s, computers became faster and smaller. By the mid-1960s silicon chips had arrived, so that circuits designed in 1970 incorporated a complete computer microprocessor on a single chip. Today microchips are used not only in personal computers but also in embedded systems in domestic appliances, automobiles, and industrial robots.

Early computers used punched cards as a means of inputting data and computer programs.

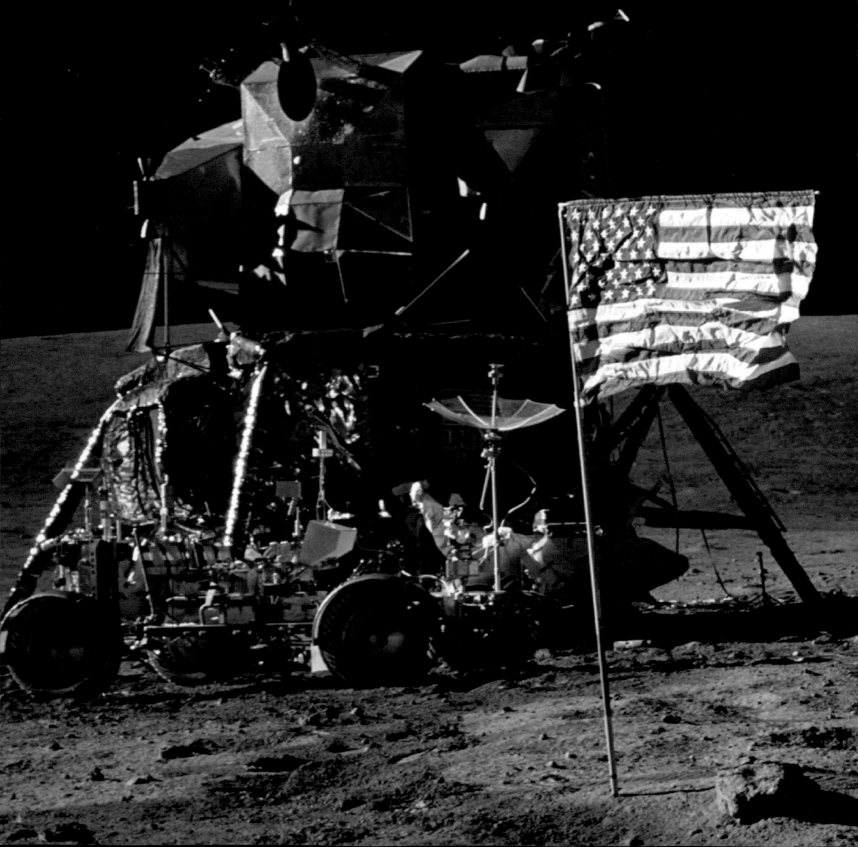

AFTER 1950 TWO OF THE MAJOR TECHNOLOGICAL DEVELOPMENTS OF WORLD War II (1939–45)—radar and rockets—were put to a wide range of uses. Radar employs very-high-frequency radio waves, and in the 1940s it was radar engineers who first began detecting radio waves from space. After the war their converted radar sets became radio telescopes, and the new science of radio astronomy began. Soon invisible objects were detected emitting radio waves from the remotest regions of the universe. These objects are now identified as quasars—first identified by American astronomer Allan Sandage (1926–) in 1960—and pulsars, observed by Northern Irish astronomer Jocelyn Bell Burnell (1943–) and English astronomer Anthony Hewish (1924–) in 1967.

Rockets left over from the German war effort were adapted to explore the upper atmosphere and space. In 1957 the Soviets launched the world's first artificial satellite, Sputnik 1, and a "space race" soon developed between the Soviet Union and the United States as a technological manifestation of the ideological stand-off known as the Cold War. In 1961, the Soviets claimed the distinction of putting the first human into space: cosmonaut Yuri Gagarin (1934–68). In responses, a major U.S. effort culminated in the National Aeronautics and Space Administration's (NASA) Apollo Program.

Deoxyribonucleic acid (DNA) was first isolated in 1869 by Swiss physician Friedrich Miescher. However, it was not until 1952 that scientists proved that DNA was the hereditary material of most life-forms. Its molecular structure—an elegant double helix—was elucidated in 1953 by Francis Crick, Maurice Wilkins, and James Watson.

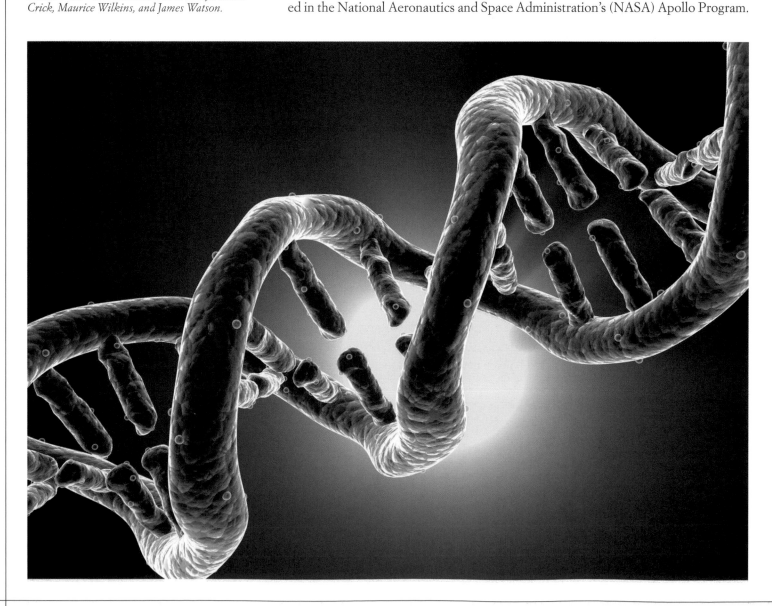

Astronaut Eugene Cernan, Apollo 17 commander, approaches the parked Lunar Roving Vehicle on the lunar surface in December 1972. Cernan was the last man to walk on the moon. NASA aims to send another piloted spacecraft to the moon by 2018 and also to put the first astronaut on Mars by 2037.

In 1969 astronaut Neil Armstrong (1930–) was the first human to walk on the moon, closely followed by Buzz Aldrin (1930–). By the end of 1972 another ten American astronauts had walked on the surface of the moon.

In life sciences attention was focused on the microscopic level with the development of molecular biology. The new branch of science studies the structures and functions of large molecules found in living organisms, such as proteins and nucleic acids. American chemist Linus Pauling (1901–94) made many advances in this new scientific field, but the breakthrough came in 1953 when English biophysicist Francis Crick (1916–2004), New Zealand-born biophysicist Maurice Wilkins (1916–2004), American biophysicist James Watson (1928–), and British physical chemist Rosalind Franklin (1920–58) discovered the structure of the deoxyribonucleic acid (DNA) molecule: the famous double helix. It is a major component of chromosomes in the cell nucleus, the genetic material that determines an organism's hereditary characteristics.

Another major scientific development during this period was the invention of the laser. In 1960 American physicist Theodore Maiman (1927–2007) created the first laser, using an artificial crystal of aluminium oxide (ruby) to emit light. Lasers are now widely used to read compact discs (CDs) and digital versatile discs (DVDs), to measure distances, to cut tissue in delicate surgery, and even to saw through metal.

	1950	1953	1956	1959	1962	
EUROPE	**1950** English physicians Richard Doll and Bradford Hill establish a link between smoking and lung cancer. **1950** English ophthalmologist Harold Ridley implants an artificial lens in an eye to treat cataract. **1952** English physiologists Alan Hodgkin and Andrew Huxley discover the ionic mechanisms of nerve-cell activity.	**1953** English engineer Christopher Cockerell begins work on the hovercraft. **1953** English biophysicist Francis Crick, American biophysicist James Watson, New Zealand-born biophysicist Maurice Wilkins, and English physical chemist Rosalind Franklin determine the structure of deoxyribonucleic acid (DNA).	**1956** Romanian cell biologist George Palade identifies ribosomes. **1957** Soviet scientists launch the first artificial satellites to orbit Earth, Sputnik 1 and Sputnik 2. **1957** The rotary Wankel engine is put into production in West Germany. **1958** Scottish surgeon Ian Donald introduces the use of an ultrasound scan to examine unborn babies.	**1959** French physician Jérôme Lejeune establishes that Down syndrome is caused by the presence of an extra chromosome. **1959** The German company Voigtlander produces a zoom lens for its cameras. **1959** The British Austin Motor Company launches the Mini car. **1961** Soviet cosmonaut Yuri Gagarin becomes the first man in space.	**1962** Scottish biochemist James Black prepares beta-blockers. **1963** Soviet cosmonaut Valentina Tereshkova becomes the first woman in space. **1964** Scottish physicist Peter Higgs predicts the existence of the Higgs boson. **1964** Kidney dialysis in the home is introduced in Britain and the United States.	
THE AMERICAS	**1950** American surgeon John Gibbon, Jr. develops the heart–lung machine. **1951** German-born American physicist Erwin Müller invents a microscope that can produce images of single atoms. **1951** German-born American physicist Polykarp Kusch builds a cesium atomic clock. **1951** Austrian-born American physician Carl Djerassi synthesizes norethindrone, the basis of the oral contraceptive pill for women. **1952** American geneticist Joshua Lederberg identifies plasmids in bacteria. **1952** U.S. government scientists explode the first hydrogen bomb.	**1953** American surgeon John Gibbon, Jr. performs the first successful open-heart surgery on a human patient using his heart–lung machine. **1953** U.S. military engineers develop a surface-to-air missile (SAM). **1954** American engineer Richard Buckminster Fuller patents the geodesic dome for roofing large buildings. **1955** The first computer using transistors instead of vacuum tubes is built in the United States by Bell Laboratories. **1955** Italian-born American physicist Emilio Segrè and American Owen Chamberlain discover the antiproton.	**1956** American physicists Clyde Cowan and Frederick Reines discover the neutrino. **1956** The company Ampex markets a videotape recorder. **1956** American computer programmers devise the FORTRAN language. **1958** American scientists launch Explorer 1, the first American Earth satellite. **1958** The National Aeronautics and Space Administration (NASA) is founded. **1958** American physician Clarence Lillehei invents a heart pacemaker, which has to be worn outside the patient's body. **1958** American electronic engineers invent integrated circuits.	**1960** Hungarian-born American biophysicist Georg von Békésy shows how sound waves stimulate the cochlea in the inner ear. **1960** American astronomer Allan Sandage makes the first optical identification of a quasar. **1960** American physicist Theodore H. Maiman invents the ruby laser. **1961** American astronaut Alan Shepard makes a suborbital flight in the spacecraft Freedom 7. **1961** The American company Texas Instruments produces the first silicon chips. **1962** American physicist Leon Lederman discovers the muon neutrino.	**1962** American communications satellite Telstar 1 relays live TV transmissions. **1962** American physicist Leon Lederman discovers the muon neutrino. **1962** American electronic engineer Nick Holonyak invents the light-emitting diode (LED). **1962** American electronic engineer Paul Weimer invents thin-film transistors. **1964** NASA's space probe Mariner 4 makes a successful flyby of Mars. **1964** American theoretical physicist Murray Gell-Mann predicts the existence of the quark. **1964** American computer programmers invent the BASIC language.	
ASIA & OCEANIA	**1952** Australian astronomer Colin Gum locates the nearby Gum nebula, the remains of a supernova explosion.	**1955** Indian scientist Narinder Kapany develops optical fibers for carrying light over long distances.	**1957** Japanese physicist Leo Esaki describes how electrons can penetrate a "barrier" in a semiconductor. **1958** Australian engineer David Warren invents the "black box" flight data recorder.	**1960** Felt-tip pens are first made by the Japan Stationery Company (later called Pentel).	**1962** French-born Australian immunologist Jacques Miller works out the role of the thymus in the immune system of infants. **1964** Bullet trains begin service in Japan.	
AFRICA & THE MIDDLE EAST				**1959** The Kariba Dam is completed in Africa. **1960** Kenyan anthropologist Jonathan Leakey discovers remains of *Homo habilis* in Tanzania.		

1965

1965 Soviet cosmonaut Aleksei Leonov is the first person to walk in space.

1966 The Soviet Luna 9 spacecraft soft-lands on the moon.

1966 An electronic fuel-injection system for automobile engines is developed in Britain.

1967 Northern Irish astronomer Jocelyn Bell Burnell and English astronomer Antony Hewish detect the first pulsar.

1965 American geneticist Charles Yanofsky and coworkers establish that the sequence of codons in a gene determines the sequence of amino acids in a protein.

1966 NASA's space probe Surveyor 1 soft-lands on the moon.

1966 American geneticist Richard Lewontin develops gel electrophoresis (now routinely used in genetic fingerprinting).

1966 American inventor Stephanie Kwolek invents Kevlar.

1967 Domestic microwave ovens are marketed in the United States.

1967 American biochemist Arthur Kornberg uses DNA polymerase to make "synthetic" DNA.

1965 Japanese astronomers discover the bright sun-grazing comet Ikeya-Seki.

1966 Chinese electronics engineer Charles Kao helps invent the fiber-optic cable.

1967 South African surgeon Christiaan Barnard performs the first successful heart transplant.

1968

1968 Swiss biophysicist Werner Arber isolates restrictive enzymes, which cut DNA.

1969 The British-French supersonic airliner Concorde makes its maiden flight in France.

1970 Swiss computer programmer Niklaus Wirth invents PASCAL programming language.

1970 Soviet space probe Luna 16 returns lunar soil samples to Earth.

1968 Italian-born American inventor Candido Jacuzzi invents the whirlpool bath named for him.

1968 American computer engineer Douglas Engelbart invents the computer mouse.

1969 Canadian electronic engineer Willard Boyle and American electronic engineer George Smith invent the charge-coupled device (CCD).

1969 The U.S. Boeing Company flies its 747 jet for the first time.

1969 NASA's Apollo 11 makes the first piloted moon landing. Astronaut Neil Armstrong becomes the first man to walk on the moon's surface. Buzz Aldrin joins him.

1970 China and Japan launch artificial Earth satellites.

1970 The Japanese company Canon Business Machines markets a pocket calculator with a printout.

1968 The power plant at the Aswan High Dam in Egypt goes into operation.

1971

1971 The Swiss company Hoffmann-LaRoche presents a liquid-crystal display.

1972 Soviet space probe Venera 8 soft-lands on Venus and returns data from the surface.

1972 Swiss biochemist Jean-François Borel develops the immunosuppressive drug cyclosporin-A, which prevents rejection following organ transplants.

1971 American electronic engineer Ted Hoff and coworkers make a single-chip microprocessor (Intel 4004).

1971 American electronic companies produce pocket calculators.

1971 The American company Centron markets a dot matrix printer.

1973 American and English physicists begin to develop nuclear magnetic resonance imaging (MRI) scanning.

1973 NASA space probe Pioneer 10 flies by Jupiter.

1973 Physicists at Bell Laboratories produce a continuous-wave laser that can be tuned to different wavelengths.

1972 In Australia astronomer B. J. Harris provides evidence that most unidentified radio sources in space are compact.

1972 Kenyan anthropologist Richard Leakey finds an intact skull of *Homo habilis* in Africa.

1974

1975 Argentine-born British molecular biologist César Milstein, English-born Danish immunologist Niels Jerne, and German immunologist Georges Köhler develop monoclonal antibodies.

1976 The British-French supersonic airliner Concorde enters service.

1976 Engineers complete the pilot bore for the new road tunnel through the St. Gotthard Pass in the Swiss Alps.

1974 NASA space probe Mariner 10 reaches Mercury.

1975 American engineer Edward Roberts markets the first commercial personal computer in kit or assembled form, the Altair 8800.

1975 The American company IBM markets a laser printer for computers.

1976 American virologists identify oncogenes, which can convert normal cells into cancer cells.

1976 American physicist Martin Perl discovers the tau subatomic particle.

1976 American computer designers Steven Jobs and Stephen Wozniak found the computer company Apple.

1974 Japanese chemist Hideki Shirakawa produces a flexible film that has metallic properties.

1976 The Japanese company Matsushita introduces the VHS format for video cassettes.

1976 The Ebola virus is first identified after outbreaks in Africa.

1977–1979

1977 English biochemist Frederick Sanger and coworkers elucidate the first full genome (of a virus).

1978 The first "test-tube" baby is born in England.

1979 German physicists announce the discovery of the gluon.

1979 The Swedish company Ericsson markets the first cellular telephones.

1977 American astronomers observe the rings of Uranus.

1977 Molecular biologists discover that some genes contain sequences of "nonsense" DNA that appear to have no genetic function. They are named introns.

1977 American government scientists develop a neutron bomb.

1977 American physicist Leon Lederman identifies the short-lived upsilon particle.

1978 Chlorofluorocarbons (CFCs) are banned as aerosol-can propellants by the U.S. government.

1979 The earliest recognized cases of acquired immunodeficiency syndrome (AIDS) occur in California and Florida.

1977 Soviet scientists unearth a baby mammoth that has been frozen in the permafrost of Siberia.

1979 Matsushita introduces a liquid-crystal flat-screen television receiver.

1978 The world's longest floating bridge is completed on the Demerara River in Guyana.

1950–1952

CONCISE HISTORY OF SCIENCE AND INVENTION

ASTRONOMY & MATH	BIOLOGY & MEDICINE	PHYSICAL SCIENCES

1950 Dutch astronomer Jan Oort (1900–92) postulates the existence of the Oort cloud, a spherical region centered on the sun that contains all the long-period comets; it extends into space a third of the way to the next nearest star.

1950 English physicians Richard Doll (1912–2005) and Bradford Hill (1897–1991) establish a link between tobacco smoking and lung cancer.

1951 Danish biochemist Kaj Linderstrøm-Lang (1896–1959) classifies proteins into three structural levels: chains; helices and pleated sheets; and folded sheets.

1952 English physiologists Alan Hodgkin (1914–98) and Andrew Huxley (1917–) discover the ionic mechanisms of nerve cell activity.

1950 German-born French physicist Alfred Kastler (1902–84) develops optical pumping, which excites atoms to emit radiation—a key step toward making a laser.

1951 German chemist Ernst Fischer (1918–) investigates ferrocene and later shows it to be a "sandwich" compound with an iron atom between two five-sided carbon organic rings.

1952 Soviet physicists Aleksandr Prokhorov (1916–2002) and Nikolai Basov (1922–2001) work out the principle of the maser and the laser.

Jonas Salk, in his laboratory, examines virus samples that were used to develop the polio vaccine.

1951 German-born American astronomer Walter Baade (1893–1960) detects visible objects that coincide with radio sources in space.

1951 American astronomer William Morgan (1906–94) provides evidence that Earth's galaxy (the Milky Way) is a typical spiral galaxy.

1950 American surgeon John Gibbon, Jr. (1903–73), develops the heart–lung machine, later used in the open-heart surgery.

1950 American biochemists George Hitchings (1905–98) and Gertrude Elion (1918–99) develop the antimalarial drug pyrimethamine (Daraprim). A year later they synthesize 6-mercaptopurine (6MP), used for treating leukemia.

1951 Austrian-born American physician Carl Djerassi (1923–) synthesizes the compound norethindrone, the basis of the oral contraceptive pill for women.

1952 American geneticist Joshua Lederberg (1925–) identifies plasmids, circular pieces of DNA in bacteria.

1952 American physician Jonas Salk (1914–95) develops a vaccine against polio.

1952 American surgeon Charles Hufnagel invents an artificial heart valve.

1950 American physicist James Rainwater (1917–86) and colleagues propose a new model of the atomic nucleus, whose shape is not perfectly spherical but distorted.

1951 American chemist Linus Pauling (1901–94) discovers the spiral structure of some proteins, soon to be important in understanding the DNA (deoxyribonucleic acid) molecule.

1951 Canadian-born American physicist Walter Zinn (1906–2000) designs the first experimental breeder reactor near Idaho Falls, Indiana. A breeder reactor creates more fissionable material than it consumes.

1951 American researchers Fred Joyner and Harry Coover (1919–) at the Eastman Kodak Company rediscover cyanoacrylate (first found in 1942 in a search for materials to make clear plastic gunsights during World War II). It is marketed in 1958 and becomes known as "superglue."

1952 American government scientists explode the first hydrogen bomb. A year later Soviet scientists successfully test their own hydrogen bomb.

1952 Australian astronomer Colin Gum (1924–60) locates the Gum Nebula, the largest and nearest nebula, the remains of a supernova explosion of 11,000 years ago.

This image taken by the Hubble Space Telescope shows Messier 81, a spiral galaxy about 12 million light-years away from Earth.

ENGINEERING & INVENTION	WORLD EVENTS
1950 Britain's first electricity-generating nuclear reactor becomes operational at Windscale (later renamed Sellafield) in northwestern England.	**1950** France, West Germany, Italy, the Netherlands, Belgium, and Luxembourg form the European Coal and Steel Community, an important precursor of the European Union.
1950 English mathematician and logician Alan Turing (1912–54) proposes the Turing test to determine whether or not a computer has real intelligence (whether it can "think").	
1950 English ophthalmologist Harold Ridley (1906–2001) implants an artificial lens in a patient's eye to treat blindness caused by a cataract.	
1952 A De Havilland Comet makes the first scheduled flight by a jet airliner (from London to Johannesburg).	

1950 The United States Air Force establishes the Semi-Automatic Ground Environment (SAGE) system to collect radar and other data and process it in real time, using the Whirlwind computer at the Massachusetts Institute of Technology.	**1950** Senator Joseph McCarthy (1908–1957) publishes claims of communist infiltration in the U.S. State Department. This begins a period of anticommunist purges in many areas of American public life.
1950 The first jet fighter aerial combats take place between U.S. F-86s and Soviet MIG-15s in the Korean War.	**1952** The United Nations building is completed in New York City.
1950 English-born American physicist William Shockley (1910–89) and coworkers build the first working junction transistor.	
1951 German-born American physicist Erwin Müller (1911–77) invents the field ion microscope, which can produce images of single atoms.	
1951 German-born American physicist Polykarp Kusch (1911–93) constructs a cesium atomic clock—the most accurate device for measuring time.	
1952 American engineer Fred Waller (1886–1954) presents the Cinerama widescreen system for movies, using three projectors. It is largely superseded a year later by the CinemaScope system, which uses a single projector with a special lens.	*Linus Pauling demonstrates the chemical bonds that hold molecules together.*

1952 Prolific Japanese inventor and computer engineer Yoshiro Nakamatsu (1928–) patents many important features of the floppy disk drive.	**1950** Chinese troops invade Tibet.
	1950 The Korean War begins between the communist North, aided by Chinese forces, and the south, backed by a U.S.-led United Nations force.
	1952 Japan regains its independence as the postwar U.S. occupation ends.

	1952 A group of army officers in Egypt overthrow the monarchy and establish a republic.
	1952 With UN approval Ethiopia takes over the neighboring state of Eritrea.

LINUS PAULING

Linus Pauling was an American chemist whose main work concerned the bonding of atoms in molecules. Born in Portland, Oregon, he studied chemical engineering at Oregon State Agricultural College and received his doctorate from the California Institute of Technology (Caltech). After studying in Europe, he became associate professor of chemistry at Caltech in 1927, rising to full professor four years later. He remained there until 1963.

From 1928 Pauling researched crystal structure and developed the idea of ionic radius to describe the space occupied by ions in crystals. He investigated the structure of molecules in general and proposed the valence bond theory. In 1931 he wrote his most important paper, "The Nature of the Chemical Bond." In it he accounted for the shapes of molecules by introducing the idea of hybrid orbitals, in which the atomic orbitals (the space around an atom in which electrons orbit) of combining atoms "blend" to form a new orbital encompassing the atoms and representing the chemical bond between them. In organic chemistry he studied hemoglobin and other proteins. In 1951 he showed that some proteins have a helical (spiral) structure. After World War II (during which he was consultant to the explosives division of the National Defense Research Commission) Pauling campaigned against nuclear weapons. His campaigning was influential in the discontinuation of aboveground nuclear tests, which led to the signing of the Partial Test Ban Treaty by the United States, the Soviet Union, and the United Kingdom in 1963.

Pauling was the first person to receive two unshared Nobel prizes—Chemistry (1954) and Peace (1962).

ASTRONOMY & MATH

BIOLOGY & MEDICINE

PHYSICAL SCIENCES

EUROPE

1954 Soviet engineers begin development of multistage ICBMs (intercontinental ballistic missiles), culminating three years later with the 100-foot (30.5-m) R-7 missile. Known to NATO as the SS-6, code name "Sapwood," it has a range of 5,000 miles (8,000 km). It is utilized in space exploration and is used to launch Sputnik 1 in 1957 and cosmonaut Yuri Gagarin into space in 1961. This rocket gives the Soviets their early lead in the space race.

1955 English astronomer Martin Ryle (1918–84) builds a large radio interferometer for detecting radio sources in outer space. (His first, two-instrument interferometer, with which he detected the radio source Cassiopeia A, was made in 1948.)

1953 English biophysicist Francis Crick (1916–2004), New Zealand-born British biophysicist Maurice Wilkins (1916–2004), and American biophysicist James Watson (1928–) determine the structure of the deoxyribonucleic acid (DNA) molecule. Their findings owe much to the work of English physical chemist Rosalind Franklin (1920–58), who produced images of the double helix using x-ray crystallography.

1953 Austrian-born British biochemist Max Perutz (1914–2002) modifies hemoglobin with mercury atoms in order to make x-ray diffraction studies of its structure.

1953 German chemist Karl Ziegler (1898–1973) develops the Ziegler process for making polyethene.

1955 English biochemist Frederick Sanger (1918–) sets out the sequence of amino acids in the hormone insulin (a protein).

1955 English crystallographer Dorothy Hodgkin (1910–94) works out the structure of cyanocobalamin (vitamin B_{12}) using a computer.

THE AMERICAS

1953 U.S. military engineers develop a 35-foot (10.7-m) surface-to-air missile (SAM), with a range of 25 miles (40 km)—later named Nike Ajax. The same year, personnel from the Redstone Arsenal first launch the U.S. Army's Redstone Rocket. The rocket is later adapted for use in early U.S. space missions.

1954 Alongside the development of ICBMs to compete with Soviet military hardware, American rocketeers plan a series of satellite launchers. The program eventually leads to the Scout of 1960—length 73 feet (22 m), range 1,000 miles (1,610 km)—preceded by the four-stage Jupiter and two-stage Vanguard of 1958. The 1961 Atlas satellite launcher is also designed for use as an ICBM—length 73 feet (22 m), range 11,000 miles (17,700 km).

1955 American radioastronomer Kenneth Franklin (1923–) detects radio emission from Jupiter.

1953 American surgeon John Gibbon, Jr. (1903–73), performs the first successful open-heart surgery on a human patient, using his heart–lung machine to supply oxygen.

1953 American biochemist Vincent du Vigneaud (1901–78) synthesizes oxytocin, the pituitary-gland hormone that causes contractions of the womb in childbirth; it is the first artificially made human hormone.

1954 A mass field trial of the polio vaccine, developed by Jonas Salk (1914–95), is conducted in the United States. It is injected by needle and found to be safe and effective in reducing the incidence of polio.

1955 Spanish-born American geneticist Severo Ochoa (1905–93) discovers an enzyme in bacteria that enables him to synthesize ribonucleic acid (RNA). (It is later found to be a catalyst for breaking down RNA, not synthesizing it.)

1953 American chemist Stanley Miller (1930–) produces simple amino acids and other "life chemicals" by exposing a mixture of gases similar to those in Earth's early atmosphere to ultraviolet light and electric sparks (to simulate lightning).

1955 American chemist Albert Ghiorso (1915–) and coworkers isolate the new radioactive element mendelevium by bombarding einsteinium-253 with alpha particles. Three years later they discover nobelium by bombarding curium with carbon ions.

1955 Italian-born American physicist Emilio Segrè (1905–89) and American Owen Chamberlain (1920–2006) discover the antiproton (a particle with the same mass as a proton but with a negative charge).

1955 Scientists at American company General Electric produce small synthetic diamonds from graphite, following experimentation by American physicist Percy Bridgman (1882–1961).

ASIA & OCEANIA

AFRICA & THE MIDDLE EAST

A De Havilland Comet, flown by the British Overseas Airways Corporation, was the world's first jet airliner.

ENGINEERING & INVENTION	WORLD EVENTS
1953 English engineer Christopher Cockerell (1910–99) begins work on the hovercraft (air-cushion vehicle), patented two years later.	**1953** On the death of Joseph Stalin (1878–1953), Nikita Khrushchev (1894–1971) becomes leader of the Soviet Union. He quickly begins dismantling Stalin's cult of personality.
1953 Radial ply tires for production-line cars are introduced by the Pirelli company in Italy and the Michelin company in France.	**1953** The Allies end their postwar occupation of West Germany and Austria; West Germany joins NATO (North Atlantic Treaty Organization).
1954 The first Soviet experimental nuclear power plant opens at Obinsk.	**1953** The Soviet controlled countries of Eastern Europe form the Warsaw Pact in response to NATO.
1954 French inventor Marc Grégoire invents the nonstick cooking pan.	
1955 The British company Rolls-Royce continues development of an experimental VTOL (vertical take-off and landing) aircraft, nicknamed the "Flying Bedstead."	

1953 Chinese-born American computer engineer An Wang (1920–90) constructs a computer with a magnetic-core memory.	**1953** Dwight D. Eisenhower (1890–1969) is inaugurated as U.S. president in succession to Harry S. Truman (1884–1972).
1953 American physicists Gerald Pearson (1905–87), Calvin Fuller (1902–94), and coworkers at Bell Laboratories develop the silicon solar cell for electricity production.	**1953** A military coup in Argentina deposes Juan Perón (1895–1974).
1953 The American F-100A Super Sabre becomes the U.S. Air Force's first supersonic fighter airplane.	**1955** In Montgomery, Alabama, Rosa Parks (1913–2005) is arrested for violating race laws after refusing to give up her bus seat to a white passenger.
1954 American truck operator Malcolm MacLean (1914–2001) introduces standard containers for transporting goods by truck, train, or ship.	
1954 American engineer Richard Buckminster Fuller (1895–1983) patents the geodesic dome for roofing large buildings.	
1954 The nuclear-powered submarine USS *Nautilus* is commissioned in the United States.	
1955 The first computer using transistors instead of vacuum tubes is built in the United States by Bell Laboratories.	

The nonstick pan was first designed by French inventor Marc Grégoire.

1955 Indian scientist Narinder Kapany (1927–) develops optical fibers for carrying light over long distances with little loss in intensity.	**1953** A CIA-backed coup in Iran deposes Mohammed Mossadegh (1882–1967) and his nationalist government and reinstates Reza Pahlavi (1919–1980) as shah.
	1953 The Korean War (1950–53) ends; North and South Korea remain divided along the cease-fire line. The two sides have never signed a formal peace treaty ending the war.
	1954 Rebels organized by the *Front de Libération Nationale* (National Liberation Front) launch a war of independence against French rule in Algeria.

HOVERCRAFT

The hovercraft, or air-cushion vehicle (ACV), is a craft capable of traveling swiftly over water, land, or other treacherous surfaces such as marshes and ice sheets. The vehicle works by floating on a cushion of air, which is produced by large fans that force air through vents around the outer edge of the craft. A flexible rubber skirt traps the air in place, while the fans act like propellers to move the craft along. The vehicle is steered by rudders resembling those used on airplanes. Small ACVs have gasoline engines, while most commercial and military ACVs have powerful gas turbine engines. Large ACVs can carry a 70-ton (64-tonne) load at speeds of up to 45 miles (72 km) per hour.

The first experimental hovercrafts were constructed during World War I (1914–18), and several other prototypes were built and tested in Europe during the first half of the 20th century. These early craft were not practical, nor were they reliable or easy to control. The first ACVs to demonstrate that the craft had practical uses were designed by British inventor Christopher Cockerell and built by British aviation firm Saunders–Roe, which had previously specialized in manufacturing flying boats. Innovations such as the flexible sideskirts were added, and the first full-size prototype was built in 1959. This ACV was capable of carrying four passengers, a pilot, and a copilot.

Within ten years, massive hovercraft capable of carrying hundreds of people, and also vehicles, were making scheduled trips across the English Channel between England and France. However, the use of ACVs as high-speed passenger ferries has now largely stopped.

Military hovercraft are still widely used because they can travel equally well on land and water. Since ACVs hover above the surface, they are also used for safely crossing areas rendered impassable to conventional vehicles by land mines. The largest military hovercraft is the Russian Zubr class LCAC, first built in 1988. It can hold three tanks or up to 500 troops.

Describing the moment when he and Crick made their discovery, Watson (left) said, "When we saw the answer, we had to pinch ourselves. We realized it probably was true because it was so pretty."

DNA—THE DOUBLE HELIX

PRIOR TO THE 1950s SCIENTISTS ALREADY understood that genes carried on chromosomes were the units of inheritance. They also knew that chromosomes were made up of a mixture of proteins and a complex compound known as deoxyribonucleic acid, or DNA.

In 1951 American chemist Linus Pauling (1901–94) developed a technique for resolving the structures of large biological molecules. He described a class of proteins whose molecules took the form of a helix—a three-dimensional spiral. Well aware that genes were "the next big thing" in scientific research, Pauling soon turned his attention to identifying the structure of DNA.

For biology graduate Francis Crick (1916–2004) at Cambridge University, England, the structure of DNA was something of an obsession. Crick was supposed to be researching hemoglobin, the iron-containing, oxygen-carrying molecule found in red blood cells. But his enthusiasm for DNA outweighed his interest in his formal studies, and he found a willing accomplice in James Watson (1928–), an American biophysicist who arrived at Cambridge in 1951. Together Watson and Crick began informally working on the problem. Their work had to be low key because at the time competition between the great research institutes was frowned on by the scientific community, and deciphering the structure of DNA

KEY DATES

1951
Helical proteins

1952
Pauling model

1953
Watson and Crick papers describing the double helix structure of DNA

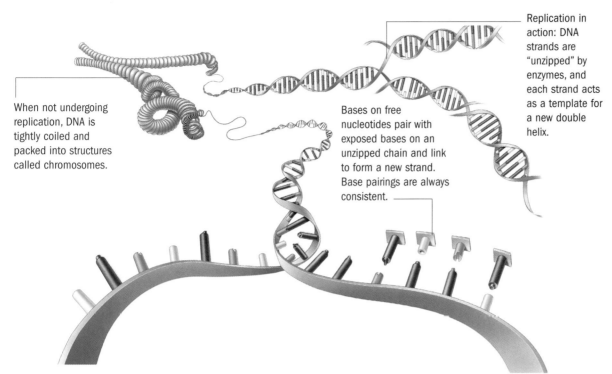

When not undergoing replication, DNA is tightly coiled and packed into structures called chromosomes.

Replication in action: DNA strands are "unzipped" by enzymes, and each strand acts as a template for a new double helix.

Bases on free nucleotides pair with exposed bases on an unzipped chain and link to form a new strand. Base pairings are always consistent.

The structure of DNA resembles the shape of a twisted ladder—the famous "double helix." The sides of the ladder are made up of sugar (deoxyribose) molecules linked by phosphate groups. The "rungs" of the ladder are made of pairs of bases. To replicate itself, DNA molecules "unzip" lengthwise. Spare nucleotides (units of DNA structure made up of a base, a sugar, and a phosphate group) are drawn to the two unzipped strands and link up to form new DNA strands.

was the stated aim of another group, at Kings College, London. There New Zealand-born biophysicist Maurice Wilkins (1916–2004) and British physical chemist Rosalind Franklin (1920–58) were involved in a series of complex experiments using x-ray diffraction to determine the structure of DNA. Franklin had all but dismissed the idea that DNA might be a helix, but Watson and Crick thought otherwise. In 1951 they produced a model of DNA as a triple helix. Franklin was among the first to disagree—the structure did not conform to her x-ray diffraction data. Watson and Crick admitted their mistake and went back to the drawing board. In 1952 Linus Pauling presented his own model of DNA. His model too showed the molecule as a helix with three intertwined strands. However, Pauling too had got it wrong—as other scientists were quick to point out.

Breakthrough

DNA contains four different chemical compounds—adenine, thiamine, guanine, and cytosine—known as bases. The realization that these molecules naturally pair off in a predictable way set Watson and Crick on the right track. On learning from the work of a scientist at Columbia University, Austrian-born chemist Erwin Chargaff (1905–2002), that the base adenine always paired with thiamine, and that guanine paired

with cytosine, Watson and Crick made their breakthrough in understanding not only the structure of DNA—a double helix—but also the way in which the molecule is able to replicate. They published their results in the journal *Nature* in April 1953 and accepted the Nobel Prize for Physiology or Medicine in 1962, together with Maurice Wilkins (Franklin had died from cancer in 1958).

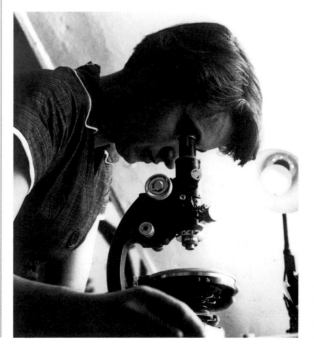

Rosalind Franklin's x-ray crystallography of DNA was crucial to Watson and Crick's discovery of its structure.

ASTRONOMY & MATH	BIOLOGY & MEDICINE	PHYSICAL SCIENCES

EUROPE

1957 The Jodrell Bank radio telescope, with a steerable dish 250 feet (76.2 m) across, is completed in the north of England.

1957 Soviet scientists launch the first artificial satellites to orbit Earth, Sputnik 1 and Sputnik 2 (meaning "fellow traveler"). Sputnik 1 weighs 184 pounds (83.6 kg) and orbits in 96 minutes. Sputnik 2 carries the dog Laika, the first living creature in space.

1958 Soviet scientists launch Sputnik 3, carrying scientific instruments, into Earth orbit. There were ten Sputniks in all: Sputniks 4, 5, and 6 tested reentry procedures, 7 and 8 were failed flights to the planet Venus, and 9 and 10 were test flights for the piloted Vostock program.

1956 Romanian cell biologist George Palade (1912–2008) identifies ribosomes, the small cellular structures that are responsible for assembling the proteins in cells.

1958 Scottish surgeon Ian Donald (1910–87) uses an ultrasound scan to examine an unborn baby in its mother's womb.

1957 Commercial production of polypropene (polypropylene) plastic begins in Italy, using a process developed by Italian chemist Giulio Natta (1903–79) and German chemist Karl Ziegler (1898–1973). It is quickly utilized in a variety of applications from automobile parts to household packaging.

1957 German physicist Rudolf Mössbauer (1929–) discovers the Mössbauer effect, which is a nuclear process concerning the recoil-free emission of gamma rays by atomic nuclei in a crystal lattice.

THE AMERICAS

1956 American astrophysicist Herbert Friedman (1916–2000) discovers that solar flares produce x-rays.

1957 American physicist Eugene Parker (1927–) discovers the solar wind, streams of particles ejected from the sun.

1958 American scientists launch Explorer 1, the first American Earth satellite, using a four-stage Jupiter rocket. It is the first of more than 70 Explorers launched up to the end of the year 2000.

1958 The National Aeronautics and Space Administration (NASA) is founded.

1958 American physicist James Van Allen (1914–2006) confirms the presence of the Van Allen radiation belts, using data from a Geiger counter on board NASA's Explorer 1. The two belts are made up of energetic charged particles trapped by Earth's magnetic field. Later that year Explorer 4 maps the trapped radiation.

1956 American chemist Robert Woodward (1917–79) synthesizes reserpine, a drug used to treat high blood pressure and psychotic behaviors.

1956 Chinese-born American biochemist Choh Hao Li (1913–87) and coworkers determine the order of the 39 amino acids in molecules of adrenocorticotropic hormone (ACTH).

1958 American physician Clarence Lillehei (1918–99) invents a heart pacemaker, which has to be worn outside the patient's body. An internal pacemaker, implanted into the patient's body, is invented a year later by Swedish surgeon Åke Senning (1915–2000).

The massive radio telescope at Jodrell Bank, in northwestern England

1956 American physicists Clyde Cowan (1919–74) and Frederick Reines (1918–98) discover the neutrino, a subatomic particle with no charge and zero mass at rest.

1956 American physicist Leon Cooper (1930–) identifies Cooper pairs, which are pairs of electrons in a superconductor (accounting for its lack of electrical resistance).

1957 Japanese physicist Leo Esaki (1925–) describes the tunnel effect, by means of which electrons can penetrate a "barrier" in a semiconductor. Three years later he produces a tunnel diode that makes use of the effect.

ASIA & OCEANIA

AFRICA & THE MIDDLE EAST

HOW THINGS WORK

Solar Wind

The solar wind, discovered by Eugene Parker in 1957, consists of an endless current of high-energy charged particles that stream out from the sun's corona into interplanetary space. By the time they reach Earth, the particles are traveling at between 125 and 160 miles (200 and 260 km) per second. They distort Earth's magnetosphere (the area of space around Earth controlled by the planet's magnetic field) into a teardrop shape leading away from the sun. It is the solar wind that causes the tails of comets to always face away from the sun, regardless of the direction of travel. The interaction between the solar wind and the magnetosphere is the cause of the auroras seen in the skies near the North Pole (northern lights) and South Pole (southern lights).

ENGINEERING & INVENTION	WORLD EVENTS
1956 The world's first commercial nuclear power plant is commissioned at Calder Hall in Britain.	**1956** The Soviet Union sends armored units into Hungary to suppress an attempted anticommunist uprising.
1957 The rotary Wankel engine, invented by Felix Wankel (1902–88), is put into production in West Germany.	**1957** The European Economic Community (EEC), later the European Union (EU), is created by the Treaty of Rome.
1957 A fire at Windscale (later Sellafield) nuclear power plant in Britain causes a radiation leak.	**1958** Summoned back to power from retirement, General Charles de Gaulle (1890–1970) founds France's Fifth Republic, modernizing the constitution and establishing the stable political system still in use today.
1957 English engineer Lionel Pilkington (1920–95) develops the float glass process for making large sheets of plate glass.	
1958 English engineer Alex Moulton (1920–) develops a folding bicycle, designed to fit in the trunk of a car.	

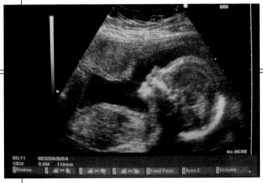

An ultrasound image of a fetus in the womb. Unlike x-ray imaging, ultrasound scans pose no potential threat to a developing fetus.

1956 The company Ampex markets a videotape recorder, designed by Russian-born American electronics engineer Alexander Poniatoff (1892–1980).	
1956 American computer programmer John Backus (1924–2007) and coworkers at IBM Corporation devise the FORTRAN (Formula Translator) computer language. It becomes commercially available the following year.	
1957 American physicist Clarence Zener (1905–93) invents the Zener diode, a type of semiconductor used in voltage-limiting circuits.	**1956** Cuban revolutionary Fidel Castro (1926–) launches a guerrilla campaign to overthrow the dictatorship of Fulgencio Batista (1901–73).
1957 Russian-born American physicist Vladimir Zworykin (1889–1982) creates a color television device that uses ultraviolet light to observe living cells.	**1956** "In God We Trust" is adopted as the national motto of the United States.
1957 The American company Smith Corona markets a portable electric typewriter.	**1957** The governor of Arkansas, Orval Faubus (1910–94), calls out the National Guard to prevent black students from enrolling at a high school in Little Rock.
1958 American electronic engineers Jack Kilby (1923–2005) and Robert Noyce (1927–90) independently invent integrated circuits, which greatly reduce the size and increase the reliability of circuits for computers and other electronic devices.	
1958 Australian engineer David Warren (1925–) invents the "black box" flight data recorder (it is, in fact, orange to make it easy to find at a crash site).	**1956** Pakistan becomes the world's first Islamic Republic.
	1958 In China Mao Zedong (1893–1976) initiates the Great Leap Forward—a three year plan for accelerated economic development that ends in disaster and famine following failed harvests.
	1956 Egypt's leader, Gamal Abdel Nasser (1918–70), nationalizes the Suez Canal; in the ensuing Suez Crisis Britain and France send troops to Egypt, but international pressure forces them to withdraw.
	1957 Ghana becomes the first British colony in Africa to gain independence.

NEW CHEMICAL ELEMENTS

Until 1937 there were only four gaps in the periodic table up to element number 92 (uranium). The gaps were at elements 43, 61, 85, and 87. That changed when scientists began to use particle accelerators such as the cyclotron, invented in 1932 by U.S. physicist Ernest Lawrence (1901–58).

At first scientists used particle accelerators as "atom smashers" to split elements into smaller components. Atoms of elements such as molybdenum, bismuth, or neodymium were bombarded with nuclei of deuterium (heavy hydrogen) or helium. Experiments using these techniques led to the discovery of technetium (atomic number 43) in 1937, astatine (85) in 1940, and promethium (61) in 1945. (Francium—atomic number 87—was discovered from the radioactive decay of another element in 1939.)

Experiments using particle accelerators to force atoms and particles together led to the discovery of yet more elements. In 1940 U.S. physical chemists Edwin McMillan (1907–91) and Philip Abelson (1913–2004) bombarded uranium-238 with slow neutrons to make neptunium (93). Also in 1940 McMillan, U.S. scientist Glenn Seaborg (1912–99), and coworkers bombarded uranium-238 with deuterium nuclei and created plutonium (94). Other elements followed in rapid succession: curium (96) and americium (95) in 1944, berkelium (97) in 1949, and californium (98) in 1950. Decades later more elements were isolated using these techniques, including seaborgium (106) in 1974, meitnerium (109), isolated in 1982 and named in 1997, and hassium (108) in 1984.

There are now about 116 chemical elements, but there—for the time being —the list ends. Scientists have created only a few atoms of the heaviest elements, which last for no more than a few seconds. Even heavier atoms are theoretically possible, but anything after element 120 would be so unstable that it could have only a fleeting existence.

ASTRONOMY & MATH	BIOLOGY & MEDICINE	PHYSICAL SCIENCES

EUROPE

1959 Soviet scientists launch three Lunik space probes to the moon; Lunik 1 flies past the moon, Lunik 2 crashes on the moon's surface, and Lunik 3 orbits the moon and sends back photographs of the far side. They are the first of 24 such probes.

1960 The Soviet Union launches two dogs, Belka and Strelka, on a 24-hour flight into space in Sputnik 5; they return safely to Earth.

1961 Soviet cosmonaut Yuri Gagarin (1934–68) becomes the first man in space on an 108-minute flight in his spacecraft Vostok (meaning "east"); the spacecraft parachutes back safely to Earth.

1961 Soviet Venera 1 space probe flies by Venus and records scientific data.

1959 Austrian-born British biochemist Max Perutz (1914–2002) determines the structure of the hemoglobin molecule.

1959 Northern Irish surgeon Denis Burkitt (1911–93) describes Burkitt's lymphoma, a disfiguring cancerous condition that most commonly affects children in Africa.

1959 French physician Jérôme Lejeune (1926–94) establishes that Down syndrome is caused the presence of an extra chromosome.

1960 French biologists François Jacob (1920–) and Jacques Monod (1910–76) coin the term *messenger ribonucleic acid* (mRNA) to describe the molecule that carries genetic code from DNA to sites in the cell where proteins are assembled.

1960 English biochemist John Kendrew (1917–97) deciphers the structure of the myoglobin molecule.

1960 English physicist Charles Oatley (1904–96) and coworkers develop the scanning electron microscope.

THE AMERICAS

1959 Researchers at the Stanford Research Institute in California make radar contact with the sun.

1960 American astronomer Allan Sandage (1926–) makes the first optical identification of a quasar (quasistellar object), an active celestial object more luminous than dozens of galaxies. In 1963 Dutch-born American astronomer Maarten Schmidt (1929–) measures its enormous redshift and proves it is billions of light-years away.

1960 The National Aeronautics and Space Administration (NASA) launches Pioneer 5 space probe to investigate the solar wind.

1960 NASA launches TIROS 1, the first weather satellite, into Earth orbit.

1961 American radio astronomer Frank Drake (1930–) formulates the Drake equation, which estimates the number of planets in our galaxy (the Milky Way) that may have technologically advanced civilizations.

1961 American astronaut Alan Shepard (1923–98) makes a suborbital flight in his spacecraft Freedom 7.

1960 American biochemist Lyman Craig (1906–74) isolates and purifies parathormone, the hormone produced by the parathyroid glands in the neck that controls calcium levels in the blood.

1960 American biologist James Bonner (1910–96) ascertains that RNA is synthesized on chromosomes.

1960 American cardiologist Paul Zoll (1911–99) develops the implant pacemaker to enable a damaged heart to beat normally.

1960 American zoologists John Prescott (1935–98) and Kenneth Norris (1924–98) discover that bottlenose dolphins produce ultrasonic pulses in a form of echolocation to detect objects under water.

1960 Hungarian-born American biophysicist Georg von Békésy (1899–1972) shows how sound waves stimulate the cochlea in the inner ear.

1961 American surgeon Judah Folkman (1933–2008) proposes (correctly) the existence of a substance called angiogenesis factor that cancerous tumors secrete to stimulate the growth of blood vessels and thereby the blood supply to a growing tumor.

1960 American chemist Robert Woodward (1917–79) synthesizes the green plant pigment, chlorophyll.

1961 American chemist Albert Ghiorso (1915–) and coworkers isolate the new radioactive element lawrencium.

Bathyscaphes, such as the Trieste *above, are designed to withstand the enormous pressures that exist at the depths of the ocean. The two-person crew sits in the steel sphere beneath the main hull.*

ASIA & OCEANIA

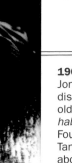

Russian cosmonaut Yuri Gagarin reclines strapped into the capsule of his Vostok spacecraft prior to making his historic first orbit of Earth.

AFRICA & THE MIDDLE EAST

1960 Kenyan anthropologist Jonathan Leakey (1940–) discovers remains of the oldest-known human, *Homo habilis* ("handy man"). Found at Olduvai Gorge, Tanzania, the fossils are about 2 million years old.

I can see the clouds, and their shadow over the Earth. It is beautiful.

YURI GAGARIN, SPEAKING FROM *VOSTOK 1*

ENGINEERING & INVENTION	WORLD EVENTS
1959 The German company Voigtlander produces a zoom lens for its cameras, providing a range of focal lengths with a single lens.	**1961** High-profile Russian ballet star Rudolf Nureyev (1938–93) requests asylum in France while touring with the Kirov Ballet.
1959 The United Kingdom Atomic Energy Authority commissions a fast-breeder nuclear reactor.	**1961** The Non-Aligned Movement comes into being at a conference in Belgrade, Yugoslavia, hosted by President Tito (1892–1980). It is comprised of nations, mostly from the developing world, that refuse to align themselves with either the United States or the Soviet Union.
1959 The British Austin Motor Company launches the Mini, an automobile designed by Greek-born British engineer Alec Issigonis (1906–88).	
1961 A 200,000-volt cable under the English Channel joins the electricity systems of England and France to enable them to "share" power during off-peak periods.	
1959 The nuclear-powered cargo vessel *Savannah* is named by First Lady Mamie Eisenhower in the U.S.; the completed ship is launched in 1962.	**1959** Fidel Castro (1926–) overthrows the dictatorship of Fulgencio Batista (1901–73) and turns Cuba into a socialist state.
1960 U.S. Navy bathyscaphe *Trieste*, guided by Swiss explorer Jacques Piccard (1922–2008) and U.S. Navy officer Don Walsh (1931–), descends the 35,810-ft (10,916-m) Marianas Trench in the Pacific Ocean.	**1961** John F. Kennedy (1917–63) is inaugurated as the 35th president of the United States.
1960 American nuclear-powered submarine U.S.S. *Triton* makes a submerged circumnavigation of the world.	**1961** The U.S.-backed invasion of Cuba at the Bay of Pigs ends in failure. The majority of the Cuban exiles who took part in the invasion are imprisoned or executed by Fidel Castro's government, and attempts to conceal the extent of U.S. involvement fail.
1960 American Digital Equipment Corporation markets the PDP-1, the precursor of the mini computer. It has a keyboard and TV-type monitor.	**1961** Freedom Riders challenging segregation laws on interstate transportation are attacked by angry mobs in Alabama and Mississippi.
1960 American physicist Theodore H. Maiman (1927–2007) invents the ruby laser—the first operable laser.	
1961 U.S. Navy *Strato-Lab V* balloon rises to 113,740 feet (34,667 m), piloted by Malcolm Ross (1919–85) and Victor Prather (1923–61), and achieves a world-record altitude for an air balloon.	
1961 The American company Texas Instruments produces the first silicon chips.	
1960 The Japan Stationery Company (later known as Pentel) markets the first felt-tip pens.	**1959** Fleeing Chinese communist rule, the 14th Dalai Lama (r. 1950–), the spiritual and political leader of Tibet, seeks asylum in India, where he establishes a government in exile.
	1961 Kuwait gains independence from the United Kingdom.
1959 The 420-foot- (128-m-) high Kariba Dam is completed on the Zambia/Zimbabwe border.	**1960** South African police fire on antiapartheid demonstrators in the black township of Sharpeville, killing 69 people.
	1961 Wars of independence begin in the Portuguese colonies of Angola and Mozambique.

NASA

The "Space Race" began when the Soviet Union launched Sputnik 1, which became the first human-made object in space. This turned a previously secret arms race with the United States into a public technological rivalry, with both sides seeking to score space "firsts" as symbols of technical superiority.

Explorer 1, the first satellite launched by the United States, reached orbit in February 1958, four months after Sputnik. Concerned that the United States had fallen behind technologically, Congress passed the National Aeronautics and Space Act, establishing the National Aeronautics and Space Administration (NASA) and allocating a large budget for the development of space technology.

The new government agency, headquartered in Washington, D.C., assumed control of all space research being conducted by the military. Along with these projects, NASA gained a group of the German rocket experts who had moved to the United States after World War II, including Wernher von Braun (1912–77).

In 1961 Alan Shepard (1923–98) became the first American in space. By 1969 NASA's Apollo program had put Neil Armstrong (1930–) and Buzz Aldrin (1930–) on the moon. NASA has also sent out many unpiloted probes to explore the solar system. Several of these have landed on and explored other planets. In the 1970s NASA launched the space station Skylab. In the 1980s and 1990s the Space Shuttle was NASA's main focus. Future projects include building a Shuttle replacement, completion of the International Space Station, and putting a human on Mars by 2037.

ASTRONOMY & MATH	BIOLOGY & MEDICINE	PHYSICAL SCIENCES

EUROPE

1962 Italian-born American physicists Riccardo Giacconi (1931–), Bruno Rossi (1905–94), and coworkers discover the first nonsolar x-ray source (the star Scorpius X-1). Two years later American astrophysicist Herbert Friedman (1916–2000) discovers another x-ray source in the Crab Nebula.

1963 Soviet cosmonaut Valentina Tereshkova (1937–) becomes the first woman in space on a 48-orbit flight in her spacecraft Vostok 6.

1964 American radio astronomers Arno Penzias (1933–) and Robert Wilson (1936–) accidentally detect cosmic background microwave radiation. Their discovery convinces most astronomers that the big bang theory is correct.

1962 Scottish biochemist James Black (1924–) prepares beta-blockers, drugs used in the treatment of patients with angina and hypertension (high blood pressure).

1964 Kidney dialysis in the home is introduced in Britain and the United States.

1962 Welsh physicist Brian Josephson (1940–) identifies the Josephson effect, in which an electric current flows through two superconductors separated by a very thin layer of insulator.

1964 Scottish theoretical physicist Peter Higgs (1929–) and coworkers predict the existence of the Higgs boson, a zero-spin subatomic particle with nonzero mass.

1964 Northern Irish physicist John Bell (1928–91) proposes Bell's theorem, which resolves apparent disagreements between relativity and quantum theory.

THE AMERICAS

1962 American astronaut John Glenn (1921–) is the first American to orbit the Earth on a three-orbit flight in Friendship 7 (part of the Mercury space program).

1962 The National Aeronautics and Space Administration's (NASA) space probe Mariner 2 flies by Venus.

1962 American communications satellite Telstar 1 (Bell Telephones/NASA) relays live TV transmissions between the United States and Europe.

1964 NASA's lunar space probe Ranger 7 takes 4,000 high-quality video pictures of the moon's surface before crash-landing on the moon.

1964 NASA's space probe Mariner 4 makes the first successful flyby of Mars, sending back photographs of the planet's surface.

1964 NASA starts the Gemini space program, which will launch 12 spacecraft (ten with two-person crews) on Titan II rockets.

1962 In her book *Silent Spring* American naturalist Rachel Carson (1907–64) awakens public awareness of the effects of chemical pesticides on the environment.

1962 American microbiologist Thomas Weller (1915–2008) develops a vaccine against rubella (German measles).

1962 British-born American chemist Neil Bartlett (1932–2008) makes the first compound of a rare gas (xenon).

1962 American physicist Leon Lederman (1922–) discovers the muon neutrino, a subatomic particle with zero charge and zero mass.

1962 American chemist Charles Pedersen (1904–89) synthesizes crown ethers, molecules that selectively bind specific metal ions in solution.

1963 American chemist Howard Rogers (1915–95) and researchers at the Polaroid Corporation led by Elkan Blout (1919–2006) develop the chemistry for producing "instant" color photographs.

1964 American theoretical physicist Murray Gell-Mann (1929–) predicts the existence of the quark, a fundamental subatomic particle with a fractional (i.e., nonintegral) charge.

ASIA & OCEANIA

1962 French-born Australian immunologist Jacques Miller (1931–) determines the role of the thymus in the immune system of infants.

AFRICA & THE MIDDLE EAST

The more clearly we can focus our attention on the wonders and realities of the universe about us, the less taste we shall have for destruction.

RACHEL CARSON, *SILENT SPRING* (1962)

Robert Moog poses with an early Moog synthesizer. Although large, expensive, and difficult to operate, the instrument soon attracted many high-profile musicians.

ENGINEERING & INVENTION	WORLD EVENTS
1962 The Bendorf Bridge—a concrete double cantilever with a central span of 673 feet (202 m)—is completed over the Rhine River in Germany. Its designer is German engineer Ulrich Finsterwalder (1897–1988). **1963** British company Courtaulds develops a method of manufacturing carbon fibers. **1963** The Dutch company Philips introduces audio cassette tapes. **1964** The German company NSU markets the Spider, the first mass-produced Wankel-engined car.	**1963** During a visit to Berlin U.S. President John F. Kennedy (1917–63) emphasizes his support for the people of West Berlin, stating, "*Ich bin ein Berliner*" ("I am a citizen of Berlin"). **1964** Premier Nikita Khrushchev (1894–1971) is ousted from power in the Soviet Union.
1962 American electronic engineer Nick Holonyak, Jr. (1928–) of the General Electric Company invents the light-emitting diode (LED). **1962** The seven-bit 128-character American Standard Code for Information Interchange (ASCII) is introduced in the States. **1962** American electronic engineer Paul Weimer (1914–2005) of the RCA Corporation invents thin-film transistors, an important contribution to solid-state circuits. **1963** South African-born American engineer Allan Cormack (1924–98) invents the CAT (computerized axial tomography) scanner. **1964** American computer programmers John Kemeny (1926–92) and Thomas Kurtz (1928–) invent the computer language BASIC (Beginner's All-purpose Symbolic Instruction Code). **1964** American engineer Robert Moog (1934–2005) invents a music synthesizer. **1964** The Verrazano-Narrows Bridge, linking Brooklyn with Staten Island, opens. At the time it is the world's longest suspension bridge, with a span of 4,260 feet (1,298 m).	**1963** Martin Luther King, Jr. (1929–68) delivers his "I have a dream" speech at the Lincoln Memorial during a civil rights march on Washington, D.C. **1963** President John F. Kennedy is assassinated in Dallas, Texas, and is succeeded by Vice President Lyndon B. Johnson (1908–73). **1964** The Civil Rights Act opposing racial discrimination becomes law in the United States. *The Verrazano-Narrows Bridge in New York links Staten Island with Brooklyn.* 
1964 In Japan the Tokaido Shinkansen train line opens. It links Tokyo and Osaka and deploys the new 100-mile- (160-km-) per-hour bullet trains.	**1962** Chinese troops occupy the Aksai Chin region of Kashmir, provoking hostilities with India. **1964** An alleged torpedo attack on two U.S. destroyers in the Gulf of Tonkin leads to U.S. entry into the Vietnam War (1959–75).
	1962 Algeria gains independence from France, with Ahmed Ben Bella (1918–) as its first prime minister (later president). **1964** Nelson Mandela (1918–) is sentenced to life imprisonment in South Africa for sabotage and treason.

ECHOLOCATION

In 1938 two young researchers at Harvard University, Donald Griffin (1915–2003), and Robert Galambos (1914–), were trying to find out how bats could see and hunt in the dark. Using special recording equipment that shifted the pitch of the bats' calls down into the range of human hearing, they were able to hear the rapid clicks that the bats made as they flew. They correctly identified these sounds as evidence of the bats' ability to detect the size and location of objects by the sound of their own reflected calls, a process called "echolocation."

In 1960 another pair of researchers, zoologists John Prescott (1935–98) and Kenneth Norris (1924–98), discovered that dolphins and many other types of whales navigate and hunt using the same method. The clicks, along with other ambient sounds, generate sound waves that reflect off solid objects. The click is generated by a complex system of reverberating chambers and airways around the animals' blowholes. It can be focused in a particular direction in order to give a more accurate idea of the location of an object. The vibrations of the reflected sound are transferred through the jawbone to the ear. There are features in the jaws of some dolphins that are not symmetrical. They may allow dolphins to judge the direction from which reflected sound has come.

The process of interpreting the information received from the clicks is believed to take place at a subconscious level, in much the same way as the sensory information from eyes and ears. Some research has suggested that dolphins are able to "see," or build up three-dimensional visualizations of the objects that they detect through echolocation.

Echolocation has since been discovered in other animals, including some shrews and tenrecs and two types of bird.

ASTRONOMY & MATH

BIOLOGY & MEDICINE

PHYSICAL SCIENCES

EUROPE

1965 Soviet cosmonaut Aleksei Leonov (1934–) is the first person to walk (tethered) in space; he leaves space capsule Voskhod 2 for 12 minutes.

1966 The Soviet Luna 9 becomes the first spacecraft to make a soft landing on the moon. Later that year Luna 10 becomes the first to go into orbit around the moon.

1966 French astronomer Audouin Dollfus (1924–) locates Janus, one of Saturn's moons. Its existence is later confirmed in 1980 by Voyager 1 photographs.

1967 Northern Irish astronomer Jocelyn Bell Burnell (neé Bell, 1943–) and English astronomer Antony Hewish (1924–) detect the first pulsar.

1965 English biophysicist Francis Crick (1916–2004) and South African-born British microbiologist Sydney Brenner (1927–) identify the codons that signal "stop" messages in deoxyribonucleic acid (DNA). These termination codons complete the protein-building process.

1967 German physicist Bernd Matthias (1918–80) and coworkers produce a superconducting alloy that functions at 20 K, the highest temperature so far achieved for a superconductor.

TURNING POINTS

Microwave Ovens

Self-taught American engineer Percy Spencer (1894–1970), who worked for the company Raytheon, had the idea for a microwave oven after noticing that a candy bar had melted while he was making a radar set in the 1940s. Raytheon patented his idea in 1947. A few cumbersome models were made, but it was not until 1967 that the first domestic microwave was marketed. Microwave ovens use microwave radiation to heat water and other polarized molecules in food. They cook quickly, efficiently, and safely. Since the late 1960s, the ovens have become smaller, more powerful, and easier to use. More than 90 percent of U.S. households now have a microwave oven.

THE AMERICAS

1965 The National Aeronautics and Space Administration (NASA) achieves several high-profile sucesses: Ranger 8 returns over 8,000 photographs before crashing on the moon; Pioneer 6 orbits and monitors the sun; two Gemini spacecraft rendezvous in Earth orbit.

1965 NASA launches the world's first commercial communications satellite *Early Bird* (later Intelsat 1).

1966 NASA's space probe Surveyor 1 soft-lands on the moon and sends back more than 11,000 photographs. Lunar Orbiter 1 and Lunar Orbiter 2 send back photographs of the far side of the moon.

1967 NASA's space probe Mariner 5 makes a close flyby of Venus. In the same year a fire kills three Apollo astronauts during a ground test.

1965 American geneticist Charles Yanofsky (1925–) and coworkers establish that the sequence of codons in a gene determines the sequence of amino acids in a protein.

1967 American biochemist Arthur Kornberg (1918–2007) uses DNA polymerase, the enzyme that assembles nucleotides, to make biologically active "synthetic" DNA.

1967 In the United States, Argentine-born surgeon René Favaloro (1923–2000) conducts a successful coronary bypass operation.

1967 Greek-born American physician George Cotzias (1918–77) introduces the use of the drug L-dopa as a treatment for Parkinsonism.

1965 American physicists Moo-Young Han (1934–) and Yoichiro Nambu (1921–) introduce the idea of "color" as a way of classifying one aspect of the new subatomic articles known as quarks.

1966 American geneticist Richard Lewontin (1929–) develops the technique of gel electrophoresis for separating proteins (a method now routinely used in genetic fingerprinting).

1966 Construction of the powerful linear accelerator at the Stanford Linear Accelerator Center (SLAC) is completed.

1966 The American Atomic Energy Commission announces that Weston, Illinois, is the site chosen for the new National Accelerator Laboratory, housing a 200 GeV particle accelerator.

1967 American physicist Steven Weinberg (1933–) and Pakistani physicist Abdus Salam (1926–96) independently state versions of the electroweak theory, which unifies the electromagnetic and weak nuclear forces.

1967 The National Accelerator Laboratory is commissioned in Batavia (formerly Weston), Illinois.

ASIA & OCEANIA

1965 Japanese astronomers Ikeya Kaoru (1926–) and, independently, Seki Tsutomu (1930–) discover the bright sun-grazing comet Ikeya-Seki. It splits in three as it passes the sun.

South African surgeon Christiaan Barnard performed the first human-to-human heart transplant.

AFRICA & THE MIDDLE EAST

1967 South African surgeon Christiaan Barnard (1922–2001) performs the first successful heart transplant. The patient lives for 18 days with his new heart.

ENGINEERING & INVENTION	WORLD EVENTS
1965 The Soviet Antonov An-22 jet airliner, the world's largest military and freight-carrying aircraft, makes its maiden flight. **1965** The Mont Blanc road tunnel between France and Italy is opened. **1966** An electronic fuel-injection system for automobile engines is developed in Britain. **1967** The first production model of the British Hawker Harrier GR Mark I V/STOL (Vertical/Short Take-Off and Landing) combat airplane makes its maiden flight. **1967** The ocean liner *Queen Elizabeth 2* is launched in Britain.	**1966** Concerned that membership is impairing French sovereignty, France withdraws from the North Atlantic Treaty Organization (NATO).

RADIO TELESCOPES

American radio engineer Karl Jansky (1905–50) first detected radio waves from outer space in 1931. He used an improvised antenna of wood and wire. Six years later American engineer Grote Reber (1911–2002) built a radio telescope in his backyard and became the world's first radio astronomer. The telescope had a dish-shaped antenna 31 feet (9.4 m) across and received signals at a wavelength of 1.9 meters. Because radio wavelengths are so much longer than those of light, radio telescopes have to be considerably larger than the mirrors of reflecting telescopes to get similar resolution. By 1942 Reber, using the shorter wavelength of 60 centimeters, had built up a radio map of the universe.

The first big single radio telescope was constructed in 1957 for Manchester University at Jodrell Bank, in England, under the supervision of English radio astronomer Bernard Lovell (1913–). The 250-foot (76.2-m) dish achieved fame almost immediately when it tracked Earth's first artificial satellite, the Soviet Sputnik 1. Cornell University completed the largest single radio telescope over a natural depression in the ground at Arecibo in Puerto Rico. It consists of an aluminum metal mesh 1,000 feet (305 m) across with a radio receiver suspended on wires at its focus.

The resolving power of even such huge dishes is limited, and to obtain greater detail astronomers used the principle of the interferometer (using two widely separated telescopes). Scientists mount two or more radio telescopes on railroad tracks to easily vary the distances between them. Communications cables carry the signals from the telescopes to a computer, which analyzes the signals. Radio astronomers employ a few widely separated telescopes in the technique known as a very large array (VLA). In 1980 the National Radio Astronomy Observatory completed a VLA near Socorro, New Mexico. This array has 27 antennas on a Y-shaped track extending for a total of 19 miles (32 km). It is the equivalent of a single dish 22 miles (36 km) across.

ENGINEERING & INVENTION	WORLD EVENTS
1965 American Digital Equipment Corporation introduces the first mini computer. **1966** American inventor Stephanie Kwolek (1923–) invents the ultrastrong synthetic fiber Kevlar. Five times stronger than steel, it is used in a wide variety of industrial products today, including fiber-optic cables, aircraft parts, canoes, and bullet-proof vests. **1966** American electronic engineer Ray Dolby (1933–) devises the Dolby noise-reduction system (type A) for sound recordings. **1967** Scientists at Bell Laboratories develop the bubble memory for computers. **1967** American engineer Joseph Engelberger (1925–) at General Motors perfects a reprogrammable computer-controlled industrial robot. **1967** The American company Raytheon markets the first domestic microwave oven.	**1965** Militant black leader Malcolm X (1925–65) is assassinated in New York City. **1967** Guerrilla leader Che Guevara (1928–67) is killed in Bolivia. **1967** During a visit to Montreal, Canada, French President Charles De Gaulle (1890–1970) declares his support for the independence of Quebec.

Modern body armor contains the ultrastrong fiber Kevlar, which can stop bullets.

1966 Chinese electronics engineer Charles Kao (1933–) and George Hockham of British company Standard Telecommunications Laboratories invent fiber-optic cable. **1967** Chinese scientists explode a hydrogen bomb over Lop Nor in western China.	**1965** India and Pakistan go to war for a second time over the province of Kashmir. **1965** American bombing of targets in North Vietnam begins. **1965** Civil war divides Nigeria as the eastern province of Biafra attempts to break away. The conflict continues until 1970.

ASTRONOMY & MATH	BIOLOGY & MEDICINE	PHYSICAL SCIENCES

EUROPE

1969 English astrophysicist Donald Lynden-Bell (1935–) proposes that there are supermassive black holes at the centers of galaxies.

1970 Soviet space probe Luna 16 returns lunar soil samples to Earth. Luna 17 lands a roving vehicle, Lunokhod 1, on the moon's surface. Soviet Venera 7 lands on Venus and is the first spacecraft to transmit data from the surface of another planet.

1968 Swiss biophysicist Werner Arber (1929–) isolates enzymes that cut the deoxyribonucleic acid (DNA) of viruses that infect bacteria. They become known as restrictive enzymes and are important later in genetic engineering experiments.

1969 English physiologist Robert Edwards (1925–) and English obstetrician Patrick Steptoe (1913–88) fertilize the first human eggs in vitro.

1969 English chemist Dorothy Hodgkin (1910–94) uses x-ray crystallography and computers to determine the molecular structure of insulin.

HOW THINGS WORK

In Vitro Fertilization

When a woman who wants to have a baby has difficulty becoming pregnant, doctors may recommend in vitro fertilization (IVF). In vitro, Latin for "in glass," describes any procedure that is carried out in the laboratory, for example in a test tube, rather than within a patient's body. For this reason, babies born using the technique have become known as "test-tube" babies. The physician first gives the woman a hormone injection to stimulate the production of eggs and then recovers the eggs from her ovary using a suction device. Next the eggs are fertilized by a sample of the father's sperm. The fertilized eggs continue to grow in a nutrient solution until they have divided repeatedly to form a ball of cells called a blastocyst. This early embryo is then implanted in the mother's womb, where it develops in the usual way into a baby. Although eggs were first successfully fertilized in vitro in 1969, the first baby produced using the technique was not born until 1978.

THE AMERICAS

1968 The National Aeronautics and Space Administration (NASA) launches a UV observatory satellite, OAO-2, into Earth orbit.

1968 NASA's Apollo 7 spacecraft (the first piloted Apollo mission) makes 163 Earth orbits, and Apollo 8 orbits the moon.

1969 NASA's Apollo 9 spacecraft makes 151 Earth orbits, testing docking and undocking of modules. Apollo 10 orbits the moon, and Apollo 11 makes the first piloted moon landing. Astronaut Neil Armstrong (1930–) becomes the first man to walk on the moon's surface. Buzz Aldrin (1930–) joins him, while Michael Collins (1930–) remains orbiting the moon in the command module. Later that year Apollo 12 also lands on the moon.

1970 NASA's Apollo 13 mission is aborted without a moon landing because of an onboard explosion, but the crew returns safely.

1970 Large reflecting telescopes are installed at observatories at Mauna Kea, Hawaii (88 inches/2.24 m), and Kitt Peak, Arizona (158 inches/4 m).

1968 American physician Norman Shumway (1923–2006) performs the first heart transplant in the United States.

1969 American geneticist Jonathan Beckwith (1935–) and coworkers isolate a single gene, lacZ.

1969 In the United States a report suggesting a link between cyclamates and cancer leads to a ban on their use as artificial sweeteners a year later.

1970 American paleontologist Edwin Colbert (1905–2001) discovers in Antarctica fossils of Lystrosaurus (a prehistoric reptile also found in India and Africa), providing evidence for the theory of continental drift (because these landmasses must once have been joined).

1970 American molecular biologists Howard Temin (1934–94) and David Baltimore (1938–) identify reverse transcriptase, an enzyme that transcribes RNA (ribonucleic acid) into DNA and later becomes important in genetic engineering.

1969 American chemist Robert Woodward (1917–79) and Polish-born American chemist Roald Hoffmann (1937–) propose the Woodward–Hoffmann rules concerning the formation of products in organic reactions.

1969 American biochemist Gerald Edelman (1929–) works out the sequence of amino acids in the immunoglobulin molecule.

ASIA & OCEANIA

1970 Artificial Earth satellites are launched by China and Japan.

American astronaut Edwin "Buzz" Aldrin stands on the surface of the moon in a photograph taken by fellow astronaut Neil Armstrong.

AFRICA & THE MIDDLE EAST

1968 South African surgeon Christiaan Barnard (1922–2001) carries out his second heart transplant operation. This time the patient, Philip Blaiberg (1909–69), lives for 19 months after the successful operation.

ENGINEERING & INVENTION	WORLD EVENTS
1968 The Soviet Tu-144 supersonic airliner, conceived by Russian designer Andrei Tupolev (1888–1972), makes its maiden flight.	**1968** Student unrest spreads across Europe, protesting the Vietnam War (1959–75) and local grievances; students' and workers' strikes almost topple the French government.
1969 The British-French supersonic airliner Concorde makes its maiden flight in France.	**1968** The Czech government, led by Alexander Dubchek (1921–92), institutes the Prague Spring of liberal reforms, quickly crushed by Warsaw Pact troops.
1969 A nuclear-powered cargo vessel, the 29,000-ton (26,000-tonne) *Otto Hahn*, is launched in West Germany. (It is named for the German chemist whose work led to the discovery of nuclear fission.)	**1968** In Northern Ireland violence between the majority Protestant community and demonstrators demanding enhanced civil rights for the Catholic minority sparks a 30-year period of violence known as the "Troubles."
1970 Swiss computer programmer Niklaus Wirth (1934–) invents PASCAL programming language, named in honor of French scientist Blaise Pascal (1623–62).	

PULSARS

In 1967 two British astronomers, Jocelyn Bell Burnell (1943–) and Anthony Hewish (1924–), were using a radio telescope to study quasars—the centers of galaxies. Bell noticed a source of radiation that was pulsing on and off about once a second. Unable to explain the source of this mysteriously regular radio signal, the astronomers named it LGM–1, a reference to the "little green men"—a light-hearted nickname for extraterrestrial intelligent life.

In 1968, other astronomers proposed that LGM–1 was a rotating neutron star. Such stars are very dense and small—about 12.4 miles (20 km) across—and spin rapidly. They emit a beam of electromagnetic radiation. If the beam points toward Earth while the star spins, it can be detected by radio telescopes as pulses of radio waves. The name *pulsar*—a contraction of "pulsating star"—was coined to describe this type of star. Other pulsars were soon discovered, with pulse rates varying from a few milliseconds to several seconds.

Most pulsars are thought to have been formed after the explosions of stars (supernovas) and are sometimes found in remnants of supernovas (the clouds of gas and plasma thrown out by exploding stars).

ENGINEERING & INVENTION	WORLD EVENTS
1968 The Lockheed C-5 Galaxy makes its maiden flight in the United States and becomes the world's largest airplane.	**1968** U.S. civil rights leader Martin Luther King Jr. (1929–68) is assassinated in Memphis, Tennessee.
1968 Italian-born American inventor Candido Jacuzzi (1903–86) invents the whirlpool bath named for him.	**1968** Democratic presidential hopeful, Robert Kennedy (1925–68), brother of assassinated President John F. Kennedy (1917–63), is shot dead after a campaign rally in Los Angeles.
1968 American computer engineer Douglas Engelbart (1925–) devises the computer mouse.	**1970** As opposition to the Vietnam War gains momentum in the United States, four student protesters are shot dead by the National Guard on the campus of Kent State University, Ohio.
1969 Canadian electronic engineer Willard Boyle (1924–) and American electronic engineer George Smith (1930–) invent the charge-coupled device (CCD). It soon replaces photographic film in many applications.	
1969 In the United States the Boeing Company flies its 747 (Jumbo) jet for the first time.	
1970 American Gary Gabelich (1940–84) sets a world land speed record of 622.287 miles (1,001 km) per hour in the rocket-powered car *Blue Flame* at Bonneville Salt Flats, Utah.	
1970 The 400-seater Boeing 747 Jumbo jet goes into service on the transatlantic run. Two years later an air cargo version goes into service, carrying freight between New York and Frankfurt, West Germany.	

At the heart of the Crab Nebula is the Crab Pulsar, a neutron star that spins 30.2 times each second.

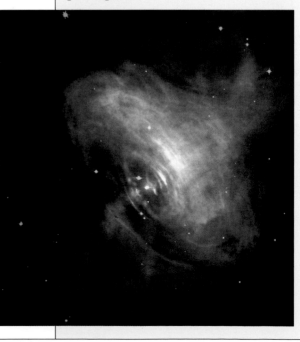

ENGINEERING & INVENTION	WORLD EVENTS
1970 The Japanese company Canon Business Machines markets a pocket calculator with a printout.	**1968** Vietcong insurgents launch the Tet offensive against South Vietnam, almost capturing the capital, Saigon, before retreating.
	1970 Civil war breaks out in Jordan when King Hussein (r. 1952–1999) expels the Palestine Liberation Organization.
1968 In Egypt the power plant at the new Aswan High Dam goes into operation.	**1969** Colonel Muammar al-Gadhafi (1942–) overthrows the monarchy and proclaims himself Libya's leader.
	1970 Biafra surrenders to Nigerian forces, giving up its three-year struggle.

ASTRONOMY & MATH

EUROPE

1971 Soviet space probe Mars 2 goes into orbit around Mars (two weeks after Mariner 9), and Mars 3 lands on the surface but its TV camera fails. Soviet spacecraft Soyuz 10 docks with Salyut 1, the first space station in Earth orbit. Later that year three Soviet cosmonauts die as they reenter Earth's atmosphere onboard Soyuz 11.

1972 Soviet space probe Venera 8 soft-lands on Venus and returns data from the surface for 50 minutes.

1973 Czech astronomer Lubos Kohoutek (1935–) discovers (photographically) the nonperiodic comet Kohoutek.

THE AMERICAS

1971 American astronomer Irwin Shapiro (1929–) identifies so-called superluminal sources—quasar components that seem to move apart faster than the speed of light.

1971 The National Aeronautics and Space Administration's (NASA) Apollo 14 makes the third piloted lunar landing and returns with rock samples. Apollo 15 lands the Lunar Rover Vehicle. Mariner 9 goes into orbit around Mars, eventually sending back more than 7,000 detailed pictures.

1972 NASA launches Landsat 1, the first Earth resources satellite. It also launches space probe Pioneer 10. Apollo 16 and Apollo 17 make the final landings on the moon.

1973 NASA space probe Pioneer 10 flies by Jupiter. NASA launches Pioneer 11 and four Skylab space station missions.

1973 Using data from the Vela Earth satellite, American astronomers detect bursts of gamma rays originating in outer space. One of the sources is later nicknamed "Geminga" (in Milanese dialect meaning "it's not there").

ASIA & OCEANIA

1972 In Australia astronomer B. J. Harris (1925–75) provides evidence that most unidentified radio sources in space are compact, when he discovers that 60 percent of them scintillate (as in the "twinkling" of stars).

AFRICA & THE MIDDLE EAST

BIOLOGY & MEDICINE

1972 Scottish biochemist James Black (1924–) develops the drug cimetidine, which blocks the secretion of stomach acids and is used to treat ulcers.

1972 Swiss biochemist Jean-François Borel (1933–) develops the immunosuppressive drug cyclosporin-A, used to prevent rejection of organs following transplant operations.

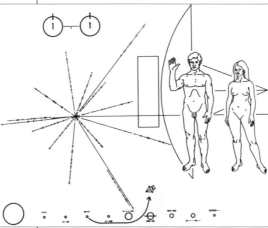

1972 American authorities restrict the use of DDT insecticide because of its effects on the environment and its inhabitants.

1972 American molecular biologist Paul Berg (1926–) produces hybrid deoxyribonucleic acid (DNA).

1972 American psychiatrist David Janowsky and coworkers propose that bipolar disorder ("manic depression") is caused by an imbalance between two kinds of chemical neurotransmitters in the brain.

1973 American and English physicists begin to develop nuclear magnetic resonance imaging (MRI scanning), later used in medical diagnosis.

1973 American biologists Stanley Cohen (1935–) and Herbert Boyer (1936–) invent a way of cloning genetically engineered molecules in foreign cells.

The development of the continuous-wave laser and the rapidly pulsing laser at Bell Laboratories in 1973 was important in the development of lasers for surgical purposes, such as eye surgery, pictured here.

1972 Kenyan anthropologist Richard Leakey (1944–) finds an intact skull of 1.9 million-year-old human ancestor *Homo habilis* in Africa.

PHYSICAL SCIENCES

1972 French mathematician René Thom (1923–2002) introduces catastrophe theory, which soon has applications in physics and other sciences.

This design was etched onto a plaque on the Pioneer 10 space probe. It contains a picture of a man and woman with an image of the probe in the background. It also gives the location of Earth relative to the sun, and of the sun relative to nearby pulsars in a way which scientists believe could be decoded by other intelligent life.

1971 Chinese-born American biochemist Choh Hao Li (1913–87) synthesizes the human growth hormone.

1972 The National Accelerator Laboratory in Weston (now eastern Batavia), Illinois, commissions its 200 GeV accelerator, later upgrading it to 400 GeV. In 1974 the laboratory is renamed Fermilab.

1972 American theoretical physicist Murray Gell-Mann (1929–) begins formulating a new branch of physics, quantum chromodynamics (QCD). It describes nuclear interaction in terms of quarks.

1973 Physicists at Bell Laboratories produce a continuous-wave laser that can be tuned to different wavelengths. A year later they have lasers that can produce light pulses of less than a trillionth of a second.

ENGINEERING & INVENTION

1971 The Swiss company Hoffmann–LaRoche presents a liquid-crystal display.

1971 Experimental electric power plants employing magnetohydrodynamic (MHD) generators go into service in West Germany and the Soviet Union.

1972 The A300B Airbus large-bodied jet airliner, built by a European consortium, makes its maiden flight at Toulouse, France.

1973 A Soviet Tu-144 supersonic airliner crashes at the Paris Air Show. Tu-144s begin carrying mail and cargo two years later, but the aircraft is retired in 1979.

1971 American electronic engineer Ted Hoff (1937–) and coworkers introduce a single-chip microprocessor (Intel 4004).

1971 American electronic engineers Jack Kilby (1923–2005) at Texas Instruments and Robert Noyce (1927–90) at Intel Corporation produce pocket calculators.

1971 The American company Centron markets a dot matrix printer.

1972 American computer engineer Nolan Bushnell (1943–) founds the computer company Atari, Inc., and creates the popular video game Pong, which employs a liquid crystal screen.

1973 The 1,368-foot (417-m) World Trade Center—a complex of buildings including the famous Twin Towers—officially opens in New York City, designed by American architect Minoru Yamasaki (1912–86).

1973 Construction work begins on the CN Tower in Toronto, Canada. When completed three years later, this radio and TV mast becomes the world's tallest structure at 1,815 feet (553 m) tall.

WORLD EVENTS

1971 Women win the right to vote in Switzerland, the last European country to introduce universal suffrage.

1972 At the Munich Olympics in Germany Palestinian terrorists from the Black September group kill two Israeli athletes and take nine others hostage; a bungled police rescue attempt results in their deaths.

1972 Intruders, all either indirectly or directly employed by the re-election campaign team for Republican President Richard Nixon (1913–94), are caught breaking into the offices of the Democratic National Committee in the Watergate Hotel, Washington, D.C. They are carrying cameras and electronic surveillance equipment.

1973 With the help of the CIA, right-wing military forces under General Augusto Pinochet (1915–2006) overthrow the elected socialist government in Chile; its leader Salvador Allende (1908–73) commits suicide. Many prominent supporters of Allende are gathered up and executed before the end of the year.

1973 The former dictator to Argentina, Juan Perón (1895–1974), returns to Argentina after 18 years in exile. Aged 77, he resumed the presidency as head of the Justicialita Party but dies the following year; his second wife, Isabel (1931–), succeeds him in power.

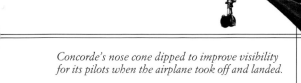

Concorde's nose cone dipped to improve visibility for its pilots when the airplane took off and landed.

CONCORDE

In the spring of 1969 a new kind of airliner capable of traveling at supersonic speeds took to the skies over Toulouse, southern France. The new Aérospatiale–BAC (British Air Corporation) Concorde was designed to fly at an altitude of 60,000 feet (18.3 km) and reach speeds of up to 1,320 miles (2,090 km) per hour—more than twice the speed of sound. Concorde's first flight was the culmination of about 20 years of research and development in France and Britain.

In 1962 Aérospatiale in France and BAC in Britain—using funding and technical assistance supplied by their respective governments—began to cooperate on a new concept. This new supersonic airliner design would incorporate features from previous supersonic projects. The resulting design had an elegant delta wing layout and engines that could maintain supersonic speeds with relative fuel efficiency.

Two other rival planes were developed in the 1960s. The first, the Soviet Tupolev Tu-144, resembled Concorde in many respects but could fly neither as fast nor as high and was marred by technical faults. The other, the Boeing 2707, never advanced beyond the planning stage.

Concorde was not the success its designers had initially hoped for, however. The rising price of oil, combined with political issues and the aircraft's deafening engine noise, discouraged many prospective operators from buying the airplanes. Despite its initial promise, it was only ever sold with government subsidies to the national airlines of Britain and France, beginning service in 1976. In 2000 a tire exploded on an Air France Concorde during takeoff, damaging one of the engines. The plane crashed, killing all passengers and crew. The fleet was grounded while the crash was investigated. Although a limited commercial service briefly resumed, Concorde was retired in Britain and France in 2003.

LASERS

LASER BEAMS CAN CUT METAL MUCH MORE precisely than saws and are also used in delicate eye surgery. Surveyors use lasers to measure distances, and lasers mounted on aircraft produce the detail needed to make highly accurate maps of the ground surface. Some computer printers use lasers, and without them there would be no CDs, DVDs, or Blu-ray Discs.

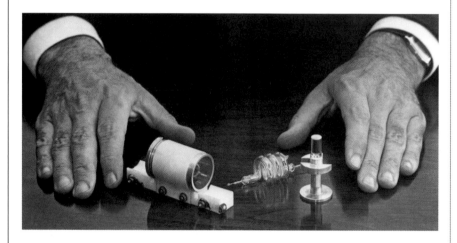

Theodore H. Maiman disassembles the world's first laser, which he made in 1960. The key component is inside the glass vessel—the ruby crystal that emits the laser beam.

In 1917 German-born physicist Albert Einstein (1879–1955) recognized that it should be possible to stimulate atoms and molecules so that they emit light. That is the principle behind the laser, but it was not until the 1950s that physicists suggested a device that could generate a laser beam. In 1952 American physicist Charles H. Townes (1915–) described a way to stimulate molecules of ammonia to emit microwave radiation using the principle of the maser—**m**icrowave **a**mplification by **s**timulated **e**mission of **r**adiation. Townes built the first maser in 1953. Masers are used in atomic clocks and radio telescopes and to amplify weak signals from satellites.

Microwave radiation is invisible, but in 1958 Townes and Arthur Schawlow (1921–99), another American physicist, published a paper showing that it was theoretically possible to make a device that would emit visible light. It would produce **l**ight **a**mplification by **s**timulated **e**mission of **r**adiation—the laser. Townes and Schawlow did not make any such device, however. It was American physicist Theodore H. Maiman (1927–2007) who made the first laser in 1960.

KEY DATES

1917
Einstein proposes stimulated emission

1952
Maser conceived

1958
Laser proposed in theory

1960
Maiman's ruby laser invented

When a substance absorbs energy such as heat, its atoms or molecules jump from a low-energy level to a high-energy level. As they drop back to the low-energy level, they emit surplus energy in the form of light. Ordinarily, each of the atoms or molecules emits light independently of the others and at different wavelengths. But if the substance is exposed to very intense light of a particular wavelength during the brief instant it is at its high-energy level, it will emit light at the same wavelength as the light shining on it. That is how the substance is stimulated, and stimulation further intensifies the light. The next step is to amplify the light by the use of mirrors. A mirror at one end of the device reflects light back through the substance being stimulated. A half-silvered mirror at the opposite end reflects some of the light but allows the remainder to escape as a laser beam. A laser emits a narrow beam of coherent light, that is, light of a single wavelength and therefore color, in which all the waves are in step.

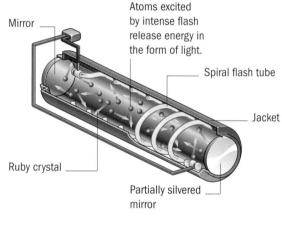

Mirror

Atoms excited by intense flash release energy in the form of light.

Spiral flash tube

Jacket

Ruby crystal

Partially silvered mirror

As atoms release more energy, the energy is reflected backward and forward between the mirrors until it is powerful enough to break through the partially silvered mirror in the form of a concentrated beam.

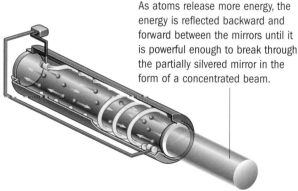

In the ruby laser, both ends of a cylindrical rod of ruby crystal are polished flat and coated with silver to make a mirror at one end and a partial mirror at the other. The ruby is enclosed in a jacket to keep it cool. A spiral tube surrounding the ruby emits flashes of light. Atoms in the ruby absorb energy from the tube and emit light. The beam emerges from the partially silvered end.

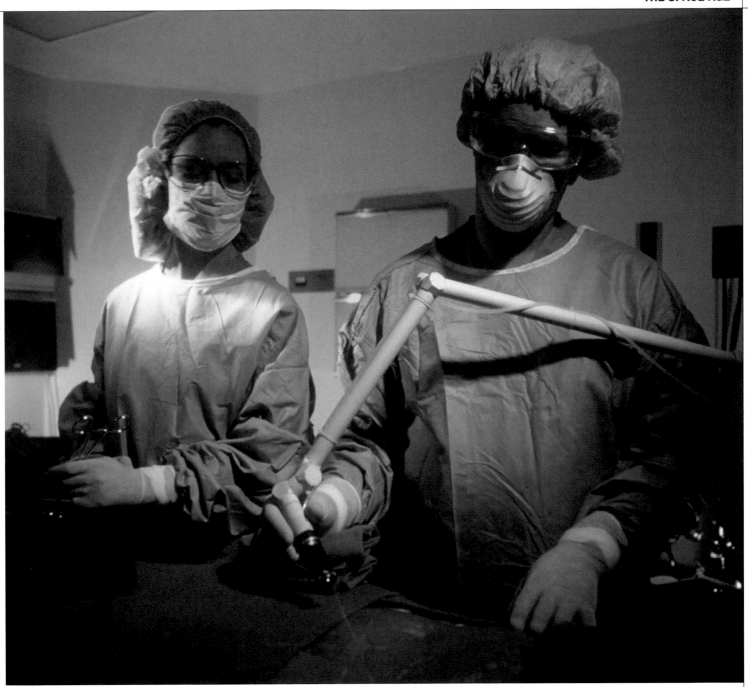

Many substances can be stimulated to emit coherent light. In his laser Maiman used a ruby crystal—an artificial crystal of aluminum oxide. Neodymium has also been used in lasers, as have liquids and gases such as carbon monoxide and a mixture of helium and neon.

The light beam from a flashlight diverges, so it illuminates a large area. A laser beam is more focused. By passing the beam through the wrong end of a telescope, the divergence is reduced further. Lasers of this type are used to guide machines that lay pipelines and drill tunnels. A ruby laser can drill through a diamond.

When a laser beam strikes a surface, the surface absorbs some of its energy and its temperature rises. Lasers produce such strong heat over such a small area that they can be used to trim excess material from electronic components and even to perform surgery.

Narrow laser beams can also be used to measure distances. When a pulse strikes a surface, some of it is reflected. Since the speed of light is always the same, distance is calculated from the time that elapses between the emission of the pulse and the arrival of its reflection. This is called lidar (light radar).

Watched by the theater nurse, a surgeon uses a laser during an operation. The laser beam allows the surgeon to make a much smaller and more precise incision than would be possible with a scalpel or knife, thereby reducing the trauma suffered by the patient.

ASTRONOMY & MATH	BIOLOGY & MEDICINE	PHYSICAL SCIENCES

EUROPE

1974 Soviet probe Mars 4 flies by Mars. Mars 5 enters orbit. Mars 6 ejects a lander that crashes onto the planet. The lander from Mars 7 misses the planet.

1975 Soviet Venera 9 and Venera 10 space probes land on Venus and send back pictures of the surface.

1975 The European Space Agency (ESA) is formed. In its first year it launches Cos-B, a gamma-ray observatory satellite, into Earth orbit; during its seven-year lifetime the satellite detects 25 gamma-ray sources.

1975 Argentine-born British molecular biologist César Milstein (1927–2002), English-born Danish immunologist Niels Jerne (1911–94), and German immunologist Georges Köhler (1946–95) develop monoclonal antibodies, used to produce antibodies with predetermined specificities.

1975 German-born Scottish pharmacologist Hans Kosterlitz (1903–96) and British pharmacologist John Hughes (1942–) discover enkephalins, chemicals produced in the brain that control pain and other sensations.

1976 An accident at a pesticide plant at Seveso, Italy, releases a cloud of poisonous dioxin gas that kills hundreds of farm animals.

THE AMERICAS

1974 American astrophysicists Joseph Taylor (1941–) and Russell Hulse (1950–) observe the first binary pulsar while working at the Arecibo radio telescope in Puerto Rico.

1974 American astronomer Charles Kowal (1940–) discovers Leda, the 13th moon of Jupiter to be found.

1974 The National Aeronautics and Space Administration (NASA) space probe Mariner 10 (launched in 1973) reaches Mercury.

1975 American astronomer Vera Rubin (1928–) measures the proper motion of our galaxy (the Milky Way) as 310 miles (500 km) per second.

1975 In a mission known as Apollo–Soyuz Test Project NASA's Apollo 18 and the Soviet Soyuz 19 space capsules link up in Earth orbit.

1976 NASA's Viking 1 and Viking 2 space probes soft-land on Mars and send back data and pictures. The landscape is seen to consist mostly of rocks and boulders.

1974 American biochemist Gertrude Elion (1918–99) and coworkers produce the antiherpes drug acyclovir, the first successful antiviral medicine, but do not announce the fact until 1978.

1974 American paleoanthropologist Donald Johanson (1943–) unearths fossils of the hominid *Australopithecus afarensis* (a female, nicknamed "Lucy") in Ethiopia. She is known to have walked upright.

1976 French-born American physiologist Roger Guillemin (1924–) reports the existence of endorphins, morphinelike chemicals released in the brain that relieve pain after injury to the body.

1976 The first known outbreak of Legionnaire's disease occurs in the United States. Two years later the bacteria that cause it (*Legionella*) are isolated.

1976 American virologists J. Michael Bishop (1936–) and Harold Varmus (1939–) and coworkers identify oncogenes, which can convert normal cells into cancer cells.

1976 Indian-born American chemist Har Khorana (1922–) and coworkers insert an artificial gene into a living cell (*Escherichia coli*) and observe that it functions fully.

1974 Mexican-born American scientist Mario Molina (1943–) and American scientist F. Sherwood Rowland (1927–) issue warnings about the damaging effect CFCs (chlorofluorocarbons) are having on the Earth's ozone layer.

1974 American physicists Samuel Ting (1936–) and Burton Richter (1931–) discover independently the J/psi particle, a type of long-lived meson.

1975 Chemists at the American company DuPont perfect the production of polyethylene terephthalate (PET) plastic for making beverage bottles.

1976 American physicist Martin Perl (1927–) discovers a subatomic particle that he names the tau particle (or tauon). It is a massive lepton with a negative charge.

ASIA & OCEANIA

A view of the surface of Mars taken by the Viking 2 robotic lander.

1974 Japanese chemist Hideki Shirakawa (1936–) produces a flexible film that has metallic properties by (accidentally) adding a concentrated catalyst solution while synthesizing polymers.

AFRICA & THE MIDDLE EAST

1976 The Ebola virus (Filoviridae family) is first identified after outbreaks in western Sudan and Zaire (now the Democratic Republic of the Congo).

ENGINEERING & INVENTION	WORLD EVENTS
1974 Architects propose making buildings with windows of electrochromic glass that darkens when a low-voltage electric current is applied, thereby reducing a building's energy loss.	**1974** A bloodless military coup in Portugal, led by General Antonio de Spinola (1910–96), brings more than 40 years of dictatorship to an end.
1976 The British–French supersonic airliner Concorde enters service in January. The first flights begin to operate between Paris and Rio de Janeiro and between London and Bahrain. Flights to Washington, D.C., begin later the same year.	**1975** General Francisco Franco (1892–1975), dictator of Spain since 1939, dies. The monarchy is restored under his chosen successor, Juan Carlos (r. 1975–), grandson of Spain's last king, who immediately sets about reintroducing democratic politics.
1976 Construction engineers complete the 10.2-mile (16.4-km) pilot bore for the new road tunnel through the St. Gotthard Pass in the Swiss Alps. It opens four years later, becoming the longest road tunnel in the world.	

SEMICONDUCTORS

A semiconductor is a substance that sometimes has the properties of an insulator (which conducts electricity poorly) but under some conditions allows an electric current to flow through. The best-known semiconductor is silicon. It is used to make microchips inside computers and domestic appliances.

ENGINEERING & INVENTION	WORLD EVENTS
1974 The 1,450-foot (442-m) Sears Tower, at the time the world's tallest building, is completed in Chicago.	**1974** U.S. President Richard Nixon (1913–94) resigns under threat of impeachment for authorizing illegal bugging of his political opponents at the Watergate complex in Washington, D.C.
1974 The American company General Motors introduces catalytic converters for cars.	**1976** Democratic candidate Jimmy Carter (1924–) is elected 39th president of the United States.
1974 American chemical engineer Arthur Fry (1931–) invents the semiadhesive Post-it Note.	
1975 The American company IBM markets a laser printer for computers. A year later it introduces an inkjet printer.	
1975 American engineer Edward Roberts (1941–) markets the first commercial personal computer (PC) in kit or assembled form, the Altair 8800.	
1975 American computer programmers Bill Gates (1955–) and Paul Allen (1953–) found the Microsoft Corporation.	
1975 NASA's Jet Propulsion Laboratory begins to employ charge-coupled devices (CCDs) instead of photographic film to record images in astronomical telescopes.	
1976 American computer designers Steven Jobs (1955–) and Stephen Wozniak (1950–) found the computer company Apple.	

Apple 1 computers, made in 1976, were sold as a complete circuit board; the owner had to purchase a case, keyboard, and monitor separately.

The first semiconductor applied in a device was a crystal of galena. It was used to make a rectifier (a device that allows current to flow in just one direction) in early radio sets.

In 1958, American electronic engineer Jack Kilby (1923–2005) realized that rather than making transistors one at a time several could be made together and placed on the same semiconductor by overlaying different impurities (which were found to improve a semiconductor's properties). Other components, such as diodes, capacitors, and resistors, could then be added. Kilby had invented the integrated circuit. A year later planar technology was developed. This process spreads different layers onto a wafer of silicon to make a flat transistor, and then evaporates metal strips onto the surface to make the necessary connections.

ENGINEERING & INVENTION	WORLD EVENTS
1974 India announces that it has successfully tested its first atomic bomb, becoming the sixth nation to develop nuclear weapons.	**1974** Floods and a devastating famine grip the new country of Bangladesh.
1976 The Japanese company Matsushita introduces the VHS (video home system) format for video cassettes.	**1975** North Vietnamese troops enter the South Vietnamese capital, Saigon, reuniting the country under communist rule.
	1976 Mao Zedong (1893–1976), China's leader since 1949, dies.
	1974 Ethiopia's long-term emperor Haile Selassie I (r. 1930–74) is deposed in a communist-led military coup.
	1974 Protests against the apartheid regime in South Africa break out in the black township of Soweto, near Johannesburg; police kill 176 demonstrators.

Much smaller than postage stamps, the chips in computers, digital cameras, and all other modern electronic devices are plastic cases enclosing layers of transistors and related components, together with the wiring linking them, on the surface of a sliver of silicon.

ASTRONOMY & MATH

EUROPE

1979 The European Space Agency (ESA) launches its first space rocket, Ariane 1, from the Guiana Space Center, French Guiana.

In the 1970s, scientists realized that chlorofluorocarbons (CFCs), which were used in aerosol cans, were damaging the ozone layer.

THE AMERICAS

1977 American astronomers on the Kuiper Airborne Observatory observe the rings of Uranus.

1977 American astronomer Charles Kowal (1940–) discovers Chiron, an outer solar system body. At first thought to be an asteroid, then a comet, it is now classified as a centaur object.

1977 The National Aeronautics and Space Administration (NASA) launches Voyager 1 and Voyager 2 space probes toward Jupiter and the outer planets.

1978 American astronomers James Christy (1938–) and Robert Harrington (1942–93) locate Pluto's moon Charon.

1978 NASA's Pioneer Venus space probes reach Venus; the Orbiter goes into orbit around the planet, and the multiprobe drops four probes into the atmosphere.

BIOLOGY & MEDICINE

EUROPE

1977 English biochemist Frederick Sanger (1918–) and coworkers elucidate the first full sequence of deoxyribonucleic acid (DNA) bases (of a virus).

1978 The first "test-tube" baby is born in England.

1979 English biologist James Lovelock (1919–) publishes *Gaia: A New Look at Life on Earth*, in which he hypothesizes that Earth can be regarded as a self-regulating superorganism.

THE AMERICAS

1977 American molecular biologist Phillip Sharp (1944–) and, independently, English-born molecular biologist Richard Roberts (1943–) discover that some genes contain sequences of "nonsense" DNA that appear to have no genetic function. They are named introns. They separate sequences of exons, which do code for part or all of the gene product or for one of its control functions.

1979 The earliest recognized cases of the disease that later becomes known as AIDS occur in California and Florida. In the 1990s examination of medical reports and blood samples suggests that the actual first AIDS case in the United States probably occurred in 1969.

ASIA & OCEANIA

1977 Soviet scientists unearth a baby mammoth that has been frozen in the permafrost of Siberia for 40,000 years.

PHYSICAL SCIENCES

EUROPE

1977 Research chemists in the Soviet Union discover a way of making graphite-free synthetic diamonds directly from methane gas.

1978 German physicist Wolfgang Paul (1913–93) and coworkers trap neutrons in a magnetic storage ring and measure the lifetime of a neutron, which is found to be about 15 minutes.

1979 A group of German physicists announce the discovery of the gluon, a particle postulated to carry the strong nuclear force.

THE AMERICAS

1977 American physicist G. Samuel Hurst (1927–) and coworkers report the use of a laser-based technique to detect a single cesium atom among 1019 argon atoms.

1977 New Zealand-born American chemist Alan MacDiarmid (1927–2007), American chemist Alan Heeger (1936–), and Japanese chemist Hideki Shirakawa (1936–) produce electrically conducting polyethyne (polyacetylene) by incorporating iodine into the plastic's structure.

1977 American physicist Leon Lederman (1922–) identifies the short-lived upsilon particle (a type of meson with a mass about ten times that of the proton).

1978 The U.S. government plans banning lead antiknock additives to gasoline.

1978 The U.S. government bans the use of chlorofluorocarbons (CFCs) as propellants in aerosol cans because they damage the Earth's ozone layer.

INSIDE STORY

AIDS

Acquired immune deficiency syndrome (AIDS) occurs when the immune system is damaged by the human immunodeficiency virus (HIV) and cannot fight infections and cancers. The earliest known cases of HIV and AIDS came from central Africa. Scientists believe that the disease originally was transferred to humans through contact with infected blood from chimpanzees (killed as "bush meat"). AIDS is believed to have reached the United States in the late 1960s via African migrant workers living in the Caribbean island of Haiti. The disease was not identified and named until 1982, although it first came to the attention of U.S. physicians in the late 1970s when groups of gay men began dying of opportunistic infections, pneumonia, and the cancer Kaposi's sarcoma.

Geological change usually takes thousands of years to happen, but we are seeing the climate changing not just in our lifetimes but also year by year.

JAMES LOVELOCK

AFRICA & MIDDLE EAST

ENGINEERING & INVENTION	WORLD EVENTS
1978 The first optical fiber telephone link in Europe goes online between two towns in East Anglia, England.	**1977** Czech dissidents found the prodemocracy Charter 77 reform movement, one of the first organizations to openly challenge government authority in a Warsaw Pact nation.
1979 The British company Post Office Telecommunications introduces the world's first viewdata service, Prestel.	**1979** Margaret Thatcher (1925–) leads the Conservative Party to electoral victory, becoming Britain's first woman prime minister.
1979 The Swedish company Ericsson markets the first cellular telephones (mobile phones); cellphone networks are tested in Tokyo and Chicago.	
1979 Dutch engineer Joop Sinjou of the Philips company and Japanese engineer Toshi Tada Do of Sony independently develop digital compact discs (CDs). Used at first for music and images, they are soon adopted by the computer industry as storage devices.	
1977 American inventor Paul MacCready (1925–2007) wins $95,000 for building a pedal-powered airplane, *Gossamer Condor*. Piloted by American cyclist Bryan Allen (1952–), it makes a 1.15-mile (1.9-km) controlled flight. Allen makes the first human-powered flight across the English Channel in *Gossamer Albatross* two years later.	**1978** In Jonestown, Guyana, 914 members of a religious cult run by the reverend Jim Jones (1938–78), including 260 children, commit suicide by taking poison.
1977 American Interactive Systems Corporation makes the UNIX computer operating system commercially available. (It was first developed in 1969 by American company Bell Laboratories.)	**1979** Nicaraguan dictator Anastasio Somoza Debayle (1925–80) is overthrown after a sustained guerrilla campaign by left-wing Sandinista rebels.
1977 American government scientists develop a neutron bomb. Rather than a powerful explosion, neutron bombs release a massive blast of deadly ionizing radiation.	
1978 The American helium balloon *Double Eagle II*, with three pilots aboard, flies across the Atlantic Ocean.	
1979 An accident at the nuclear plant at Three Mile Island, Pennsylvania, results in a radiation leak.	
1979 The Japanese company Matsushita introduces a liquid-crystal flat-screen television receiver.	**1979** Amid growing civil unrest and economic instability Shah Mohammad Reza Pahlavi (r. 1941–79), who has ruled Iran with the backing of western intelligence agencies since 1941, is forced to step down; the Muslim religious leader Ayatollah Ruhollah Khomeini (1902–89) returns from exile to establish an Islamic state.
1978 The world's longest floating bridge, spanning 6,074 feet (1,851 m), is completed across the Demerara River in Guyana.	**1978** War breaks out between Ethiopia and Somalia over the disputed Ogaden region.

The famous "Blue Marble" photograph taken of Earth on the return voyage of Apollo 17, the last piloted moon mission.

THE APOLLO PROGRAM

In May 1961 American president John F. Kennedy (1917–63) pledged that the United States would land a man on the moon within the next ten years. In July 1969 two American astronauts fulfilled that promise and stepped onto the lunar surface. The spacecraft that took them there—Apollo 11—represented the culmination of an eight-year project, a technological endeavor on a scale never before seen.

The purpose of earlier Apollo missions had been to test the various launch procedures, rockets, and modules before making the final landing. In January 1967 the first planned Apollo flight ended in disaster. Three astronauts died in a fire during a launch-pad test. In early 1968 the National Aeronautics and Space Administration (NASA) made three unpiloted launches. In October 1968 Apollo 7 took three astronauts on a 163-orbit flight around Earth. Two months later Apollo 8 carried three astronauts to the moon, where they made ten orbits. March 1969 saw the testing of the lunar module in Earth orbit by Apollo 9, and later that year in a low orbit around the moon.

Then came Apollo 11. Launched in July 1969 and crewed by Neil Armstrong (1930–), Edwin "Buzz" Aldrin (1930–), and Michael Collins (1930–), it reached the moon without a hitch. Armstrong and Aldrin descended to the surface in the lunar module on July 20 and spent two hours taking photographs and collecting samples. Collins remained in orbit around the moon in the command module.

The Apollo program continued for another six years after Apollo 11 and returned to the moon a further six times before being cancelled in 1975.

CHAPTER 10

THE MODERN WORLD

A maglev, or magnetic levitation, train streaks through Shanghai, in China. Maglev transportation uses powerful magnets to lift and propel trains along the tracks. The vehicles are faster and smoother than conventional trains and can reach speeds of up to 310 miles (500 km) per hour.

SCIENCE AND TECHNOLOGY CONTINUE TO BUILD ON THE KNOWLEDGE accumulated over many centuries, as described in the previous chapters of this book. Astronomy continues to advance with the aid of the Hubble Space Telescope and other instruments placed in Earth orbit by reusable space shuttles. Space travel has become so "routine" that some missions carry fee-paying space "tourists." In physics, scientists carry on searching for superconductors that will function at ever higher temperatures, investigating molecule-sized machines in nanotechnology, and refining solid-state devices to make computers smaller but more powerful.

Physicists at the European Organization for Nuclear Research, known as CERN, are attempting to re-create the conditions just after the big bang at the beginning of the universe with the largest particle accelerator ever built, known as the Large Hadron Collider. Chemists continue to study the effects of greenhouse gases on the atmosphere and to investigate possible links with global warming, while governments around the world pledge to reduce their countries' carbon emissions.

The space shuttle Columbia *touches down at Edwards Air Force Base, in California, after its first orbital mission in 1981. The story of the space shuttle is one of triumph and tragedy. It was involved in some of the National Aeronautics and Space Administration's (NASA) greatest achievements, such as placing the Hubble Space Telescope in Earth orbit, as well as in its two worst disasters, in 1986 and 2003, when all crew members perished.*

In biology, research remains concentrated on cloning animals with a view to finding a source of stem cells for treating various human disorders. The techniques of genetic fingerprinting have been perfected and, thanks to the Human Genome Project, the complete human genome has been published. Biologists have studied sequences of DNA from the remains of extinct animals, such as the dodo, solitaire, woolly mammoth, and even from Neandertals. Gene therapy—the insertion of a functional gene into body cells to replace a faulty version of the gene—is still in its infancy and is seen as controversial by its opponents, but it may hold the promise of treating and curing certain genetic disorders, such as cystic fibrosis. Unfinished business includes the production of vaccines against disorders such as human variant Creutzfeldt–Jakob disease (CJD) and acquired immune deficiency syndrome (AIDS), and the elusive cure for cancer.

Many current developments in technology involve the Internet and the World Wide Web. Personal computers (PCs) have become more and more versatile, enabling people to contact each other and have access to information anywhere in the world almost instantly. Most people now carry cell phones, many of which can be used to send text messages, surf the Internet, play music, and take digital photographs, in addition to verbal communication. And with a modern satellite navigation system, we can pin down a person's location to within a couple of yards. But despite all this, science has so far proved unable to come up with adequate defenses against natural disasters such as tsunamis, tornadoes, and hurricanes.

A highway of cables links routers and servers in an Internet exchange point and data center in Los Angeles. Such facilities are necessary to cope with today's levels of Internet traffic

THE WORLD AT A GLANCE

CONCISE HISTORY OF SCIENCE AND INVENTION

	1980	1984	1988	1992	1996	
EUROPE	**1980** A treatment for kidney stones that uses ultrasound waves to break them up is introduced in Germany. **1980** English engineer Clive Sinclair designs the ZX80 computer. **1981** The high-speed TGV (*Train à Grande Vitesse*) is introduced in France. **1983** French virologist Luc Montagnier and American physician Robert Gallo discover the human immunodeficiency virus (HIV).	**1984** Danish reproductive physiologist Steen Willadsen clones the first mammal, a sheep. **1985** Danish-born computer programmer Bjarne Stroustrup invents the programming language C++. **1986** The Soviet Union launches space station Mir into Earth orbit. **1987** British surgeons in England carry out the first heart/lung/liver triple transplant operation.	**1988** Greek cyclist Kanellos Kanellopoulos pilots a human-powered aircraft across the Aegean Sea. **1991** Researchers in England briefly achieve controlled nuclear fusion. **1990** The two opposite halves of the Channel Tunnel meet under the English Channel. **1990** English computer scientist Tim Berners-Lee begins to devise the World Wide Web.	**1992** Scientists at the University of Pisa, Italy, make the most accurate determination so far of the acceleration of free fall (acceleration due to gravity). **1992** Experimental digital FM radio broadcasts begin in France. **1994** English mathematician Andrew Wiles offers a proof of Fermat's last theorem. **1994** The Channel Tunnel rail link opens between England and France.	**1996** Medical researchers establish a link between bovine spongiform encephalopathy (BSE) and Creutzfeldt–Jakob Disease (CJD). **1996** Scottish biologist Ian Wilmut at the Roslin Institute, Edinburgh, Scotland, clones a sheep named Dolly. **1996** Physicists at the European Organization for Nuclear Research (CERN) in Switzerland produce the first example of antimatter.	
THE AMERICAS	**1980** The Very Large Array (VLA) system of radio telescopes begins operation in New Mexico. **1981** The National Aeronautics and Space Administration's (NASA) first space shuttle, *Columbia*, makes its maiden flight. **1981** IBM Corporation introduces the first personal computer (PC), using MS-DOS (Microsoft disk-operating system). **1982** Eli Lilly & Company produces genetically engineered insulin. **1983** NASA's space probe Pioneer 10 passes Pluto. **1983** American biochemist Kary Mullis invents the polymerase chain reaction (PCR) to multiply small samples of deoxyribonucleic acid (DNA).	**1984** American Microsoft Corporation launches the Windows computer applications program. **1984** American company Apple markets the Macintosh computer, which uses screen icons. **1987** Engineers from American company AT&T install the first fiber-optic telecommunications cable under the Atlantic Ocean. **1985** American researchers isolate the first gene that (when faulty) is responsible for a cancer (retinoblastoma, which affects the eye). **1985** Chemists in the United States produce a new allotrope of carbon called buckminsterfullerene.	**1988** American climatologist James Hansen predicts that increased levels of "greenhouse gases" will lead to global warming. **1989** NASA's Voyager 2 space probe reveals that Neptune has rings. **1989** Boeing company's High Technology Center produces a photocell that converts more than a third of incident solar radiation into electricity. **1990** NASA's space shuttle *Discovery* places the Hubble Space Telescope into orbit around the Earth. **1990** The Human Genome Project gets under way, directed by American biophysicist James Watson.	**1992** Anticancer drug taxol gets official approval in North America. **1993** American physicians introduce gene therapy for cystic fibrosis. **1993** American company Intel markets the Pentium microprocessor chip. **1994** Fragments of comet Shoemaker–Levy 9 are observed colliding with Jupiter. **1994** A genetically modified tomato called Flavr Savr is marketed in the United States. **1994** American scientists announce the discovery of the subatomic particle called the top quark. **1995** American computer programmer James Gosling introduces Java as a programming language.	**1996** NASA's space shuttle *Atlantis*, docks in space with Russian space station Mir. **1996** American astronomer David McKay and coworkers find traces of what might be primitive microscopic life in a meteorite that originated from Mars. **1996** American researchers Theodore Poehler and Peter Searson develop an all-plastic battery. **1997** The Hubble Space Telescope locates the brightest known star in the universe. **1997** American geneticist Huntington Willard assembles an artificial human chromosome.	
ASIA & OCEANIA	**1980** Japanese company Sony Corporation markets the compact disc (CD). **1982** Australian bacteriologist Barry Marshall isolates *Helicobacter pylori*, a cause of stomach ulcer.	**1985** The 33.5-mile (53.9-km) Seikan Tunnel is completed in Japan. **1985** Japanese company Seiko-Epson markets a television set that uses a liquid crystal display for its screen.	**1990** Japanese scientists launch a space probe to the moon. **1991** Japanese researcher Sumio Iijima makes carbon nanotubes.	**1992** Japanese chemists use palladium atoms to make stable polymers of buckyballs. **1994** Japanese rocket engineers launch their new heavy-lifting rocket, H-2.	**1996** Japanese research chemists synthesize cellulose. **1997** Paleontologists in China discover fossils of *Protarchaeopteryx*, a reptilian creature with birdlike characteristics.	
AFRICA & THE MIDDLE EAST	**1983** English-born Kenyan anthropologist Meave Leakey finds fossils of 16-million-old hominoid *Silvapithecus*.	**1984** Kenyan anthropologist Richard Leakey and coworkers find a 1.6-million-old skeleton of *Homo erectus*. **1984** Israeli physicists produce quasicrystals.	**1988** Israel makes its first successful space launch. **1988** Anthropologists discover a 92,000-year-old fossil of *Homo sapiens* in Israel.	**1993** Anthropologists from Berkeley discover remains of the oldest known hominoid, *Ardipithecus ramidus*. **1994** A new Ebola virus is identified in Africa.		

1998 | 2000 | 2002 | 2004 | 2006–PRESENT

1998	2000	2002	2004	2006–PRESENT
1998 A team of international scientists determines the entire genetic code, or genome, for a nematode. **1998** Swiss scientists produce a titanium dioxide solar cell that is twice as efficient as standard solar cells. **1999** Swiss balloonist Bertrand Piccard and English balloonist Brian Jones circumnavigate the world in their hot-air balloon, *Breitling Orbiter 3*.	**2000** Russia launches a service module that together with two other modules already in orbit form the new International Space Station (ISS). **2000** The world's longest road tunnel (15.2 miles/24.5 km) is completed in Norway. **2000** The Pyrenean ibex becomes extinct. **2001** Gray wolves are found living wild in Germany (they have not been seen in the wild for 150 years).	**2002** English inventor David Baker patents the Land Shark, a high-speed amphibious car. **2003** Austrian sportsman Felix Baumgartner jumps from an airplane and skyglides across the English Channel. **2003** 350,000-year-old footprints of an upright-walking human are discovered in Italy. **2003** Chemist Leonid Khryashtchev makes an organic compound that contains krypton.	**2005** Scientists extract and decode DNA from two cave bears that died 40,000 years ago. **2005** After a seven-year trip, the Cassini–Huygens space probe—a joint venture between the European Space Agency and NASA—reaches Saturn. **2005** European consortium Airbus Industrie's Airbus 380 makes its maiden flight from Toulouse, France.	**2007** A 405-year-old clam is discovered by Welsh researchers off the coast of Ireland. **2008** Researchers in England create human–cow embryos, which survive for three days. **2008** The Large Hadron Collider at CERN begins its experiments.
1998 Zoologists discover five new species of small salamanders in Mexico. **1998** American researchers at Johns Hopkins University successfully grow human stem cells in the laboratory. **1998** Astronomers in Hawaii discover a near-Earth asteroid that passes within the Earth's orbit. **1998** American dentists first use lasers for "drilling" teeth. **1999** Computer virus Melissa spreads rapidly by e-mail to infect more than 100,000 computers around the world. **1999** The Hubble Space Telescope is serviced by astronauts in the space shuttle *Discovery*.	**2000** Scientists working on the Human Genome Project produce a rough draft of the sequence of the human genome. **2000** American paleontologist Dale Russell discovers a fossilized dinosaur heart. **2000** Geneticists figure out the complete genome of the fruit fly *Drosophila*. **2000** American surgeon Robert Jarvik begins work on the Jarvik–2000 artificial heart. **2001** The uncrewed *Southern Cross II* (Global Hawk spy plane) crosses the Pacific Ocean. **2001** American researchers clone a human embryo.	**2002** NASA's space probe Mars Odyssey begins mapping the surface of Mars. **2002** Researchers at Texas A&M University unveil their clone of a domestic cat. **2002** American researchers at the University of New York at Stony Brook make a synthetic virus. **2002** American chemists Lester Andrews and Bruce Bersten make a compound of uranium and the rare gas neon. **2003** NASA's Wilkinson Microwave Anisotropy Probe satellite analyzes microwave background radiation to reveal that the universe is 13.7 billion years old.	**2004** The first commercial spaceflight occurs when SpaceShipOne takes to the air. **2004** Physicists from Penn State University announce a helium-based "supersolid" that flows through another material without friction. **2005** American geophysicist Joseph Dwyer and coworkers discover that flashes of lighting also produce x-rays. **2005** Astronomer Michael Brown announces the discovery of a large remote object (Eris) in the solar system. **2005** American scientists make the smallest measurement of mass ever made when they weigh a cluster of xenon atoms.	**2006** The dwarf planet Eris is found to be larger than Pluto. **2006** NASA's spacecraft New Horizons is launched on its journey to Pluto. **2006** Analysis of a fossil found in Canada shows it to be a "missing link" between fish and four-legged vertebrates. **2007** A chlorophyll-producing bacterium is discovered in hot springs at Yellowstone National Park. **2007** U.S scientists create flexible batteries by weaving carbon nanotubes into paper.
1998 The world's largest passenger airport opens in Hong Kong, China. **1998** Two Japanese satellites in Earth orbit carry out the first automatic docking.	**2000** Japanese chemist Katsuyoshi Hoshino and coworkers announce a new way of "fixing" nitrogen in air to produce ammonium perchlorate.	**2003** Yang Liwei becomes the first Chinese astronaut to orbit the Earth. **2003** An outbreak of the severe acute respiratory syndrome (SARS) virus in Asia spreads worldwide.	**2004** Scientists in South Korea clone human embryos for stem cells. **2004** An 18,000-year-old skeleton of a 3-foot (1-m) tall humanoid is found in Indonesia. It is named *Homo floresiensis*.	**2007** The Baiji, or Chinese river dolphin, is now thought to be extinct. **2008** The Indian Space Research Organization launches Chandrayaan-1, an unpiloted lunar spacecraft.
1998 A whole skeleton of a 36-foot (11-m) fish-eating dinosaur is found in Niger, Africa.		**2003** A new group of insects, named Mantophasmatodea, is discovered in Africa.	**2005** Two new species of mouse lemurs are found in Madagascar.	

ASTRONOMY & MATH	BIOLOGY & MEDICINE	PHYSICAL SCIENCES

EUROPE

1980 French astronomers Pierre Laques (1934–), Raymond Despiau, and Jean Lecacheux (1944–) discover Helene, a small moon of Saturn that takes only 2.7 days to orbit the planet.

1980 Russian cosmonauts from the Soyuz 35 spacecraft set an endurance record by spending 185 days aboard the orbiting Salyut 6 space station.

1980 German company Dornier Medical Systems announces a treatment for kidney stones that uses ultrasound waves to break them up painlessly inside the patient. The technique, called ultrasonic lithotripsy, replaces the need for intrusive surgery.

1980 German physicist Klaus von Klitzing (1943–) discovers the quantum Hall effect, in which the production of a voltage in material carrying a current in a magnetic field at very low temperatures takes place in "steps" rather than continuously.

THE AMERICAS

1980 Data from the National Aeronautics and Space Administration's (NASA) Voyager 1 space probe enable American astronomers to identify Saturn's moons Pandora, Prometheus, Telesto, Atlas, and Calypso.

1980 Polish-born American mathematician Benoit Mandelbrot (1924–) continues his research into fractals, which are mathematical curves generated by successive subdivision.

1980 The Very Large Array (VLA), a system of 27 radio telescopes at Socorro, New Mexico, begins operation.

1981 American astronomer Joseph Cassinelli and coworkers identify the star R136a, which is 2,500 times more massive than the sun.

1981 American astronomer Harold Reitsema and coworkers identify Neptune's inner moon Larissa.

1981 NASA's first space shuttle, *Columbia*, makes its maiden flight, proving that a reusable spacecraft is feasible.

1981 NASA's space probe Voyager 2 flies by Saturn and sends back pictures of the planet and its moons.

1980 American experimental physicist Luis Alvarez (1911–88) and his son Walter (1940–), a geologist, put forward the theory that a meteorite collision with Earth gave rise to the K-T event, which probably led to the extinction of the dinosaurs.

1980 American researchers at Harvard synthesize interferon, a substance that shows promise as a treatment for viral diseases and some forms of cancer.

1980 The U.S. Supreme Court rules that genetically engineered life-forms can be patented.

1981 Researchers at the Merck Institute for Therapeutic Research, Pennsylvania, produce a vaccine against the hepatitis-B virus.

1981 The American Center for Disease Control and Prevention (CDC) first acknowledges acquired immune deficiency syndrome (AIDS) as a communicable disease.

1980 A device called an undulator is installed in the SPEAR storage ring of Stanford Radiation Laboratory's synchrotron to increase its power.

1981 Romanian-born American physicist Adam Heller (1933–) and American Ferdinand Thiel (1933–) construct a liquid-junction solar cell.

ASIA & OCEANIA

AFRICA & THE MIDDLE EAST

The Very Large Array in New Mexico combines 27 radio telescopes in a Y-shaped configuration.

ENGINEERING & INVENTION	WORLD EVENTS
1980 The 10-mile (16-km) St. Gotthard Tunnel in Switzerland is opened, making it the world's longest road tunnel. **1980** English engineer Clive Sinclair (1940–) designs an inexpensive computer, the ZX80. **1981** French railway company SNCF introduces its new high-speed train, the TGV (*Train à Grande Vitesse*). **1981** *Solar Challenger*, a solar-powered aircraft, crosses the English Channel. **1981** The 4,626-foot- (1,410-m-) long suspension bridge across the Humber River in northeastern England becomes the world's longest single-span bridge.	**1980** President Tito of Yugoslavia (1892–1980) dies. **1980** Polish workers led by Lech Walesa (1943–) establish the independent Solidarity trade union; the organization will play a pioneering role in the downfall of communism in Eastern Europe. **1980** The Summer Olympics in Moscow are boycotted by 50 nations, including the United States, in protest at the Soviet invasion of Afghanistan. **1981** Pope John Paul II (1920–2005) is seriously injured by a gunman in St. Peter's Square, Rome.
1980 Microsoft Corporation, founded by Bill Gates (1955–) and Paul Allen (1953–), develops MS–DOS (Microsoft disk-operating system), a computer operating system, and licenses it to IBM Corporation. **1980** American company Hughes Aircraft makes a machine that uses a laser for cutting cloth, reducing costs for the mass production of garments. **1981** American company Hewlett-Packard launches a 32-bit silicon chip for its computers. **1981** IBM Corporation introduces the first personal computer (PC), using Microsoft's MS-DOS operating system. Within a year Compaq and Columbia Data Products produce "clones," machines that will run the same programs as the IBM.	**1980** Former Hollywood actor Ronald Reagan (1911–2004) defeats Jimmy Carter (1924–) in the race for the White House; Carter's reelection chances are seriously damaged by the disastrous failure of a mission to rescue U.S. hostages held in Iran. **1980** Bolivia is taken over by a military junta backed by cocaine barons. **1980** More than 120,000 Cubans are allowed to immigrate to the United States. **1980** Ex-Beatle John Lennon (1940–80) is shot and killed by an obsessed fan in New York. **1980** MTV begins transmission on U.S. television.
1980 A wind-assisted commercial vessel, the *Shin-Aitoku-Maru*, is launched in Japan. It has computer-controlled vertical sails. **1980** The Japanese Sony Corporation and Dutch company Philips market the audio compact disc (CD) for commercial use. Later (1985) it is adapted as the CD-ROM.	**1980** Japan becomes the world leader in manufacturing, surpassing the United States as the leading automaker. It also has eight out of the ten largest banks in the world. **1981** Sikhs begin fighting for independence in the Punjab.
	1980 The Iran–Iraq War (1980–88) breaks out. **1980** Zimbabwe gains independence under Robert Mugabe (1924–). **1981** President of Egypt Anwar el-Sadat (1918–1981) is assassinated.

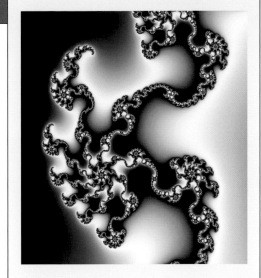

BENOIT MANDELBROT

Benoit Mandelbrot (1924–) is a Polish-born American mathematician who is best known for developing fractals. He was born in Warsaw, the son of a Lithuanian Jewish merchant, but moved with his family to Paris in 1936 to escape persecution by the Nazis. Forced to move again in 1939, they lived in Tulle in southern France during World War II. Despite a very patchy education, after the war Mandelbrot attended the École Polytechnique in Paris, and in 1952 obtained his doctorate from the University of Paris.

After several brief appointments in the United States, Switzerland, and France, Mandelbrot went in 1958 to the IBM Research Center, at Yorktown Heights, New York. He remained there until 1987, when he became professor of mathematics at Yale. He developed the idea of fractals while considering how to measure the length of a coastline. Every inlet has smaller inlets, which also have tiny inlets of their own. He pointed out that tree bark is not smooth, and mountains are not perfect cones, so how do you measure them? He outlined his ideas (first developed in 1980) in his 1982 book *The Fractal Geometry of Nature*. Fractals have applications in various areas of science (such as the growth of crystals), in chaos theory, in cartography, and in computer graphics.

	ASTRONOMY & MATH	BIOLOGY & MEDICINE	PHYSICAL SCIENCES

EUROPE

1982 Soviet Venera 13 and Venera 14 space probes reach Venus and release landers that collect data as they descend through the corrosive atmosphere.

1982 Soviet cosmonaut Svetlana Savitskaya (1948–), in a Soyuz spacecraft, becomes the second woman in space, 19 years after Valentina Tereshkova (1937–) orbited the Earth.

1983 The Soviet Venera 15 space probe reaches Venus and orbits the planet, using a radar scanner to map the surface.

1982 Biologist Karl Stetter (1941–) discovers bacteria living in hot seawater near black smokers on the seabed.

1982 Biochemists Louis Chedid and Michael Sela (1924–) prepare the first totally synthetic vaccine (against diphtheria).

1983 French virologist Luc Montagnier (1932–) and American physician Robert Gallo (1937–) discover the human immunodeficiency virus (HIV) that causes AIDS.

1983 Swiss biologist Walter Gehring (1939–) and coworkers discover the homeobox gene —a sequence of about 180 base pairs common to most eukaryote organisms— that controls their development.

1982 German physicist Peter Armbruster (1931–) and coworkers at the Institute for Heavy Ion Research in Darmstadt, Germany, make a few atoms of element 109 (later named meitnerium) by bombarding bismuth-209 with nuclei of iron-58.

1983 The meter is redefined in terms of the distance light travels in a vacuum in a particular time (1/299,792,458 of a second).

1983 Italian physicist Carlo Rubbia (1934–) and coworkers discover W and Z particles (belonging to the group known as intermediate vector bosons and carriers of the weak force).

THE AMERICAS

1982 American astronomer Eleanor Helin discovers the slow-moving, near-Earth asteroid Nereus (asteroid 4660).

1982 The National Aeronautics and Space Administration's (NASA) space shuttle *Columbia* is first used for commercial purposes on its fifth mission, when it places two communications satellites into Earth orbit.

1983 Data from the Infrared Astronomical Satellite (IRAS) reveals a new asteroid (no. 3200) that passes close to the sun. It is named Phaethon and is the first asteroid to be discovered by instruments in space.

1983 American mathematicians Leonard Adleman (1945–) and Robert Rumely announce a new way of finding prime numbers (numbers that can be divided only by 1 and themselves).

1983 NASA's space probe Pioneer 10 passes Pluto and becomes the first human-made object to leave the solar system.

1983 U.S. astronaut Sally Ride (1951–) becomes the first American woman in space.

1983 NASA launches its second space shuttle, *Challenger*.

1982 Eli Lilly & Company begins producing genetically engineered insulin (used in the treatment of diabetes).

1982 American biochemist Stanley Prusiner (1942–) introduces the term *prions* to describe the infective agents responsible for scrapie and other spongiform encephalopathy diseases such as Creutzfeldt–Jakob Disease.

1982 American physician William DeVries (1943–) and coworkers in Salt Lake City, Utah, implant the first Jarvik-7 artificial heart (made of aluminum and plastic); the patient lives for 112 days. The use of the Jarvik heart is discontinued in 1990.

1983 American biochemist Kary Mullis (1944–) invents the polymerase chain reaction (PCR), a method of multiplying small samples of DNA (deoxyribonucleic acid) that will become important in genetic fingerprinting.

1983 The immunosuppressive drug cyclosporine is approved for use in the United States, making transplant operations much safer. Three years later Japanese researchers discover an alternative immunosuppressive—FK506—produced by a fungus.

Sally Ride, the first American woman in space, was one of the five crew of the space shuttle Challenger's *second flight.*

ASIA & OCEANIA

1982 Australian bacteriologist Barry Marshall (1951–) isolates and cultures *Helicobacter pylori*, a bacterium that causes peptic ulcers.

It's easy to sleep floating around—it's very comfortable. But you have to be careful that you don't float into somebody or something!

AFRICA & THE MIDDLE EAST

1983 English-born Kenyan anthropologist Meave Leakey (1942–) finds fossils of the hominoid *Sivapithecus*, dated at about 16 million years old.

SALLY RIDE

ENGINEERING & INVENTION	WORLD EVENTS
1982 The Thames Barrier is completed downstream of London, England. Normally lowered to allow the passage of shipping, it can be raised if exceptionally high tides threaten to cause flooding in the city. It is raised for the first time the following year. **1983** English driver Richard Noble (1946–) takes the land speed record at 633.468 miles (1,019.44 km) per hour in his jet car *Thrust 2* at Black Rock Desert, Nevada.	**1983** Buoyed by success in the Falklands War (1982), Britain's Prime Minister Margaret Thatcher (1925–) wins a landslide general election victory. **1983** The United States deploys Cruise missiles in Britain and Pershing missiles in West Germany.

CELL PHONES

The development of cellular telephones and their associated technology has been rapid since the 1980s. The cellular telephone network divides a geographical area into cells. Because cell phones and base stations use low-power transmitters, the same frequencies (indicated by matching colors in the diagram below) can be reused in nonadjacent cells. At first, all transmissions were analog (meaning that signals were sent as a continuous stream or wave). From about 1990 service providers began to use digital technology, which breaks up the wave and sends it in short bursts that are better suited to carry data quickly and without distortion.

Early cell phones were heavy and bulky. The first truly portable commercial cell phone was produced by Motorola in 1983 and weighed 16 ounces (450 g). The latest phones now weigh as little as 3 ounces (85 g). Most modern cell phones have other uses than just as a means of verbal communication. These include text messaging (texting), taking photographs and videos (and sending and receiving them), sending and receiving emails, playing music, and accessing the Internet.

ENGINEERING & INVENTION	WORLD EVENTS
1982 Engineers in California complete Solar One, the world's largest solar power plant, which can produce 10 megawatts of electric power. **1982** American computer programmer Mitchell Kapor (1950–) founds the American Lotus Corporation and produces the Lotus 1-2-3 software. **1983** In the United States the first mobile telephones, or cellphones, are introduced in Chicago, Illinois. **1983** American IBM Corporation launches the PC-XT, a personal computer with a built-in 10-megabyte hard disk drive. **1983** American company Apple markets a consumer computer that uses a mouse and pull down menus. **1983** The 4,150-foot- (1,265-m-) long dam across the American River in California becomes the world's largest thin-arch dam. **1983** Japanese physicist Akio Sasaki invents an optical transistor.	**1982** Argentina and Britain go to war over sovereignty of the Falkland Islands (Malvinas) and South Georgia; the British forces prevail. **1983** U.S. Marines are sent to Grenada to reverse a leftist military coup.

The Thames Barrier, completed in 1982, can be raised to prevent high tides from the North Sea from flooding London, England.

ENGINEERING & INVENTION	WORLD EVENTS
	1982 Israel occupies Lebanon. **1983** Drought in Ethiopia results in millions of deaths through starvation.

PERSONAL COMPUTERS

THE PERSONAL COMPUTER (PC) IS A FAMILIAR item in many homes all over the world. People use PCs to play games, write letters, and manage domestic and business accounts. E-mail takes only seconds to deliver messages and pictures to the other side of the globe. PCs are used to shop, make travel arrangements, book hotels, and buy theater and concert tickets. It is hard to imagine a world without PCs.

Yet PCs are relatively new. The first fully electronic computer was built in 1946 at the University of Pennsylvania. Called ENIAC (Electronic Numerical Integrator and Calculator), it contained 18,000 vacuum tubes and used 100 kilowatts of power.

All the early computers used vacuum tubes, or valves. Those machines were so huge that they filled a large room, and so unreliable (because of tube failures) that teams of engineers had to remain constantly on hand to keep them working. The invention of the transistor in 1947 offered a smaller, more dependable replacement for the vacuum tube, and the invention of the integrated circuit in 1958 opened up the possibility of miniaturization. Computers began to shrink in size.

IBM launched its first personal computer in 1981. The IBM PC 5150 was fitted with an Intel 8088 microprocessor. The machine used magnetic tape to load data and had an optional floppy disk drive and printer.

Even so, it was not until 1975 that a computer appeared that was both affordable and small enough to use at home. Micro Instrumentation and Telemetry Systems (MITS) of Albuquerque, New Mexico, sold the Altair 8800 for $495 assembled, and in kit form for just $395. The Altair 8800 measured 17 x 18 x 7 inches (43 x 46 x 18 cm) and was based on a 2-MHz Intel 8080 processor. It had no monitor, keyboard, or printer and only 256 bytes of memory. The user programmed it by means of switches along the front of the box, and read the output from a pattern of flashing lights on a front panel. In 1976 MITS equipped their computers with an 8-inch (20-cm) floppy-disk drive for storing data.

Operating Systems

Computer software—the programs that run useful applications such as word processing or games—will work only if the computer is able to communicate with a storage device such as a disk drive. This process requires special software in the form of an operating system. In 1972 American computer scientist Gary Kildall (1942–94) devised PL/M (Programming Language/Microprocessor). It allowed engineers to write programs that were burned into the ROM (read-only memory) of the Intel 4004 processor. These processors were used to control devices such as traffic lights and domestic appliances such as washing machines. The following year Kildall wrote software that allowed the user to read data files stored on a disk and write files onto the disk. He called it CP/M (Control Program/Microcomputer), and it was the first operating system for small computers. CP/M was instantly successful, but when International Business Machines Corporation (IBM) needed an operating system for its

small computers, the company offered both CP/M and DOS (Disk Operating System). DOS was a rival system developed by American computer programmer Bill Gates (1955–) of Microsoft in 1980. As MS-DOS, the Microsoft operating system eventually came to dominate the market, although some computer enthusiasts still use CP/M. WordStar, launched in 1979, was the first popular word-processing program. At first, it ran on CP/M, although later versions ran on MS-DOS.

Affordable Computers

Computers remained expensive, however, until 1980, when English engineer Clive Sinclair (1940–) designed the ZX80. In the United States it cost $199.95 ready made. The ZX80 measured about 8 x 8 inches (20 x 20 cm), had 1 kilobyte of RAM (random-access memory), and a membrane keyboard. It connected to a TV receiver. Sinclair followed the ZX80 a year later with the ZX81. It used audio cassette tapes for storage.

IBM introduced its first small computer in 1981, calling it a "personal computer" (PC). Within a year

In a modern computer, backup memory is stored on hard disks inside the disk drive. A large memory store consists of a stack of hard disks, mounted on the same spindle and accessed simultaneously.

Disks can rotate at speeds of 100 miles (160 km) per hour or more. Data is stored as magnetic fields in areas of the disk as small as 40 millionths of an inch (1 micrometer) across.

A read/write head is mounted on the end of a carriage. It swings in and out across each disk as required. The head "flies" a few millionths of an inch above the disk surface.

or two, rival manufacturers were marketing cheaper imitations, known as "IBM clones." All of them resembled the IBM PC and used MS-DOS. Modern PCs are the direct descendants of those "clones."

Computers respond to instructions in machine code written in binary, and a computer program comprises page after page of zeros and ones. Machine code is difficult to write and check for errors. Computer programmers needed a simpler code. The first of them became available in 1957. It had been devised by American programmer John Backus (1924–2007) at IBM and was called FORTRAN (FORmula TRANslator). It was the first high-level programming language, but it was designed for scientists. Teachers still needed a language that students could master easily, and in 1964 American computer programmers John Kemeny (1926–92) and Thomas Kurtz (1928–) at Dartmouth College, New Hampshire, announced their solution to the problem: the Beginner's All-Purpose Symbolic Instruction Code, or BASIC.

The power of a PC depends on the speed of its processor and the amount of memory it has. Both have increased rapidly, and are still doing so, allowing modern computers to perform tasks far beyond the capacity of their predecessors. The first multimedia PC appeared in 1991, and English computer scientist Tim Berners-Lee (1955–) created the World Wide Web in 1990. Broadband Web access now allows users to download music and movies.

The Altair 8800 of 1975 was the forerunner of today's personal computers. Advertised to enthusiasts through Popular Electronics magazine, its designers envisaged sales of a few hundred. However, it proved so popular that they sold more than ten times that number within one month.

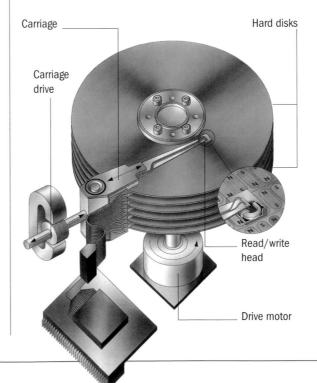

Carriage

Carriage drive

Hard disks

Read/write head

Drive motor

ASTRONOMY & MATH

1984 Soviet cosmonaut Svetlana Savitskaya (1948–) becomes the first woman to walk in space, on a Soyuz mission.

1985 The Soviet Union launches its first two-stage Zenit rocket. By 2001 this type of rocket launches a total of 28 satellites into orbit around Earth.

1984 Astronomers at the European Southern Observatory in Chile discover that Neptune has a partial ring system.

1984 American astronaut Bruce McCandless (1937–) makes the first untethered space walk, from the space shuttle *Challenger*.

1985 Astronomers at Cornell University report eight infrared galaxies revealed by the Infrared Astronomical Satellite (IRAS).

1985 Images from the National Aeronautical and Space Administration's (NASA) Voyager 2 reveal Puck, the largest of the inner moons of Uranus. It is named for a mischievous sprite of folklore.

1985 NASA's space probe International Cometary Explorer (ICE) flies through the tail of comet Giacobini–Zinner. A year later it flies by Halley's comet.

1985 NASA launches its fourth space shuttle, *Atlantis*.

1984 Indian astronomer J. Bhattacharyya (1950–) and team observe two new rings of Saturn when they occlude (block the light from) a distant star.

BIOLOGY & MEDICINE

1984 The 2,000-year-old body of Celtic "Lindow Man" is found preserved in a peat bog in northern England.

1984 Danish reproductive physiologist Steen Willadsen (1944–) clones the first mammal, a sheep, using the nucleus of an embryonic sheep cell.

1984 English geneticist Alec Jeffreys (1950–) perfects the technique of genetic fingerprinting, which involves identifying sequences of deoxyribonucleic acid (DNA).

1985 The first case of the disease bovine spongiform encephalopathy (BSE) is diagnosed in cattle in Britain.

1984 American anthropologist Andrew Hill finds a fossil jawbone of the hominid *Australopithecus afarensis* in Kenya.

1984 American biologist Robert Sinsheimer proposes the Human Genome Project.

1985 American researchers isolate the first gene that (when it malfunctions) is responsible for a type of cancer called retinoblastoma (a malignant tumor affecting the eye).

This Cray 2 supercomputer installed at NASA's Ames Research Center, Moffett Field, California, had a memory capacity of 2 billion bytes and contained about 240,000 computer chips.

HOW THINGS WORK
Genetic Fingerprinting
Genetic fingerprinting is the name commonly given to the technique of identifying sequences of nucleotides along a molecule of deoxyribonucleic acid (DNA). This pattern is unique to each individual because no two people have identical DNA (aside from identical twins). As a result, the technique can be used as a method of identification, for example, in forensic examinations. Scientists obtain the DNA from small samples of body tissue, such as blood, saliva, hair, sperm, or cells scraped from the inside of the mouth.

1984 Kenyan anthropologist Richard Leakey (1944–) and coworkers, working near Lake Turkana in northern Kenya, discover the 1.6-million-year old skeleton of *Homo erectus* (nicknamed "Turkana boy").

PHYSICAL SCIENCES

1984 German physicist Peter Armbruster (1931–) and coworkers at the Institute for Heavy Ion Research in Darmstadt, Germany, using a linear accelerator, produce atoms of element 108 (hassium) by bombarding lead-208 with nuclei of iron-58. Russian scientists at Dubna, Moscow, also produce hassium by the same method.

1985 Several chemists, including Robert Curl (1933–) and Richard Smalley (1943–2005) in the United States, produce a new allotrope of carbon called buckminsterfullerene (also known as "buckyballs").

1984 An accidental escape of toxic methyl isocyanate from the Union Carbide pesticide plant in Bhopal, India, kills thousands of people.

1984 Israeli physicist Dany Shechtman (1941–) and coworkers produce quasicrystals, which are solids with some long-range internal order but lacking the symmetry of true crystals.

EUROPE · THE AMERICAS · ASIA & OCEANIA · AFRICA & THE MIDDLE EAST

ENGINEERING & INVENTION	WORLD EVENTS

1985 A Concorde supersonic airliner flies from London, England, to Sydney, Australia, in the record time of 17 hours, 3 minutes.

1985 German physicist Gerd Binnig (1947–) and coworkers develop the atomic force microscope.

1985 Danish-born computer programmer Bjarne Stroustrup (1950–) at Bell Laboratories invents C++, a high-level computer programming language.

1985 British company Inmos introduces the T414 transputer (for use in parallel computers).

1984 American physicist Dennis Matthews invents an x-ray wavelength laser.

1984 American Microsoft Corporation launches the Windows computer applications program for the IBM PC and compatible computers.

1984 American company Apple markets the Macintosh computer, which uses screen icons, a mouse, and a graphical user interface.

1985 American undersea explorer Robert Ballard (1942–) uses the remote-controlled robot Argo to film the wreck of S.S. *Titanic*, the British liner that sank on its maiden voyage in 1912 after hitting an iceberg in the North Atlantic Ocean.

1985 American company Adobe Systems introduces PostScript, a page-description computer language.

1985 American company Cray Research markets the Cray-2 supercomputer, followed three years later by the twice-as-fast Cray Y-MP.

1985 The world's longest railroad tunnel, the 33.5-mile (53.9-km) Seikan Tunnel, is completed between the islands of Honshu and Hokkaido in Japan.

1985 Japanese company Seiko-Epson markets a small television set that uses a liquid crystal display for its screen.

1984 More than a million marchers force the French government to abandon its challenge to the independence of religious schools.

1985 Mikhail Gorbachev (1931–) comes to power in the Soviet Union following the death of Konstantin Chernenko; Gorbachev adopts a reformist agenda based on *glasnost* (openness) and *perestroika* (reconstruction).

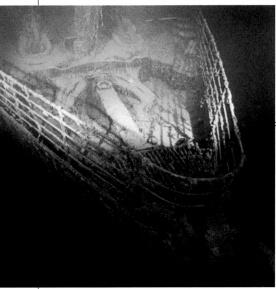

Underwater explorer Robert Ballard located the wreck of the Titanic *in 1985. The ship lay at a depth of 12,000 feet (3,660 m) off the coast of Newfoundland.*

1984 A group of top popular music artists come together as U.S.A. for Africa to record the song "We Are The World," written by Michael Jackson (1958–) and Lionel Richie (1949–). The record is sold to raise funds for drought and famine victims in Ethiopia.

1984 Indian troops storm the Golden Temple, a Sikh holy site at Amritsar, where armed militants seeking an independent Punjab ("Khalistan") have taken refuge; more than 700 rebels are killed.

1984 India's premier Indira Gandhi (1917–84) is assassinated by members of her bodyguard.

1984 A famine strikes Ethiopia and Sudan in East Africa, claiming about 100,000 lives. In 1985 Live Aid rock concerts in Philadelphia, London, Moscow, and Sydney raise $60 million for famine victims.

OZONE LAYER AND CFCs

Ozone (O_3) is a molecule that consists of three oxygen atoms. (Such molecules are called triatomic.) It is less stable than diatomic oxygen (O_2), which is the most common form of the gas in the air at ground level. Ground-level ozone is a pollutant, and high levels can damage the respiratory system of animals. In the upper atmosphere—between 6 and 31 miles (10–50 km) above Earth's surface—a layer of ozone blocks harmful ultraviolet (UV) radiation produced by the sun.

The ozone layer was discovered in 1913 by French physicists Charles Fabry (1867–1945) and Henri Buisson (1873–1944). British meteorologist G. M. B. Dobson (1889–1976) began to monitor ozone levels in the late 1920s.

In 1985, British scientists working in Antarctica reported a 40-percent depletion of ozone in the layer over the continent. Monitoring of the depletion has led to a worldwide phase-out of chemicals called chlorofluorocarbons (CFCs). These chemicals, invented by American chemist Thomas Midgley (1889–1944) in 1928, are mainly used as refrigerants. Once released into the atmosphere, CFCs slowly diffuse up to the ozone layer. There, UV rays from the sun cause them to react with ozone, breaking it down. This leads to a higher amount of UV reaching ground level, increasing the risk of skin cancer.

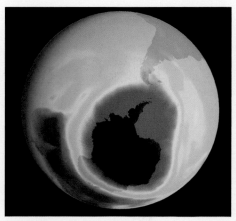

The purple area shows the ozone hole above the South Pole, in Antarctica.

315

ASTRONOMY & MATH	BIOLOGY & MEDICINE	PHYSICAL SCIENCES

EUROPE

1986 The Soviet Union launches space station Mir into Earth orbit. It becomes the first permanently crewed space station.

1986 European Space Agency's (ESA) probe Giotto passes within 375 miles (600 km) of Halley's comet. The same year a Japanese probe passes within 93,210 miles (150,000 km) of the comet and Soviet probes pass within about 5,280 miles (8,500 km).

1987 Soviet cosmonaut Yuri Romanenko (1944–) returns to Earth after a record 326 days in space station Mir.

1987 The British-Dutch William Herschel Telescope is completed at Roque de los Muchachos Observatory in the Canary Islands. The 13.8-foot (4.2-m) reflecting telescope is fitted with spectroscopes and cameras.

1987 British surgeons John Wallwork and Roy Calne (1930–) at Papworth Hospital, Cambridge, England, carry out the first heart/lung/liver triple transplant operation. The patient survives for ten years.

1987 German zoologist Hans Fricke uses a submersible to observe coelacanths (*Latimeria chalumnae*)—for a long time thought to be extinct—swimming in their natural habitat deep in the Indian Ocean.

1986 German physicist Georg Bednorz (1950–) and Swiss physicist Alex Müller (1927–) make "high-temperature" superconductors that function at 35 K (–460.67°F; –238.15° C). In 1987 Chinese physicist Ching-Wu Chu (1941–) and coworkers make one that superconducts at 98 K (–347.27°F; –175.15°C).

1986 An explosion at the Chernobyl nuclear reactor in the Ukraine releases radioactivity that produces widespread poisonous fallout in Europe and the Soviet Union.

1987 German chemist Herbert Naarmann and coworkers make an electrically conducting plastic by "doping" polyethyne (polyacetylene) with iodine.

THE AMERICAS

1986 More data from the National Aeronautical and Space Administration's (NASA) Voyager 2 reveal a new set of inner moons of Uranus, named Belinda, Cordelia, Cressida, Desdemona, Juliet, Ophelia, and Portia (after Shakespearian characters).

1986 NASA's space shuttle *Challenger* explodes soon after launch, killing all seven crew members.

1986 NASA's space probe Voyager 2 flies by Uranus.

1987 Canadian astronomer Ian Shelton (1958–) discovers the supernova SN1987A in the Large Magellanic Cloud galaxy, the brightest since 1604.

1987 Astronomer R. Brent Tully announces his discovery of the Pisces–Cetus supercluster of galaxies, the largest feature so far found in the Universe.

1986 American pharmacologist Louis Ignarro (1941–) identifies the substance EDRF (endothelium-derived relaxing factor)—named in 1980 by American pharmacologist Robert Furchgott (1916–)—as nitric oxide.

1986 American geneticist Louis Kunkel (1949–) identifies a gene for Duchenne muscular dystrophy.

1986 American biotechnology company Agracetus carries out field trials of genetically engineered tobacco.

1986 Physician Fred Turck introduces the use of diazepine tranquilizers, soon to become some of the most prescribed drugs in Western society.

1987 The last wild Californian condor (*Gymnogyps californianus*) is captured and placed in a breeding program.

1987 Paleontologist Kevin Aulenback finds a "nest" of fossilized dinosaur eggs in Alberta, Canada. In the same year American paleontologist Wade Miller discovers a 150-million-year-old dinosaur egg containing a fossilized embryo (detected by x-rays).

1986 Physicists at Lawrence Livermore National Laboratory in the United States bring about laser-induced nuclear fusion.

1987 American physicists discover the longest-lived radioisotope found so far, selenium-32, with a half-life of 1.1×10^{20} years.

In 1986 the world's fishing nations introduced a world ban on killing whales (with a few exceptions for traditional societies).

ASIA & OCEANIA

AFRICA & THE MIDDLE EAST

The first disposable or single-use cameras were marketed in 1987.

ENGINEERING & INVENTION	WORLD EVENTS
1986 European consortium Airbus Industrie announces the Airbus A320, the first commercial aircraft to use "fly-by-wire" (computer-controlled) technology. **1986** English businessman Richard Branson (1950–) makes a record-breaking trip across the Atlantic Ocean in his speedboat *Virgin Atlantic Challenger II.* **1987** Richard Branson and Swedish aeronautical engineer Per Lindstrand (1948–) make the first crossing of the Atlantic Ocean in a hot-air balloon, *Virgin Atlantic Flyer.* **1987** French company Agrotechnic devises a process for making a synthetic milk substitute from soybeans.	**1986** Spain and Portugal join the European Community, bringing the membership to 12 countries (Greece having joined in 1981). **1987** British Prime Minister Margaret Thatcher (1925–) leads the Conservative Party to a third successive victory, the first such achievement in 20th-century British politics. **1987** On a visit to Berlin, U.S. President Ronald Reagan (1911–2004) calls on Soviet leader Mikhail Gorbachev (1931–) to "tear down" the Berlin Wall.
1986 A bicycle ridden by Fred Markham establishes a human-powered land speed record of 65.48 miles (105.38 km) per hour. **1986** American pilots Dick Rutan (1938–) and Jeana Yeager (1952–) complete a nine-day nonstop flight around the world in their airplane *Voyager.* **1986** The 1,525-foot (465-m) Alex Fraser Bridge in Canada becomes the world's longest cable-stayed bridge. **1987** Engineers from American company AT&T install the first fiber-optic telecommunications cable (TAT-8) under the Atlantic Ocean. **1987** American company Kodak and Japanese company Fuji market 35mm disposable cameras. **1987** American researchers James Van House and Arthur Rich (1937–90) develop the positron microscope, which works in a similar way to an electron microscope but instead of electrons makes use of positrons ("positive electrons") produced by a radioactive isotope.	**1986** On Black Monday (October 19) stock markets in New York and then around the world experience a major crash, wiping billions of dollars off the value of shares. **1987** At a New York auction, "Irises" by Vincent van Gogh (1853–90) becomes the most expensive piece of art in history, selling for US$40 million. **1987** The United States and the Soviet Union sign the first ever nuclear arms reduction treaty, covering the two countries' medium- and short-range arsenals. **1987** Condom commercials run on U.S. television to combat the spread of AIDS.
1986 Japanese manufacturers demonstrate a digital audio tape (DAT) system. **1987** Japanese Airlines introduces telephones on their airplanes that employ communications satellites to link calls to land lines.	**1986** President Ferdinand Marcos (1917–89) of the Philippines is deposed by a "people power" movement led by Corazon Aquino (1933–), widow of Benigno Aquino (1932–83). **1986** Martial law, first imposed in 1949, is finally lifted in Taiwan.
	1986 Tripoli is attacked by U.S. warplanes flying from British bases in retaliation for the support of international terrorism by Libyan leader Colonel Muammar al-Gaddafi (1942–).

THE SPACE SHUTTLE

Plans for the space shuttle date back to 1972. The National Aeronautics and Space Administration (NASA) wanted a cargo-carrying rocket that could go into space, carry out its mission, return to base, and be used again and again.

At launch, the shuttle consists of three parts: an airplanelike orbiter, a large external tank that holds extra fuel, and two solid rocket boosters. The flight deck has seats for seven crew, and the mid-deck serves as a wardroom, kitchen, and gym, and has a bathroom. The payload bay can carry up to 27.6 tons (25 tonnes). The bay also has a robot arm called the Remote Manipulator System. It deploys and retrieves payloads and acts as a "ladder" for space-walking astronauts.

After launch, the boosters fall off; the external tank is jettisoned once the shuttle is in Earth orbit. At the end of a mission, the crew retrofire the maneuvering rockets to slow it down. As it reenters the Earth's atmosphere, thermal tiles on the wings and fuselage glow red hot with the heat generated by friction with the air.

NASA has built six space shuttles and made more than 120 trips. Two disasters, in 1986 and 2003, resulted in the deaths of both crews. The shuttle program was due to finish in 2010, when it would be replaced by a new kind of spacecraft.

ASTRONOMY & MATH	BIOLOGY & MEDICINE	PHYSICAL SCIENCES

EUROPE

1988 English theoretical physicist and mathematician Stephen Hawking (1942–) publishes a popular account of cosmology, *A Brief History of Time*, which becomes an international best-seller.

1988 The first Soviet space shuttle, *Buran*, makes an uncrewed test flight.

1989 The European Space Administration (ESA) launches astrometry satellite Hipparcos (High Precision Parallax Collecting Satellite) for measuring precisely the locations of stars. By 1993 it locates 120,000 selected stars.

1988 Dutch company CCA Biochem introduces polylactide biodegradable polymer for making surgical sutures (stitches) and artificial skin to treat burns.

A genetically modified mouse, or OncoMouse, was patented in the United States in 1988.

1988 At Imperial College, London, physicists Paul French and Roy Taylor produce a short-pulse x-ray laser.

1988 English physicist Richard Friend makes a diode entirely of plastic using polyethyne (polyacetylene).

THE AMERICAS

1988 The National Aeronautical and Space Administration's (NASA) space shuttle program restarts with a successful launch of *Discovery*.

1989 NASA's Voyager 2 space probe reveals that Neptune has a system of rings and discovers five inner moons—Despina, Galatea, Proteus, Thalassa, and Naiad— and rediscovers Larissa (first seen 1981).

1989 NASA launches space probes Galileo (to Jupiter) and Magellan (to Venus). The following year Magellan makes a radar map of the surface of Venus.

1988 The U.S. Patent Office grants a patent for a genetically engineered mouse (the first issued for a vertebrate animal).

1988 American climatologist James Hansen (1941–) predicts that increased levels of "greenhouse gases," such as carbon dioxide, in the Earth's atmosphere will lead to global warming.

1988 American physicians at the Presbyterian Hospital in Pittsburgh, Pennsylvania, begin performing double-lung transplant operations.

1989 Virologist Qui-Lim-Choo and coworkers confirm their earlier (1987) discovery of the virus that causes the liver disorder hepatitis-C.

1989 Scientists find the Chicxulub meteor crater on the floor of the Gulf of Mexico. It is thought to be the impact site of a meteorite that gave rise to the K-T event, which may have led to the extinction of the dinosaurs.

1989 Physicians in the United States use fetal brain tissue to treat Parkinson's disease.

1988 American physicist Frank Filisko (1942–2008) prepares a fluid whose viscosity (stickiness) can be varied by applying an electric field to it.

This false-color image of the surface of Venus was created from data collected by the Magellan space probe. The probe used radar-imaging to map the cloudy planet's surface.

ASIA & OCEANIA

1988 Japanese mathematician Yoichi Miyaoka offers a proof of Fermat's last theorem (that the equation $x^n + y^n = z^n$ has no solutions in positive integers x, y, and z if n is an integer greater than 2). Later it is found to be insufficiently rigorous. A valid proof finally comes in 1994.

1988 The Human Genome Organization (HUGO), with headquarters in Singapore, is established to promote international collaboration in the field of human genetics.

AFRICA & THE MIDDLE EAST

1988 Israel makes its first successful space launch from its site at Palmachim.

1988 Anthropologists from France and Israel discover in an Israeli cave fossils of a 92,000-year-old *Homo sapiens*, the oldest anatomically modern human to be found.

ENGINEERING & INVENTION	WORLD EVENTS	STEPHEN HAWKING

ENGINEERING & INVENTION

1988 Greek cyclist Kanellos Kanellopoulos (1957–) pilots the human-powered aircraft *Daedalus* across the Aegean Sea from Crete to Santorini. The 74.6-mile (120-km) crossing takes him 3 hours, 54 minutes.

1988 An explosion on Piper Alpha, an oil-drilling platform in the North Sea, results in a fire in which 167 people are killed.

1988 The F-117A Nighthawk Stealth fighter, which is "invisible" to radar, is revealed to the public, five years after being procured by the U.S. Air Force.

1988 A wind-powered 3-megawatt electricity generator with a single propeller blade 320 feet (97.5 m) across is installed in Hawaii.

1988 American IBM Corporation researchers use a scanning tunneling microscope to produce an image of a benzene molecule.

1988 The U.S. National Oceanic and Atmospheric Administration begins operations in Aquarius, an underwater habitat in the Caribbean, inside which a crew of six can work for nine hours a day.

1989 The Bell/Boeing V-22 Osprey tilt-rotor airplane with vertical take-off and landing makes its maiden flight.

1989 Boeing company's High Technology Center produces a photocell that converts more than a third of incident solar radiation into electricity.

1989 American computer engineer Seymour Cray (1925–96) establishes a company to build the Cray 3 supercomputer; it goes out of business in 1995.

1988 Integrated services digital network (ISDN) is launched in Japan as a world standard for digital data communications.

WORLD EVENTS

1988 A U.S. airliner is destroyed by a terrorist bomb over the Scottish town of Lockerbie, killing 270 people; a Libyan agent will eventually be convicted of the atrocity.

1989 Across Europe the communist regimes of Soviet satellite countries (Czechoslovakia, East Germany, and Poland) collapse as their citizens demand democratic reform.

1989 In Romania communist dictator Nicolae Ceaucescu (1918–1989) is deposed and executed.

1988 Vice President George H. W. Bush (1924–) is elected 41st president of the United States.

1988 The United States and Canada sign a comprehensive free-trade agreement, becoming effective on January 1, 1989.

1988 Use of crack—a derivative of cocaine—becomes increasingly popular.

1989 U.S. troops invade Panama and arrest military dictator Manuel Noriega (1934–) on drug-trafficking, racketeering, and money laundering charges.

1989 General Colin Powell (1937–) becomes the first African-American chairman of the U.S. Joint Chiefs of Staff.

1989 Oil tanker *Exxon Valdez* runs aground on reefs in Prince William Sound, Alaska, spilling an estimated 10 million gallons (40 million l) of crude oil.

STEPHEN HAWKING

Stephen Hawking is an English theoretical physicist and mathematician best known for his popular account of cosmology, *A Brief History of Time*. He was born in Oxford, England, and graduated from the university there, although he received his doctorate from Cambridge University in 1966. He became professor of gravitational physics at Cambridge in 1977 and two years later was appointed Lucasian Professor of Mathematics. At this time his main interest was relativity and its implications for the big bang (at the start of the universe) and black holes (in which enormous gravitational fields result from the collapse of stars).

Hawking showed mathematically that only angular momentum, electric charge, and mass are conserved when a black hole forms, although in 1974 he proposed that black holes could also evaporate and release heat radiation. Mass is lost by what is called the Hawking process. His "no-boundary proposal" of 1983 states that both space and time are infinite and have no physical boundaries.

In 1963 Hawking developed the incurable degenerative neuromuscular disease amyotrophic lateral sclerosis and since then has spent his life in a wheelchair. He communicates through a computer speech synthesizer.

Stephen Hawking floats free in a zero-gravity flight in April 2007.

ASTRONOMY & MATH

EUROPE

1991 Britain's first astronaut, chemist Helen Sharman (1963–), goes into Earth orbit on board a Soviet spacecraft.

THE AMERICAS

1990 Using nine-year-old data from the National Aeronautical and Space Administration's (NASA) Voyager 2 space probe, American astronomer Mark Showalter (1957–) locates Saturn's tiny innermost moon Pan—just 12 miles (20 km) across.

1990 NASA's Voyager 1 space probe returns photographs from deep space showing the whole of the solar system.

1990 NASA's space shuttle *Discovery* places the Hubble Space Telescope into orbit around the Earth. Over the next 15 years the telescope will provide astronomers with detailed images of the solar system, the galaxy, and distant objects in the universe.

1991 NASA uses the space shuttle *Atlantis* to place the Compton Gamma Ray Observatory (CGRO) satellite into Earth orbit; it operates until 2000.

1991 NASA sends its Upper Atmosphere Research Satellite into orbit around Earth. It studies the effects of chlorofluorocarbons (CFCs) on the ozone layer.

ASIA & OCEANIA

1990 Japanese scientists launch a space probe to the moon, where it releases a small satellite into lunar orbit.

AFRICA & THE MIDDLE EAST

English computer scientist Tim Berners-Lee devised the World Wide Web in 1990.

BIOLOGY & MEDICINE

1990 British geneticists Peter Goodfellow (1951–) and Robin Lovell-Badge (1953–) discover the male sex-determining gene on the human Y chromosome.

An engineer checks one of the boring machines used to make the Channel Tunnel, which provides a rail link between England and France.

1990 The Human Genome Project gets under way, directed by American biophysicist James Watson (1928–).

1991 Canadian scientists discover fossils of the oldest known multicellular animal (a sponge). It is 600 million years old.

1991 American electronics engineer Kenneth Matsumura invents a small portable electrocardiograph machine that gives its wearer advanced warning of heart problems. In the same year American physicists William and Jean Bennett (father and daughter) develop an electrocardiograph triggered by heartbeat sounds (the dynamic spectral phonocardiograph, or DSP).

PHYSICAL SCIENCES

1990 British company ICI introduces a biodegradable plastic, called Biopol. It also invents Klea 134a, a harmless hydrocarbon substitute for chlorofluorocarbons (CFCs).

1990 French molecular biologist Jean-Marie Lehn (1939–) prepares synthetic compounds called nucleohelicates, which mimic natural deoxyribonucleic acid (DNA).

1990 The nuclear physics research facility at the European Organization for Nuclear Research (CERN) in Switzerland commissions the new Large Electron–Positron Collider (LEP) for carrying out particle experiments.

1991 Researchers at the Joint European Torus (JET) project in England briefly achieve controlled nuclear fusion.

1990 American researchers make the lightest known solid, a silicon dioxide aerogel with a density of only 5 ounces per cubic foot—a cubic yard would weigh only 8 pounds (5 kg per cu m).

1991 Japanese researcher Sumio Iijima (1939–) makes carbon nanotubes (microscopically small tubes of carbon).

ENGINEERING & INVENTION

1990 British and French workers greet each other when the two opposite halves of the new Channel Tunnel meet in the rock under the English Channel.

1990 A Concorde supersonic airliner flies from London, England, to New York, United States, in the record time of 2 hours, 53 minutes.

1990 From this year all new cars sold in Europe have to be capable of running on nonleaded gasoline.

1990 English computer scientist Tim Berners-Lee (1955–) begins to devise the World Wide Web.

1991 With a central span of 1,739 feet (530 m), the Skarnsundet Bridge in Norway is the world's longest cable-stayed bridge.

1990 American Northrop/McDonnell Douglas consortium reveals the prototype of its new YF-23 Advanced Tactical Fighter (ATF) aircraft. Two months later Lockheed/General Dynamics/Boeing unveil their competing YF-22 design.

1990 American Microsoft Corporation releases the Windows 3 computer operating system.

1990 American company Kodak announces the invention of a Photo CD disc.

1990 Nanotechnology researchers at American IBM Corporation use an atomic force microscope to manipulate 35 xenon atoms on a nickel plate to draw the letters "IBM."

1990 The amount of electricity generated in the United States by nuclear power plants rises to 20 percent of total output (it is nearly 75 percent in France).

1991 American engineer Alvon Elrod (1928–) invents a car engine that has a camshaft with variable cams, to minimize fuel consumption at any engine speed.

1990 A new section of the trans-Siberian railroad opens in Russia between Baikal and Amur, with four large tunnels and 3,000 bridges.

1990 The world's largest church, the Basilica of Our Lady of Peace, is completed in Yamoussoukro, Côte d'Ivoire (Ivory Coast), West Africa.

WORLD EVENTS

1990 Boris Yeltsin (1931–2007) becomes the first freely elected president of Russia.

1990 East and West Germany are reunited.

1990 Margaret Thatcher (1925–) quits as British prime minister after 11 years.

The Japanese maglev (magnetically levitated) train uses powerful superconducting magnets to reach speeds of up to 310 miles (500 km) per hour.

1990 General Pinochet (1915–2006) steps down as military ruler of Chile, restoring civilian rule after 17 years.

1990 Nicaragua's communist Sandinista government is voted out of power with the election of Violetta Chamarro (1929–).

1990 Benazir Bhutto (1953–2007) is relieved of her post as prime minister of Pakistan after being accused of corruption.

1990 Democracy campaigner Aung San Suu Kyi (1945–) wins Myanmar's general election; the ruling military junta declares the result void and places her under house arrest.

1990 After 27 years in jail veteran South African antiapartheid leader Nelson Mandela (1918–) is freed from detention.

1991 A U.S.-led coalition of forces under a UN mandate undertakes to liberate Kuwait, which was invaded by Iraq in 1990; Iraqi forces crumble in the ensuing Gulf War (1990–91).

SUPERCONDUCTORS

A superconductor is a substance that offers no resistance to the flow of electricity. Superconductors were first discovered in 1911, and for many years scientists thought that superconductivity occurs only at temperatures that are very close to absolute zero (0 K = –459.67°F, or –273.15°C). The temperature below which superconductivity occurs is known as the transition temperature (Tc). Until 1985 the highest Tc known at ordinary atmospheric pressure was 23.2 K (–481.91°F, or –249.95°C) for an alloy of niobium.

Breakthroughs in the 1980s and 1990s came with the discovery of a "high-temperature" ceramic superconductor with a Tc of about 35 K (–460.67°F; –238.15°C). Although 35 K is still an extremely low temperature, the discovery raised the possibility of much higher Tcs, and it stimulated more research. In 1993, a Tc of 153 K (–248.27°F; –120.15°C) was found in a mercury-based ceramic subjected to high pressure.

Wires made from superconducting material are used to make superconducting magnets. They have several uses in magnetic separation and medical imaging and also in magnetically levitated (maglev) trains. Magnets make the train float, eliminating friction between train and track. In 2003 a test vehicle reached a speed of 361 miles (581 km) per hour on the Yamanashi Maglev Test Line in Japan.

ASTRONOMY & MATH	BIOLOGY & MEDICINE	PHYSICAL SCIENCES

EUROPE

1992 The Roman Catholic Church reverses the verdict of the 1633 trial of Italian scientist Galileo Galilei (1564–1642) at which he was convicted of heresy.

1992 The European Space Administration's (ESA) space probe Giotto passes within 124 miles (200 km) of comet Grigg–Skjellerup.

1992 The space probe Ulysses, a joint venture between the National Aeronautics and Space Administration (NASA) and ESA, passes within 236,000 miles (380,000 km) of Jupiter, inside the orbit of its moon Io, on its way to the sun.

1992 Scientists at the University of Pisa, Italy, make the most accurate determination so far of the acceleration of free fall (acceleration due to gravity), not far from where Italian scientist Galileo Galilei is said to have first measured it in about 1602.

Princeton University's Tokamak Fusion Test Reactor is used to research nuclear fusion. Many scientists see nuclear fusion as a possible power source of the future.

THE AMERICAS

1992 Astronomers discover an object that crosses the orbits of Saturn, Uranus, and Neptune. An estimated 93 miles (150 km) across, it is probably an asteroid (assigned no. 5145) but may be a comet. They name it Pholus.

1992 NASA's space shuttle *Endeavour* makes its first flight. In 1993 it carries out repairs to the Hubble Space Telescope in Earth orbit.

1992 NASA launches its Extreme Ultraviolet Explorer (EUVE) satellite into Earth orbit to study the heavens at very short ultraviolet wavelengths (between 1 and 100 nanometers).

1992 NASA's space probe Pioneer Venus 1 burns up on entering the atmosphere of Venus.

1993 Radio astronomers make the first observations with the complete Very Long Baseline Array (VLBA) series of ten radiotelescopes, located across the United States and its overseas territories.

1993 American astronomers Carolyn Shoemaker (1929–) and David Levy (1948–) discover a new comet, which is named Shoemaker–Levy 9.

1992 Anticancer drug taxol, extracted from the bark of yew trees, gets official approval in North America by the U.S. Food and Drug Administration. It is used mainly for treating ovarian cancer.

1992 Surgeons at the University of Pittsburgh Medical Center perform a transgenic transplant of a baboon's liver into a human patient.

1993 American physicians introduce gene therapy for the congenital disorder cystic fibrosis.

1993 American physicians develop a way of detecting acquired immune deficiency syndrome (AIDS) in newborns and young infants.

1993 American physician Susan Perrine and coworkers carry out trials using the fatty acid derivative butyrate as a new treatment for sickle-cell anemia.

1992 Research scientists at the American company General Electric report making extrahard diamonds using the isotope carbon-13 (natural diamonds are made of carbon-12).

1993 Soviet-born American physicist Alexei Abrikosov (1928–) explains the workings of type-II superconductors (which, unlike type-I, remain superconducting even in a strong magnetic field). They depend on an arrangement of atoms known as an Abrikosov vortex lattice.

1993 The Tokamak fusion reactor at the Princeton Plasma Physics Laboratory produces 5.6 megawatts of power (in a one-second burst) but requires more than this amount of energy to operate it.

1993 American research chemists discover a way of making liquid methanol (methyl alcohol) from the gas methane (natural gas) using a low-temperature mercury vapor catalyst. It could provide a way of making a liquid fuel from a gaseous one.

ASIA & OCEANIA

1992 The space probe *Geotail* (developed by Japanese scientists and managed by NASA) is launched to examine the Earth's magnetosphere (the pear-shaped magnetic field that surrounds the Earth and extends into space).

1992 The world population reaches 5.4 billion people, with about 1.2 billion in China alone.

1992 Japanese chemists use palladium atoms to make stable polymers of buckyballs (the C_{60} allotrope with a spherical arrangement of carbon molecules).

AFRICA & THE MIDDLE EAST

1993 American anthropologist Tim White (1950–) and coworkers from Berkeley discover in Africa remains of *Ardipithecus ramidus*, the oldest hominoid australopithecine fossil found so far.

ENGINEERING & INVENTION	WORLD EVENTS
1992 The 223-foot (68-m) *Destriero* establishes a new powerboat record for crossing the Atlantic Ocean in 2 days and 10 hours.	**1993** Czechoslovakia separates into two states, the Czech Republic and Slovakia, after a peaceful plebiscite approves this "Velvet Revolution."
1992 Dutch company Philips markets the CD-i interactive computer disk.	**1993** Nations of the European Community (now renamed the European Union) sign the Maastricht Treaty, committing them to a program of ever closer union.
1992 Experimental digital FM radio broadcasts begin in France.	

A photograph from the Hubble Space Telescope reveals a spiral galaxy deep within the universe.

1992 The U.S. Air Force and U.S. Navy finance construction in Alaska of the High Frequency Active Auroral Research Program (HAARP) to try to reduce the effects of the aurora borealis (northern lights) on satellite communications.

1992 In Davis, California, the Advanced Photovoltaic Systems company assembles a huge array of thin-film photovoltaic cells that produce 400 kilowatts of electrical power.

1993 American engineers produce two cost-effective "free-swimming" submersible robots: the *Odyssey* (designed by James Bellingham), deployed in Antarctica, and the Autonomous Benthic Explorer (ABE), developed originally by Albert Bradley and deployed off Bermuda.

1993 The state of Iowa interlinks all of its 99 counties with a fiber-optic cable network.

1993 Researchers at the University of Colorado construct the first all-optical programmable computer.

1993 American company Intel markets the Pentium microprocessor for computers.

1992 Bill Clinton (1946–) becomes the 42nd President of the United States.

1993 A terrorist bomb explodes in the World Trade Center in New York.

1993 Toni Morrison (1931–) becomes the first African-American woman awarded the Nobel Prize in Literature.

1992 Japanese Sony Corporation introduces transistors made from ceramic semiconductors. The same year it markets the first digital audio MiniDisc.

1993 Japanese company Mazda announces plans to construct a fuel-efficient car using a Miller-cycle internal combustion engine.

1992 Hindu militants destroy a 16th-century mosque on an ancient Hindu holy site at Ayodhya in India; more than 1,000 die in the ensuing Hindu–Muslim rioting.

1993 The Third River irrigation canal is completed in Iraq, linking the Tigris and Euphrates Rivers near Baghdad.

1992 A UN peacekeeping mission to Somalia ends in conflict between U.S. forces and troops loyal to warlord General Mohamed Farrah Aidid (1934–96). The conflict continues until 1995.

HUBBLE SPACE TELESCOPE

The Hubble Space Telescope (HST) is named for American astronomer Edwin Hubble (1889–1953). It was completed by the National Aeronautics and Space Administration (NASA) in 1985 and placed in orbit by the space shuttle *Discovery* in 1990. It follows an orbit 377 miles (607 km) above Earth and is designed to be serviced and updated from time to time by the space shuttle.

The HST is an aluminum cylinder 43 feet (13 m) long and 14 feet (4.3 m) across. Electric power comes from two 40-foot (12-m) solar panels. Two high-gain antennas transmit signals to ground control at the Goddard Space Flight Center. The cylinder houses a reflecting telescope with a prime mirror 94.5 inches (2.4 m) across. There are also five detectors of various types.

HST can photograph objects 50 times fainter than anything visible from the ground. In 1994 HST photographed fragments of the comet Shoemaker–Levy 9 crashing into Jupiter. By the end of 1995 it took photographs of some of the most distant objects in the universe, recording faint galaxies 12 billion light-years away. In 1998 the HST directly imaged an extrasolar planet orbiting a star in the constellation Taurus. A more powerful telescope is currently being developed to replace HST.

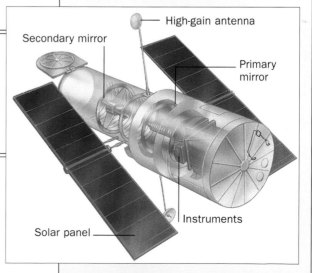

ASTRONOMY & MATH	BIOLOGY & MEDICINE	PHYSICAL SCIENCES

EUROPE

1994 English mathematician Andrew Wiles (1953–) offers a proof of Fermat's last theorem.

1995 The European Space Agency (ESA) launches the French Infrared Space Observatory (ISO) into a highly elliptical Earth orbit.

1995 Russian cosmonaut Valeri Polyakov (1942–) clocks the longest space mission to date, returning after 438 days aboard the space station Mir.

1995 Swiss astronomers Michael Mayor (1942–) and Didier Queloz (1966–) discover an extrasolar planet (orbiting the star 51 Pegasi).

Genetically Modified Plants

Plants can be genetically engineered to modify their properties, for example, to make them grow faster, tolerate cold and drought better, or simply taste nicer. Genetically engineered crops can have their own inbuilt insecticides or be made resistant to high doses of sprayed-on pesticides. Similar crops engineered to grow in arid or salty soils can boost farming productivity in developing countries. The first genetically engineered food to be granted a licence for human consumption was the Flavr Savr tomato, which was first sold in 1994. The fruit ripens on the vine without going soft (and so does not get damaged during shipping to the supermarket) because of the presence of a gene that blocks the action of the enzyme polygalacturonase, which causes fruit to soften naturally.

THE AMERICAS

1994 The National Aeronautics and Space Administration's (NASA) and U.S. Strategic Defense Initiative Organization's space probe Clementine goes into orbit around the moon and maps the surface. Its intended later trip to the near-Earth asteroid Geographos is abandoned after a rocket malfunctions.

1994 The Hubble Space Telescope confirms the existence of the Kuiper belt, a spherical region at the edge of the solar system where comets originate.

1994 Fragments of comet Shoemaker–Levy 9, first seen in 1993, collide with Jupiter.

1995 NASA's space probe Galileo sends its own probe into Jupiter's atmosphere. It radios back data for an hour before being crushed by the pressure.

1995 American Norman Thagard (1943–) becomes the first U.S. astronaut aboard a Russian spacecraft when he joins the crew of a Soyuz craft to reach the Mir space station. He returns 105 days later on the space shuttle *Atlantis*.

1994 A genetically modified tomato called Flavr Savr is marketed by the company Calgene in the United States.

1995 American company Thermo Cardiosystems introduce the LVAD (left ventricular assist device), an implanted pump for heart patients.

1994 American scientists at Fermilab announce the discovery of the evasive subatomic particle called the top quark.

1995 American geophysicists Xiaodong Song and Paul Richards detect the rotation of the Earth's solid inner core through computer analysis of seismic waves.

1995 American physicist Eric Cornell (1961–) and coworkers produce a Bose–Einstein condensate, a fourth state of matter.

ASIA & OCEANIA

1994 Japanese rocket engineers launch their new heavy-lifting rocket, H-2.

1994 Paleontologists from Pakistan and the United States discover fossils of a whale that had hind limbs.

1994 Scientists record the first giant muntjac (a type of deer) in northern Vietnam. It is given the scientific name *Muntiacus vuquangensis*.

AFRICA & THE MIDDLE EAST

1994 A new Ebola virus (Ebola hemorrhagic fever) is identified in Côte d'Ivoire (Ivory Coast) and Gabon in Africa; other outbreaks occur in 1995 in Zaire (now the Democratic Republic of the Congo).

ENGINEERING & INVENTION

1994 The Channel Tunnel rail link opens between England and France for freight, cars and trucks (carried in railroad wagons), and passengers. It is the longest tunnel under the sea at that time.

1994 The 16,800-ton (15,000-tonne) ferry *Estonia* sinks in the Baltic Sea off Finland with the loss of almost 900 lives.

1994 Scottish inventor Jonathan Copus invents the biogun, a device that uses a stream of negatively charged ions to kill bacterial and fungal infections.

1995 The 2,808-foot (856-m) Pont de Normandie in Le Havre, France, is completed and is for a few years the world's longest cable-stayed bridge.

1994 American businessman Jon Zeeff launches the world's first Internet shopping mall with Grant's Flowers and Greenhouses.

1995 American company Lockheed introduces the Athena rocket launcher vehicle, originally called the Lockheed Martin Launch Vehicle (LMLV), for placing satellites into low Earth orbit.

1995 For the first time the number of trucks and cars in the United States exceeds 200 million—more than one for every adult member of the population.

1995 American computer programmer James Gosling (1955–) of Sun Microsystems company introduces the Java computer-programming language.

Eurostar trains carry passengers between England and France or via the Channel Tunnel. The trains can reach speeds of 186 miles (300 km) per hour.

WORLD EVENTS

1994 Cheychnya's attempt to break away from the Russian government is thwarted by the Russian army.

1995 The Dayton Peace Accord brings the bloody civil war in Bosnia to an end; the state is divided between a Muslim–Croat federation and a Bosnian Serb republic.

1994 The North American Free Trade Agreement (NAFTA) links the United States, Canada, and Mexico in an enlarged free-trade zone.

1995 A truck bomb planted by right-wing extremists destroys a federal building in Oklahoma City, killing 168 people.

1995 Despite international protests, France resumes nuclear weapons testing at Muroroa Atoll in French Polynesia.

1995 The Japanese port of Kobé suffers extensive damage in a major earthquake; 6,000 people die.

1994 Interethnic violence in Rwanda claims more than one million lives.

1994 Nelson Mandela (1918–) is elected president of South Africa.

1995 Israeli Prime Minister Yitzhak Rabin (1922–95) is assassinated by an extreme nationalist opposed to his policies.

FERMAT'S LAST THEOREM

Pierre de Fermat (1601–65) was a French mathematician who made many important contributions to number theory, geometry, and the development of calculus and probability theory. Fermat posed the theorem that the equation $x^n + y^n = z^n$ has no solutions in positive integers x, y, and z if n is an integer greater than 2. If $n = 3$, for example, the theorem states that there are no positive integers x, y, and z such that $x^3 + y^3 = z^3$. No mathematicians could prove or disprove the theorem (although proofs for specific values of n were devised), which became known as Fermat's last theorem. Fermat himself claimed to have found a proof, which he never published. After seven years of work, English mathematician Andrew Wiles proposed his proof in 1993. After finding an error, Wiles with help from Richard Taylor (1962–) revised the proof. He published his now watertight proof in 1995.

Andrew Wiles outlines his first attempt to prove Fermat's last theory to fellow mathematicians in Cambridge, England, in 1993.

325

1996–1997
CONCISE HISTORY OF SCIENCE AND INVENTION

ASTRONOMY & MATH	BIOLOGY & MEDICINE	PHYSICAL SCIENCES
EUROPE		
1996 Ariane 5, the new uncrewed space rocket of the European Space Administration (ESA), explodes on its first launch.	**1996** Medical researchers establish a link between bovine spongiform encephalopathy (BSE) and Creutzfeldt–Jakob Disease (CJD), a human brain disorder that generally affects middle-aged and elderly people. A year later the diseases are shown to have the same cause by Moira Bruce working in Edinburgh, Scotland, and, independently, John Collinge and coworkers in London, England. **1996** Scottish biologist Ian Wilmut (1944–) at the Roslin Institute, Edinburgh, Scotland, clones a sheep named Dolly. Two years later Dolly gives birth to a lamb in the normal way.	**1996** Physicists at the laboratories at the European Organization for Nuclear Research (CERN) in Switzerland produce antihydrogen (consisting of hydrogen atoms with positrons instead of electrons and antiprotons instead of protons as their nuclei). It is the first example of antimatter.
THE AMERICAS		
1996 The National Aerospace and Space Administration's (NASA) space shuttle *Atlantis*, carrying American astronaut Shannon Lucid (1943–), docks in space with Russian space station Mir. Lucid returns to Earth on Atlantis six months later—the most time spent in space by a woman. **1996** American scientists launch the astronomical satellite Polar into Earth orbit. It carries 11 instruments for studying (among other things) the Earth's magnetosphere, the solar winds, and the aurora. **1997** The Hubble Space Telescope locates the brightest star in the universe; it is ten million times as bright as the sun. **1997** Canadian astronomer Brett Gladman (1966–) and coworkers at the Palomar Observatory, California, discover a small outer moon of Uranus, which they name Caliban. In the same year Philip Nicholson (1951–) discovers another small outer moon, Sycorax. **1997** NASA's space probe Mars Pathfinder soft-lands on Mars and releases a small six-wheel rover vehicle called Sojourner. About 16,500 images are sent back to Earth.	**1996** American astronomer David McKay (1936–) and coworkers at the Johnson Space Center, Houston, find traces of what might be primitive microscopic life in a meteorite that originated from Mars. **1997** American geneticist Huntington Willard (1952–) assembles an artificial human chromosome that successfully replicates. *NASA's rover Sojourner hitched a ride on the space probe Mars Pathfinder. The rover was used to study the geology of the surface of Mars.*	**1997** Following their work of 1995 on Bose–Einstein condensates, American physicist Eric Cornell (1961–) and coworkers produce an atomic laser.
ASIA & OCEANIA		
1996 Japanese amateur astronomer Yuji Hyakutake (1950–2002) discovers a new long-period (14,000 years) comet, named Comet Hyakutake. It passes within 9 million miles (14.9 million km) of Earth.	**1997** The avian influenza ("bird flu") virus is isolated from a human patient in Hong Kong. After six patients die, the entire chicken population of Hong Kong is slaughtered. **1997** Paleontologists in China discover fossils of *Protarchaeopteryx*, a reptilian creature with birdlike characteristics.	**1996** Japanese research chemists synthesize cellulose.
AFRICA & THE MIDDLE EAST		

ENGINEERING & INVENTION	WORLD EVENTS

1996 The company DaimlerChrysler produces its second experimental vehicle powered by fuel cells, a car (the first, in 1994, was a panel truck).

1997 British fighter pilot Andy Green (1962–) sets the supersonic land speed record when he reaches 763.035 miles (1,227.99 km) per hour in the twin-jet car *Thrust SSC*.

1997 British author and inventor Ian Harrison files a patent for a dual-hinged refrigerator door that can be opened from either the left- or the right-hand side.

1996 Boris Yeltsin (1931–2007) becomes president of Russia.

1997 Conservative rule in Britain ends after 18 years when the Labour Party under its young leader Tony Blair (1953–) wins a landslide general election victory.

1997 Diana, Princess of Wales (1961–97), is killed in a car accident in Paris. About two billion people across the world watch her funeral on television.

Ian Wilmut and Dolly the sheep.

CLONING ANIMALS

Early animal cloning experiments involved splitting sea urchin and salamander embryos so that two identical twins, or clones, developed. By the late 1950s scientists could create frog clones by transferring a nucleus from an

1996 American researchers Theodore Poehler and Peter Searson develop an all-plastic battery.

1997 Edible food packaging is introduced in the United States.

1997 NASA's solar-powered airplane *Pathfinder* reaches a record altitude of 71,490 feet (21,790 m) during a flight over Hawaii.

1996 The United States increases its efforts to restrict illegal immigration from Mexico by hiring more U.S. Border Patrols and erecting 40 miles (65 km) of 14-foot (4.25-m) fence along its border with Mexico.

1996 Bill Clinton (1946–) is reelected, the first Democrat president to win a second term since 1936.

1997 American Tiger Woods (1975–) becomes the youngest golfer to win the U.S. Masters tournament in Augusta, Georgia.

1997 U.S. tobacco companies pay out $368.5 billion in claims made against them by former smokers.

1997 Bill Clinton apologizes to almost 400 African-American men in Alabama who were left untreated for the sexually transmitted infection syphilis as part of a government experiment between 1932 and 1972.

adult cell into an egg cell from which the original nucleus had been removed, creating an exact replica of the animal from which the nucleus was taken. Using the nucleus of fully mature cells proved that adult cells keep a full set of genetic material, despite only expressing part of that material. The nucleus of a cell from a frog's intestine still "knew" how to make all the other cell types in a whole frog.

Making clones of mammals is much trickier because mammalian cells are much smaller than amphibian cells. But in 1996 Scottish scientist Ian Wilmut (1944–) created "Dolly the sheep." He fused an enucleated sheep's egg cell with an udder cell from an adult ewe. The resulting cell became an embryo, which was implanted into the uterus of a mature ewe. The ewe subsequently gave birth to a lamb that became an animal celebrity. Dolly went on to bear six lambs of her own in the normal way, but her health was poor. In 2001 she developed premature arthritis, and in 2003 she was diagnosed with lung disease and had to be put down. There was speculation as to whether Dolly's ill health was the result of her unusual origin.

Completed in 1996 the 241-foot (73.5-m) Petronas Towers in Kuala Lumpur, Malaysia, become the world's tallest buildings.

1996 The Tabilan overrun the Afghan capital Kabul.

1997 Hong Kong reverts to Chinese rule after 155 years of British sovereignty.

1997 Reformist Mohammed Khatami (1943–) is elected president of Iran.

Since Dolly, many more mammals have been cloned. In 1997 Wilmut and his team created Polly, a sheep cloned from fetal cells genetically altered to include a human gene. Other cloned animals include pigs, cattle, mice, and, in 2005, a racehorse.

CONCISE HISTORY OF SCIENCE AND INVENTION

ASTRONOMY & MATH	BIOLOGY & MEDICINE	PHYSICAL SCIENCES

EUROPE

1998 Dutch astronomers detect a large galaxy 20 million light-years away in a region previously thought to be nearly empty.

1998 The Astronomical Technology Centre (ATC) is established at the Royal Observatory, Edinburgh, for the design and production of astronomical instruments and associated technology for terrestrial observatories and space missions.

1999 The European Space Agency (ESA) launches XMM-Newton, the X-Ray Multi-Mirror Observatory, into Earth orbit. It consists of three aligned telescopes for making observations at x-ray wavelengths.

1999 Russia abandons its Mir space station, after 13 years of occupation.

1998 After 15 years' work a team of international scientists, including English biologist John Sulston (1942–), determines the genome for a whole animal, *Caenorhabditis elegans*, a tiny nematode worm.

1999 The British government bans the advertising of tobacco products on television and on roadside billboards.

1999 French paleontologists unearth fossils of 30 million-year-old *Baluchitherium* (also known as *Paraceratherium*). The largest ever land mammal, the rhinoceroslike beast stood 18 feet (5.5 m) tall.

1999 According to the World Health Organization (WHO), AIDS becomes the primary cause of death in Africa.

1999 Russian researchers at the Joint Institute for Nuclear Research in Dubna, Moscow, create element 114 by bombarding plutonium-244 with calcium-48 nuclei.

In 1999 the hot-air balloon Breitling Orbiter 3 *circumnavigated the world in 19 days, 21 hours, and 55 minutes.*

THE AMERICAS

1998 The National Aeronautics and Space Administration (NASA) launches its space probe Deep Space 1, the first of the New Millennium Program missions, using new technology such as ion propulsion rockets.

1998 Astronomers at the University of Hawaii discover a 130-foot (40-m) near-Earth asteroid that passes within Earth's orbit.

1999 The Hubble Space Telescope has its second service since being placed in orbit in 1990. The mission is carried out by astronauts in the space shuttle *Discovery*.

1999 Canadian astronomers Matthew Holman (1967–), J. J. Kavelaars, and Brett Gladman (1966–) find three outer moons of Uranus.

1999 American astronaut Eileen Collins (1956–) is the first woman to command a space shuttle when *Columbia* is launched to place the Chandra X-ray Observatory (CXO) into an elliptical Earth orbit.

1999 NASA launches its Stardust space probe to rendezvous with comet Wild-2 in 2004. It returns to Earth with samples of dust from the comet in 2006.

1998 Zoologists discover five new species of small salamanders in tropical Mexico. They are assigned to the genus *Thorius*.

1998 American researchers at Johns Hopkins University successfully grow human stem cells in the laboratory (stem cells may one day be used to treat various cellular disorders).

1998 Researchers in Hawaii clone 50 mice from adult cells, and Japanese scientists clone eight calves.

1998 American dentists first use lasers for "drilling" teeth.

1999 American scientists create element 118 by fusing lead-208 with krypton-86, but it decays to form element 116.

ASIA & OCEANIA

1998 Two Japanese satellites in Earth orbit carry out the first automatic docking, using laser sensors. The Japanese Institute of Space and Astronautical Sciences also launches its Planet-B space probe to Mars.

1999 Chinese archaeologists uncover 4,000-year-old human remains with evidence of a healed craniotomy (also known as trepanning, a surgical operation to make a hole in the skull).

AFRICA & THE MIDDLE EAST

1998 Paleontologists find a whole skeleton of a 36-foot (11-m) fish-eating dinosaur in a desert in Niger, Africa.

INSIDE STORY

Caenorhabditis elegans

The first multicellular animal to have its genome—its hereditary information encoded in deoxyribonucleic acid (DNA)—sequenced was the nematode roundworm *Caenorhabditis elegans* in 1998 by a team of international scientists. The worm's genome is about 100 million base pairs long, with about 20,000 genes. Research into this free-living, transparent worm, which grows to about 0.04 inches (1 mm) in length, was first begun by South African biologist Sydney Brenner (1927–) in 1974, and it soon proved to be a very useful biological model. Adult *C. elegans* worms have about 1,000 body cells and scientists learned what each cell does. About 300 of the cells are neurons, and scientists have studied the neurons involved in many of the worm's behaviors, including mating and chemotaxis—movement toward chemicals in the worm's environment. Scientists have also found it relatively easy to block specific genes to elucidate their function in the worm.

ENGINEERING & INVENTION	WORLD EVENTS
1998 Swiss scientists produce a titanium dioxide solar cell. It is twice as efficient as standard solar cells. **1998** The Paris subway opens a new route, Meteor (Métro Est-Ouest Rapide), with fully automated driverless trains. **1999** Swiss psychiatrist and balloonist Bertrand Piccard (1958–) and English balloonist Brian Jones (1947–) circumnavigate the world in their hot-air balloon, *Breitling Orbiter 3*.	**1998** Voters in Northern Ireland and the Irish Republic endorse the Good Friday Agreement, bringing the prospect of peace after 30 years of paramilitary violence. **1998** Serbian paramilitaries ravage the Yugoslav province of Kosovo, conducting ethnic cleansing against the Albanian populace, but withdraw after the North Atlantic Treaty Organization (NATO) orders airstrikes against Serbia. The conflict continues into 1999. **1998** Germany establishes a pension fund to compensate Jewish Holocaust survivors in Central and Eastern Europe. **1999** Poland, Hungary, and the Czech Republic join NATO.

Millennium Bug

Toward the end of the 1990s computer experts predicted that a phenomenon known as the "millennium bug," or the Y2K problem, would automatically take effect at midnight on December 31, 1999. They had realized that the Basic Input Output System (BIOS) programs in most computers contained a fundamental error. It meant that the computer would not recognize the date 2000 and would set the time back to an incorrect date, usually January 1, 1900. It was said that, unless corrected by expensive software, the "bug" would erase memories or make computers crash, with terrible consequences for homes and businesses worldwide. Air-traffic control and transportation systems would malfunction; machines in hospitals would suddenly stop; and domestic appliances containing microchips would fail. Many organizations took precautions to prevent or lessen the effects, often at considerable cost. But on January 1 nothing happened: The millennium bug did not exist.

At about the same time computer viruses that were started deliberately became a problem. They generally spread as attachments to e-mails, hence the advice from experts not to open any attachments from unknown senders.

People in Hong Kong, worried about the millennium bug, withdraw money from their bank accounts on December 30, 1999.

1999 Computer virus Melissa spreads rapidly by e-mail to infect more than 100,000 computers wordwide. Other viruses of the year that wreak havoc are called Chernobyl and ExploreZip. 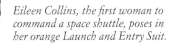	**1998** The weather phenomenon El Niño causes high temperatures, drought, and tornadoes in the United States. **1999** U.S President Bill Clinton (1946–) and Mexican President Ernesto Zedillo (1951–) work together to combat drug trafficking. **1999** A Senate trial acquits President Bill Clinton of perjury and obstruction of justice. **1999** The founder of Amazon.com, Jeff Bezos (1964) is named *Time* magazine's Man of the Year for his significant input into launching the online shopping revolution.
	Eileen Collins, the first woman to command a space shuttle, poses in her orange Launch and Entry Suit.
1998 The world's largest passenger terminal opens at the new Chek Lap Kok Airport in Hong Kong, China.	**1998** The government of Pakistan is overthrown in a military coup; General Pervez Musharraf (1943–) becomes head of state. **1999** East Timor votes for independence from Indonesia; after much violence it will achieve its goal in 2002.
	1998 The terror group al-Qaeda bombs U.S. embassies in Kenya and Tanzania, killing more than 200 people. **1999** A major earthquake in northern Turkey claims 17,000 lives.

THE GREENHOUSE EFFECT AND GLOBAL WARMING

KEY DATES

1827
Fourier describes the greenhouse effect

1896
Arrhenius publishes a theory of global warming linked to human-made emission of greenhouse gases

1939
Callendar observes a rise in both global temperatures and CO_2 levels

1979
First World Climate Conference

1985
First international conference on the greenhouse effect

1988
United Nations sets up the Intergovernmental Panel on Climate Change (IPCC)

1998
The hottest year in the hottest decade in the hottest century of the millennium

2005
Kyoto Protocol comes into effect

IN THE MINDS OF MOST PEOPLE THE GREENHOUSE effect is inextricably linked with the phenomenon of global warming, but it is also one of the fortuitous natural phenomena that make the planet habitable. The Earth has benefited from it for billions of years. The overall effect is an insulating one—the natural greenhouse effect keeps the Earth's average temperature about 60°F (32°C) higher than it would otherwise be. The principles of the phenomenon and the term *greenhouse effect* were first described by French mathematician Jean Fourier (1768–1830) in 1827. Experimental evidence supporting Fourier's ideas was provided by Irish physicist John Tyndall (1820–93) in 1859. Tyndall demonstrated that gases including water vapor and carbon dioxide (CO_2) could trap heat.

During the early 20th century scientists were aware that the Earth's climate had previously undergone dramatic changes and that it was currently enjoying a period of relative warmth, called an interglacial period. Aware of the greenhouse role of CO_2, Swedish physical chemist Svante Arrhenius (1859–1927) suspected that ice ages might have been caused by reduced levels of atmospheric CO_2. Then he thought of something else. He calculated the amount of CO_2 being released into the atmosphere by human activities and realized that such output could eventually begin to have the reverse effect. In 1896 he was the first to suggest that, instead of facing global cooling, the world may experience global warming as a result of industrial emissions. But the prospect was a distant one, and even Arrhenius was not concerned by it.

Rising Levels of Carbon Dioxide

The idea was revived four decades later in 1939 by English hobby meteorologist Guy Stewart Callendar (1989–1964). After reviewing historical records, he suggested that increases in temperatures and CO_2 levels were linked. The suggestion was rejected by many climatologists, who thought that natural checks and balances, such as the absorption of excess CO_2 by oceans, would render such changes impossible.

But Callender's suggestion had sown a seed of doubt, and the idea refused to go away. The evidence, however, remained thin and open to question. Climatologists desperately needed better models and more data. Over the latter part of the 20th century, they gradually became available.

Global warming has reduced the sea-ice habitat of polar bears. With a shrinking range to find sufficient food, the species is now under serious threat.

In the 1960s it became possible to measure accurately atmospheric carbon dioxide levels, and over the ensuing years it became apparent that they were indeed rising rapidly. Throughout the late 20th century scientists were uncovering layers of complexity relating to the way the Earth's climate systems work, making it almost impossible to give firm predictions.

During the 1980s records from around the world showed an increase in temperatures, but an enhanced greenhouse effect remained only one of many proposed causes. Climate models began to take account of variables such as ocean absorption and clouds. The year 1988 marked something of a turning point. Globally, it was the hottest year on record (there have been many hotter ones since), and it was the year that public awareness of the possibility of global warming took off. American climatologist James Hansen reiterated that increased levels of CO_2 in the atmosphere would lead to global warming.

Between 1890 and 1990 the amount of CO_2 in the atmosphere rose by a quarter, from 280 to 345 parts per million by volume. By the early 1990s human civilization was churning out 6.6 billion tons (6 billion tonnes) of CO_2 gas a year—5.5 billion tons (5 billion tonnes) from the burning of fossil fuels and 1.1 billion tons (1 billion tonnes) from burning down rain forests. At the same time, other greenhouse gases were increasing at an even greater rate: methane at 1 percent a year and chlorofluorocarbons (CFCs) at 6 percent each year. Both gases are markedly more efficient at trapping solar radiation than CO_2.

By the end of the 20th century, scientists reached a general consensus that the world is undergoing a significant warming and that the trend is the result of human activities contributing to an enhanced greenhouse effect. Climate models were providing alarming predictions about what these changes would mean: rising sea levels, violent storms, floods, and droughts

In natural conditions most carbon dioxide is absorbed by phytoplankton in the sea and by forest trees. As humans create more and more carbon dioxide, excess amounts accumulate in the atmosphere. This absorbs the solar energy that is radiated back from the surface of the Earth, trapping the heat so that global temperatures begin to rise. This creates the so-called "greenhouse effect."

Most scientists now agree that curbing the emissions of greenhouse gases, such as those that result from burning fossil fuels, is vital in combating climate change.

in quick succession. Some governments had already begun taking steps to limit their national output of greenhouse gases and, in 1997, 84 nations made a firm commitment to curb emissions by signing up to the Kyoto Protocol, which came into effect in 2005.

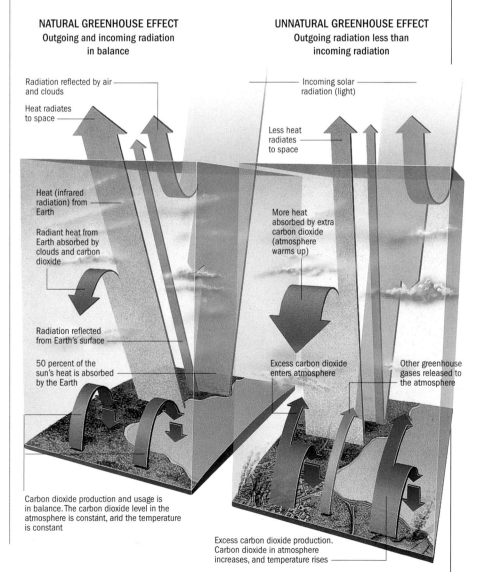

NATURAL GREENHOUSE EFFECT
Outgoing and incoming radiation in balance

Radiation reflected by air and clouds

Heat radiates to space

Heat (infrared radiation) from Earth

Radiant heat from Earth absorbed by clouds and carbon dioxide

Radiation reflected from Earth's surface

50 percent of the sun's heat is absorbed by the Earth

Carbon dioxide production and usage is in balance. The carbon dioxide level in the atmosphere is constant, and the temperature is constant

UNNATURAL GREENHOUSE EFFECT
Outgoing radiation less than incoming radiation

Incoming solar radiation (light)

Less heat radiates to space

More heat absorbed by extra carbon dioxide (atmosphere warms up)

Excess carbon dioxide enters atmosphere

Other greenhouse gases released to the atmosphere

Excess carbon dioxide production. Carbon dioxide in atmosphere increases, and temperature rises

ASTRONOMY & MATH	BIOLOGY & MEDICINE	PHYSICAL SCIENCES

EUROPE

2000 The European Space Administration (ESA) launches four Cluster satellites to explore the Earth's magnetosphere.

2000 Russia launches the Zvezda service module that (together with Zarya and Unity, which are already in orbit) forms the basis of the new International Space Station. Later that year an American astronaut and two Russian cosmonauts travel in a Russian Soyuz spacecraft to become the first crew of the new space station.

2001 Russia's abandoned space station Mir reenters the Earth's atmosphere and largely burns up.

2000 The Pyrenean ibex (*Capra pyrenaica*) goes extinct when the last individual dies in Ordesa National Park, Spain.

2001 Gray wolves (*Canis lupus*) are found living wild in Germany (they have not been seen in the wild for 150 years).

2001 An epidemic of foot-and-mouth disease leads to the slaughter of thousands of cattle in Britain.

We are here to celebrate the completion of the first survey of the entire human genome. Without a doubt, this is the most important, most wondrous map ever produced by humankind.

PRESIDENT BILL CLINTON

THE AMERICAS

2000 The National Aeronautics and Space Administration's (NASA) space probe Galileo passes close to Jupiter's moon Io.

2000 A carbonaceous chondrite meteorite crashes near Tagish Lake in the Yukon. Its composition is thought to be similar to the materials from which the sun and solar system evolved.

2000 A camera on NASA's Cassini space probe reveals a new asteroid (no. 2685), which is named Masursky for American planetary scientist Harold Masursky (1922–90), who worked on most of NASA's missions from the 1960s to the 1980s.

2001 NASA's orbiter Mars Odyssey enters orbit around Mars.

2001 NASA launches its Genesis probe to collect samples of the solar wind.

2001 NASA's space probe NEAR (Near Earth Asteroid Rendezvous), later renamed NEAR Shoemaker, lands on and photographs the surface of the asteroid Eros.

2001 The fourth of the 323-inch (8.2-m) reflecting telescopes is added to complete the Very Large Telescope (VLT) at Paranal Observatory in the Atacama desert, Chile.

2000 Scientists on the Human Genome Project produce a rough draft of the sequence of the human genome (using more than 3 billion characters).

2000 American paleontologist Dale Russell discovers a fossilized dinosaur heart.

2001 American researchers clone a human embryo but do not allow it to develop further.

2001 Surgeons in New York City use computers and "telepresence" to operate on a woman in France.

2000 Geneticists figure out the complete genome sequence of the fruit fly *Drosophila*, the most widely used experimental animal in the study of genetics.

2001 NASA's Trans-Iron Galactic Element Recorder (TIGER) makes its first ascent on the helium-filled Ultra Long Duration Balloon (ULDB) on a 30-day flight over Antarctica. Its mission is to detect heavy elements from iron to zirconium in cosmic rays originating in outer space.

ASIA & OCEANIA

2000 Japanese chemist Katsuyoshi Hoshino and coworkers announce a new way of "fixing" nitrogen in air using bright light and composite plastics to produce ammonium perchlorate (meaning that the nitrogen is converted to ammonium).

AFRICA & THE MIDDLE EAST

On September 11, 2001, Islamic terrorists flew airliners into the World Trade Center in New York City and the Pentagon in Washington, D.C.; a fourth plane crashed in Pennsylvania.

ENGINEERING & INVENTION

2000 In Norway the 15.2-mile (24.5-km) Lærdal Tunnel is completed, making it the world's longest road tunnel.

2000 British inventor Matthew Allwork (1963–2003) perfects a gyrostabilized camera that runs along tracks to televise athletics events. It is first used at the Olympic Games in Sydney, Australia.

2001 British inventor Ron Northedge patents a valve for controlling fluid flow that uses a rare-earth magnet, with no springs or continuous electricity supply.

2000 Divers in South Carolina raise the wreck of the Confederate submarine *H. L. Hunley*, which sank in 1864 during the American Civil War.

2000 American surgeon Robert Jarvik (1946–) begins work on the Jarvik–2000 artificial heart.

2001 The uncrewed *Southern Cross II* (Global Hawk spy plane) crosses the Pacific Ocean.

2001 International Launch Services, a joint U.S.–Russian venture, introduces the two-stage Proton M rocket, which can place a payload of 3.2 tons (2.9 tonnes) directly into a geostationary orbit around Earth.

2001 The twin towers of the World Trade Center in New York City, the world's second largest building, are destroyed by terrorist attacks.

WORLD EVENTS

2000 Serbia's president Slobodan Milosevic (1941–2006) is ousted in a popular uprising; he will later be indicted for war crimes and put on trial by an international court.

2000 Vladimir Putin (1952–) is elected president of Russia.

2000 Republican George W. Bush (1946–) emerges the winner in a disputed U.S. presidential election. He is reelected in 2004.

2000 Hilary Clinton (1947–) becomes the first First Lady elected to public office, winning a U.S. Senate seat in New York.

2000 Vicente Fox (1942–) becomes president of Mexico.

2001 The United States leads an invasion of Afghanistan, whose government is accused of harboring terrorists.

2000 The first-ever meeting takes place between the leaders of North and South Korea.

2001 Pakistan is a major ally in the U.S. invasion of Afghanistan.

2000 Israel ends its occupation of Southern Lebanon.

2000 The United States endorses the creation of a Palestinian state.

INSIDE STORY

"Love Bug"

Early in 2000 a computer virus known as the "Love Bug" forced computer systems across Europe to close down. It spread to the United States within a few hours. Possibly the reason why it spread so fast was because it originated in an attachment to an e-mail entitled "I love you... ." As soon as the attachment was opened, copies of the same e-mail were sent automatically to each name listed in the user's address book. Not only did the "bug" overload e-mail servers, it also infected certain files on the victim's machine. Within a few months at least 13 variants of the original virus had been identified. Since then a range of new antivirus products have been introduced to prevent future infections.

THE HUMAN GENOME PROJECT

A genome is a compete set of genes or genetic instructions that make up an organism. Because all organisms inherit their genes from the previous generation, the genome also provides important information about that organism's ancestry. In humans, as in other organisms, faults or mutations in the genetic code often lead to medical conditions known as genetic disorders.

Genes are instructions carried on chromosomes. Chromosomes are made of deoxyribonucleic acid (DNA). The human genome is a code spelled out in four letters: A, T, C, and G. The letters represent the chemical bases adenine, thiamine, cytosine, and guanine, which link up to form the "rungs" of DNA's twisting ladderlike structure.

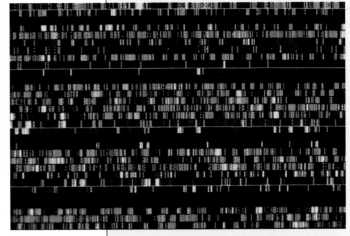

This computer screen display shows a sequence of human DNA as a series of colored bands. Each color represents a specific base.

The Human Genome Project was launched in 1990, with research institutes in several countries collaborating. Its aims were to sequence the letters of the human genetic code and identify all the genes. The project took 13 years to complete, with most of the sequencing done in laboratories in the United States. Advances in sequencing techniques pioneered by entrepreneurial scientist J. Craig Venter (1946–) helped speed up the project. In February 2001 the first draft of the genome, a list of about three billion bases, was published. The full sequence—containing about 25,000 different genes—was published in 2003.

ASTRONOMY & MATH	BIOLOGY & MEDICINE	PHYSICAL SCIENCES

EUROPE

2003 The Netherlands reports an epidemic of avian influenza ("bird flu").

2003 Footprints of an upright-walking human that lived 350,000 years ago are reported to have been discovered in Italy.

"Copycat" or "CC" was the first successfully cloned cat.

2002 German chemist Hans Gerd-Boyen at the University of Ulm discovers a new isotope of gold that resists powerful oxidizing agents and holds out promise for use as a catalyst.

2003 Chemist Leonid Khryashtchev at Helsinki University, Finland, makes an organic compound of a rare gas by reacting ethyne (acetylene) with krypton.

THE AMERICAS

2002 The National Aeronautic and Space Administration's (NASA) space probe Mars Odyssey begins mapping the surface of Mars, using thermal emission imaging.

2002 Astronomers at the observatory at Mauna Kea in Hawaii locate 11 new moons of Jupiter (bringing the total number to 39).

2002 The crew of NASA's space shuttle *Columbia* upgrades the Hubble Space Telescope in orbit around the Earth.

2003 NASA's space shuttle *Columbia* is destroyed when it breaks up 16 minutes before it is due to land on Earth, killing all of the crew. Shuttle flights are suspended until 2005.

2003 NASA's Wilkinson Microwave Anisotropy Probe satellite makes a detailed cosmic microwave background radiation map of the universe. The map reveals the universe to be 13.7 billion years old.

2002 Researchers at Texas A&M University reveal their clone of a domestic cat, which they name "Copycat."

2002 American researchers at the University of New York at Stony Brook produce a synthetic virus.

2002 The U.S. Food and Drug Administration approves clozapine as the first drug to reduce the risk of suicidal behavior.

2002 American chemists Lester Andrews and Bruce Bersten synthesize a compound of uranium and the rare gas neon.

The crew of the space shuttle Columbia *died in 2003 when the shuttle disintegrated during reentry into Earth's atmosphere. The incident was a result of damage to the shuttle's thermal protection system during its launch.*

ASIA & OCEANIA

2002 Astronomers in China and Japan observe the reappearance of Comet Ikeya-Zhang, which has not been seen for 341 years.

2003 Astronaut ("taikonaut" in China) Yang Liwei becomes the first Chinese astronaut to orbit the Earth in a 21-hour flight in China's first crewed spacecraft, Shen Zhou 5.

2003 An outbreak of the severe acute respiratory syndrome (SARS) virus in Asia spreads worldwide.

AFRICA & THE MIDDLE EAST

2003 A new group of insects called Mantophasmatodea is discovered in southern Africa.

ENGINEERING & INVENTION

2002 English inventor David Baker patents the Land Shark, a high-speed amphibious car.

2003 Austrian "extreme" sportsman Felix Baumgartner jumps from an airplane and skyglides across the English Channel. He makes the 22-mile (35-km) crossing in 14 minutes.

2003 Concorde makes its last flight.

2003 The last old-style Volkswagen Beetle is made in Puebla, Mexico.

Austrian Felix Baumgartner tests his carbon glider before his successful attempt to cross the English Channel in 2003.

WORLD EVENTS

2002 The Euro—the new currency of the European Union—begins circulating.

2002 Queen Elizabeth (1900–2002), the Queen Mother, of Britain dies aged 101.

2003 Energy company Enron declares bankruptcy, the largest bankruptcy case in U.S. history.

2003 The United States launches an attack on Iraq.

INSIDE STORY

Synthetic Virus

In 2002 a team of of scientists from the State University of New York at Stony Brook made a synthetic poliovirus. The researchers downloaded the genome sequence of the virus from the Internet, ordered it in fragments from a mail-order supplier, and then assembled it into the complete genome. The scientists injected their virus into mice, which became paralyzed and died. Synthetic viruses could be an important tool for gene therapy, in which viruses are used to carry genes into the cells of people with genetic disorders to replace or correct faulty genes. The creation of a synthetic virus also led to fears that bioterrorists would be able to make and spread lethal viruses such as smallpox.

2002 Islamic terrorists bomb nightclubs in Bali, Indonesia, killing about 200 people.

2002 The dispute between India and Pakistan over the Kashmir region threatens to turn into a nuclear war.

2003 Unrest breaks out in the Darfur region of Sudan, where government troops and their allies kill some 180,000 people and displace two million.

2003 An earthquake in Iran kills more than 40,000 people.

SARS

Severe acute respiratory syndrome, or SARS, was the first serious new contagious disorder of the 21st century. SARS is caused by a virus and affects the respiratory tract. Symptoms include high fever, chills, headache, cough, and diarrhea. Most infected people also develop pneumonia and breathing difficulties. In the SARS outbreak of 2002–03, which affected about 8,000 people, almost 800—about 1 in 10 sufferers—died. The disease originated in China and soon spread outside the country. The virus is passed on via the coughs and sneezes of those infected or by touching a contaminated object, such as a door handle, that had been touched by an infected person. The virus may also be able to travel in the air.

As with many other viral infections—including common cold, influenza, and HIV infection—medical scientists have not found a cure for SARS. Treatment aims at relieving symptoms, such as fever and breathing difficulties. With effective isolation of affected people, an outbreak of the disease can be contained. Chinese scientists produced a vaccine against SARS virus in 2004.

Schoolchildren in Hong Kong wear masks to protect themselves against SARS infection.

	ASTRONOMY & MATH	BIOLOGY & MEDICINE	PHYSICAL SCIENCES

EUROPE

2004 The Russian Soyuz TMA-4 spacecraft with a three-man crew docks with the International Space Station (ISS).

2004 The European Space Agency's (ESA) Beagle II lander, carried aboard the National Aeronautical and Space Administration's (NASA) Mars Express space probe, vanishes during its landing attempt on Mars.

2005 After a seven-year trip, the Cassini–Huygens space probe reaches Saturn. NASA's Cassini orbits the planet, while ESA's Huygens probe parachutes onto the surface of Saturn's massive moon Titan. It sends back data and pictures of what looks like an ice-strewn landscape.

2005 Scientists extract and decode the deoxyribonucleic acid (DNA) of two cave bears that died 40,000 years ago in the Austrian Alps.

An artist's impression shows the moment when a projectile from NASA's Deep Impact space probe collided with Comet Tempel 1.

THE AMERICAS

2004 NASA scientists obtain images of a "planetoid," named Sedna, orbiting beyond Neptune at the edge of the solar system.

2004 The first commercial spaceflight takes place when SpaceShipOne, funded by American computer programmer and entrepreneur Paul Allen (1953–), takes to the air and reaches a height of 337,600 feet, or 63.9 miles (103 km).

2005 Astronomer Michael Brown (1965–) announces the discovery of a remote object larger than Pluto. It becomes a candidate to be the tenth planet in the solar system.

2005 A projectile dispatched from NASA's Deep Impact space probe successfully collides with Comet Tempel 1, throwing out a huge plume of icy debris. Deep Impact is unharmed and redirected toward another comet.

2005 Astronomers discover 12 new moons orbiting Saturn.

2005 NASA space shuttle *Discovery* restarts the shuttle program with a successful flight to the International Space Station (ISS). It returns 14 days later after delays due to problems with heat-shield tiles. NASA grounds the shuttle fleet indefinitely.

2005 American researchers at Knoxville, Tennessee, grow human eggs in the laboratory by culturing ovarian stem cells in a hormone-rich solution.

2005 The Genographic Project is announced —a project spanning five continents that aims to map the history of human migration using DNA.

2005 Brazilian government figures indicate that the Amazon rain forest is being destroyed at record levels.

2004 Physicists from Penn State University announce a helium-based "supersolid" that flows through another material without friction.

2005 American geophysicist Joseph Dwyer and coworkers discover that lightning flashes also produce bursts of x-rays.

ASIA & OCEANIA

2005 The National Space Development Agency (NASDA) of Japan launches a weather satellite into Earth orbit, providing Japan with an independent weather forecasting facility.

2004 Medical researchers in South Korea clone human embryos to obtain stem cells for therapeutic purposes.

2004 Paleontologists announce the discovery of an 18,000-year-old skeleton of a 3-foot (1-m) tall humanoid on Flores Island, Indonesia. They name it *Homo floresiensis*.

AFRICA & THE MIDDLE EAST

2005 German zoologists on the Indian Ocean island of Madagascar identify two new tiny species of mouse lemurs (*Microcebus*).

ENGINEERING & INVENTION	WORLD EVENTS

2005 European consortium Airbus Industrie's Airbus 380 makes its maiden flight from Toulouse, France. At 240 feet (73 m) long, with a wingspan of 239 feet (72.8 m) and able to carry an average of 550 passengers, it is the world's largest passenger plane. It can fly nonstop between any of the world's major airports.

2005 The International Thermonuclear Experimental Reactor project is announced to build a nuclear fusion reactor in France; the project is expected to run for 35 years.

2004 Terrorist attacks on trains in Madrid kill 190 people.

2004 Ten more countries join the European Union: Poland, Lithuania, Latvia, Estonia, the Czech Republic, Slovakia, Slovenia, Hungary, Malta, and Cyprus.

2004 The Russian army ends a terrorist siege at a school in Beslan, North Ossetia-Alania. More than 330 people are killed and at least 700 more are injured.

2005 Pope John Paul II (1920–2005) dies.

2005 Four explosions on public transport in London kill 56 people and injure more than 700 others.

2005 American company Boeing launches the Boeing 777-200LR airliner, designed to carry 300 passengers across the world nonstop in 18 hours.

2005 American adventurer Steve Fossett (1944–) lands at Salina, Kansas, after a 67-hour solo nonstop flight around the world in a jet-powered plane.

2005 American scientists use highly sensitive scales to measure the mass of a cluster of xenon atoms at just a few billionths of a trillionth of a gram—the smallest measurement of mass ever made.

2005 American researchers produce the world's smallest brushes, with bristles more than a thousand times finer than a human hair.

2004 George W. Bush (1946–) begins a second term as the U.S. President.

2005 Hurricane Katrina hits the Gulf Coast of the United States, resulting in one of the worst natural disasters in U.S. history.

2005 American cyclist Lance Armstrong (1971–) wins the Tour de France for an unprecedented seventh consecutive time.

2004 An undersea earthquake triggers a tsunami that devastates Indonesia and other parts of southern Asia, killing about 300,000 people.

The Airbus A380 test crew wave from a platform in front of the world's biggest airliner after its four-hour maiden flight from Toulouse Blagnac airport in France.

2004 The first municipal elections in 40 years are held in Saudi Arabia. Woman are not allowed to vote or run for office.

2004 The first free elections in 50 years are held in Iraq.

THE HOBBIT

In 2003, a team of Australian and Indonesian paleontologists found skeletal remains, including a skull, of a previously unknown hominoid species in the Liang Bua cave in Flores, an island in Indonesia. The team named the species *Homo floresiensis*, for the island of Flores. *H. floresiensis* lived until about 18,000 years ago and is thought to be a descendant of *H. erectus*, which lived in Africa, Asia, and Europe and also gave rise to modern humans, *H. sapiens*.

H. floresiensis grew to about 40 inches (100 cm) tall, had long arms, and a small skull—similar to the size of a chimpanzee's skull but with more humanlike features. The team published their findings in 2004, and the press soon nicknamed the species "hobbits," for the race of short humanlike creatures featured in the novels of J. R. R. Tolkien.

Some scientists disputed whether *H. floresiensis* was a species in its own

Archaeologist Tony Djubiantono holds the skull of Homo floresiensis.

right. They believe that the skull that was found belonged to a modern human with a disease, such as the genetic disorder microcephaly, which results in a small brain and skull. Others believe *H. floresiensis* was a population of slender (gracile) modern humans. However, the skeletal remains seem unlikely to provide any deoxyribonucleic acid (DNA) that would help resolve the relationship of *H. floresiensis* to modern humans.

THE WORLD WIDE WEB

ABOVE: *More than
70 percent of people
in the United States
use the Internet.*

THE WORLD WIDE WEB ALLOWS USERS ACROSS the world access to a vast amount of data and enables rapid communication with other users at the click of a mouse. It uses telephone lines or radio to link computers into a network that extends across the world. It allows computer users to gain access to billions of Web pages as well as video, movies, and music. English computer scientist Tim Berners-Lee (1955–) devised the Web in 1990.

Computer links had existed since the 1970s. They were developed originally for the use of scientists working for the Advanced Research Projects Agency (ARPA) of the U.S. Department of Defense as a network known as ARPANET. Stanford University set up a commercial version of ARPANET in 1974.

In 1981 the City University of New York launched BITNET. It could be used by university scientists throughout the eastern United States, provided they used IBM mainframe computers. European versions soon followed: EUNET in 1982 and the European Academic and Research Network (EARN) in 1984.

These networks were limited by the difficulty of generating information on one computer in a form that could be read by other computers. The problem was solved within each network, but there were so many systems that computers belonging to one network were unable to communicate with computers from another.

As early as 1974, however, computer scientists at ARPA and Stanford University had devised a system called a transmission control protocol/internet protocol (TCP/IP) to allow computers to send data between networks. ARPA adopted TCP/IP in 1982. Networks could finally be linked: The Internet had been born and, with it, e-mail. Messages between

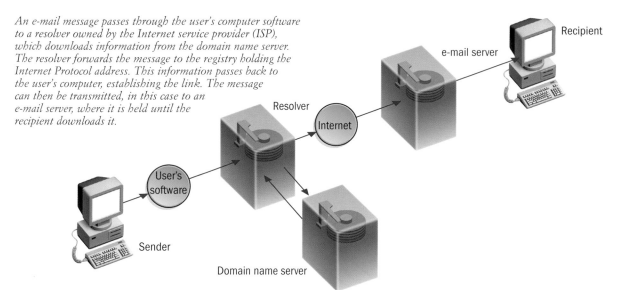

An e-mail message passes through the user's computer software to a resolver owned by the Internet service provider (ISP), which downloads information from the domain name server. The resolver forwards the message to the registry holding the Internet Protocol address. This information passes back to the user's computer, establishing the link. The message can then be transmitted, in this case to an e-mail server, where it is held until the recipient downloads it.

Recipient

e-mail server

Resolver

Internet

User's software

Sender

Domain name server

KEY DATES

1980
Tim Berners-Lee releases Enquire

1981
BITNET launched

1982
EUNET launched; Internet born

1984
EARN launched; domain names introduced; JANET launched

1985
NSFNET launched

1990
Tim Berners-Lee names the World Wide Web

1991
NSFNET opened to the public; the Web released to the public

1992
"Information superhighway project"

1993
Mosaic X, the first Web browser, introduced

1993
World Wide Web certified by CERN as being in the public domain

computers had to be routed. This meant that each host (any computer linked to a network) had to be allotted a unique address. At first, it was sufficient to allocate a name to each host, but in 1984 the system became more sophisticated with the introduction of domain name servers. A domain name server is a computer that stores lists of domain names and can route requests accordingly. Domain names include http:// (hypertext transfer protocol), www (World Wide Web), ac (academic), edu (education), com (commercial), and gov (government), as well as national identifiers, such as uk (United Kingdom) and nl (Netherlands).

The Internet received a further boost when, also in 1984, British government backed the Joint Academic Network (JANET) to serve British universities. In 1985 the U.S. National Science Foundation set up NSFNET to extend Internet use to all authorized persons on every American campus. NSFNET concluded agreements with the owners of other networks and made TCP/IP mandatory for all participants. In 1991 NSFNET allowed access to private computers.

Tim Berners-Lee

Since 1980 Tim Berners-Lee had been searching for a way to allow physicists to communicate with one another using different computer systems. His first program, devised in 1980, was called "Enquire-Within-Upon-Everything." It allowed certain types of computers to exchange data using hypertext transfer protocol, which links documents on different computers, allowing the user to move swiftly from one to

another. It was not until 1990, however, that Berners-Lee developed Enquire into the World Wide Web.

In 1991 the program was published on the Internet, free for anyone to use. The World Wide Web was born. It grew slowly. By the end of 1993 there were no more than about 150 sites connected to it. But 1993 was the year American Mark Andreessen (1971–) of the National Center for Supercomputing Applications in Illinois released the first browser, Mosaic X (later renamed Netscape). A browser hides the links between documents. Instead of typing in the address of a required document, the user simply clicks on a hypertext link indicated by words in a different color. Where the Internet linked computers, the World Wide Web linked documents. Today there are more than 20 million Web sites and more than 20 billion Web pages.

An employee wanders through Amazon.com's depot in Seattle. Founded in 1994, Amazon.com is the biggest online retailer in the United States.

2006–Present

CONCISE HISTORY OF SCIENCE AND INVENTION

ASTRONOMY & MATH	BIOLOGY & MEDICINE	PHYSICAL SCIENCES

EUROPE

2006 A space mission led by the French Space Agency launches COROT (COnvection ROtation and planetary Transits), a telescope with spectroscopic detectors, to look for extrasolar planets. It finds its first planet, COROT-Exo-1b, in 2007.

2008 Jules Verne, an unpiloted European cargo spacecraft, is launched to resupply the International Space Station.

2007 A team at Roslin Institute in Scotland develop genetically modified chickens that lay eggs containing proteins that can fight cancer.

2007 Researchers from Wales discover a 405-year-old clam off the coast of Ireland.

2008 Researchers at Newcastle University in England create human–cow embryos, which survive for three days. The hybrid embryos—which would provide stem cells to develop therapies for neurological disorders such as Alzheimer's—were made by injecting human deoxyribonucleic acid (DNA) into enucleated cow egg cells.

2008 The Large Hadron Collider at the European Organization for Nuclear Research (CERN) begins its experiments, with about one billion people watching the switch-on live worldwide. Nine days later the collider develops a fault and is shut down for repairs.

THE AMERICAS

2006 The dwarf planet Eris (discovered the previous year by astronomers at the Palomar Observatory in California) is found to be larger than Pluto.

2006 The National Aeronautics and Space Administration's (NASA) spacecraft New Horizons is launched on its nine-year journey to Pluto.

2006 Genesis I, an experimental space habitat designed and built by American firm Bigelow Aerospace, is launched into Earth orbit.

2007 American astronomer Travis Barman at the Lowell Observatory in Arizona detects water vapor on extrasolar planet HD 209458 using spectroscopy.

2008 NASA's Messenger spacecraft makes two flybys of Mercury, with a third and final flyby in late 2009.

2006 Analysis of a 375-million-year-old fossil found in the Canadian territory of Nunavut shows it to be a "missing link" between fish and tetrapods (four-legged vertebrates). The animal is given the name *Tiktaalik roseae* and nicknamed the "fishapod."

2007 Geneticist J. Craig Venter (1946–) publishes his entire genetic sequence—the first genome published of a single person.

2007 Scientists sequence protein fragments found in soft tissue recovered from the fossil bones of a 68 million-year-old *Tyrannosaurus rex* and a half-million-year-old mastodon.

2007 A chlorophyll-producing bacterium—which transforms light into chemical energy like plants—is discovered in several of the hot springs at Yellowstone National Park.

2008 A previously unknown species of uakari monkey is discovered in the Amazon and named C*acajao ayresii*.

2007 A team of researchers from Massachusetts Institute of Technology light a 60-watt bulb by transferring energy through the air from a power source not physically connected to the bulb. The team refers to the transfer of energy as "WiTricity" (wireless electricity).

2008 Former NASA scientist John C. Mankins uses radio waves to transmit solar power between two Hawaiian islands.

2008 Scientists from Princeton University propose that a series of volcanic eruptions in India may have killed the dinosaurs, rather than a meteor impact in the Gulf of Mexico.

ASIA & OCEANIA

2008 The Indian Space Research Organization launches Chandrayaan-1, an unpiloted lunar spacecraft.

2007 Clouded leopards on Borneo and Sumatra are declared a separate species from the clouded leopards on mainland Asia after DNA studies.

2007 Last seen in 2004 the Baiji, or Chinese river dolphin (*Lipotes vexillifer*), is now believed to be extinct.

AFRICA & THE MIDDLE EAST

Scientists think that Tiktaalik roseae *lived in shallow water and used its fins to prop itself up.*

ENGINEERING & INVENTION

2007 The Airbus A380 makes its first commercial flight, from Singapore to Sydney.

2009 British engineer Richard Jenkins breaks the world land-speed record when his wind-powered *Greenbird* car reaches 126.1 miles (202.9 km) per hour in Nevada.

2006 The Boeing 747 Large Cargo Freighter (LCF), known as the *Dreamlifter*, makes its maiden flight.

2007 Apple markets its iPhone, a multimedia smartphone with a touch screen.

2007 U.S scientists create printable, flexible batteries by weaving black carbon nanotubes into paper.

2008 Wind power—a growing source of energy—now accounts for just over 1 percent of total electricity in the United States.

WORLD EVENTS

2007 Bulgaria and Romania join the European Union.

2007 Gordon Brown (1951–) replaces Tony Blair (1953–) as prime minister of Britain.

2008 Dmitry Medvedev (1965–) becomes president of Russia, replacing Vladimir Putin (1952–).

A scientist tests the magnets that bend and focus the beams of particles in the Large Hadron Collider.

2008 Barack Obama (1961–) becomes the first African-American president of the United States.

2008 More than 133,000 people are killed in Myanmar by Cyclone Nargis.

2008 Robert Mugabe (1924–) is reelected as president of Zimbabwe after a controversial election.

INSIDE STORY

The Baiji

Also called the Chinese river dolphin, the baiji is now thought to be extinct (or with too few alive to maintain the species). Historically, this freshwater dolphin was found in a 1,000-mile (1,700-km) stretch of the Yangtze (Chang Jiang) River, from Yichang in the west to the mouth of the river, near Shanghai. Many factors have led to its demise in recent decades, including pollution, habitat loss due to dam building, entanglement in fishing nets, collisions with boats, illegal electric fishing, and low stocks of its fish prey. A six-week survey in 2006 failed to find any baijis, and the last unattested sighting was in 2004. Its extinction makes it the first aquatic mammal to disappear since the Japanese sea lion and Caribbean monk seal in the 1950s.

THE LARGE HADRON COLLIDER

The Large Hadron Collider (LHC) is the world's largest particle accelerator. Built by the European Organization for Nuclear Research (CERN), LHC is located in an underground circular tunnel with a circumference of 17 miles (27 km) near Geneva, Switzerland.

Protons were circulated in the collider for the first time on September 19, 2008. Nine days later an electrical fault in the collider led to problems, and it was shut down for several months.

More than 10,000 scientists and engineers from all over the world are involved in LHC's setup and experiments. Planned experiments will help solve many unanswered questions in high-energy physics. For example: Does the Higgs boson exist? What are dark matter and dark energy? Are there extra dimensions?

The circular tunnel of the collider contains two beam pipes that run parallel but intersect at four different points. In the experiments, each pipe contains a beam of particles; in one pipe the particles travel clockwise, in the other counterclockwise. In most of the experiments protons from opposing beams, traveling at 99.99 percent of the speed of light, will collide at the intersection points. Other planned experiments will collide heavy ions, such as lead ions.

The collisions release concentrated energy and simulate the conditions immediately after the big bang at the beginning of the universe, when there are thought to have been various types of short-lived particles and quark-gluon plasma. Particle detectors—located at LHC's intersection points—will look for new types of particles, the origins of mass, extra dimensions, quark-gluon plasma, and antimatter.

ILLUSTRATIONS CREDITS

Pages 2 & 3 Shutterstock/Bernhard Lelle.
Page 9 NASA/MSFC.

Chapter 1: Origins of Science Prehistory-850 B.C.E.
12-13, TopFoto/Charles Walker; 14, NGS Image Collection; 15, Corbis/Werner Forman; 18b, Shutterstock/MaxPhoto; 23, Corbis/Roger de la Harpe/Gallo Images; 24, Corbis/Christie's Images; 25, Corbis/Kazuyoshi Nomachi; 27, TopFoto/J. Irwin/ClassicStock; 28, Shutterstock/Kmiragaya; 30t, Shutterstock/IPK Photography; 30b, Shutterstock/Cora Reed; 31, 32-33, Photos.com; 34, Shutterstock/Sculpies; 36, Shutterstock/Timo Kohlbacher; 37, Corbis/Bojan Brecelj; 38, Photos.com; 40, Shutterstock/Graeme Dawes; 41, Photos.com.

Chapter 2: Classical and Early Medieval Science 849 B.C.E.-999 C.E.
42-43, Shutterstock/Jonathan Larsen; 44, Shutterstock/Styve Reinek; 45t, Shutterstock/Giovanni Beninstende; 45b, Shutterstock/Alex Stiop; 48, Photos.com; 49, Shutterstock/Vangelis; 50-51, Shutterstock/Daniel Loncarevic; 52t, Shutterstock/Gary Yim; 52b, Shutterstock/Zhouhui8525; 54, 55, Photos.com; 56b, NASA; 57, Shutterstock/Curtis Kautzer; 59, Shutterstock/Elena Elisseeva; 60, Shutterstock/Luisa Fernandez Gonzalez; 62, Shutterstock/WizData, inc.; 64t, Shutterstock/Martin Ezequiel Gardeazabal; 64b, Shutterstock/Irene Kofman; 66, Shutterstock/YKh; 67, TopFoto/Granger Collection; 68t, Photos.com; 68b, Shutterstock/Rafael Ramirez Lee.

Chapter 3: Late Medieval and Renaissance Science 1000-1624
70-71, Corbis/Derek Croucher; 72, Shutterstock/Janaka; 73t, Corbis/I. Vanderhaust/Robert Harding World Imagery; 73b, Shutterstock/Scott Rothstein; 76, Shutterstock/Stephen Strathdee; 77, Shutterstock/PixAchi; 78, Shutterstock/Holger Mette; 79, 80, 81, Photos.com; 82, Shutterstock/Asier Villafranca; 83, Science Photo Library/Sheila Terry; 84, Shutterstock/Vesilio; 86, Shutterstock/Ricardo Manuel Silva de Sousa; 87, Getty Images/Hulton; 88l, Shutterstock/Arogant; 89, 90t, Photos.com; 90b, Photodisc; 91, Shutterstock/c.; 92, Art Archive/University of Gottengen/Eileen Tweedy; 93, Art Archive/Bibliotheque Nationale Paris; 96l, Science Photo Library/J.L. Chaumet; 96r, Shutterstock/Johanna Goodyear.

Chapter 4: The Scientific Revolution 1625-1774
98-99, Corbis/The Gallery Collection; 100, iStock/Lawrence Sawyer; 101, Photos.com; 104t, Shutterstock/Aleksandr Ugovenkow; 105t, 105b, Photos.com; 107t, Art Archive/Private Collection/Eileen Tweedy; 107b, Photos.com; 108, NASA; 109, Shutterstock/Pnicoledolin; 110, Shutterstock/Cathy Keifer; 111, Photos.com; 112, Science Photo Library/Biophoto Associates; 113, Shutterstock/Stephen Finn; 114, Corbis/Bettmann; 115, Photos.com; 116b, Science Photo Library/CCI Archives; 117, Getty Images/Time & Life Pictures; 118t, Photos.com; 118b, Corbis/ Bettmann; 119, Shutterstock/Picsfive; 121t, Photos.com; 122, NASA; 123, Shutterstock/Frank Heritage; 124r, Getty Images/Time & Life Pictures; 125, Science Photo Library/Maria Platt-Evans; 126, Science Photo Library; 127t, Science & Society Photo Library; 128t, 128b, 129, Photos.com; 130, Corbis/Philadelphia Museum of Art; 131, 132, 133, Photos.com; 134l, Shutterstock/Kevin Britland; 135, Photos.com.

Chapter 5: The Industrial Revolution 1775-1839
136-137, Science and Society Picture Library; 138, Art Archive/Tate Gallery London/Eileen Tweedy; 139t, Photos.com; 139b, Shutterstock/Michael Zysman; 142, Photos.com; 143l, 143r, Science Photo Library/Sheila Terry; 144, Shutterstock/John A. Anderson; 145, Shutterstock/Eric Isselee; 146, 147, Photos.com; 148l. Corbis/Bettmann; 148r, Corbis/DK Ltd.; 150, Shutterstock/Vladimir Vitek; 151t, Photos.com; 151b, Shutterstock/Russell Shirley; 151-152, 152t, Photos.com; 153t, Science Photo Library; 154, Shutterstock/dinadesign; 155t, Shutterstock/John R. Smith; 155b, Science Photo Library/Ben Johnson; 156, NASA/JPL; 157, Photos.com; 158, Photos.com; 159t, Corbis/Bettmann; 160t, Shutterstock/Konstantin Mironov; 160b, Science Photo Library/Science, Industry & Business Library/New York Public Library; 162t, TopFoto/Novosti; 162b, TopFoto/Picturepoint; 163, Shutterstock/Pete Hoffman; 165, 166t, Photos.com.

Chapter 6: The Age of Steam 1840-1884
168-169, Bridgeman Art Library/Bristol City Museum & Art Gallery; 170, Corbis; 171, Corbis/Steve Raymer; 174, NASA/SOHO; 175t, Shutterstock/psamtik; 175b, Photos.com; 176, Shutterstock/John Keith; 177, Getty Images/Time & Life Pictures; 178l, Science Photo Library; 178r, Shutterstock/Keith Sponsler; 179, Shutterstock/Gail Johnson; 180, Science Photo Library/Dr. Paul Andrews, University of Dundee; 181, Science Photo Library/Tom McHugh; 182t, Science Photo Library; 183, Getty Images/Hulton; 184t, Shutterstock/Jens Stolt; 185, Photos.com; 186, Shutterstock/Christophe Testi; 187t, Science Photo Library/Charles D. Winters; 188, Library of Congress; 189, iStock/onfilm; 190, Shutterstock/Maksym Gorpenyuk; 192-193, Photos.com; 194, Science Photo Library/Dr. Kari Lounatmaa; 195, 196, Photos.com; 197t, Getty Images/Boyer/Roger Viollet.

Chapter 7: The Age of Electricity 1885-1919
198-199, Corbis/Sergey Konenkov/Sygma; 200, Getty Images/Bob Thomas/Popperfoto; 201, Corbis/Bettmann; 204, NASA/ESA; 205t, TopFoto/Picturepoint; 205b, Getty Images/Time & Life Pictures; 207, Photos.com; 208, Shutterstock/Kuzma; 209, Shutterstock/Dvoretskiy Igor Vladimirovich; 210, 211, Science Photo Library; 212l, Science Photo Library/Tony & Daphne Hallas; 212r, Photos.com; 214l, Science Photo Library/American Institute of Physics; 215, Science Photo Library/Omikron; 216, Photos.com; 217t, Shutterstock/Sebastian Kaulitzki; 217b, Getty Images/Hulton; 218, Shutterstock/Margo Harrison; 219, Photos.com; 220, Shutterstock/Judy Whitton; 221t, Photos.com; 221b, Getty Images/Hulton; 222, Corbis/Bettmann; 223t, Library of Congress; 223b, Getty Images/Hulton; 224-225, Topfoto/ClassicStock; 224b, Getty Images/Hulton; 226t, TopFoto/Novosti; 226b, Photos.com; 227, Library of Congress; 229t, Photos.com; 229b, Shutterstock/Johnny Tran; 230, Getty Images/Jens Schlueter; 231t, Photos.com; 233t, TopFoto/Ullsteinbild; 233b, TopFoto; 234, Shutterstock/Glen Jones; 235, Photos.com.

Chapters 8: The Atomic Age 1920-1949
236-237, Cern; 238, Corbis/Bettmann; 239, NASA/USAF/Lt. Robert A. Hoover; 242, Science Photo Library/David A. Hardy; 243, Shutterstock/StillFX; 244t, TopFoto/Photri; 245, Cern; 246, Getty Images/Kurt Hu Han; 247l, 247ml, 247mr, NASA/HSTI; 247r, Science Photo Library/American Institute of Physics; 248, TopFoto; 249b, Science Photo Library/Sheila Terry; 250, Corbis/Bettmann; 251, Photos.com; 252, Shutterstock/Ben C; 253l, Corbis/Hulton-Deutsch; 254, Corbis/Visuals Unlimited; 255, Robert Hunt Library; 256, Science Photo Library/Robin Scagell; 257, Science Photo Library/Photo Researchers; 258l, iStock/Kathy's Pictures; 258r, Shutterstock/Mike Flippo; 260, Robert Hunt Library; 261t, iStock/George Cairns; 261b, Shutterstock/Rob Wilson; 262, Science Photo Library/National Archives; 263, Robert Hunt Library; 264, Getty Images/Time & Life Pictures; 265l, TopFoto; 266, Getty Images/Hulton; 267t, Getty Images/Time & Life Pictures; 268, Science Photo Library/Des Bartlett; 269t, Public Health Image Library/CDC/Dr. J.D. Miller; 270, TopFoto; 271t, Science Photo Library/U.S. Army; 271, Shutterstock/c.

Chapter 9: The Space Age 1950-1979
272-273, NASA; 274, Science Photo Library/Medical RF.com; 275, NASA; 278t, Science Photo Library/National Library of Medicine; 278b, NASA/ESA/Hubble Heritage Team; 279, Science Photo Library/Thomas Hollyman; 280, Getty Images/Popperfoto; 281, Shutterstock/Robert Zywucki; 282, Science Photo Library/Barrington Brown; 283b, Science Photo Library/Science Source; 284, Shutterstock/David Woods; 285, Shutterstock/Simon Pederson; 286l, Science Photo Library/RIA Novosti; 286r, Getty Images/Time & Life Pictures; 287, NASA; 288, Getty Images/Hulton; 289t, Shutterstock/Steve Noakes; 289b, Shutterstock/Vladimir Korostyshevskiy; 290, TopFoto; 291, Shutterstock/Dmitry Tereshchenko; 292, NASA; 293, NASA/CXC/ASU/J.Hester; 294t, NASA; 294b, Science Photo Library/NIHI Custom Medical Stock; 295, Shutterstock/Graham Bloomfield; 296l, Science Photo Library/Corning Inc./Emilio Segre Visual Archives/American Institute of Physics; 297, TopFoto/Phottri; 298, NASA/JPL; 299t, Shutterstock/Dariush M.; 299b, Science Photo Library/Volker Steger; 300, Shutterstock/Paul Laragy; 301, NASA/JSC.

Chapter 10: The Modern World 1980-Present
302-303, Getty Images/AFP; 304t, Corbis/Keren Su; 304b, NASA; 307, Corbis/Bob Sacha; 308, Shutterstock/Jonathan Larsen; 309, Photos.com; 310, NASA/JCS; 311, Shutterstock/Rui Saraiva; 312, Science and Society Picture Library; 313t, Public Domain; 314, Science Photo Library/Dale Boyer; 315t, Corbis/Ralph White; 315b, NASA/GSFC; 316l, Photos.com; 316r, Shutterstock/Brett Atkins; 317, NASA; 318l, Shutterstock/Eric Isselee; 318r, NASA/JPL; 319, NASA/KSC/Byron Lichtenberg; 320t, Corbis/Francois Pugnet; 320b, Science Photo Library/Hank Morgan; 321, Shutterstock/Petronillo G. Dangoy Jr.; 322, Science Photo Library/U.S. Department of Energy; 323t, Nasa/Hubble Heritage Team; 324, Corbis/Jeremy Horner; 325t, Photos.com; 325b, Science Photo Library/Professor Peter Goddard; 326, NASA/JPL; 327l, Science Photo Library/GustoImages; 328, Corbis/Fabrice Coffrini/EPA; 329l, NASA/Robert Markowitz; 329r, Getty Images/AFP; 330, iStock/Coldimages; 331t, Photos.com; 332, iStock/Markus Seidel; 333, Science Photo Library/James King-Holmes; 334t, Getty Images; 334b, NASA/JSC; 335t, 335b, Getty Images/AFP; 336t, NASA/JPL/Pat Rawlings; 336b, Getty Images; 337, Science Photo Library/Laurant Orloc; 338, iStock/Sean Locke; 339b, TopFoto/Imageworks/Barry Sweet; 340, Science Photo Library/National Science Foundation; 341, Science Photo Library/David Parker.

All Artworks The Brown Reference Group.

General Reference

Allaby, Michael, and Derek Gjersten, eds. *Makers of Science*. New York: Oxford University Press, 2002.

Asimov, Isaac. *Asimov's Biographical Encyclopedia of Science and Technology*. Garden City, New York: Doubleday, 1972.

Boorstin, Daniel J. *The Discoverers*. New York: Random House, 1983.

Boyle, David. *The Tyranny of Numbers*. London: HarperCollins, 2000.

Bryson, Bill. *A Short History of Nearly Everything*. New York: Broadway Books, 2003.

Bunch, Bryan H., and Alexander Hellemans. *The History of Science and Technology*. Boston: Houghton Mifflin, 2004.

Carey, John, ed. *The Faber Book of Science*. Boston: Faber and Faber, 1995.

Carruth, Gorton. *The Encyclopedia of American Facts and Dates*. New York: HarperCollins, 1997.

Crystal, David, ed. *The Cambridge Biographical Dictionary*. New York: Cambridge University Press, 1996.

Daintith, John, ed. *A Dictionary of Chemistry*. New York: Oxford University Press, 2000.

Daintith, John, ed. *A Dictionary of Scientists*. New York: Oxford University Press, 1999.

Daintith, John, and R. Rennie, eds. *The Facts on File Dictionary of Mathematics*. New York: Facts on File, 2005.

Darton, Mike, and John Clark. *The Macmillan Dictionary of Measurement*. New York: Macmillan, 1994.

Day, Lance, and Ian McNeil, eds. *Biographical Dictionary of the History of Technology*. New York: Routledge, 1996.

Diamond, Jared. *Guns, Germs and Steel*. New York: W. W. Norton and Co., 1997.

Dyson, James, and Robert Uhlig, ed. *A History of Great Inventions*. New York: Carroll and Graf Publishers, 2001.

le Fanu, James. *The Rise and Fall of Modern Medicine*. New York: Carroll and Graf Publishers, 2000.

Giscard d'Estaing, Valerie, A. *The Book of Inventions and Discoveries*. London: Queen Anne Press, 1990.

Glover, Linda K., *et al. National Geographic Encyclopedia of Space*. Washington, D.C.: National Geographic Society, 2005.

Gribbin, John. *Science, A History, 1543–2001*. New York: Allen Lane, 2002.

Harrison, Ian. *The Book of Inventions*. Washington, D.C.: National Geographic Society, 2004.

Hoskin, Michael, ed. *The Cambridge Concise History of Astronomy*. New York: Cambridge University Press, 1999.

The Hutchinson Dictionary of Scientific Biography. Abingdon, England: Helicon, 2007.

Inventions that Changed the World. Pleasantville, New York: Reader's Digest Association, 1999.

Kagan, Nick, ed. *National Geographic Concise History of the World: An Illustrated Time Line*. Washington, D.C.: National Geographic Society, 2006.

Luck, Steve, ed. *Philip's Science and Technology Encyclopedia*. London: George Philip Limited, 1998.

McLeish, John. *Number*. New York: Fawcett Columbine, 1992.

Margotta, Roberto. *The History of Medicine*. Feltham: Hamlyn, 1968.

Meadows, Jack. *The Great Scientists*. New York: Oxford University Press, 1997.

Messadié, Gerald. *Great Inventions through History*. New York: Chambers, 1991.

Messadié, Gerald. *Great Scientific Discoveries*. New York: Chambers, 1991.

Millar, David, *et al. The Cambridge Dictionary of Scientists*. New York: Cambridge University Press, 1996.

Muir, Hazel, ed. *Larousse Dictionary of Scientists*. New York: Larousse, 1996.

Philip's Astronomy Encyclopedia. London: George Philip Limited, 2002.

Philip's Science and Technology People, Dates and Events. London: George Philip Limited, 1999.

Porter, Roy. *The Greatest Benefit to Mankind*. New York: W. W. Norton and Co., 1998.

Rockwood, Camilla, ed. *Chambers Biographical Dictionary*. Edinburgh: Chambers, 2007.

Silver, B. L. *The Ascent of Science*. New York: Oxford University Press, 1998.

Smith, Jacqueline. *The Facts on File Dictionary of Earth Science*. New York: Facts on File, 2006.

Tallack, Peter, ed. *The Science Book*. London: Weidenfeld and Nicolson, 2003.

Trefil, James. *Cassell's Laws of Nature*. London: Cassell, 2002.

Waites, Gillian. *The Cassell Dictionary of Biology*. London: Cassell, 1999.

Waller, John. *Fabulous Science*. New York: Oxford University Press, 2004.

Webster's New Biographical Dictionary. Springfield, Massachusetts: Merriam-Webster, 1983.

Whitfield, Peter. *Landmarks in Western Science*. London: The British Library, 2004.

Williams, E. T., and C. S. Nicholls, eds. *The Dictionary of National Biography*. New York: Oxford University Press, 1981.

Williams, Trevor I., ed. *A Biographical Dictionary of Scientists*. New York: Wiley, 1974.

Williams, Trevor I. *A History of Invention*. New York: Checkmark Books, 2000.

Chapter 1: Origins of Science Prehistory-850 B.C.E.

Burrell, Roy E. C. *First Ancient History*. Oxford: Oxford University Press, 1994.

Duncan, David E. *Calendar: Humanity's Epic Struggle to Determine a True and Accurate Year*. New York: Bard, 1998.

Haywood, J. *World Atlas of the Past*. New York: Oxford University Press, 1999.

James, Peter, and Nick Thorpe. *Ancient Inventions*. New York: Ballantine Books, 1994. (Also used for Chapters 2 and 3.)

Landels, J. G. *Engineering in the Ancient World*. Berkeley: University of California Press, 2000. (Also used for Chapters 2 and 3.)

Romer, John. *The Great Pyramid: Ancient Egypt Revisited*. New York: Cambridge University Press, 2007.

Wells, Spencer. *The Journey of Man: A Genetic Odyssey*. Princeton, New Jersey: Princeton University Press, 2002.

What Life Was Like on The Banks of the Nile: Egypt, 3050–30 B.C. Alexandria, Virginia: Time-Life Books, 1996.

Zimmer, Carl. *Smithsonian Intimate Guide to Human Origins*. New York: Collins, 2005.

Chapter 2: Classical and Early Medieval Science 849 B.C.E.-999 C.E.

Brockman, John, ed. *The Greatest Inventions of the Past 2,000 Years*. New York: Simon and Schuster, 2000. (Also used for Chapters 3, 4, 5, 6, 7, 8, and 9.)

Coes, Michael D. *The Maya*. New York: Thames and Hudson, 2005.

Fagan, Brian M., ed. *The Seventy Great Inventions of the Ancient World*. London: Thames and Hudson, 2004.

Hill, Donald R. *A History of Engineering in Classical and Medieval Times*. New York: Routledge, 1996. (Also used for Chapter 3.)

Kaplan, Robert. *The Nothing that Is: A Natural History of Zero*. New York: Oxford University Press, 2000.

Martin, Sean. *Alchemy and Alchemists*. Harpenden, Hertfordshire: Pocket Essentials, 2006. (Also used for Chapters 3 and 4.)

Pearson, Anne. *Ancient Greece*. New York: DK Publishing, 2007.

What Life Was Like When Longships Sailed. Alexandria, Virginia: Time-Life Books, 1998.

Wilkinson, Philip. *What the Romans Did for Us*. London: Boxtree, 2000. (Also used for Chapter 3.)

Woodman, Richard. *The History of the Ship*. New York: Lyons Press, 1997. (Also used for Chapters 4, 5, 6, 7, 8, and 9.)

Chapter 3: Late Medieval and Renaissance Science 1000-1624

Clegg, Brian. *The First Scientist: A Life of Roger Bacon*. New York: Carroll and Graf Publishers, 2003.

Gately, Iain. *Tobacco: The Story of How Tobacco Seduced the World*. New York: Grove Press, 2001.

Gravett, Christopher. *Castles and Fortifications from around the World*. Ludlow, England: Thalamus Publishing, 2006.

Kelly, Jack. *Gunpowder*. New York: Basic Books, 2004.

Kelly, John. *The Great Mortality: An Intimate History of the Black Death, the Most Devastating Plague of All Time*. New York: HarperCollins Publishers, 2005.

Ochoa, George, and Carter Smith. *Atlas of Hispanic-American History*. New York: Facts On File, Inc., 2008.

Peterson, Harold L. *The Book of the Gun*. London: Paul Hamlyn, 1962. (Also used for Chapters 4 and 5.)

Thompson, Logan. *Guns in Colour*. London: Octopus, 1981. (Also used for Chapters 4, 7, and 8.)

White, Michael. *Leonardo: The First Scientist*. New York: St. Martin's Press, 2000.

Zuckerman, Larry. *The Potato: How the Humble Spud Rescued the Western World*. New York: North Point Press, 1999.

Chapter 4: The Scientific Revolution 1625-1774

Blunt, Wilfrid. *The Compleat Naturalist: A Life of Linnaeus*. New York: Viking Press, 1971.

Clark, David H., and Stephen P. H. Clark. *Newton's Tyranny*. New York: W. H. Freeman and Company, 2001.

Cleempoel, Koenradd van. *Astrolabes at Greenwich: A Catalogue of the Astrolabes in the National Maritime Museum, Greenwich*. New York: Oxford University Press, 2005.

Emsley, John. *The Shocking History of Phosphorus*. London: Macmillan, 2000. (Also used for Chapter 5.)

Gleick, James. *Isaac Newton*. New York: Pantheon Books, 2003.

Holmes, Richard. *The Age of Wonder: How the Romantic Generation Discovered the Beauty and Terror of Science*. New York: Pantheon Books, 2009.

Inwood, Stephen. *The Man Who Knew Too Much: The Strange and Inventive Life of Robert Hooke, 1635–1703*. London: Macmillan, 2002.

Lane, Nick. *Oxygen: The Molecule that Made the World*. New York: Oxford University Press, 2002.

Sobel, Dava. *Galileo's Daughter*. New York: Walker and Co., 1999.

Sobel, Dava. *Longitude: The True Story of a Lone Genius Who Solved the Greatest Scientific Problem of His Time*. New York: Walker and Co., 1995.

Chapter 5: The Industrial Revolution 1775-1839

Benton, Michael J. *When Life Nearly Died*. New York: Thames and Hudson, 2003. (Also used for Chapter 6.)

Burton, Anthony. *Thomas Telford*. London: Aurum Press, 1999.

Cadbury, Deborah. *The Dinosaur Hunters*. London: Fourth Estate, 2000.

Chambers, Paul. *Bones of Contention*. London: John Murray, 2002. (Also used for Chapter 6.)

Faraday, Michael. *The Philosopher's Tree: A Selection of Michael Faraday's Writings*. Philadelphia: Institute of Physics Publishing, 1999.

Morus, Iwan. R. *Michael Faraday and the Electrical Century*. London: Icon Books Ltd, 2004. (Also used for Chapter 6.)

Osborne, Roger. *The Floating Egg*. London: Random House, 1999. (Also used for Chapter 6.)

Vaughan, Adrian. *Isambard Kingdom Brunel*. London: John Murray, 1993. (Also used for Chapter 6.)

Wall, John. *First in the World: The Stockton & Darlington Railway*. Stroud, England: Sutton Publishing, 2001.

Chapter 6: The Age of Steam 1840-1884

Auerbach, Jeffrey A. *The Great Exhibition of 1851: A Nation on Display*. New Haven, Connecticut: Yale University Press, 1999.

Emsley, John. *Nature's Building Blocks*. New York: Oxford University Press, 2001. (Also used for Chapters 7, 8, and 9.)

Fant, Kenne. *Alfred Nobel: A Biography*. New York: Arcade, 1993.

Friedel, Robert, and Paul Israel. *Edison's Electric Light*. New Brunswick, New Jersey: Rutgers University Press, 1986.

Henig, Robin M. *A Monk and Two Peas*. London: Weidenfeld and Nicholson, 2000.

Parrish, Thomas D. *The Submarine: A History*. New York: Viking, 2004.

Shrenk, Friedemann, and Stephanie Müller. *The Neanderthals*. New York: Routledge, 2008.

Stewart, Gail B. *The Suez Canal*. San Diego, California: Lucent Books, 2001.

Strathern, Paul. *Mendeleyev's Dream*. London: Hamish Hamilton, 2000.

Uglow, Jenny. *The Lunar Men*. New York: Farrar, Straus, and Giroux, 2002.

Chapter 7: The Age of Electricity 1885-1919

Ballard, Robert. *Titanic: The Last Great Images*. Philadelphia, Pennsylvania: Running Press, 2008.

Brian, Denis. *Einstein*. New York: John Wiley and Sons, 1996.

Garfield, Simon. *Mauve*. London: Faber and Faber, 2000.

Grant, R. G. *Flight: 100 Years of Aviation*. New York: DK Publishing, 2002.

Kramer, Peter D. *Freud: Inventor of the Modern Mind*. New York: HarperCollins, 2006.

Messadié, Gerald. *Great Modern Inventions*. New York: Chambers, 1991. (Also used for Chapters 8 and 9.)

Parker, Matthew. *Panama Fever: The Epic Story of One of the Greatest Human Achievements of All Time—the Building of the Panama Canal*. New York: Doubleday, 2007.

Weightman, Gavin. *Signor Marconi's Magic Box*. London: HarperCollins, 2003.

Weinberg, Steven. *The Discovery of Subatomic Particles*. New York: Cambridge University Press, 2003.

Who's Who in the Twentieth Century. New York: Oxford University Press, 1999. (Also used for Chapters 8 and 9.)

Chapter 8: The Atomic Age 1920-1949

Bird, Kai, and Martin J. Sherwin. *American Prometheus: The Triumph and Tragedy of J. Robert Oppenheimer*. New York: A. A. Knopf, 2005.

Buderi, Robert. *The Invention that Changed the World*. New York: Simon and Schuster, 1996.

Close, Frank. E. *Particle Physics: A Very Short Introduction*. New York: Oxford University Press, 2004.

Fisher, David E., and Marshall. J. Fisher. *Tube: The Invention of Television*. Washington, D.C.: Counterpoint, 1996.

Hege, John. B. *The Wankel Rotary Engine: A History*. Jefferson, North Carolina: McFarland and Co., 2001.

Jackson, R., ed. *Helicopters: Military, Civilian, and Rescue Rotorcraft (The Aviation Factfile)*. San Diego, California: Thunder Bay Press, 2005.

Lee, Kelley. *World Health Organization (WHO)*. New York: Routledge, 2008.

Macfarlane, Gwyn. *Alexander Fleming: The Man and the Myth*. Cambridge, Massachusetts: Harvard University Press, 1984.

Ward, Bob. *Dr. Space: The Life of Wernher von Braun*. Annapolis, Maryland: Naval Institute Press, 2005.

Chapter 9: The Space Age 1950-1979

Beniada, Frédéric, and Michel Fraile. *Concorde*. St. Paul, Minnesota: Zenith Press, 2006.

Gribbin, John. *In Search of the Double Helix*. New York: McGraw-Hill, 1985.

Lagerkvist, Ulf. *DNA Pioneers and Their Legacy*. New Haven, Connecticut: Yale University Press, 1998. (Also used for Chapter 10.)

Pauling, Linus. *Scientist and Peacemaker*. Corvallis: Oregon State University Press, 2001.

Reynolds, D. W. *Apollo: The Epic Journey to the Moon*. New York: Harcourt, 2002.

Thomas, Jeanette, A., Cynthia F. Moss, and Marianne Vater, eds. *Echolocation in Bats and Dolphins*. Chicago: The University of Chicago Press, 2004.

Watson, James, D. *The Double Helix: A Personal Account of the Discovery of the Structure of DNA*. New York: Atheneum, 1968.

Chapter 10: The Modern World 1980-Present

Campbell-Kelly, Martin, and William Aspray. *Computer: A History of the Information Machine*. Boulder, Colorado: Westview Press, 2004.

Cossons, Neil, ed. *Making of the Modern World*. London: John Murray, 1997.

DeVorkin, David, H., and Robert W. Smith. *Hubble: Imaging Space and Time*. Washington, D.C.: National Geographic Society, 2008.

Global Warming. New York: Time Home Entertainment, 2007.

Hawking, Stephen W. *A Brief History of Time: From the Big Bang to Black Holes*. New York: Bantam Books, 1988.

Lincoln, D. *The Quantum Frontier: The Large Hadron Collider*. Baltimore: Johns Hopkins University Press, 2009.

Mandelbrot, Benoit B. *The Fractal Geometry of Nature*. San Francisco: W. H. Freeman, 1982.

Morwood, Mike J., and Penny van Oosterzee. *The Discovery of the Hobbit: The Scientific Breakthrough that Changed the Face of Human History*. Milsons Point, New South Wales: Random House Australia, 2007.

Riordan, Michael, and Lillian Hoddesdon. *Crystal Fire: The Birth of the Information Age*. New York: W. W. Norton and Co., 1997.

Singh, Simon. *Fermat's Enigma: The Epic Quest to Solve the World's Greatest Mathematical Problem*. New York: Walker, 1997.

INDEX

CONCISE HISTORY OF SCIENCE AND INVENTION

PUBLISHED BY THE NATIONAL GEOGRAPHIC SOCIETY

John M. Fahey	*President and Chief Executive Officer*
Jr. Gilbert M. Grosvenor	*Chairman of the Board*
Tim T. Kelly	*President, Global Media Group*
John Q. Griffin	*Executive Vice President; President, Publishing*
Nina D. Hoffman	*Executive Vice President; President, Book Publishing Group*

PREPARED BY THE BOOK DIVISION

Barbara Brownell Grogan	*Vice President and Editor in Chief*
Marianne R. Koszorus	*Director of Design*
Carl Mehler	*Director of Maps*
R. Gary Colbert	*Production Director*
Jennifer A. Thornton	*Managing Editor*
Meredith C. Wilcox	*Administrative Director, Illustrations*

STAFF FOR THIS BOOK

Susan Straight	*Editor*
Elizabeth Thompson	*Editorial Assistant*
Caitlin Mertzlufft	*Intern*

THE BROWN REFERENCE GROUP LTD

Erin Dolan	*Consultants*
Leon Gray	
Jolyon Goddard	*Text Editor*
David Poole	*Design Manager*
Dave Allen	*Designers*
Joan Curtis	
Steve McCurdy	
Ben Hollingum	*Assistant Editor*
Sophie Mortimer	*Picture Manager*
Andrew Webb	*Picture Researcher*
Lindsey Lowe	*Editorial Director*
Alastair Gourlay	*Production Director*
Richard Berry	*DTP Design*
Heather Dunleavy	
Indexing Specialists (UK) Ltd	*Indexer*
Tim Cooke	*Managing Editor*

MANUFACTURING AND QUALITY MANAGEMENT

Christopher A. Liedel	*Chief Financial Officer*
Phillip L. Schlosser	*Vice President*
Chris Brown	*Technical Director*
Nicole Elliott	*Manager*
Rachel Faulise	*Manager*

The National Geographic Society is one of the world's largest nonprofit scientific and educational organizations. Founded in 1888 to "increase and diffuse geographic knowledge," the Society works to inspire people to care about the planet. It reaches more than 325 million people worldwide each month through its official journal, *National Geographic*, and other magazines; National Geographic Channel; television documentaries; music; radio; films; books; DVDs; maps; exhibitions; school publishing programs; interactive media; and merchandise. National Geographic has funded more than 9,000 scientific research, conservation and exploration projects and supports an education program combating geographic illiteracy. For more information, visit nationalgeographic.com.

For more information, please call 1-800-NGS LINE (647-5463) or write to the following address:

National Geographic Society
1145 17th Street N.W.
Washington, D.C. 20036-4688 U.S.A.

Visit us online at www.nationalgeographic.com

For information about special discounts for bulk purchases, please contact National Geographic Books Special Sales: ngspecsales@ngs.org

For rights or permissions inquiries, please contact National Geographic Books Subsidiary Rights: ngbookrights@ngs.org

LIBRARY OF CONGRESS CATALOGING-IN-PUBLICATION DATA

Concise history of science & invention : an illustrated time line / edited by Jolyon Goddard.
    p. cm.
    Includes index.
    ISBN 978-1-4262-0544-6 (trade)
    1. Science--History--Chronology. 2. Inventions--History--Chronology. I. Goddard, Jolyon. II. Title: Concise history of science and invention.
    Q125.C576 2009
    509--dc22
    2009018460

Printed in China

09/BRG/1